Lecture Notes in Computer Science 7539

Commenced Publication in 1973
Founding and Former Series Editors:
Gerhard Goos, Juris Hartmanis, and Jan van Leeuwen

Radu Calinescu   David Garlan (Eds.)

Large-Scale Complex IT Systems

Development, Operation and Management

17th Monterey Workshop 2012
Oxford, UK, March 19-21, 2012
Revised Selected Papers

 Springer

Volume Editors

Radu Calinescu
University of York
Department of Computer Science
Deramore Lane, Heslington
York YO10 5GH, UK
E-mail: radu.calinescu@york.ac.uk

David Garlan
Carnegie Mellon University
School of Computer Science
5000 Forbes Avenue
Pittsburgh, PA, 15213, USA
E-mail: garlan@cs.cmu.edu

ISSN 0302-9743   e-ISSN 1611-3349
ISBN 978-3-642-34058-1   e-ISBN 978-3-642-34059-8
DOI 10.1007/978-3-642-34059-8
Springer Heidelberg Dordrecht London New York

Library of Congress Control Number: 2012949191

CR Subject Classification (1998): D.2, C.2, H.4, K.6.5, C.2.4, D.3, H.3, F.3

LNCS Sublibrary: SL 2 – Programming and Software Engineering

Typesetting: Camera-ready by author, data conversion by Scientific Publishing Services, Chennai, India

Printed on acid-free paper

Springer is part of Springer Science+Business Media (www.springer.com)

Preface

It is a great pleasure to introduce the proceedings of the 17th Monterey Workshop, held in Oxford, UK, during March 19–21, 2012. Attended by leading researchers from academia and industry, the workshop explored the challenges associated with the development, operation, and management of large-scale complex IT systems.

Large-scale complex IT systems underpin key critical applications in domains ranging from health care and financial markets to manufacturing and defence. Such systems are created and evolved dynamically through the integration of independently built and controlled heterogeneous components. As a result, traditional techniques, which assume complete control over the parts of a system, are inadequate in supporting the dependable engineering of important safety-, security-, and business-critical requirements.

The revised and significantly extended papers included in this volume incorporate the insights gained from the productive and lively discussions at the workshop, and the feedback from the post-workshop peer reviews. The volume has three parts. Part I focuses on identifying the challenges and risks faced by the developers, operators, and users of large-scale complex IT systems. The papers in this part examine the current and envisaged use of such systems in domains including cyber-physical systems, global financial markets, health care, teams of autonomous vehicles, and air traffic control.

Part II of the volume covers the model-based engineering of different aspects of large-scale complex IT systems. The papers included in this part explore a broad range of approaches to addressing the uncertainty, continual change, large scale, security concerns, and compositional and distributed nature that characterize these systems. Multi-view, multi-disciplinary, domain-specific, security, and multi-agent responsibility modelling approaches are identified as promising in handling such hard problems, and research agendas for turning them into fully fledged solutions are laid out by these papers.

Finally, Part III explores avenues for extending the use of formal specification, analysis, and verification to large-scale complex IT systems. The approaches envisaged to help achieve this ambitious objective include formal techniques that are incremental, modular, compositional, or which exploit extreme symmetries, quantitative steering, and independent viewpoint implementability.

We would like to thank UK's national research and training initiative in the science and engineering of Large-Scale Complex IT Systems (LSCITS) and its Director, Dave Cliff, for their generous sponsorship of the workshop. We are also grateful to the General Chairs, Luqi and Bill Roscoe, for their support in the organization and smooth running of a very successful workshop.

July 2012

Radu Calinescu
David Garlan

Message from the Monterey Workshop
General Chairs

Oxford, in Strachey, Hoare and others, has an outstanding history in advancing programming language semantics, program verification, and the theory of concurrent computing. It maintains its strength in these areas and newer ones such as security and information systems, all of which made it natural to hold the 17th Monterey Workshop there between 19th and 21st March 2012.

Awareness of the importance of system integration has spread, and the economy and society of our interconnected world has become increasingly dependent on complex interacting systems. Such systems may incorporate networked multitudes of people, information services, physical components, sensors, software controllers, and actuators that affect the physical components. Examples of sectors relying on such systems include energy, transportation, manufacturing, defense, and medicine.

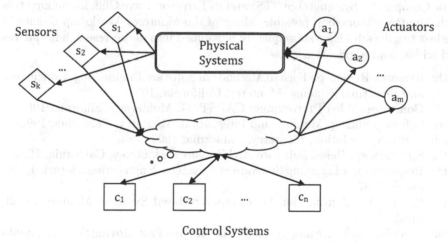

Control Systems

Cyber Physical Systems (CPS) are engineered systems comprising interacting physical and computational components [1]. Emerging CPS will be coordinated, distributed, and connected, and must be robust and responsive [2]. Potential applications span an amazing variety of contexts, from swarms of nano quadrotors to robotic surgery. Many of these applications impact the safety and well-being of societies and individuals. Therefore high integrity, predictable operation, compositional and iterative verification, and complex systems in the cloud are all relevant.

The need for dependable operation of systems that integrate heterogeneous components, continuously evolve, and have decentralized ownership and control has expanded yet again the challenges that the field of software engineering must address, introducing connections to subjects beyond its traditional scope, such as complexity in organizations, socio-technical engineering, and cyber-security.

The workshop itself was held in the Randolph Hotel, the setting of numerous episodes of Inspector Morse. It brought together a wide range of research relevant to complex heterogeneous systems, including approaches to developing them, securing them, verifying them, and taming their complexity. Others dealt with design and specification of systems with respect to multiple viewpoints, and how to combine these. It was natural that several of the papers addressed healthcare issues since healthcare IT provides some of the most complex and important examples of cyber-physical systems and complex distributed information systems.

It was wonderful to see the interactions and integration of advances from software engineering and many related fields coming together, following the culture and tradition of the Monterey Workshop series. We thank the program committee chairs Radu Calinescu from York and David Garlan from CMU for putting together a fascinating workshop program. Janos Sztipanovits initiated CPS as the workshop topic, Fabrice Kordon produced the beautiful website and years of collectable posters, and the Oxford hosts handled innumerable details.

The Monterey Workshop steering committee would like to thank the sponsors for their support of the Monterey Workshops, with special thanks to the UK's national research and training initiative in the science and engineering of Large-Scale Complex IT Systems (LSCITS) and its Director, Dave Cliff, for making this 17th Monterey Workshop possible. Many of the Monterey Workshop themes in the last two decades have subsequently blossomed into major research initiatives and widespread applications:

0th: Research Review on Formal Methods in Software Engineering: Concurrent and Real-time Systems, Monterey, California, 1991

1st: Computer-Aided Prototyping: CAPSTAG, Monterey, California, 1992

2nd: Software Slicing, Merging and Integration, Monterey, California, 1993

3rd: Software Evolution, Monterey, California, 1994

4th: Specification Based Software Architectures, Monterey, California, 1995

5th: Requirements Targeting Software and Systems Engineering, Bernried, Germany, 1997

6th: Engineering Automation for Computer Based Systems, Monterey, California, 1998

7th: Modeling Software and System Structure in a Fast Moving Scenario, Santa Margherita Ligure, Italy, 2000

8th: Engineering Automation for Software Intensive System Integration, Monterey, California, 2001

9th: Radical Innovations of Software and Systems Engineering in the Future, Venice, Italy, 2002

10th: Software Engineering for Embedded Systems: From Requirements to Implementation, Chicago, Illinois, 2003

11th: Software Engineering Tools: Compatibility and Integration, Vienna, Austria, 2004

12th: Realization of Reliable Systems on Top of Unreliable Networked Platforms, Irvine, California, 2005

13th: Composition of Embedded Systems: Scientific and Industrial Issues, Paris, France, 2006

14th: Innovations for Requirement Analysis: From Stakeholders' Needs to Formal Designs, Monterey, California, 2007

15th: Foundations of Computer Software, Future Trends and Techniques for Development, Budapest, Hungary, 2008

16th: Modeling, Development and Verification of Adaptive Systems, Redmond, Washington, 2010

17th: Development, Operation and Management of Large-Scale Complex IT Systems, Oxford, UK, 2012

18th: Cyber Intelligence and Security, Washington DC, 2013

The coming 18th Monterey Workshop will discuss challenges associated with the modeling, design, evaluation, and monitoring of cyber and cyber-physical systems, assess engineering techniques, and explore future research topics. Cyber- is a prefix derived from "cybernetic," which comes from the Greek adjective κυβερνητικός meaning skilled in steering or governing [3]. Cyber and cyber-physical systems are being networked to perform critical functions and to evolve into the global superstructure:

- Accurately modeling the cyber-social context is a prerequisite for systems aimed at gathering, processing, storing, analyzing and using cyber data intelligently to support decisions.
- Document processing and data synchronization are needed to derive real-time intelligence from ongoing events in complex networked systems.
- Secure architecture and firm technical foundations are necessary to enable such systems to adapt to a changing world while maintaining reliable operation.
- Establishing abstractions to understand, predict, and build systems with optimized security and real-time intelligence should facilitate security and reliability of cyber and cyber-physical systems.

Prof. Sadie Creese, Director of the Oxford Cyber Security Center, and Dr. Doug Lange will be the program committee chairs of the 18th Monterey Workshop on Cyber Intelligence and Security in 2013.

July 2012   Luqi & Bill Roscoe

References

1. Sztipanovits, J., Stankovic, J., Corman, D.: Industry – Academy Collaboration in Cyber Physical Systems Research, http://cra.org/ccc/docs/CPS-White%20Paper-May-19-2009-GMU-v1.pdf
2. Cyber-Physical Systems, National Science Foundation, USA
3. http://en.wikipedia.org/wiki/Internet-related_prefixes

Table of Contents

Part III: Formal Specification, Analysis and Verification

Cyber-Physical Systems: Imminent Challenges*

Manfred Broy[1], María Victoria Cengarle[2], and Eva Geisberger[2]

[1] Technische Universität München
broy@in.tum.de

[2] fortiss GmbH
{cengarle,geisberger}@fortiss.org

Abstract. A German project is presented which was initiated in order to analyse the potential and risks associated with Cyber-Physical Systems. These have been recognised as the next wave of innovation in information and communication technology. Cyber-Physical Systems are herein understood in a very broad sense as the integration of embedded systems with global networks such as the Internet. The survey aims at deepening understanding the impact of those systems at technological and economical level as well as at political and sociological level. The goal of the study is to collect arguments for decision makers both in business and politics to take actions in research, legislation and business development.

1 Introduction

The vision of Cyber-Physical System (CPS) is that of open, ubiquitous systems of coordinated computing and physical elements which interactively adapt to their context, are capable of learning, dynamically and automatically reconfigure themselves and cooperate with other CPS (resulting in a compound CPS), possess an adequate man-machine interface, and fulfil stringent safety, security and private data protection regulations. Nowadays CPS are being conceived and chances are high that they will be widely used in the near future. Forerunners can already be found in as dissimilar areas as automotive, avionics, energy, health, environmentalism and consumer electronics. So for instance a car equipped with an intelligent parking assist system combined with a navigation system as well as the (suppositional) road traffic management is a CPS. This vision poses extraordinary challenges particularly regarding technology, organisation and human-system cooperation. It also entails a huge potential both for economy as well as for tackling problems of modern society.

A first step towards CPS is given by networked embedded systems whose operations are monitored, coordinated, controlled and integrated by a distributed computing and communication core. CPS potentially can change the way individuals and organisations interact with and control the physical world, and be as revolutionary as the internet technology was and still is. The transition of economy and society seems inexorable and disruptively leads to value-added chains and economic ecosystems spanning over diverse domains.

---

* This work has been partially sponsored by the BMBF project "Integrierte Forschungsagenda Cyber-Physical Systems" under the patronage of acatech, the National Academy of Science and Engineering.

R. Calinescu and D. Garlan (Eds.): Monterey Workshop 2012, LNCS 7539, pp. 1–28, 2012.

Peculiarities, prospects and obstacles of CPS, and opportunities, risks and acceptance factors to be raised by the envisioned systems were pinpointed in a survey which is the outcome of a collaborative analysis carried out by experts in the related fields and working in industry and academia, including both basic and applied research; see [GBC⁺12]. Trends of CPS were identified and charaterised; by means of (contrived) future scenarios further developments gone through; and social, economic and technical challenges and new opening possibilities discussed.

Starting from this cognisance, a guidance can be implied for the evolution of core technologies, exploration of user demands (be they end users or companies), inter- and transdisciplinary research and development, economic ecosystems, social guidelines and stipulations, participatory conformation and analysis of the techniques. Preliminary recommendations for action can be found in [BGC⁺12].

In this paper we present the characteristics of the envisaged CPS, namely their capabilities plus the demands they must fulfil. In the course of the project we also discussed different issues of CPS including security as well as social acceptance and usability; see [GBC⁺12]. Here we limit ourselves to highlight the challenges for the formal modelling and engineering of requirements and systems, and to enumerate some issues regarding, on the one hand, social acceptability of CPS and, on the other, the role of CPS in innovation as well as successful business models.

Outline. Firstly in Sec. 2 we discuss the key drivers of the incipient evolution. Then in Sec. 3 we present the method employed to characterise CPS and single out the challenges they bear, and sum up this characterisation. Afterwards in Secs. 4 and 5 we list some of the issues of CPS regarding technologies and society, respectively. Finally in Sec. 6 we summarise the implications that CPS bring along.

2   Towards Cyber-Physical Systems

The information and communication technologies progress faster and faster. At a dizzying pace circuits become even more miniaturised and speedier every day, networks allow more rapid and reliable communication, mobile phone coverage expands, to mention only a couple of examples. These technologies, at the same time, become less and less expensive. This way, ubiquitous computing becomes a reality thanks to the proliferation of netbooks, tablet computers, smartphones, and the like. Furthermore, more and more computing systems are embedded into physical devices, like home applicances, vehicles, or medical devices, providing additional intelligence. Proprietary closed systems, as embedded systems and devices, increasingly become open and dynamically linked to other systems, they are more flexible, more interactive, more networked, and seamlessly connect the physical systems of actuator and sensor technology with virtual software systems.

CPS are the result of further development and integrated use of two dominant areas of innovation: systems with embedded software, on the one hand, and global data networks like the Internet with distributed and interactive application systems on the other. There exists a powerful infrastructure of sensors, actuators and communications networks, employed by cooperating global companies. The following technologies and trends act thereby as key drivers:

- The use of powerful intelligent embedded systems, mobile services and ubiquitous computing.
- The use of the Internet as business web, that is, as a platform for economic cooperations, with two complementary forms:
  - traditional IT management tasks are increasingly transferred to the "cloud", i.e., outsourced to external service providers worldwide distributed,
  - especially in trade and logistics but also in application areas such as remote support, components find use that are intelligent, networked and equipped sensors, as for instance RFID technology.
- The use of the Semantic Web and of techniques of Web 2.0 as well as of interactive design of integrated services through
  - user-defined interaction and the corresponding configuration of knowledge and communication network, and
  - communities of developers typically around open source initiatives like Firefox, Android and MediaWiki, but also around application distribution platforms like iOS.

We envisage CPS as the convergence of those trends. These forthcomming systems enable services and functionalities far beyond the scope of the capabilities of present-day networked embedded systems. CPS are distributed and interactive, location-independent as well as aware of their context of use and adaptable, capable of learning and (semi-)autonomous.

In the next section, we presente a method which characterises CPS.

3   Characteristics of CPS

In the first place future scenarios were conceived that both reinforced the desirability of CPS and helped identify the further course of action with the purpose of making the vision of CPS a reality. Indeed, they allowed the reification of goals and requirements of CPS and their engineering as well as the deduction of CPS-specific capabilities. Requirements and capabilities, on the one hand, permit the detection of challenges and implications of CPS engineering and, on the other, the derivation of essential core technologies.

Scenarios were concocted in various domains including automotive, traffic management, health care system, mobile communications, medical technology, manufacturing, procurement and logistics, industry and building automation, plant construction and engineering, smart grid. Figs. 1 and 2 delineate two sample scenarios in the areas of health and mobility, respectively.

The smart mobility scenario in Fig. 2 makes apparent the need for connecting CPS of different domains: The convoy of fully autonomous cars abandons the premium track in order to give way to an ambulance. This situation lies in the intersection of CPS specific for traffic management and CPS specific for health care system or, more precisely, demands CPS dedicated to different domains to interact and coordinate. A similar case is given by CPS for smart home and/or smart building in cooperation with CPS for smart health and/or ambient assisted living. Simultaneously, CPS are open thus dynamically adaptable systems and services. Therefore, according to social and spatial network topologies, CPS operate across different nested spheres of uncertainty (see Fig. 3):

Smart health

Ms Huber is 70 years old, retired and lives alone in an old farmhouse in Munich East. She never made the driver's license since she always used to ride with her husband. Since his death a few years ago, Ms Huber suffers from mild depression. Although she still is able to manage everything, her concern is to helplessly fall into a dangerous situation. Because of this reason she acquired a smart health system. This system passively monitors her vital values, assists her in medical matters, and calls for help in case of emergency. The passive monitoring controls Ms Huber's weight and reminds her of taking her medicine. These are only the basic functions, the system can be adapted to changing needs.

After some time and with the help of sensors installed in the farmhouse, the system has recorded Ms Huber's habits in particular regarding how she moves around and created a profile. She no longer perceives the small devices. The daily jump on the bathroom scales has become routine. And the guidance as how to prepare her weekly medication has stilled her fear of confusion.

Ms Huber used to meet her friends on a regular basis, but for some time now their encounters are less frequent. The smart health system detects weight gain. Given that this change has occurred relatively fast, the system recommends Ms Huber to contact her family physician prior to her next regularly scheduled visit. The system allows the arrangement of an appointment directly with the physician's surgery. The physician recommends Ms Huber more exercise and to also control daily her blood pressure. Ms Huber gets on prescription a blood pressure measuring device as well as a motion sensor, that are integrated to her smart health system. After a couple of days Ms Huber's situation has further deteriorated, so her family physician refers her to a specialist who can closer examine her. For this to be possible, Ms Huber had previously granted approval the monitoring of her data regularly in the cloud.

A couple of days later, Ms Huber suffers a slight stroke, which is quickly treated. For the smart health system stores instructions as what is to be done in case of emergency. Not only an ambulance is immediately sent to Ms Huber's farmhouse. Ms Huber's family members are informed via SMS, the newspaper subscription is suspended and the alarm system of the farmhouse is activated.

Fig. 1. Scenario "smart health" (excerpt)

1. a *controlled* area of closed large-scale infrastructure systems and services,
2. a *defined* area of cooperative, social infrastructure systems and services run by skilled users, and
3. a *demarcated* area of social application systems and services, including businesses, spanning over diverse domains, open to individual application systems and utilisation processes, employed in everyday life, that make use of services of the controlled and of the defined areas.

CPS' services (co-)operate across all three areas in open and unforeseen physical and social environments.

The analysis of the scenarios resulted in a number of characteristics shown by the hypothetical CPS. Those characteristics allowed the derivation of goals and requirements of CPS as well as their capabilities, which were sorted in benefit and system abilities. Out of these, on the one hand challenges and implications and, on the other, indispensable technologies and engineering skills were inferred. In sum, CPS characteristics are portrayed in Fig. 4.

Smart mobility

Ms Müller records a visit to her mother on Friday morning in her mobile device: she gives only departure time as well as from and to locations, and a maximum cost amount for the entire route. The mobile device is connected to various providers and makes her suggestions for the trip from her home in Munich West to pick up her children at their school in the center of Munich and onward to her mother in Munich East. Ms Müller decides to use public transportation to the children's school, as this is the most energy-efficient and least expensive alternative. There, Ms Müller intends to continue the journey with her children to her mother with a car-sharing vehicle (CSA). To this end, she explicitly decides in favor of a hybrid vehicle with autonomous driving capabilities. The necessary travel documents such as public transport ticket and CSA authorisation are transmitted to the mobile device of Ms Müller.

Prior to departure, Ms Müller is informed via her mobile device of a defective signal box and thus significant delays of her public transport connection are to be expected. Via her mobile device, again, she receives the suggestion to book a CSA already from her home. Ms Müller accepts the proposal, consequently and automatically her public transport ticked is cancelled and her CSA authorisation from her home is transferred on her mobile device. Shortly thereafter, Ms Müller is informed about the impending arrival of the CSA. Simultaneously, the children are informed that their mother will pick them up with a CSA at the school.

During her car ride and while the CSA autonomously drives in a convoy on the highway, on her mobile device Ms Müller answers e-mails and reads the newspaper. Meanwhile, the convoy leaves the premium track –a fee-based fast track for fully autonomous vehicles– to give way to an ambulance, and then joins the premium track again.

Shortly thereafter the CSA abandons the convoy, leaves the highway, and returns the control to Ms Müller. She drives the vehicle toward her children's school. As the CSA is networked with a back-end infrastructure and with other vehicles, Ms Müller is supported in a high degree during this trip. For example, the CSA automatically reduces its speed to the prescribed speed limit. When driving past a stopped school bus with activated warning lights in the immediate vicinity of the school, suddenly the CSA halts: a child runs from behind the school bus over the street and in front of the CSA, which in time comes to a stop. A glance in the rearview mirror convinces Ms Müller that the vehicles behind her were also warned in time.

Once the children get on the car and they set off to Ms Müller's mother, the CSA is notified of the fine dust pollution limit being exceeded and that only emission-free vehicles are allowed to proceed. The vehicle checks whether the existing battery capacity is sufficient and switches to electric mode.

Fig. 2. Scenario "smart mobility" (excerpt)

Capabilities associated with this characterisation can be found in Tab. 1. Essentially, CPS are required to be

- x-aware and assimilable to their physical/social context,
- capable of learning (of evolving) and adaptable,
- transparent, equipped with predictable human-machine interaction,
- reliable, cooperative, strategic,
- subject to risk, target and quality analysis as well as quality of service (QoS) assurance.

Once goals, characteristics and capabilities of the envisioned CPS were determined, the research and development landscape in science and industry, as far as relevant

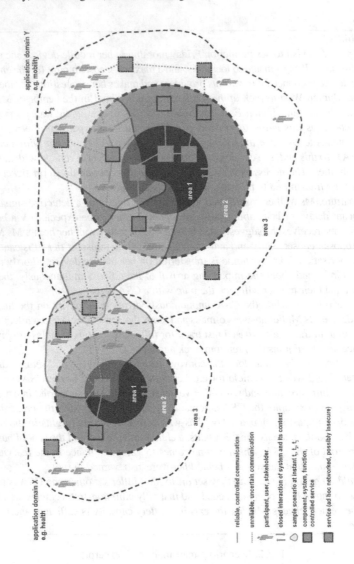

Fig. 3. CPS domain structure

information is available and/or put at disposal, both at national and international level, was examined and the abilities of today's systems gathered. This information and the capabilities of CPS inferred were contrasted. This way, some shortcomings could be identified. These results were validated within workshops with experts, interviews and polls, which where systematically iterated.

Example: Evolution of a Vehicle's Brake System

The development stages of braking systems in vehicles illustrate the technology evolution and the increasing complexity of embedded systems, and hint at the sophisticated

By CPS,

- physical and virtual, locally/globally networked systems are fused into
- systems of systems with dynamically shifting boundaries that are
- context-adaptive, partially or completely autonomous, and capable of active real-time control,
- cooperative with each other under distributed, alternating control, and
- able of comprehensive human-system cooperation.

CPS include embedded systems, logistics, coordination and management processes as well as Internet services that, using sensors, directly capture physical data and, through actuators, act on physical processes that are interconnected by means of digital networks, use globally available data and services, and have multimodal human-system interfaces. CPS are open socio-technical systems that provide a range of new functionalities, services and features which go far beyond the current capabilities of embedded systems with controlled behaviour.

Fig. 4. CPS characteristics

requirements on the way to open CPS. The development stages are graphically represented in Fig. 5.

In order to avoid traffic accidents the automobile industry, in the development of safety-critical functions as for instance the braking function, resorts to classical embedded systems and, increasingly, to CPS. Milestones in this development are the anti-lock braking system (ABS) introduced in 1978, the electronic stability control (ESP) introduced in 1995, and the active brake assist (ABA) as extension of the adaptive cruise control (ACC), introduced in 2003. The ABS allows the wheels on a motor vehicle to continue interacting tractively with the road surface as directed by driver steering inputs while braking. The ESP actively allocates a deceleration torque to individual wheels thus preserving the steerability. An ABA may warn the driver, precharge the brakes, among others; the Honda brake collision mitigation system uses a radar-based system to monitor the situation ahead and automatically brakes if the driver does not react to a warning.

These three milestones show the gradual evolution from basic (physical) funtionality via information processing through automatic control. Associated with ABS the physical causal chains (brake pedal – hydraulic line – cylinder) is partially substituted by causal chains supported by information technology (brake pedal – position sensor – bus – controller – bus – actuator – cylinder). While ABS only considers wheel revolutions and braking power, ABA additionally deals with the vehicle environment in the form of obstacles. This evolution goes from an individual monofunctional system (braking in the case of ABS) over cooperative, i.e., closed and networked, embedded systems (braking and steering in the case of ESP) to a system of systems (braking, steering, dashboard, and context via sensors in the case of ABA).

The example clearly shows the increasing demands on the ability of systems to investigate their surroundings. The requirements range from the acquisition of simple physical data and their fusion into physical environment information such as distance, location or speed (physical awareness), over the identification of the situational importance of this information (situation awareness), to the inclusion of extensive contextual

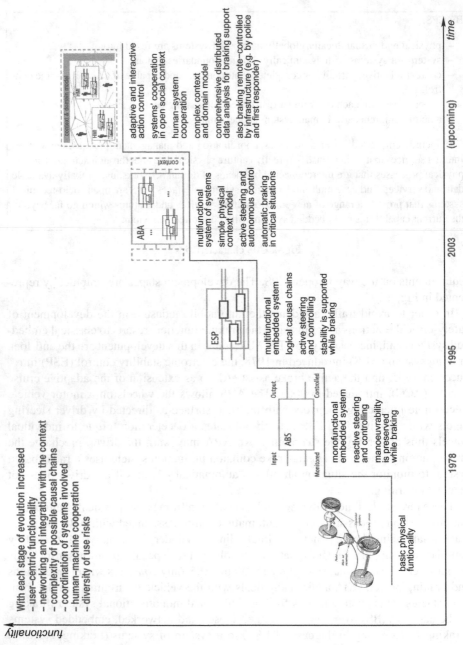

Fig. 5. Evolution of the brake system in a vehicle

information for the proper assessment of the situation (context awareness) and action control, and this in cooperation with other systems. In order to meet these complex requirements, and in addition to physical environmental models, increasingly complex situation and context models are required on the part of the systems.

In the next sections, some topics of technical and social nature for (further) development of CPS are presented.

4 Technological Challenges

As explained above, on the one hand, describing characteristics of the envisioned CPS (see Fig. 4) were inferred using the future scenarios devised. On the other and as detailed in Tab. 1, associated goals, requirements and capabilities were derived, which were then arranged in a taxonomy comprising the taxa benefit, system-inherent capability, technology, and engineering competence; see [GBC+12]. Characteristics and capabilities pose a number of challenges, require novel and/or improved technologies, and entail a series of implications; Fig. 6 shows the approach followed by the project. In this section, the technological challenges are addressed. In particular because of the increasing openness of the systems and the capabilities listed in columns (3)–(5) of Tab. 1 (which are also reflected in the evolution of braking systems exemplarily exposed in Sec. 3 above), the prospective demands go beyond the possibilities of current technologies. There is thus increased demand for research and development. On the basis of the those capabilities, we reflected upon the needed apparatus, examined the state of the art, and tried to identify both the difference or distance between available and required technologies as well as the associated challenges.

4.1 Individual Technologies

Out of the distinctive nature and features of CPS, necessary advances in technology were recognised that can be either individually intended for the implementation of CPS capabilities or address engineering issues. This section focuses on the first ones.

Among individual technologies is sensor fusion, that allows physical situation awareness, provided improved sensor and actuator technologies together with communication networks are available. A step beyond sensor fusion is multi-criterial situation assessment, which permits decision making even if the information at disposal is uncertain or contradictory. Furthermore, CPS must be aware not only of their physical and situation context but also of their own situational capabilities, and adapt accordingly. They moreover must be able to learn from, e.g., the way they have been used so far, and accommodate to their user putting a comprehensive human-system interface at disposal. And what is more, they must be able to organise themselves and evolve. These issues, among others, are dealt with in the next section.

In what follows, we give an overview of the surveyed techniques and technologies. Basic techniques and technologies already available –which as a matter of fact address capabilities under (1) and (2)– that can be sophisticated include

- domain modelling, ontologies and domain-specific languages,
- sensor and actuator technology,
- communication infrastructure and communication platform,
- efficient parallel processing units, and
- distributed stable controlling;

Table 1. CPS capabilities

(1) Sensor and actuator technology, virtual, locally/globally networked, with real-time management	(2) Systems of systems (SOS), controlled network with dynamic boundaries	(3) Context-adaptive and (partially) autonomous systems	(4) Cooperative systems with distributed, alternating control	(5) Comprehensive human-system cooperation	Central abilities and non-functional requirements, quality in use, quality of service (QoS)
• Parallel acquisition (through sensors), fusion, processing of physical data from the local/global environment in real time (physical awareness)	• Interpretation of data from context and situation over several levels, depending on application situations	• Extensive, continuous context awareness	• Distributed, cooperative and interactive perception and evaluation of the situation	• Intuitive, multimodal, active and passive HMI support (simplified control)	• "X" awareness through correct perception and interpretation of ○ situation and context ○ self, third party, and human (state, objectives, intentions, ability to act)
• Interpretation of the situation w.r.t. the goal achievement and job completion of the CPS	• Targeted selection, incorporation, coordination and use of services—depending on situation, local and global goal, and behaviour	• Continual collection, observation, selection, processing, evaluation, decision making, communication of context data, situation data and application data (often in real time)	• Distributed, cooperative and interactive determination of the steps to be carried out—depending on the evaluation of the situation, the goals of individual participants and the goals of the community	• Support of a further (time and space) and enlarged perception, support of an extended capacity to act of individual and several persons (groups)	• Learning and adaption (behaviour)
• Acquisition, interpretation, deduction, prediction of faults, obstacles, risks	• Service composition and integration, decentralised control: recognition, active search and dynamic incorporation of missing services, data and functions	• Targeted adaptation of the interaction, coordination, control with/of other systems and services	• Coordinated processing of mass data	• Recognition and interpretation of human behaviour including feelings, needs and intentions	• Self-organisation
• Interaction, integration, rules and control of CPS components and functions	• Evaluation of components and services to be incorporated regarding required use and quality for the application (QoS, overall quality) as well as possible risks	• Recognition, analysis and interpretation of plans and intentions of systems and participating users	• Coordinated estimation and negotiation of the decision ultimately taken, i.e., own and shared control and decision-making autonomy	• Acquisition and evaluation of state and context of human and system (extension of perception and of evaluation skills)	• Cooperation, negotiation and decision-making (within precise boundaries—compliance)
• Globally distributed, networked real-time control	• Reliability and compliance w.r.t. guaranteed QoS	• Model creation for application field, application domain, available services, tasks, and participants incl. their roles, goals and demands	• Decision with uncertain knowledge	• Integrated and interactive decision making and action of systems and individual persons or multitudes	• Decisions with uncertain knowledge
	• Controlled access to system's own data and services	• Assessment of goals and steps to achieve them, taking into consideration alternatives concerning costs and risks	• Cooperative learning and adaptation to situations and needs	• Ability to learn	• Policy-making and, if applicable, compliance with QoS guarantees
		• Self-awareness in terms of knowledge about own situation, status and options for action	• Estimation of the quality of own and external services and abilities		• Comprehensive reliability, safety and security policies
		• Learning of e.g. modified work processes, logistics, habits, interaction, etc., and corresponding behaviour adaption	• Self-organisation in clusters		• Transparent HMI, shared control—integrated situation evaluation and assessable behaviour
					• Risk management
					• Proactive, strategic and reliable action
					• Privacy protection

→ → Increasing openness, complexity, autonomy, "smartness" and evolution of the systems (with disruptive effects in the fields of application) → →

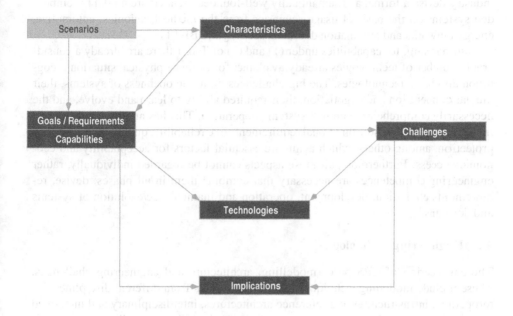

Fig. 6. Project plan

see, e. g., [Len97, Dmi04, RLM⁺06, KS03, GMA09, BHGZ09, MM06, HSMS07, ABB⁺09, Arb11, CPS08]. Additional technologies to be further developed are

- for physical situation recognition: sensor fusion, pattern recognition, situational maps (see, e. g., [Rab08, Web02, Mat03, Thi10]);
- for planning and anticipatory, partially or completely autonomous behaviour: multi-criterial situation assessment, artificial intelligence (see, e. g., [RN09, FN71, PB03, GMP⁺06]);
- for cooperation and negotiation: multi-agent systems (see, e. g., [MVK06, KNR⁺11, Osb03, Wei00, Woo09]);
- for human-machine interaction and shared control: human-machine interface and interaction modalities, intention and plan recognition, user modelling, human aware-ness (see, e. g., [Nor96, Sad11, SS11, Hua11]);
- for learning: machine learning and data mining (see, e. g., [Bis07, BKS11, MCS11]);
- for evolution, strategies of self organisation and adaption: self organising manufac-ture, multi-agent systems, self organising communication networks (see, e. g., [BS00, SB01, SMS11, BCHM06, SAL⁺03, WS10]).

Both general and domain-specific reference architectures were already developed; see [DoD09a, DoD09b, DoD09c, NAF07, TOG09] and [ABD⁺10, AUT10, Dra10, Gif07, GP09, MLD10], respectively. Essentially, the reference architectures are struc-tured in three abstraction levels: (a) functional, (b) logical, and (c) technical (from ab-stract to concrete). Within SPES 2020 –a research project dedicated to a methodology for the model-based development of embedded systems– partners from academia and industry devise a formal and semantically well-founded architecture model for embedded systems on the basis of usage scenarios from the medical, avionics, automotive, energy networks and automation domains; see, e. g., [BBB$^+$11].

Summarising, for capabilities under (1) and (2) of Tab. 1 there are already a considerable number of technologies already available, for instance physical situation recognition and basic technologies. The big challenges lie in the openness of systems, their mutual cooperation and negotiation, their required ability to learn and evolve, and the necessarily comprehensive human-system cooperation. This has an immediate impact in the realisability of non-functional requirements like reliability, quality in use, privacy protection, among others, which again are essential factors for acceptability and economic success. Furthermore, all those aspects cannot be regarded individually, rather engineering competences are necessary that combine them in all phases: devise, requirements elicitation, development, operation and maintenance/evolution of systems and domains.

4.2 Engineering Technologies

The engineering of CPS poses modelling, architecture and engineering challenges. These include modelling techniques integrating aspects from different disciplines, interoperable infrastructures and reference architectures, interdisciplinary and integrated engineering and evolution, enhanced non-functional requirements elicitation and privacy protection policies. A detailed analysis of these issues can be found in [GBC$^+$12, Secs. 5.2 and 5.3].

Integrated Models. Since CPS applications have the potential to pervade all spheres of life, a deep analysis of the nexus between today's and future application domains must be conducted. This analysis needs embrace users, involved persons and participating systems as well as the human-system cooperation. Comprehensive and integrated formal models for humans, systems and architectures are necessary. In order to integrate those models, the CPS must be engineered using harmonised requirement models and architectural concepts, which are moreover structured according to abstraction level, system design phase and functional modelling view; see e.g. [BGK$^+$07, GBB$^+$06, GS07, Sch04]. This applies to the description and modelling of (statements of) problems, stakeholders' viewpoints and objectives, and related requirements as well as to their mapping to system design(s) and their overall integration, validation, horizontal and vertical traceability, evolution and coordination between all stakeholders—users, customers, business and solution engineers from different disciplines.

On the one hand, there is the need to clarify how physical (continuous) models of the mechanical and related engineering disciplines can be integrated with digital models of the software and system engineering. Especially in the context of control theory, classical models and modelling techniques in software and systems engineering as well as engineering design in mechanical engineering, there is a plethora of challenges. For example, different disciplines have made their contributions to the Smart Grid: computer science, information and communication technology, but also energy networks and devices (such as smart metering).

On the other hand, it is important to investigate which models, methods, and interdisciplinary research efforts are needed to understand and analyse the profound changes in human-system interaction that are triggered by information and communication technologies, Internet, and CPS. The comprehensive social and political implications must be investigated, so that useful and acceptable (both for users and society) CPS applications and services can be designed.

For the engineering tasks, integrated hybrid system and architectural models are required. Here, by hybridity are meant socio-technical infrastructures encompassing, e. g., cognition models and actor-network theory; see [Lat87]. Domains and models, on the one hand, and systems engineering, on the other, determine and influence each other in this integrated view procured by CPS. Fig. 7 shows an attempt to make this mutual influence pictorially perceptible.

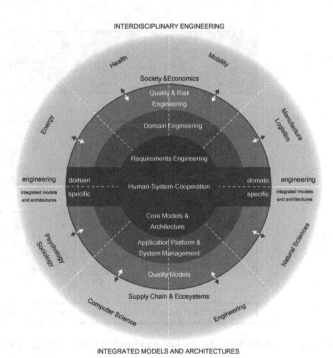

Fig. 7. Integrated engineering models and methods, interdisciplinary and participative development, interactive use and evolution of CPS

Interoperable Infrastructures and Reference Architectures. A technique that obviously needs be updated is the infrastructure: CPS must be interoperable and their services and the cooperation with each other must be reliable. Thus, appropriate platform and middleware are indispensable, and reference architectures need be built up.

Because the scope of operation of CPS may easily extend across country boundaries, communication and interoperability standards become absolutely necessary—on technical level as well as on semantical and user-visible levels. Interoperable and compatible

CPS' components and services with the relevant interfaces and protocols require a gradual construction of standardised, flexible infrastructures and communication platforms, as illustrated in Fig. 8. At the lowermost level the communication infrastructure with basic services as well as the middleware are located. On top of them, application-specific platforms exchange their data via interfaces; services for targeted access are provided on these platforms. To this end, technical interoperability is needed. Moreover, in order for CPS to cooperate beyond application boundaries, information from different applications must be consistently interpreted. Thus, a decisive factor is semantic interoperability, that ultimately enables the interplay of applications. The top layer shows the application layer accessed by the users. At this level, user-visible interoperability allows users to visualise and comprehend behaviour as well as interaction and options of communication and cooperation of CPS and, furthermore, to interactively engage in the utilisation process.

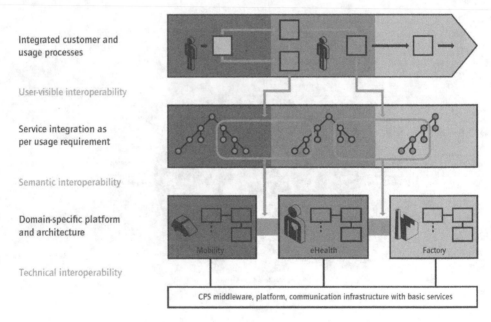

Fig. 8. Levels of abstraction, design, integration and interoperability of CPS

CPS are expected to be open, that is, to provide some combination of interoperability, portability, and open software standards. Specific installations can be furthermore configured to allow unrestricted access by people and/or other computers. An immediate aftermath are conflict as well as reconciliation handling; see [Lev95, EBJ03]. Connected with these issues, a further and non-trivial one is posed by the human-system cooperation and shared control. There are high-level requisite and expectations to be fulfiled by CPS with respect to this matter. This question is briefly examined in the next section.

Interdisciplinary and Integrated Engineering and Evolution. Knowledge across different domains of application must be synthetised. This calls for sophisticated domain and requirement engineering disciplines. A source of inspiration for this purpose surely is to be found in product line engineering (see, e. g., [Ber07, CN08, PBvdL05a]), system of systems engineering (see, e. g., [SC01, JSE+08]), model-based requirement engineering (see, e. g., [BGK+07, KS98]). Also comprehensive and integrated models for humans as well as for systems and their architecture are needed. In particular, the formal methods community is asked to contribute with well-founded approaches that enable specification and modelling of crucial aspects of the novel characteristics of CPS that are not addressed by conventional techniques. These characteristics include context and environment as well as the already mentioned different levels of interoperability (see Fig. 8).

In order to improve present-day engineering concepts and competences, broad initiatives in the following areas are needed:

- user-centered and participatory, virtual methods for the collection, the design and the evaluation of requirements (see, e. g., [ABB+09, EBJ03, MOS08]),
- comprehensive and integrated human-system models (see, e. g., [FFM05, Soc07, Soc07]),
- integrated and interoperable system architectures and domain models (see [Sch04, TOG09, NAF07]),
- domain engineering and system management including requirements traceability (see, e. g., [LLYL08, AZM09, PBvdL05b]),
- quality engineering at every level of development,
- living labs and controlled fields for experimentation.

Domain engineering involves the acquisition of domain-specific knowledge as a foundation for the development and the evolution of systems, products and services within a domain. This includes methods of requirements analysis and modelling, and also design and modelling of generic architectures for product families, the conception of reusable components, functions and services of the architecture, as well as the evolution of the domain, of the architecture and of implementation models. Particularly significant for the domain engineering of CPS are the definition of appropriate domain models (inclusive scoping), the development of interoperable architecture and composition patterns, suitable tailoring and reuse principles, and the management of complex domain and application platforms. In addition to the issue of evolution of CPS application architectures and platforms, it is important to develop models, methods and procedures for the engineering of autonomous, self-organising and learning systems. With regard to the engineering of quality five approaches can be distinguished: the transcendent, the product-based, the user-based, the manufacturing-based, and the value-based ones; see [Gar84]. The quality of a product or a service is therefore not uniformly determined: it is certainly the result of many comparisons and cost-benefit considerations, both in the supply chain as well as among users. Today's quality in use and quality of service criteria are not aligned with the new challenges pose by the networked intelligent technology of CPS. Rather, advanced quality models and integrated methods of validation and verification, interdisciplinary and integrated research efforts, as well as social debate and interactive evolution of technology and society are necessary.

Non-functional Requirements and Privacy Protection. In the following the challenges are analysed that need to be faced in order to ensure the observance of non-functional requirements in terms of safety/security, validation/verification and privacy protection. Those challenges are about features of systems that are relevant for the safe use of CPS under specific conditions.

Major success factors of CPS are their usability, transparency, controllability and dependability for users that sustain the claim of self-determination. The observation (compliance) of non-functional requirements, like for instance trustworthiness, reliability, availability, confidentiality, integrity and maintainability, constitutes an extreme difficult task. An essential question here is raised by the dependability of CPS, which may (help to) control delicate and complex situations, in which e.g. human lives are at risk, while having incomplete or uncertain information; this is especially critical if the decisions must be taken in real time. Sensible criteria must therefore be codified in fast algorithms that make use of reliable communications. Previous works addressing these subjects are, e. g., [CES10, ISO11]. CPS may moreover access, manage and/or transmit sensitive data. As computer systems and networks become more capable, their security also becomes more vulnerable. Ubiquitous distributed systems, like ad hoc networks of handheld computers, sensor networks for directly interacting with the world, and radio-frequency identification (RFID) tags which instantiate real-world objects with elements in our virtual computer systems, face security challenges. Security properties can be distilled to a core set, including confidentiality meaning secrecy of communication between parties, integrity in the sense that data has not been modified by an unauthorised party, authenticity which ensures that a message originated from a known other party, etc. Works on these matters include [ALRL04, BSI10, ABCS05, CMK+11, HV08, MOS08, WS10].

By dependability usually a combination of classical aspects concerning safety and security is understood, typically comprising functional safety, reliability, availability, confidentiality, integrity, maintainability. Crucial for dependability are the aspects safety, security and maintainability, especially significant because of the longevity of CPS. To this end, steady mechanisms are necessary for maintenance, servicing and development at runtime as well as integrated view of operational security and data integrity. On the one hand, current mechanisms for the servicing, maintenance and development provide procedures for the exchange of system components without taking a whole system out of service (for example in telecommunications). However, in general no procedures are provided for examining the impact on the safety and security requirements, and thus no aspects of "safety@runtime" and "security@runtime" are addressed. Today only a small degree of self reflection and self documentation of systems can be found, for example in machinery and plant engineering. On the other hand, methods for guaranteeing safety and data integrity share techniques like for instance identification of threats and definition of protection goals and protection levels, the combination into an integrated approach is nevertheless still missing.

Security is an issue that needs be considered during development of CPS (secure by design) and during operation as well. This raises questions with respect not only to systems engineering but also to systems characteristics. In this regard, efficient and lightweight cryptographic algorithms and protocols, component protection by dedicated security hardware, secure execution environments, procedures for determining the trustworthiness of other CPS, security engineering for CPS, security management, new methods for test and analysis are indispensable.

Regarding (functional) safety, today's technologies offering limited support for robustness and fault tolerance are multicore processors, component description and testing at runtime, cross-platforms with integrated high-quality safety/security mechanisms, advanced standards of development and of safety/security regulations, scalable security concepts and theories.

Privacy protection is defined in [Wes67] by "the claim of individuals, groups, or institutions to determine for themselves when, how, and to what extent information about them is communicated to others"; see also [RBB+08]. Thus, an essential security standard to be observed by CPS is personal data protection. Privacy protection observance by CPS should be guaranteed by design (cf. [Cav09, RB11]). The protection goals identified are intervenability, unlinkability, and transparency; see [HT12]. By intervenability it is understood that the persons concerned actually have the possibility to exercise their rights. Data is unlinkable when it is impossible to gather information from different sources and to infer out of this information further facts worthy of protection. A system is transparent to the persons concerned as well as the persons who run it if its functionality and its effect are intelligible to a sufficient grade and, moreover, provided those persons can retrieve the data available to the system with reasonable expenditure. Other thoughts on these topics can be found in, e. g., [Bra00, CMPB03, Cav09, FHDH+11, KSWK10, RBB+08, RB11, RP09, Sch07a, Wes67, WMKP10], some regulations can be found in [Eur50, Eur95, Eur02, Eur09].

5 Social Challenges

CPS can only unfold their full benefit and be given favourable response if they can seamlessly adapt to different contexts of use and safely integrate in these contexts, and also address the needs of users and customers, who must experience those systems and services as manageable and trustworthy. (It cannot be ruled out that existing regulations concerning liability and privacy protection be revised and updated to the new facts and circumstances.[1]) But it also happens that the requirements of customers and markets are difficult to assess and subject of continuous shifts and changes due to the diversity and dynamics of social transformation, which itself is influenced by the progress of ICT among other factors.

One of the biggest challenges for devising useful and widely accepted CPS is the design of a suitable human-system cooperation. This goes far beyond ordinary man-machine interaction. There is quite a number of criteria to be fulfilled by the interface of CPS to their users: it must be appropriate for the task the CPS has to perform and also manageable, it must explain itself and be tailorable at the same time, it must answer

---

[1] With respecto to liability, especially to functional safety but also to security, existing regulations (including [IEC10]) do not cope with those integration capabilities, substantially limiting design, implementation, commissioning, and maintenance of CPS. These approaches often achieve dependability by limiting access to the system, and thus contract essential properties of CPS.

the user's expectation and learn from the user's behaviour, and it must be fault tolerant. These features must moreover coexist with additional properties: a CPS must be aware of and assess its context of use, its state and the user's situation, it must be acquainted of other CPS with which it can or even must interact and share its own control, and it must not overstrain users who a priori show dissimilar characteristics. And as if that were not enough, some CPS must be open and easily extendable and connectable; cf. mobile apps' markets.

Considerations regarding human-system cooperation are driven by the increasing complexity of systems, and furthermore draw our attention to the so-called human factors. These are physical or cognitive properties of humans that influence functioning of technological systems as well as human-environment equilibria. The understanding of human capability can help the development of systems that are ergonomic, i.e., that optimise human well-being and overall system performance. The study of human factors resorts to many disciplines including anthropometry, physiology, sociology and psychology. Such considerations lead to the conclusion that inter- and transdisciplinary research and development are absolutely necessary.

In addition, no special skills or specific training can be demanded of CPS users. For instance, not every car driver can always be trained in the latest version of a route planning service. In order to avoid any danger that can arise due to inexperienced use of CPS, concepts for intuitive and transparent user interaction are required that ensure a secure shared control.

Particularly critical because fatiguing for the user are systems, or more precisely interfaces, that operate in different modes; see e.g. [LPS+97, Wey06, Sch07b]. It may frequently happen that the user forgets what state the interface is in, performs an action that is appropriate to a different mode, and gets an unexpected and undesired response.[2] That is, reality and mental model behave diversely, and this can moreover be the case in relation to a safety aspect. A mode error can be quite startling and disorienting as the user copes with the sudden violation of his/her expectations. This has an impact not only on the user experience with the interface; the violation of his/her expectations can have drastic consequences, especially in the application of safety-critical and highly automated systems like aircrafts. For these reasons, modes are often disfavoured.

A further topic to be considered is the fact that there surely will exist individuals that do not want to or cannot afford the new technologies. A meaningful road traffic management, for instance, must be operable even if there are vehicles driving out there that are not networked. It will moreover be undesirable if fellow citizen feel marginalised because of not having access to CPS; see e.g. [CSH04].

Distributed control of systems raises some questions. For example systems, which differ in the nature of their coordination (central and closed vs. decentralised and open) and must cooperate, in some situations may stay in conflict to each other. Also the governance of hybrid systems, that is, of systems distributedly handled by humans and by machines, may face the dilemma of optimisation vs. fairness; e. g., traffic management in cities or energy distribution and control in smart energy nets (see [CW07, KPM11,

---

[2] A very simple example is given by caps lock key, which is a common source of mode errors. Very annoying are modes that do not or only counter-intuitively allow to restore the old system state.

Ram03, RSS02b, Sch11]). The design of CPS and the analysis of consequences of their use should be subject of participatory discussion.

Concerning economical ecosystems, open platform strategies with transparent architectures, open interfaces, and experimental living labs are required—in particular, in order to use the increased potential for innovation through interactive and participatory involvement of customers, new external technology-based companies and developers communities, but also in order to bring the essential quality and acceptance requirements of the customer off such that individual usefulness and usability are met as well as protection and security of the systems is provided with transparent, trustworthy and reliable structures. A platform strategy, as opposed to a product strategy, "[. . .] requires an external ecosystem to generate complementary innovations and build 'positive feedback' between the complements and the platform" and, moreover, "the effect is much greater potential for growth and innovation than a single firm can generate alone"; see [Cus10].

6 Conclusions

We have presented short overview of the study that has been worked out during 2010/11. The study takes a very comprehensive view, starting from what we can expect from technology and the implied changes in business, society, legislation, and politics. The result of the study is that the convergence of embedded systems, global networks, business web and interactive CPS' service crecation by users, will bring a new wave of innovations and changes.[3] We expect disruptive changes in business and application domains. Therefore, it is of utmost significance to discuss the consequences for research and development of ICT systems.

The smart mobility scenario describes the future of mobility of our society. Prerequisites are a comprehensive ascertainment of environment and the integration of vehicles, transportation infrastructure and individuals. This creates innovative ways to consider both individual needs as well as socio-political aspects and here to make contributions to, among other things, accident prevention, intelligent use of limited resources and reduction of environmental impact. Similar and likewise desirable consequences can be drawn from other scenarios as e.g. smart grid.

Summarising, engineering challenges include

– human-system cooperation, usability and safety:
  • shared control, transparency/controllability, integrated models for human-machine interaction, cooperative and strategic task and action modelling, conflict and reconciliation handling;
– formal and integrated system and architecture models:
  • integrated requirements, context, domain, system modelling,
  • hybrid system and architecture: analog-digital control models, human-machine, socio-technical interaction and network models,
  • interoperable reference architectures, domains and platforms;

---

[3] Those could constitute (or be aligned with) the much cited and discussed sixth wave of innovation; see e.g. [Kle90, Mar80, SV03, Šmi10].

- expanded quality modelling and engineering standards:
  - models for quality in use, quality of service, compliance, technical and organisational models and methods for quality assurance,
  - elicitation and negotiation of acceptance requirements and corresponding system concepts (e. g., governance and fairness).

Social challenges imply new engineering strategies, so

- acceptance, which calls for participatory analysis and design of
  - systems and services that are manageable, tailorable, trustworthy, fault tolerant, accountable,
  - capable of learning from user's behaviour,
  - self-determined usable and controllable by the users,
  - compatible with non-networked systems and services (as well as dropouts);
- inter-, transdisciplinary and explorative research and development, which require integrated models and methods of virtual engineering;
- interactive innovations by means of economic ecosystems and platforms, regional and international innovation systems, which
  - integrate different life-cycles, business models and engineering cultures of CPS' components and services,
  - find complementary concepts of competition, cooperation and distributes value creation.

The great opportunity opened by CPS for industry, business and economy in general, cannot be missed. As stated in [HW11], "The cultural change must take place mainly on the provider side. The willingness to make radical changes in business processes or even new business models can only come from here. If the market forces them, then it is usually too late." Inter- and transdisciplinarity, value creation and innovation in corporate networks and in business ecosystems are required that face the above challenges and take a leading role.

Acknowledgement. The authors are indebted to Bernhard Schätz for his comments on a previous version of this work and particularly for his support in the illustration of the evolution of the braking system in the automotive domain.

References

[ABB⁺09]   Achatz, R., Beetz, K., Broy, M., Dämbkes, H., Damm, W., Grimm, K., Liggesmeyer, P.: Nationale Roadmap Embedded Systems. ZVEI (Zentralverband Elektrotechnik und Elektronikindustrie e. V.), Kompetenzzentrum Embedded Software & Systems, Frankfurt/Main (December 2009), https://www.zvei.org/fileadmin/user_upload/Forschung_Bildung/NRMES.pdf

[ABCS05]   Anderson, R., Bond, M., Clulow, J., Skorobogatov, S.: Cryptographic processors – a survey. Technical Report UCAM-CL-TR-641, University of Cambridge, Computer Laboratory (August 2005),
http://www.cl.cam.ac.uk/techreports/UCAM-CL-TR-641.pdf

[ABD⁺10] Armenio, F., Barthel, H., Dietrich, P., Duker, J., Floerkemeier, C., Garrett, J., Harrison, M., Hogan, B., Mitsugi, J., Preishuber-Pfluegl, J., Ryaboy, O., Sarma, S., Suen, K.K., Williams, J.: The EPCglobal Architecture Framework. In: Traub, K. (ed.) Technical report, GS1 (2010) (final version 1.4 approved December 15, 2010), http://www.gs1.org/gsmp/kc/epcglobal/architecture/architecture_1_4-framework-20101215.pdf

[ALRL04] Avižienis, A., Laprie, J.-C., Randell, B., Landwehr, C.: Basic Concepts and Taxonomy of Dependable and Secure Computing. IEEE Transactions on Dependable and Secure Computing 1(1), 11–33 (2004)

[Arb11] Arbeitskreis Multicore. Relevanz eines Multicore-Ökosystems für künftige Embedded Systems: Positionspapier zur Bedeutung, Bestandsaufnahme und Potentialermittlung der Multicore-Technologie für den Industrie- und Forschungsstandort Deutschland (December 2011), http://www.bicc-net.de/workspace/uploads/subfeatures/downloads/positionspapier_multicore_oekosys-1323952449.pdf

[AUT10] AUTOSAR – Demonstration of Integration of AUTOSAR into a MM/T/HMI ECU V1.0.0. Technical report, AUTOSAR (AUTomotive Open System ARchitecture) (2010), http://www.autosar.org/download/informaldocuments/AUTOSAR_TR_IntegrationintoMMTHMIECU.pdf

[AZM09] Aziz, R.A., Zowghi, D., McBride, T.: Towards a Classification of Requirements Relationships. In: 21st International Conference on Software Engineering & Knowledge Engineering (SEKE 2009, Proceedings), pp. 26–32. Knowledge Systems Institute Graduate School (2009)

[BBB⁺11] Baumgart, A., Böde, E., Büker, M., Damm, W., Ehmen, G., Gezgin, T., Henkler, S., Hungar, H., Josko, B., Oertel, M., Peikenkamp, T., Reinkemeier, P., Stierand, I., Weber, R.: Architecture modeling. Technical report, Oldenburger Forschungs- und Entwicklungsinstitut für Informatik (OFFIS) (March 2011)

[BCHM06] Bernon, C., Chevrier, V., Hilaire, V., Marrow, P.: Applications of self-organising multi-agent systems: An initial framework for comparison. Informatica 30(1), 73–82 (2006)

[Ber07] Berger, T.: Softwareproduktlinien-Entwicklung – Domain Engineering: Konzepte, Probleme und Lösungsansätze. Diplomarbeit, Universität Leipzig (April 2007)

[BGC⁺12] Broy, M., Geisberger, E., Cengarle, M.V., Keil, P., Niehaus, J., Thiel, C., Thönnißen-Fries, H.-J.: Cyber-Physical Systems: Innovationsmotor für Mobilität, Gesundheit, Energie und Produktion. acatech BEZIEHT POSITION, vol. 8. Springer, Berlin (2012), http://www.springer.com/computer/book/978-3-642-27566-1

[BGK⁺07] Broy, M., Geisberger, E., Kazmeier, J., Rudorfer, A., Beetz, K.: Ein Requirements-Engineering-Referenzmodell. Informatik Spektrum 30(3), 127–142 (2007)

[BHGZ09] Brand, L., Hülser, T., Grimm, V., Zweck, A.: Internet der Dinge: "Übersichtsstudie. Technical report, Zukünftige Technologien Consulting der VDI Technologiezentrum GmbH (March 2009), http://www.vdi.de/fileadmin/vdi_de/redakteur/dps_bilder/TZ/2009/Band%2080_IdD_komplett.pdf

[Bis07] Bishop, C.: Pattern Recognition and Machine Learning. Springer, New York (2007), Corr. 2nd printing

[BKS11]   Brecher, C., Kozielski, S., Schapp, L.: Integrative Produktionstechnik für Hochlohn-
            länder, pp. 47–70. Springer, Berlin (2011),
            http://www.acatech.de/fileadmin/user_upload/Baumstruktur
            _upload/Baumstruktur_nach_Website/Acatech/root/de/
            Publikationen/acatech_diskutiert/acatech_diskutiert
            _Wertschoepfung_WEB.pdf

[Bra00]   Brands, S. (ed.): Rethinking Public Key Infrastructures and Digital Certificates;
            Building in Privacy. MIT Press, Cambridge (2000)

[BS00]   Bussmann, S., Schild, K.: Self-Organizing Manufacturing Control: An Industrial
            Application of Agent Technology. In: Fourth International Conference on Multi
            Agent Systems (Proceedings), pp. 87–94 (2000)

[BSI10]   Leitfaden Informationssicherheit – IT-Grundschutz kompakt. Techni-
            cal Report BSI-Bro10/311, Referat 114 Sicherheitsmanagement und IT-
            Grundschutz, Bundesamt für Sicherheit in der Informationstechnik (2010),
            https://www.bsi.bund.de/SharedDocs/Downloads/DE/BSI
            /Grundschutz/Leitfaden/GS-Leitfaden_pdf.pdf?_blob=
            publicationFile

[Cav09]   Cavoukian, A.: Privacy by Design. Technical report, Office of the Information and
            Privacy Commissioner, Ontario (2009),
            http://www.privacybydesign.ca/content/uploads/2010/03/
            PrivacybyDesignBook.pdf

[CES10]   Definition and exemplification of RSL and RMM. Deliverable D_SP2_R2.1_M1,
            Cost-efficient methods and processes for safety relevant embedded systems (CE-
            SAR) (April 2010),
            http://www.cesarproject.eu/fileadmin/user_upload/
            CESAR_D_SP2_R2.1_M1_v1.000.pdf

[CMK+11]   Checkoway, S., McCoy, D., Kantor, B., Anderson, D., Shacham, H., Savage, S.,
            Koscher, K., Czeskis, A., Roesner, F., Kohno, T.: Comprehensive Experimental
            Analyses of Automotive Attack Surfaces. In: 20th USENIX Security Symposium
            (Proceedings), pp. 77–92 (2011),
            http://www.autosec.org/pubs/cars-usenixsec2011.pdf

[CMPB03]   Mont, M.C., Pearson, S., Bramhall, P.: Towards Accountable Management of Iden-
            tity and Privacy: Sticky Policies and Enforceable Tracing Services. In: 14th Interna-
            tional Workshop on Database and Expert Systems Applications (DEXA 2003, Pro-
            ceedings), pp. 377–382. IEEE Computer Society (September 2003), Long version
            http://www.hpl.hp.com/techreports/2003/HPL-2003-49.pdf

[CN08]   Cusumano, M., Nobeoka, K.: Thinking Beyond Lean: how multi-project manage-
            ment is transforming product development at Toyota and other companies. In: MIT
            International Motor Vehicle Program. Free Press (May 2008)

[CPS08]   Cyber-Physical Systems Summit "Holistic Approaches to Cyber-Physical Integra-
            tion". Report, CPS Week (April 2008),
            http://iccps2012.cse.wustl.edu/_doc/CPS_Summit_Report
            .pdf

[CSH04]   Capurro, R., Scheule, R., Hausmanninger, T. (eds.): Vernetzt gespalten: Der Digital
            Divide in ethischer Perspektive. Wilhelm Fink, Paderborn (2004)

[Cus10]   Cusumano, M.: Staying Power: Six Enduring Principles for Managing Strategy and
            Innovation in an Uncertain World. Oxford University Press, Oxford (2010)

[CW03]   Christaller, T., Wehner, J. (eds.): Autonome Maschinen. Westdeutscher Verlag,
            Wiesbaden (2003)

[CW07]   Cramer, S., Weyer, J.: Interaktion, Risiko und Governance in hybriden Systemen.
           In: Dolata, Werle [DW07], pp. 267–286,
           http://www.techniksoziologie-dortmund.de/Mitarbeiter/
           Cramer/K%C3%B6lnpdf.pdf
[Dmi04]   Dmitriev, S.: Language Oriented Programming: The Next Programming Paradigm.
           onBoard (November 1, 2004),
           http://www.jetbrains.com/mps/docs/Language_Oriented_
           Programming.pdf
[DoD09a]   Department of Defense Architecture Framework Version 2.0 (DoDAF V2.0) –
           Volume 1: Introduction, Overview, and Concepts – Manager's Guide. Technical
           report, Department of Defense Chief Information Officer (May 2009),
           http://cio-nii.defense.gov/docs/DoDAF%20V2%20-
           %20Volume%201.pdf
[DoD09b]   Department of Defense Architecture Framework Version 2.0 (DoDAF V2.0) –
           Volume 2: Architectural Data and Models – Architect's Guide. Technical report,
           Department of Defense Chief Information Officer (May 2009),
           http://cio-nii.defense.gov/docs/DoDAF%20V2%20-%20Volume
           %202.pdf
[DoD09c]   Department of Defense Architecture Framework Version 2.0 (DoDAF V2.0) – Vol-
           ume 3: DoDAF Meta-model, Physical Exchange Specification – Developer's Guide.
           Technical report, Department of Defense Chief Information Officer (May 2009),
           http://cio-nii.defense.gov/docs/DoDAF%20V2%20-%20Volume
           %203.pdf
[Dra10]   Drath, R. (ed.): Datenaustausch in der Anlagenplanung mit AutomationML: Integra-
           tion von CAEX, PLCopen XML und COLLADA. VDI-Buch. Springer, Heidelberg
           (2010)
[DW07]   Dolata, U., Werle, R. (eds.): Gesellschaft und die Macht der Technik:
           Sozioökonomischer und institutioneller Wandel durch Technisierung. Schriften aus
           dem Max-Planck-Institut für Gesellschaftsforschung Köln, vol. 58. Campus Verlag,
           Frankfurt (2007)
[EBJ03]   Endsley, M., Bolte, B., Jones, D.: Designing for Situation Awareness: An Approach
           to User-Centered Design. CRC Press (July 2003)
[Eur50]   European Convention on Human Rights (Convention for the Protection of Human
           Rights and Fundamental Freedoms. Article 8 "Right to respect for private and
           family life" (as amended by the provisions of Protocol No. 14 (CETS no. 194) as
           from its entry into force on June 1, 2010 (November 4, 1950),
           http://www.echr.coe.int/NR/rdonlyres/D5CC24A7-DC13-4318
           -B457-5C9014916D7A/0/CONVENTION_ENG_WEB.pdf
[Eur95]   European Community. Directive 95/49/DC of the European Parliament and of the
           Council of 24 October 1995 on the protection of individuals with regard to the
           processing of personal data and on the free movement of such data. Official Journal
           of the European Communities L 281, 31–50 (1995),
           http://eur-lex.europa.eu/LexUriServ/LexUriServ.do?uri=
           OJ:L:1995:281:0031:0050:EN:PDF

[Eur02]   European Community. Directive 2002/58/EC of the European Parliament and of the Council of 12 July 2002 concerning the processing of personal data and the protection of privacy in the electronic communications sector (Directive on privacy and electronic communications). Official Journal of the European Communities L 201, 37–47 (2002), http://eur-lex.europa.eu/LexUriServ/LexUriServ.do?uri= OJ:L:2002:201:0037:0047:EN:PDF

[Eur09]   European Union. Directive 2009/136/EC of the European Parliament and of the Council of 25 November 2009 amending Directive 2002/22/EC on universal service and users' rights relating to electronic communications networks and services, Directive 2002/58/EC concerning the processing of personal data and the protection of privacy in the electronic communications sector and Regulation (EC) No 2006/2004 on cooperation [...] for the enforcement of consumer protection laws. Official Journal of the European Union L 337, 11–36 (2009), http://eur-lex.europa.eu/LexUriServ/LexUriServ.do?uri= OJ:L:2009:337:0011:0036:EN:PDF

[FFM05]   Fischer, K., Florian, M., Malsch, T. (eds.): Socionics. LNCS (LNAI), vol. 3413. Springer, Heidelberg (2005)

[FHDH⁺11] Fischer-Hübner, S., Duquenoy, P., Hansen, M., Leenes, R., Zhang, G. (eds.): Privacy and Identity Management for Life. IFIP AICT, vol. 352. Springer, Heidelberg (2011)

[FN71]   Fikes, R., Nilsson, N.: STRIPS: A new approach to the application of theorem proving to problem solving. Artificial Intelligence 2(3-4), 189–208 (1971)

[Gar84]   Garvin, D.: What does "product quality" really mean? MIT Sloan Management Review, 25–45 (1984)

[GBB⁺06]   Geisberger, E., Broy, M., Berenbach, B., Kazmeier, J., Paulish, D., Rudorfer, A.: Requirements Engineering Reference Model (REM). Technical Report TUM-I0618, Technische Universität München (November 2006)

[GBC⁺12]   Geisberger, E., Broy, M., Cengarle, M.V., Keil, P., Niehaus, J., Thiel, C., Thönnißen-Fries, H.-J.: agendaCPS: Integrierte Forschungsagenda Cyber-Physical Systems. Springer, Berlin (2012), http://www.fortiss.org/ fileadmin/user_upload/downloads/agendaCPS_Studie.pdf

[Gif07]   Gifford, C. (ed.): The Hitchhiker's Guide to Manufacturing Operations Management: ISA-95 Best Practices Book 1.0. ISA (2007)

[GMA09]   Roadmap "Prozess-Sensoren 2015+". Technical report, NAMUR und VDI/VDE-Gesellschaft Mess- und Automatisierungstechnik (GMA) (November 2009), http://www.vdi.de/fileadmin/vdi_de/redakteur_dateien/ gma_dateien/Prozess-Sensoren_2015+.pdf

[GMP⁺06]   Geib, C., Mourão, K., Petrick, R., Pugeault, N., Steedman, M., Krueger, N., Wörgötter, F.: Object Action Complexes as an Interface for Planning and Robot Control. In: Humanoids 2006 Workshop Towards Cognitive Humanoid Robots, Proceedings (2006)

[GP09]   Garside, R., Pighetti, J.: Integrating modular avionics: A new role emerges. Aerospace and Electronic Systems Magazine (IEEE) 24(3), 31–34 (2009)

[GS07]   Geisberger, E., Schätz, B.: Modellbasierte Anforderungsanalyse mit AutoRAID. Informatik – Forschung und Entwicklung 21(3-4), 231–242 (2007)

[HSMS07]   Hirvonen, J., Sallinen, M., Maula, H., Suojanen, M.: Sensor Networks Roadmap. Research notes 2381, VTT Tiedotteita (2007), http://www.vtt.fi/inf/pdf/tiedotteet/2007/T2381.pdf

[HT12]   Hansen, M., Thiel, C.: Cyber-Physical Systems und Privatsphären-Schutz. Datenschutz und Datensicherheit (DuD) 36(1) (2012)

[Hua11]   Huang, J.-D.: Kinerehab: a kinect-based system for physical rehabilitation: a pilot study for young adults with motor disabilities. In: 13th International ACM SIGAC-CESS Conference on Computers and Accessibility (ASSETS 2011, Proceedings), pp. 319–320 (2011)

[HV08]   Hogg, S., Vyncke, E.: IPv6 Security: Information assurance for the next-generation Internet Protocol. Cisco Press, Indianapolis (2008)

[HW11]   Heuser, L., Wahlster, W. (eds.): Internet der Dienste. acatech DISKUTIERT. Springer,   Berlin   (2011),   http://www.acatech.de/fileadmin/
user_upload/Baumstruktur_nach_Website/Acatech/root/de/
Publikationen/acatech_diskutiert/acatech_Diskutiert
_Internet-der-Dienste_WEB_02.pdf

[IEC10]   Functional safety of electrical/electronic/programmable electronic safety-related systems. Technical Report IEC/TR 61508 Part 0-7, International Electrotechnical Commission (IEC) (2010)

[ISO11]   Road vehicles – Functional safety – Part 1: Vocabulary. Technical Report ISO 26262-1:2011, International Organization for Standardization (ISO) (November 2011),
http://www.iso.org/iso/iso_catalogue/catalogue_tc/
catalogue_detail.htm?csnumber=43464

[JSE+08]   Joordens, M., Shaneyfelt, T., Eega, S., Jaimes, A., Jamshidi, M.: Applications and prototype for system of systems swarm robotics. In: Systems, Man and Cybernetics, 2008 (SMC 2008, Proceedings) (2008)

[Kle90]   Kleinknecht, A.: Are there Schumpeterian waves of innovations? Cambridge Journal of Economics 14(1), 81–92 (1990)

[KNR+11]   Krewitt, W., Nienhaus, K., Roloff, N., Weeber, R., Reeg, M., Weimer-Jehle, W., Wassermann, S., Fuchs, G., Kast, T., Schmidt, B., Leprich, U., Hauser, E.: Analyse von Rahmenbedingungen für die Integration erneuerbarer Energien in die Strommärkte auf der Basis agentenbasierter Simulation (Abschlussbericht). Technical report, Deutsches Zentrum für Luft- und Raumfahrt e.V. (DLR), Inter-disziplinärer Forschungsschwerpunkt Risiko und nachhaltige Technikentwicklung (ZIRN), Thomas Kast Simulation Solutions, Institut für ZukunftsEnergieSysteme (IZES), gefördert mit Mitteln des Bundesministeriums für Umwelt, Naturschutz und Reaktorsicherheit unter dem Förderkennzeichen 0325015 (February 2011),
http://www.dlr.de/Portaldata/41/Resources/dokumente/st/
AMIRIS-Pilotvorhaben.pdf

[KPM11]   Koukoumidis, E., Peh, L.-S., Martonosi, M.: SignalGuru: leveraging mobile phones for collaborative traffic signal schedule advisory, pp. 127–140. ACM (2011)

[KS98]   Kotonya, G., Sommerville, I.: Requirements Engineering: Processes and Techniques. Wiley (September 1998)

[KS03]   Kalfoglou, Y., Schorlemmer, M.: Ontology mapping: The state of the art. The Knowledge Engineering Review 18(1), 1–31 (2003)

[KSWK10]   Könings, B., Schaub, F., Weber, M., Kargl, F.: Towards territorial privacy in smart environments. In: Genesereth, M., Vogl, R., Williams, M.-A. (eds.) Intelligent Information Privacy Management Symposium (AAAI Spring Symposium, Proceedings), pp. 113–118, Technical Report SS-10-05. Stanford University (March 2010),
http://www.aaai.org/ocs/index.php/SSS/SSS10/paper/view/
1043/1496

[Lat87]   Latour, B.: Science in Action: How to Follow Scientists and Engineers through Society? Open University Press (1987)

[Len97]   Lenat, D.: From 2001 to 2001: Common Sense and the Mind of HAL, pp. 305–332. MIT Press, Cambridge (1997)

[Lev95]   Leveson, N.: Safeware: System Safety and Computers. Addison-Wesley (September 1995)

[LLYL08]   Li, Y., Li, J., Yang, Y., Li, M.: Requirement-Centric Traceability for Change Impact Analysis: A Case Study. In: Wang, Q., Pfahl, D., Raffo, D.M. (eds.) ICSP 2008. LNCS, vol. 5007, pp. 100–111. Springer, Heidelberg (2008)

[LPS⁺97]   Leveson, N., Denise Pinnel, L., Sandys, S.D., Koga, S., Reese, J.D.: Analyzing Software Specifications for Mode Confusion Potential. In: Workshop on Human Error and System Development (Proceedings), pp. 132–146 (March 1997), http://sunnyday.mit.edu/papers/glascow.pdf

[Mar80]   Marchetti, C.: Society as a Learning System: Discovery, Invention, and Innovation Cycles Revisited. Technological Forecasting and Social Change 18(4), 267–282 (1980)

[Mat03]   Mattern, F. (ed.): Total vernetzt: Szenarien einer informatisierten Welt (7. Berliner Kolloquium der Gottlieb Daimler- und Karl Benz-Stiftung, Tagungsband). Xpert Press, Springer, Heidelberg (2003)

[MCS11]   International Workshop on Multiple Classifier Systems (MCS, Proceedings). LNCS. Springer (2000-2011)

[MLD10]   Mahnke, W., Leitner, S.-H., Damm, M.: OPC Unified Architecture. Springer (2010)

[MM06]   Marrón, P.J., Minder, D. (eds.): Embedded WiSeNts Research Roadmap. Logos Verlag, Berlin (2006), ftp://ftp.informatik.uni-stuttgart.de/pub/library/ncstrl.ustuttgart_fi/BOOK-2006-03/BOOK-2006-03.pdf

[MOS08]   Pilot gaze performance in critical flight phases and during taxiing. Technical report, Deutsches Zentrum für Luft- und Raumfahrt (DLR), Results from the Project MOSES (More Operational Flight Security through increased Situation Awareness) (July 2008), http://www.dlr.de/fl/en/Portaldata/14/Resources/dokumente/abt27/MOSES_results.pdf

[MVK06]   Monostori, L., Váncza, J., Kumara, S.R.T.: Agent-Based Systems for Manufacturing. CIRP Annals - Manufacturing Technology 55(2), 697–720 (2006)

[NAF07]   NATO Architecture Framework Version 3.0 (NAF V2.0). Technical report, North Atlantic Treaty Organization (NATO) (November 2007), http://www.nhqc3s.nato.int/ARCHITECTURE/_docs/NAF_v3/ANNEX1.pdf

[Nor96]   Norman, D.: Dinge des Alltags: Gutes Design und Psychologie für Gebrauchsgegenstände. Campus Verlag (March 1996)

[Osb03]   Osborne, M.: An Introduction to Game Theory. Oxford University Press (August 2003)

[PB03]   Petrick, R.P.A., Bacchus, F.: Reasoning with Conditional Plans in the Presence of Incomplete Knowledge. In: ICAPS 2003 Workshop on Planning under Uncertainty and Incomplete Information' (Proceedings), Trento, pp. 96–102. Università di Trento (June 2003)

[PBvdL05a] Pohl, K., Böckle, G., van der Linden, F.: Software Product Line Engineering: Foundations, Principles and Techniques. Springer (August 2005)

[PBvdL05b] Pohl, K., Böckle, G., van der Linden, F.: Software Product Line Engineering: Foundations, Principles and Techniques. Springer (2005)

[Rab08]   Rabaey, J.: A brand new wireless day, p. 1. IEEE Computer Society Press, Los Alamitos (2008)

[Ram03]   Rammert, W.: Technik in Aktion: Verteiltes Handeln in soziotechnischen Konstellationen. In: Christaller, Wehner [CW03], pp. 289–315

[RB11]   Rost, M., Bock, K.: Privacy By Design und die Neuen Schutzziele. Datenschutz und
            Datensicherheit (DuD) 35(1), 30–35 (2011)
[RBB+08]   Roussopoulos, M., Beslay, L., Bowden, C., Finocchiaro, G., Hansen, M., Langhein-
            rich, M., Le Grand, G., Tsakona, K.: Technology-induced challenges in Privacy &
            Data Protection in Europe. Technical report, Ad Hoc Working Group on Privacy
            & Technology, European Network and Information Security Agency (ENISA)
            (October 2008),
            http://www.enisa.europa.eu/act/rm/files/deliverables/
            technology-induced-challenges-in-privacy-data-protection
            -in-europe/at_download/fullReport
[RLM+06]   Rubin, D., Lewis, S., Mungall, C., Misra, S., Westerfield, M., Ashburner, M., Sim,
            I., Chute, C., Solbrig, H., Storey, M.-A., Smith, B., Day-Richter, J., Noy, N., Musen,
            M.: National Center for Biomedical Ontology: Advancing Biomedicine through
            Structured Organization of Scientific Knowledge. OMICS: A Journal of Integrative
            Biology 10(2), 185–198 (2006),
            http://www.liebertonline.com/doi/pdf/10.1089/omi.2006.
            10.185
[RN09]   Russell, S., Norvig, P.: Artificial Intelligence: A Modern Approach, 3rd edn. Prentice
            Hall (December 2009)
[RP09]   Rost, M., Pfitzmann, A.: Datenschutz-Schutzziele – revisited. Datenschutz und
            Datensicherheit (DuD) 33(6), 353–358 (2009)
[RSS02a]   Rammert, W., Schulz-Schaeffer, I. (eds.): Können Maschinen handeln?: Soziolo-
            gische Beiträge zum Verhältnis von Mensch und Technik. Campus Wissenschaft,
            Frankfurt/Main (2002)
[RSS02b]   Rammert, W., Schulz-Schaeffer, I.: Technik und Handeln – Wenn soziales Handeln
            sich auf menschliches Verhalten und technische Abläufe verteilt. In: Rammert, W.,
            Schulz-Schaefer, I. [RSS02a], pp. 11–64
[Sad11]   Sadri, F.: Logic-Based Approaches to Intention Recognition. In: Chong, N.-Y., Mas-
            trogiovanni, F. (eds.) Handbook of Research on Ambient Intelligence and Smart En-
            vironments: Trends and Perspectives, pp. 346–375. IGI Global (May 2011)
[SAL+03]   Stankovic, J., Abdelzaher, T., Lu, C., Sha, L., Hou, J.: Real-time communication
            and coordination in embedded sensor networks. Proceedings of the IEEE Real-Time
            Systems 91(7), 1002–1022 (2003)
[SB01]   Sundermeyer, K., Bussmann, S.: Einführung der Agententechnologie in einem pro-
            duzierenden Unternehmen – Ein Erfahrungsbericht. Wirtschaftsinformatik 43(2),
            135–142 (2001)
[SC01]   Sage, A., Cuppan, C.: On the Systems Engineering and Management of Systems
            of Systems and Federations of Systems. Information-Knowledge-Systems Manage-
            ment 2(4), 325–345 (2001)
[Sch04]   Schätz, B.: AutoFocus – Mastering the Complexity. In: Kordon, F., Lemoine, M.
            (eds.) Formal Methods for Embedded Distributed Systems: How to Master the Com-
            plexity, ch. 7, pp. 215–257. Kluwer Academic Publishers (2004)
[Sch07a]   Schaar, P.: Das Ende der Privatsphäre: Der Weg in die "Uberwachungsgesellschaft.
            C. Bertelsmann (September 2007)
[Sch07b]   Schulz, A.: Driving without awareness – Folgen herabgesetzter Aufmerksamkeit im
            Straßenverkehr. VDM Verlag Dr. Müller (2007)
[Sch11]   Schwan, B.: Grüne Welle dank Smartphone. Technical report, Technology Review
            (Oktober 7, 2011),
            http://www.heise.de/tr/artikel/Gruene-Welle-dank-
            Smartphone-1353408.html

[Šmi10]   Šmihula, D.: Waves of technological innovations and the end of the information revolution. Journal of Economics and International Finance 2(4), 58–67 (2010)

[SMS11]   Schleipen, M., Münnemann, A., Sauer, O.: Interoperabilität von Manufacturing Execution Systems (MES): Durchgängige Kommunikation in unterschiedlichen Dimensionen der Informationstechnik in produzierenden Unternehmen. Automatisierungstechnik 59(7), 413–425 (2011),
           http://www.iosb.fraunhofer.de/servlet/is/4893/
           auto.2011.0936.pdf?command=downloadContent&filename=
           auto.2011.0936.pdf

[Soc07]   Special section: Socionics. Journal of Artificial Societies and Social Simulation (January 2007),
           http://jasss.soc.surrey.ac.uk/10/1/contents.html

[SS11]   Stone, E., Skubic, M.: Evaluation of an Inexpensive Depth Camera for Passive In-Home Fall Risk Assessment. In: 5th International Conference on Pervasive Computing Technologies for Healthcare (PervasiveHealth 2011, Proceedings), pp. 71–77 (2011) (Best Paper Award),
           http://eldertech.missouri.edu/files/Papers/StoneE/
           Evaluation%20of%20an%20Inexpensive%20Depth%20Camera.pdf

[SV03]   Silverberg, G., Verspagen, B.: Breaking the waves: a Poisson regression approach to Schumpeterian clustering of basic innovations. Cambridge Journal of Economics 27(5), 671–693 (2003)

[Thi10]   Thiel, C.: Multiple classifier systems incorporating uncertainty. Verlag Dr. Hut, München (2010)

[TOG09]   TOGAF Version 9, Enterprise Edition. Technical report, The Open Group (February 2009),
           https://www2.opengroup.org/ogsys/jsp/publications/
           PublicationDetails.jsp?catalogno=g091

[Web02]   Webb, A.: Statistical Pattern Recognition, 2nd edn. John Wiley & Sons (October 2002)

[Wei00]   Weiss, G. (ed.): Multiagent Systems: A Modern Approach to Distributed Artificial Intelligence. MIT Press (July 2000)

[Wes67]   Westin, A.F.: Privacy and Freedom, 1st edn. Atheneum, New York (1967)

[Wey06]   Weyer, J.: Die Zukunft des Autos – das Auto der Zukunft. Wird der Computer den Menschen ersetzen? Soziologische Arbeitspapiere 14, Universität Dortmund (March 2006),
           http://www.wiso.tu-dortmund.de/wiso/is/Medienpool/
           Arbeitspapiere/ap-soz14.pdf

[WMKP10]   Wiedersheim, B., Ma, Z., Kargl, F., Papadimitratos, P.: Privacy in Inter-Vehicular Networks: Why simple pseudonym change is not enough. In: 7th International Conference on Wireless On-demand Network Systems and Services (WONS 2010, Proceedings), pp. 176–183. IEEE Computer Society Press (2010)

[Woo09]   Wooldridge, M.: An Introduction to Multi Agent Systems, 2nd edn. John Wiley & Sons (May 2009)

[WS10]   Wood, A., Stankovic, J.: Security of Distributed, Ubiquitous, and Embedded Computing Platforms. In: Voeller, J. (ed.) Wiley Handbook of Science and Technology for Homeland Security, John Wiley & Sons (March 2010)

The Global Financial Markets:
An Ultra-Large-Scale Systems Perspective

Dave Cliff[1] and Linda Northrop[2]

[1] UK Large Scale Complex IT System Initiative,
Department of Computer Science, University of Bristol, Bristol BS8 1UB, U.K.
dc@cs.bris.ac.uk
[2] Research, Technology, and System Solutions Program,
Software Engineering Institute, Carnegie-Mellon University, Pittsburgh PA 15213, USA
lmn@sei.cmu.edu

Abstract. We argue here that, in recent years, the world's financial markets have become a globally interconnected complex adaptive ultra-large-scale socio-technical system-of-systems, and that this has important consequences for how the financial markets should be engineered and managed in future. Major failures in the financial markets can now occur at super-human speeds, as was witnessed in the "Flash Crash" of May 6th 2010. Events such as the Flash Crash may become more commonplace in future, unless lessons are learned from other fields where complex adaptive socio-technical systems-of-systems have to be engineered for high-integrity, safety-critical applications. In this document we review the literature on failures in risky technology and high-integrity approaches to safety-critical SoS engineering. We conclude with an argument that, in the specific case of the global financial markets, there is an urgent need to develop major national strategic modeling and predictive simulation capabilities, comparable to national-scale meteorological monitoring and modeling capabilities. The intent here is not to predict the price-movements of particular financial instruments or asset classes, but rather to provide test-rigs for principled evaluation of systemic risk, estimating probability density functions over spaces of possible outcomes, and thereby identifying potentially high-consequence failure modes in the simulations, before they occur in real life, by which time it is typically too late.

Keywords: Large-scale complex IT systems, ultra-large-scale systems, financial markets, algorithmic trading, high-frequency trading, normalization of deviance, flash crash.

1   Introduction

For what events will the date of May 6th, 2010 be remembered? In Britain, there was a general election that day, which ousted the ruling Labour Party after 13 years and led to the formation of the UK's first coalition government since 1945. Nevertheless, it seems likely that in financial circles at least, May 6th will instead long be remembered for dramatic and unprecedented events that took place on the other side of the Atlantic, in the US capital markets. May 6th is the date of what is now widely known as the "Flash Crash".

On that day, in a period lasting roughly 30 minutes from approximately 2:30pm to 3:00pm EST, the US equity markets underwent an extraordinary upheaval: a sudden

R. Calinescu and D. Garlan (Eds.): Monterey Workshop 2012, LNCS 7539, pp. 29–70, 2012.
© Springer-Verlag Berlin Heidelberg 2012

catastrophic collapse followed by an equally unprecedented meteoric rise. In the space of only a few minutes, the Dow Jones Industrial Average dropped by over 600 points, representing the disappearance of more than 850 billion dollars of market value. In the course of this sudden downturn, the share-prices of several blue-chip multinational companies went haywire, with shares in companies that had previously been trading at a few tens of dollars plummeting to $0.01 in some instances, and rocketing to values of $100,000 in others. Seeing prices quoted by some major exchanges suddenly going crazy, other major exchange-operators declared "self-help" (that is, they invoked a regulation allowing them to no longer treat the price-feeds from the other exchanges as valid), thereby decoupling the trading on multiple venues that had previously been unified by the real-time exchange of reference price data.

Then as suddenly as this downturn occurred it reversed, and over the course of another few minutes most of the 600-point loss in the Dow was recovered, and share prices returned to levels within a few percentage points of the values they had held before the crash. That recovery took less than twenty minutes.

Two weeks after the Flash Crash, the US Securities and Exchange Commission (SEC) and the US Commodity Futures Trading Commission (CFTC) jointly released an interim report into the events of May 6th (CFTC&SEC, 2010a) that established very little, other than dispelling rumours of the flash crash having been caused by a "fat-finger" error (where a trader mis-keys an order) or terrorist action. After that, for more than four months there was open speculation on the cause of the Flash Crash, and senior figures in the markets voiced their growing exasperation at the lack of a straightforward explanation. Identifying the cause of the crash was made difficult by the "fragmentation of liquidity" (trading taking place simultaneously on a number of independent but interconnected exchange-venues); by the lack of a single unifying "consolidated audit trail" showing synchronized timestamps for all events in all the markets with identifiers of the originators of those events; and by the widespread use of algorithmic trading systems: autonomous adaptive software systems that automate trading jobs previously performed by human traders, many operating at super-human speeds. Various theories were discussed in the five months that it took the SEC and CFTC to produce their joint final report on the events of May 6th. Many speculated on the role of high-frequency trading (HFT) by investment banks and hedge funds, where algorithmic traders buy and sell blocks of financial instruments on very short timescales, sometimes holding a position for only a few seconds or less.

When the SEC/CFTC final report on the Flash Crash was eventually published on September 30th, nearly five months after the event, (CFTC&SEC, 2010b), it made no mention of a "bug" anywhere in the system being a causal factor. Instead, the story it told was that the trigger-event for the crash was a single block-sale of $4.1bn worth of futures contracts, executed with uncommon urgency on behalf of a traditional fund-management company. It was argued that the consequences of that trigger event interacting with HFT systems rippled out to cause the system-level failures just described. The SEC/CFTC report was met with very mixed responses. Many readers concluded that it left more questions unanswered than resolved, and a subsequent much more detailed analysis of the time-series "tapes" of market event data conducted by Nanex Corp.[1] offered an alternative story that many market

---

[1] See www.nanex.net

practitioners found more plausible: see Meerman *et al.* (2010) and Easley *et al.* (2011) for further details of the extent to which the CFTC/SEC version of events is disputed.

Ten months after the event, in February 2011, a specially convened panel of regulators and economists, the Joint CFTC-SEC Advisory Committee on Emerging Regulatory Issues, released a report (CFTC&SEC, 2011) urging a number of rule changes, some of them fundamental and potentially far-reaching. At the time of writing this Foresight review, the extent to which the report's recommendations will be acted upon is unclear (see, e.g., Demos, 2011a, 2011b, 2011c).

Now the fact that there was such a rapid recovery immediately after the down-spike meant that, by the close of business on May 6th the overall inter-day price change on the previous day was nothing particularly dramatic. To someone focused only on daily market-close prices, this may look like just another day of a downward-trending market in a time of significant political and economic uncertainty: on that day, the Greek national debt crisis was threatening to destabilize the entire Euro-zone single-currency economic union; and the indeterminate outcome of the UK general election was a further distraction. For sure, the intra-day dynamics on May 6th were unlike anything ever seen before, but the market pulled back, so what is there to worry about?

We contend that there are two significant reasons to be worried by the Flash Crash. The first worry is that at the micro-level there was a clear market failure: whether a trader was richer or poorer by the end of that disorderly day was in many cases not much more than a lottery. The second worry is the macro-level observation that, with only a very slight change in the sequence of events, the global financial markets could plausibly have gone into meltdown, with May 7th 2010 (i.e, the *next* day) becoming the date of a global collapse that dwarfed any previous stock-market crash. We'll expand on these two worries in the next two paragraphs.

The first worry, on the micro-level, is that while some equity spot and derivatives trades that took place at the height of the mayhem were subsequently "busted" (declared to be invalid on the basis that they were clearly made on the basis of erroneous data) by the exchanges, the means by which trades were selected for busting was argued by many to be arbitrary, after-the-fact rule-making. Some traders who had lost large amounts of money did not have their trades busted; some who had made handsome profits found their gains taken away. The flash-crash chaos had rippled beyond the equity markets into the foreign exchange (FX) markets where certain currency exchange rates swung wildly on the afternoon of May 6th as the markets attempted to hedge the huge volatility and risk that they were suddenly seeing explode in equities. There is no provision to retrospectively bust trades in FX, and so those deals were left to stand. Sizeable fortunes were made, and sizeable fortunes were lost, by those caught in the storm; the issue of who lost and who gained was in too many cases almost random.

The second worry is a much more significant concern: the Flash Crash could have occurred any time that day. Certainly the specific time-period during which the Flash Crash occurred, roughly 2:30pm to 3:00pm, was not cited as a causal factor in the official CFTC/SEC report on the events of May 6th, nor in the much more detailed analysis performed by Nanex Corp. This is a point recently explored in public statements by Bart Chilton, head of the CFTC, who said the following in a public lecture given in March 2011: "…Think about it. There are stocks and futures, which are arbitraged internationally. If the Flash Crash had taken place in the morning on

May 6th, when E.U. markets were open, it could have instigated a global economic event. Since it took place in the mid-afternoon, it was primarily limited to U.S. markets…" (Chilton, 2011). Although we respect Commissioner Chilton's view, we think that in fact the much, much bigger worry is not what would have happened if the Flash Crash had occurred in the morning of May 6th, but instead what would have happened if it had occurred a couple of hours or so *later* that day. Specifically, we think that the true nightmare scenario would have been if the crash's 600-point down-spike, the trillion-dollar write-off, had occurred immediately before market close: that is, if the markets had closed just after the steep drop, before the equally fast recovery had a chance to start. Faced with New York showing its biggest ever one-day drop in the final 15 minutes before close of business on May 6th, and in the absence of any plausible public-domain reason for that happening, combined with the growing nervousness that the Greek government would default on its sovereign debt and throw the entire Euro-zone economic union into chaos, traders in Tokyo would have had only one rational reaction: sell. The likelihood is that Tokyo would have seen one of its biggest ever one-day losses. Following this, as the mainland European bourses and the London markets opened on the morning of May 7th, seeing the unprecedented sell-offs that had afflicted first New York and then Tokyo, European markets would have followed into precipitous freefall. None of this would have been particularly useful in strengthening confidence in the Greek debt crisis or the future of the Euro, either. And, as far as we can tell, the only reason that this sequence of events was not triggered was down to mere lucky timing. Put simply, on the afternoon of May 6th 2010, the world's financial system dodged a bullet.

Although the Flash Crash was a particularly extreme event, similar phenomena have been witnessed in various markets in the period since May 2010. Some notable examples are listed here, but this is by no means an exhaustive list:

- On 28th September 2010, share-prices of major technology stocks Apple, Dell, Hewlett-Packard, IBM, Microsoft, and Oracle all experienced sudden severe spike-transitions before returning to normal price ranges.[2]
- On May 2nd, 2011, the market price of gold spiked sharply downwards by $20 and then immediately recovered more than $15 of that loss. The graph of price against time for this event is strongly reminiscent of the graph of the Dow Jones Industrial Index during the Flash Crash. Unlike the Flash Crash, which unfolded over a period of roughly 30 minutes, this down-spike and recovery in the price of gold took less than 10 minutes.[3]
- The next day, on May 3rd, 2011, the price of silver dropped dramatically in after-hours trading, an event that was again attributed to algorithmic trading systems.[4]
- On June 8th 2011 the price of natural gas in the USA commodity markets had been trending flat (i.e. showing neither a rise or a fall for the day) over a period of

---

[2] http://ftalphaville.ft.com/blog/2010/09/28/355081/market-on-edge-after-apple-drops-like-a-stone/

[3] See http://www.zerohedge.com/article/golden-flash-crash

[4] See http://www.zerohedge.com/article/and-now-todays-mini-silver-flash-crash-same-time-same-place

several hours, when the price suddenly started to oscillate in a pattern strongly reminiscent of a smooth sine-wave, with the amplitude of the oscillations (the height of the peaks and the depths of the troughs) growing steadily in a short space of time, and then the price crashed dramatically. This event was also attributed to an erroneously programmed algorithmic trading system.[5]

• On July 7th 2011, there were sizeable swings in the price of crude oil futures on the New York Mercantile Exchange (one of the world's primary exchanges for trading of commodities and commodity derivatives). According to the analysis published by Nanex Corp, these swings appear to have been the result of a "massive arbitrage algorithm" running at a significant speed advantage for a period of around five seconds.[6]

• On March 23rd 2012, the initial public offering (IPO) of shares in the company *BATS Global Markets* was marred by an astonishingly fast collapse in its share price. BATS (an acronym for "Better Alternative Trading Systems") was founded in 2005 and is the owner and operator of popular electronic trading venues in major economies such as the USA and UK, that are alternatives to the traditional, longer-established stock exchanges. At 11:14 am on the day of the IPO, BATS' shares commenced trading at a price of $15.25. Within 0.9 seconds of the start of trading, the price had dropped to $0.2848; and at +1.5 seconds, the price was $0.0002. A total of 567 orders had been executed by the time trading in BATS was halted, and BATS subsequently cancelled its IPO, thereby depriving the company of the capital that would otherwise have been raised by the sale of its shares that day. Subsequent reports in the financial media quoted BATS as blaming this collapse on "problems" and "bugs" in their own exchange software,[7] but analysis of market data subsequently released by Nanex Corp[8] indicated that the collapse in BATS' share price had been driven primarily by so-called *intermarket sweep orders* originating from a trader or traders operating on the Nasdaq exchange. Nanex's analysis also demonstrated that the collapse in BATS' price traced an almost-perfect logarithmic decay curve, strong evidence that a computerized system was driving the price down by a fixed percentage with each successive trade. In the days that followed, there was open speculation that BATS' crash had been caused by a rogue trading system, and that perhaps someone had deliberately programmed a system to inflict this grief on BATS.

In each of these cases, there is evidence to suggest that computer-based trading systems were involved in the transactions that played causal roles in these events, but unlike the events of May 6th 2010, there have been no official investigations launched by regulatory bodies such as the CFTC and the SEC. There is frequent open discussion among market practitioners (especially on the anonymously-sourced but very well-informed website www.zerohedge.com) that current markets are too often

---

[5] See http://www.zerohedge.com/article/story-berserk-nat-gas-algo-just-got-really-strange and for the supporting data analysis see http://www.nanex.net/StrangeDays/06082011.html

[6] See http://www.nanex.net/StrangeDays/07072011.html

[7] See T. Demos (2012), "IPO Software Behind BATS' Failure", *The Financial Times*, March 26th 2012.

[8] See http://www.nanex.net/aqck/2970.html

showing price movements for which the only plausible explanation is that a computerised system is operating in an unexpected or unanticipated fashion, giving market dynamics that deviate from expectations based on experience of markets populated by human traders, or from rational economic argument.

We argue here that market disorder such as the May 6th 2010 Flash Crash, and the mini-flash-crashes that have been recorded since then in various markets, are *deviant events* that are best understood as evidence of *"normal failure"* in an *ultra-large-scale complex adaptive socio-technical system-of-systems*.

Unpacking that assertion requires some care, so in the following sections we'll start first with a discussion of notable technology failures, then bring the conversation back to discussion of failures of the financial markets.

Systems, such as the financial markets, that are themselves composed of constituent stand-alone systems that are each operationally and managerially independent, are very often the result of incremental, sporadic, organic growth and unplanned accretion rather than clean-sheet engineering design. They thereby involve or acquire significant degrees of variability in components and heterogeneity of constituent systems, and their make-up changes dynamically over multiple timescales. For this reason traditional engineering techniques, which are predicated on very different assumptions, cannot necessarily be trusted to deliver acceptable solutions. And, therefore, new approaches are required: new engineering tools and techniques, new management perspectives and practices.

In the main text and the appendices of this review, we survey some recently developed approaches that look likely to grow into promising new engineering techniques in the coming decade and beyond, better suited to current and future systems than our traditional engineering practices, which owe more to the mid-twentieth-century than they can offer the early-twenty-first.

2   Background: Failures in Risky Technology

The global financial markets are not the only area in which the application of new technologies has led to failures. Although operator error can be attributed to many failures, as technological systems grow in complexity the prospect of failure-modes being inadvertently designed-in also grows. Take, for example, bridge building. As an engineering activity this is something that dates at least as far back as ancient Rome (c.150BC) and so probably doesn't figure as a risky technology for many people.

Yet for decades, engineering students have been taught the story of the Tacoma Narrows suspension bridge, opened in July 1940, which collapsed four months later, where the designers did not anticipate the prospect of wind-flows over the bridge deck reinforcing the deck's natural mode of vibrations, leading to the bridge shaking itself apart. Presumably, current and future students will also be taught the story of the London Millennium Bridge, which opened in June 2000 and two days later was closed for two years to remedy destabilizing swaying motions induced when groups of people walked over it. A significant difference between Tacoma Narrows and London Millennium is that in the latter case, it was the interaction of people, the users, with the engineered system that caused the problem. The Millennium Bridge on its own, as a piece of engineering, was a fine and stable structure; but when we consider the interaction dynamics of the larger system made up of the bridge *and* its many simultaneous users, there were serious unforeseen problems in those dynamics that only came to light when it was too late.

As engineered systems become more complex, it becomes more reasonable to argue that no one person or group of users is responsible for failures, but rather that the failures are inherent, latent, in the system; this seems especially so in the case of *socio-technical systems*, i.e. systems (like the Millennium Bridge, when in use) whose dynamics and behaviour can only be properly understood by including human agents (such as operators and/or users) within the system boundary.[9]

This is perhaps most clear in some of the more famous technology failures of the past 40 years. The oxygen-tank explosion that crippled the *Apollo 13* Lunar Service Module as it was en route to the moon in 1970, and subsequent safe return of her crew, has been rightly popularized as a major triumph of bravery, skill, teamwork, and engineering ingenuity. Nevertheless, the fact remains that NASA very nearly suffered the loss of *Apollo 13* and her crew, due to the compounding effect of several independent small failures of process rather than malign intent or major error from one or more individuals. The successful return of *Apollo 13*'s crew owed an awful lot to the availability of accurate simulation models, physical replicas on the ground of key components of the spacecraft, where emergency procedures could be invented and rehearsed and refined before being relayed to the astronauts. The value of simulation models is something that we will return to in depth, later in this paper.

While loss of a space vehicle is undoubtedly a tragedy for those concerned, the number of fatalities is small in comparison to the potential losses in other high-consequence systems, such as petrochemical plants and nuclear power stations. The release of toxic gas at the Union Carbide plant in Bhopal in December 1984 immediately killed over 2,000 people, with estimates of the subsequent delayed fatalities running at 6,000-8,000. The partial meltdown at the Three Mile Island nuclear plant in 1979 was successfully contained, but the reactor-core fire at Chernobyl in 1986 was not, and estimates of the number of deaths resulting from that event range from many hundreds to several thousand.

High-risk technology failures including *Apollo 13* and Three Mile Island were the subject of serious scholarly analysis in Charles Perrow's seminal work *Normal Accidents* (Perrow, 1984). Perrow argued that in tightly-coupled systems with sufficiently complex internal interactions, accidents and failures, including catastrophic disasters of high-risk systems with the potential to end or threaten many lives, are essentially inevitable – such accidents are, in that sense, to be expected as "normal", regardless of whether they are common or rare.

In Perrow's terms, the losses of the NASA space shuttles *Challenger* in January 1986 and *Columbia* in February 2003 were also normal accidents. However, the sociologist Diane Vaughan argued for a more sophisticated analysis in her classic study *The Challenger Launch Decision* (1997), in which she presented a detailed analysis of transcripts, covering the hours immediately preceding *Challenger*'s launch, of interactions between NASA staff and the staff of Morton Thiokol, manufacturers of the shuttle's solid-fuel rocket booster (SRB) that failed leading to loss of the vehicle and her crew.

---

[9] For an early, but very insightful, discussion of the dynamics of socio-technical systems, see Bonen (1979).

The transcripts had been released as part of the official Presidential Commission on the Space Shuttle *Challenger* Accident, led by William Rogers. A shocking finding of the Rogers investigation was that the specific failure-mode (burn-through of rubber O-ring seals in a critical joint on the SRB) had been known since 1977 and the consequent potential for catastrophic loss of the vehicle had been discussed at length by NASA and Thiokol, but the shuttle had not been grounded. Vaughan concluded that while the *proximal* cause of disaster was the SRB O-ring failure, the *ultimate* cause was a social process that Vaughan named *normalization of deviance*.

Put simply, normalization of deviance occurs when the safe-operating envelope of a complex system is not completely known in advance, and where events that were *a priori* thought to be outside the envelope, but which do not then result in failures, are taken after the fact as evidence that the safe envelope should be extended to include those events. In this way, deviant events become normalized: the absence of a catastrophe thus far is taken as evidence that in future catastrophes are less likely than had previously been thought. The flaw in this line of reasoning is starkly revealed when a catastrophe then ensues. In Vaughan's analysis, the loss of *Challenger* was not a purely technical issue but rather was an organizational failure in the *socio-technical system* comprised of the (technical) shuttle hardware systems and the (social) human individuals, teams, and organizations that had to interact appropriately to ensure safe launch and return of the shuttle.

Vaughan's analysis of the *Challenger* accident came more than a decade after the official inquiry into that 1986 event. In contrast, because of her work on *Challenger*, following the loss of *Columbia* in 2003 Vaughan was immediately invited onto the Columbia Accident Investigation Board (CAIB) and subsequently authored a chapter of the CAIB official report. It was argued that once again an organizational failure at NASA had resulted in loss of a vehicle, once again via a long-standing process of normalization of deviance.

For *Columbia*, the *proximal* cause of disaster was a lump of insulating foam that broke away from the external fuel tank and struck the leading edge of the orbiter's left wing, damaging its thermal insulation: on re-entry, this damage allowed atmospheric gases, compressed in the bow-wave at the wing edge and hence heated to more than 1,500 degrees Celsius, to penetrate the wing; and the vehicle then broke up at high speed. But the *ultimate* cause was an organizational culture that had once again engaged in normalization of deviance, despite the warnings from Vaughan's analysis of the *Challenger* disaster.

Prior to the loss of *Columbia*, sixty-four previous missions had suffered strikes from insulating material breaking away during launch and hitting the orbiter, and yet each such strike was technically a violation of the shuttle's design requirements: the shuttle had simply not been designed to withstand impacts from breakaway insulating material. Most notably, in 1988 on mission STS-27, insulation broke away from an SRB during launch and damaged 700 of the heat-insulating tiles on shuttle *Atlantis*, and the crew on board believed they would very likely be killed on re-entry; nevertheless, they weren't, and post-mission repairs to the shuttle's damage from insulation strikes became increasingly seen as nothing more than a routine maintenance issue (Mullane, 2006).

Vaughan discussed the similarities between the *Challenger* and *Columbia* losses in a book chapter (Vaughan, 2005) and has documented her experience on the CAIB and her subsequent interactions with NASA in a 40-page journal article (Vaughan, 2006). The CAIB report is probably the first major US government accident investigation that explicitly states the cause of the disaster to be a socio-technical system failure.

The approaches exemplified by the writings of Perrow and Vaughan are not the only ones. Studies of what are known technically as High-Reliability Organizations (such as emergency rooms in hospitals, firefighter teams, and the flight-deck operations crews on aircraft carriers) have revealed that there are social and organizational, as well as technical, solutions to creating resilient socio-technical systems: see, for example, Roberts (1990); Weick & Sutcliffe (2007); and Reason (2008). The results from these studies indicate that there is no traditional, "pure" engineering approach that is suitable for ultra-large-scale systems. Multi-disciplinary approaches, that integrate the social with the technical, need to be developed: so-called *socio-technical systems engineering*.

But what does this academic literature on the study of technology failures offer to teach us about the events of May 6th, 2010?

Of course, the Flash Crash was by no means the first failure in a major financial market. As anyone reading this paper must surely be aware, in July 2007 the investment bank Bear Stearns was the first in what turned out to be a sequence of major financial institutions to signal that it had suffered significant losses on subprime hedge funds, triggering a sudden dramatic reassessment of counterparty risk in most major financial institutions around the world which led, *inter alia*, to the UK's Northern Rock consumer bank being the first to suffer a full-scale public bank run in 150 years; and to the US government bailing out insurance giant AIG, mortgage providers Freddie Mac and Fannie Mae, and yet famously not extending a lifeline to Lehman Brothers, which turned out not to be too big to fail, and duly went bust.

Taking a longer historical perspective, the crisis of 2007-08 was just one in a sequence that stretches back through the collapse of the LTCM hedge-fund in 1998; the "black Monday" crash of October 1987; the US savings-and-loan crisis of the mid-1980's; the Wall Street Crash of October 1929; the South-Sea Bubble of the 1720s; and the Tulip Mania of the 1630s.

This history of financial crises has been documented in a popular text by Kindleberger (2001), and with more academic rigour by Gorton (2010). The events of 2007-08 have been recounted from a number of journalistic perspectives, of which Lewis's (2010) and Tett's (2009) are notably thorough and well written. Tett's perspective is particularly insightful: she is a senior executive journalist for the *Financial Times* but has a PhD in social anthropology, and this clearly influences her analysis. Tett was one of the few journalists to warn of the impending crisis before it came to pass, and notes various events that are clear instances of normalization of deviance. Lewis's brilliant book tells the story of the few individuals who recognized that deviance, and bet on the markets failing. For more scholarly, academic, studies of the sociology of the financial markets, see the works of Edinburgh sociologist Donald MacKenzie and his colleagues (MacKenzie 2008a, 2008b; MacKenzie *et al.* 2008), although all of those pre-date the turmoil of the subprime crisis.

One significant difference between previous financial crises and the Flash Crash is the speed at which they played out. In the past quarter of a century, financial-market trading has shifted from being a largely human, face-to-face activity, to being phone-and-screen-based rather than face-to-face, but still largely requiring a human at each end of the phone or screen. But within the past decade a fundamental technology-led shift has occurred. Increasingly, the counterparties at either end of the trade, at each end of the telecoms cable, are pieces of software rather than humans. Algorithmic trading systems are increasingly trusted to do trading jobs that were previously done by human traders, and to do jobs that would require super-human data-integration abilities in a person.[10] As was seen on May 6th, the system-wide interaction between multiple independently-engineered, independently operated, and independently managed automated trading systems had at least one unknown catastrophic failure mode. A major proportion of traders in the markets are still human, but to understand today's markets it is necessary to study the interaction of these human traders with their automated counterparts; that is, we need to study the socio-technical system.

The danger that normalization of deviance posed in high-frequency automated trading systems in the global financial markets, and the possibility of major catastrophe happening within very short time-scales, was discussed in a strategic briefing paper written by one of us for the UK Government's Office of Science, first draft of which was submitted in January 2010 and the final version of which (Cliff, 2010) was submitted to the government nine days *before* the Flash Crash. Similarly, in the US at least one academic was repeatedly warning the SEC of the likelihood of a Flash Crash type of event in the year running up to May 6th 2010 (Angel, 2009a, 2009b, 2009c; Angel *et al.*, 2010; Angel 2010a, 2010b).

We think it is reasonable to argue that the Flash Crash was, at least in part, a result of normalization of deviance. For many years, long before May 6th 2010, concerns about systemic effects of rapid increases in the price volatility of various instruments had led several exchanges to implement "circuit breaker" rules, requiring that trading in a security be suspended for some period of time if the price of that security moved by more than some percentage within a sufficiently short time-period. For instance, the London Stock Exchange first adopted circuit-breakers, now known there as Automated Execution Suspension Periods (AESPs) and Price Monitoring Extensions (PMEs), shortly after the 1987 Black Monday crash; and Chi-X Europe enforces "order-entry controls" that prevent orders being entered that are more than 20% away from the current price (Flinders, 2007; Grant, 2010). In response to the Flash Crash, the USA's SEC has now enforced similar mechanisms in the US markets with the aim of preventing such an event re-occuring. In fact the move toward introducing circuit-breakers in the US pre-dates the Flash Crash by more than two years: it had been proposed in an influential report on the sub-prime crisis from the Institute of International Finance (IIF, 2008) but seems to have been actively resisted until the events of May 2010. Thus, it seems plausible to argue that before the Flash Crash occurred there had been some significant degree of normalization of deviance: high-speed changes in the prices of equities had been observed, market participants were well aware that that could lead to a high speed crash, but these warning signals were ignored and the introduction of safety measures that could have prevented them was resisted.

---

[10] The history of the spread of technology innovations in the financial markets, and some likely future developments, are discussed in a recent review by Cliff, Brown, & Treleaven (2011).

Moreover, it could plausibly be argued that normalization of deviance has continued to take place in the markets *since* the Flash Crash. The SEC's introduction of circuit breakers seems to have been offered, and largely accepted, as the one necessary solution for preventing another similar event; and (so the story goes) all is now well. We are told that adding circuit breakers firmly shuts the stable door. Admittedly, this was done only after the Flash Crash horse had bolted, but at least the door is now shut.

Now, for sure, the introduction of circuit breakers means that the US markets today are not the same markets as they were on May 6th 2010. With circuit breakers added, those markets, and the other markets around the world that they are coupled to (i.e., the entire global financial market system) should be in a new dynamic regime – that is, their market dynamics are different now. But the new dynamics are still not entirely known, and so the new regime is certainly not yet guaranteed to be safe. Despite the circuit breakers, the next Flash Crash could be lurking just around the corner.

There are anecdotal stories that the speed of price fluctuations occurring *within* the limits of circuit breaker thresholds seems to be increasing in some markets (See, e.g., Blas, 2011); and there is evidence to suggest that another Flash Crash was "dodged" on September 1st 2010, in a similarly bizarre period when quote volumes exceeded even those seen at peak activity on May 6th 2010 (Steiner, 2010), but no official investigation was commissioned to understand that latter event. Furthermore, the circuit-breaker mechanisms in each of the world's major trading hubs are not harmonized, exposing arbitrage opportunities for exploiting differences; computer and telecoms systems can still fail, or be taken down by enemies of the system, and the systemic effects of those failures may not have been fully thought through.

Of course, the next Flash Crash won't be exactly the same as the last one, the SEC's circuit breakers will probably see to that. But there are no guarantees that another event, just as unprecedented, just as severe, and just as fast (or faster) than the Flash Crash cannot happen in future. Normalization of deviance can be a very deep-running, pernicious process. After *Challenger*, NASA addressed the issue with the SRB O-ring seals, and believed the Shuttle to be safe. That was no help to the crew of *Columbia*.

Reassurances from regulators that all is now well are likely to sound somewhat hollow for as long as people can remember the near-total failure of the regulatory bodies to have anything useful to say about the subprime crisis until shortly after its severity was clear to even the most casual of observers. Light-touch regulation and its consequence for financial markets in the UK were discussed in the 2009 Turner Review[11], and the parallel systemic failure of the economics profession is discussed at length by Colander *et al.* (2009) and by Bootle (2009). The next market failure may well be a failure of risky technology that, like the Flash Crash, has no clear precedent.

The global financial markets, considered as a single ultra-large-scale super-system, is made up of components, of constituent systems. These constitutents include the human traders and their trading procedures; the various electronic exchanges; the automated trading systems operated by the various investment banks and hedge funds; and their associated clearing, settlement and risk-management systems. All of these constituent systems have been developed, procured, operated and managed independently, although for some of them the development and procurement processes were informal, organic

---

[11] http://www.fsa.gov.uk/pubs/other/turner_review.pdf

growth rather than pre-specified projects. That is, the current global financial markets are, from a technology perspective, *systems of systems* (SoS). We explore the definition of "system of systems" in some detail in Appendix A.2.

A key issue with SoS is that the effects of failure in one or more of the constituents may be contained, or may ripple out in a domino-effect chain reaction, analogous to the crowd-psychology of contagion. Furthermore, SoS are often used in unanticipated circumstances and by unanticipated users. In such situations, the response of the constituent systems may not result in local failure but rather the combined local responses can trigger a global failure: this seems to be what happened in the Flash Crash. In this very definite sense, the global financial markets have become high-consequence socio-technical systems of systems, and with that comes the risk of problems occurring that are simply not anticipated until they occur, by which time it is typically too late, and in which minor crises can escalate to become major catastrophes at timescales too fast for humans to be able to deal with them. The extent to which the SEC/CFTC report attributes cause to a single rushed block-sale as a $4.1bn hedge as the trigger-event in the Flash Crash seems comparable to the way in which the *Challenger* accident investigation report identified failed SRB O-rings: there is a wider socio-technical perspective that should not be ignored, and which was already being pointed to by some authors prior to the events of May 6th 2010 (Haldane, 2009; Cliff, 2010).

That the global financial markets have become ultra-large-scale complex IT-centric socio-technical systems is perhaps no surprise, given the wider context that IT systems have moved from back-office support (for payroll processing, say) firmly onto the critical path for very many enterprises and organizations, to the point where failure of the IT system can incapacitate an organization. For example, ten years ago a failure of the IT servers in a hospital would not have a major negative effect; whereas in the near future, once all data is digitized at the point of capture and integrated with patient's historical data before delivery in an appropriate form to a healthcare practitioner, then when a hospital's servers go down it will cease to be a functioning hospital and instead be a big building full of sick people, with highly trained professionals frantically tapping the touch screens on their PDAs/tablet-computers, wondering where the data went. Similar stories can be told, or are already plausibly foreseeable, in very many private-sector, public-sector, and defence organizations in most industrialized economies.

Most notably, such issues have for some time been a growing, major concern in those areas of systems engineering where system failures can result in hundreds or thousands of fatalities or where, in the limit, system failures pose existential threats to entire nations: the engineering research literature in aerospace, nuclear, and defence systems may well be a source of experiences and new tools and techniques that could be applicable to the financial markets, although it is doubtful that any techniques yet exist that address the unique characteristics of ultra-large-scale systems. The manifestly dire consequences of failure in aerospace, nuclear, and defence systems, and also of course in automotive systems, has led to the development of engineering teaching and practices specific to the development and maintenance of safety-critical, high-integrity systems: a field known as high-integrity systems engineering (HISE), which we briefly review in Appendix A.1 of this document.

So, the concerns expressed here about modern computer-based trading in the global financial markets are really just a detailed instance of a more general story: it seems likely, or at least plausible, that major advanced economies are becoming increasingly reliant on large-scale complex IT systems (LSCITS): the complexity of these LSCITS is increasing rapidly; their socio-economic criticality is also increasing rapidly; our ability to manage them, and to predict their failures before it is too late, may not be keeping up. That is, we may be becoming critically dependent on LSCITS that we simply do not understand and hence are simply not capable of managing. This is something that we illustrate, purely notionally, as a single three-line graph, shown in Figure 1.

We, the authors of this review, each work for major national strategic initiatives intended to address these issues. In the UK, the National Research and Training Initiative in the Science and Engineering of LSCITS was started in 2007 as a strategic investment with the primary aim being to foster the formation of a new community of researchers and practitioners with the training and experience appropriate for dealing with future software-intensive systems engineering dominated by LSCITS issues (Cliff *et al.* 2006). At pretty much exactly the same time as the UK LSCITS Initiative was being planned and set up, entirely independently, in the USA the US Army

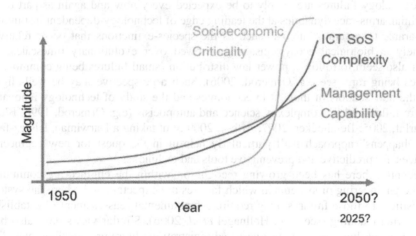

Fig. 1. The Complexity Crossover Crisis. The complexity of information and communications technology (ICT) socio-technical systems of systems (SoS) has increased dramatically since ICT was first commercialized in the 1950s, and in recent years the socio-economic criticality of ICT SoS has also sharply increased, as very many enterprises and organizations in advanced economies have become dependent on the availability of ICT functionality as a key component on the critical paths of their operations. Over the same period, there is increasing concern (and growing evidence) that our ability to manage and predict the behavior of these critical ICT SoS is not increasing at the same pace, and so at some point in time there is the potential for crisis, where major socio-economic systems are critically dependent on ICT SoS whose complexity is beyond that which we can manage. We are deliberately non-committal on the precise timing of this crossover point: for some companies or industrial sectors it could be a decade or more away, for others it could have happened already.

commissioned a team of world-class researchers led by the Software Engineering Institute (SEI) at Carnegie Mellon University to conduct a study of ultra-large-scale systems software. The study resulted in a major report that argued the necessity for the USA to invest in ultra-large-scale systems engineering research, to safeguard its international dominance in information systems; this authoritative report marked the first major output from the SEI Ultra-Large-Scale (ULS) Systems Project (Northrop *et al.*, 2006). For a brief overview of the ULS Systems project, the UK LSCITS Initiative, and other related projects, see Goth (2008).

3   Where Next for the Financial Markets?

One criticism that is sometimes leveled at the academic study of technology failures is that there is perhaps a tendency to be wise after the event. That is, a large amount of the work is descriptive (saying what happened) but not sufficiently predictive (saying what could happen next) or prescriptive (saying what should be done differently in future, to predict or prevent such failures from re-occurring).

One possible approach, which side-steps the need for specific predictions, is to accept that technology failures are simply to be expected every now and again as part of the Darwinian arms-race dynamics at the leading edge of technology-dependent institutions, comparable to natural "failures" such as the species-extinctions that occur relatively routinely in biological ecosystems, when viewed over evolutionary timescales, and which also seem to follow a power-law distribution (small failures being common, big failures being rare: see e.g. Ormerod, 2006). Such a perspective may be well-aligned with the new schools of thought in economics and the study of technology innovation that are influenced by complexity science and autopoeisis (e.g. Ormerod, 1998; Blume & Durlaf, 2005; Beinhocker, 2007; Arthur, 2009), but taking a Darwinian, laissez-faire, "stuff happens" approach isn't particularly helpful in the quest for new engineering practices, for predictive and preventative tools and techniques.

Recently, there has been growing recognition within the engineering community that the engineering of systems in which failures are expected, and where the systems are resilient to those failures, may require a fundamental reassessment of established engineering teaching (see, e.g., Hollnagel *et al.* 2006). Similar views have also been expressed, earlier, in the business administration literature dealing with the management of large-scale technology-driven projects (Collingridge, 1992). It seems reasonable to suggest that changes are necessary both in engineering practices, and in the coordination, incentivization, and management of projects, for all LSCITS including those underlying the global financial markets. But such changes are likely to take time, and while we wait for them to take effect it would be good to have a viable near-term strategy, one that would potentially offer major payoff within five to seven years (seven years is long enough to achieve quite a lot, given enough resources: the US Apollo programme took seven years, from John F. Kennedy's famous speech to Neil Armstrong's famous small step.) In the following pages, we outline one such strategy. It will require national-scale investment, to create a national-scale strategic resource (or, perhaps, international collaboration to create a shared multinational resource, rather like the CERN Large Hadron Collider or the European Space Agency's *Arianne* space rocket).

The proposed strategy is simple enough to state: build a predictive computer simulation of the global financial markets, as a national-scale or multinational-scale resource for assessing systemic risk. Use this simulation to explore the "operational envelope" of the current state of the markets, as a hypothesis generator, searching for scenarios and failure modes such as those witnessed in the Flash Crash, identifying the potential risks before they become reality. Such a simulator could also be used to address issues of regulation and certification. Doing this well will not be easy and will certainly not be cheap, but the significant expense involved can be a help to the project rather than a hindrance.

Explaining and justifying all that was written in that last paragraph will take up the next several pages.

For most engineering and scientific domains, in recent years it has become increasingly commonplace to rely on high-precision computer simulation as a means of studying real-world systems. Such simulations offer the possibility of evaluating the performance of proposed systems that have not yet been physically constructed, and of exploring the response of existing real-world systems to different operating-environment conditions, and to alterations of the system itself, allowing "test-to-destruction" without actually destroying anything. Engineers interested in aerodynamic flows over aeroplanes and cars, or around buildings, or hydrodynamic flows around a ship's hull, can routinely call upon highly accurate computational fluid dynamics (CFD) models to evaluate these flows in simulation, rather than building physical models to test in wind-tunnels or test-tanks. Almost all silicon chip designs are evaluated in microelectronics circuit-simulators such as SPICE (e.g. Tuinenga, 1988) before the chip-producers make the final (and most expensive) step of committing their design to fabrication. Fissile nuclear reactions can be simulated with sufficient accuracy that designs for nuclear power stations, and for nuclear weapons, can be evaluated in simulation without splitting a single atom. In most advanced economies, weather forecasts are produced by national agencies on the basis of detailed sensor readings, and advanced computer simulations, that allow for accurate short-term and medium-term predictions of the future. Similar stories can be told in computational drug design, computational systems biology, and so on. Advocates of the use of predictive computer simulations in science and engineering have argued that this approach now represents a well-established third paradigm within science, in addition to the two long-established paradigms of empirical observation and theoretical modeling/generalization (see e.g. Gray, 2009, p.xviii).[12]

It's important to be clear about the nature of the predictive simulation models that we are advocating here. Meteorological simulations are predictive in the sense that they make weather-forecasts, specific projections about the likely future state or states that the real-world weather system may find itself in; that is, they say what is about to happen, or what would be likely to happen under specific circumstances. This is the most familiar practical use of simulation modeling. But there is a second use to which simulation modeling can be put: simulating a model of some system allows the model itself to be explored; in this sense, the model is an embodiment, an implementation in computer-code, of a theory of how the thing being modeled works. This second type of simulation

---

[12] The use of predictive simulations in engineering safety-critical complex systems-of-systems is discussed further in Appendix A.4.

modeling often starts out as essentially exploratory, with the intention of delivering explanatory insights that would otherwise have been difficult or impossible to come by.

One illustrative example of this kind of simulation-as-explanation is Schelling's (1971) model of racial segregation, where a very simple iterative process (i.e., an algorithm) operating on black or white markers positioned on a grid of square cells arranged chessboard-like over a two-dimensional space (i.e., an abstract model of the real world) was used to explore and explain how groups of people expressing only very weak preferences for wanting to live near to neighbours of the same race could lead over time to total segregation with large spatial clusters all of one race or the other. That is, the Schelling model, when simulated, showed in its dynamics an emergent behavior at the system-level that was unexpected and difficult to predict from mere inspection of the set of rules that the simulated people (the "agents" in the model) were specified to follow; Schelling was subsequently awarded the 2005 Nobel Memorial Prize in Economic Sciences. For a recent collection surveying such exploratory and explanatory simulation modeling in social sciences research, an approach now widely known as agent-based modeling, see Epstein (2007); and for a review of foundational work in agent-based computational finance, see LeBaron (2000).

Of course, computational simulations are currently also routinely used by financial institutions: Monte-Carlo techniques are used to solve and explore options-pricing models, to evaluate value at risk, to back-test trading algorithms on historical data, and to perform stress-tests on individual financial instruments or on portfolios of such instruments. But historically it has been much less commonplace to simulate entire markets at a fine-grained level to study issues in overall system behaviour in an exploratory fashion.

In an excellent book, Darley & Outkin (1997) give a detailed description of how they used complex adaptive systems (CAS)[13] agent-based simulation-modeling techniques to explore the consequences of the Nasdaq exchange's move from quoting prices expressed as multiples of sixteenths of a dollar to fully decimalized prices, expressed as multiples of one hundredth of a dollar (i.e., as dollars and cents). In the language of the markets, this was exploring the effects of a reduction in the Nasdaq "tick size" from \$0.0625 to \$0.01. Nasdaq had previously changed its tick-size from \$1/8th to \$1/16th in 1997, and there was evidence to suggest that at the same time there had been a change of strategies among the market participants trading on Nasdaq. Nasdaq commissioned Darley & Outkin to construct a detailed simulation model to evaluate possible effects of changing the tick-size to \$0.01, in advance of the actual decimalization which was completed in April 2001; that is, Darley & Outkin were dealing in predictions, not postdictions. Darley & Outkin's book recounting this predictive-simulation CAS work was published several years later. In it, they state:

> "While building the simulated model of the market, we interacted
> extensively with many market participants: market-makers, brokers,
> traders, large investors, etc. We found this interaction invaluable – as a
> source of information in particular on often subtle details of market
> operations, as a venue for verifying our assumptions and simulations

---

[13] The definition of a "complex adaptive system" is explored in more depth in Appendix A.3.

results, and at times as a source of constructive criticism. One conversation with a market maker still stays clear in our minds. He was supportive, but skeptical. The core of his skepticism lay in this question: how one can model the fear and greed often ruling the market behavior? This is a valid point: while fear and greed affect markets immensely, as has been time and again demonstrated by numerous booms and busts, understanding of underlying individual and mass psychology is lacking.

"In our approach we address this problem by explicitly modeling strategies of individual market participants, by allowing those strategies to evolve over time due to individual learning or evolutionary selection, and by allowing to [sic] investigate various what-if scenarios by using user-defined strategies."

(Darley & Outkin, 1997, pp.5-6)

Darley & Outkin report that the results from their CAS simulations led them to make six substantive predictions before decimalization was enacted, and that events subsequent to the actual decimalization largely supported all of those predictions, except one (concerning the upper bound on the increase in trading volume, which had not yet been reached by the time that Darley & Outkin published their book).

Darley & Outkin's book describes a simulation model of one specific real-world exchange, and was the first to do so in such detail. For other studies of using CAS simulation-modeling techniques to explore how the collective behaviour of individual trader-agents can give rise to certain market-level phenomena, see e.g. Palmer *et al.*, 1994; Cliff & Bruten, 1999; LeBaron, 1999; Levy *et al.*, 2000; and Tesfatsion & Judd, 2006.

Given the success of Darley & Outkin's work, which is now over a decade old, it seems entirely plausible to propose that a similar complex-adaptive-systems, evolutionary agent-based, predictive simulation model could be constructed to assess the dynamics and behavior of individual financial markets, or indeed of the entire global financial market system. Obviously, it would be a major endeavour to create such a model, requiring national-scale levels of investment and ongoing funding to provide appropriate resources of human capital and computing power.

Nevertheless, there is an obvious precedent in most advanced economies: very many countries fund, as a national utility, a meteorological agency such as the UK's Met Office[14]. Combining real-time sensor data from satellites and ground-based observation stations with historical data and advanced, highly compute-intensive, predictive simulation models, the Met Office is able to give accurate near-term weather forecasts with a high spatial precision.

The famously chaotic nature of weather systems (Lorenz, 1963) means that accurate longer-term predictions remain more problematic, and the same is very likely to be true of long-term predictive models of the financial markets, but there is a well-established technique used in meteorological forecasting that should also be of use modeling the markets: so-called *ensemble forecasting*, where the same model is re-run many hundreds or thousands of times, with each fresh run having minor variations in the initial conditions, and/or a different sequence of random numbers generated in the modeling of stochastic factors (see, e.g., Smith, 1995, 2002). From a thousand runs

---

[14] http://www.metoffice.gov.uk

(say) of a model aimed at predicting the weather 48 hours into the future, it may be that 243 of the simulations show snowfall on a particular area, 429 show rain, and the rest predict no precipitation; with these results, the forecast for two day's time would be a 24% chance of snow, a 43% chance of rain, and a 33% chance of it staying dry. In this sense then, the forecast is a probability function over the space of possible outcomes. Here we have only three mutually exclusive outcomes; a more sophisticated model might give a probability density function (PDF) over the space of possible precipitation levels measured to the nearest millimeter per unit of area, and also a separate PDF over the space of possible ambient temperatures, measured to the nearest degree Celsius; taken together, the two PDFs would form a prediction of whether water would fall from the sky, and whether it would fall as rain or as snow.

So, the chaotic nature of financial markets is not necessarily an impediment to the development of predictive simulation models, so long as sufficient computing resources are made available to allow for ensemble forecasting. In fact, it is likely that the real value of the ensemble forecasting work would be in running very many simulations (perhaps tens or hundreds of thousands or more) in the search for those extremely rare but devastatingly problematic combinations of circumstances that have become widely known as *Black Swan* events (Taleb, 2007). It seems reasonable to describe the May 6th Flash Crash as a Black Swan event, and maybe the likelihood of such an event could have been predicted in advance, if a suitably detailed simulation model had been available beforehand. Of course the simulation would not have predicted that the crash would occur on May 6th, and would probably not have identified the precise trigger event. But it does seem entirely reasonable to argue that an appropriate model may have identified in advance the existence of a nonzero probability that if a certain type of order is executed in sufficiently large volume with certain (lack of) constraints on its execution pattern, that order could interact with the existing population of traders (both human and machine) to cause a "hot-potato" dynamic leading to a sudden, largely irrational, mass sell-off, exposing stub-quote values as reference prices, and leading major exchange-operators to declare self-help against each other, which is the current official story (CFTC & SEC, 2010a,b).

The possibility of such a sequence of events does not seem to have been much discussed prior to May 6th; perhaps if an appropriate national-level or international-level modeling facility had been operational, people would have been aware of the latent risk. Central government treasury departments in most economies have for many years (since before the advent of electronic computers) run large-scale macro-economic models for forecasting, but as far as we are aware there are no mature models used to understand and predict issues of systemic risk in the financial markets. Such a systemic-risk market simulator system could also be used for training market practitioners and regulators in dealing with rare but extreme situations, in much the same way as civil and combat aeroplane pilots are trained to deal with various rare but serious aircraft system failures by flying many hours of simulator practice, so that in the unlikely event of such a failure occurring on a real flight, the pilot can rely on her lessons learned and experience gained in the simulator. The rescue of *Apollo 13* owed an awful lot to the availability of accurate simulation models (physical electro-mechanical ones rather than purely virtual computer simulations) at NASA Mission Control. The simulators had been developed to train the astronauts in dealing with various mid-mission failure situations, including using the Lunar Excursion Module as a "lifeboat", as was necessary on *Apollo 13*; after the explosion on *Apollo 13* the simulators also became the test-bed for evaluating novel procedures necessary to keep the crew safe and the crippled ship on its return course.

Simulation models used in complex systems engineering are typically not intended for training humans *within* the socio-technical system being simulated; rather, any human agents within the real system are *also* simulated in the model of that system. Nevertheless, the use of simulation models as scientific evaluation and training tools for humans dealing with unusual complex situations has a long history: see, e.g., Sloan (1981) and Dorner (1990, 1997), yet there is currently very little in the way of comparable use of personnel training/evaluation simulators in the financial markets. Trainee traders typically learn the ropes by running "dummy" accounts, keeping a record of trades that they would have made, but did not actually execute, so that any losses are merely on paper; this can be done using live market data, and trading strategies can also be back-tested on historical data. A notably more sophisticated simulator, integrating real-time price feeds, was developed in a collaboration between the University of Pennsylvania and Lehman Brothers, the Penn-Lehman Automated Trading project, described by Kearns & Ortiz (2003).

While techniques such as these work well as training for situations where the trader's activity has no immediate effect on the prices of the securities being traded, they cannot readily model *market impact*, where the mere act of revealing the intent to buy or sell a large quantity of a security means that other traders in that security (potential counterparties to the trade) alter their prices before the transaction occurs, in anticipation of the change in price that would otherwise result after the transaction has executed. Furthermore, simulators based on regurgitating historical data offer essentially nothing toward understanding the current or future overall system-level dynamics of the system: they can tell you what happened, but not what might happen next, nor what might have happened instead. Simulators for evaluating trading strategies on historical data are sometimes referred to as financial-market "wind-tunnels" (e.g. Galas *et al.*, 2010). A financial-market wind-tunnel is certainly useful in refining the dynamics of an individual trading strategy, in much the same way as a traditional engineer's wind tunnel is useful in refining the aerodynamics of a new aeroplane or car. But financial-market wind-tunnel simulators are of zero help in understanding systemic issues such as financial stability, for much the same reason that an aerodynamicist's wind tunnel can tell you nothing about system-level phenomena such as traffic congestion in a city's street, nor air safety in a nation's skies.

More fancifully, it may also be worth exploring the use of advanced simulation facilities to allow regulatory bodies to act as "certification authorities", running new trading algorithms in the system-simulator to assess their likely impact on overall systemic behavior before allowing the owner/developer of the algorithm to run it "live" in the real-world markets. Certification by regulatory authorities is routine in certain industries, such as nuclear power or aeronautical engineering. We currently have certification processes for aircraft in an attempt to prevent air-crashes, and for automobiles in an attempt to ensure that road-safety standards and air-pollution constraints are met, but we have no trading-technology certification processes aimed at preventing financial crashes. In the future, this may come to seem curious.

We're not arguing here that predictive simulation models are a "silver bullet", an easily achievable panacea to the problem of assessing systemic risk and identifying black-swan failure modes: developing and maintaining such models would be difficult, and would require a major research investment. It seems very likely that quantitative analytical techniques such as probabilistic risk assessment (see e.g. Stamatelatos *et al.,* 2002a, 2002b; Dezfuli *et al.*, 2009; Hubbard, 2009) and probabilistic model-checking (e.g. Calinescu & Kwiatkowska, 2010; Calinescu, Kikuchi, & Kwiatkowska, 2010) would also need to be involved, in sufficiently extended forms, to help constrain the (otherwise impossibly vast) space of possible situations and interactions that would need to be explored by the simulations.

While there is no shortage of challenges in simulating the technical entities in socio-technical systems, simulating the social entities is almost always even more problematic, and this is something that doesn't have to be addressed by meteorological forecasting systems. Whether individual human agents, or groups of humans operating and interacting as teams or large organizations, the social entities in a socio-technical system are frequently present in virtue of the fact that they are needed to perform roles and discharge responsibilities with levels of flexibility, adaptability, and subtleness that are beyond the capability of automated systems. Modelling those kind of issues certainly presents a large number of deep technical challenges, and it is fair to say that the representations of social entities in many HISE models are often quite primitive: simple probabilistic models of humans switching from "safe" to "error" status are not uncommon. More sophisticated nondeterministic behavioural models such those based on Markov chains (e.g. Haccou & Meels, 1994; Benveniste *et al.*, 2003), and computational implementations of models of behaviour and motivation from the ethology literature (such as Lorenz's well-known hydraulic model explained in his 1966 book *On Aggression*) have all been explored in the research field that studies mechanisms for the generation or simulation of adaptive behaviour in animals (including humans) and synthetic agents, including those that are needed to model human ingenuity and adaptivity in predictive simulation models. One of the biggest drivers for this research is the need for creating believable synthetic agents in virtual environments such as computer games, yet the work presents deep challenges and is also directly relevant to simulations of real-world scenarios for training and evaluation purposes (so-called "serious games")[15]: see, e.g., Blumberg, 1996; Ivanov, 2002; Tomlinson & Blumberg, 2002; Horswill 2009. In some limited domains, for instance the modeling of emergency egress by crowds of humans from stricken structures (such as burning buildings or sinking ships), where there is reasonable data for how humans do behave in such circumstances, such

---

[15] See, for example, the Serious Games Institute at http://www.seriousgamesinsti tute.co.uk, the Serious Games Initiative at http://www.seriousgames.org/, and the various research outputs from FutureLab on Games and Learning, Serious Games in Education, Game-Based Experience in Learning, and Teaching with Games, all available at http://www.futurelab.org.uk/projects/. An extensive report on the use of serious games in military education and training was produced by Caspian Learning for the UK Ministry of Defence:http://www.caspianlearning.co.uk/MoD_Defence_ Academy_Serious_games_Report_04.11.08.pdf.

models have proven to be genuinely insightful (see, e.g., Johnson, 2005, 2006, 2008; Johnson & Nilsen-Nygaard, 2008)[16].

The significant cost of constructing and operating such a simulation facility could possibly be met from the public purse via general taxation, or could perhaps be funded by direct contributions from the major financial corporations (banks, fund-management companies, exchange operators, insurers, etc.) operating in a particular country or group of countries. If funded as a public-sector project, it would of course be necessary to recognize that in addition to the significant technical challenges, the establishment of such a simulator facility also present significant budgetary challenges and the entire endeavour would need to stand up to a thorough cost-benefit analysis: this is an issue expanded upon by Bullock (2011).

However, it is not the case that the only way of building or running such a simulation facility is via public-sector financing. It is possible that a group of financial institutions could collaborate on, and co-fund, the necessary capital expenditure at start-up and ongoing operational costs. A UK precedent for this, albeit in a different industry sector, is the independent non-profit company CFMS Ltd[17] that is jointly owned and operated by founding partners Airbus, BAE Systems, Frazer-Nash Consultancy, MBDA UK, Rolls-Royce, and Williams Formula 1 Engineering. CFMS exists to advance the theory and practice of simulation-based design processes, and has invested in its own high-performance computing facilities available in its Advanced Simulation Research Centre (ASRC). Given the importance of aerodynamics to many of the founding partners, there is a focus on computational fluid dynamics modeling in CFMS/ASRC, which is of no direct relevance to the world of finance. Nevertheless, the success of CFMS and ASRC shows that independent companies can indeed come together to co-found and co-run shared facilities as an investment in pre-competitive research and development capability.

If a major simulation facility was constructed, revenue could be generated from levying charges for anyone wanting access to it, and also possibly from using it as a training or certification facility. The potentially massive cost involved is not necessarily a disincentive: if the simulator was constructed on a minimal budget of (say) several hundred thousand pounds, it would be reasonably easy for financial corporations such as a hedge funds or investment banks to fund their own rival internal projects, probably much better-resourced, which would then detract from the public-good shared-utility nature of what is proposed here.

But, if the national-level simulator was funded by tens or hundreds of millions of pounds (and assuming that these pounds were spent wisely) then it is plausible that it would be so well resourced, and hence so much more detailed and/or accurate, that no private corporation could reasonably hope to compete with it, then all private corporations reliant on its results would have an incentive to contribute to the running costs, and the intellectual content, of the simulator facility as a common good. The facility would then be a pre-competitive shared resource: all contributing corporations would have access to details of its design and construction, and all would have access to its facilities for running experiments. Corporations would nevertheless be free to

---

[16] See also http://www.massivesoftware.com/real-world-simulation-gallery/.
[17] See www.cfms.org.uk

compete on the basis of what questions they ask of the simulator (details of each corporation's specific experiments could be kept confidential), and in how they then use the results from their experiments.

Of course the counterargument to developing a single utility facility is that this would concentrate risk: if the one national simulator is wrong, and everyone is using results from that simulator, then everyone's expectations or predictions are wrong at the same time. This is also manifestly true of national weather-system simulator facilities, and there is no shortage of examples of entire nations being taken by surprise when their state-funded monopoly weather-forecasting services got it wrong.[18]

One approach to mitigating this risk may be to enforce so-called "n-plex redundancy", as is common in the design of controllers for aerospace and defence systems, where the same control-system functionality is implemented by n multiple parallel systems, each designed and implemented by different independent suppliers, often constrained to not use the same core technologies (such as particular processor chips, programming languages and compilers, third-party suppliers, etc). The rationale for such an approach is that, while each of the n redundant systems may have one or more failure modes, the likelihood of all n systems having the same (or overlapping) vulnerabilities is greatly reduced by the active prevention of them sharing common components and/or development paths. Thus, so the argument goes, while one or more of the individual systems may fail from time to time, the remaining parallel redundant systems will most probably remain operational, and thereby coherent control will be maintained. So, maybe the best approach is for a national agency to commission some small number n of competing predictive simulation models, adopting or guided by the principle of n-plex redundancy, in the hope that the collective indications from the suite of n independent simulations can be trusted more than the lone voice of a single model.

A more thorny issue is the effect of the feedback loop from the model(s) back to the market systems being modeled. Results from a predictive simulation model of the weather do not actually alter the weather, but results from a market simulation may have a significant effect on the subsequent behavior of agents within the real-world markets that the simulator is a model of. There is prior evidence of self-fulfilling prophecies driving market dynamics, such as the theory that market activity is somehow affected by the number of sunspots. There is no *a priori* causal mechanistic explanation for why sunspots might affect market activity, but someone once proposed that there was at least a correlation between sunspot numbers and markets rising or falling; all that was then required was for enough people to believe in the correlation and to allow that belief to alter their trading activity in the markets. This

---

[18] On October 15th, 1987, a UK Met Office forecaster reassured viewers on the BBC prime-time evening weather broadcast that there was not a hurricane coming, in an attempt to quell earlier speculation. Later that night the south of England was hit by the worst hurricane-force windstorm for over 250 years, with speeds gusting to 120mph for several hours, causing huge amounts of damage and unprecedented levels of disruption for days afterwards. Other nations' meteorological forecasting services on mainland Europe, using different monitoring and prediction models, had given more accurate forecasts of the windy weather that night.

shared belief then *became* the causal link: if enough people are counting sunspots and using that to drive their market behaviour, then an increase in the number of sunspots will indeed affect the market in the manner that was "predicted" by their belief, thereby reinforcing the conviction of those who already hold the belief and helping to convert non-believers. The causal feedback loop from predictive simulations back to the real-world markets is something that will need to be handled well, but it is not necessarily a problem: the feedback could have a positive effect, dampening unwelcome dynamics.

To conclude, we observe that there is an old saying: "if it ain't broke, don't fix it". This is certainly wise guidance in very many situations. But it is important to remember that for some systems, when they do actually break, they go so catastrophically wrong so superhumanly fast that the safest option for such a system really is to fix it while it ain't broke, because that is the only decent chance you'll get. This is the case for many large-scale complex IT systems (LSCITS). Ensemble forecasting via *n*-plex redundant predictive simulation models is not cheap, is not easy, and is certainly far from perfect, but it may just be the best option currently available.[19]

The novelty of this proposal can perhaps be judged by the fact that the most recent comprehensive UK industry-focused review examining mechanisms for achieving supervisory control of systemic risk (Bonisch & Di Giammarino, 2010) mentions predictive simulation modeling only obliquely, in passing; but that same report also mentions the Flash Crash only once, in passing, too, as if such a manifestly deviant event was already normalized.

Nevertheless, we are certainly not the only people to be making such proposals: see, e.g. (Farmer & Foley 2009; Economist, 2010; Harford, 2011; Salmon, 2011), and the UK Government Office for Science's recent *Foresight* project exploring the future of computer trading in the financial markets has commissioned two excellent reviews that discuss aspects of the idea in more detail: see Bullock (2011) and Farmer & Skouras (2011). The UK already has significant investments in university research centres that could make valuable contributions to this approach.[20]

In his April 2009 speech *Rethinking the Financial Sector*, Andy Haldane, Executive Director for Financial Stability at the Bank of England, argued that three steps were necessary to safeguard against another series of events like the 2007/08 subprime crisis: all three steps deal with the global network of interacting financial institutions. Haldane's argument was that we should work first to map that network; then take steps to better manage and regulate the existing network; and then explore useful ways in which the network could be restructured or otherwise modified. We contend that all three of these steps (map, manage, & modify) could, and in fact should, be performed

---

[19] In the interests of balance, for recent counterarguments to the use of simulation models, see Turkle (2009).

[20] Major UK academic research centres that could be involved include: the Bristol Centre for Complexity Science (http://bccs.bristol.ac.uk); the Bristol/Bath Systems Engineering Centre (www.bristol.ac.uk/eng-systems-centre/); the Southampton Institute for Complex Systems Simulation (www.icss.soton.ac.uk); the UCL PhD Centre for Financial Computing (http://fc.cs.ucl.ac.uk/phd-centre); the York Centre for Complex Systems Analysis (www.yccsa.org); and the UK Large-Scale Complex IT Systems Initiative (www.lscits.org).

via an appropriate simulation-model-based engineering approach: creating and maintaining the model would be Haldane's mapping exercise; once operational, the effects of different regulatory actions, and any potential restructuring of the financial network could be explored and evaluated in the model too.

4   Summary

The Flash Crash of May 6th 2010 was a sudden and dramatic failure in a ultra-large-scale software-intensive socio-technical system (the US financial markets) with prices running wild at a speed and magnitude of volatility that were without historical precedent. The fact that there was not major lasting damage to the global financial markets is perhaps more due to luck than judgement: if the down-spike in the Flash Crash had occurred five minutes before market close in New York, it's plausible that could have triggered a contagious global sell-off that then went on to wrap around the world.

Yet from a broader perspective it is clear that the Flash Crash was just one more in a sequence of failures of risky technology, and quite plausibly such an event was made more likely via a prior process of financial-market practitioners becoming increasingly tolerant of unexpected events, previously thought to be unacceptable, not resulting in disasters: that is, via a process of normalization of deviance.

The problems posed by attempting to engineer and manage reliable ultra-large-scale complex adaptive socio-technical systems of systems are becoming ever more clear, but further research is needed to develop appropriate tools and techniques. System-of-systems issues of scaling, normal failure, heterogeneity via organic growth, and emergent behavior all have to be addressed. Parallel running of multiple redundant predictive simulation models is one approach that may now be applicable for assessing and controlling systemic risk in the financial markets.

The engineering of LSCITS and ULS socio-technical ecosystem system-of-systems is in its infancy: it has significant differences from traditional engineering of smaller-scale systems, and developing rigorous trusted approaches may turn out to be a long haul. The UK's LSCITS Initiative and the USA's Ultra-Large-Scale (ULS) Systems Initiative are each articulations of national strategic concerns. Both represent a sizeable step toward developing a new community of practitioners and researchers who are conversant with all the necessary subfields that can contribute to addressing issues in the science and engineering of such systems, forming those communities of practice will take several years of sustained investment. Without doubt this is not merely responding to a national need but an international one. We, the authors of this report, welcome any researchers, practitioners, regulators, policy-makers or sponsors who would like to become involved in the LSCITS and/or the ULS Systems initiatives. The intellectual challenges are significant, but not insurmountable; the potential societal savings are massive, and the scale is truly global.

Acknowledgements. This chapter is slightly revised and extended/updated from a report that we co-authored in early 2011 for the UK Government Office for Science's *Foresight* project on the future of computer trading in the financial markets. We thank the following people for valuable conversations and/or for their comments on previous versions of this document: Prof. Philip Bond, University of Bristol and University of

Oxford; Prof. Seth Bullock, University of Southampton; Andy Haldane, Bank of England; Kevin Houston, FIX Protocol Ltd; Prof. David Parkes, Harvard University; Lucas Pedace, UK Government Office for Science; Dr. John Rooksby, University of St Andrews; Tim Rowe and his colleagues at the UK Financial Services Authority; Prof. Ian Sommerville, University of St Andrews; Dr. Gillian Tett, *The Financial Times*; and Nigel Walker, UK Financial Services Knowledge Transfer Network.

Appendix: High-Integrity Large-Scale Complex Ecosystems

In this Appendix we take a quick tour through the concepts and approaches from current systems engineering that are relevant to the discussion just presented, but for which going into detailed explanation or definition would have been a distracting diversion from the flow of our argument. In sequence, here we briefly review high-integrity approaches to systems engineering (Appendix A.1); the definitions of Systems-of-Systems (A.2) and Complex Adaptive Systems (A.3); and then selected current leading-edge approaches to the high-integrity engineering of complex adaptive systems-of-systems (A.4).

A.1 High-Integrity Systems Engineering

High-integrity engineering techniques for safety-critical systems have a long heritage, and it's simply beyond the scope of this document to provide a comprehensive review of all the relevant background literature; for detailed surveys, see the review chapters in the recent PhD theses by Alexander (2007, pp.29-55), Despotou (2007, pp.41-76), and Hall-May (2007, pp.33-72).

It is commonplace in real-world engineering situations to be dealing with systems that simply cannot be guaranteed to be *absolutely* safe because key components in the system are known not to be *absolutely* reliable. If one of the key components is known to be 99.99999% reliable, that is an admission that there is a 0.00001% chance of failure; if failure of that component compromises the safety of the overall system, then there is a risk (small, but nonzero) that the system will become unsafe. Safety engineering has developed techniques for estimating the causal chains of events leading to failure, the attendant risks of failure, the effects of failure, and for reducing those risks and limiting their effects; in this sense then, risk and reliability are two sides of the same coin.

One of the earliest forms of risk and reliability assessment method, developed in the 1960's US aerospace and missile programs, is fault-tree analysis (FTA). FTA operates by the engineer first identifying "basic events" such as a fuse blowing or a relay-switch failing to open. Significant combinations of these basic events are then aggregated into a graph structure much like a family tree: compound events are formed via "gate" nodes that link basic events. It may be that basic events E1 and E2 and E3 *all* have to occur for a particular output fault F1 to occur: on the graph the event nodes E1, E2, and E3 would be shown as "daughters" of F1, with F1 denoted as an "and" gate. Other types of gate include: "or" (any one or more of the daughters triggers the compound fault);"combination" (the compound fault is triggered by any n

or more of the daughters occurring, for $n>1$); "exclusive or" (exactly one daughter will act as the trigger); "priority and" (the daughter events have to all occur in a specific sequence); and "inhibit" (the daughter event occurs as the same time as some enabling condition). The daughter nodes of a compound event are not required to be basic events: they can be other compound events, and so it is possible to construct deep trees showing how basic events, combinations of basic events, and combinations of those combinations, can each combine to contribute to particular faults or failures in the system under analysis. Fault-tree analysis distinguishes between failure *effects* (such as a switch failing to make contact), failure *modes* (such as the switch's contacts being broken, or the contacts having a very high resistance), and failure *mechanisms* by which those modes may come about (such as high resistance on the switch contacts being caused by corrosion of the contact surfaces, or by an insulating coating having been spilled onto them); this well-known safety-critical engineering practice is known as Failure Modes and Effects Analysis (FMEA). For further details, see e.g. Stamatelatos *et al.* (2002b).

FMEA and FTA, as just described, are essentially qualitative, deterministic, approaches. In recent years, there has been a concerted move toward developing quantitative approaches where numeric values represent measures of risk. An obvious, intuitive, risk metric is the probability of failure, and so the field is widely known as probabilistic risk assessment (PRA).[21] Over much the same period, the field of mathematical statistics has undergone something of a revolution in the rapid adoption of the so-called *Bayesian* approach as an alternative to the long-established, traditional, *frequentist* approach, and this has been reflected in the PRA literature. For instance, in 2002 NASA published a 323-page guide to PRA procedures for its managers and practitioners (Stamatelatos *et al.*, 2002a) based on traditional frequentist statistics, but then in 2009 it published a new 275-page guide to PRA using Bayesian methods (Dezfuli *et al.*, 2009). Some authors, most notably Hubbard (2009), have argued forcefully that PRA should be the only game in town, but PRA is not without its critics and detractors: see, for example: Parry (1996); Slovik (1999); and Apostolakis (2004).

The opening page of NASA's 2002 guide to PRA neatly summarises the history of its adoption in that organization:

> "Legend has it that early in the Apollo project the question was asked about the probability of successfully sending astronauts to the moon and returning them safely to Earth. A risk, or reliability, calculation of some sort was performed and the result was a very low success probability value. So disappointing was this result that NASA became discouraged from further performing quantitative analyses of risk or reliability until after the Challenger mishap in 1986. Instead, NASA decided to rely on the Failure Modes and Effects Analysis (FMEA) method for system safety assessments. To date, FMEA continues to be required by NASA in all its safety-related projects.

---

[21] Some authors (e.g. Apostolakis, 2004) instead refer to Quantitative Risk Assessment, to cover the possibility that the numerical values being manipulated are not strictly interpretable as probabilities.

"In the meantime, the nuclear industry picked up PRA to assess safety almost as a last resort in defense of its very existence. This analytical method was gradually improved and expanded by experts in the field and has gained momentum and credibility over the past two decades, not only in the nuclear industry, but also in other industries like petrochemical, offshore platforms, and defense. By the time the Challenger accident occurred, PRA had become a useful and respected tool for safety assessment. Because of its logical, systematic, and comprehensive approach, PRA has repeatedly proven capable of uncovering design and operation weaknesses that had escaped even some of the best deterministic safety and engineering experts. This methodology showed that it was very important to examine not only low-probability and high-consequence individual mishap events, but also high-consequence scenarios which can emerge as a result of occurrence of multiple high-probability and nearly benign events. Contrary to common perception, the latter is oftentimes more detrimental to safety than the former." (Stamatelatos *et al.*, 2002a, p.1)

NASA's series of public-domain guides on FTA, frequentist PRA, and Bayesian PRA (Stamatclatos *et al.*, 2002a; Stamatclatos *et al.*, 2002b; Dczfuli *et al.*, 2009, respectively) talk in terms of estimating and assuring *system* safety/reliability: they do not involve themselves in the distinction between systems, and systems-of-systems (SoS), which was informally introduced earlier. However, for the discussion that follows, we need to take a brief diversion into a more precise definition of what precisely we mean here by "SoS".

A.2 Systems-of-Systems: Directed, Collaborative, Coalition, and Ecosystem

Probably the most-cited paper in the SoS literature is Maier's "Architecting Principles for Systems of Systems" (1998), and we will use Maier's careful definition of a SoS here. Maier proposed two primary characteristics that distinguish a SoS: a system that did not exhibit these two characteristics was, in his terms, not to be considered as a SoS "...*regardless* of the complexity or geographic distribution of its components." (Maier 1998, p.271, original emphasis). Maier's definition reads as follows:

> "A system-of-systems is an assemblage of components which individually may be regarded as systems, and which possess two additional properties:
>
> > "Operational Independence of the Components: If the system-of-systems is disassembled into its component systems the component systems must be able to usefully operate independently. That is, the components fulfill customer-operator purposes on their own.
> >
> > "Managerial Independence of the Components: The component systems not only *can* operate independently, they *do* operate independently. The component systems are separately acquired and integrated but maintain a continuing operational existence independent of the system-of-systems."
>
> (Maier, 1998, p.271, original emphasis)

A strict interpretation of Maier's definition of SoS would argue that the US Space Shuttle, even at one second before launch, is not a system of systems. The Orbiter, its external fuel tank, its left and right SRBs, and the launch-pad and support-tower that they all lift off from, do not have immediate *operational independence*: that is, they were all intimately designed to work with each other. It might perhaps be argued that with a little tinkering the SRBs could be re-engineered to usefully operate independently (as warhead-carrying long-range missiles, perhaps), but that would be clutching at straws: even if that were true, there is no real sense in which any of the Shuttle's component systems exhibit Maier's second property, of *managerial independence*, and on that basis the Shuttle at launch is simply not an SoS. At launch, each of the shuttle's component systems is under the collective, coordinated, combined command of NASA (the precise nexus of that command is something that is constructed by the interaction of, and shifts dynamically between, Mission Control on the ground, and the astronauts onboard the Shuttle).

Precisely because of Maier's definition, earlier in Section 2 of this paper we were careful not to describe the Shuttle as a SoS. Nevertheless, it is clear that the global financial markets network, or even "just" the financial markets operational in one of the major global hubs such as London or New York, satisfy both the operational independence and managerial independence criteria. Maier goes on to note that SoS can be classified as *Directed* (built and managed to fulfill specific purposes), or *Collaborative,* or *Virtual*. His definition of collaborative SoS reads as follows:

> "Collaborative systems-of-systems are distinct from directed systems in that the central management organization does not have coercive power to run the system. The component systems must, more or less, voluntarily collaborate to fulfill the agreed upon central purposes."
> (Maier, 1998, p.278).

In Maier's terms, a virtual SoS is then a SoS that is neither directed nor collaborative, i.e. it is one for which there is no central management authority, and also no agreed upon central purposes. Maier is explicit that he considers national economies to be virtual SoS; and it seems obvious that in Maier's terms the global financial markets are also virtual SoS. But classifying the markets as a virtual SoS simply because of their *absence* of central management and centrally agreed purpose glosses over some important richness in the network of interacting institutions within the financial markets. The markets involve varying numbers of various types of institution (e.g., investment banks, hedge funds, exchange operators, insurers, technology providers). The organizations that participate in the markets (and those that regulate them too) serve different purposes; some of them are in direct competition with other institutions (sometimes in zero-sum terms), others are in collaborative relationships with one or more other institutions; and such institutions come and go over time. Sommerville *et al.* (2012) have recently coined the term "Coalition of Systems" to describe this class of SoS; before that, Valerdi *et al.* (2008) referred to "No Single Owner SoS", and Northrop *et al.* (2006) coined the term *socio-technical ecosystems*, to capture the same notion that these SoS can be represented as a web of interacting constituents: in some cases the interactions are collaborative, in others they are competitive, all within the one SoS. It seems unarguable that the technology-enabled global financial markets of today, and in the future, are ecosystem-SoS.

The development of techniques for maintaining and managing high-integrity large-scale ecosystem-SoS is a new and significantly under-researched field. Fewer than five years ago, eight authors from industry and academia co-authored a paper (De Laurentis *et al.*, 2007) calling for an international consortium on SoS engineering to be established, to better understand the problems and solution strategies associated with SoS, yet their conception of a SoS was phrased in terms of "...heterogeneous independently operable systems to achieve a unique purpose" (p.68) – that is, they concentrated on a conception of SoS that is better suited to Maier's directed/collaborative SoS than the ecosystem-SoS of Northrop *et al.* Books and research papers exploring how to engineer robustly scalable socio-technical systems are currently few and far between (but see Abbot & Fisher, 2009; Rooksby, Rouncefield, & Sommerville, 2009; Baxter & Sommerville 2010).

The primary reason for that is because the development of reliable practices, and engineering teaching, for ensuring or assuring the integrity or safety of a SoS is a current research challenge; one that is being actively pursued by the world's leading research groups in high-integrity systems engineering, and even those leading researchers would admit that it is not yet a solved problem. In contrast to traditional engineering teaching, with its emphasis on designing "from scratch", starting (metaphorically at least) with a clean sheet of paper, most SoS instead arise from organic processes of aggregation and accretion, where pre-existing systems are integrated as constituents into the SoS. In almost all large-scale SoS, there is significant heterogeneity (which itself changes over time) because different constituents in the SoS were added at different stages in the development of the SoS and arrived via differing design and implementation paths. In their 2008 book *Eating the IT Elephant: Moving from Greenfield Development to Brownfield*, senior IBM staff Richard Hopkins and Kevin Jenkins made the analogy between the greenfield/brownfield distinction in civil engineering, and modern-day large-scale complex IT projects. A greenfield engineering project is one in which construction takes place on a previously undeveloped site, allowing a "clean-sheet" approach at the design stage, with relatively little preparatory work required on-site before construction, and with relatively few constraints on the construction process. A brownfield project is one in which the site has previously been built on and hence may require significant clearing operation before construction, with the possibility of the added complexity from the requirement that existing structures must be retained and their viability maintained during the construction phase (Hopkins & Jenkins, 2008).

Even if a large-scale SoS *was* the product of a clean-sheet engineering design process and was initially constructed from homogeneous constituents, sheer largeness-of-scale implies that at any one time it is almost definite that some of those constituents will have failed and be needing replacement (so-called *normal failure*). Those replacement constituents may not be exactly identical to the originals, and so the SoS becomes a heterogeneous, brownfield engineering problem.

The challenge of determining the safety of a SoS is neatly summarized by Alexander, Kazakov, & Kelly (2006):

> "In a conventional system, ...the system boundary is well defined and the components within that boundary can be enumerated. When a safety analyst postulates some failure of a component, the effect of that failure can be propagated through the system to reveal whether or not the failure results in a

hazard. This is not always easy, because of the complexity of possible interactions and variability of system state, hence the need for systematic analysis techniques, automated analysis tools and system designs that minimize possible interactions. To make the task more tractable, most existing hazard analysis techniques.... deal with only a single failure at a time; coincident failures are rarely considered.

"In an SoS, this problem is considerably worse. The system boundary is not well defined, and the set of entities within that boundary can vary over time, either as part of normal operations... or as part of evolutionary development... Conventional tactics to minimize interactions may be ineffective, because the system consists of component entities that are individually mobile. In some cases... the entities may be designed to form ad-hoc groupings amongst themselves. Conventional techniques may be inadequate for determining whether or not some failure in some entity is hazardous in the context of the SoS as a whole."

The prospect of component entities being "individually mobile" was relevant to Alexander *et al.* because their work concentrated on SoS in defence applications, where the constituent entities in the SoS are often individual battlefield units (e.g., troops, tanks, unmanned vehicles, etc). While there is no direct *physical* correlate of spatial mobility in the computerized global financial markets, there is a reasonable equivalent in the *virtual* space defined by the network of current interactions between agents in the markets: just as a tank might physically move from one location to another on a battlefield in order to engage with the enemy or withdraw to a position of safety, so a trading agent (human or machine) might establish a connection with a potential counterparty, or terminate an existing connection. In both the tank battle and the trading scenario, the key factor that is altered is the network of links from the node in question (the tank, the trader), to other nodes in the network (enemy units, other traders) with which that node might have meaningful interactions (exchange of fire, exchange of bids/offers).

But this "mobility" issue of the network of meaningful interactions changing dynamically is not the only issue that confuses the task of understanding or managing an ecosystem SoS. Each of the nodes in the network, i.e. each of the constituent entities, is likely to be both *nonlinear* and *adaptive*. For the sake of the argument here, we'll simply define "nonlinearity" as a meaning that the entity's "outputs" (i.e., its responses or behavior) are not a simple linear function of its "inputs" (i.e., readings from its sensors, say); and we'll adopt a similarly simple definition of "adaptive": the entity is adaptive if its "outputs" may change over time, in consequence of the particular time-sequence of "inputs" that the entity is exposed to. Readers familiar with the mathematical economics literature will recognize this notion of adaptation as similar to "path-dependency"; colloquially we can think of the entity "learning from experience" or "evolving its response over time". In recent decades, a new set of scientific tools and techniques has been developed to study systems composed of networks of interacting nonlinear adaptive entities. That field is known as Complexity Science, and the networked nonlinear adaptive systems are known as Complex Adaptive Systems.

A.3 Complex Adaptive Systems

In complexity science, *complex systems* are commonly defined as systems that are composed from large numbers of components, where each component interacts with some number of other components, and where there are nonlinearities in the nature of the component interactions and/or in the responses of the components themselves, which compound across the entire system in such a way that the overall system-level behaviour is difficult or perhaps impossible to predict accurately, even when one is given complete or near-complete information about the individual components and their interactions. The system-level behaviour is said to *emerge* from the network of interacting components and their constituent behaviours, forming a whole that is in some reasonable sense more than the sum of its parts. Substituting the word "constituent" for "component" in that description and it is clear that for very many SoS of practical importance, the SoS is manifestly a complex system. In addition to exhibiting emergent behaviour, many complex systems of significant interest are *adaptive* (in the sense informally introduced in the previous paragraph), and this also is surely true of many constituents in SoS, hence many SoS are instances of Complex Adaptive Systems (CAS). Since the late 1980's a growing number of scientists have been attempting to understand the financial markets as CAS, and have been exploring the links between the financial markets and other CAS, both naturally-occurring and engineered artefacts. There is growing evidence that the emergent behaviour, phase changes, instabilities, and hysteresis seen in many other complex systems are also to be found in the financial markets: see, for example: Anderson, Arrow, & Pines (1989); Arthur, Morrison, *et al.* (1997); Johnson, Jefferies, & Hui (2003); Challet, Marsili, & Zhang (2004); and Blume & Durlaf (2005).

A small but growing number of researchers in the (systems-of-) systems engineering community have, in recent years, turned their attention to whether tools and techniques from complexity science can help in the brownfield engineering of robust, scalable, large-scale, systems: that is, they are exploring the consequences of taking a CAS approach to the creation and management of such large-scale systems and SoS: see, for example, Bar-Yam (2005); Braha *et al.* (2006); Sheard, & Mostashari (2008); Polacek, & Verma, (2009); and Sillitto (2010). Thus far, only a small amount of this work has addressed issues directly relevant to the financial markets but some notable work has been produced; see, e.g.: Harman & Bar-Yam, 2008; and the Nasdaq study by Darley & Oatkin (1997), which was discussed in more detail in Section 4.

Very often, such approaches involve exploring the system using so-called Multi-Agent Simulation (MAS) models, where a computer simultaneously models each of the constituents (or "agents") in the network of interacting adaptive nonlinear entities, resolving the consequence of each entity's interaction with its environment (which in most cases will include one or more other such entities), often using fine time-slicing or discrete-event simulation techniques. The agents in the simulation may adapt their responses over time either by implementing machine-learning techniques (for learning "within the lifetime" of the agent) and/or by implementing a process inspired by Darwinian evolution, a so-called *genetic algorithm* (a simulated population of agents, adapting to its niche over successive generations via a process of random variation and "survival of the fittest" directed selection: each agent's behaviour or performance at the task at hand being determined at least in part by "genes" that can be passed on to successor agents: see e.g. Goldberg, 1987). Very often, the reliance on computer simulation models is a consequence of the mathematical nonlinearities in the system being analytically intractable: that is, they are sufficiently complicated and complex that the tools for expressing them as a set of equations and then deriving formal proofs of certain statements about the system, via manipulation of the equations, is simply not possible.

For introductions to the use of CAS/MAS models in understanding social, economic, and socio-technical systems, see the texts by Epstein & Axtell (1996) and Axelrod & Cohen (2000). For examples of early machine-learning adaptive trading agents, see Cliff (1997) & Gjerstad & Dickhaut (1998), for the story of how those agents beat human traders, see Das et al. (2001). With regard to the application of evolutionary approaches, there has been heavy use of "replicator dynamics" (a technique pioneered in the theoretical study of evolution in biological systems) for exploring the interactions between different types of trading strategies, and identifying stable equilibria in the interaction dynamics (e.g., Walsh et al., 2002; Vytelingum, Cliff, & Jennings 2008); and also various researchers have used genetic algorithms to create trading agents, and the market-mechanisms they operate in, co-adapted to each other by evolution (e.g., Phelps et al., 2002; Cliff, 2003; Byde, 2003; Cliff, 2009; Phelps et al., 2010). Evolutionary adaptation and co-adaptation in biological systems has served as a productive metaphor for economic dynamics at various levels for several decades (see, e.g., Nelson & Winter, 1982; Hodgson, 1993; Ormerod, 2006; Stephens & Waelbroeck, 2009); and there are other aspects of biological systems, such as the interconnected web of dependencies in natural ecosystems, that can offer fruitful insights into the functioning of financial systems (see, e.g., May et al., 2008; Haldane & May, 2011; also Johnson, 2011). Sources of inspiration are not limited to biological systems: studies of the complex dynamics and size-vs-frequency distributions of earthquakes also offer insights for students of markets crashes: see Sornette (2002).

CAS and MAS approaches are not limited to the exploration of economic and financial systems: the approach is now pretty-much a standard item in the toolboxes of biologists, urban planners, military strategists, movie animators, safety architects, and practitioners of many more application areas in science and engineering. Several research teams have worked on developing general-purpose simulators (with associated visualization and analysis tools) for exploring CAS and MAS: for details of an example generic simulator and reviews of related work see Polack, Andrews, & Sampson (2009); and Polack et al. (2010).

In the course of this section's discussion thus far, we've briefly surveyed high integrity systems engineering, and the definitions of systems of systems (SoS) and of complex adaptive system. Now we draw those three strands together and explore the current state, and future prospects for, high-integrity safety-critical engineering of complex adaptive ecosystem SoS.[22]

---

[22] We recognize that this is a long and cumbersome phrase. A shorter alternative might be "wicked systems", first coined as a technical term in information systems engineering by Metcalf (2005) in direct reference to Rittel & Webber's (1973) notion of "wicked problems". But, given the current widespread disaffection in the media and general public with the banking sector, it seems prudent to avoid the potential confusion between the technical sense of "wicked" and the morally judgmental one, confusion that might arise in talking about trying to develop new engineering approaches for dealing with the "wicked systems of the financial markets".

A.4 Engineering High-Integrity Complex Adaptive Ecosystem System-of-Systems

All approaches to risk assessment and safety-critical engineering involve the notion of a *model*. Rather than attempting to observe and manipulate the real physical system in its real operating environment, the model is instead an abstract representation of those aspects of the system that the engineers believe to be necessary and sufficient to reason about in order to achieve the task at hand. So, in this sense, a fault-tree diagram for some system is a model of that system. The fault-tree can be reasoned about, argued over, and altered to make it a better or worse representation of the real system, and the fault-tree can be manipulated to arrive at specific answers to specific questions, without having to touch the real system. The fault-tree is an explicit, diagrammatic, model of the system, suitable for risk assessment. But, as we have seen, the same system's risk assessment could instead be approached via Bayesian PRA, in which case the model will be a set of coupled equations and the associated prior probabilities.

In high integrity systems engineering, it is recognized that all models are developed iteratively, that they pass through a lifecycle: after an initial model is proposed, experience with the real system may reveal that the model needs refinement and improvement, the model is altered appropriately, but subsequent experience may again reveal the need for additional alterations. Eventually, it is hoped, the model will stabilize as more is known of the system. Of course, if the system itself is changing over time (as is almost definite in a socio-technical ecosystem SoS), the safety-engineer's model is forever playing catch-up; there will always be a strong likelihood that some aspect of the SoS is not yet known, not yet captured in the safety model.

Recognizing this, in recent years many researchers and practitioners involved in the engineering of high-integrity systems of systems have turned to predictive computer simulation models as a way of exploring "what if" scenarios. Such simulations are typically highly compute-intensive, and it is only with the ongoing Moore's-Law reductions in the real costs of computer power that such approaches have become practicable. In a predictive simulation, the model is expressed as interacting processes within the computer: such simulations may involve manipulating numeric values according to given equations (as in PRA); and they may also represent the model, or its outputs, via explicit diagrammatic visualizations (as in fault-tree analysis). Computer simulations offer the advantage of taking exhaustive "brute force" approaches to exploring system safety: for some systems, it is feasible to simulate the system in every possible combination of values for all variables of interest – the entire "state-space" of the system (that is, the space of all possible states it could ever find itself in) can be explored by the computer, given enough time. If the entire state-space is explored, and no unanticipated failures are discovered in the model, then (so long as the model is an accurate representation of the real system) the system's reliability is known completely. This technique of brute-force simulation has been particularly successful in the microelectronics industry, where the responses of new designs for silicon chips are explored exhaustively in simulation before the chip is fabricated for real: mistakes discovered at the simulation stage are *much* cheaper to fix than if the error is discovered only after the chip has been manufactured.

However, for many real-world systems, the state-space is sufficiently large that brute-force exhaustive searching is simply not possible. The combinatorics of state-spaces often involve exponentials-of-exponentials: equations of the form v=w-to-the-power-(x-to-the-power-(y-to-the-power-z))), and numbers such as v can grow astronomically huge, much larger than the number of atoms in the known universe, for only moderate values of w, x, y, and z. Attempting exhaustive search of such vast state-spaces is possible in theory, but the sun will burn out long before the search is over. So, for many real systems, sophisticated techniques are required to cleverly sample only selected points or areas in the system's state-space. Developing such techniques is a current research issue, even in microelectronics where the state-spaces of current chips have now grown to routinely be beyond the size where exhaustive search is practicable (see, e.g. Hsueh & Eder, 2006).

Researchers concerned with risk assessment and safety assurance in SoS have developed increasingly sophisticated simulation modelling techniques (see, e.g., De Laurentis & Han, 2006; Parisi et al., 2008; Clymer, 2009; Kewley & Tolk, 2009), and researchers interested in developing generic simulation tools for the study of complex adaptive systems have learnt from the methods developed in high-integrity systems engineering (Polack, Andrews, & Sampson, 2009). Some recent work has explored the possibility of feeding the outputs of simulation models directly into machine learning (ML) algorithms, so that the ML system can discover or learn rules and regularities that can neatly summarise the behavior of the system (see, e.g., Eder, Flach, & Hsueh, 2006; Alexander, 2007). Nevertheless, researchers remain cautiously aware that the model is only that: only a model, an abstraction. The models are used to explore possible circumstances and situations that may be very rare, and/or disastrous, in the real system. Alexander et al. (2006) comment that this approach is one that Dewar et al. (1996) refers to as "weak prediction":

> "[Dewar et al., 1996] note that *subjective judgement is unavoidable in assessing credibility*" and that when such a simulation produces an unexpected result "it has created an interesting hypothesis that can (and must) be tested by other means". In other words, when a simulation reveals a plausible system hazard, other, more conventional analyses must be carried out to determine whether it is credible in the real system. Therefore, the role of the simulation analysis is to narrow down a huge analysis space into one that is manually tractable." (Alexander et al., 2006)

One of the biggest challenges at present concerns modeling the *social* elements in socio-technical SoS: people and groups of people can be surprisingly sophisticated (and surprisingly stupid), and representing their relevant nonlinear, adaptive, nondeterministic behavior in a simulation model is certainly not easy.

Although it is undoubtedly difficult to capture human ingenuity and adaptivity, there are well-developed techniques in the CAS literature that can serve as good proxies: most notable of these is the use of co-evolution as a process for driving stochastic search through a space of possible designs or strategies, giving rise to what can appear to be a form of "artificial creativity".

The seminal example of this approach was described in a paper by Hillis (1990): Hillis used simulated evolution, a genetic algorithm (GA), to automatically design algorithms for sorting lists of numbers into numeric order; each "individual" in his

GA's population was a particular algorithm, and the sequence of steps in each individual's algorithm were specified by its "genes" (each step involved comparing a pair of numbers, and if necessary swapping their places in the list to make them be in the right numeric order); each individual's probability of reproduction (i.e., its *fitness*) was determined by how many test-lists it sorted successfully.

Initially, Hillis worked with a set-up where the test-lists were fixed in advance: when he did this, his GA could reliably evolve individual algorithms that did well at sorting the specific lists in the test set, but did poorly when presented with a novel list, one that was not in the test set. To counteract this, Hillis re-worked his system so that the test-lists were *also* an evolving population: the test-set was a population of lists, the particular numbers in each list were specified via its "genes" and the "fitness" of each list was determined by how "difficult" it was, i.e., by how many of the sorting algorithms failed to sort it. Thus the population of sorting algorithms, and the population of test-lists, made up a competitive co-evolutionary system, much like a predator-prey or parasite-host dynamic: the fitness of each sorter-algorithm depended on how many lists it could sort; the fitness of each list depended on how many sorter-algorithms it could defeat; and the two populations co-evolved over time. The co-evolutionary system was much more productive, and readily discovered sorting algorithms that rivalled the best-known human-designed ones.

Since Hillis' paper, several CAS researchers have demonstrated the power of co-evolution as a force for generating novel solutions and designs (see, e.g. Sims, 1994; Funes & Pollack 1999; Cartlidge & Bullock, 2004; Cliff & Miller 2006; Stuermer *et al.* 2009), it seems entirely plausible that co-evolutionary processes could be used to approximate the effects of human ingenuity and creativity in socio-technical systems. Perhaps more importantly, co-evolutionary processes could also be used to explore the state-space of simulated ecosystems SoS, in the search for conditions that reveal unanticipated failure modes, in much the same way as Hillis's population of test-lists searched for methods of "failing" his population of sorting algorithms. This would allow semi-automated generation of hypotheses about how the real system might fail.

References

1. Abbot, M., Fisher, M.: The Art of Scalability: Scalable Web Architecture, Processes, and Organizations for the Modern Enterprise. Addison-Wesley (2009)
2. Alexander, R., Kazakov, D., Kelly, T.: System of Systems Hazard Analysis Using Simulation and Machine Learning. In: Górski, J. (ed.) SAFECOMP 2006. LNCS, vol. 4166, pp. 1–14. Springer, Heidelberg (2006)
3. Alexander, R.: Using Simulation for Systems of Systems Hazard Analysis. PhD Thesis, Department of Computer Science, University of York, UK (2007)
4. Anderson, P., Arrow, K., Pines, D. (eds.): The Economy as an Evolving Complex System. Addison-Wesley (1989)
5. Angel, J.: Opening Remarks at SEC Roundtable on Shortselling (May 5, 2009a), http://www.sec.gov/comments/4-581/4581-2.pdf
6. Angel, J.: Letter to the Securities and Exchange Commission (June 19, 2009b), http://www.sec.gov/comments/s7-08-09/s70809-3758.pdf
7. Angel, J.: Letter to the Securities and Exchange Commission (September 21, 2009c), http://www.sec.gov/comments/s7-08-09/s70809-4658.pdf
8. Angel, J., Harris, L., Spratt, C.: Trading in the 21st Century (2010) (unpublished manuscript), http://www.sec.gov/comments/s7-02-10/s70210-54.pdf

9. Angel, J.: Letter to the Securities and Exchange Commission (April 30, 2010a), http://www.sec.gov/comments/s7-02-10/s70210-172.pdf
10. Angel, J.: Testimony to the US Senate (December 8, 2010b), http://msb.georgetown.edu/story/1242666871500.html
11. Apostolakis, G.: How Useful is Quantitative Risk Analysis? Risk Analysis 24(3), 515–520 (2004)
12. Arthur, B.: The Nature of Technology: What it is and how it evolves. Allen Lane (2009)
13. Arthur, B., Morrison, V., Durlauf, S., Lane, D. (eds.): The Economy as an Evolving Complex System II. Addison Wesley (1997)
14. Axelrod, R., Cohen, M.: Harnessing Complexity: Organizational Implications of a Scientific Frontier. Free Press (2000)
15. Bar-Yam, Y.: Making Things Work: Solving Complex Problems in a Complex World. Knowledge Press (2005)
16. Baxter, G., Sommerville, I.: Socio-technical Systems: From design methods to systems engineering. Interacting with Computers 23(1), 4–17 (2010)
17. Benveniste, A., Fabre, E., Haar, S.: Markov Nets: Probabilistic Models for Distributed and Concurrent Systems. IEEE Transactions on Automatic Control 48(11), 1936–1950 (2003)
18. Beinhocker, E.: The Origin of Wealth: Evolution, Complexity, and the Radical Remaking of Economics. Harvard Business School Press (2007)
19. Blas, J.: High-speed trading blamed for sugar rises. The Financial Times (February 8, 2011), http://www.ft.com/cms/s/0/05ba0b60-33d8-11e0-b1ed-00144feabdc0.html#axzz1JIx0tWXK
20. Blumberg, B.: Old Tricks, New Dogs: Ethology and Interactive Creatures. Ph.D. Thesis, MIT Media Lab. (1996)
21. Blume, L., Durlaf, S.: The Economy as an Evolving Complex System, III. Addison-Wesley (2005)
22. Bonen, Z.: Evolutionary Behavior of Complex Socio-Technical Systems. Working Paper #1056-79. Alfred P. Sloan School of Management, MIT (1979)
23. Bonisch, P., Di Giammarino, P.J.: Achieving Supervisory Control of Systemic Risk. Report jointly produced by UK Financial Services Knowledge Transfer Network, JWG, and Paradigm Risk (October 2010), http://www.jwg-it.eu/library.php?typeId=11
24. Bootle, R.: The Trouble with Markets: Saving Capitalism from Itself. Nicholas Brealey Publishing (2009)
25. Braha, D., Minai, A., Bar-Yam, Y.: Complex Engineered Systems: Science Meets Technology. Springer (2006)
26. Bullock, S.: Prospects for Large-Scale Financial Systems Simulation. Driver Review DR14, Foresight Project on the Future of Computer Trading in the Financial Markets. UK Government Office for Science (2011), http://www.bis.gov.uk/assets/foresight/docs/computer-trading/11-1233-dr14-prospects-for-large-scale-financial-systems-simulation.pdf
27. Byde, A.: Applying Evolutionary Game Theory to Auction Mechanism Design. In: Proceedings of the 2003 ACM Conference on E-Commerce, pp. 192–193 (2003)
28. Calinescu, R., Kwiatkowska, M.: Software Engineering Techniques for the Development of Systems of Systems. In: Choppy, C., Sokolsky, O. (eds.) Monterey Workshop 2008. LNCS, vol. 6028, pp. 59–82. Springer, Heidelberg (2010)
29. Calinescu, R., Kikuchi, S., Kwiatkowska, M.: Formal Methods for the Development and Verification of Autonomic IT Systems. In: Cong-Vinh, P. (ed.) Formal and Practical Aspects of Autonomic Computing and Networking: Specification, Development and Verification. IGI Global (2010) (to appear)
30. Cartlidge, J., Bullock, S.: Combating Coevolutionary Disengagement by Reducing Parasite Virulence. Evolutionary Computation 12(2), 193–222 (2004)

31. CFTC & SEC. Preliminary Findings Regarding the Market Events of May 6, 2010. Report of the staffs of the CFTC and SEC to the Joint Advisory Committee on Emerging Regulatory issues (May 18, 2010a), http://www.sec.gov/sec-cftc-prelimreport.pdf

32. CFTC & SEC. Findings Regarding the Market Events of May 6, 2010. Report of the staffs of the CFTC and SEC to the Joint Advisory Committee on Emerging Regulatory issues (September 30, 2010b), http://www.sec.gov/news/studies/2010/marketevents-report.pdf

33. CFTC & SEC. Recommendations Regarding Regulatory Responses to the Market Events of May 6, 2010. Summary Report of the Joint CFTC and SEC Advisory Committee on Emerging Regulatory issues (February 18, 2011)

34. Challet, D., Marsili, M., Zhang, Y. (eds.): Minority Games: Interacting agents in financial markets. OUP (2004)

35. Chilton, B.: Stopping Stammering: Overcoming Obstacles in Financial Regulatory Reform. In: Speech of Commissioner Bart Chilton to the Goldman Sachs Global Commodity Conference, London (2011), http://www.cftc.gov/pressroom/speechestestimony/opachilton-43.html

36. Cliff, D., Keen, J., Kwiatkowska, M., McDermid, J., Sommerville, I.: Large Scale Complex IT Systems (LSCITS) Research Programme. Research proposal to the UK Engineering and Physical Sciences Research Council (2006), http://lscits.cs.bris.ac.uk/docs/LSCITSproposalRP1.pdf (submitted December 2006, commenced April 2007)

37. Cliff, D.: Minimal-intelligence agents for bargaining behaviors in market- based environments. Technical Report HPL-97-91, Hewlett Packard Labs (1997)

38. Cliff, D., Bruten, J.: Animat Market-Trading Interactions as Collective Social Adaptive Behavior. Adaptive Behavior 7(3&4), 385–414 (1999)

39. Cliff, D.: Explorations in evolutionary design of online auction market mechanisms. Journal of Electronic Commerce Research and Applications 2(2), 162–175 (2003)

40. Cliff, D., Miller, G.: Visualising Coevolution with CIAO plots. Artificial Life 12(2), 199–202 (2006)

41. Cliff, D.: ZIP60: Further Explorations in the Evolutionary Design of Trader Agents and Online Auction-Market Mechanisms. IEEE Transactions on Evolutionary Computation 13(1), 3–18 (2009)

42. Cliff, D.: Networked Governance in the Financial Markets. Foresight strategic briefing paper, for UK Government Office of Science & Technology, Department of Business, Innovation, and Skills (2010), http://www.cs.bris.ac.uk/home/dc/Foresight_NetGov_v2a.pdf

43. Cliff, D., Brown, D., Treleaven, P.: Technology Trends in the Financial Markets: A 2020 Vision. Driver Review DR3, Foresight Project on the Future of Computer Trading in the Financial Markets. UK Government Office for Science (2011), http://www.bis.gov.uk/assets/foresight/docs/computer-trading/11-1222-dr3-technology-trends-in-financial-markets.pdf

44. Clymer, J.: Simulation-Based Engineering of Complex Systems, 2nd edn. Wiley-Blackwell (2009)

45. Colander, D., Föllmer, H., Haas, A., Goldberg, M., Juselius, K., Kirman, A., Lux, T., Sloth, B.: The Financial Crisis and the Systemic Failure of Academic Economics. Kiel Working Paper 1489, Kiel Institute for the World Economy (2009)

46. Collingridge, D.: The Management of Scale: Big Organizations, Big Decisions, Big Mistakes. Routeledge (1992)

47. Darley, V., Outkin, A.: A NASDAQ Market Simulation: Insights on a Major Market from the Science of Complex Adaptive Systems. World Scientific (2007)

48. Das, R., Hanson, J., Kephart, J., Tesauro, G.: Agent-Human Interactions in the Continuous Double Auction. In: Proceedings IJCAI 2001 (2001)
49. De Laurentis, D., Dickerson, C., DiMario, M., Gartz, P., Jamshidi, M., Nahavandi, S., Sage, A., Sloane, E., Walker, D.: A Case for an International Consortium on System-of-Systems Engineering. IEEE Systems Journal 1(1), 68–73 (2007)
50. De Laurentis, D., Han, E.: System-of-Systems Simulation for Analyzing the Evolution of Air Transportation. In: Proceedings of the 25th International Congress of the Aeronautical Sciences, pp. 1–10 (2006)
51. Demos, T.: US panel on flash crash urges rule changes. The Financial Times (February 18, 2011a), http://www.ft.com/cms/s/0/417134ea-3b84-11e0-9970-00144feabdc0.html#axzz1EOx4E4Gg
52. Demos, T.: Quick View: Blown away by the flash crash report. The Financial Times (February 19, 2011b), http://www.ft.com/cms/s/0/bf6017b0-3baa-11e0-a96d-00144feabdc0.html#axzz1EOx4E4Gg
53. Demos, T.: Plans to avert 'flash crash" draw opposition. The Financial Times (March 22, 2011c), http://www.ft.com/cms/s/0/3a3e52a0-54a9-11e0-b1ed-00144feab49a.html#axzz1Ht6fUrUu
54. Despotou, G.: Managing the Evolution of Dependability Cases for Systems of Systems. PhD Thesis, Department of Computer Science, University of York, UK (2007)
55. Dewar, J., Bankes, S., Hodges, J., Lucas, T., Saunders-Newton, D., Vye, P.: Credible Uses of the Distributed Interactive Simulation (DIS) System. Technical Report MR-607-A, RAND (1996)
56. Dezfuli, H., et al.: Bayesian Inference for NASA Probabilistic Risk and Reliability Analysis. NASA SP-2009-569 (2009), http://www.hq.nasa.gov/office/codeq/doctree/SP2009569.pdf
57. Dorner, D.: The logic of failure. Philosophical Transactions of the Royal Society of London, Series B 327(1241), 463–473 (1990)
58. Dorner, D.: The Logic of Failure: Recognizing and Avoiding Error in Complex Situations. Perseus (1997)
59. Easley, D., Lopez de Prado, M., O'Hara, M.: The Microstructure of the Flash Crash: Flow Toxicity, Liquidity Crashes and the Probability of Informed Trading. The Journal of Portfolio Management 37(2), 118–128 (2011)
60. Economist. Agents of Change. The Economist 396(8692), 76 (2010) (Note that The Economist has a standard policy of not showing author bylines for articles written by regular staff journalists)
61. Eder, K., Flach, P.A., Hsueh, H.-W.: Towards Automating Simulation-Based Design Verification Using ILP. In: Muggleton, S., Otero, R., Tamaddoni-Nezhad, A. (eds.) ILP 2006. LNCS (LNAI), vol. 4455, pp. 154–168. Springer, Heidelberg (2007)
62. Epstein, J., Axtell, R.: Growing Artificial Societies: Social Science from the Bottom Up. MIT Press (1996)
63. Epstein, J.: Generative Social Science: Studies in Agent-Based Computational Modelling. Princeton University Press (2007)
64. Farmer, D., Foley, D.: The economy needs agent-based modeling. Nature 460, 685–686 (2009)
65. Farmer, D., Skouras, S.: An ecological perspective on the future of computer trading. Driver Review DR6, Foresight Project on the Future of Computer Trading in the Financial Markets. UK Government Office for Science (2011), http://www.bis.gov.uk/assets/foresight/docs/computer-trading/11-1225-dr6-ecological-perspective-on-future-of-computer-trading.pdf
66. Flinders, K.: The Evolution of Stock Market Technology. Computer Weekly (November 2, 2007), http://www.computerweekly.com/Articles/2007/11/02/227883/The-evolution-of-stock-market-technology.htm

67. Funes, P., Pollack, J.: Computer Evolution of Buildable Objects. In: Bentley, P. (ed.) Evolutionary Design by Computers, ch. 17. Morgan Kauffman (1999)

68. Galas, M., Brown, D., Treleaven, P.: ATRADE Platform: Algorithmic Trading & Risk Analytics Development Environment. Unpublished manuscript, Department of Computer Science, University College London (2010), http://fc.cs.ucl.ac.uk/mscfc/virtual-trading-floor

69. Gjerstad, S., Dickhaut, J.: Price Formation in Double Auctions. Games and Economic Behavior 22, 1–29 (1998)

70. Grant, J.: Quick View: US looks at European-style circuit breakers. The Financial Times (May 19, 2010), http://cachef.ft.com/cms/s/0/139ddd44-6325-11df-99a5-00144feab49a.html#axzz1Ij5j9zds

71. Goldberg, D.: Genetic Algorithms in Search, Optimization, and Machine Learning. Addison-Wesley (1987)

72. Gorton, G.: Slapped by the Invisible Hand: The Panic of 2007. OUP (2010)

73. Goth, G.: Ultralarge Systems: Redefining Software Engineering? IEEE Software 25(3), 91 (2008)

74. Gray, J.: On eScience: A Transformed Scientific Method. In: Hey, T., Tansley, S., Tolle, K. (eds.) The Fourth Paradigm: Data-Intensive Scientific Discovery, pp. xvii–xxxi. Microsoft Press (2009)

75. Haccou, P., Meelis, E.: Statistical Analysis of Behavioral Data: An Approach Based on Time-Structured Models. Oxford University Press (1994)

76. Haldane, A.: Rethinking the Financial Network. Text of a speech given at the Financial Student Association, Amsterdam (April 2009), http://www.bankofengland.co.uk/publications/speeches/2009/speech386.pdf

77. Haldane, A., May, R.: Systemic risk in banking ecosystems. Nature 469, 351–355 (2011)

78. Hall-May, M.: Ensuring Safety of Systems of Systems. PhD Thesis, Department of Computer Science, University of York, UK (2007)

79. Harford, T.: What we can learn from a nuclear reactor? The Financial Times (January 14, 2011), http://www.ft.com/cms/s/2/cea7b256-1def-11e0-badd-00144feab49a.html#axzz1DN62IXnB

80. Harman, D., Bar-Yam, Y.: Technical Report on SEC Uptick Repeal Pilot. NECSI Technical Report 2008-11, New England Complex Systems Initiative (2008)

81. Hillis, D.: Co-evolving parasites improve simulated evolution as an optimization procedure. Physica D 42, 228–234 (1990)

82. Hodgson, G.: Economics and Evolution: Bringing life back into economics. Polity Press (1993)

83. Hollnagel, E., Woods, D., Leveson, N. (eds.): Resilience Engineering: Concepts and Precepts. Ashcroft (2006)

84. Hopkins, R., Jenkins, K.: Eating the IT Elephant: Moving from Greenfield Development to Brownfield. IBM Press (2008)

85. Horswill, I.: Very Fast Action Selection for Parameterized Behaviors. In: Proceedings of the Fifth International Conference on Foundations of Digital Games (FDG 2009), Orlando (2009)

86. Hsueh, H., Eder, K.: Test Directive Generation for Functional Coverage Closure Using Inductive Logic Programming. In: Proc. IEEE International High Level Design Validation and Test Workshop (HLDVT), pp. 11–18 (2006)

87. Hubbard, D.: The Failure of Risk Management. Why It's Broken and How to Fix It. John Wiley (2009)

88. Institute for International Finance. Interim Report of the IIF Committee on Market Best Practices (April 2008), http://www.iif.com/download.php?id=SDzcEc8juCI=://

89. Ivanov, Y.: State Discovery for Autonomous Learning. Ph.D. Thesis, MIT Media Lab. (2002)

90. Johnson, C.: Lessons from the Evacuation of the World Trade Center, September 11, 2001, for the Future Development of Computer Simulations. Cognition, Technology, & Work 7, 214–240 (2005)

91. Johnson, C.: Using Evacuation Simulations to Ensure the Safety and Security of the 2012 Olympic Venues. Safety Science 46(2), 302–322 (2008)

92. Johnson, C., Nilsen-Nygaard, L.: Extending the Use of Evacuation Simulators to Support Counter-Terrorism: Using Models of Human Behaviour to Coordinate Emergency Responses to Improvised Explosive Devices. In: Simmons, R., Mohan, D., Mullane, M. (eds.) Proceedings of the 26th International Conference on Systems Safety (2008)

93. Johnson, C.: The Application of Computational Models for the Simulation of Large-Scale Evacuations Following Infrastructure Failures and Terrorist Incidents. In: Proceedings of NATO Research Workshop on Computational Models of Risk to Infrastructure, May 9-13. NATO (2006)

94. Johnson, N., Jefferies, P., Hui, P. (eds.): Financial Market Complexity. OUP (2003)

95. Johnson, N.: Proposing Policy by Analogy is Risky. Nature 469, 302 (2011)

96. Kearns, M., Ortiz, L.: The Penn-Lehman Automated Trading Project. IEEE Intelligent Systems, 22–31 (November/December 2003)

97. Kewley, R., Tolk, A.: A Systems Engineering Process for Development of Federated Simulations. In: SpringSim 2009: Proceedings of the 2009 Spring Simulation Multiconference. Society for Computer Simulation International (2009)

98. Kindleberger, C.: Manias, Panics, and Crises: A History of Financial Crises. John Wiley (2001)

99. LeBaron, B.: Agent Based Computational Finance: Suggested Readings and Early Research. Journal of Economic Dynamics and Control 24, 679–702 (2000)

100. LeBaron, B., Arthur, B., Palmer, R.: The Time Series Properties of an Artificial Stock Market. Journal of Economic Dynamics and Control 23, 1487–1516 (1999)

101. Levy, M., Levy, H., Solomon, S.: Microscopic Simulation of the Financial Markets: From Investor Behavior to Market Phenomena. Academic Press (2000)

102. Lewis, M.: The Big Short: Inside the Doomsday Machine. Allen Lane (2010)

103. Lorenz, E.: Deterministic Nonperiodic Flow. Journal of Atmospheric Science 20, 130–141 (1963)

104. Lorenz, K.: On Aggression. Routledge Classics (1966/2002)

105. MacKenzie, D.: An Engine, Not a Camera: How Financial Models Shape Markets. MIT Press (2008a)

106. MacKenzie, D.: Material Markets: How Economic Agents are Constructed. Oxford University Press (2008b)

107. MacKenzie, D., et al. (eds.): Do Economists Make Markets? On the Performativity of Economics. Princeton University Press (2008)

108. Maier, M.: Architecting Principles for Systems of Systems. Systems Engineering 1(4), 267–284 (1998)

109. May, R., Levin, S., Sugihara, G.: Ecology for Bankers. Nature 451, 893–895 (2008)

110. Meerman, M., et al.: Money and Speed: Inside the Black Box. Documentary produced by VPRO (Dutch public broadcaster) (2011), available as an iPad application http://itunes.apple.com/us/app/money-speed-inside-black-box/id424796908?mt=8&ls=1#

111. Metcalfe, M.: Strategic knowledge sharing: a small-worlds perspective. In: Hart, D., Gregor, S. (eds.) Information System Foundations: Constructing and Criticizing, Australian National University Press (2005)

112. Mitchell, M.: Complexity: A Guided Tour. OUP (2009)

113. Mullane, R.: Riding Rockets: The Outrageous Tales of a Space-Shuttle Astronaut. Simon & Schuster (2006)

114. Nelson, R., Winter, S.: An Evolutionary Theory of Economic Change. Harvard University Press (1982)
115. Northrop, L., et al.: Ultra-Large-Scale Systems: The Software Challenge of the Future. Technical Report. Carnegie Mellon University Software Engineering Institute (2006)
116. Ormerod, P.: Butterfly Economics: A New General Theory of Economic and Social Behaviour. Faber (1998)
117. Ormerod, P.: Why Most Things Fail: Evolution, Extinction, & Economics. Faber (2006)
118. Palmer, R., Arthur, B., Holland, J., LeBaron, B., Tayler, P.: Artificial economic life: a simple model of a stockmarket. Physica D: Nonlinear Phenomena 75(1-3), 264–274 (1994)
119. Parry, G.: The Characterization of Uncertainty in Probabilistic Risk Assessments of Complex Systems. Reliability Engineering and System Safety 54, 119–126 (1996)
120. Parisi, C., Sahin, F., Jamshidi, M.: A discrete event XML based system of systems simulation for robust threat detection and integration. In: Proc. 2008 IEEE International Conference on System of Systems Engineering (2008)
121. Perrow, C.: Normal Accidents: Living with High-Risk Technologies. Basic Books, New York (1984)
122. Phelps, S., McBurney, P., Parsons, S., Sklar, E.: Co-evolutionary Auction Mechanism Design: A Preliminary Report. In: Padget, J., Shehory, O., Parkes, D., Sadeh, N., Walsh, W.E. (eds.) AMEC 2002. LNCS (LNAI), vol. 2531, pp. 123–142. Springer, Heidelberg (2002)
123. Phelps, S., McBurney, P., Parsons, S.: Evolutionary Mechanism Design: A Review. Autonomous Agents and Multi-Agent Systems 21(2), 237–264 (2010)
124. Polack, F., Andrews, P., Sampson, A.: The Engineering of Concurrent Simulations of Complex Systems. In: Proc. 2009 IEEE Congress on Evolutionary Computation, pp. 217–224 (2009)
125. Polack, F., Andrews, P., Ghetiu, T., Read, M., Stepney, S., Timmis, J., Sampson, A.: Reflections on the Simulation of Complex Systems for Science. In: Proc. International Conference on Engineering of Complex Computer Systems (ICECCS 2010), pp. 276–285. IEEE Press (2010)
126. Polacek, G., Verma, D.: Requirements Engineering for Complex Systems: Principles vs. Rules. In: Proceedings of the Seventh Annual Conference on Systems Engineering Research, CSER 2009 (2009)
127. Reason, J.: The Human Contribution: Unsafe Acts, Accidents, and Heroic Recoveries. Ashgate (2008)
128. Rittel, H., Webber, M.: Dilemmas in a General Theory of Planning. Policy Sciences 4, 155–169 (1973)
129. Roberts, K.: Some Characteristics of One Type of High Reliability Organization. Organization Science 1(2), 160–176 (1990)
130. Rooksby, J., Rouncefield, M., Sommerville, I.: Testing in the Wild: The Social and Organisational Dimensions of Real-World Practice. Journal of Computer Supported Cooperative Work 18(5-6), 559–580 (2009)
131. Salmon, F.: Algorithmic trading and market-structure tail risks. Reuters (January 13, 2011), http://blogs.reuters.com/felix-salmon/2011/01/13/algorithmic-trading-and-market-structure-tail-risks/
132. Schelling, T.: Dynamic Models of Segregation. Journal of Mathematical Sociology 1, 143–186 (1971)
133. Sheard, S., Mostashari, A.: Principles of Complex Systems for Systems Engineering. Systems Engineering 12(4), 295–311 (2008)
134. Sillitto, H.: Design Principles for Ultra-Large-Scale Systems (2010) (unpublished draft manuscript)
135. Sims, K.: Evolving 3D Morphology and Behavior by Competition. In: Brooks, R., Maes, P. (eds.) Artificial Life IV Proceedings, pp. 28–39. MIT Press (1994)
136. Sloan, S.: Simulating Terrorism. University of Oklahoma Press (1981)

137. Slovik, P.: Trust, Emotion, Sex, Politics, and Science: Surveying the Risk-Assessment Battlefield. Risk Analysis 19(4), 689–701 (1999)
138. Smith, L.: Accountability and Error in Ensemble Forecasting (1995) (manuscript), http://people.maths.ox.ac.uk/lenny/ecmwf96.pdf
139. Smith, L.: What might we learn from climate forecasts? Proceedings of the National Academy of Sciences of the United States of America 99, 2487–2492 (2002)
140. Stamatelatos, M., et al.: Probabilistic Risk Assessment Procedures Guide for NASA Managers and Practitioners. V1.1 (2002a), http://www.hq.nasa.gov/office/codeq/doctree/praguide.pdf
141. Stamatelatos, M., et al.: Fault Tree Handbook with Aerospace Applications. Version 1.1. (2002b), http://www.hq.nasa.gov/office/codeq/doctree/fthb.pdf
142. Sommerville, I., Cliff, D., Calinescu, R., Keen, J., Kelly, T., Kwiatkowska, M., McDermid, J., Paige, R.: Large-Scale Complex IT Systems. Communications of the ACM (July 2012)
143. Sornette, D.: Why Stock Markets Crash: Critical Events in Complex Financial Systems. Princeton University Press (2002)
144. Steiner, C.: Did We Dodge Another Flash Crash on September 1? (2010) Forbes blog, http://blogs.forbes.com/christophersteiner/2010/09/02/did-we-just-dodge-another-flash-crash-yesterday/
145. Stephens, C., Waelbroeck, H.: Algorithm Switching: Co-Adaptation in the Market Ecology. Journal of Trading, 1–15 (Summer 2009)
146. Stuermer, P., Bucci, A., Branke, J., Funes, P., Popovici, E.: Analysis of coevolution for worst-case optimization. In: Proceedings GECCO 2009, the 11th Annual Conference on Genetic and Evolutionary Computation (2009)
147. Taleb, N.: The Black Swan: The Impact of the Highly Improbable. Allen Lane (2007)
148. Tesfatsion, L., Judd, K. (eds.): The Handbook of Computational Economics. Agent-Based Computational Economics, vol. 2. North-Holland (2006)
149. Tett, G.: Fool's Gold: How Unrestrained Greed Corrupted a Dream, Shattered Global Markets, and Unleashed a Catastrophe. Little, Brown (2009)
150. Tomlinson, B., Blumberg, B.: Social Synthetic Characters. Computer Graphics 26(2) (2002)
151. Tuinenga, P.: SPICE: A Guide to Circuit Simulation and Analysis Using PSpice. Prentice Hall (1988)
152. Turkle, S.: Simulation and its Discontents. MIT Press (2009)
153. Valerdi, R., Axelband, E., Baehren, T., Boehm, B., Dorenbos, D., Jackson, S., Madni, A., Nadler, G., Robitaille, P., Settles, S.: A research agenda for systems of systems architecting. International Journal of System of Systems Engineering 1(1&2), 171–188 (2008)
154. Vaughan, D.: The Challenger Launch Decision: Risky Technology, Culture and Deviance at NASA. University of Chicago Press (1997)
155. Vaughan, D.: On Slippery Slopes, Repeating Negative Patterns, and Learning from Mistakes. In: Starbuck, W., Farjoun, M. (eds.) Organization at the Limit: Lessons from the Columbia Disaster, pp. 262–275. Wiley Blackwell (2005)
156. Vaughan, D.: NASA Revisited: Theory, Analogy and Public Sociology. American Journal of Sociology 112(2), 353–393 (2006)
157. Vytelingum, K., Cliff, D., Jennings, N.: Strategic bidding in continuous double auctions. Artificial Intelligence 172(13), 1700–1729 (2008)
158. Waldrop, M.: Complexity: The Emerging Science at the Edge of Order and Chaos. Simon & Schuster (1992)
159. Walsh, W., Das, R., Tesauro, G., Kephart, J.: Analyzing Complex Strategic Interactions in Multi-Agent Games. In: Proceedings of AAAI 2002 Game Theoretic and Decision Theoretic Agents Workshop, Edmonton, Canada (2002)
160. Weick, K., Sutcliffe, K.: Managing the Unexpected. Jossey Bass (2007)

What Is a Care Pathway?

Justin Keen

Leeds Institute of Health Sciences, University of Leeds, England
j.keen@leeds.ac.uk

Abstract. This paper argues that it is possible to develop useful generic representations of care pathways, drawing on evidence and argument about clinical teams, about the ability of teams to cope with radical uncertainty and about the influence of institutional arrangements on the journeys that patients take through health systems. The arguments are used to identify a mismatch between current practices in the design of large scale digital systems and doctors' and other health professionals' needs for information about patients' risks and outcomes to support their work.

Keywords: health care, care pathways, requirements.

1   Introduction

The rate of innovation and diffusion of digital services in health care is low, relative to other sectors, in developed countries. There are many reasons for this, but one stems from our poor understanding of the fundamental processes in health care, variously termed patient journeys or care pathways, which are broadly equivalent to industrial and commercial production processes.

While some have argued that we are now in a world where requirements are no longer needed – in part because users can configure their own services – this cannot be the case in health care. There is clear evidence that poor requirement and specification processes are still leading to failures in procurement, design and implementation. [1,2] Further, legacy systems in primary and hospital settings will not, at present, allow users to tailor services to their own needs.

This chapter argues that it is possible to identify flaws in the prevailing assumptions about the role of IT systems in health care, to develop useful generic representations of care pathways, and to use those representations to chart a more productive direction of travel. It is concluded that problems with the design and use of systems are due, at least in part, to a combination of the flawed thinking and lack of attention to identification of hardware and software requirements.

2   Two Ideas

The author Victor Hugo observed that there is nothing as powerful as an idea whose time has come. In the last decade or so, health systems around the world have been exposed to two such ideas. The first is that service delivery is becoming ever more

R. Calinescu and D. Garlan (Eds.): Monterey Workshop 2012, LNCS 7539, pp. 71–80, 2012.

complex, in the sense that it requires more intensive and more frequent co-ordination between different professionals, or across a number of organisations, or both. We need to find ways of managing this complexity, and in practice this means finding new ways for clinicians, managers and others to collaborate with one another. It has always been difficult to link inputs, outputs and outcomes in health care, and the complexity – reflected in highly modularised, but poorly co-ordinated, care – only makes the task harder. In practice professionals have to be involved in the identification and implementation of strategies for designing services that reconcile them, and thus achieving better control of resources. Similarly, safety improvements are most likely to be effective when clinicians work collaboratively, co-ordinating their work with one another.

The second idea is that health systems need to manage risks pro-actively. The argument, in a nutshell, is that no country can afford to run reactive illness services any longer, cost pressures are increasing all the time, and all countries must find ways of managing costs more effectively. In England, for example, 30% of the population has one or more chronic health problems, and consumes about 70% of the budget.

Historically, health services have been reactive, responding to people as they became ill. Today people still get ill, but the policy focus now is on preventing, or at least delaying, the problems associated with getting older, or with poor lifestyle choices (smoking, lack of exercise, consuming too much salt or refined sugar). This has two notable consequences, namely that health systems have to identify effective strategies for managing risks, and that those risks often arise outside health care systems – lifestyle choices occur out in civil society.

3   The Challenges

These two ideas have major implications for the organisation of health care. Health systems have traditionally been organised along functional lines, with family doctors, community services and hospital departments operating separately from one another. This made sense, at a time when the over-riding need was to ensure that each of these services was as efficient as possible. This organisational model served us reasonably well for a long time, when many problems could be solved by visiting one or two services, when the co-ordination challenge was relatively modest.

It has become clear, though, that traditional organisational forms cannot deliver the co-ordination needed in the new environment. Many people need support from several services, often over months and years. Many of them are older people, and people with chronic health problems such as heart disease, stroke, diabetes, asthma and some cancers. Maximising the efficiency of each service is no longer the primary task. Rather, there is a need to manage patients' clinical risks, arising from their own problems and from the complexity of modern health systems.

Similarly, traditional organisations are not set up to manage demand, and hence control costs – that is, control organisational risks. The idea, the belief, is that this can be achieved by identifying problems early, or before they occur, either by encouraging healthier lifestyles or by screening populations and identifying individuals at risk of developing preventable problems (eg stopping smoking reduces the probability of lung cancer).

The need to respond to the two new ideas prompts a question about IT systems. How are health care IT managers, suppliers and policy makers responding to them? The answer seems to be – barely at all. This point will be discussed once care pathways have been examined.

4   Care Pathways

A single idea, the care pathway, appears to make sense of the challenges set out in the last section. A care pathway is really an idea, a high level representation, of the journeys that people take through health systems. People should be encouraged to avoid getting too far down any pathway (through health promotion and prevention). They should take responsibility for decisions about their own care where possible, and make others in consultation with professionals. Professionals need to co-ordinate effectively with one another to ensure that the journey goes smoothly from a clinical perspective. Note here that the focus is on patients – a major shift from the focus on services in traditional models.

In formal guidance, and in the research literature, care pathways are typically represented as sequences of discrete decisions and actions, where recommendations are based on the best available evidence from experimental studies. [3,4] Sometimes flow diagrams are included in guidance, which show how assessments, diagnostic tests and decisions should be linked chronologically. This focus on decisions and actions, and on patients 'flowing' between decision-makers, will seem intuitively reasonable to many software engineers.

This said, an obvious question arises: how are the many discrete events actually linked to one another? The short answer is: we don't know. Leading commentators point out that we are in the early stages of understanding care pathways. [5-7] We know that dynamics of patient journeys are clearly different from industrial production processes such as car assembly or bottling plants [8]. Patients do not travel down pre-determined 'assembly lines'. There is, rather, substantial unexplained variation in access to, and utilisation of, health care in all countries. The flow diagrams in official guidance are ideals, and do not represent actual processes on the ground. One important consequence is that clinicians and managers are not in a position to help software engineers to identify requirements that will improve the quality and safety of patients' journeys.

Further, it is at best unclear how to include patients into thinking about pathways. Prevention and health promotion cannot be imposed – people cannot be ordered to change their lifestyles - and citizens have to be properly involved in decisions about their lives. So, rather than being consumers, citizens need to be active collaborators in their health and health care.

We can make some progress, though, and start by identifying two important problems. The first, which could be called the process problem, stems from the point just made. We need to work out how patients actually move through health systems, and why. The second problem concerns governance – what management infrastructure will help to improve co-ordination along pathways. Even short journeys involve co-ordination between teams, and there is good evidence that the organisation of services can affect both the quality and the outcomes of care.

5   Teams That Expect the Unexpected

In many areas of a health system, specialist knowledge is concentrated in teams – general practice teams, emergency department teams, community-based mental health teams and so on. This starting point – the clinical team - resonates with the thinking behind total quality management, where each team involved in a production process manages its own affairs, co-ordinates its work with other teams locally, and is subject to 'light touch' regulation by a senior management team.[9] It is also reminiscent of Piore and Sabel's concept of flexible specialisation, where teams work relatively independently of one another, each specialising in a particular activity, and building up a deep understanding of that activity over time.[10]   This arrangement has important long-run advantages for organisations, because individual teams can change the way they work without significantly disrupting the work of other teams. At the same time, the specialised nature of a team's work can make it difficult for outsiders – often managers, in practice – to intervene or to co-ordinate the activities of different teams with one another.

One of the keys to understanding patient journeys lies in appreciating the capacity of clinical teams to cope with uncertainty. This is what distinguishes health care from car production and processing insurance claims. Let us consider an example of an elderly woman, Mrs B., who is living in her own home, who feels unwell and makes an emergency call. An ambulance is dispatched, the paramedics assess her, and drive her to the emergency department at the local hospital. The process can be conceptualised as occurring in discrete phases, with different teams taking primary responsibility at different points in time. It turns out that there is nothing that needs immediate attention, but the episode has taken place in the context of her on-going health problems, including some heart problems and a recent history of falls. Hospital doctors recommend assessments when Mrs B. gets home.

Analyses of this (relatively simple) sequence of events, and others like it, typically focus on strategies for reducing clinical uncertainty – on arriving at a diagnosis and making decisions about the appropriate course of treatment. But it seems more realistic to argue that there are two distinct types of team, with the difference between the two highlighted by their responses to uncertainty.

There are two distinct types of uncertainty in any patient journey. First, there is task uncertainty – uncertainty about the appropriate course of action for the patient. Second, there is environmental uncertainty.[11] This occurs, in part, because teams are specialized – they do not know, in any detail, how other teams do what they do. More generally, teams cannot anticipate developments in their wider environments, which in the case of health care might include epidemics or a major incident leading to many injuries. Suppose, for the sake of making the arguments clear, that uncertainty can be either high or low, so that there are four possible combinations of high and low task and environmental uncertainty. In the first case there is high certainty about both the specific clinical actions and the best way of co-ordinating them over the next few days or weeks. This is found, for example, in care following the diagnosis of some cancers, or following a suspected heart attack. It may be that our elderly patient, Mrs B., is able to go home the same day, with no need to change any of the support she receives in her own home. The main co-ordination challenge is to get her home safely.

Second, there can be certainty about the treatment that is needed now, but not about the environment that a patient will have to cope with later on in a journey. Mrs B. might be able to go home, but it may not be clear to hospital staff whether she will be able to cope without additional help when she gets there. Third, there can be low certainty about the necessary treatment, but high certainty about the general environment. This situation might occur with many of us, where there is clearly something wrong, but it is difficult to pin down what it is. While we and our doctors are working out what is wrong, though, at least we know we have our friends and family to support us. Fourth and finally, there are many circumstances where both task and environmental uncertainty are high. It is necessary to rely on local discretion – of both clinicians and patients - about the combinations of clinical inputs needed to help navigate care journeys. In this context it may well be appropriate for individuals with similar medical needs, but who differ in other respects (such as the extent of family support), to receive different services.[12] This diversity should not be confused with the unwarranted variations observed in studies of practice variations.[13] Finally, there is a fourth combination, of high task uncertainty and low environmental uncertainty.

Drawing on these arguments, we can sketch out two theoretical ideals, one based on teams optimizing efficiency and the other on them maximizing the capacity to respond flexibly – to expect the unexpected. The first is, in essence, total quality management. Total quality thinking is based on the relative certainty of industrial production, where there are always major challenges, not least in continuously reducing costs and improving quality, and in ensuring that quality improvements in one part of a process do not disrupt processes elsewhere. This type of thinking is entirely appropriate in many services, where there is high certainty about most patients and there are well established routines, for example in maternity services or high volume elective surgery.

The second ideal is based on a capacity to expect the unexpected, and on having knowledge of the referral options available for each patient. When Mrs B. arrives at the emergency department, the clinicians do not know what is wrong with her. They should be able to assess her and take the appropriate actions, whatever is wrong with her – whether she has a nasty cold coming on, or needs cardiac surgery in the next few hours. That is, the emergency team should be able to mobilize whatever resources they need. These will vary from patient to patient, so that the system as a whole needs to be designed to provide resources in different combinations at any one point in time. The emergency team should, further, be able to ensure that Mrs B. is referred to the right teams – in her case, back to her GP, nursing and therapist teams near her home.

More generally, we can say that this second type of team exhibits, (i) the ability to respond to each patient individually, mobilizing different combinations of services for each one as necessary, and, (ii) an ability to refer patients to the right team or teams, which requires knowledge of the options that are available, and an ability to make the right decision even when it is not clear what the problem is. This is qualitatively different from total quality initiatives, and from the concept of flexible specialization described earlier. The second model is not concerned with continuous improvement, or at least with continuous improvement alone. Rather, the key qualities are flexibility of response and robustness – teams can cope with a very wide range of problems that come through their doors.

6   Institutions Shape Journeys

We have some useful sketches, but they are only part of our story. During Mrs B's hospital visit, her care needed to be co-ordinated. The ambulance needed to arrive quickly, and warn the emergency department about Mrs B's problems. Doctors in the emergency department needed to order tests and get results in a reasonable period of time. And so on.

Many researchers, including those working in the field of computer supported co-operative work (CSCW), would focus quite properly on the role of communication in the co-ordination of Mrs B's care. But sociologists and political scientists point out that institutional arrangements substantially influence the decisions and actions of clinicians working in any given environment. These arrangements have been established over years, or even decades. Individuals within teams have established ways of working with one another, and also established ways of managing their relationships with other teams, so that those teams are able to co-ordinate their work with one another. Much of the time, teams do not need to communicate with one another directly, or can communicate using brief messages – a referral form, a brief telephone conversation. That is, these norms can help to increase efficiency.

The point here is that institutional relationships shape patient journeys. That is, patient journeys are not simply sequences of rational decisions, taken in the face of greater or lesser uncertainty. Decisions taken by both clinicians and patients are influenced by the prevailing institutional arrangements. In the context of our arguments here, there are two useful indicators of the importance of this point, and key weaknesses in many health systems around the world, namely the extent to which patient journeys are the journeys that patients want and need to take, and the safety of patients in the course of their journeys.

Taking the patterns of patient journeys first we can say, on the positive side, that there is good evidence that patients are often satisfied or very satisfied with the services they receive. The level of satisfaction varies from country to country, and over time, but it seems reasonable to infer that many patients receive the services they need. Their expectations are met and their health problems are successfully addressed. Less positively, as noted earlier, there is evidence of systematic variation in many areas of health care, for example in referrals by family doctors to hospitals, in prescribing practices and in access to mental health, physiotherapy and other services. There is also evidence that people with multiple problems – typical of many older people – receive fragmented and incomplete services.[14] The variation can be attributed, at least in part, to differences between professionals. If some GPs refer more than others, and issue more prescriptions than others, then it is likely that their own behavioural norms are influencing the services that patients receive.

The second indicator is the safety of patients. Adverse events are a reasonable, if general, indicator of the integrity of a health system, covering both events that occur within teams and between them. The Institute of Medicine's report, *To Err Is Human*, stressed the importance of designing safe systems of care – or safe patient journeys in the context of this discussion.[15] There have been very substantial efforts, in many countries, to improve the safety of services since the publication of that report, and other reports conveying similar alarming messages. There have undoubtedly been improvements in many services. Consider the following passage by Leape and colleagues:

"Too many healthcare organisations fit James Reason's definition of the "sick system syndrome." They are hierarchical and deficient in mutual respect, teamwork and transparency. Blame is still a mainstay solution. Mechanisms for ensuring accountability are weak and ambiguous. Few have the capacity to learn and change that is characteristic of the so-called high reliability industries. Most do not recognise that safety should be a precondition, not a priority... Many physicians do not know how to be team players and regard other health workers as assistants ... Too many practitioners—doctors, nurses, pharmacists, therapists, technicians—function in "silos," focusing on their own performance and communicating with others in fragmented and inefficient ways that inhibit teamwork. Patients are seldom included in organisational planning or in the analysis of adverse events that have harmed them." [16]

The 'safety movement' in health care has grown substantially in the last ten years, but there is clearly still a long way to go. The main implication, for this paper, is that improving patients' journeys requires the proactive management of those journeys, taking into account their preferences, so that they go on appropriate journeys. This point is reinforced by another trend, around the world, away from the provision of reactive illness services to the management of long-term conditions (such as asthma, diabetes or neurological conditions such as Parkinson's Disease). There is also a trend towards the management of a range of known risks, such as the risk of developing pressure ulcers, of experiencing a fall (and breaking a hip or other bone), or of a heart attack or stroke if one smokes, has a poor diet or fails to exercise. In short, when patient journeys are inherently uncertain – or open-ended - in nature, and there are concerns about the governance of services, the best strategy is to proactively manage those journeys.

7   Implications for IT Systems

Current IT design practice tends to focus on the collection of detailed activity information. This is reasonable. The recording of clinical information has a long history, stretching back into antiquity. Counting, and aggregating, information for managing services and for accountability to governments or insurers has a shorter history, but it has had a major influence of thinking about information in the last 30 or so years. Data collection on the ground has long had to include data required by others, who are not directly involved in treatment and care. Indeed, in many countries this 'machine bureaucracy' thinking dominates thinking about the design of digital services. The result is that digital services have long been designed and used principally for recording and counting purposes.

In the last decade or so, there have been two significant trends. One involves the progressive linking together of formerly separate IT systems – family doctor systems to hospital systems, hospital systems to one another, and so on. The other is the 'colonisation' of people's personal lives, under the banner of so-called telehealth applications. Most of these applications are designed to gather data from individuals, living in their own homes, purportedly to monitor their health status remotely. It has to be said that there is little evidence that such applications are effective, still less cost-effective. It is also striking that the ethical implications of these two trends have barely been explored. Linking systems together, by its nature, raises concerns about privacy and confidentiality. Colonisation raises questions about the relationship between health care providers and individuals going about their private business. But governments around the world are enthusiastic about telehealth, and suppliers are happy to provide technical solutions.

The important point here is that there is a mismatch between most current practices in designing and implementing digital services and important trends in the management of patient journeys. The implication of the arguments set out in this chapter is that it is difficult to turn 'machine bureaucracy' information, that has been collected in silos, into information that can be used to actively manage patient journeys. Indeed, managing risks in the course of patient journeys will often require quite different types of information. The information that helps nurses to monitor Mrs B's risk of a fall or of developing a pressure ulcer is different in kind to the information that is routinely collected on a ward or in a community setting in most countries.

There is some evidence about this mismatch. One person who has thought hard about this problem is Dr. Aksel Tjora, a Norwegian emergency physician and researcher.[17] He makes a straightforward observation: in his hospital, he has access to a number of departmental systems at a single terminal. And yet, even though he has access to far more information than he used to, it does not help him very much with the management of processes of care.

8   Concluding Comments

We can put the arguments set out in this chapter together. They point to the need to develop information systems for managing clinical and organisational risks. Thinking and practice in this area is still in its infancy. But there are signs that thinking is changing. There has, for example, recently been a great deal of interest in the use of checklists for managing both known risks and to encourage clinical teams to 'expect the unexpected', for example by checking that procedures are in place should anything go wrong (conceptually, the equivalent of having fire extinguishers in place in the unlikely, but plausible, event of fire). There has, similarly, been substantial interest in capturing patients' assessments of the outcomes of the services they receive. By and large the tools and procedures for monitoring risk and outcomes have not been automated: but the existence of valuable research and practice suggests that automation is now possible.

Thinking about the systems that will enable patients – and their carers – to become actively involved in their journeys is for the future. One obvious move is to ensure that patients can access their own records – and this is already possible in several countries. The problem here, of course, is that existing systems are not focused on patients' risks – on the extent to which they, or their clinicians, are successfully managing risks, as opposed to treating them reactively.

From a patient perspective, there is also an argument for implementing systems to ensure that risks and outcomes are being routinely monitored, and signs of problems acted upon. That is, there are arguments for ensuring that systems are designed in patients' interests – not just that they are engaged in their own journeys. If patients cannot trust the institutions looking after them, then they need assurance processes to be built in. The results would look very different from much current practice, emphasizing risks and outcomes rather than the recording and counting of activity.

This chapter has argued that it is possible to identify a generic approach to representing health care pathways. The approach is based on three building blocks, namely clinical teams (as opposed to decision-makers or idealized patient 'flows'), the ability of teams to cope with radical uncertainty, and taking into account the ways in which institutional arrangements influence the journeys that patients take through health systems. In practice, few suppliers in the sector have begun to incorporate checklists and other risk management tools into their systems. There is, then, a mismatch between much current requirements and design practice and the need on the ground, for information systems that are oriented towards the pro-active management of clinical and organizational risks.

Acknowledgment. This paper reports on research funded by the UK Engineering and Physical Sciences Research Council, the Large Scale Complex IT Systems Programme, EP/F001096/1.

References

1. Office of the National Coordinator for Health Information Technology. Update on the adoption of health information technology and related efforts to facilitate the electronic use and exchange of health information. A Report to Congress (January 2012)
2. National Audit Office. The National Programme for IT in the NHS: an update on the delivery of detailed care records systems. HC 888, Session 2010-12. The Stationery Office, London (2010)
3. Pearse, R., Holt, P., Grocott, M.: Managing peri-operative risk in patients undergoing elective non-cardiac surgery. BMJ 343, d5759 (2011)
4. Davis, M., Rogers, S., Rudolf, M., Hughes, M., Lip, G.: Patient care pathway, implementation and audit criteria for patients with atrial fibrillation. Heart 93, 48–52 (2007), doi:10.1136/hrt.2006.099937
5. Wachter, R.: Patient Safety At Ten: Unmistakeable Progress, Troubling Gaps. Health Affairs 29, 165–173 (2010), doi:10.1377/hlthaff.2009.0785
6. Morton, A., Cornwell, J.: What's the difference between a hospital and a bottling factory? BMJ 339 (2009), doi:10.1136/bmj.b2727
7. Leape, L., Berwick, D.: Five years after 'To Err Is Human', what have we learned? JAMA 293, 2384–2390 (2005), doi:10.1001/jama.293.19.2384
8. Stevens, D.: Safe healthcare: we're running out of excuses. Qual. Saf. Health Care 18, 418 (2009), doi:10.1136/qshc.2009.038778
9. Anderson, J.: The Evolution of the health care quality journey. Journal of Legal Medicine 31, 59–72, doi:10.1080/01947641003598252
10. Piore, M., Sabel, C.: The Second Industrial Divide. Basic, London (1984)

11. Helper, S., MacDuffie, J., Sabel, C.: Pragmatic Collaborations: Advancing Knowledge While Controlling Opportunism. Industrial and Corporate Change 9, 443–488 (2000)
12. Keen, J., Moore, J., West, R.: Pathways, networks and choice in health care. International Journal of Health Care Quality Assurance 19, 316–327 (2006)
13. Wennberg, J.: Unwarranted variations in healthcare delivery: implications for Academic Medical Centres. BMJ 325, 961–964 (2002), doi:10.1136/bmj.325.7370.961
14. Boult, C., Wieland, G.: Comprehensive primary care for older patients with multiple chronic conditions. JAMA 304, 1936–1943 (2010), doi:10.1001/jama.2010.1623
15. Kohn, L., Corrigan, J., Donaldson, M.: To Err Is Human. Institute of Medicine, Washington DC (1999)
16. Leape, L., Berwick, D., et al.: Transforming healthcare: a safety imperative. Qual. Saf. Health Care 18, 424–428 (2009), doi:10.1136/qshc.2009.036954
17. Tjora, A., Scambler, G.: Square pegs in round holes: Information systems, hospitals and the significance of contextual awareness. Socl. Sci. Med. 68, 519–525 (2009)

Command and Control of Teams of Autonomous Systems

Douglas S. Lange[*], Phillip Verbancsics, Robert S. Gutzwiller,
John Reeder, and Cullen Sarles

Space and Naval Warfare Systems Center Pacific
San Diego, CA 92152
doug.lange@navy.mil

Abstract. The command and control of teams of autonomous vehicles provides a strong model of the control of cyber-physical systems in general. Using the definition of command and control for military systems, we can recognize the requirements for the operational control of many systems and see some of the problems that must be resolved. Among these problems are the need to distinguish between aberrant behaviors and optimal but quirky behaviors so that the human commander can determine if the behaviors conform to standards and align with mission goals. Similarly the commander must able to recognize when goals will not be met in order to reapportion assets available to the system. Robustness in the face of a highly variable environment can be met through machine learning, but must be done in a way that the tactics employed are recognizable as correct. Finally, because cyber-physical systems will involve decisions that must be made at great speed, we consider the use of the Rainbow framework for autonomics to provide rapid but robust command and control at pace.

Keywords: cyber-physical, command and control, autonomic, machine learning.

1 Introduction

Teams that include heterogeneous autonomous unmanned systems (AUS) are good generalizations of complex cyber-physical systems. They contain autonomous units connected by a network, involving distributed computation, and to further complicate matters may have cooperative intelligent behavior among changing subsets of the systems components. As the elements of these networked systems exist in and interact with the physical environment, the physical nature of AUS is obvious. Even the network can be influenced by the environment given the use of wireless communications.

Controlling such a complex system requires several critical capabilities. First, the goals and constraints for the AUS team must be communicated to the various decision making nodes. This may include all of the AUS, as they all may possess sufficient autonomous capability to decide how to act under many situations given the goals. A central controller, or more generally several distributed controllers, must have

---

[*] Corresponding author.

R. Calinescu and D. Garlan (Eds.): Monterey Workshop 2012, LNCS 7539, pp. 81–93, 2012.
© Springer-Verlag Berlin Heidelberg 2012

confidence (particularly if human operated) that the goals and constraints have been received and correctly interpreted by the autonomous units. Second, the control units must have sufficient situational awareness of the environment and the behaviors of the team members in order to decide if changes to orders are required. The control must have the ability to determine if any error conditions are present and must be able to distinguish between aberrant behavior and what may be a plausible but unpredicted solution. Finally, team strategies must be selected to accomplish goals, and these strategies may need to be altered as the environment changes.

This paper explores the control of complex cyber-physical systems. In particular we look at the requirement for human controllers to influence the operation of these systems as well as addressing the need for autonomic control in situations where time constraints do not allow human decision making. This combination of requirements poses interesting demands on how cyber-physical systems are constructed and how they incorporate adaptation.

2   Control of Complex Systems

The control exercised by a military commander over forces is described as "…guiding the operation" [1]. The presumption is that there is a mission statement, a set of assets with which to perform the mission, and an environment to operate in that may include an opposing force. There are several ways in which a commander guides an operation.

Maintain alignment: The commander must ensure that all decisions remain aligned with the operation's mission and the commander's intent.

Provide situational awareness: The commander must assess the status of plan execution constantly, utilizing a common operational picture (COP).

Advance the plan: The commander must monitor the status of plan execution against the plan's timeline.

Comply with procedure: The commander oversees compliance with warfighting procedures to avoid mistakes (e.g., friendly fire engagements or collateral damage) and achieve efficiencies.

Counter the enemy: The commander must be responsive to emerging intelligence, surveillance, and reconnaissance information that differ significantly from expectations.

Adjust apportionment: Changes to asset availability or changes to requirements and priorities may require reapportionment of assets.

Military organizations are essentially complex cyber-physical systems. The end – nodes may be aircraft with pilots, or aircraft without pilots. These units whether manned or unmanned can be viewed as autonomous systems that cooperate to achieve a mission under the command of a human commander.

The tasks of the military commander are also clearly analogous to what would be required in many non-military systems. The only difference may be that no enemy exists, but the environment is nevertheless capable of surprising, therefore emerging information that alters assumptions is still possible. Units may become inoperable just as in military operations, and adjustments to plans must often be made.

As the complexity of the system increases, the commander must work at higher, more abstract levels. The units of the system must also exhibit higher levels of autonomy so that decision making is moved further down and is more immediate [2]. Based on the level of autonomy exhibited by the units, we can model the size of an operation that a single person can manage, provided the situation can be adequately described to the commander.

3   Control of Systems by Humans

Automation can easily be called ubiquitous. We interface with it daily, even if we do not immediately recognize it. In years past for example, elevators required human operators, but now we simply press a button to reach our floor. Even highly complex systems integrate automation; commercially flown airplanes have autopilots that are capable of landing the plane, and some models of cars have automated systems which bypass the driver if safety is in doubt (i.e., automatic braking systems, vehicle headway monitoring). These systems integrate automation, but still rely heavily on a human component for routine performance and supervision. While automation is becoming more common, and more reliable, it rarely replaces or removes a human with experience from the overall task [3].

Automation has also been shown to result in phenomena such as complacency which results in operators failing to detect failures of automated systems [4,5,6] and automation bias, which results in operators blindly following automation recommendations or failing to act unless the automation requests the human action in decision making systems [7,8,9,10,11].

Leli and Filskov [12] suggest that it is specifically the integration that plays a large role in determining the effectiveness of a system outcome. In their work, automated diagnostic systems consistently outperformed clinicians when in isolation; however decision accuracy decreased as a direct result of integrated clinician use of the aid to diagnose psychological conditions. This suggests that perhaps the most critical aspect of automation is not the engineering behind the automation itself, but the interaction between any automation and the operator who is expected to work together with it.

Parasuraman and Wickens [3] also identified issues related to the ability of human operators to understand the actions of the automation. The operators trust and ability to evaluate the performance of autonomous systems comes, in part, from an ability to recognize behaviors as correct or incorrect. AUS that have been programmed to perform in a particular fashion may or may not exhibit behaviors that are recognizably correct while optimal for the given situation. Knowing that such situations can exist may also push an operator to show complacency when observing odd behaviors because they can be explained as possibly correct if not humanlike.

4   The Roles for Learning

4.1   Developing Team Tactics

A common approach to the design of autonomous systems is to design the entire system to be scripted. That is, a human decides on the action the autonomy takes for any given state the system is in. Such systems face many challenges. The first is the significant investment in human resources in the design because every part of the autonomy must be thought out and scripted. Furthermore, the autonomous capability is dependent upon the incorporated knowledge. Therefore, the investment of human resources necessarily includes subject matter experts in the task the autonomy is addressing. Another difficulty is that scripted autonomy is brittle, e.g. unexpected situations can cause the autonomy to not work. This lack of robustness is due to the expansive state space that exists in the real world. Human designers will not be able to test or even anticipate every situation the autonomous system will be exposed to, resulting in a number of states that will not be addressed by the autonomy or be addressed with limited effectiveness. For example, consider a scripted autonomous system designed to deter piracy that assumes there exists only a single pirate threat at any given time. Once such autonomy encounters a situation where there exists more than one pirate, the script will degrade in effectiveness because the situation was not anticipated. Furthermore, once the autonomous system is introduced, pirates can adapt their tactics to counter the system and render ineffective the specific design of the autonomy. Finally, scripted systems often lack scalability. In particular, the designs will be tied to a particular number of autonomous agents, or a particular autonomous system, meaning each time the number of types of unmanned vehicles change, the autonomy for the system must be redesigned.

In a proof of concept experiment, such a scripted system was compared to a cutting edge multiagent learning method, *Multiagent HyperNEAT*. Multiagent HyperNEAT approaches the problem of multiagent learning by focusing on the geometric relationships among agent policies [13]. The policy geometry is the relationship among policies located at particular positions and the team behavior. Because multiagent HyperNEAT is built upon HyperNEAT, it can exploit the same patterns that HyperNEAT is able, such as regularities. Furthermore, because HyperNEAT can encode repetition with variation, it can encode agent policies that share skills and vary in significant ways. Conventional multiagent learning cannot capture such regularities to enable sharing of skills and variation of policy. For a full description of how multiagent HyperNEAT encodes a team of policies see [13,14]. The main idea is to place a whole set of policies within a team geometry and compute their individual policies as a function of their location within the team.

Moving from simulated domains to real robots will mean that situations may occur where the number of agents varies, such as malfunctions or replacements and therefore ideally team size should be dynamically adjustable. The multiagent HyperNEAT approach allows such scaling because it represents team policies indirectly as a function of team geometry. Thus new agents can be added by simply generating the policy for their assigned team position.

The results of the proof of concept experiment are illustrated in the figure below.

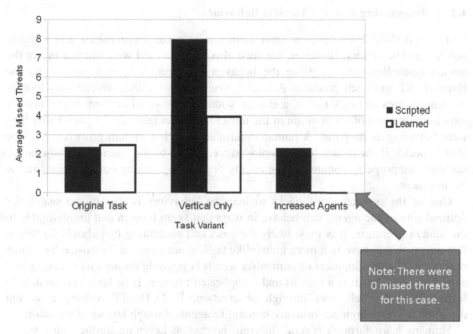

Fig. 1. Performance of Scripted Search versus Learned Policy

Overall, the results show that policies created by multiagent learning approaches are more robust to change. The scripted parallel search and learned multiagent HyperNEAT policies are compared on three variations of a threat detection task. In each of the variations, the policies are tested over 100 evaluations and the results averaged. The learned policy tested is trained solely on the first variation. The first variation is the training task for multiagent HyperNEAT, in which there are seven simulated unmanned vehicles patrolling and the threats can randomly appear along any of the four edges of the operational area. In this task, the learned policy has statistically the same performance as the scripted policy, resulting in the patrols missing 2.37 threats, and the learned patrol policy missing 2.47.

In the second variation, the tactics employed by the threats are altered such that they now appear from two of the four sides at random, thus increasing the density of the attacks along that vector and testing the robustness of the approaches. The learned policy missed 3.94 threats, significantly (p < 0.001) outperforming the scripted policy, which decreased significantly in performance to 7.98 threats missed.

In the third variation, threats can appear along all four edges, but the number of simulated unmanned vehicles in the team is increased from seven to eleven. The learned policy exploits the increased number of vehicles, decreasing the missed threats to 0. However, the scripted policy is unable to take advantage of the new vehicles and only insignificantly decreased missed threats to 2.32. These results demonstrate that learning can produce more robust and scalable policies.

4.2   Recognizing Correct Tactical Behavior

Using HyperNEAT to develop team tactics will create more robust and scalable policies and behaviors. However, we must also be concerned with whether or not the human controller will recognize the behaviors as being safe and correct. As the HyperNEAT approach produces Artificial Neural Nets (ANN), we can only look at the team tactics as black boxes, and even within the proof of concept experiment, it took a fair amount of observation of the units to interpret (essentially guess) why they were behaving as they did. A human controller in such a system however, must be able to decide if the tactics being employed are aligned to the mission and whether or not they are properly countering the enemy or handling arising complications in the environment.

One of the primary draw backs to learning behaviors is that in the search for optimal actions the agents can behave in ways that seem foreign and unintelligible to the human operators. It is most likely the case, and something that should be tested, that agents that behave in a more humanlike fashion are more easily trusted by human observers. The development of humanlike agents is possible through hand coding and expert systems, but it is a tedious and complicated process. It is, however possible to learn humanlike behaviors through observation. FALCONET is such a system designed to create high performance humanlike agents through human observation.

Humans learn through several different processes. Learning through observation entails watching the process as performed by some other individual or agent. Learning through experience involves repetitive practice of the process with feedback on performance. Learning can and does occur under each process individually, but it is the combination of observation and experience that generally leads to the highest levels of performance. For instance when learning a new sport humans typically observe others already proficient in the activity before beginning to practice themselves. Observation bootstraps the learning process of experience enabling faster learning speed and higher peak performance.

There is a long history in Machine learning of borrowing from biological systems. Examples include knowledge representations like neural networks, optimization algorithms such as genetic algorithms and ant colony optimization, and learning paradigms like reinforcement learning. In the particular method discussed below the observational-experiential learning cycle is replicated in machine learning to achieve the same goals for simulated learning that are achieved in biological learning.

FALCONET is a method of agent training that follows the biologically inspired cycle of observation and experiential learning. It was designed to enable the creation of high performing, humanlike agents for real time reactionary control systems [15]. Typically, the building of humanlike agents involves the complicated process of interviewing knowledge experts and then codifying that knowledge into a format that is machine readable. This process is complicated and time consuming and has led to the slow adoption of this technique in real world systems, despite the success that can be achieved. This problem is known as the "knowledge engineering bottleneck" [16]. FALCONET was designed to automate the agent creation process from human observation thereby sidestepping the bottleneck.

Previous work has been done using observational data alone to train agents, stopping once an acceptable level of performance is reached on training and validation sets [17,18,19,20,21]. While this might produce humanlike agents, it ignores the possibility that the observational agents will perform poorly in situations not covered in the observational data. The agents when presented with novel situations could perform in unpredictable and unintelligent ways. The experiential phase can fill in these gaps by providing feedback on the agent's performance in novel situations.

The training in FALCONET follows a two phase training approach. First a supervised observational phase, followed by an unsupervised experiential phase. During the observational phase the objective of the learning is to be similar to the actions of a human trainer. Human trainers run through the selected tasks starting from many different scenarios to generate the observational training set. The agents are then trained on this data set while being graded on how closely they mimic the decisions of the human. In the experiential phase the agents are trained further using a measure of performance on the task. In FALCONET all training is done by a hybrid genetic algorithm (GA) particle swarm optimization (PSO) algorithm called PIDGION-alternate. This is an ANN optimization technique that generates efficient ANN controls from simple environmental feedback. FALCONET has been tested showing that it can produce agents that perform as well or better than experiential training alone while incorporating humanlike behaviors. The results from FALCONET also state that unique human operator traits can be incorporated and evident in the final highest performance controls, that is to say that agents sourced from different trainers have slightly different behavioral quirks.

As part of the validation of the FALCONET method experiments were conducted using only the experiential learning phase. High performance controls were created in this manner, but they showed several "improper" quirks, that while more optimal in the performance metric, seem foreign to human operators. These quirks, like driving backward or slamming the controls left and right very quickly, can be programmed out by a human designer, but it requires the a priori knowledge of all "improper" behaviors that would be undesirable. The FALCONET method bypasses this need by bootstrapping the process with human training.

5   Autonomic Control

So far, we have discussed the basic needs that will allow a human commander/controller to exercise command and control over a network of autonomous units that include highly autonomous unmanned systems (AUS). We have recognized that the controller must be able to develop adequate situational awareness of the environment, any enemies, and the behaviors and status of assets available. This SA requires the commander to recognize the behaviors being displayed as aligned with the mission, commander's intent, and applicable procedures. It also requires that these behaviors be robust to the variation found in the environment.

We have also recognized that the human controller is subject to many difficulties inherent to managing automation. Humans are prone to complacency and automation bias. They also can only work at human speeds and can only handle a finite level of complex information. Abstraction and supervisory control are therefore essential to success if many rapid decisions will need to be made in controlling the network.

We are beginning to model AUS teams utilizing the Rainbow Framework [22] from Carnegie Mellon University. Rainbow groups commands into tactics and strategies and directs the system with those instead of individual actions. This approach allows an automated controller to move the system out of local maximums that it may encounter in utility functions. Additionally, the grouping of actions into tactics and strategies allows for the system to leverage learning techniques and previous human experience in dealing with situations.

Rainbow will provide an autonomic command and control in the sense that it assists with the same set of six tasks, only faster.

Maintain alignment: The mission goals and the commander's intent will be modeled as a set of utility functions within Rainbow. Rainbow evaluates current readings from probes and gauges as well as tactics for changing the resource allocations against these utility functions to select an action.

Provide situational awareness: Rainbow's framework of probes and gauges provides situational awareness into how well the current plan is meeting mission goals.

Advance the plan: The autonomic systems is continuously evaluating the readings from the probes and gauges against the plan and makes changes to adjust in the event that desired goals are not being met.

Comply with procedure: Procedural guidelines can be coded in the tactics employed by Rainbow in the stitch language. It is our intention to also link tactical procedures to learned behaviors.

Counter the enemy: As the environment or enemy actions impinge on success of the goal, Rainbow adjusts the operation based on evaluating tactics against the likelihood of success. The evaluation processes will need to be robust enough to estimate how the changes will effect operations.

Adjust apportionment: The basic types of tactics employed in Rainbow to date have been apportionment decisions. In [22] experiments were done on video teleconferencing services where additional servers were brought online to solve problems that occurred during operations.

In the application of Rainbow, AUS teams are represented in a similar fashion as a network of servers would be. However, we include probes into the physical world providing information both on the AUS and on the environment. Many of these probes relate directly to the sensors that are onboard typical AUS. Strategy decisions involving costs include physical costs of fuel as well as risks found only in systems that interact with the physical world. Likewise, rewards are based on the ability of the AUS to effect a positive change on the environment, often in the form of achieving a probability of detection of other physical entities in a portion of the environment.

We have developed an initial proof of concept in autonomic control of unmanned systems by applying the Rainbow Framework to a simulated domain. In this domain, a number of AUS must maximize the probability of detection, $P(d)$, in an environment by maximizing sensor coverage across the area. In this case, $P(d)$ is a simple metric defined as the fraction of horizontal and vertical paths across the space that do not have sensor coverage across them, i.e. straight paths that can be traversed without detection. Thus each AUS has a location (x,y-coordinate) and sensor range along with other parameters. Because AUS are conceptually similar to computational services (e.g. servers), they can be similarly modeled in the Acme architecture model language that defines a system architecture in the Rainbow Framework. A simple AUS architecture definition is as follows:

```
Component Type AUST extends ArchElementT with {
    Property x : float <<  default : float = 0.0; >> ;
    Property y : float <<  default : float = 0.0; >> ;
    Property fuel : float <<  default : float = 1.0; >> ;
    Property fuelExpendRate : float <<  default : float = 1.0E-4; >> ;
    Property speed : float <<  default : float = 0.01; >> ;
    Property sensorRadius : float <<  default = 0.1; >> ;
    Property cost : float <<  default : float = 1.0; >> ;
}
```

Properties, such as the geographic location and fuel state, represent values that are probed from the (simulated) world. Such values inform the Rainbow model manger, allowing it to accurately reflect and gauge the real system within the Rainbow defined model.

A key feature of Rainbow is the definition of constraints that the system must follow. For example, a web business may desire the minimization of response time for its customers and define a constraint that the response time experienced by any customer if below some threshold. In turn, Rainbow would probe these response time values from the real system and then evaluate the model for constraint violations. If a constraint is violated, Rainbow adapts the model through predefined strategies and then executes these strategies on the real system through effectors. In this proof of concept, the constraint is that the value P(d) must be above a given threshold of 0.8. To satisfy this constraint, Rainbow implements a simple strategy.

```
strategy BruteDetection
[styleApplies && cViolation] {
    t0: (overlapExists) -> move(){
        t0a: (default) -> done;
    }
    t1: (cViolation  && ! overlapExists) -> enlistAUS() {
        t1a: (overlapExists) -> move();
    }
```

In brief, the strategy states that if an overlap in sensor coverage exists, move the active AUS to minimize the overlapping coverage. If there is no overlap, but the constraint is still violated, then add a new AUS to the domain. This strategy implements two tactics that we described in stitch: move and *enlistAUS*. As an example of how these tactics are defined, *enlistAUS* is as follows:

```
tactic enlistAUS () {
    condition {
    // Probability of detection is below a threshold
    ModelAlt.probabilityDetection(M.components) <M.MIN_PDETECT;
    // there should be enough available AUS
    ModelAlt.availableServices(T.AUST) >= 1;
    }
    action {
    set aus = Set.randomSubset(ModelAlt.findServices(T.AUST), 1);
    for (T.AUST freeAUS : aus) {
        S.activateAUS(freeAUS);
        }
    }
    effect {
    // Probability of detection rising should result
    ModelAlt.probabilityDetection(M.components) >= M.PDETECT;
    }
}
```

In the *enlistAUS* tactic, the condition first checks whether the constraint is violated and then if there are any AUS not currently active. If both these conditions are satisfied, a random free AUS is chosen and activated. The effect being that the addition of the new AUS increases the sensor coverage, thus improving P(d) over the current levels.

In the domain, the AUS exist in a two-dimensional plane with coordinate values in the range [0,1]. Initially, no AUS are active, thus the constraint is violated at the start. This compels Rainbow to adapt the system with the above strategies and tactics to achieve the pre-determined desired P(d) level. When each AUS is activated, they are placed at location (0,0) and then move from there. Each AUS moves at the same fixed speed of 0.01, have a sensor range of 0.1, and begin with 100% fuel.

Results demonstrate that Rainbow can be implemented to effectively control such systems. Figure 2 shows that the system begins at a low P(d), indicative of the initial state of the system. However, by time step 150, Rainbow has successfully adapted the system to achieve the desired P(d) value.

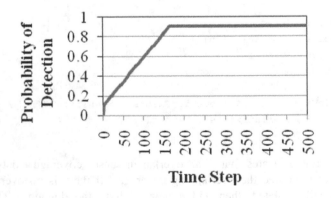

Fig. 2. Probability of Detection in Proof-of-Concept Experiment

Not only is the result interesting, but the behavior of the system is as well. Figure 3 shows the final configuration of the system, when it achieves the P(d) threshold required. Each circle represents an AUS sensor coverage.

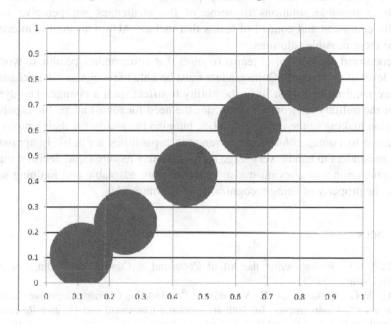

Fig. 3. Final AUS Positions with Sensor Radii

Through the composition of simple strategies and tactics, organization emerges that effectively minimizes the probability of anyone passing through the region undetected. In this simulation, utility of the system is equal to the probability of detection. However, Rainbow includes the capability to calculate system utility as a function of multiple variables. For example, maintaining sensor coverage may be only one important aspect; another may be reducing fuel consumption or minimizing the AUS required. Rainbow weights each of these contributions of utility to determine the overall utility of the system. Through these relative weightings, different aspects can be emphasized. A suite of strategies to address these differing concerns may be required, forming a pareto-front of performance depending on particular user needs.

The ability of Rainbow to automatically and quickly implement strategies frees up the controller to focus on macro level concerns, such as overall probability of detection, fuel levels, and costs, rather than micro-managing individual AUS. Thus the controller can make decisions about required detection levels versus preferred fuel levels and leave it up to Rainbow and its strategies to implement the decisions. Many avenues remain for exploration in the Rainbow Framework including, but not limited to, performance with "human-in-the-loop" changing the system constraints and goals, integrating machine learning into tactics and strategies, extending Rainbow to be able to dynamically acquire system architecture, and evaluating robustness to failures in the system, such as an AUS malfunctioning, being destroyed, running out of fuel, or being reassigned.

6   Conclusions

We have both found and produced, proof-of-concept level experiments that demonstrate possible solutions to some of the challenges we perceive for the successful command and control of teams that include AUS. Our goal is to continue to pursue these possible solutions.

The command and control of teams requires that commanders be able to work at a suitable level of abstraction. Commanders must be able to recognize when changes to a plan are required and must have the ability to affect such a change. The dynamic nature of the military environment indicates the need for robust adaptable capabilities for decision making in the individual AUS, but also the ability for their actions to be recognizable to human controllers. Autonomic capabilities are a likely approach to allow commanders to handle very large teams that may require rapid decision making, but the autonomic strategies must also be made more adaptable and in doing so also maintain the property of being recognizable by a commander.

References

1. Willard, R.F.: Rediscovering the Art of Command & Control. Proceedings of the US Naval Institute (2002)
2. Rodas, M.O., Szatkowski, C.X., Veronda, M.C.: Modeling Operator Cognitive Capacity in Complex C2 Environments. In: 16th International Command and Control Research and Technology Symposium (2011)
3. Parasuraman, R., Wickens, C.D.: Humans: Still vital after all these years of automation. Human Factors 50(3), 511–520 (2008)
4. Parasuraman, R., Molly, R., Singh, I.L.: Performance consequences of automation induced "complacency". The International Journal of Aviation Psychology 3(1), 1–23 (1993)
5. Wiener, E.L.: Cockpit automation. In: Wiener, E.L., Nagel, D.C. (eds.) Human Factors in Aviation, pp. 433–461. Academic, San Diego (1988)
6. Parsasuraman, R., Manzey, D.H.: Complacency and Bias in Human Use of Automation: An Attentional Integration. Human Factors 52, 381–410 (2010)
7. 32nd Army Air and Missile Defense Command: Patriot Missile Defense Operations during Operation Iraqi Freedom, Washington, DC (2003)
8. Chen, T.L., Pritchett, A.R.: Development and evaluation of a cockpit decision-aid for emergency trajectory generation. Journal of Aircraft 38, 935–943 (2001)
9. Johnson, K., Ren, L., Kuchar, J., Oman, C.: Interaction of automation and time pressure in a route replanning task. In: International Conference on Human-Computer Interaction in Aeronautics, pp. 132–137 (2002)
10. Layton, C., Smith, P.J., McCoy, E.: Design of a cooperative problem-solving system for en-route flight planning: An empirical evaluation. Human Factors 36, 94–119 (1994)
11. Mosier, K.L., Skitka, L.J., Dunbar, M., McDonnell, L.: Aircrews and automation bias: The advantages of teamwork? The International Journal of Aviation Psychology 11(1), 1–14 (2001)
12. Leli, D., Filskov, S.: Clinical detection of intellectual deterioration associated with brain damage. Journal of Clinical Psychology 40(6), 1435–1441 (1984)
13. D'Ambrosio, D.B., Stanley, K.O.: Generative encoding for multiagent learning. In: Proceedings of the Genetic and Evolutionary Computation Conference (2008)

14. D'Ambrosio, D.B., Lehman, J., Risi, S., Stanley, K.O.: Evolving policy geometry for scalable multiagent learning. In: Proceedings of the Ninth International Conference on Autonomous Agents and Multiagent Systems (2010)

15. Stein, G.: FALCONET: Force-feedback approach for learning from coaching and observation using natural and experiential training. Ph.D. Thesis, University of Central Florida (2009)

16. Feigenbaum, E.A.: Knowledge Engineering: The Applied Side of Artificial Intelligence. Annals of the New York Academy of Sciences 426(1 Computer Culture: The Scientific, Intellectual, and Social Impact of the Computer), 91–107 (1984)

17. Dejong, G., Mooney, R.: Explanation-based learning: An alternative view. Machine Learning 1(2), 145–176 (1986)

18. Lee, S., Shimoji, S.: Machine acquisition of skills by neural networks. In: IEEE International Joint Conference on Neural Networks, vol. II, pp. 781–788 (1991)

19. Sammut, C., Hurst, S., Kedzier, D., Michie, D.: Learning to fly. In: Proceedings of the Ninth International Workshop on Machine Learning, pp. 385–393 (1992)

20. Henninger, A.E., Gonzalez, A.J., Georgipoulos, M., DeMara, R.F.: The limitations of static performance metrics for dynamic tasks learned through observation. Ann Arbor 1001, 43031 (2001)

21. Fernlund, H.K.G., Gonzalez, A.J., Georgiopoulos, M., DeMara, R.F.: Learning tactical human behavior through observation of human performance. IEEE Systems, Man, and Cybernetics, Part B: Cybernetics 36(1), 128–140 (2006)

22. Garlan, D., Cheng, S., Huang, A., Schmerl, B., Steenkiste, P.: Rainbow: Architecture-Based Self Adaptation with Reusable Infrastructure. Computer 37(10), 46–54 (2004)

The Risks of LSCITS:
The Odds Are Stacked against Us

John A. McDermid

Department of Computer Science, University of York,
Deramore Lane, York, YO10 5GH

Abstract. Complex IT Systems are often used in applications which can pose a
risk to their owners or to the public. Many of these are subject to extensive risk
assessment before they are deployed and operated yet, despite this, undesired
events do arise, leading to financial loss or loss of life. This paper investigates
the role of existing risk assessment methods and draws the conclusion that they
do not effectively predict the causes of actual loss events. The paper then
suggests an alternative approach, which has the potential to offer a unified
approach to risk assessment across a number of domains, and across different
system properties, e.g. safety and financial risk. It concludes with observations
on similar methods and research results, especially from accident analysis, and
makes suggestions for future research directions.

Keywords: Large Scale Complex IT Systems, Risks, Safety, Security.

1 Introduction

Many Large-Scale Complex IT Systems (LSCITS) are used in roles where
organisations depend on them for a key aspect of their business. As a consequence,
these systems may be safety, security or mission (business) critical. It is common to
assess such systems in terms of the risks they pose – whether to the organisation that
owns them or to third parties – but different approaches to risk analysis are used in
different domains. This paper analyses some "loss events" associated with a range of
LSCITS (and one comparatively simple system) then uses the "signatures" of these
events both to question current approaches to risk analysis and as a source of ideas
and inspiration for an alternative model.

Serious failures of the more "critical" LSCITS are relatively rare, and that might
suggest that "all is well" in terms of our ability to design and assess such systems.
However a cursory assessment of a range of "loss events", e.g. accidents or financial
losses, suggests that the current approaches to risk assessment do not throw much
light on the actual causes of the loss events. The paper considers a range of "loss
events" which illustrate safety, financial and availability issues. It shows that the risk
assessment methods used, explicitly or implicitly, in these different domains do not
provide a good basis for gaining an understanding of these events.

This analysis also shows that the events studied have remarkably similar "signatures"
in the sense that the "confluence of events" which leads to the loss are very similar in

R. Calinescu and D. Garlan (Eds.): Monterey Workshop 2012, LNCS 7539, pp. 94–117, 2012.

nature, although they are in different technologies, systems and domains. As LSCITS are increasingly depended on for multiple critical properties, e.g. safety and security, the availability of a "unified" approach to risk assessment has the potential to be valuable in the design and assessment of future generations of LSCITS.

It should be noted that these initial findings are tentative, and need further and more rigorous study. Observations on methodological issues are presented in the next section, followed by a brief, textual, analysis of five loss events. The "signature" of each loss event is discussed, and some observations are made which are intended to help in developing a methodological approach to assessing LSCITS risk. This is followed by a discussion of risk analysis. This discussion first outlines the risk analysis processes typically used in several different domains, and then discusses how well these processes reflect the signatures of the loss events described previously. Next, the paper outlines an alternative perspective on risk analysis, believed to be suitable for assessing LSCITS. The paper then considers related research, before drawing conclusions and proposing directions for future work.

2   Methodological Remarks

It is not possible to do an exhaustive, scientific, analysis of LSCITS and their risks. In some domains the allowable failure/loss rates are so low that the expectation would be that there would no failures in the operational life of the system – and that is many decades. Further, there are far too many systems, and the numbers deployed are increasing at a rate that defies analysis.

Thus our approach reflects an approach developed in social and management sciences, e.g. by Van der Ven [1], which provides a framework for observing, modelling and (ultimately) intervening in real-world applications. This approach is outlined in Fig. 1 overleaf.

The framework can be "entered" anywhere but, for our purposes, it is easiest to think of it starting with observations of reality (the bottom of Fig. 1) to produce a problem formulation. From the problem formulation and the observations, it is then possible to develop theories and models which provide explanations of the observed phenomena (which are better than current theories in this regard). The framework then proceeds to build a "research design" enabling an intervention – changing reality – which can then be re-assessed to seek to confirm or refine the theory and model. At this stage in our work, we are firmly in the (early) stages of theory and model building.

Van der Ven also uses the nature of the research, and the degree of engagement, to refine his research framework; this is outlined in Fig. 2 overleaf. In terms of this model, we are working in the "describe/explain" part of the framework, and within that mainly in the "detached/outside" research perspective (although one of our examples below is in the "attached/inside" quadrant, as it is a personal experience).

Thus, at this stage, the criteria for assessing the theory and model are relevance and validity; we would also say that they should give greater explanatory power than current models of risk.

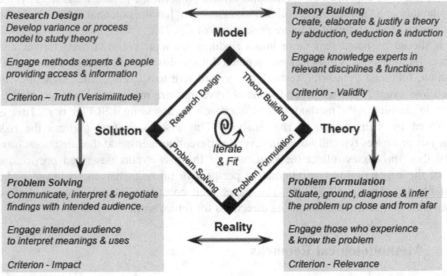

Fig. 1. Model Of Engaged Scholarship (from Van der Ven [1])

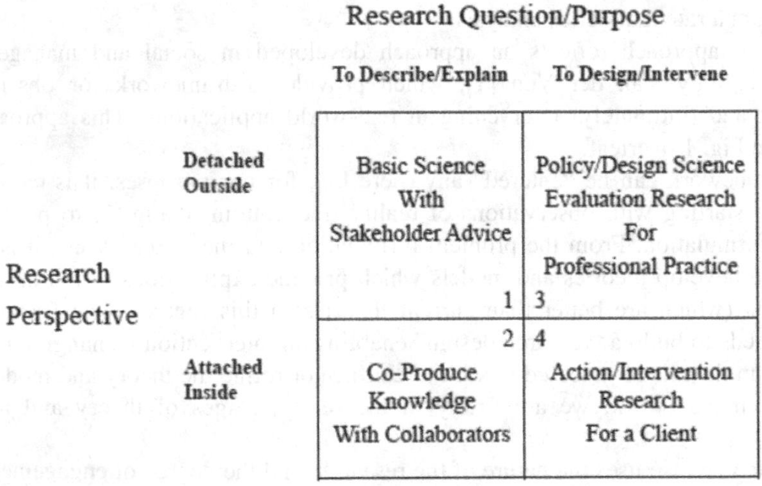

Research Question/Purpose

		To Describe/Explain	To Design/Intervene
Research Perspective	Detached Outside	Basic Science With Stakeholder Advice 1	Policy/Design Science Evaluation Research For Professional Practice 3
	Attached Inside	2 Co-Produce Knowledge With Collaborators	4 Action/Intervention Research For a Client

Fig. 2. Types Of Research (from Van der Ven [1])

This work is undertaken as part of the LSCITS programme [2]. The original LSCITS proposal divided the space of concern for LSCITS into four layers in a "stack", viz:

- PSS – Predictable Software Systems – the development and application of the most advanced scientific principles to large-scale computing problems;
- HISE – High Integrity Systems Engineering – rigorous approaches to dealing with the design and assessment of systems beyond the reach of the PSS methods, including Systems of Systems (SoS);
- STSE – Socio-Technical Systems Engineering – the analysis of systems and their failures where the causes of the difficulties arise in the interaction between technology and users, both individuals and organisations;
- CiO – Complexity in Organisations – focusing on the problems of large-scale organisations, and how they influence system success.

Also, the LSCITS programme includes orthogonal work on non-standard computational approaches to complex problems, and work on the cloud.

To help understand the risks of LSCITS, it would be possible to classify the example loss events in terms of the LSCITS stack. However, it is sometimes hard to make distinctions between the four different concerns, and as several of the loss events studied have complex causal factors, it has been decided instead classify the events on a "scale", viz:

- Pure technical – there is a clear technical cause of the loss event, and the interaction with, and behaviour of, the organisation is much as intended;
- Socio-technical – the causes of the event include erroneous interaction between the system and users, and may also include individual human errors or technical failures;
- Pure organisational – there is a clear organisational cause of the event, e.g. failure to implement separation of duty, and the system behaved according to intent (and requests from users).

This is intended to be a "sliding scale" not a hard categorisation, and it is used to "locate" the primary causal factors in each loss event on the technical-organisational axis.

In analysing loss events there is always a risk of hindsight bias – looking for evidence to prove the author's hypothesis. In part we have sought to address this risk through consideration of events which span the range from highly technical causes to those whose origins are largely organisational. Further we are seeking to build a theory and model, not to prove one. However there is always a risk of such biases, and we return to this concern in the discussion.

3   An Analysis of Some Loss Events

In order to shed light on the issues of risk assessment we consider five "loss events". Four are documented in the literature, to varying degrees; one is a personal experience. Many more examples could be chosen, but the rationale here has been to choose events which span the range from technical to organisational, and cover safety, financial risk and availability (integrity) of private data. Of course there would always be benefit in considering more loss events; see the conclusions for a discussion of future work.

It would be possible to analyse the events using methods such as Why-Because Analysis (WBA) or Why-Because Graphs (WBG) [3]. We have chosen not to do so here, partly for brevity, partly so that we can emphasise what we perceive to be key points, and partly as there is not a body of work to draw on showing how to apply the techniques outside the safety domain. However if this work is to be taken further, then it will be necessary for the analysis of these individual events to be put on a more rigorous footing (although this might require extensions to techniques such as WBA).

In each case, the description contains a brief overview of the event, primarily to set context. This is followed by a descriptive analysis of the event(s) leading to the loss, and ends with an assessment of the "signature" of the event. Following the discussion of these five loss events, some observations are presented, followed by the problem formulation, as suggested by Van der Ven's framework [1].

3.1   A Syringe Pump

This example relates to a syringe pump, that is a medical device which delivers liquid drugs on hospital wards, or anaesthetics in operating theatres. A desired delivery rate is set by a nurse, or an anaesthetist, then an electric motor drives the syringe plunger to deliver the fluid at the set rate. The flow rates set may be very low.

For safety, the initial design had diverse mechanisms for measuring movement of the plunger: a linear interference grating directly measuring plunger movement and a quadrature system measuring the rotation of the motor shaft. In initial use, the device suffered a lot of "spurious trips" where the pump stopped because the linear grating system detected inappropriate movement. Investigation showed that this was spurious, and was due to backlash in a gearbox, which was significant given the low rates at which the pump was meant to operate.

It was decided that the device should be modified so that the linear grating was not enabled until the quadrature system had confirmed that the syringe plunger was moving. Two patients were killed when the plunger emptied the syringe at high speed (it emptied a 250ml syringe in a matter of seconds). A more detailed analysis of the control loop is presented in [4], but the reference does not describe the context of use which was deemed to be sensitive at the time.

Note that this is a simple example, and can not be considered to be an LSCITS, but it is included as it is possible to give quite a detailed technical exposition of what happened, and it also shows the problems of change – which are a causal factor in many accidents and incidents.

Description of the Event. The quadrature system had a reference square wave signal (Fig. 3 a). A sensor on the motor shaft generated a square wave signal; if the rising edge from the sensor was before the rising edge on the reference signal that indicated movement in one direction (Fig. 3 b); movement in the opposite direction was indicated by the edges being in the other order (Fig. 3 c).

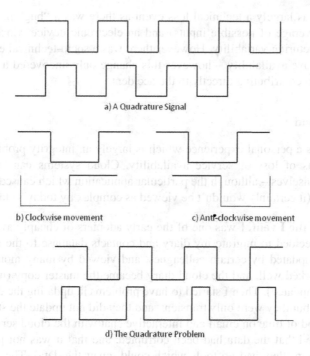

a) A Quadrature Signal

b) Clockwise movement   c) Anti-clockwise movement

d) The Quadrature Problem

Fig. 3. Critical Waveforms (adapted from [4])

The signal coming from the sensor was not "clean" and was "squared up" by means of a Schmitt trigger. Schmitt triggers vary in performance; most produce a signal which is close to square (with a mark-space ratio of 1), but some produce signals with a much higher mark-space ratio. For some devices at the limit of the manufacturing variability, the resultant signal was very distorted and the complete positive pulse was within the positive part of the reference signal (Fig. 3 d).

The logic in the software was designed on the basis that the complete overlap of signals shown at Fig. 3 d) was impossible; unfortunately rather than flagging this as an error and stopping the motor, the software looped, kept power on the motor, read the next set of inputs, and kept going waiting for a "valid" input showing that the motor was moving. Following the change, the motor control software did not enable the linear grating until it had a "valid" input, so the protection system did not stop the motor either.

Signature: The key causal factors in the loss event are:

- Intrinsic flaw (software "bug") exposed by the circumstances;
- The protection system was disabled due to a single point failure (the Schmitt trigger at the limit of tolerances); thus it was a common cause failure;
- Opportunities for further protection, i.e. detecting invalid inputs and/or stopping the device after a time had elapsed without detecting a "valid" input, were missed.

This is viewed as largely a technical loss event as there was a "bug" in the software (incomplete coverage of possible inputs) and an electronic device which was at the limit of manufacturing variability. However there was a socio-technical element – the change to improve availability – however this change only uncovered a basic design flaw, rather than contributing directly to the accident.

3.2   The Cloud

This example is a personal experience which is largely an integrity problem, but also shows problems of loss of service availability. Cloud systems can be viewed as LSCITS in themselves – although the particular application which caused the problem is quite simple (it certainly wouldn't be viewed as complex by today's standards).

Description of the Event. I was one of the early adopters of cheaply available cloud services, and decided to migrate my diary and contacts database to the cloud so that they could be updated by certain colleagues, and viewed by many more. For a few months this worked well, and the cloud diary became the master copy (my "back up" was no longer updated). Then I started to have problems in updating the diary (I could make changes, but they were only transient, and they did not update the stored diary).

After a period of time on email and interactive chat with the cloud service provider it was concluded that the data had been corrupted, and that it was not practicable to "fix" the problem (they had no tools which could repair the data). The support team agreed that they would "package up" my diary and email it back to me (so I could import it into another diary/calendar tool). Again, after an extended exchange with the cloud service provider it became clear that this "resolution" wouldn't work either – the corruption which prevented update also prevented an export being produced!

Fortunately, the diary could still be displayed and printed, thus it was possible to print out my diary (about a year and a half ahead) and to type it all back in. In total the process took 2-3 weeks during which my diary was not up to date, and it cost a significant amount of time in discussion with the service provider and in retyping the diary. (Contacts had changed very little, so there was a minimal amount of effort needed to restore them.)

Signature: The key causal factors in the loss event are:

- Intrinsic flaws (software "bug") exposed by the circumstances;
- A single point failure (the data corruption) disabled both the primary function (diary update) and the protection system (the ability to export data);
- Other protection systems, e.g. the replication of the data in the cloud, were rendered worthless as the data was corrupted not "lost".

Overall this is largely a technical failure, and clearly a detailed software design (data dependency) issue. There was a socio-technical element – the point at which the service provider decided they would stop trying to solve the problem – but as the annual charge for the system was under $100, this was understandable (they will have made a loss on my account given the amount of time they spent in helping me).

3.3   The "Flash Crash"

On May 6th 2010, there were a number of significant anomalies in the financial markets both in New York and in Chicago. Perhaps the most significant event was the drop in the Dow Jones Industrial Average by almost 10%. Unlike some accidents leading to loss of life, e.g. in the aerospace sector, the problem is not well-described in the literature, and the description here draws heavily on [5] and contemporaneous press reports, e.g. [6].

Current financial markets are operated through a mixture of highly autonomous algorithmic trading systems, referred to as algo traders, and human traders. As well as trading directly, the humans set parameters for the algo traders. The changes in the way markets work have been rapid and significant. In 2003 the human traders on the New York Stock Exchange (NYSE) handled about 80% of trading volume of stocks listed on the exchange. By the end of 2009, the proportion being traded "manually" had fallen to 25% with much of the trading moving to electronic-trading platforms, such as Direct Edge and BATS, which execute trades in milliseconds.

Further, markets are linked and some of the trading is done on "spot differences" between markets, e.g. between New York and Chicago. This sort of trading tends to be automatic (algo) as the computer systems have the speed (the millisecond trades) to capitalise on small differences in prices, by trading huge volumes of shares or other commodities.

Description of the Event. On May 6th 2010 the Dow Jones Industrial Average plunged by nearly 1,000 points, with most of the losses occurring between 2.40pm and 3.00pm, see Fig. 4. It was the largest single day decline in the market's history. Some well-known stocks, such as Accenture, briefly traded for as little as a cent. The market later rebounded, to close down by 348 points, although it was "off" by 9.2%, and over $800 billion, at worst.

There has been considerable speculation about the cause or trigger of the "Flash Crash", and it seems that what happened was a combination of general nervousness (about the state of the Greek economy and the UK general election results) and some specific trading actions. Automated systems certainly played a very big role in the rapidity at which events occurred, but human traders also influenced the markets.

First, there is evidence to suggest that human traders were active and significant participants in the market during the big drop. Also, it seems that some human traders were experiencing serious delays in their data feeds caused by the huge volume of trades being executed, so they issued orders in good faith but on the basis of bad (stale) data, and that just made things worse.

Second, humans had "rigged" their algo trading systems to get around some regulations without actually breaking the law. The regulations require that traders always offer two prices: one to buy and one to sell shares. If the traders don't want to take business, then they would offer to buy at $0.01 (1 cent) and to sell at $99,999 (the allowed limits). Whilst the human traders may not have used these prices directly, they were encoded in the algo traders, and these prices were used during the event.

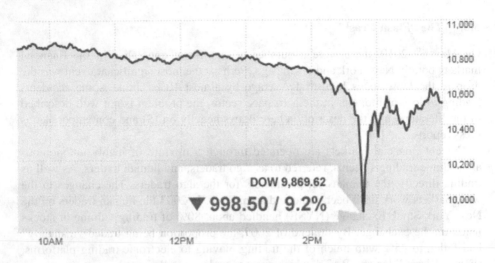

Fig. 4. The Change in the Dow Jones Industrial Average during the "Flash Crash"

In setting these values, the trading houses didn't consider that in a big panic like the "Flash Crash", that many of the traders would get out of the market, cancelling their existing (sensibly-priced) bids and offers, and so the extreme prices would then be left exposed as the best offer and bid prices in the market. At that point, other algo traders transacted at these prices because they had been programmed to automatically deal with the best bid or offer price, regardless of its absolute value (and whether or not it was sensible). Thus the "Flash Crash" is what can be viewed as an emergent property of a complex set of interacting "systems" (an SoS) – both human and automated.

Several companies such as Tradeworx, a hedge fund with a high-frequency trading business, shut off their systems. Manoj Narang, the CEO of Tradeworx said he did this when he "noticed the prices were erroneous", because he knew exchanges would cancel those trades. Many of the trades were cancelled, and the share values returned to near normal, however many companies suffered sustained losses as the trades went through before "limits" were reached where the trades were later cancelled.

Signature: The key causal factors in the loss event are:

- Intrinsic flaw (algorithmic trading at the "best price" regardless of the actual price) exposed by the circumstances;
- Protection (requirement to set buy and sell prices) rendered ineffective by setting of extreme values;
- Other protection systems (cancelling of trades) did at least partially rectify the problems, but some traders did suffer lasting damage (losses on trades which were upheld, as the prices were not deemed "erroneous").

Although much of the "damage" was done by automated trading systems this is a socio-technical issue, as human traders were still operating during the drop, and they set the algo parameters which so significantly contributed to the event.

3.4   Überlingen

In July 2002, two aircraft collided near Überlingen over the Bodensee (Lake Constance) [7]; the description here draws heavily on [8]. One aircraft was owned by DHL and was carrying freight; the other was a commercial aircraft carrying passengers, and operated by Bashkirian Airlines.

One of the roles of air traffic control (ATC) is to monitor flights and to offer guidance or instructions to aircraft so they maintain safe separation. In this case the primary control centre was Zurich. Many aircraft are also fitted with a Terminal Collision Avoidance System (TCAS) which is a "last resort" system which gives pilots "advisories" if it detects that there is another aircraft on a collision course. The TCAS systems coordinate their advisories so the two aircraft take diverging paths. Both aircraft were fitted with TCAS.

Description of the Event. In July 2002, a DHL-owned Boeing 757 aircraft collided with a Tupolev 154 operated by Bashkirian Airlines. All passengers and crew were killed. The trajectories are shown in Fig. 5, where the Bashkirian Airlines aircraft is moving South West, and the DHL aircraft is moving almost due South.

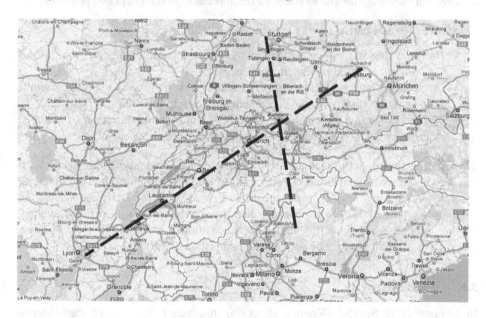

Fig. 5. Überlingen Accident

The two aircraft were initially on a collision course at 36,000 feet, and were first made aware of each other when their TCAS systems issued a traffic warning. Soon afterwards both aircraft received collision-avoidance instructions from TCAS — the B757 was to descend and the Tu-154 was to climb. Shortly after, the Tu-154 received an instruction from Zurich ATC to descend to avoid traffic. According to the cockpit voice recorder on the Tu-154, the pilot originally chose to follow the instruction from

TCAS. However, his co-pilot, a senior company executive who was on board in order to assess the pilot's performance, overruled him, and the aircraft began to descend; this was in accordance with company procedures and the Tu-154 operations manual.

At no point did Zurich ATC give any instructions to the Boeing 757 pilot, although the pilot did tell the ATC that he was descending, shortly before the collision. The two aircraft descended to 35,400 feet where they collided.

The entire accident, from the first TCAS traffic warning to the collision, took slightly less than a minute. Neither pilot was aware of the precise location of the other aircraft until a few seconds before the collision. Zurich ATC was not operating at full effectiveness on the night of the incident. Only a single controller was working, rather than the usual two, and he had to cover two frequencies and two radarscopes. In addition, upgrade work on the Zurich radar processing system meant that the system's performance was severely impaired. In particular, the STCA (Short Term Conflict Alert) function was not available. Further work on the ATC telephone network meant that it was unavailable. There was a backup line, but it was effectively useless due to technical problems.

The impending collision was noticed by a number of ATC centres in neighbouring regions, but they were unable to contact Zurich because of the telephone problems.

Signature: The key causal factors in the loss event are:

- Intrinsic flaw in that one airline took ATC as primary and the other took TCAS as primary, exposed by the circumstances;
- Protection systems (TCAS and ATC) rendered ineffective by the intrinsic flaw, and by reduced staffing and equipment problems in the Zurich ATC;
- Other protection systems, e.g. STCA and communications, rendered ineffective by the technical status of equipment at the Zurich ATC centre.

There are technical, socio-technical and organisational elements to this accident. It can be viewed as further along the spectrum towards an organisational accident, by comparison with the "Flash Crash" for at least two reasons. If DHL and Bashkirian Airlines had treated TCAS as primary, then the accident would have been averted. Further, Zurich ATC operating under such constrained conditions – low staffing, inoperative equipment – can be seen as an organisational failing.

3.5   Société Générale

In January 2008 Société Générale (SocGen) discovered that one of their agents, Jérôme Kerviel (JK), had been building up fraudulent trading positions over a number of years. The positions built up by JK amounted to about €50 Billion. These were "unwound" by SocGen resulting in a net loss of €4.9 Billion for the bank [9]. The actions taken by JK led to a court case and his being given a custodial sentence.

Description of the Event. The root of the problem came from "massive directional positions" [9], i.e. transactions assuming a massive movement of an asset's price in one direction (without any hedging); JK's activities went on over a number of years, and it was only towards the end that these positions became "massive". JK used a number of methods for hiding these positions, including a significant number (nearly 1000) of fictitious trades which both hid his fraudulent positions, and altered various parameters which were monitored by the bank to detect excessive risk-taking. JK also used intra-monthly provisions (adjusting information at month end) which hid his position. There appears to have been some collusion with a trading assistant (who would normally make such intra-monthly provisions) although this does not seem to have been proven in the Court.

The positions went undetected partly due to JK's activities to conceal them, but also apparently due to poor supervision (although the decision by the Court could be seen as exonerating SocGen in this regard). For example, in 2007 JK was without an immediate superior for about two-and-a-half months, and no effective provisions for monitoring his activities were put in place during this period. Also, the new manager coming into post in April 2007 was weak [9], and the new manager was not given much support in taking on his new role.

A further factor, related to weak supervision, is the failure to act on the numerous alerts generated by systems which monitor positions and trades, for undesirable/ suspicious activity. For example, in January 2007, an unusually high number of trades were marked as pending or with no counterparty; these were in fact fictitious, so the alert was a clear sign of the issue. In many cases the alerts were direct evidence of the fraudulent activity; it seems that they were followed up, but explanations from JK were accepted, and issues not escalated to superiors. The internal investigation [9] showed some 64 alerts which were directly linked to the fraudulent behaviour (and several more which were indirect).

A number of other factors, e.g. monitoring the growth in JK's share of the trades and profits in his division, and running a number of computer-based monitoring tools, could have helped to detect the problem. Also, it would have been possible to design the system so that JK could not make some of the trades, and his assistant would have had to, but this only increases the personal risk which would have been taken through collusion, rather than preventing the loss.

Signature: The key causal factors in the loss event are:

- Fraudulent behaviour, together with fictitious transactions which (to a degree) hid the inappropriate transactions;
- Failure of supervision, meaning that many of the systems put in place to detect such anomalous activity were either inoperative or not acted upon;
- Failure to investigate adequately alerts which indicated that fraudulent activity was taking place.

This is the closest to a "pure organisational" problem of the five examples reviewed here. Although there were technical systems which could have been used to help detect the fraud at an earlier stage than actually occurred these all appeared to work, if not perfectly, at least well enough to provide alerts and hence warnings of problems. The underlying "weakness" is that these systems were not used, for several reasons, including leaving JK without an immediate supervisor for a period of time, or because the warnings were not adequately handled.

3.6   Observations

The description of the signature of the above loss events is focused on protection, or barriers to accidents or other loss events (in the SocGen case, the supervision and alerts act as protection or barriers). One of the reasons for starting with two very simple examples is that the role (and inadequacy) of the barriers is reasonably obvious and unequivocal. Inevitably, for the more complex events, the choice of key factors is rather more selective (subjective) as there are many causal factors. Thus there is a risk of hindsight bias – but protection/barriers are introduced for a purpose, and it is thus worthwhile at least as part of our investigation considering why they were not effective, in these cases. There are some other factors that support the focus on barriers.

First, in some domains, e.g. nuclear, there are very clear design principles, e.g. [10], which are based around the idea of layers of protection. Here, the notion of protective layers and "defence in depth" seems to be fundamental to system design and risk control.

Second, even where the standards are not so explicit about protection, e.g. aviation, analysis of real system designs [11] indicates that the degree (number of levels) of protection varies with criticality. Thus it seems that design engineers "naturally" seek to introduce layered protection systems, even where this is not formally required.

Third, financial regulation also supports the idea of layers of protection, with measures both intended to reduce the likelihood of a loss event occurring, and to ameliorate a problem if it does arise [12].

Fourth, as is hopefully obvious from these examples, the notion of barriers is quite general and can apply to technical systems, to the interaction between technical systems and people (i.e. in the socio-technical space) and in organisations. Thus it seems to be a useful unifying concept.

We would thus argue that the focus on barriers is both relevant and valid as the basis for a "theory" and model of risk and loss in LSCITS (see below).

However, there is an apparently contradictory or countervailing issue which arises from standards and regulations – that is the requirement to evaluate risk, usually quantitatively. For example there are numerical targets for aircraft of 10^{-9} per flight hour for catastrophic events, and of 1.55×10^{-8} per flight hour for ATC induced accidents (e.g. mid air collisions). In other domains, e.g. financial markets, the notion of risk targets is less explicit, but there is still an expectation that risk is evaluated quantitatively (see below).

To simplify the issue, we can state that designers are often required to quantify risks "before the event". However it is less clear how useful this quantification is "after the event" (here we are thinking about it as an explanatory mechanism; it is clearly not meaningful to talk about the probability of an event arising after it has occurred).

Thus this initial assessment of these loss events leads us to a problem formulation (in the sense meant by van der Ven [1]): *what is an appropriate risk assessment method for LSCITS?*

4   Risk Analysis

The term risk is used in many different ways, but with broadly similar meanings – the chance of harm or loss. We briefly set out some of the key principles of risk analysis below then use these principles in considering risk in the five loss events described in section 3. This approach is adopted in order to throw light on the problem formulation set out above. This then leads on to the suggestion of a theory for risk in LSCITS – the next step in Van der Ven's model (see Fig. 1) to help us to reach the point where we might define models which can be evaluated via experiments and interventions.

4.1   Risk Analysis Principles

In its simplest form, risk is normally represented as follows:

$$Risk = likelihood \times severity$$

Where the likelihood is the probability of the loss event, or the frequency of the event, and the severity is the extent of the loss. This allows the risk of different events to be compared. For example, consider two risks, A and B, where:

Risk A = 10^{-7} per hour x 10 deaths
Risk B = 10^{-6} per hour x 1 death

Both have the same risk – an expectation of one fatality in a million hours, on average. Similar calculations can be done in terms of financial risk, e.g. expected loss of $10M pa.

Some models of risk don't quantify severity, but rank it qualitatively, e.g.: catastrophic, major, minor, and then risk is evaluated in terms of the probability in each risk class. In some cases, the probabilities are grouped into classes as well; when this is done, risk is evaluated via a matrix, see for example MilStd 882D [13].

In some circumstances, other factors are introduced, e.g. exposure to the risk, or the controllability of the risk by the operators. It is not uncommon for the exposure to be used to modify the probabilities, and factors such as controllability to be used in determining risk categories. Although there are many variations on a theme, the notion that risk is fundamentally a combination of probability and severity of loss is fairly universal, and that will be the focus in our analysis.

Finally, it should be noted that we are always interested in predicting or estimating risk to answer questions such as "is this system safe enough to deploy?" Even when making *post-hoc* decisions, e.g. "is this system now too insecure to continue using?", we are making predictions of future behaviour based on knowledge of the past.

4.2   Risk Analysis of Loss Events

As may be apparent from the loss event descriptions above, it is not always easy to evaluate risk. The approach taken here is to seek to identify, in broad terms, what would need to be done (or known) to evaluate risk quantitatively in each case. An assessment is made of what risk might have been estimated before the events, and what might have been estimated with hindsight. This analysis is then used to inform a discussion of an approach to risk assessment for LSCITS.

Syringe Pump: The safety risk of a device such as the syringe pump would normally be evaluated using a tool such as fault trees [14] which enable accident probabilities to be evaluated based on data about the failure probability and failure modes of basic components, e.g. motors. To the author's knowledge this wasn't done, but a rough estimate of risk can still be made. The intent was that there was triple redundancy: the motor control, primary protection (quadrature system) and secondary protection (linear grating) would all need to fail for the device to fail in a hazardous manner. A failure rate of 10^{-3} per hour for each element is not unreasonable (a "rough" figure for commercial electronics); thus the accident probability might have been estimated at circa 10^{-9} per hour. With 10,000 devices in operation, this suggests 100,000 hours, or about 11 years between accidents.

However this estimate was not appropriate, in the circumstances. Two critical factors in the syringe pump accidents were the software which ignored "impossible" inputs rather than detecting them and taking safe actions, and the Schmitt triggers which could produce "impossible" inputs, at the extreme of their manufacturing tolerances.

To estimate the likelihood of any syringe pump containing a Schmitt trigger with the undesirable behaviour requires a model of the manufacturing distribution, and hence what proportion of the production would have the "dangerous" behaviour. Based on informal data on the system and the accident, this is about 100-1000 ppm (parts per million), or one in 10,000 to one in 1,000.

The likelihood that this erroneous behaviour would give rise to the accident was:

- ~0 prior to the modification to the code which disabled the start of the linear grating checking for movement, until it was detected by the control subsystem
- 1 after this modification

Note that the post-modification probability could also have been made 0, with defensive design of the software. However, without that design change between one in 1,000 and one in 10,000 of the devices would have been flawed, giving rise to an accident rate of one-ten per annum. Assuming that the Schmitt triggers "reliably" produced poor signals, then the accidents would occur early in operational life, and the actual accident rate per operating hour would be many orders worse than the estimate of 10^{-9} per hour.

The optimism in the estimated risk arises because the model used for risk estimation did not adequately reflect the way in which the devices (syringe pump software and the Schmitt triggers) worked (and failed).

The Cloud: In the case of using the cloud to store calendars, a very informal risk evaluation was undertaken. In essence a view was taken that cloud services were highly resilient (gave good availability) and if the service proved poor, the diary could be "repatriated" to a PC without too much difficulty. Also, an informal view of security was taken – that the calendar data wasn't too sensitive (although it would allow someone to determine travel arrangements) thus password protection was sufficient. However the terms of service say "you assume all risks and costs ..." , so it should have been apparent that there were risks! Further, the terms of service do say "does not guarantee or warrant that any content you may store or access through the service will not be subject to inadvertent damage, corruption or loss". However this was viewed (perhaps naively) as an "escape clause", not a "real warning" so, informally, the view was that the risk of unauthorised access to data was low, and the risk of "losing" the data was effectively nil.

As was the case in the syringe pump example, the model used for risk estimation was inappropriate. As it turned out, the real cost of the failure was in the time to retype the calendar into a different tool (and this wasn't even identified as an issue) and the failure mechanism, i.e. inability to re-export the calendar, was not considered either although, arguably, the wording of the terms of service should have sensitised me to this possibility.

Flash Crash. Financial markets have long understood the concept of "market risk", see for example [15], and related concepts such as credit risk. These ideas are also at the basis of bank regulation; under the "Basel 2" arrangements banks have to hold reserves based on the notion of the "Value-at-Risk" (VaR). At its simplest, the requirements are for banks to maintain a level of capital which covers VaR at the 99.9[th] percentile confidence interval [16]. Whilst the details are complex, as many of the traders involved in the "Flash Crash" will have used hedging techniques (buying options to enable adverse movements in the price of assets to be offset), the majority if not all of the organisations involved will have undertaken some form of market risk analysis.

However what happened in the "Flash Crash" was not a market risk, but a systemic risk (or, perhaps better, the systemic issues meant that the market risk analysis was not accurate). The concept of systemic risk in financial markets is not new. In 2008 Long-Term Capital Management (LTCM), a US hedge fund, lost about 90% of its capital in about 9 months, for example losing $1.8 Billion in August 2008 alone. It was "rescued" as there was a concern that it could collapse and cause significant consequential business failures [17]. The root cause of the "Flash Crash" was not the same as with LTCM – instead it was a socio-technical problem caused by a combination of the use of algo trading and the way certain trading parameters were set. However the critical point here is that the classical market risk analyses were not good predictors of events – again the underlying model of risk was inappropriate.

Überlingen. The safety of air traffic management in Europe is subject to Eurocontrol regulations, specifically ESARR 4 [18]. ESARR 4 sets a quantitative target for catastrophic accidents, which includes mid-air collisions, in European controlled airspace of 1.55×10^{-8} per flight hour (the figure is derived from historical achievement). It also requires "use of a quantitative risk based-approach in Air Traffic Management when introducing and/or planning changes to the ATM System" (section 1.1). In other words, providers of ATM services are required to provide a quantified risk assessment which shows that the risk of accidents, such as that at Überlingen, are less than 1.55×10^{-8} per flight hour.

Due to the way regulation is carried out, the services at Zurich will either have been subject to this regulation, or evaluated based on similar regulations which require a quantitative risk assessment. Thus there was a belief, prior to the accident, that the risk per aircraft was of the order of 10^{-8} per flight hour. As there are many accumulated flight hours in Europe, the occurrence of this one accident does not mean that this average accident rate has been exceeded, however it is very unlikely that the models on which the risk assessment was carried out will have reflected the circumstances which arose at Überlingen.

In particular, the risk assessment models would have assumed proper staffing, working telephones, working STCA, etc. – or perhaps more accurately, the models would have assumed that where there were such deficiencies appropriate means would have been taken to mitigate risks, e.g. calling on neighbouring centres. TCAS is viewed as an aircraft system, not part of ATM, so it is unlikely that the ATM risk analysis would have considered TCAS. Further, it seems very improbable that the risk analysis would have considered the fact that ATM might have, in effect, rendered TCAS ineffective by giving instructions which over-rode this "last line of defence". So, once more, the model (which almost certainly would have been) used for the risk calculations was not representative of the situation that arose.

Société Générale. SocGen will have carried out market risk analysis but, as with the "Flash Crash", what happened was "outside" the models used to assess risk. However, what occurred at SocGen would generally be classified as operational risk, rather than systemic risk. There are, nonetheless, similarities with the "Flash Crash". The type of problem seen was not unprecedented; for example work by the Federal Reserve Bank of Boston [19] states that the "capital charge for operational risk will often exceed the charge for market risk". Put another way, the VaR for operational issues may well be greater than that due to the market.

As the causes of the SocGen issues were largely organisational, an effective risk model would have to address these issues. Some work has been done in this area, e.g. using Bayesian approaches to modelling operational risk including fraud in insurance [20], but this remains a little explored area, to the author's knowledge.

4.3   Risk Analysis for LSCITS

The examples given above show that "classical" analyses of risk do not shed much light on the causes of the loss events. Implicitly, system safety engineering methods (which apply to the syringe pump and Überlingen) assume that physical failure mechanisms reflect aleatoric or aleatory uncertainty, i.e. "randomness", which can be characterized by a stochastic model. Further, we implicitly assume ergodicity – i.e. that past failure behaviours are good predictors of the future. Based on these assumptions we can use probability density functions (PDFs) and often we approximate those functions by point probabilities, e.g. the mean of the PDF, in evaluating risk. Such approaches are good ways of modelling processes such as the tossing of coins, and the failure of simple components, e.g. resistors. They underlie the most common quantitative models of system safety, e.g. the calculations supporting fault tree analysis. Similar assumptions underlie the processes of modelling market risk (and in some approaches to software safety [21]).

However, in many cases we face epistemic uncertainty, i.e. limited knowledge of the system model or of the stochastic model. In other words we do not know the shape of the PDF, nor can we estimate its mean. In the cases above, whether sophisticated risk analysis was carried out, or it was very informal, as in the cloud example, the loss events are much better explained in terms of epistemic uncertainty – or to put it simple, the wrong model was used.

There is a further factor in some cases – that the models need to change (or be changed). In other words even if the right model was used in the initial assessment of risk, the system structure and thus the model which is used for assessing risk changes as the system operates and evolves. As markets and trading systems evolve rapidly, it is almost inevitable that, in situations typified by the "Flash Crash", any analysis done before introducing a new trading system would rapidly become inaccurate. Further, in the SocGen case, the risk controls assumed a model of the organisation with people filling key roles – the risks were very different when JK's superior left and was not replaced for over two months.

Returning to Van der Ven's framework, we can propose an *explanatory* theory: *risks and loss events in LSCITS are better explained via analysis of epistemic uncertainty than aleatory uncertainty.*

Note that this is not to say that the techniques based on aleatory uncertainty are worthless – indeed it can be argued it is because they are so effective that the epistemic factors dominate in actual loss events. However, even if it is accepted that this is a plausible explanatory theory, it does not really help us towards a model which can be used to analyse LSCITS, so we now consider some aspects of the LSCITS "stack" and consider how we might use this to build a generative theory, as a step towards a model (in Van der Ven's terms).

In an analysis of Australian defence avionics systems [11] it became clear that there are "layers of protection" against systematic (design) faults in systems, which vary with criticality – the worse the outcome the more the layers of protection. Further the "innermost" layer of protection was concerned with either avoiding or containing any systematic causes of hazards, at source, and the outer layers were concerned with detection and mitigation (of hazard causes). Barriers can be seen in all the five examples discussed above; in some cases these are technological, and in several of the cases they are organisational. This leads us back to the LSCITS "stack" – or something like it.

We can think of "barriers" in the following ways:

- Prevention of problems, at source, or managing them to a low and controlled probability of occurrence – the province of PSS, and other techniques, e.g. Six Sigma, where the processes are human and organisational, not technical;
- Detection and mitigation of technical problems – (in part) the province of HISE, especially considering the interaction of peer components (in a system or SoS);
- Prevention of socio-technical problems, and detection and mitigation of problems through socio-technical means – the province of STSE which is both concerned with good socio-technical system design, and with handling errors arising at this level;
- Prevention of organisational problems, and detection and mitigation of problems through organisational means – the province of CiO which is both concerned with good organisational design, and with handling errors arising at this level.

In general the "barriers" can be characterised in the following ways:

- Their detection and handing of failures (undesirable behaviours) which arise from lower levels;
- Their detection and handing of failures (undesirable behaviours) which arise from peer systems;
- Internally generated failures (undesirable behaviours);
- Failures (undesirable behaviours) "exported" to higher levels.

If this is an appropriate way of looking at LSCITS, in this context, then a means of evaluating risks is needed. We briefly discuss this below, but first set out a further "theory" in the sense of Van der Ven's framework. We propose a *generative* theory: *risks and loss events in LSCITS are best controlled (and risks estimated) via the design and analysis of barriers.*

In order to proceed from the above theory towards a model, in Van der Ven's terms, we need to produce means of identifying the need for barriers, for "designing" them, and for evaluating risk. For brevity, we assume here that barrier identification is possible, e.g. by using adaptations of current methods, which do identify barriers in both technical systems and organisations, and focus on risk evaluation. There are at least three possible approaches:

- Qualitative approaches, e.g. the use of tabular ways of expressing the "depth of defence" against particular potential causes of loss events – these can then be evaluated based on loss event severity, to assess the adequacy of risk controls (this is essentially a generalisation of the approach used for safety in MilStd 882D [13]);
- Quantitative approaches, perhaps by extending the Fault Propagation and Transformation Analysis (FPTA) method [22] developed in part through the LSCITS programme, to consider fault propagation between barriers;
- Quantitative approaches, building on Bayesian approaches such as those proposed for operational risk [20].

It may be practical to combine these approaches in particular ways, or to learn from them, e.g. using the scenario testing approach proposed in [20] to validate FPTA models. In practice, it might be that the quantitative approaches are best thought of as means of ranking designs (sets of barriers), than evaluating risk in the aleatory sense, or in the sense of loss per unit time, which is the underlying measure in safety and in financial risk. In practice, the idea of scenario testing may prove to be vital, as the only practicable way of handling system complexity.

Several of the examples discussed above, e.g. the financial ones and Überlingen can be viewed as SoS. A characteristic of an SoS is that the constituent systems – its configuration – changes over time, and typically faster than individual systems can be redesigned. If any change violates assumptions made about the SoS then there can be undesired behaviour – such changes can be thought of as inflection points [23]. No SoS or system design can be robust against all potential changes, but perhaps it might prove possible to use scenario testing on barrier models to demonstrate robustness against epistemic uncertainty – or at least to identify what classes of change bring about undesirable inflection points. Of course, this will only be as good as the underlying models.

5   Discussion

There has been work, particularly in the safety community, focused on the modelling and analysis of accidents. We review this work here, and draw some distinctions with the approach which we have outlined above. We then make a few further observations about the difficulties of quantification of risk for high criticality systems.

Peter Ladkin in Bielefeld has developed Why-Because Analysis (WBA) [3] as a "rigorous technique for causally analysing the behaviour of complex technical and socio-technical systems". Whilst it is also intended to assist in analysing safety requirements, to the author's knowledge it has found greatest utility in accident analysis, where its flexibility enables it to be used to address relevant causal factors. Our experience with WBA, for example [8] which analyses the Überlingen accident, and our as yet unpublished work on the Wenzhou train crash, shows its utility. Indeed, one possible step for making the ideas set out above more rigorous would be to analyse all the loss events using WBA. However our work on Wehzhou suggests that WBA is not good at dealing with influences, rather than causes, thus there may be merit in seeking to extend WBA before analysing all the above loss events.

Further, we are not aware of cases where WBA has been used proactively to drive designs and we do not see how it would help in identifying barriers, although we note that [3] refers to the use of WBA to identify requirements. As we understand it, WBA does not help to evaluate risk (at least quantitatively) although again one can envisage ways of extending the method to do this.

Nancy Leveson at MIT has developed STAMP [24] as a means of analysing both socio-technical and organisational causes of accidents – thus it gives a framework for analysing the type of loss events discussed earlier. One of the great attractions about STAMP is that it gives a generic model of factors in accident causation from low-level technical issues through organisations, up to political institutions. A number of examples using STAMP have been published. However our experience, to date, has been that it is hard to apply, and that the guidewords in the method for assessing deviation from intent do not seem to be sufficiently comprehensive. For example, one of the issues in the Wenzhou accident is that the Ministry of Railways (MoR) was both the operator of the trains and the regulator; although the STAMP model identifies operators and regulators there is no obvious way to reflect the conflict of interest (potential single point of failure) due to MoR's dual role, in that framework. As one of the key factors in some of the five loss events discussed above was single point failures which undermined multiple protective barriers, this at present seems to be a limitation of STAMP (this must be viewed as a tentative assessment as our work on Wenzhou is ongoing).

Like WBA, we have yet to see STAMP used proactively in system design although there is nothing intrinsic in the method which should prevent this. Again, like WBA, STAMP does not appear to provide a basis for evaluating risk in the sense investigated here although, again, extensions might be possible.

Recent work on resilience engineering [25] has a stronger influence on the ideas set out herein. Both in his publications on resilience engineering, and in prior work, Hollnagel emphasises the importance of designing barriers, and the need to assess human behaviour and cognitive processes, in designing systems and barriers. As we develop the ideas set out above we need to draw on the insights from resilience engineering, but note that the scope of our endeavour is broader – seeking to take a unified view of critical systems, rather than the focus on safety in Hollnagel's work.

Other work in LSCITS is addressing issues relevant to the approach outlined here, for example the use of responsibility modelling as an aid to risk analysis in socio-technical systems [26]. As currently defined, this work would most naturally form part of the qualitative risk analysis approach identified above (indeed we have used it this way in our Wenzhou analysis).

There is some literature, for example [27], which is casting doubt on the validity of quantitative risk assessment. This can be read two ways: as supporting our analysis here, by confirming that real-world risk assessments are often flawed, or contradicting it by implying that trying to quantify risk is impractical. We hope, in time, to be able to support a third view; that taking an approach, informed by quantitative analysis, can lead to more robust designs (e.g. better and better-placed barriers) and more resilience to changes in models, than achieved by current approaches. Separately, we are working on approaches to assessing whether or not risk predictions are valid, or trustworthy.

As indicated earlier, there is a risk of hindsight bias, including finding examples which confirm the author's hypothesis. Also identifying "root causes" of a loss event is always judgemental – in other words, when do you stop looking for prior causes of events? In the cases considered, several are the subject of existing public domain analyses, so this helps avoid hindsight bias. Further, barriers are intended to stop the propagation of faults and errors – so it is not biased to observe that they weren't effective, once a loss event has occurred.

Further, the author's "foresight bias" was that the loss events would be explained by change – in the technical system, in usage, etc. In some of the examples, e.g. the syringe pump (technical) and Überlingen (organisational) there are clear changes (if only temporary in the case of Überlingen) which have a causal influence on the loss event, but the other cases are less clear-cut. Arguably, they all involve change – with the "cloud" example it was moving a calendar, with the "Flash Crash" and SocGen there were changes in behaviour. However these can be viewed as changes in usage within design parameters, not a change in the intended usage. Partly for this reason, and also because change can be thought of as one of the possible reasons why the models used for analysis do not reflect the system (in the broadest sense) as used, it was decided to treat epistemic uncertainty as the primary factor in the explanatory theory. Whilst we cannot prove that there is no hindsight bias, the fact that this is an explanatory theory, and it is not used directly to produce the generative theory and any solutions, makes the problem of hindsight bias less of a concern than it might otherwise be.

Finally, we believe that the observation we have made about the limitations of risk analysis because the causation of loss events is based more on epistemic than aleatory uncertainty to be a distinctive, if not unique viewpoint. There are, for example, criticisms of ESARR 4, e.g. [27], which challenge the underlying safety models in ATM (especially for setting targets), but this, and all the other examples we know, focus on a particular system or scenario. However, if nothing else, this analysis of ESARR 4 serves to show how important it is to analyse the models behind standards, as well as systems designs, to ensure that they are effective in their role.

6   Conclusions

There are growing numbers of LSCITS in operation, many of which are critical, e.g. those supporting ATM and the financial markets. Also more "classical" safety-critical applications are becoming more extensively networked. The failure or misbehaviour of such LSCITS could lead to harm, be it in terms of loss of life or financial impact. This paper has sought to demonstrate, by means of examples, that classical approaches to assessing risks of critical systems have severe limitations in practice, and do not seem to be effective for LSCITS. In general this is because the basis on which the risk assessment is done is not representative of the causal mechanisms in actual loss events.

Our approach in this paper has been influenced by Van der Ven's approach to research in social sciences, building research problems and theories from empirical observations. Although this is perhaps unusual, it seems justified in that the social sciences deals with very complex situations where experimentation (in the classical scientific sense) is not possible – and the same problems exist in assessing the effectiveness and risks of LSCITS. It is our intent to take this on further, to build models from which we can then plan and conduct experiments to help refine our ideas. To do this requires at least three areas of exploration:

- Assessment of the signatures of a larger set of loss events;
- More rigorous assessment of the causal structures and signatures of a number of loss events, e.g. using WBA;
- Construction of a prospective model for system risk analysis and design refinement, perhaps based on work on FPTA and Bayesian approaches to risk analysis (to rank risks, if not to evaluate them accurately).

An underlying assumption in the approach we have sketched here is that the concept of barriers is a useful abstraction in LSCITS. It has several merits:

- The concept is already used in technical systems, e.g. aviation and nuclear, and in organisations, e.g. the financial sector, and is one of the underlying principles in resilience engineering;
- The concept applies independent of implementation technology;
- It offers a significant abstraction away from the detail of an LSCITS;
- Analysis of "integrity of barriers" may give a way of assessing the continued robustness and resilience of a system (or SoS) following change.

In extending this work, one of the key challenges will be to demonstrate that the concepts are effective in the presence of change, especially in SoS, as this is central to the challenges of constructing and assuring LSCITS.

Finally, the LSCITS principals have recently set out their views on the engineering of LSCITS [29], and identified several challenges. It is hoped that the work set out here will contribute to providing solutions to two of these challenges: 5 ("how can systems be designed to recover from failure?") and 6 ("how can we mange complex, dynamically changing system configurations?"). If we can do this, then we will have made a significant contribution to the understanding of how to design and assess LSCITS for critical applications.

Acknowledgements. In producing this paper I have been influenced by the work of colleagues in York and in the LSCITS partner Universities, and by discussions with other collaborators.

I am grateful for input made by my LSCITS colleagues, especially Dave Cliff and Ian Somerville. In York I have benefited from discussions and contributions from Rob Alexander, Georgios Despotou, Giaocheng Xe, Tim Kelly, Andrew Rae, Derek Reinhardt and Niu Ru.

I have also had some useful and stimulating discussions with Mark Connelly and Mark Rodbert of Neural Insights, and Maurice Perks of IBM. I am particularly grateful to Mark Connelly for identifying some relevant literature on practices in the financial sector. Further, I am grateful for the brief but helpful discussions with Robert Cowell of City University, the lead author of [20], during a visit to York.

Finally, I should like to acknowledge the support to this work by the EPSRC through the LSCITS programme, ref. EP/F001096/1.

References

1. Van der Ven, A.H.: Engaged Scholarship: A Guide for Organizational and Social Research. Oxford University Press (2007)
2. LSCITS research programme (last accessed February 3, 2012), http://lscits.cs.bris.ac.uk/research.html
3. Ladkin, P.B.: Why-Because Analysis (last accessed February 4, 2012), http://www.rvs.uni-bielefeld.de/research/WBA/
4. Clarke, S.J., Coombes, A., McDermid, J.A.: The Analysis of Safety Arguments in the Specification of a Motor Speed Control Loop, YCS 136, Department of Computer Science, University of York (1990)
5. Cliff, D.: Private Communication (January 2012)
6. The Economist (on-line edition), A Few Minutes of Mayhem (May 13, 2010)
7. Bundesstelle für Flugunfalluntersuchung (BFU: German Federal Bureau of Aircraft Accidents Investigation), Accident on 1 July 2002, Near Überlingen/Lake Constance, Germany Involving Boeing B757-200 and Tupolev TU154M, Investigation Report AX001-1-2/02 (May 2004)
8. Alexander, R., Hall-May, M.: Modelling and Analysis of System of Systems Accidents, DARP/TN/2003/19, University of York (February 2004)
9. Société Générale, General Inspection Department, Mission Green, Summary Report (May 20, 2008) (English version, translated from the French)
10. Health and Safety Executive, Safety Assessment Principles for Nuclear Facilities, Revision 1 (2006)
11. Reinhardt, D.W., McDermid, J.A.: Assuring against Systematic Faults using Architecture and Fault Tolerance in Aviation Systems. In: Proc. Improving Systems and Safety Engineering, Brisbane, Australia (August 2010)

12. The Basel Committee on Banking Supervision of the Bank for International Settlements (last accessed February 4, 2012), http://www.bis.org/bcbs/about.htm
13. US DoD, MilStd 882D Standard Practice for System Safety (2002)
14. Roberts, N.H., Vesely, W.E., Haasl, D.F., Goldberg, F.F.: Fault Tree Handbook, Systems and Reliability Research Office of U.S. Nuclear Regulatory Commission, Washington, DC, 20555 (1981)
15. Alexander, C.: Market Risk Analysis, vol. I-IV. Wiley, New York (2008)
16. Basel Committee on Banking Supervision, International Convergence of Capital Management and Capital Standards (Basel II), Bank for International Settlements (2004)
17. US General Accounting Office, Long-term Capital Management: Regulators Need to Focus Greater Attention on Systemic Risk, GAO/GDD-00-3 (October 1999)
18. Eurocontrol Safety Regulatory Requirement (ESARR) 4, Risk Assessment and Mitigation in ATM. Eurocontrol (2001)
19. de Fontnouvell, P., DeJesus-Reuff, V., Jordan, J., Rosengren, E.: Using Loss Data to Quantify Operational Risk. Federal Reserve Bank of Boston (April 2003)
20. Cowell, R.G., Verrall, R.J., Yoon, Y.K.: Modelling Operational Risk with Bayesian Networks. Journal of Risk and Insurance 74(4), 795–827 (2007)
21. McDermid, J.A.: Risk, Uncertainty and Software Safety. In: Proc 28th International System Safety Conference. International System Safety Society, Vancouver (2008)
22. Ge, X., Paige, R.F., McDermid, J.A.: Probabilistic Failure Propagation and Transformation Analysis. In: Buth, B., Rabe, G., Seyfarth, T. (eds.) SAFECOMP 2009. LNCS, vol. 5775, pp. 215–228. Springer, Heidelberg (2009)
23. Perks, M.: Private Communication (February 2012)
24. Leveson, N.G.: A New Accident Model for Engineering Safer Systems. Safety Science 42(4), 237–270 (2004)
25. Hollnagel, E., Woods, D.D., Leveson, N.G.: Resilience Engineering: Concepts and Precepts. Ashgate Publishing (2006)
26. Sommerville, I., Lock, R., Storer, T.: Responsibility Modeling for Risk Analysis. In: Proc. ESREL 2009, Prague (September 2009)
27. Hansson, S.O.: Seven Myths of Risk. Risk Management 7(2), 7–17 (2005)
28. Brooker, P.: Air Traffic Management Accident Risk, Part 2: Repairing the Deficiencies of ESARR 4. Cranfield Research report PB/5/05 (May 2005)
29. Sommerville, I., Cliff, D., Calinescu, R., Keen, J., Kelly, T.P., Kwiatkowska, M., McDermid, J.A., Paige, R.F.: Large-Scale Complex IT Systems. Communications of the ACM 55(7), 71–77 (2012)

Integration Architecture Synthesis
for Taming Uncertainty in the Digital Space

Marco Autili, Vittorio Cortellessa, Davide Di Ruscio, Paola Inverardi,
Patrizio Pelliccione, and Massimo Tivoli

Università dell'Aquila
Dipartimento di Ingegneria e Scienze dell'Informazione e Matematica
L'Aquila, Italy
{marco.autili,vittorio.cortellessa,davide.diruscio,paola.inverardi,
patrizio.pelliccione,massimo.tivoli}@univaq.it

Abstract. The abundance of software that will be more and more available will promote the production of appropriate integration means (architectures, connectors, integration patterns). The produced software will need to be able to evolve, react and adapt quickly to a continuously changing environment, while guaranteeing dependability through (on-the-fly) validation. The strongest adversary to this view is the lack of information about the software, notably about its structure, behavior, and execution context. Despite the possibility to extract observational models from existing software, a producer will always operate with software artifacts that exhibit a degree of uncertainty in terms of their functional and non functional characteristics. Uncertainty can only be controlled by making it explicit and by using it to drive the production process itself. This calls for a production process that explores available software and assesses its degree of uncertainty in relation to the opportunistic goal G, assists the producer in creating the appropriate integration means towards G, and validates the quality of the integrated system with respect to the goal G and the current context. In this paper we discuss how goal-oriented software systems can be opportunistically created by integrating under uncertainty existing pieces of software.

1 Introduction

Increasingly, software applications will be produced following a production process paradigm that will be based on the reuse of non-proprietary software, often black-box and on software integrator systems that will ease the collaboration of existing software for the realization of new functionalities. The produced software will be inherently dynamic since it needs to operate in a continuously changing environment and must be able to quickly react and adapt to different types of changes, even unanticipated, while guaranteeing the dependability today's users expect.

This evidence promotes the use of an *experimental* approach, as opposed to a *creationistic* one, to the production of dependable[1] software. In fact, software

---

[1] We refer to the general notion of dependability, as defined by IFIP Working Group 10.4: *"the trustworthiness of a computing system which allows reliance to be justifiably placed on the service it delivers"*.

R. Calinescu and D. Garlan (Eds.): Monterey Workshop 2012, LNCS 7539, pp. 118–131, 2012.
© Springer-Verlag Berlin Heidelberg 2012

development has been so far biased towards a *creationist view*: a producer is the owner of the artifact, and with the right tools she can supply any piece of information (interfaces, behaviors, contracts, etc.). The Digital Space promotes a different *experimental view*: the knowledge of a software artifact is limited to what can be observed of it. The more the observations will be powerful and costly the more the knowledge will be deep, but always with a certain degree of uncertainty. Indeed, there is a theoretical barrier that limits, in general, the power and the extent of observations.

The big challenge underlying this scenario is therefore to accept that this immense software resources availability corresponds to a lack of information about the software, notably about its behavior and on its execution context. A software producer will less and less know the precise behavior of a third party software service, nevertheless she will use it to build her own application. This means that the producer will operate in an environment in which the available services, and hence their related software artifacts (e.g., behavioral models, interface descriptions), exhibit a degree of uncertainty in terms of their functional and non functional characteristics (e.g., approximated behavioral models, incomplete interfaces, inaccuracy of performance parameters). We borrow Galbraith's definition of uncertainty, as taken from [35]: it "*defines uncertainty as the difference between the amount of information required to perform a task and the amount of information already possessed*". Indeed, in the software domain we see a flourishing of tools and methods to elicit approximated behavioral models of running systems. This problem recognized in the software engineering domain [23] is faced in many other computer science domain, e.g., exploratory search [45] and search computing [15], as well as software risk management [12], economics and other social domains [35]. In order to face this problem and provide a producer with a supporting framework to engineer the future software applications we envision a process that implements a radically new perspective.

In this paper we move some steps in the definition of EAGLE [4], an integrated model-based framework of theories, models, model-driven techniques, and tools to support the perpetual explore-integrate-validate production process of dependable software in the digital space, i.e., goal-oriented software systems that are opportunistically created by integrating under uncertainty existing software and that are dynamically evolving within a perpetually changing context. Specifically, we focus on the integration synthesis phase that aims at producing integration means to compose the explored software together in order to produce an application that satisfies the goal and that is able to tames uncertainty. The idea is that the integration solution compensates the lack of knowledge of the composed software by adding integration logic like connectors, mediators and adapters.

The paper is structured as follows: Section 2 presents the state of the art and motivates the work. Section 3 recalls the EAGLE approach while Section 4 explains the integration synthesis promoted by EAGLE. Final remarks are discussed in Section 5, while the paper concludes in Section 6.

2   State-of-the-Art Overview

EAGLE calls for uncertainty-aware and partial models. Uncertainty here corresponds to a measure, in a given metric system, of the incompleteness and inaccuracy of the models with respect to the goal G, which is due to the nature of the elicitation technique, its cost, and the operative context of the software system. EAGLE systems opportunistically integrate pieces of software as available in a non-ideal world: this leads to accept incomplete information, hence accepting systems that represent the strictly necessary solution for satisfying the specified goal, possibly also in face of risks identification and prioritization. Thus, goal-oriented validation is another key aspect for EAGLE. As discussed below, there exist many methods and techniques to account for uncertainty while developing software systems. All of them operate within different domains and consider uncertainty at different abstraction levels by also exploiting different software models. In this direction, one of the aims of EAGLE is to combine/extend existing techniques and methods into a unified uncertainty-aware framework. Therefore, our state-of-the art overview is organized in several parts: Section 2.1 discusses approaches addressing the problem of deriving partial models from implemented systems. Section 2.2 presents the models@runtime approach and Section 2.3 concentrates on automatic connector synthesis to support software integration and coordination. Finally, Section 2.4 focuses on functional and non-functional Verification and Validation (V&V) under uncertainty.

2.1   Derivation of Partial Models

Many reverse engineering techniques have been applied to recover software architectural information from software systems. These techniques result in different structural models that describe approximations of the system internal structure [42]. Several approaches have recently addressed the problem of deriving partial behavioral models from implemented systems. In [8] we propose a method that combines synthesis and testing techniques in order to automatically derive the behavior protocol of a web-service out of its WSDL interface. In [22] the authors propose an approach to construct partial models for representing sets of alternatives and to use those alternatives for reasoning. In [44] the authors propose a synthesis technique that constructs partial behavioral models in the form of Model Transition Systems (MTS), a combination of safety properties and scenarios. In [32] the authors describe a technique to automatically generate behavioral models from (object-oriented) system execution traces. The work described in [25] aims to infer a formal specification of stateful black-box components that behave as data abstractions by observing their run-time behavior. In [18] the authors propose tools and techniques to automatically derive models from running open source software systems in order to enable the simulation of their upgrades and to detect possible configuration inconsistencies.

2.2   Models@runtime

The models@runtime approach [9] seeks to extend the applicability of models produced in Model Driven Development (MDD) [39] approaches to the run-time environment. An example of design models application at run-time has been proposed by the PLASTIC project[2]. The PLASTIC development process [3,2] relies on model-based solutions to build adaptable context-aware service-oriented applications. It encompasses methodologies and software tools to generate QoS models and adaptable application code from UML-based specifications. In this setting, opportunistic reuse of heterogeneous pieces of software, context aware-ness, run-time evolution, adaptiveness and uncertainty represent challenges that can be addressed by adopting a models@runtime approach [9]. Modeling tech-niques coupled with MDD capabilities, such as model transformation and code generation, provide viable means to enable system monitoring, model analysis and adaptation at run-time [27]. In [16] variability models are reused at run-time to support self-reconfiguration of systems when triggered by changes in the en-vironment. In [34] run-time models of a system are used to reduce the number of configuration and reconfigurations to be considered when planning adaptations of the application. In [24] the use of configuration graphs is investigated as a means for monitoring and recording information about the system adaptations. As discussed in [31], meta-models allowing the definition of models where design- and run-time concepts are combined represent another key aspect for the cre-ation and exploitation of effective run-time models. In the context of free and open source software systems, we use models@runtime to manage the upgrade of system configurations [18]. These approaches recognize the need to produce, manage and maintain software models all along the software's life time in order to assist the realization and validation of system's adaptations while the system is in execution.

2.3   Automatic Connector Synthesis to Support Software Integration and Coordination

The first approaches to connector synthesis appeared in the 90s in the control theory domain [38] and, thereafter, they have been revised to fit the domain of software (embedded) systems [1,5]. The aim of these approaches is to automati-cally synthesize a controller that restricts the system behavior so as to satisfy a given specification. In [14,37] LTSs are used to model the I/O behavior of com-ponents and automatically synthesize a set of constraints on the components' environment that allow deadlock avoidance. In [43] we show how to automati-cally derive either a centralized or distributed connector from a specification of the components' interaction and of the requirements that the composed system must fulfill. However, these approaches do not take into account both possible run-time changes in the environment and non-functional requirements of the system to be integrated. The CONNECT project[3] overcomes these limitations

---

[2] FP6 IST EU PLASTIC, http://www.ist-plastic.org/
[3] FP7 FET EU CONNECT, http://connect-forever.eu/

promoting the development of automatic connector synthesis approaches that can be efficiently performed at run-time [29]. EAGLE aims at tackling the problem of automatically synthesizing integrators at run-time under uncertainty.

2.4 Functional and Non-functional Verification and Validation under Uncertainty

The idea of moving V&V activities at run-time [6] has been often realized by introducing monitoring activities both for functional and non-functional properties, and more recently by moving testing to on-line [7]. Uncertainty in EAGLE calls for compositional V&V techniques that permit to perform partial V&V (based on the information currently available) and to instrument the system so to be able to support on-line V&V. Many works have been proposed in compositional verification and, in particular, in assume-guarantee reasoning [17,26,19]. Bayesian models (such as Bayesian Networks [36]) can be considered as the stochastic counterpart of the assume-guarantee paradigm. In this direction, an example of bayesian approach for modeling the reliability of a software component-based system, given the reliability of its components, has been presented in [40]. More sophisticated stochastic models can be used to take into account uncertainty in non-functional validation processes. Hidden Markov Models (HMM) [20] are typically used to model systems that have Markovian characteristics in their behavior, but that also have some states (and transitions) for which only limited knowledge is available. Finally, theories [28] and techniques [10] for compositional approaches to testing have been investigated.

3   The EAGLE Approach

The EAGLE approach promotes a novel production process (see Figure 1) that builds around three iterative phases explore-integrate-validate as follows [4]:

(i) **Explore:** explore available software services with the aim of extracting models as much complete as possible with respect to an opportunistic goal G. This means that, within the proposed software production process, we admit to deal with models that may exhibit a high degree of incompleteness, provided that they are accurate enough to satisfy user needs and preferences. For sake of validation, we will consider behavioral models annotated with quantitative non-functional parameters (e.g., Probabilistic Automata, UML+MARTE models, Queueing Networks, etc.);

(ii) **Integrate:** assist the producer in creating the appropriate integration means to compose the explored software together in order to produce an application that satisfies G (e.g., from specific architectural integration patterns to solutions enforcing suitable architectural constraints). The integration solution can indeed compensate the lack of knowledge of the composed software by also adding integration logic like connectors, mediators and adapters.

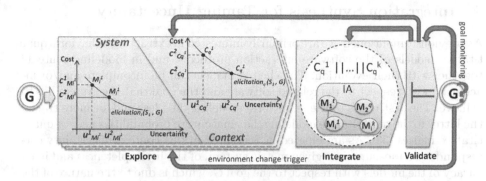

Fig. 1. Explore, Integrate, and Validate cycle

(iii) **Validate:** dynamically validate the integrated system to assess its quality
with respect to the goal G and the current context. This also requires to
check whether a change in the goal or in the context occurs, so to seamlessly
re-enact the explore-integrate-validate process to adapt to the change(s).

Feedbacks coming from validation and goal monitoring activities (see Figure 1)
will instruct the process on whether proposing a new integration architecture
(e.g., with the aim to act on the integration means, such as connectors, to avoid
interactions that prevent the achievement of the goal), or reiterating the entire
process to incrementally elicit more accurate software models (a specific lack
of information in the considered models may lead to a meaningless validation).
The explore-integrate-validate iteration is terminated once the validation step
shows that the goal is achieved. Indeed, whenever changes in the monitored
environment occur, the reiteration of the entire cycle might also be triggered (as
new context may invalidate the goal).

In more details, according to Figure 1, if $S_1, \cdots, S_k$ are (with respect to the
goal G) the candidate pieces of software that are being elicited by an explorative technique i, the result of an explorative phase, $elicitation_i(S_1, G), \ldots,$
$elicitation_i(S_k, G)$, is a set of models $M = \{M_i^1, \ldots, M_i^k\}$. Each model shall have
associated its own accuracy, and hence its own metric for measuring the degree
of uncertainty $u_{M_i^j}$. Moreover, each elicited model M_i^j has a cost $c_{M_i^j}$ that represents a quantitative measure of the effort to elicit M_i^j with an uncertainty degree
$u_{M_i^j}$. The *Explore* box of Figure 1 shows a curve for the explorative technique i,
that is able to elicit the model M_i^1 with different costs and uncertainty degree
(along the curve). In general, a piece of software can have associated different
models, as derived from different observations performed by different elicitation
techniques. That is, the *Explore* box has a certain multiplicity (as represented
by the dashed box boundaries) given by the multiplicity of the pieces of software under observation and of the explorative techniques. Similarly, different
models of context $C = \{C_1, \ldots, C_n\}$ can be elicited and analogous definitions of
uncertainty and cost metrics can be introduced for them.

4   Integration Synthesis for Taming Uncertainty

As previously mentioned, we are primarily interested in extracting behavioral quantitative models of the software interaction protocols, and in modeling contexts together with their evolution. The elicited models can be incomplete and/or inaccurate with respect to the related software and the goal that the system has to achieve. The first refers to the behavioral modeling, i.e., less and/or more traces, the latter to the quantitative modeling, i.e., inaccurate probabilities and/or quantitative indices [33]. As anticipated in Section 2, in this context uncertainty corresponds to a measure, in a given metric system, of the incompleteness and inaccuracy of the models with respect to the goal G, which is due to the nature of the elicitation technique, its cost, and the operative context of the software system. Analogously to testing where the notion of coverage is pivotal to any metrics to assess the effectiveness of testing, reasoning about the quality of the elicited observational models needs similar notions. Indeed, in the EAGLE scenario we are interested in developing systems by opportunistically integrating pieces of software and in assessing costs subsequent to choices, as in the "value-based" paradigm [11], so to achieve the goal most effectively. For the elicitation techniques, it shall therefore be possible to: (i) establish what portion of the goal specification can be fulfilled by the system under exploration, possibly under some assumptions on the environment; and (ii) select the suitable exploration techniques and establish a convenient strategy for their usage according to the cost of the elicitation process, as specified by the user preferences and needs.

To better explain how the integration synthesis promoted by EAGLE tames uncertainty, let us introduce a hypothetical scenario of EAGLE at work. Let us consider an e-commerce web service, *EcommerceWS*, with the aim of eliciting a behavioral model of it. The goal G is a combination of functional and non-functional properties, that can be informally expressed as follows: (i) to achieve a successful interaction among *EcommerceWS* and a client of it, i.e., to ensure that the client always progresses on buying items, (ii) to achieve a certain level of reliability of the whole system, where this attribute is given by the combination of the client and the web service reliabilities.

The **explore** step might use different techniques to elicit behavioral models of the software under exploration, e.g., from standard analysis techniques complemented with statistical inference to machine learning techniques [21,13]. An elicited model M has a degree of uncertainty with respect to the system S and the goal G. In general, different models, each with its own degree of uncertainty, may exist. This is shown in the *Explore* box of Figure 1, where S can have associated different models obtained through elicitation techniques with different costs and uncertainty degrees. Similarly, different models of context can be elicited and analogous definitions of uncertainty and cost metrics can be introduced for them. As a possible technique to be used in the **explore** step, we consider a version of the `StrawBerry` tool [8] that, for the EAGLE purposes, is enhanced to deal with the uncertainty degree of the elicited models.

Coming back to the example, clients of *EcommerceWS* can open a session, add a product to a shopping cart and buy items added to the cart. When an item is

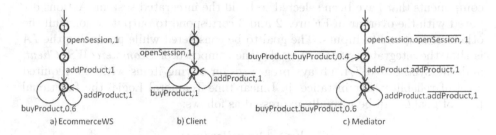

Fig. 2. *EcommerceWS* sample: explore and integration

bought, it is removed from the cart. The operation used to buy a product, named *buyProduct*, is successfully concluded only if the shopping cart connected to the current session is not empty, an error will be raised otherwise. By taking as input the WSDL of *EcommerceWS*, the current version of StrawBerry produces a finite state automaton modeling the interaction protocol that a client has to follow in order to correctly interact with *EcommerceWS*. For the sake of the scenario, the enhanced version of StrawBerry shall produce the probabilistic automaton [41] for *EcommerceWS* in Figure 2.a. This automaton is potentially incomplete and the probabilities represent the uncertainty of the elicitation technique. Indeed, the operation *buyProduct* has a probability 0.6 to happen and to loop on state 3 (e.g., the case of successfully buying an item). The incompleteness of the model concerns the remaining cases in which *buyProduct* happens with a probability 0.4. In these cases, the model does not express what the behaviour of *EcommerceWS* may be, i.e., which states may be reached (e.g., when trying to buy an item from an empty cart). For instance, there might be other two *buyProduct* transitions from state 3, both with probability 0.2, going to state 1 and 2 respectively. The reason for this incompleteness of the model may depend on limits to the cost of the elicitation process as specified by user preferences and needs. Uncertainty on the behavior can also affect the estimate of reliability for sake of goal satisfaction, along with the uncertainty on the values of fundamental reliability parameters, such as the probability of failure of the *buyProduct* operation.

The **integration** step shall support the producer in creating the most effective (to the goal G) integration means that takes into account the uncertainty degree, and the associated cost, of each single elicited model. During the integration step, by reasoning on their elicited models and further accounting for the tradeoff between uncertainty degree and cost, the candidate pieces of software are selected. Then, an integration architecture IA is synthesized, possibly automatically (see the Integrate box of Figure 1). IA is synthesized by making assumptions on the uncertain behavior of the selected pieces of software, as well as on the uncertain reliability parameter values, in order to achieve the goal G. That is, the integrated system satisfies G only if the assumptions hold. As detailed later, the validation step is responsible to check such assumptions. Thus, IA plays a crucial role in influencing the overall uncertainty degree of the final integrated system S, as different IAs may result in different uncertainty degrees for S. By continuing our example, *EcommerceWS* and *Client* are the components that have been selected to build the integrated system. Actions denoted with the overbar in Figures 2 and 3 correspond to output actions, all the others correspond to inputs. The goal to be considered while producing the IA is that the integrated system, i.e., the one composed of *EcommerceWS*, *Client*, and the synthesized IA, always progresses on buying items with the required level of reliability. For instance, in Linear-time Temporal Logic, the functional part of goal G can be formally expressed as follows:

$$G =!(<>[\,](buyProduct))$$

whereas the non-functional one (in a simplified formulation) as follows:

$$Rel(Client) * Rel(EcommerceWS) >= targetrel$$

where *targetrel* is the required level of reliability. In this example, IA assumes the form of a mediator (see Figure 2.c), which is an additional software entity that can be synthesized[4] [30]. It suitably mediates the interaction between *EcommerceWS* and *Client* in order to achieve G provided that some assumptions on the incomplete behavior and the reliability parameters of *EcommerceWS* hold. By referring to Figure 2.c, *Mediator* assumes that *EcommerceWS* reaches state 2 after a failure occurred while buying items. The transitions of the mediator model are labeled according to the following template:

<Client operation>.<*EcommerceWS* operation>, <probability to happen>

The mediator copes with the inherent uncertainty of the *EcommerceWS* model that concerns the case(s) in which *buyProduct* happens with a probability of 0.4. To this aim, *Mediator* assumes that *EcommerceWS* reaches state 2 after performing *buyProduct*,0.4. This assumption is reflected by the transition labeled *buyProduct.buyProduct*,0.4 in Figure 2.c. This transition is added during mediator synthesis to enforce the integrated system to perform *addProduct* once *buyProduct* has been executed with an empty shopping cart. For the non-functional part of the goal, assumptions are made on the reliabilities of service components, under a certain level of uncertainty.

A **validation** step shall then assess the quality of the integrated system with respect to the assumptions made by IA. If the final assessment is not satisfying then the process shall iterate either to select different pieces of software, or to reduce the uncertainty degree of models (some already in place), or to modify the overall IA. For instance, back to the example, a new iteration of the explore-integrate-validate process is required when, upon validation, the above behavioral assumption made by *Mediator* does not hold. The new explore step will incrementally refine the elicited model by exploiting the feedbacks of the validation phase and the results of the previous explore step. In particular,

---

[4] The CONNECT project (http://connect-forever.eu/, Grant agreement no. 231167) concerns the definition of theories and techniques to drop interoperability barriers by synthesizing on the fly the connectors via which networked systems communicate.

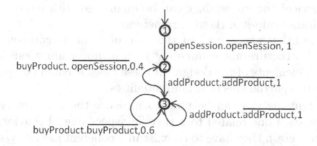

Fig. 3. *EcommerceWS* sample: validation

the *EcommerceWS* model, of Figure 2.a, is refined by adding the transition *buyProduct*,0.4 from state 3 to 1. Consequently, a new mediator needs to be synthesized as shown in Figure 3. In general, although still incomplete with respect to the modeled software, the refined models might be accurate enough to achieve the functional part of *G*. In particular, the new mediator detects the failure of *buyProduct* and, by exploiting authentication information previously stored, simulates an access of Client to *EcommerceWS* by performing *openSession*. The non-functional validation of the integrated system can also report an uncertain result, such as "the system reliability is within an interval of 10% around *targetrel*", for example due to incomplete information about the reliability of some software components. In this case, either the process is reiterated, or (if feasible) the goal can be loosened and the integration acceptable.

5 Discussion

In this section we discuss some aspects that merit to be further investigated.

– **Metrics to quantify/qualify the uncertainty** - The metrics adopted to reason on uncertainty should be different depending on the sources of uncertainty they refer to. Furthermore, in some cases uncertainty cannot be quantified due to the source domain it stems from, thus it has to be qualified in non-ambiguous terms. Hence, uncertainty can be quantified/qualified in different ways. In the following we propose some examples:

1. The uncertainty can be originated by a set of available alternatives (such as static, dynamic, or deployment alternatives) when more than one alternative can be suitable with respect to the goal *G*. In this case the uncertainty can be quantified (i) either with a probability assigned to each suitable alternative, when knowledge is sufficient to generate a set of values that sum up to 1, (ii) or with a non-stochastic metric that represents the level of preference/priority associated to each suitable alternative.

2. When uncertainty stems from functional or non-functional parameters of the model (e.g., maximum multiplicity of a component, resource demand

of a service) the uncertainty can be quantified with intervals that bind the suitable values of these parameters.

3. In some other cases, e.g., in the case of a macro-component with an internal structure not completely known, uncertainty can be qualified through elements of the design. In these cases it could be appropriate to define/use partial specification modalities.

Since different metrics can be used to measure the uncertainty of a piece of software, each one related to a specific aspect (e.g., behavior, reliability, performance, etc.), they have to co-exist in a coherent metric system. Therefore, such system should also contain relations and dependencies among these different metrics.

- **Tradeoffs between different metrics** - As anticipated, the uncertainty of a system is measured by means of a metric system. Then, this calls for tradeoffs between the different functional or non-functional aspects to be considered, each related to a suitable metric of uncertainty. In other words, within a suitable space of solutions determined by all uncertainties still in place, often a designer has to take decisions that decrease uncertainty in one direction whereas increase uncertainty in other directions. For example, in order to increase the reliability a higher number of (replicated and differently designed) components are put in place, whereas this choice, at the same time, increases the uncertainty about the resource demand of this system because many more components' demands have to be estimated.

- **Uncertainty estimation** - The explore phase of EAGLE produces a model of a software artifact specialized to represent some aspects. Quite often this model is defined under uncertainty that is associated to one or more metrics. Now a question raises, that is: *how to estimate the value of uncertainty metrics?* Referring to the example in Section 4, StrawBerry makes use of testing to extract the model, thus in this case the metric of uncertainty can be estimated by considering the number of positive and negative tests that have been performed. The knowledge of the designer can help during the explore phase since she can be aware, for instance, that a piece of software requires an amount of CPU that is in the range of $[x, y]$, with x and y belonging to the real numbers, event though no exact value is known.

- **Uncertainty of composed systems** - While building a system composed of several components or subsystems, the uncertainty metric system might be derived out of the uncertainty metric systems of the single components or subsystems. This calls for mechanisms to create a new metric system out of existing ones. Thus, relations and dependencies of the component metric systems have to be exploited, and/or new relations and dependencies among metrics must be inferred. Let us now focus on a single metric. The measure of uncertainty related to this metric for a composed system can be calculated by suitably combining the metrics of uncertainty associated to the single components or subsystems. Thus, a suitable operator must be aptly adopted. In the example described in Section 4, the composition is simply performed by multiplying the probabilities associated to *Client* and *ECommerceWS*.

6 Conclusion

EAGLE proposes a model-based framework for supporting the perpetual explore-integrate-validate cycle that will be realized by exploiting model-driven techniques. This integrated framework will support the engineering of goal-oriented software systems that are opportunistically created by integrating, under uncertainty, existing software and that are dynamically evolving within a perpetually changing context.

Reaching this goal requires to put at work different expertises and skills together, hence asking for a multi-domain research and development work on functional and non functional system modeling, verification and validation, model-driven development, context-aware programming, connector synthesis, and techniques for run-time monitoring and reconfiguration. As a by-product of this approach we expect that EAGLE results should be exploitable in a multitude of contexts both research-wise and industrial-wise.

Acknowledgment. This work is supported by the European Community's Seventh Framework Programme FP7/2007-2013 under grant agreements: number 257178 (project CHOReOS - Large Scale Choreographies for the Future Internet - www.choreos.eu), and number 231167 (project CONNECT - Emergent Connectors for Eternal Software Intensive Networked Systems - http://connect-forever.eu/).

References

1. Asarin, E., Maler, O., Pnueli, A.: Symbolic Controller Synthesis for Discrete and Timed Systems. In: Antsaklis, P., Kohn, W., Nerode, A., Sastry, S. (eds.) HS 1994. LNCS, vol. 999, pp. 1–20. Springer, Heidelberg (1995)
2. Autili, M., Di Benedetto, P., Inverardi, P.: Context-Aware Adaptive Services: The PLASTIC Approach. In: Chechik, M., Wirsing, M. (eds.) FASE 2009. LNCS, vol. 5503, pp. 124–139. Springer, Heidelberg (2009)
3. Autili, M., Berardinelli, L., Cortellessa, V., Di Marco, A., Di Ruscio, D., Inverardi, P., Tivoli, M.: A Development Process for Self-adapting Service Oriented Applications. In: Krämer, B.J., Lin, K.-J., Narasimhan, P. (eds.) ICSOC 2007. LNCS, vol. 4749, pp. 442–448. Springer, Heidelberg (2007)
4. Autili, M., Cortellessa, V., Di Ruscio, D., Inverardi, P., Pelliccione, P., Tivoli, M.: Eagle: engineering software in the ubiquitous globe by leveraging uncertainty. In: Proceedings of the 19th ACM SIGSOFT Symposium and the 13th European Conference on Foundations of Software Engineering, ESEC/FSE 2011, pp. 488–491. ACM, New York (2011)
5. Baier, C., Größer, M., Leucker, M., Bollig, B., Ciesinski, F.: Controller synthesis for probabilistic systems (extended abstract). In: IFIP TCS 2004, vol. 155 (2004)
6. Bertolino, A., De Angelis, G., Frantzen, L., Polini, A.: The PLASTIC Framework and Tools for Testing Service-Oriented Applications. In: De Lucia, A., Ferrucci, F. (eds.) ISSSE 2006-2008. LNCS, vol. 5413, pp. 106–139. Springer, Heidelberg (2009)
7. Bertolino, A., De Angelis, G., Polini, A.: (role)CAST: A Framework for On-line Service Testing. In: Proc. of WEBIST 2011 (2011)

8. Bertolino, A., Inverardi, P., Pelliccione, P., Tivoli, M.: Automatic synthesis of behavior protocols for composable web-services. In: Proc. of ESEC/FSE 2009 (2009)
9. Blair, G., Bencomo, N., France, R.B.: Models@run.time. Computer 42, 22–27 (2009)
10. Blundell, C., Giannakopoulou, D., Păsăreanu, C.S.: Assume-guarantee testing. Softw. Eng. Notes 31 (2005)
11. Boehm, B.: Value-based software engineering: reinventing. SIGSOFT Softw. Eng. Notes 28, 3 (2003)
12. Boehm, B.W.: Software risk management: Principles and practices. IEEE Softw. 8, 32–41 (1991)
13. Calinescu, R., Johnson, K., Rafiq, Y.: Using observation ageing to improve markovian model learning in qos engineering. In: ICPE, pp. 505–510 (2011)
14. Canal, C., Poizat, P., Salaün, G.: Synchronizing Behavioural Mismatch in Software Composition. In: Gorrieri, R., Wehrheim, H. (eds.) FMOODS 2006. LNCS, vol. 4037, pp. 63–77. Springer, Heidelberg (2006)
15. Ceri, S., Braga, D., Corcoglioniti, F., Grossniklaus, M., Vadacca, S.: Search Computing Challenges and Directions. In: Dearle, A., Zicari, R.V. (eds.) ICOODB 2010. LNCS, vol. 6348, pp. 1–5. Springer, Heidelberg (2010)
16. Cetina, C., Giner, P., Fons, J., Pelechano, V.: Autonomic computing through reuse of variability models at runtime: The case of smart homes. Computer 42, 37–43 (2009)
17. Cobleigh, J.M., Giannakopoulou, D., Păsăreanu, C.S.: Learning Assumptions for Compositional Verification. In: Garavel, H., Hatcliff, J. (eds.) TACAS 2003. LNCS, vol. 2619, pp. 331–346. Springer, Heidelberg (2003)
18. Di Cosmo, R., Di Ruscio, D., Pelliccione, P., Pierantonio, A., Zacchiroli, S.: Supporting Software Evolution in Component-Based FOSS Systems. Science of Computer Programming 76(12) (2011)
19. Dingel, J.: Computer-Assisted Assume/Guarantee Reasoning with VeriSoft. In: Proc. of ICSE 2003 (2003)
20. Ephraim, Y., Merhav, N.: Hidden markov processes. IEEE Transactions on Information Theory 48, 1518–1569
21. Ernst, M.D., Perkins, J.H.: Learning from executions: Dynamic analysis for software engineering and program understanding. Tutorial at ASE 2005 (2005)
22. Famelis, M., Salay, R., Chechik, M.: Partial models: Towards modeling and reasoning with uncertainty. In: Proceedings of the 34th International Conference on Software Engineering, ICSE (2012)
23. Garlan, D.: Software engineering in an uncertain world. In: Proc. of FSE/SDP 2010, pp. 125–128 (2010)
24. Georgas, J.C., van der Hoek, A., Taylor, R.N.: Using architectural models to manage and visualize runtime adaptation. Computer 42, 52–60 (2009)
25. Ghezzi, C., Mocci, A., Monga, M.: Synthesizing intensional behavior models by graph transformation. In: Proc. of ICSE 2009, pp. 430–440 (2009)
26. Giannakopoulou, D., Pasareanu, C.S., Barringer, H.: Component verification with automatically generated assumptions. ASE Journal 12(3), 297–320 (2005)
27. Goldsby, H.J., Cheng, B.H.C.: Automatically Generating Behavioral Models of Adaptive Systems to Address Uncertainty. In: Czarnecki, K., Ober, I., Bruel, J.-M., Uhl, A., Völter, M. (eds.) MODELS 2008. LNCS, vol. 5301, pp. 568–583. Springer, Heidelberg (2008)
28. Hamlet, D.: Composing Software Components: A Software-testing Perspective, 1st edn. Springer Publishing Company, Incorporated (2010)

29. Inverardi, P., Issarny, V., Spalazzese, R.: A Theory of Mediators for Eternal Connectors. In: Margaria, T., Steffen, B. (eds.) ISoLA 2010, Part II. LNCS, vol. 6416, pp. 236–250. Springer, Heidelberg (2010)
30. Inverardi, P., Spalazzese, R., Tivoli, M.: Application-Layer Connector Synthesis. In: Bernardo, M., Issarny, V. (eds.) SFM 2011. LNCS, vol. 6659, pp. 148–190. Springer, Heidelberg (2011)
31. Lehmann, G., Blumendorf, M., Trollmann, F., Albayrak, S.: Meta-modeling Runtime Models. In: Dingel, J., Solberg, A. (eds.) MODELS 2010. LNCS, vol. 6627, pp. 209–223. Springer, Heidelberg (2011)
32. Lorenzoli, D., Mariani, L., Pezzè, M.: Automatic generation of software behavioral models. In: Proc. of ICSE 2008, pp. 501–510 (2008)
33. Mishra, K., Trivedi, K.: Uncertainty propagation through software dependability models. In: 2011 IEEE 22nd International Symposium on Software Reliability Engineering (ISSRE), November 29-December 2, pp. 80–89 (2011)
34. Morin, B., Barais, O., Jezequel, J.-M., Fleurey, F., Solberg, A.: Models@ run.time to support dynamic adaptation. Computer 42, 44–51 (2009)
35. Mula, J., Poler, R., Garcia-Sabater, J., Lario, F.: Models for production planning under uncertainty: A review. IJPE 103(1), 271–285 (2006)
36. Neil, M., Fenton, N., Tailor, M.: Using bayesian networks to model expected and unexpected operational losses. Risk Analysis 25(4), 963–972 (2005)
37. Passerone, R., de Alfaro, L., Henzinger, T.A., Sangiovanni-Vincentelli, A.L.: Convertibility verification and converter synthesis: two faces of the same coin. In: Proc. of ICCAD 2002, pp. 132–139 (2002)
38. Ramadge, P., Wonham, W.: The control of discrete event systems. Proceedings of the IEEE 77(1), 81–98 (1989)
39. Schmidt, D.C.: Guest Editor's Introduction: Model-Driven Engineering. Computer 39(2), 25–31 (2006)
40. Singh, H., Cortellessa, V., Cukic, B., Gunel, E., Bharadwaj, V.: A bayesian approach to reliability prediction and assessment of component based systems. In: Proc. of ISSRE 2001 (2001)
41. Stoelinga, M.: An introduction to probabilistic automata. Bulletin of the European Association for Theoretical Computer Science 78, 176–198 (2002)
42. Stringfellow, C., Amory, C.D., Potnuri, D., Andrews, A., Georg, M.: Comparison of software architecture reverse engineering methods. Information and Software Technology 48(7), 484–497 (2006)
43. Tivoli, M., Inverardi, P.: Failure-free coordinators synthesis for component-based architectures. Sci. Comput. Program. 71(3), 181–212 (2008)
44. Uchitel, S., Brunet, G., Chechik, M.: Synthesis of partial behavior models from properties and scenarios. IEEE Trans. Softw. Eng. 35, 384–406 (2009)
45. White, R.W., Roth, R.A.: Exploratory Search: Beyond the Query-Response Paradigm. Synthesis Lect. on ICRS. Morgan & Claypool Publishers (2009)

Social Networks
for Importing and Exporting Security

Bangdao Chen and A.W. Roscoe

Oxford University Computer Science Department
James Martin Institute for the Future of Computing
{Bangdao.Chen,Bill.Roscoe}@cs.ox.ac.uk

Abstract. Online social networks are rapidly changing our lives. Their growing pervasiveness and the trust that we develop in online identities provide us with a new platform for security applications. Additionally, the integration of various sensors and mobile devices on social networks has shortened the separation between one's physical and virtual (i.e. web) presences. We envisage that social networks will serve as the portal between the physical world and the digital world. However, challenges arise when using social networks in security applications; for example, how can one prove to a friend (or Friend) that your Facebook page belongs to you and not a man in the middle? Once you have proved this, how can you use it to create a secure channel between any device belonging to you and one belonging to your friend? We show how human interactive security protocols (HISPs) can greatly assist in both these areas and in general create a decentralised and user-oriented model of security. And we demonstrate that by using this security model we can quickly and efficiently bootstrap security for sharing information within a large group.

1   Introduction

Online social networks (OSNs), such as Facebook, Google+, Foursquare, Twitter, and LinkedIn, have enjoyed phenomenal growth in recent years. The authors of [13] analysed relationships and communication on Twitter, and pointed out that Twitter also plays the role of a social medium: information can spread widely and quickly. For example, in less than 12 hours after the first tweet of Osama Bin Laden being killed, there were 2.2 million tweets related to this event [3]. OSNs therefore not only help to create and maintain a large amount of relationships between humans, they also provide efficient and convenient platforms for sharing and spreading data amongst a large audience.

The future of OSNs is changing with the growing pervasiveness of device connections. For example, the CEO of Ericsson [2] has forecast that there will be 50 billion device connections by 2020, which will create a "connected society". Sensors are often used to make data about physical objects available online, for example, to display the sensory data on OSNs. An IBM researcher connected his

R. Calinescu and D. Garlan (Eds.): Monterey Workshop 2012, LNCS 7539, pp. 132–147, 2012.
© Springer-Verlag Berlin Heidelberg 2012

house with Twitter[1]: a set of sensors are used to generate tweets about power consumption, water usage and the temperature of the house. We also notice that there are plenty of body-monitoring sensors [1] with mobile connectivity in the market today.

The integration of OSNs on mobile devices has further shortened the separation between our virtual presences on the web and our physical existence. By using a mobile device, OSNs have the opportunity to collect more private data; for example, location data or medical data from on-body medical sensors. There is already a clear need for a solid security model for social networking, and the more we use them for, the more we need them to be secured.

Given that the social network providers are increasingly making their applications available as secure web sites, there remain two primary concerns:

A How can we know that a given OSN page belongs to a given user: the *identification*, or *authentication* problem? In general such knowledge may be absolute or come with some identified confidence level.

B The provision of appropriate security models for collecting, using and sharing data from the local user and his or her devices including sensors.

In this paper we concentrate on A, and furthermore show how security developed for social networking can be used to conveniently bootstrap other secure connections.

We imagine that in general solutions to A might involve any one, or combinations of (i) pre-existing security infrastructures such as PKIs, (ii) reputational models based on trust ratings by other network users, and (iii) bootstrapping security by person-to-person contact by interaction outside the social network. In this paper we concentrate on (iii) and show how *Human-Interactive Security Protocols* (HISPs) can be used to do this efficiently when there is a means for getting a small amount of information from the owner of the page that is to be authenticated to the person who wants to authenticate it. This transmission might be via personal contact or using a second medium that is trusted as authentic.

In this paper we make the following contributions:

1. We propose a security model that exploits the trust on social networks by using HISPs. This model can be used to authenticate online identities and create secure connections between devices.
2. We demonstrate these by implementing a prototype system. It can efficiently bootstrap security for a large group. It shows the practicability of using our security model in future mobile computing.

2 Using a HISP

A typical HISP relies on the assumption that there is an empirical channel in a specific application, in which one or more humans can compare a short

---

[1] http://stanford-clark.com/andy_house.html

authentication string (SAS) received from the empirical channel. An empirical channel is a human-based, non-fakeable channel, for example, face-to-face conversations, video calls or voice calls. The best of these protocols, for example those of [14,15,16,17,18,19,20,22,23], enable assurance to these humans that there is no attack that would allow an intruder to get the system into an insecure state (where the connections established are other than what the humans believe), with probability meaningfully greater than 2^{-b}, where b is the number of bits in the check-string. In addition, to have such a chance, the attacker will have a $1 - 2^{-b}$ chance of his presence being revealed by the difference between the strings.

HISPs can be thought of as tools that enable one (perhaps informal) authentic channel to efficiently authenticate, and then secure another one. This means that they have two complementary potential uses in social networking.

1. We can use a HISP to authenticate online identities by using existing connections (typically personal or telephone conversations between the humans involved). In this case, we import security from existing social relationships to social networks.
2. We can use a HISP to create secure connections between devices, in this case, we can use authenticated social network accounts as proxies to display SASs. This can significantly improve the usability of HISPs. We therefore export security from social networks to other applications. This also provides a new channel of sharing information directly between devices, which is useful especially when the OSN providers cannot guarantee the privacy of information posted online.

In the following sections we will introduce two HISPs that we use in our implementation.

2.1   Pair-Wise HISP

Below is the pair-wise HISP we use:

1. $A \longrightarrow B : hash(0 : hk_A), hash(k), Info_A,$
2. $B \longrightarrow A : hash(1 : hk_B), pk, Info_B,$

Each party creates a *hash*, or *digest* key: we call these hk_A and hk_B. These are needed to randomise the final check-string. A creates a session key k. B either creates freshly, or re-uses, an asymmetric key pair (pk, sk). There is no need for the "public" key pk to be certified. The length of these keys will depend on the desired level of security[2], the amount of available computing power, and the crypto-system in use.

In the first pair of steps of the protocol, A and B both commit each other without knowledge to values of hk_B or hk_A. The only one of the four parameters

---

[2] The key certainly needs to be strong enough so that there is no realistic chance of it being broken during the life of the session being established. Further strength is required to ensure that the contents of that session remain secret after it ends.

hk_A, hk_B, pk and k communicated openly is B's public key pk. $Info_A$ and $Info_B$ are the information A and B wants to authenticate. In our example, when Alice wants to verify Bob's OSN account, $Info_B$ contains Bob's social network account profile; similarly, $Info_A$ contains Alice's social network account profile when Bob wants to verify Alice's OSN account.

The protocol now proceeds:

3. $A \longrightarrow B : hk_A, \{k\}_{pk}$

4. $B \longrightarrow A : hk_B$

The second part of Message 3 is to tell B the actual value of the session key, which is now checked against the hash. It is the transmission of the unencrypted keys hk_A and hk_B at this stage that represents the core of the protocol. Firstly, of course, the participants must check that these are the same values that were represented in Messages 1 and 2. If not, the run is abandoned. Secondly, they (and anyone else who has been listening in) can compute a value for

$$digest(hk_A \oplus hk_B, (pk, hash(k), Info_A, Info_B))$$

where $\oplus$ is bit-wise exclusive or and (X, Y) is an ordered pair. The protocol completes successfully if A (or A and B) are convinced that their two versions of the value – the check-string of this protocol – are equal: in becoming convinced they must not use a channel which can be "spoofed" by an intruder. Typically one will read their value to the other, or A will read B's value directly and compare it with her own. Whichever knows that the two values are equal can conclude that the link is authenticated. Typically this is either A or both of them. It is this comparison that makes it a HISP.

Naturally, if the protocol has proceeded uninterfered with, A's and B's values will be equal. If, however, an intruder has imposed his own values onto the receivers of Messages 1–4, A and B will not agree on all four parameters. For security, what is important is that they agree on pk and $hash(k)$, so we will concentrate on what happens if the intruder interferes with these.

The digest function [17,18] is designed so that, as hk varies, the probability that $digest(hk, X) = digest(hk, Y)$ for $X \neq Y$ is less than ϵ, where typically ϵ is very close to the theoretically optimal value of 2^{-b} for b the number of bits in the output of $digest$. It must also have the property that for any fixed value d, the chance that $digest(hk, X) = d$ as hk varies is less than ϵ also. More details of this protocol can be found in [9]. Formal verification of this protocol is presented in [21].

An important quality a HISP must have is that it protects the SAS that the users compare from combinatorial searching by potential attackers: analysis must be able to show that no matter what conceivable amount of computing an attacker uses, he has no better chance of getting lucky and persuading the users to agree on an SAS in inappropriate circumstances than if it had made a single guess. All the HISPs we see in this paper have that property.

2.2   Group HISP

The Symmetric HCBK (SHCBK) protocol [18] is used in our implementation. This, the general description, connects an arbitrary-sized group. Good examples of group authentication using HISPs are GAnGs [7] and SPATE [24].

1. $\forall A \longrightarrow_N \forall A' : A, INFO_A, hash(A, hk_A)$
2. $\forall A \longrightarrow_N \forall A' : hk_A$
3. users compare $digest(hk^*, \{INFO'_A | A \in G\})$, where hk^* is the XOR of all hk_A's for $A \in G$

SHCBK has each node "publish" its name and a collection of information that it wishes to be authentically connected with that name. It also sends a hash[3] of a randomly generated key hk_A coupled with the name. Once it has received that information from all nodes, and therefore become committed to the set of identities, $INFO$ and hashed keys it will use, it publishes its previously secret hk_A. The point is that by the time of this last publication, it was in fact *committed* to all the data used in the above protocol, even though it does not yet *know* all the hk_As. HCBK stands for Hash Commitment Before Knowledge. A careful security analysis of this protocol (see [18], for example) demonstrates that any attacker is unable to profit from combinatorial analysis aimed at getting the SASs (i.e. digests) to agree even though nodes have different views of the authenticated information. Good HISPs such as SHCBK therefore offer maximum security for a given amount of human effort.

We can reduce the number of human interactions if there is a trustworthy Initiator I, consider the rest of the group as G', then the above protocol can be modified as following: in the process of comparing digest values, I compares digest value published by $\forall A$ ($A \in G'$), $\forall A$ compares the digest value published by I; I then publishes the final result of digest comparison, $\forall A$ checks this result. We call it Semi-SHCBK protocol. Therefore the total number of messages to be exchanged via empirical channels changes from $N(N-1)/2$ to $3N - 3$. If there is a trustworthy Initiator, when $N > 6$, Semi-SHCBK protocol is more efficient than SHCBK protocol.

The key generation is simple: we include a copy of an uncertified Diffie-Hellman public key in $INFO_A$, then after a successful run of SHCBK or Semi-SHCBK protocol, each user generates $N-1$ shared pair-wise secret keys sk. For example, $sk_{\alpha\beta}$ means a shared secret key between user α and user β. To generate a group key sk_G, the following group key protocol is used ($\longrightarrow_S$ means sending encrypted information using a corresponding pair-wise secret key):

1. $\forall A \longrightarrow_S \forall A' : Nonce_A$
2. $sk_G = Nonce^*$, where $Nonce^*$ is the XOR of all $Nonce_A$'s for $A \in G$

Each member also generates an anonymous ID. It can be used to publish information anonymously on OSNs. The anonymous ID is created by $hash(Nonce_A,$

---

[3] Hash means a standard cryptographic hash function that has two main properties: collision resistance, and inversion resistance.

A's social network ID) $mod \ 10^{15}$. This will generate a 15-digit[4] ID for each group member.

2.3   Improving the Usability and Security of HISPs

The practicability of using HISPs is in inverse proportion to the cost of human effort. For example, factors that determine the practicability are: the availability of empirical channels; the length of information to be compared; and the times of comparison required in one run.

In order to reduce the amount of human effort without compromising security, one solution is to allow automated comparison of SASs online. For example, when OSN pages are being used to display SASs in HISPs there is clearly also the the option for these same pages to compare the SASs provided they are connected securely to the local device that is participating in the HISP.

If all participants have this property we could use a longer SAS, but in general we assume that there is likely to be some human participant creating the link in person. The primary motivation for using HISPs is, after all, allowing this.

3   Proving Online Identities

In order to use OSNs as empirical channels we must answer the following question: *"how do I know that what I am seeing on the page comes from the person or other entity that I think it does"*. To better analyse this problem, we divide it into two sub-questions: how do I know the (e.g. Facebook) page I am seeing is authentic within the OSN? and how do I know it belongs to the person I think it does? The first of these questions can be solved by conventional computer security, for example, the *https* service on OSNs. It is therefore assumed that all relevant interactions with the OSNs are via their *https* interfaces.

The second question can be converted into the following one: "is this an established Friend for which you are certain of the link between page and person?" If the answer is yes, then secure access to that page is clearly a good empirical channel. This is the most common way of authentication in our daily life. For example, one may have experiences in interacting with a social network account, one may authenticate a social network account by the number of common Friends, or one can authenticate a social network account by viewing its profile, Friends list, photos, history of participated events and other context information.

If we can not make our decision based on past experiences, we may use telephony or physical interactions to accomplish this task. A HISP can therefore be used to authenticate OSN accounts. For example, Alice wants to know that the social network account of Bob is authentic; if Alice has a phone number of Bob and she is certain of the authenticity of this phone number, she then runs a HISP with Bob to verify his account by using telephony as the empirical channel.

---

[4] We use the same length of digits as Facebook ID.

Note that the availability of HISPs provides us with the flexibility to bootstrap security from any existing authentic connection, whether one derived from physical proximity or other means such as telephony.

And there are other alternatives of authenticating online identities in practice, for example:

1. Centralised authentication. For example, Twitter provides authentication service. The verified account will display a special indicator (a small icon or a "badge"). However this service is limited to celebrities on Twitter. A similar situation can be found in other OSNs.

2. Introducing decentralised authorities. For example, we can publish OSN accounts of a group on a company's *https* web-page. In this case, the company acts as an authority which authenticates a group. Similarly, a trusted organisation or a trusted individual can also play the role of an authority. For example, a community leader may only keep Friends that belong to the community, therefore his or her Friend-list can be used to help authenticate the community members. This can be used to replace the human effort of authenticating group members and can greatly improve the application in authenticating a group when its size is large. In our implementation, when prompting users to verify the member-list of a group, we provide an option for users to use a trusted authority (in the form of an *https* web-page). Details of this approach are presented in Section 5.

3. Introducing trust ratings. Rating by trust is a common practice in OSN research, for example, [12] describes a semantic web-based OSN, and they developed algorithms to rate the inferred reputation of a node. Another distinct example is PGP. It exploits ratings to determine the level of authenticity of downloaded public keys. A rating scale of 1 to 4 is used: full (complete trust), marginal (partial trust), untrustworthy and don't know. The most distinct advantage of this method is that it provides pervasive automated authentication. We have implemented a demonstration rating system by using the same ratings introduced in PGP (see Section 5).

4. Blackballing. Blackballing[5] is a voting method used in many gentleman's clubs: members have a large number of white and black balls and each member casts a single ball into the ballot box to vote for a proposition, if there are one or more black balls in the ballot box, everyone will immediately know this proposition has been vetoed. In our implementation, each member checks the list objects one-by-one, if one object is "vetoed" by one member, then list L is "vetoed". This is also a form of utilising "crowd knowledge" which effectively reduces the security mistakes when members manually authenticate each other.

4   Bootstrapping a Large Group by Using OSNs

An important assumption has to be made before bootstrapping security for a group: members of a group are capable of verifying the legitimacy of each other

---

[5] http://en.wikipedia.org/wiki/Blackballing

within the group. This is supported by the methods introduced in Section 3. It allows us to start our discussion of how to bootstrap a large group by using OSNs. The insecure state we will address is where one trustworthy user believes he has an authenticated connection to another but is in fact connected to a third party (e.g. the attacker).

In some cases when bootstrapping a HISP group the identities (however defined) of those participating will be obvious. Perhaps this will be because all know each other well and have agreed to connect, or perhaps it will be because they are together is some easily identifiable context such as sitting around a table. In these cases all that is necessary for them to start the protocol is the number of them. For small groups this will be obvious; for large ones they might either organise a count themselves or build up a list to which they agree.

In other cases – for example where some members of the group do not have a direct link – it will certainly be necessary to establish the list of participants in advance. In this case the names on the list will need to be authenticated. Each intended party can check if his/her name is on the list, but it may be more difficult to establish that no undesirables are on it.

The correctness of bootstrapping a group can be defined as follows: all members acknowledge a list L, which contains details of all members; the resulting group G contains exactly the same number of members recorded in L and no one, except for the members included in L, can be allowed to join G. To fulfill this task, we need to identify and overcome the following challenges:

- Collecting group information. This is to create list L. [7] presents two solutions for collecting information from group members when they are in the same room: the first solution is to use an untrusted projector as a central node by displaying its Bluetooth address as a 2D barcode; all members connect their mobile phones to the projector by reading this barcode and send their details to this projector which then broadcasts list L to the group. The second solution is to create a tree structure of collecting member's information one-by-one by reading 2D barcodes of Bluetooth addresses. These methods are too cumbersome and inconvenient when the size of the group is large. In remote scenarios, collecting group information becomes more difficult since group information is often discrete and inconsistent.
- Counting and authentication. Counting is to check whether the size of group G matches with the size of list L. Authentication is to check whether members included in list L are legitimate. In general, there are two types of attacks: (i) man-in-the-middle (MITM) or outsider attacks; (ii) Sybil [10] or insider attacks. Counting and authentication is to detect attacks of (i) and (ii). Normally, if authentication is prudent, authentication alone can detect attacks of (i). However, an insider may be capable of providing multiple fake identities[6] to get access to more resources, therefore counting is necessary to detect attacks of (ii). Depending on physical interactions to perform counting and authentication has many limitations. For example, members of a group

---

[6] The fake identities can be different copies of the insider's identity or fake identities of others.

may be distributed and remote, and physical interactions may be unavailable; humans can be lazy and careless, for instance, they may not correctly count a group, or they may not correctly perform actions of authentication.

To simplify our discussion, we assume group formations are presented in the form of events; for example, the Department of Computer Science creates a list of their staff and students in order to share their project data; they arrange an event (e.g. a Facebook event) by informing all members within the department via emails or by posting a notice to the public. We generalise these events of group formation into the following two events:

A. Pre-emptive event: group members know each other and they all trust the Initiator before the event runs, therefore, the Semi-SHCBK protocol is used.
B. Non-pre-emptive event: except for the Initiator, the rest of the group does not know of the event in advance and they may not know each other. The Initiator sends out invitations to ask for participation. Those who accept it join the event. Members may not all trust the Initiator and the SHCBK protocol is used.

In our solution, all functions are achieved and performed by using a mobile application installed on users' mobile phones.

4.1   Collecting Group Information

OSNs provide two functions that make collecting group information convenient and efficient: (i) information on OSNs is rich and well formatted which is convenient for exporting information to other applications; (ii) OSN accounts are managed according to social relationships; for example, we can create and manage different groups[7], and we can create an event (e.g. a Facebook event or a Google+ page) and invite Friends to join.

In Event A, we can assume that group members are already Friends of the Initiator on OSNs, therefore the Initiator can simply create a group by selecting accounts from his/her Friend list, and then export the group information to our mobile application. In Event B, we assume that group members may not be Friends with each other. The Initiator can simply create an event and then notify all others. For example, the Initiator can introduce this event by sending emails or by publishing it on posters. Others can easily identify and join this event on OSNs. In the end we can export group information from this event.

This process can also be made via physical interactions, for example, one can display an event's OSN page address as a 2D barcode and others can read this barcode to join this event. Therefore by using OSNs, we can support group formation when group members are collocated, remote to each other, or a mixture of the former two situations.

---

[7] On Google+ a group is presented as a "circle".

4.2 Counting and Authenticating Members

Counting, if made by humans, has limitations. For example, one may make mistakes when the size of the group is large. [7] assumes humans can accurately count less than ten individuals via physical interactions. They randomly divide a large group into small subgroups in order to allow humans to count and verify members correctly. This action provides greater usability but leads to weaker security: there may be the chance that attackers are allocated to the same subgroup. The probability of attack detection [7] is less than the value of $1 - 2^{-b}$ assumed by the HISP (b is the bit-length of the SAS). In addition, subgrouping can be laborious and inconvenient since it has to be randomised.

Authentication normally requires more human efforts. For example, in [7] they use visual channels (created by mobile phone display screens and cameras) to check the presence of identities. Since visual channels of reading 2D barcodes on mobile phones are normally unidirectional, a symmetric authentication of a group of size N requires $N(N-1)/2$ interactions. This number increases quickly when the size of the group increases.

When using OSNs as empirical channels, we can first divide the authentication process into the following two steps:

1. Authenticate OSN accounts included in list L are legitimate. We call it the authentication of online identities.
2. Read and compare digest values displayed on members' OSN pages. We call it the authentication of connections.

Step 1 is to ensure that we can use OSN accounts as proxies of our physical presences. Step 2 is to test the presence of MITM attackers by using a HISP, which is to authenticate that the electronic connection is correctly connected to the intended device represented by the OSN account. This strategy can remove the requirement for physical interactions in Step 2.

In [7], counting is important because an insider can create multiple fake identities and then perform physical interactions of authentication multiple times. In our solution, the only chance of successful insider attacks is to add fake identities in list L and pass the authentication in Step 1. In Section 3 we have discussed various techniques of proving online identities. These allow humans to conveniently and efficiently adapt their authentication strategy according to different scenarios. In addition, we can conveniently run a program to automatically count and check whether the number of responsive[8] (or active) OSN accounts is equal to the number of accounts included in list L. We therefore conclude that counting is unnecessary in our solution and there is no need of subgrouping. This improves both security and usability.

More importantly, once we have authenticated that OSN accounts included in list L are legitimate, Step 2 can be made automatically since we use OSN accounts as proxies of our physical presences. This is a significant improvement which provides more capacity for large groups, for example, groups with size

---

[8] Those who display the digest value.

over 100. In addition, we can display long digest values without increasing the cost of human efforts.

It is worth noticing that on OSNs, the cost of Sybil attacks of creating multiple fake accounts are higher because OSN providers, for example, Facebook[9], Google+, require unique identifiers (email addresses or mobile phone numbers) to register, and they keep records of online interactions which can be used as indicators of authenticity. We also notice that by reducing physical interactions, we can reduce impacts from other uncontrolled factors; for example, the luminous intensity, the physical distances, the quality of mobile phone cameras or display screens, and most importantly, the human complacency.

Another significant improvement in usability may be that we can allow delayed running of HISPs. Experiments of relying on physical interactions to run HISPs have one implicit assumption that all members have to finish the process of authentication within a short period of time. And it is the reason that reducing time is critical for improving usability. However, in practice, the cost of coordination can be high and humans may not necessarily be available of carrying out the same physical action at the same time. This problem can be more significant[10] when humans are remote to each other. By using OSN accounts as proxies of our physical presences, we can divide the authentication process into two separate steps discussed earlier in this section. Because Step 2 of reading and comparing digest values can be automatically completed by using a program, and Step 1 of authenticating the legitimacy of OSN accounts in list L can be carried out asynchronously, the running of HISPs can be delayed until the last member completes the authentication in Step 1.

This allows more useful security applications. For example, a department sends out notifications of bootstrapping a secure network for internal communication to its employees. Some employees are traveling abroad and they are not responding immediately. By using our solution, the program keeps waiting until the last employee responds which triggers the authentication process. After the authentication process has been finished, the program displays results to all employees.

5   Demonstration Implementation

We have implemented a secure location sharing service to demonstrate the use of our security model. We have developed three versions of mobile applications: RIM (Blackberry), Android, and iOS (iPhone, iPad and iTouch). One server SO is used as the coordination server. All devices are connected to SO. After they have successfully bootstrapped security for the group, they start to share their locations with each other.

---

[9] In our investigation, we discover that Facebook normally requires at least one mobile phone number to register; and accounts registered by email addresses will later be required to be authenticated via a mobile phone number.

[10] Our experiment shows evidence of high cost of coordination.

The mobile phone application first checks the ratings; if there are accounts which fail to pass the rating check, it will prompt the user with a dialogue calling for authentication resource (from a decentralised authority), it will automatically remove the authenticated objects from the stack of the member list; the objects that are left on the stack will be verified by empirical authentication, for example, by using a HISP. Figure 1 shows the flow chart of the authentication process.

Note that while the current practices of implementing a rating system are mostly experimental, we observe that the presence of a decentralised authority is strong in scenarios with security demands. For example, in a conference scenario, the organiser can manage the "guest list" of the conference's Facebook event. He or she can either remove those illegal "guests" or set this event to be visible only to the "guests" on a given "guest list". In an online community, the community leader can manage the legitimate list of community members on his or her social web-page (for example, he or she keeps the list as a group in the Friends-list).

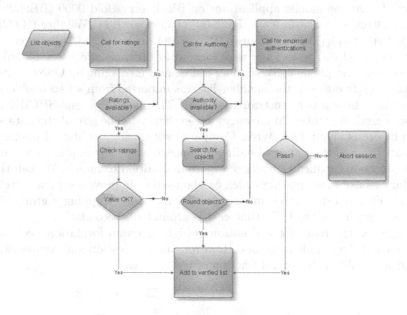

Fig. 1. The flow chart of the authentication process

If the entire member list has been verified, the protocol starts to run. The user will start to share his or her data of locations on Facebook (or directly between devices) if the protocol has been finished successfully. Figure 2 shows the screen shots of the application on Android.

We use Bouncy Castle Crypto Java API on RIM and Android; and OpenSSL C Library for iOS. We use 1024-bit Diffie-Hellman public keys to generate shared secret keys; 128-bit AES is used to encrypt data.

Fig. 2. Screen shots of the mobile application

6   Performance Analysis

We have tested the mobile applications on Blackberry Bold 9000 (BB9000) (4 devices), Blackberry Storm 9500 (BB9500) (1 device), HTC Wildfire (HTC) (1 device), Dell Streak (Dell) (1 device), iPhone 3 (1 device), iPad 1 (2 devices). 10 volunteers joined this test. They were located at different addresses. Coordination was made via phone calls, sending SMSs, and messaging on OSNs. Note in order to simplify our test, the member-list was imported from a Facebook event. We assumed there was a trustworthy leader. Therefore, the semi-SHCBK protocol was used. A total of 20 messages are exchanged. The size of the data sent by one device is about 18 KBytes. Compared with using traditional public key certificates, our method allows binding of contextual data (e.g. photos, voices or videos) to the uncertified public key we use in addition to names. We call these secondary security information which can be used to improve security as well as usability. Figure 3 shows the time consumption of bootstrapping a group of all the devices we have. The total time cost is around 193 seconds.

We can see the cost of coordination is high in group formation because of many uncontrolled random factors. However, the verification and comparison is efficient and only takes a small fraction of the total time.

Table 1. Facts and statistics

Device	Time	Ratio	Speed1	Speed2
BB9000	3.69s	99%	1.72kb/s	4.32kb/s
BB9500	4.49s	99%	1.35kb/s	3.75kb/s
HTC	3.74s	99%	1.56kb/s	4.80kb/s
Dell	0.85s	99%	2.42kb/s	7.15kb/s
iPhone	0.11s	99%	4.38kb/s	8.74kb/s
iPad	0.08s	99%	4.06kb/s	13.7kb/s

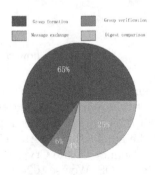

Fig. 3. Time consumption

Table 1 shows the facts and statistics of different devices. The second column is the time of computing DH secret; the third column is the ratio of the time of computing DH secret against the time of total on-device computing (excluding communication); the fourth column is the speed of connection between the device and the coordination server; the last column is the speed of the connection between the device and the Facebook server. We can see the time of on-device computation mostly originates from the DH secret computation.

According to the above analysis, we can identify two challenges for the future: (A) providing more convenient methods for large ad hoc group formation; (B) increasing the speed of mobile connections to allow including more contextual data in the protocol. Challenge A requires research on both security and usability. For example, should a group be formed using a single initiator, a tree structure, broadcasting over a fully connected graph, or some other topology? Challenge B is less significant since there are continuous developments in improving the speed of mobile connections; for example, the deployment of 4G network.

7 Related Research

WhozThat [4] is a system making use of OSN IDs among mobile phones: two users exchange their OSN IDs using Bluetooth, and it then introduces social context into the local context; for example, one may play the favourite music of the other. This is similar to our solution of binding OSN IDs with mobile devices while our intention is to facilitate identification and connection rather than interaction between humans. CenceMe [11] is a more advanced mobile OSN system which detects users' social activities by analysing sensory data on mobile phones. It demonstrates a well designed integration of OSNs on mobile phones: automated input of social information (deducted from sensory data) replaces traditional manual input. This is similar to our vision for future OSNs; for example, sensor networks like on-body sensor networks can be exploited by OSNs to automatically generate and display social patterns.

In [8] the authors presented a concrete implementation of Cloud Computing Service (for storage) on Facebook. However, there is no description as to actually utilise the Cloud after creation. Our solution gives a clear data flow between different interfaces and it can be put in use instantly.

Security is a key enabling factor for the above practices. In [5] the authors suggested OSN operators should not be trusted and data should be encrypted before posting online. They provided an example of creating a peer-to-peer system by using a pair-wise HISP to distribute public keys. A similar example was discussed in [6], which proposed a completely decentralised peer-to-peer system by storing data on user devices.

We notice that although there is much research on creating decentralised systems to improve security, practices without using a PKI or existing security infrastructures can be difficult. And such peer-to-peer systems are not efficient when the scale of sharing increases. Practices introduced in [7,24] reveal the high complexity of group HISPs when using physical interactions to collect group information and authenticate members, therefore they are not practical when bootstrapping a large ad hoc group.

8   Conclusions

We have revealed the challenges of authenticating online identities and bootstrapping security for a large ad hoc group. The model of social networks for importing and exporting security we have presented can be used to (i) exploit existing social relationships to authenticate online identities and (ii) exploit existing online relationships to efficiently bootstrap security for a large ad hoc group. This provides a way of incorporating social context into security which can be used to deal with changing security requirements emerging from new applications. The secure location sharing service we have implemented demonstrates these features of this model.

The security of social networks remains an interesting problem on which more work is required. Its attack models based on technology are likely to be similar to those of other online services, but there is also a social/psychological dimension to investigate. We believe that in the future the growing investment in security by social network companies will make our solution more secure when exporting security to other applications, and the development of computing power on mobile devices will make it more efficient in supporting security services.

References

1. Body-monitoring sensors, http://store.runkeeper.com/
2. CEO to shareholders: 50 billion connections 2020,
   http://www.ericsson.com/thecompany/press/releases/2010/04/1403231
3. How Fast the News Spreads Through Social Media, http://blog.sysomos.com/2011/05/02/how-fast-the-news-spreads-through-social-media/
4. Beach, A., et al.: Whozthat? evolving an ecosystem for context-aware mobile social networks. IEEE Network 22(4), 50–55 (2008)
5. Anderson, J., Diaz, C., Bonneau, J., Stajano, F.: Privacy-enabling social networking over untrusted networks. In: Proc. WOSN 2009 (2009)
6. Buchegger, S., Datta, A.: A Case for P2P Infrastructure for Social Networks - Opportunities & Challenges. In: Proc. WONS 2009 (2009)
7. Chen, C.-H.O., et al.: GAnGS: gather, authenticate 'n group securely. In: The 14th ACM International Conference on Mobile Computing and Networking (2008)
8. Chard, K., Caton, S., Rana, O., Bubendorfer, K.: Social cloud: Cloud computing in social networks. In: Proc. IEEE CLOUD 2010 (2010)
9. Chen, B., Nguyen, L., Roscoe, A.W.: Reverse authentication in financial transactions and identity management. To appear in Wireless Networks, Mobile Networks and Applications (2012)
10. Douceur, J.: The Sybil Attack. In: Druschel, P., Kaashoek, M.F., Rowstron, A. (eds.) IPTPS 2002. LNCS, vol. 2429, pp. 251–260. Springer, Heidelberg (2002)
11. Miluzzo, E., et al.: Sensing meets mobile social networks: the design, implementation and evaluation of the cenceme application. In: Proc. ACM SenSys 2008 (2008)

12. Golbeck, J., Hendler, J.: Accuracy of metrics for inferring trust and reputation. In: 14th Int'l Conf. on Knowledge Engineering and Knowledge Management (2004)
13. Kwak, H., Lee, C., Park, H., Moon, S.: What is Twitter, a social network or a news media? In: Proc. the 19th Int'l Conf. on World Wide Web (2010)
14. Laur, S., Nyberg, K.: Efficient Mutual Data Authentication Using Manually Authenticated Strings. In: Pointcheval, D., Mu, Y., Chen, K. (eds.) CANS 2006. LNCS, vol. 4301, pp. 90–107. Springer, Heidelberg (2006)
15. Lindell, A.: Comparison-Based Key Exchange and the Security of the Numeric Comparison Mode in Bluetooth v2.1. In: RSA Conference (2009)
16. Nguyen, L. (ed.): Part 6: Mechanisms using manual data transfer
17. Nguyen, L., Roscoe, A.: Efficient group authentication protocol based on human interaction. In: Proc. FCS-ARSPA 2006, pp. 9–31 (2006)
18. Nguyen, L., Roscoe, A.: Authenticating ad hoc networks by comparison of short digests. Information and Computation 206, 250–271 (2008)
19. Nguyen, L., Roscoe, A.: Separating two roles of hashing in one-way message authentication. In: FCS-ARSPA-WITS (2008)
20. Nguyen, L., Roscoe, A.: Authentication protocols based on low-bandwidth unspoofable channels: a comparative survey. Computer Security 19(1), 139–201 (2011)
21. Roscoe, A., Smyth, T., Nguyen, L.: Model checking cryptographic protocols subject to combinatorial attack, http://www.cs.ox.ac.uk/files/4157/guess.pdf
22. Roscoe, A.W.: Human-centred computer security (2006) (unpublished draft)
23. Vaudenay, S.: Secure Communications over Insecure Channels Based on Short Authenticated Strings. In: Shoup, V. (ed.) CRYPTO 2005. LNCS, vol. 3621, pp. 309–326. Springer, Heidelberg (2005)
24. Lin, Y.-H., et al.: SPATE: Small-Group PKI-Less Authenticated Trust Establishment. IEEE Transactions on Mobile Computing 9(12), 1666–1681 (2010)

CScale – A Programming Model
for Scalable and Reliable Distributed Applications

Jose Faleiro, Sriram Rajamani, Kaushik Rajan, G. Ramalingam, and Kapil Vaswani

Microsoft Research India
{t-josfal,sriram,krajan,grama,kapilv}@microsoft.com

Abstract. Today's connected world demands applications that are responsive, always available, and can service a large number of users. However, the task of writing such applications is daunting, even for experienced developers. We propose *CScale*, a programming model that attempts to simplify this task. The objective of *CScale* is to let programmers specify their application's core logic declaratively without explicitly managing distribution. *CScale* applications have simple semantics that simplify reasoning about correctness and enable testing and debugging on the single machine. In turn, the *CScale* runtime manages all aspects of execution of a *CScale* application on large clusters, including deployment, state management (replication and data partitioning) and fault tolerance. *CScale* ensures high availability by using distributed wait-free data structures to manage state. *CScale* does impose some constraints on the kind of operations clients can perform. However, we find that many real-world web applications can be naturally expressed using *CScale*.

1 Introduction

Today's connected world demands applications that are responsive, always available, and can service a large number of users. In the last few years, cloud based platforms such as Azure, EC2 and Google App Engine have democratized the infrastructure needed to host such applications, allowing anyone with internet access to deploy applications on a large cluster of machines. At the same time, these platforms expose programmers to pitfalls of distribution, such as process and network failures, imperfect messaging, and shared mutable distributed state. Writing applications that can effectively utilize these platforms and still meet user expectations is an extremely challenging problem.

In conventional web applications, the task of dealing with pitfalls of distribution is typically delegated to (distributed) databases. Databases allow shared state and integrity constraints between parts of state to be declaratively specified and support consistent access to state via transactions. However, this convenience often comes at a cost. In conventional distributed databases, transactions are built using primitives such as 2-phase commit, which introduce blocking and reduce availability, especially under network failures.

Modern distributed databases such as Dynamo, Cassandra and Azure tables (more popularly dubbed as NoSQL databases) have emerged as viable alternatives to conventional databases. These databases use replication and data partitioning for improved

R. Calinescu and D. Garlan (Eds.): Monterey Workshop 2012, LNCS 7539, pp. 148–156, 2012.

availability and throughput but do not necessarily guarantee consistent access to data. In general, the trade-off between consistency, availability and the ability to deal with network failures often permeates through entire software stack, including business logic and increases programming complexity.

In the past, the problem of increased programming complexity is often addressed using programming models and application platforms. Application platforms incorporate best practices in dealing with generic concerns such as scalability, reliability and security and allow developers to focus on application-specific logic. MapReduce and DryadLINQ are examples of programming models that have significantly simplified the task of developing distributed batch processing applications. There is an urgent need for similar programming models to manage complex consistency, availability and partition-tolerance trade-off in real time web applications.

In this paper, we describe *CScale*, a declarative programming model for building scalable distributed web applications. The objective of *CScale* is to allow programmers to specify their application's core logic declaratively without explicitly managing distribution. As we describe later, *CScale* applications have simple semantics (serializability) that simplify reasoning about correctness and enables testing and debugging on the single machine (using an emulator). In turn, the *CScale* runtime manages all aspects of execution of a *CScale* application on clusters, including deployment, state management (including replication and data partitioning), dealing with node and network failures, message delays etc. *CScale* ensures high availability by using distributed wait-free algorithms to manage state. The use of wait-free algorithms guarantees that a *CScale* application continues to service requests even if parts of the underlying systems fail. *CScale* does impose some constraints on the kind of operations clients can perform. However, as we show, many real-world web applications can be naturally expressed using *CScale*.

2 Programming Model

2.1 Language

The *CScale* programming language is a variant of Datalog (a logic programming language) and closely related to SQL. State in a *CScale* application is modelled as a set of relations. Relations fall into two categories, *base* and *derived* (as shown in Figure 1). Base relations are collection of base tuples and derived relations are functions of one or more base relations defined using relational operators (select, project, join, aggregation), negation and recursion. Consider a simple *CScale* program representing an auction application (Figure 2).

In this application, *Items* and *Bids* are base relations whereas *ValidBids, Highest-BidAmounts* and *HigestBidders* are derived relations. As defined in line 6, a tuple <*bidId, userId, itemId, bidAmount*> belongs to *ValidBids* if there exists an item with the identifier *itemId* in the Items relation and a bid in the Bids relation such that the bid was placed before the auction end time of the item. In line 7, the relation *HigestBidAmounts* is computed by grouping valid bids by item, then selecting the maximum. Finally in line 8, the relation *HigestBidders* is derived from *HigestBidAmounts* and ValidBids a

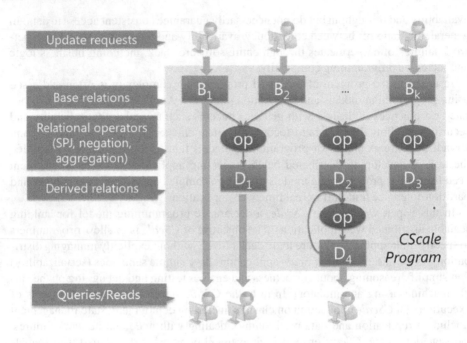

Fig. 1. *CScale* Programming Model

tuple *<bidId, userId, itemId, bidAmount>* exists in *HigestBidders* if the *bidAmount* is highest among all bids and the bid was placed by a user *userId*.

While we have adopted a language similar to Datalog, it is also possible to express *CScale* applications in other langauges such as LINQ. Unlike batch processing frameworks like MapReduce and DryadLINQ, *CScale* applications are reactive. *CScale* relations are persistent. The lifetime of a *CScale* application extends from the point at which it is deployed on a cluster to the time it is removed. Clients can interact with a *CScale* application either by updating one or more base relations (with some constraints defined later) or by querying one or more relations (base and derived). A *CScale* application performs computation to update derived relations when base relations are modified. In some sense, this computation resembles view maintenance in conventional databases. In the auction application, the relation *Items* is updated when a new item is added or removed and the relation *Bids* is updated when a new bid is placed.

CScale relations are exposed as a RESTful WCF data service. Therefore, clients may interact with a *CScale* application directly via HTTP or using the OData protocol.

2.2   Semantics

CScale applications are designed to receive and process concurrent updates from a large number of clients. Furthermore, *CScale* relations may be partitioned or replicated for throughput and availability, potentially across different geographical locations. In spite of the concurrency and distribution, *CScale* guarantees serializability. In other words,

```
1. decl Items(itemId, itemName, itemDescription, auctionEndDateTime)
2. decl Bids(bidId, userId, itemId, bidAmount, bidDateTime)
3. decl ValidBids(bidId, userId, itemId, bidAmount)
4. decl HighestBidAmounts(itemId, bidAmount)
5. decl HighestBidders(bidId, userId, itemId, bidAmount)

6. ValidBids(bidId, userId, itemId, bidAmount) :-
        Items(itemId, itemName, ItemDescription, auctionEndDateTime),
        Bids(bidId, userId, itemId, bidAmount, bidDateTime),
        bidDateTime < auctionEndDate

7. HighestBidAmounts(itemId, highestBidAmount) :-
        GroupBy(ValidBids(bidId, userId, itemId, bidAmount),
          [itemId], highestBidAmount = max(bidAmount))

8. HighestBidders(bidId, userId, itemId, bidAmount) :-
        HigestBidAmounts(itemId, bidAmount),
        ValidBids(bidId, userId, itemId, bidAmount)
```

Fig. 2. Online auctions application expressed in *CScale*

an update to a base relation (and the computation triggered to re-compute derived relations) appears to occur atomically and in isolation from other reads and updates. In the auction application, serializability ensures that clients do not observe state where a bid appears in the Bids relation but does not reflect in the highest bids (if indeed it was the highest valid bid). Constraints As described before, *CScale* relations may be replicated and/or partitioned for availability and throughput. Achieving serializability and availability in the presence of network and node failures is a hard problem. However, *CScale* is able to meet these requirements by restricting the class of applications that can be expressed in the model. Specifically, *CScale* restricts the kinds of requests clients may issue. Clients may add or remove tuples from base relations. A set of add/remove requests to base relations may be submitted as a batch. All requests in a batch appear to occur together (though not necessarily in isolation). Clients may also specify temporal dependencies between add/remove requests and reads. However, *CScale* does not support arbitrary transactions composed of reads and writes to one or more relations. For example, a transaction that performs a read-modify-write on a base tuple is not supported. Note: In SQL terms, a *CScale* program defines views over base relations. Views have transactional semantics. However, arbitrary transactions on base relations are not permitted.

2.3 Target Applications

The *CScale* programming model is naturally suited for a rich class of web applications. These include ad serving, real time search, financial data processing, real time web analytics (vulnerability and fraud detection), blogs and social networking applications, auctions and online shopping, relaxed variants of resource allocation applications such as banking and ticketing etc.

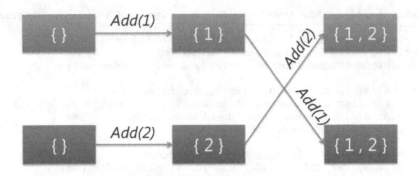

Fig. 3. A replicated set that only supports add operations

3   Implementation

An important feature of applications expressed within the *CScale* model is that they can be implemented with strong consistency and availability guarantees, even in the presence of network and process failures. *CScale* achieves this using novel distributed wait-free algorithms.

3.1   Wait-Free Data Types

CScale uses a set of distributed wait-free data types as fundamental building blocks of *CScale* applications - *CScale* relations are implemented using these data types. A key feature of these data types is that they are carefully hand-crafted to permit asynchronous, wait-free replication and still guarantee serializability. As an example, let us consider how the set data type can be implemented in this fashion. First, consider a set that only supports Add operations. Since all add operations commute, it is easy to see that if such a set were to be asynchronously replicated (i.e. operations performed on one replica are broadcast to all other replicas asynchronously), all replicas will eventually reach the same state.

Figure 3 illustrates this design. Let us assume that each replica starts with an empty state. As long as operations performed on one replica are broadcast to and applied at other replicas (in arbitrary order), all replicas are guaranteed to reach the same state (at quiescence). Hence, this set is eventually consistent. Furthermore, it can be shown that the result of all membership tests and state at quiescence can be obtained by some sequential ordering of all the add operations. Let us now try and extend this set with Remove operations. Unfortunately, Add and Remove operations on the same element do not commute. Hence, a nave implementation of the set does not satisfy the properties mentioned above because the state of the set depends on the order in which the Add and Remove operations are applied. However, in this case, these operations can be carefully designed to ensure that any two concurrent Add and Remove operations on the same element appear to occur in the same order on all replicas, irrespective of the order in which are actually applied. Figure 4 describes one such algorithm (known as the Observed Remove (OR) set) [5].

```
void Add(e) {
    S = S ∪ {e, g}
    Broadcast Add(e, g) to other replicas
}

void Remove(e) {
    G = { g | (e, g) ∈ S }
    S = S - {(e, g) | g ∈ G}
    Broadcast Remove(e, G) to other replicas
}
```

Fig. 4. Add and remove operations on a single replica in the Observed Removed set

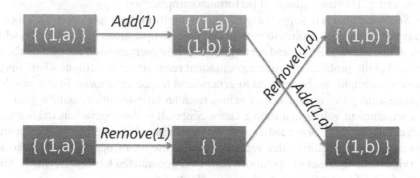

Fig. 5. An example illustrating replication in OR set

The Add operation of the OR set associates a globally unique identifier with every operation and broadcasts this identifier along with the elements. Replicas which receive the Add operation update their copy of the set in similar fashion. The Remove operation identifies the set of globally unique identifiers associated with the element (also known as the observed set) at the source replica (where it is first received from a client). It broadcasts the observed set along with the element. Replicas which receive this operation only remove tuples corresponding to the identifiers in the observed set.

Figure 5 illustrates how the OR set operates. The Remove operation on the second replica observes the identifier *a* associated with element *1* but does not observe the concurrent Add (associated with identifier *b*). The modified remove has the same effect (i.e. appears to occur before any concurrent adds) on all replicas, irrespective of the order in which it is applied. Note: Several other data types such as key-value tables and sequences can be designed to guarantee eventually consistency along the same lines as the OR set. Refer to [5] for more details.

3.2   Consistent Queries via Lattice Agreement

The set implementation described above is eventually consistent. However, intermediate queries against the set are not serializable. The example in Figure 6 shows a scenario where queries may return inconsistent values. Starting with an empty set, if queries are serviced by multiple replicas as shown, the queries may return a sequence of values $\{\}, \{1\}, \{2\}, \{1, 2\}$, which cannot be obtained by any interleaving queries with any sequential ordering of the two Add operations.

Conventional replicated databases solve this problem by requiring replicas to agree on the order in which (non-commuting) operations are processed. This is achieved using protocols such as 2PC or Paxos [4], or even pessimistic locking. However, agreement in an asynchronous distributed system in the presence of failures has been shown to be impossible [3]. This reflects in choices made in these protocols. The Paxos protocol [4], for instance, preserves safety in the presence of failures but does not guarantee progress. Furthermore, most replication protocols essentially reduce to a form of primary master replication where all operations are first sent to a special replica known as the primary, which is responsible for ensuring that all replicas process non-commuting operations in the same order. This has significant performance implications.

In *CScale* our goal is to support asynchronous, multi-master replication. This form of replication permits each replica to receive and process operations independently, which can result in better scalability and performance. Our implementation is based on the observation that the problem of ensuring consistent reads under conditions where update operations commute can be reduced to generalized lattice agreement. In this problem, each process proposes a sequence of values from an infinite lattice, and the goal is to learn a sequence of values that form a chain. Since all update operations (adds and removes) commute, they form a lattice with set inclusion as the ordering. We can achieve consistent reads by requiring that replicas propose the set of operations they receive, and service reads from set of operations learnt via generalized lattice agreement. Since the sets of values learnt form a chain, serializability follows.

In the running example, the operations Add(1) and Add(2) form the following lattice. The use of generalized lattice agreement ensures that the values replicas learn from a chain in this lattice. Thus any sequence of reads will observe only serializable values.

Recently, we have proposed a wait-free algorithm for solving generalized lattice agreement [2]. The algorithm can tolerate process failures as long as a majority of the processes survive at any point in time. The algorithm has a complexity of O(N) message delays, where N is the number of replicas. In the absence of failures, the algorithm ensures that new operations can be learnt in 2 message delays.

3.3   Incremental Evaluation and View Maintenance

In *CScale* updates to base relations trigger computation to update derived relations. Since changes to base relations at any given moment in time are likely to be small, it is possible to re-compute derived relations more efficiently by incrementally propagating changes. Incremental evaluation is challenging for several reasons. First, operators like negation and recursion require complex algorithms for detecting changes incrementally. Furthermore, if relations are partitioned and distributed, incremental evaluation must be performed without the use of primitives such as distributed transactions [6]. Many existing systems decide to offer weak consistency for derived relations [1] for better performance, which significantly complicates reasoning.

The *CScale* runtime guarantees strong consistency of derived relations using a novel incremental evaluation protocol based on lattice agreement. In this protocol, base relations participate in an agreement protocol to order all operations on base relations. Derived relations then update state according to this order. The details of this protocol are beyond the scope of this paper.

The *CScale* runtime also supports a query optimizer that analyzes a *CScale* application and generates an optimized plan for incremental evaluation. Some of the supported optimizations include early aggregation and index maintenance.

4   Current Status and Experience

CScale proposes a fundamentally different way of building distributed applications. Applications written in *CScale* are declarative and hide low level implementation details such as messaging, failures etc. At the same time, *CScale* imposes some restrictions on how clients can interact with applications and does not (yet) provide primitives to escape the model. Therefore, our first step was to evaluate if the *CScale* model is expressive enough for real world distributed applications and if the model improves programmer productivity. We built a prototype implementation of the *CScale* system (without a distributed backend) and then re-wrote a few applications (including applications from the Windows Azure patterns and practices team such as an online survey application and an online auctions application) in *CScale*.

Our initial experiences with *CScale* are very encouraging. We were able to replace the existing storage layer and most of the application logic in these applications with a simple *CScale* program significantly smaller in the number of lines of code (from a few thousand to few 10s of lines of code). Furthermore, the application expressed in *CScale* was much more understandable and maintainable as compared to the original implementation, where the application logic was spread across multiple projects (and Azure roles) and aspects of distribution such as messaging, fault tolerance etc. was handled explicitly in code. However, we recognize that much work needs to be done to fully ascertain the shortcomings and benefits of this programming model.

A distributed implementation of *CScale* consists of many pieces a programming environment (including testing and debugging support), a compiler, a runtime system (that implements replication and partitioning on a cluster and performs query evaluation), a scalable storage layer, a platform layer that supports efficient communication and provides primitives such as network and node failure detection, a query optimizer and client side interfaces amongst others. We are in the process of building these components. We would also like to ensure that *CScale* applications can be easily deployed on cloud platforms such as Azure. Finally, we are in the process of building a suite of sample applications that illustrate the best patterns and practices for building scalable and reliable *CScale* applications.

References

1. Agrawal, P., Silberstein, A., Cooper, B.F., Srivastava, U., Ramakrishnan, R.: Asynchronous view maintenance for vlsd databases. In: SIGMOD 2009, Stanford InfoLab (June 2009)
2. Faleiro, J., Rajamani, S., Rajan, K., Ramalingam, G., Vaswani, K.: Generalized lattice agreement. In: Principles of Distributed Computing (PODC) (July 2012)

3. Fischer, M.J., Lynch, N., Paterson, M.S.: Impossibility of distributed consensus with one faulty process. Journal of the ACM 32(2), 374–382 (1985)
4. Lamport, L.: The part-time parliament. ACM Transactions on Computer Systems 16, 133–169 (1998)
5. Shapiro, M., Preguiça, N., Baquero, C., Zawirski, M.: Convergent and commutative replicated data types. Bulletin of the European Association for Theoretical Computer Science (EATCS) (104), 67–88 (2011)
6. Zhuge, Y., Garcia-molina, H., Wiener, J.L.: The strobe algorithms for multi-source warehouse consistency. In: International Conference on Parallel and Distributed Information Systems, pp. 146–157 (1996)

Foundations and Tools for End-User Architecting

David Garlan, Vishal Dwivedi, Ivan Ruchkin, and Bradley Schmerl

School of Computer Science
Carnegie Mellon University
Pittsburgh, USA
{garlan,vdwivedi,iruchkin,schmerl}@cs.cmu.edu

Abstract. Within an increasing number of domains an important emerging need is the ability for technically naïve users to compose computational elements into novel configurations. Examples include astronomers who create new analysis pipelines to process telescopic data, intelligence analysts who must process diverse sources of unstructured text to discover socio-technical trends, and medical researchers who have to process brain image data in new ways to understand disease pathways. Creating such compositions today typically requires low-level technical expertise, limiting the use of computational methods and increasing the cost of using them. In this paper we describe an approach — which we term *end-user architecting* — that exploits the similarity between such compositional activities and those of software architects. Drawing on the rich heritage of software architecture languages, methods, and tools, we show how those techniques can be adapted to support end users in composing rich computational systems through domain-specific compositional paradigms and component repositories, without requiring that they have knowledge of the low-level implementation details of the components or the compositional infrastructure. Further, we outline a set of open research challenges that the area of end-user architecting raises.

Keywords: end-user architecture, end-user architecting, software architecture, end-user programming, software composition, software development tools.

1 Introduction

Increasingly users rely on computation to support their professional activities. In some cases turnkey applications and services are sufficient to carry out computational tasks. However, in many situations users must adapt computing to their specific needs. These adaptations can take many forms: from setting preferences in applications, to "programming" spreadsheets, to creating orchestrations of services in support of some business process. This situation has given rise to an interest in end-user programming [41], and, more generally, end-user software engineering [28] or end-user computing [23]. This emerging field attempts to find ways to better support users who, unlike professional programmers, do not have deep technical knowledge, but must somehow find ways to harness the power of computation to support their tasks.

One important subclass of end-user computation arises in domains where users must compose existing computational elements into novel configurations. Examples include e-science (e.g., astronomers who create new analysis pipelines to process telescopic

R. Calinescu and D. Garlan (Eds.): Monterey Workshop 2012, LNCS 7539, pp. 157–182, 2012.

158   D. Garlan et al.

data), intelligence analysis (e.g., policy planners who process diverse sources of unstructured text to discover socio-technical trends), and medicine (e.g., researchers who
process repositories of brain imaging data to discover new disease pathways).

In these domains professionals typically have access to a large number of existing
applications and data sets, which must be composed in novel ways to gain insight, carry
out "what if" experiments, generate reports and research findings, etc. For example, in
the field of brain imaging, scientists study samples of brain images and neural activity
to diagnose disease patterns. Innovative research in this domain requires that scientists
compose a large number of tools and apply them to brain-imaging data sets to diagnose
problems, such as malformations and structural or functional deformities. There also
exist dozens (if not hundreds) of brain image processing tools for image recognition,
image alignment, filtering, volumetric analytics, mapping, etc. Figure 1 illustrates a
popular neuroscience tool suite, called FSL, that is used to create scripts for analyzing
FMRI [44] data.

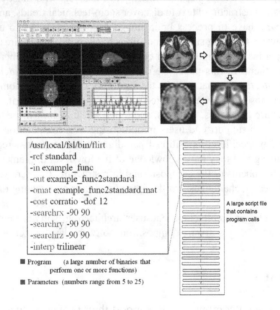

Fig. 1. Compositions in the neuroscience domain

Unfortunately, assembling such elements into coherent compositions is a non-trivial
matter. In many cases users must have detailed low-level knowledge of things like application parameter settings, application invocation idiosyncrasies, file locations and
naming conventions, data formats and encodings, ordering restrictions, and scripting
languages. In Figure 1, for example, users must create and execute detailed scripts illustrated at the bottom of the figure.

Further, it may be difficult for end users to determine whether a set of components
can be composed at all, and, if not, what to do about it. For example, differences in data
encodings may make direct component composition infeasible without the inclusion
of one or more format converters. Even when a legal composition can be achieved, it

may not have the performance (or other quality attributes) critical to the needs of the end user. And, even when a suitably performing composition can be created, it may be difficult to share it with peers or reuse it in similar but different settings.

In this paper we advocate an approach to these problems that exploits the similarity between such compositions and software architecture, and attempts to leverage the considerable advances made within that field over the past two decades. The key idea is to view the activities of these end users as engaging in architectural design within a domain-specific style and to represent those architectures explicitly. As we will see, such explicit representation allows one to raise the level of abstraction for composition, provide criteria for evaluating the soundness and quality of a composition, support reuse and parametrization, and establish a platform for a host of task-enhancing services such as program synthesis, analysis, compilation, execution, and debugging.

By approaching the problem in this way we identify a new field of concern, which we term *end-user architecting*. Similar to end-user programming [41], it recognizes up front that the key issue is bridging the gap between available computational resources and the skill set of the users who must harness them — users who typically have weak or non-existent programming skills. But unlike end-user programming, it seeks to find higher-level abstractions that leverage the considerable advances in software architecture languages, methods, and tools to support component composition, analysis and execution.

In Section 2 we revisit the problem, highlighting the cross-cutting similarities in computing needs for composition-based domains such as those mentioned above, and we outline the challenges for solving the problems of users in these domains. Section 3 makes the case for taking an architectural perspective on the problem, and outlines an approach in which software architecture tools and techniques can be incorporated into environments that support end-user architecting. Section 4 illustrates how this approach can be applied by considering three case studies. Section 5 considers related work, and Section 6 explores some of the open research challenges in this area.

2   The Problem

As noted above, an increasing number of domains are evolving to depend on composing existing components to support their tasks. Table 1 lists examples of these domains, including e-science, business processing, social science research, and electronic music synthesis.

While very different in their specific tasks and goals, the use of computation within these communities shares a number of common properties. First, it relies on compositions of existing components to accomplish computational tasks. For example, there exist large repositories of reusable components such as BioCatalogue [55] for life science web services, the BIRN Data Repository [4] for neuroscience data and analysis tools, and myExperiment [40] for scientific workflows.

Second, in many cases those compositions are complex, involving dozens of components, possibly running on many hosts. Thus, creating new compositions becomes a non-trivial task, often taking weeks to develop, test, and execute.

Third, quality attributes matter. While the specific quality attributes of concern vary from domain to domain, they typically include things like performance (time to

Table 1. Domains involving end user compositions

Type	Compositions
Astronomy	electromagnetic image processing tasks [11]
Bioinformatics	biological data-analysis services [30]
Digital music production	audio sequencing and editing [33]
Environmental Science	spatio-temporal experiments [57]
Geospatial Analysis	interactive visualization of geographical data [38]
Home Automation	home devices and services [29]
Neuroscience	brain-image processing libraries [12]
Scientific computing	transformational workflows [49]
Socio-technical Analysis	dynamic network creation, analysis, reporting and simulation [48]

complete a task), resource requirements (numbers of processors, storage requirements), availability (likelihood of crashing), privacy and security (protection of data). For example, a brain imaging composition may be of little use to a neuroscience researcher if it takes a week to execute, fails frequently, or compromises the privacy of the data.

Fourth, the socio-technical ecosystem within which these computations are used is complex, involving many roles and incentives [25]. For example, *researchers* care that their compositions produce credible outputs and that they can share their computations with their peers; *component providers* care that they are given credit for the use of their components; *regulators and funders* care that the provenance of all results is fully documented.

Today these end-user communities are not well served by existing technology and development platforms. In particular, we can identify five critical barriers.

1. **Excessive Technical Detail:** Creating compositions today often requires knowledge of myriad low-level technical details, such as data formats, parameter settings, file locations, ordering constraints, execution conventions, scripting languages, etc. As Figure 1 illustrates, brain imaging research using FSL tools requires a user to understand and create detailed execution scripts that specify how to configure each of the constituent tools, which may have dozens of configuration parameters. As another example, in the domain of intelligence analysis (cf. Section 4) a typical composition that involves two logical steps, but is executed in the context of a service-oriented architecture (SOA), requires the end user to specify a Business Processing Event Language (BPEL) script shown in Figure 2 [48]. The script requires the user to explicitly specify low-level details that handle control flow, variable assignment, exception handling, and other programming constructs.

2. **Inappropriate Computational Models:** The computational models provided by typical execution platforms, such as SOA, may require end users to map their tasks into a computational vocabulary that is quite different from the natural way of decomposing the task in that domain. For example, tasks that are logically represented in the end user's mind as a workflow may have to be translated into the very-different vocabulary of service invocations executing on a SOA, as illustrated in Figure 2.

3. **Inability to Analyze Compositions:** There may be many restrictions on legal ways to combine elements, dictated by things like format compatibility, domain-specific processing requirements, ordering constraints, and access rights to data and applications. Today, discovering whether a composition satisfies these restrictions is largely a matter of trial and error, since there are few tools to automate such checks. Moreover, even when a composition does satisfy the composition constraints, its extra-functional properties — or quality attributes — may be uncertain. For example, determining how long a given computation will take to produce results on a given data set can often be determined only by time-consuming experimentation.

4. **Lack of Support for Reuse:** An important requirement in many communities is the ability for professionals to share their compositions with others in those communities. For instance, brain researchers may want to replicate the analyses of others, or to adapt an existing analysis to a different setting (e.g., executed on different data sets). Packaging such compositions in a reusable and adaptable form is difficult, given the low-level nature of their encodings, and the brittleness of the specifications.

5. **Impoverished Support for Execution.** The execution environment for compositions is often impoverished. Compared to the capabilities of modern programming environments, end users have relatively few tools for things like compilation into efficient deployments, interactive testing and debugging (e.g., setting breakpoints, monitoring intermediate results, etc.), history tracking, and graceful handling of run-time errors. This follows in part from the fact that in many cases compositions are executed in a distributed environment using middleware that is not geared towards interactive use and exploration by technically naive users.

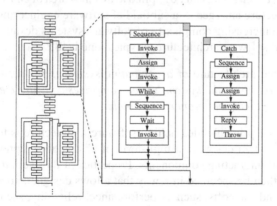

Fig. 2. A segment of BPEL orchestration of a socio-cultural analysis workflow

This gap between the needs of end users and today's technology has a number of serious consequences. The cost of producing effective compositions is excessive because end users must become experts in implementation details not relevant to their primary task. The quality is low because compositions tend to be brittle and in many cases fail to meet their extra-functional requirements. Compositions are difficult to reuse, modify, and maintain, leading to gratuitous reinvention.

Recognizing these problems, a number of research- and practitioner-based efforts have produced platforms that provide end-user tools for composition, reuse and execution within specific domains. As described in more detail in Section 5, this is typically done through the creation of component repositories, and composition environments that support computational models appropriate to the domain, such as workflow execution, widget composition, data exploration or music synthesis and composition. Examples include Taverna for life sciences, the Ozone Widget Framework (OWF) for geospatial analysis, VisTrails for data exploration and visualization, Steinberg's Virtual Studio Technology (VST) for composing music effects, etc.

While many of these platforms have been quite successful, and several are in widespread use, they are typically handcrafted for specific communities and domains — often at great cost in development time and effort. What is needed, we would argue, is a foundational understanding of the problem and a general approach to a solution that gets at the heart of the mismatch between end user needs and technologies that must be exploited. Such foundations would ideally lead to a systematic approach to developing tools that surmount the barriers outlined earlier. In the next section we outline such an approach.

3   End-User Architecture

The key to solving the problems outlined above is to recognize that the computational design activities performed by those communities are fundamentally architectural in nature. Recognizing that, one can then explore how modern techniques and tools in support of *software architecture* can be applied to this new area of *end-user architecting*.

Software architecture emerged as a subfield of software engineering in the 1990s as a way to tackle the increasing complexity of software systems design. While there are many definitions of software architecture, a typical one is [8]:

> The software architecture *of a computing system is the set of structures needed to reason about the system, which comprises software elements, relationships among them, and properties of both.*

Definitions aside, the principle idea behind software architecture is to allow software engineers to treat system design at a high-level of abstraction, representing a system as a composition of interacting components. Properties of those components and their compositions can then be specified in a way that allows designers to analyze systemic quality attributes and tradeoffs, such as performance, reliability, security, availability, maintainability, and so on [50].

Since its emergence there has been substantial development of foundations, tools, and techniques to aid software architects. These include formal and semi-formal architecture description languages (ADLs) [34], architecture-based analyses [19], architecture reconstruction tools [47], architecture evaluation methods [9], architecture handbooks [6], architecture style definition and enforcement [17], and many others.

With respect to the theme of this paper, a number of salient features of software architecture are particularly important:

- **Component Composition:** Software architecture represents a system as a composition of components, supporting a high-level view of the system and bringing to the forefront issues of assignment of function to components, component compatibility, protocols of interaction between components, and ways to package component compositions for reuse.
- **Domain-Specific Computation Models:** Software architecture allows developers to represent a system using compositional models that are not restricted by the implementation platform or programming language, but can be chosen to match the intuition of designers. Specifically, software architecture allows one to define *architectural styles*, where each style denotes a family of systems that shares a common vocabulary of composition, conforms to rules for combining components, and identifies analyses that can be applied to systems in that family [50]. Styles may represent generic computational models such as publish-subscribe, pipe-filter, and client-server. Or, they may be specialized for particular domains [35,36].
- **Analysis:** Software architecture allows developers to perform analysis of quality attributes at a systems level. This is typically done by exposing key properties of the components and their interactions, and then using those properties in support of calculations to determine expected component compatibility, performance, reliability, security, and so on [19]. This in turn allows developers to make engineering tradeoffs, for example balancing attributes like fidelity, performance, and cost of deployment to match the particular business context. Additionally, in some cases it is possible to build analytic tools that not only detect problems, but also suggest possible solutions [52].
- **Reuse:** Software architecture supports several kinds of reuse. First, architectural styles provide a basis for sharing components that fit within that style [35,36]. Modern examples of this include platforms like JEE and frameworks like Eclipse. Second, software architectures permit the definition of reusable patterns that can be used to solve specific problems [2,6]. Third, most architectural models support hierarchical description, whereby a component can be treated as a primitive building block at one level of composition, but refined to reveal its own sub-architecture.
- **Execution Support:** For some architectural styles tools can generate implementations. Typically this is done by using a repository of components that conform to the style, and then compiling the system description into executable code [18]. Additionally, software architectures can be used for run-time monitoring and debugging [58].

These properties suggest that if applied appropriately, software architecture principles, tools, and practices could directly address the five challenges outlined in Section 2. Specifically:

1. **Excessive Technical Detail:** Architectural models provide a way to develop, analyze, and execute compositional models at a high level of abstraction, suppressing details of implementation.
2. **Inappropriate Computational Models:** Architectural models can define domain-specific compositional styles to match the computational intuition of end users.

3. **Inability to Analyze Compositions:** Architectural models, suitably represented and formalized, can be analyzed by tools to gain insight into a system's expected quality attributes and to evaluate tradeoffs between alternative designs based on their support for relevant qualities.
4. **Lack of Support for Reuse:** Architectural models support reuse of components, patterns, styles, and encapsulated subsystems.
5. **Impoverished Support for Execution.** Architectures can, in principle, be used as a basis for compilation, deployment, execution, and debugging.

How can these potential benefits be realized? We would argue that the key to doing this is to use an approach in which there is an explicit architectural representation of the compositions created by end users. For a given domain the architectures that could be created would be associated with a domain-specific architectural style corresponding to natural computational models for the domain (such as some variant on workflow, publish-subscribe, or data-centric styles). Further, associated with the style and corresponding infrastructure, there would be a set of architecture services that could support analysis, execution, etc. Finally, all of these features would be made available to users through a graphical front end that supports access to component repositories, architecture construction, system execution, and various additional support services.

This leads to a general framework of system organization in support of end-user architecting, as illustrated in Figure 3. Part (a) of the figure shows the current state of affairs: users must translate their tasks into the computational model of the execution platform, and become familiar with the low-level details of that platform and the primitive computational elements (applications, services, files, etc.) — leading to the problems outlined in Section 2. Part (b) illustrates the new approach. Here, end-user architectures are explicitly represented as architectural models defined in a domain-specific architectural style. These models and the supporting infrastructure can then support a host of auxiliary services, including checking for style conformance, quality attribute analysis, compilation into efficient deployments, execution and debugging mechanisms, and automated repair — as shown in part (c).

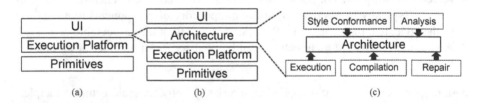

Fig. 3. End-user Architecting Approach

4   Case Studies

To investigate the potential of this approach we instantiated the general framework described above in three domains: dynamic network analysis, brain imaging, and geospatial analysis. For each we describe the nature of the domain and the forms of composition that are required within the community of use. We then consider how we adapted the end-user architecting framework to this domain in terms of (a) architecture representation, (b) architecture style, (c) architectural analysis, (d) execution support, (e) additional services, (f) reuse, and (g) user interface.

4.1 Dynamic Network Analysis

Dynamic Network Analysis (DNA) is a domain of computation that focuses on the analysis of network models, which represent entities, relations, and their properties. DNA is increasingly being used in a variety of fields, including anthropology, sociology, business planning, law enforcement, and national security, where networks capture the relationships between people, knowledge, tasks, locations, etc. [7].

End users in these fields are typically analysts who extract entities and relations from unstructured text (such as web sites, blogs, twitter feeds, email, etc.) to create network models, and who then use those models to gain insight into social, organizational, and cultural phenomena through analysis and simulation.

For example, an analyst interested in understanding disaster relief after the Haiti earthquake in 2010 [59] might build a network from open source news data provided through a source such as LexisNexis [31]. This unstructured textual data needs to be processed into a usable form, or "cleaned," to filter out headers, remove noise, and normalize concepts. From this processed data a dynamic network can be generated representing associations between people, places, resources, knowledge, tasks, and events. Using network analysis algorithms, insights can then be gained. For example, analysis can determine things like the primary organizations and people involved in the relief effort, how information about food and medical supplies propagated through the network, and how these evolved over time.

Similar kinds of analyses are routinely carried out in law enforcement (where analysts use crime reports and statistics to determine drug-related gang activities), healthcare and disease control (where analysts use medical reports from hospitals and pharmacies to understand disease vectors), and anthropology (where social scientists can understand belief systems and how they relate to demographics).

Within this broad domain of dynamic network analysis, analysts typically engage in a process of composing a variety of existing tools to extract networks, analyze them, and display results. Figure 4 illustrates a typical toolset used for such analyses consisting of the following: AutoMap for extracting networks from natural language texts, ORA for analyzing and visualizing networks, and Construct for "what-if" reasoning about the networks using simulation [48].

Conceptually the computations that analysts create can be viewed as workflows, where each step in the workflow requires the invocation of some data transformation step that consumes the data from previous steps and produces results for the next step. However, traditionally, to achieve this kind of composition analysts would need to understand the idiosyncrasies of each of tool, manually invoke them on data stored in various file locations using a variety of file naming schemes and data formats, and preserve the results of the analysis in some location that they would have to keep track of, before invoking another tool to carry out the next step.

More recently coarse-grained tools like AutoMap, ORA, and Construct have been reengineered to expose a set of services that can be composed within a SOA

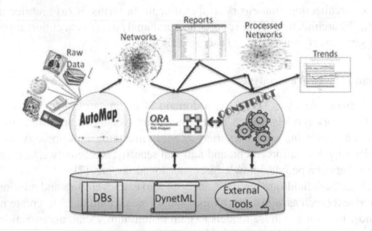

Fig. 4. Typical tools for socio-cultural analysis

framework. While the use of services reduces the burden of learning to use specific tools, and opens up the possibility of novel compositions, unfortunately the use of SOA requires end users to translate their workflow intuitions into the low-level encodings and scripting required by SOA orchestration languages such as BPEL. Figure 2 illustrated the resulting complexity of such encodings.

To apply the proposed end-user architecting approach to this domain, we adapted the end-user architecting framework of Figure 3 by creating an environment, called SORASCS (Service ORiented Architecture for Socio-Cultural Systems), for dynamic network analysis [16,48], and illustrated in Figure 5. Key features of this environment are as follows:

a. **Architecture Representation:** Architectures are explicitly represented in a system layer, called the socio-cultural analysis layer. This layer stores compositions as workflows. It also provides a repository of data transformers, which act as component building blocks for creation of new workflows.

b. **Architecture Style:** Compositions are defined using a formal workflow architectural style, which specifies the vocabulary of element types and constraints on compositions [12]. Element types include data transformers, data sources, and data sinks. Constraints of the workflow style prohibit the introduction of cycles, dangling connectors, unattached interfaces, and mismatched communication channels (where the data produced by one component is incompatible with the data consumed by a successor component).

c. **Analysis:** The SORASCS workflow style supports a number of analyses including (a) data privacy analysis, which identifies potential privacy issues in the information flows, (b) ordering analysis, which uses machine-learning to evaluate whether the ordering of transformation steps is consistent with previously constructed workflows, and (c) performance analysis, which estimates the amount of time that will be taken to complete an analysis of a specified data set.

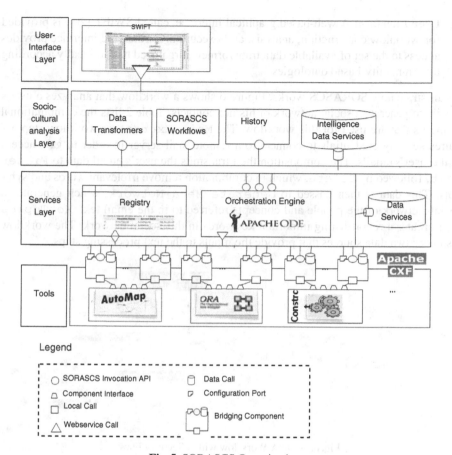

Fig. 5. SORASCS Organization

d. **Execution Support:** Workflows are compiled into BPEL scripts, which are run within the Services Layer using standard SOA infrastructure. The compilation process attempts to optimize performance by parallelizing workflow execution. Additionally, there is execution support for long-duration transformations and graceful error handling — typically not provided by baseline SOA infrastructure. Further, it is possible for a user to set breakpoints, execute the workflow one transformation at a time, and preserve intermediate data for later inspection.

e. **Services:** The SORASCS platform provides services for examining history and for repeating previously executed activities in the history list. The platform also provides data services for organizing data into projects and categories, and categorizing the data in ways that are informative to analysts. Access control is provided to check that users have appropriate rights to use data sets and transformations.

f. **Reuse:** Workflows can be encapsulated as parameterized components for later reuse and adaptation. These are stored in a repository of available data transformers, which may be used as primitives, or "opened" to reveal their substructure and possibly edited for new usage contexts.

g. **User Interface:** A web-based graphical interface, called SWiFT [20], is provided for workflow construction, analysis, and execution. Further, the interface provides access to the set of available data transformers, organized hierarchically according to community-based ontologies.

To illustrate how SORASCS works, Figure 6 shows a workflow that analyzes a user's emails to generate a social network of his/her contacts. Table 2 lists the computational elements that are used for this workflow. The `Mail Extractor` workflow step acquires security credentials to connect to a remote mail server in order to gain access to the user's emails. The composition then transmits the user's email data to `Filter Text`, followed by `Delete`, which in combination remove irrelevant words and symbols. This data is then passed to `Generate Meta-Network`, which generates a social-network of the people and concepts referred to in the email text. `HotTopics` then creates a report listing important keywords in this social network. The workflow also uses two data sources that provide the inputs to the text processing steps.

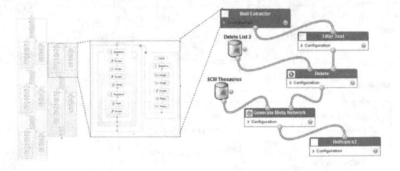

Fig. 6. A DNA Workflow with a Security Flaw

When a security analysis is run on this workflow, SORASCS detects a security problem. In this case, data security requirements mandate the use of 'token-based authentication' by all services. However the above workflow includes the `Mail Extractor` service, which uses 'password-based authentication' — indicating a security violation. The analysis flags this as a problematic workflow by highlighting the inappropriate service in red.

Once analysis is complete and the errors have been corrected, the user can compile the workflow into the BPEL script illustrated in Figure 6, which can then be executed. Although not illustrated here, as execution proceeds, the user is given feedback through the SORASCS user interface to show which workflow step is currently being executed.

4.2   Neuroscience

Functional magnetic resonance imaging (fMRI) is a common form of analysis performed by neuroscientists in the brain-imaging domain to understand the behavior of the human brain [44]. A typical fMRI analysis consists of sequences of computations over brain image data to support hypotheses or interpretations, such as assessing the

Table 2. DNA operations used in the workflow of Figure 6

Operation	Description
`Mail Extractor`	Extracts email from a server to a text file
`Filter Text`	Removes undesirable information from text files
`Delete`	Removes a set of common keywords using a standard dictionary (such as: a, an, the, etc) from a text file
`Generate Meta-Network`	Creates a dynamic network based on the information in the text file
`Hot Topics`	Creates a report about important keywords in a social network

evolution of cognitive deficits in neurodegenerative diseases [13]. Figure 7 illustrates a typical image translation process.

Neuroscientists have at their disposal large repositories of brain imaging data, such as the BIRN Data Repository [4] and the Portuguese Brain Imaging Network Project [54]. Neuroscientists also have access to a large variety of processing tools, which perform functions such as those listed in Table 3.

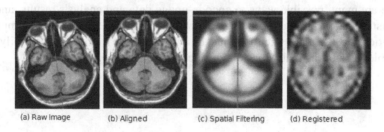

(a) Raw Image   (b) Aligned   (c) Spatial Filtering   (d) Registered

Fig. 7. Brain image data viewed after individual pre-processing steps

Professional neuroscientists can easily identify the steps required for processing brain imaging data, but because of a proliferation of possible tool implementations for each step and their idiosyncratic parameterization requirements, they find it difficult to choose and assemble tools to implement these steps. Furthermore, while these experts can debug a processing script by examining the outputs, novices are typically unable to do this. As an example of the complexity introduced by tool parameterization, Figure 1 illustrates a part of a typical script in which a single logical processing step requires the specification of 9 parameters[1].

Additional complexity arises because of implicit sequencing constraints. For example, a mandatory step in fMRI analysis is to perform pre-processing operations on brain image data to remove or control some aspects that can affect the overall analysis [53] (such as aligning one brain volume to another using linear transformations operations

---

[1] In practice, the number of parameters ranges from 5 to 25.

Table 3. Some tools for brain-imaging processing

Operation	Description	Tool name
Align	Alignment of an fMRI sequence based on a reference volume (i.e. motion correction, direction correctness)	fslmaths, fslroi, mcflirt
Segmentation	Segmentation of a brain mask from the fMRI sequence	bet2, fslmaths, fslstats
Spatial Filtering	Compute spatial density estimates for neuroscience images, and filter the volumes accordingly	fslmaths, susan
Temporal Filtering	Blur the moving parts of images, while leaving the static parts.	fslmaths
Normalize	Translating, rotating, scaling, and may be wrapping the image to match a standard image template	flirt
Register	Align one brain volume to another using linear transformation operations (such as rotation, translations, etc.) or non-linear transformations (such as warping, local distortions, etc.)	flirt, fnirt

like rotation, translation, etc.). While experts may learn these constraints through trial and error, there are no tools to guide less-expert end users.

There are many possible ways to encode image data and analysis results, and neuroscientists must ensure that encodings match between steps. This further complicates composition because neuroscientists must be aware of these formats and carefully select compatible steps or manually locate transducers that can bridge mismatches.

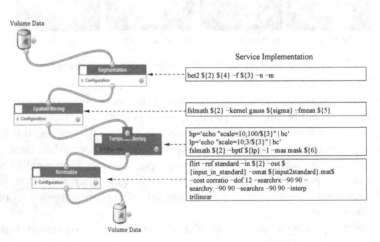

Fig. 8. A problematic neuroscience workflow that misses 'alignment' of data before 'temporal filtering'

To address these problems we adapted the end-user architecting framework to this domain as follows:

a. **Architecture Representation:** Similar to dynamic network analysis, architectures are explicitly represented in a system layer that stores compositions as workflows and provides a repository of processing steps and transducers. The main components made available in this prototype were derived from the FSL tool suite (e.g., *bet2, fslmath, flirt*) [14].

b. **Architecture Style:** Compositions are defined using a formal workflow architectural style, which is similar to the one used for dynamic network analysis.[2] The neuroscience style differs in two respects: (a) it defines computational elements specific to the neuroscience domain, and (b) it provides additional properties and domain-specific constraints (such as checking ports for different data encodings and other content of brain-image data) that allow the correct construction of workflows within the neuroscience domain.

c. **Analysis:** Similar to dynamic network analysis, the properties of the style elements are used for designing various domain-specific analyses for the brain imaging domain. An example is data mismatch analysis to support the detection of data mismatches in the neuroscience compositions and to suggest repairs that can resolve these mismatches based on an end user's quality of service requirements [56].

d. **Execution Support:** Workflows are compiled into BPEL scripts, which are executed on a service-oriented platform, identical to SORASCS, providing the similar feedback and debugging facilities.

e. **Services:** Similar to dynamic network analysis, the brain imaging platform provides services to end users tracking the history of operations performed and access to brain imaging data sets.

f. **Reuse:** Like dynamic network analysis, workflows can be encapsulated as parameterized components for later reuse and adaptation.

g. **User Interface:** A web-based graphical interface is provided for workflow construction, analysis, and execution.

Figure 8 illustrates a typical application that analyzes brain image data using some of the transformation operations listed in Table 3. To the right of the workflow the figure indicates the invocation and parameter settings that are used to invoke individual tools.

In this example analysis reveals an error in the workflow located in the `Temporal Filtering` component and its corresponding interface. The error occurs because before doing temporal filtering on brain-imaging data, it is necessary to align it. Therefore any workflow is required to have the `Align` component before the `Temporal Filtering` component. This is an example of a typical semantic problem that cannot be easily identified from scripts or BPEL-like compositions.

---

[2] In fact, using the formal architectural description language of Acme[37], we have defined a common root style for both the dynamic network analysis domain and the neuroscience domain [12].

4.3 Geospatial Analysis

Geospatial analysis tools allow analysts to explore location-based data using graphical representations such as maps and charts [51]. Examples of such data include data about infrastructure (e.g., an electrical grid), population distribution (e.g., census data), or dynamic network data that has location information associated with it (e.g., crime activities associated with a criminal network derived from police reports). End users in this field typically want to display information on one or more maps, drill down into more detail in certain views, and receive updates when information changes. In contrast to dynamic network analysis and neuroscience analysis, which is largely sequential and transformational, end users doing geospacial analysis typically explore information through a set of concurrent tools that exchange dynamically-changing data to update multiple concurrent views.

The Ozone Widget Framework (OWF) [45] – or just Ozone – is a web platform for integrating web-based tools in this domain. Web applications are represented as lightweight visual applications, called *widgets*, and OWF allows end users to open and compose a set of widgets through a web "dashboard" in their browser. Users interact with widgets, which communicate among each other using the OWF framework.

An example of an Ozone dashboard is shown in Figure 9. The right-most window is the launch menu from which end users can add widgets to their dashboard. There are four widgets displayed on the dashboard, displaying information of different types, some in chart form, others (in the background) on maps. These widgets may pass information between each other to ensure that they are focused on the same map region, for example, or to display updated information as it becomes available from a database or data stream. This dashboard and the arrangement of widgets can be shared between developers by exchanging textual configuration files.

Ozone widgets interact in a publish-subscribe style [8]: widgets can publish events to channels and subscribe to channels to receive events.[3] All widgets that have subscribed to a channel receive data published to that channel by any other widget. Widget developers who wish to integrate with other developers must agree on the names of channels to publish to, and the format of the data that is published. To offer additional control over communication, Ozone also allows end users to restrict potential communication between widgets by indicating pairs that are allowed to communicate, thereby implicitly restricting other widgets from participating in those communications.

While end users are free to choose which widgets appear in their dashboard, considerable care must be taken to ensure sensible configurations. In particular, it is important to make sure that widgets both publish and subscribe to the appropriate channels, and that the type of data published is consistent with that expected by subscribers.

Unfortunately, today it is difficult to do this because the interconnection topology is largely implicit. Specifically, to determine the interconnection structure between widgets an end user needs to either examine widget source code, or perform experiments. This problem is compounded by the use of restriction lines, because they can radically change the communication topology indicated in the code by prohibiting interactions that would otherwise be allowed.

---

[3] Events in Ozone are plain-text strings or JSON objects.

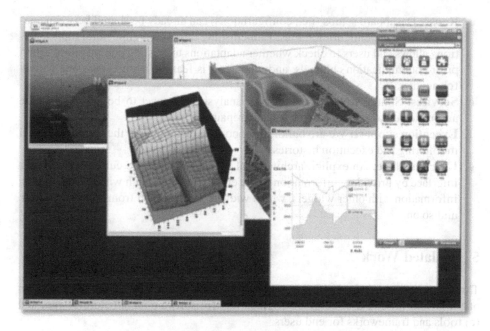

Fig. 9. An Ozone dashboard example from [24]

The existence of complex interconnection rules and behavior lead naturally to the use of architectural modeling of widget compositions, which could support the end-user architecting process through automated constraint checking. For example, a widget topology can be checked to conform to a privacy constraint that widgets containing private data do not communicate it to third-party untrusted widgets. Another application is widget topology generation: a user would specify what pairs of widgets should and should not interact, and a set of topologies would be generated.

Key features of our end-user architecting approach to this domain are:

a. **Architecture Representation:** Ozone widget configurations are represented as explicit architectural models, that indicate which widgets are involved in a composition and the communication topology.
b. **Architectural Style:** Compositions are defined using a variant of a publish-subscribe style that takes into account the idea of restrictions. Element types include Widgets, which have publish and subscribe interfaces, and two types of connectors representing public channels and private (restricted) channels.
c. **Analysis:** We are building analyses to provide insight into the widget compositions, such as which widgets are communicating, whether there are data mismatches over publish-subscribe channels, how to restrict communication to minimize event messaging, whether information is lost (e.g., because there is no widget subscribed to information on a particular channel).

d. **Reuse:** Dashboard setups (i.e., configurations) can already be shared between analysts as textual configuration files. Embellishing this with architectural representations allows end users to check whether adaptations to existing compositions retain prior communication channels, and whether it is feasible to substitute one widget for another.

e. **Services:** Similar to dynamic network analysis,we expect to be able to provide automated data mismatch detection and repair.

f. **Execution support:** We are building support for debugging in the form of channel monitoring and execution histories.

g. **User interface:** An explicit architectural model enhances the current Ozone user interface by providing information to the end user about which widgets are sharing information with other widgets, which widgets are restricted from communicating, and so on.

5 Related Work

Three primary areas of related research have influenced the formulation and direction of this work: (a) end-user software engineering, (b) software architecture design, and (c) tools and frameworks for end users.

End-User Software Engineering

End-user software engineering is a research area at the intersection of computer science and human-computer interaction. It aims to empower users who do not have deep technical expertise to harness the power of computers in support of tasks within their profession [28]. Although such users do not have (or want to have) the skills of professional software developers, often they face many of the same software engineering challenges: understanding requirements, carrying out design activities, supporting reuse, quality assurance, etc. In fact, studies have shown that across many domains, such end users spend about 40% of their time doing programming-related activities [25], but employ few of the tools and techniques used by modern software engineering. As as result, creating computations often leads to systems that are brittle, contain numerous bugs, have poor performance, cannot be easily reused or shared, and lead to a proliferation of idiosyncratic solutions to similar problems within a domain [5].

To date, most of the research in end-user software engineering has focused on end-user *programming*, where novel forms of programming languages have been developed for enhanced usability within a domain. These include visual programming languages [39], programming-by-demonstration [10], direct manipulation programming languages [26], and domain-specific languages [15].

In contrast, this paper focuses on domains in which component composition is the primary form of end-user system construction, an activity that we have termed end-user architecting. For such domains, we have argued, it makes sense to explore ways to adapt the tools and techniques of software *architecture*, rather than software *programming*.

Software Architecture

As we discussed in Section 3, there exists a large body of foundational work on software architecture that has paved the way for architecture to be used as a model to reason about a software system. In this paper we build directly on that heritage. Key influences have been architecture description languages [34], the use of architectural styles [50,37], and architecture-based analyses [19].

In this paper we have argued that these techniques have direct relevance and can be effective in solving many of the problems of end-user architecting. However, as we elaborate in Section 6, there also remain a number of gaps and challenges that require additional research and adaptation of those techniques to the needs of end users.

Tools and Frameworks for End-User Composition

The primary motivation for this paper is the fact that a large number of domains require technically-naive users to compose computational elements into novel configurations, such as workflows and scripts for experiments and analyses. Such users often form large communities that share a common set of tasks, vocabulary, and computational needs. These communities include astronomy [11], bioinformatics [30], environmental sciences [57], intelligence analysis [48], neuroscience [42], and scientific computing [49]. In such communities simple turnkey or parameterized implementations are inadequate, since it is impossible to anticipate all possible configurations — hence the need for tools that can help users in creating, executing, and sharing compositions.

As a consequence, a number of powerful composition environments have been created for particular problem domains. Examples include: Loni-pipeline [46] for brain-imaging compositions; Galaxy [21] for genomics; and Vistrails [3] for data-exploration and visualization for scientific applications. Other more generic composition environments, such as Taverna [43], Kepler [32], WINGS [22], and Ozone [38], can be used across several domains, but typically only support a specific computation model — such as workflow or publish-subscribe.

In contrast to these efforts, this paper attempts to lay the foundation for viewing this class of tools and frameworks as supporting architecture design, and argues that there are considerable benefits in taking this point of view. Among those benefits are the ability to formally define and reason about compositional models as instances of domain-specific architectural styles, create cross-domain analyses, provide systematic support for reuse and adaptation, support powerful auxiliary services (e.g., mismatch repair), and support execution, testing, and debugging.

6 Discussion

Having described an approach to end-user architecting and illustrated it through three case studies, we now consider some of the aspects of that approach in more detail and outline some of the challenges and open problems.

The centerpiece of an end-user architecting approach is the explicit representation of a composition of computational elements as an architecture, expressed within an appropriate architectural style for the domain at hand. In the case of dynamic network analysis and neuroscience we used variations on a dataflow style. In the case of geospatial analysis we used a publish-subscribe style.

But where does that style come from? In our own experience, we have found that it is often non-trivial to determine this. For example, in the case of dynamic network analysis we found that in some compositions, users wanted to include interactive tools as components in their workflows, in addition to data transformers. This led to a hybrid style that was not purely transformational (as would be the case for a pure dataflow style), but rather permitted a user to interrupt a data transformation workflow, and interactively explore data using applications running on the desktop, before continuing with successive data transformation. Formally, we had to introduce into the style a new type of component — an interactive tool component — and create execution infrastructure to permit those components to work smoothly with data transformation executing on a SOA (see [48] for details).

Similarly, we were initially unsure how to model the communication restrictions present in the Ozone Widget Framework. After exploring a number of options we eventually decided on a variant of a publish-subscribe style that includes two publish-subscribe connector types: public and private pub-sub channels.

The problem of defining an appropriate end-user architecting style is further complicated by the fact that end users may have different compositional needs at different times. For instance, in many analytical domains (including all three domains that we studied), it is the case that in early stages of development end users want to do exploratory investigation using highly interactive, manually-controlled tools. But once it is clear what kinds of computation need to be done, a more streamlined composition can be constructed that provides better performance and is easier for others to use as a packaged computation. This suggests that end users may have several modes of composition, with different architectural modeling needs.

Thankfully, today there are a number of tools that allow one to experiment with different styles. For instance, in our own work we used Acme and its supporting Acme Studio toolset [17]. Acme supports rapid design and experimentation with styles. In particular, styles can be defined using a declarative language, which can then be directly compiled into an environment for constructing systems in that style and for checking conformance with the constraints of the style. Acme Studio also provides an analysis plug-in framework that allows one to rapidly develop analyses appropriate for a given style [19].

Moreover, Acme has a rich set of base styles (client-server, publish-subscribe, etc.), which can be used as a starting point defining domain-specific styles for end-user architecting communities. For instance, both the dynamic network analysis style and neuroscience style were developed by specializing a common inherited dataflow style. Further, since Acme styles are formally defined they may also be formally analyzed as specifications in their own right to determine, for example, whether a style has the properties that one expects, or to detect inconsistencies when multiple styles are combined [27].

Another technique that helps address this problem is construction of support services that bridge the gap between different modes of composition. In SORASCS, for example, we provided tools to transition between interactive exploration and workflow.

Specifically, an end user can manually and interactively invoke operations on data sets. SORASCS keeps track of the history of these invocations. Once users are happy with the results, they can use the history to generate a workflow that captures the overall transformation that they want to package as a workflow.

A second concern that must be addressed when pursuing an end-user architecting approach is the issue of managing large component repositories. As we indicated earlier, for many domains there may be hundreds of possible elements that can be combined to produce compositions. In SORASCS, for example, there are over 100 data transformations that are available for dynamic network creation, analysis, visualization, simulation, and report generation. Thus any effective tool for end-user architecting will need to provide scalable ways to search repositories. We have experimented with several schemes for this. For example, we can use community-based ontologies to organize services into categories familiar to end users. We can provide a set of standard filters that can be used to extract components with appropriate properties along several dimensions. We can also use machine learning to recommend possible component selections, based on prior compositions. However, this remains an open problem, as few software architecture tools have addressed the problem of rich component repositories.

A third concern is whether we have raised the level of abstraction sufficiently high. While end-user architecting is a huge improvement over today's programming-based systems, it still requires end users to consider carefully how their computations are composed from the available components. For some users — particularly novice users, or users who are simply reusing existing compositions — this may still require too much expertise.

This suggests that in many cases it may make sense to provide another level above that of architecture representation that more directly supports user tasks. For instance, there might be simple domain-specific languages that can be used to define some computation task. Or, there may be simplified interfaces that automatically construct the architectures through various menus or "wizards". For example, with SORASCS we demonstrated the ability to do this by connecting it to a front-end tool, called VIBES [1], that provides a specialized interface for constructing belief network analyses.

More generally, the presence of an intermediate level of architecture simplifies the problem of providing task assistance to end users, since the gap between a task and an architecture that supports it is usually much smaller than the gap between a task and its executable. However, task-level support for end users seems a particularly rich area for future research, and many questions remain open. For example, is it possible to learn compositions by watching experts solve certain tasks? Can automated synthesis be used to achieve a computational goal based on a high-level description of the inputs and desired outputs?

A fourth concern is the engineering cost for creating end-user architecting environments. Ideally it should be possible to generate large parts of the N-tiered framework that we illustrated in Figure 3. This remains an open and active area of research.

Finally, as we noted in Section 2, one of the common elements of end-user architecting communities is that they often involve complex ecosystems. In this paper we have primarily addressed only one role within these ecosystems – the end-user architect. But there are also other roles, such as component developers, data set providers, regulatory bodies, funding agencies, etc.

We have found that when following the end-user architecting approach advocated in this paper, it is also critical that these other roles be considered. For instance, what incentives are there for people to contribute reusable components to an end-user architecting platform? If none are in place, it is unlikely that there will be a sufficiently large base of parts for end users to assemble. Has the platform been constructed in such a way that it can be certified for use in deployment environments where there may be significant privacy or security requirements? If not, the end-user architecting tools may not be usable in the target context. How can an analyst who has created a composition get credit for that design if it is used by others? In many communities people are reluctant to make their tools available or share their analyses unless they receive some professional recognition for doing this.

While the approach we have advocated above does not by itself address the entire ecosystem, it can, however, help address some of the concerns such as those mentioned. For instance, analytical outputs of some computation can be formally linked to the composition that produced those results, providing a way to acknowledge the developers of the individual components and the composition itself. Additionally, as we have indicated, style-based analyses can guarantee certain properties of a composition — such as security or privacy. Tools can enforce that such analyses are successfully completed before permitting execution of a composition. Further, the decoupling of the architecture from the execution infrastructure on which it runs allows one to select an execution platform that satisfies regulatory concerns.[4] That said, the understanding of ecosystems for end-user architecting communities remains a largely unexplored area, and a rich subject for future research.

7   Conclusion

We have argued that the computational activities of end users in many domains are analogous to that of software architects, and that rather than forcing end users to become programmers, we should instead provide architecture-based tools and techniques to support their tasks.

To make this concrete, we outlined six elements of an approach: (a) explicit representation of compositions as architectures, (b) use of domain-specific architectural styles to provide appropriate computational models, (c) the ability to analyze end-user architectures for properties such as performance, reliability, security, etc., (d) support for execution and debugging, (e) support for reuse, and (f) possibly additional services that leverage the architectural representation. We then illustrated how this approach can be used in three end-user architecting domains: dynamic network analysis, neuroscience, and geospatial analysis.

We believe that the recognition of the value of architectural modeling for end users in certain domains is an important first step towards improving the ability for myriad disciplines to leverage the power of computation without requiring its participants to

---

[4] For instance, there are certain pre-approved infrastructures for the US military. By using these, one limits the amount of certification that must be done to the parts that are built on top of it.

become programmers. However, we also acknowledge that there is much more to be done to make this a reality, and we outlined some of the possible future directions in Section 6.

Acknowledgments. This work was supported in part by the Office of Naval Research grant ONR-N000140811223, and the Center for Computational Analysis of Social and Organizational Systems (CASOS). The views and conclusions contained herein are those of the authors and should not be interpreted as representing the official policies, either expressed or implied, of the Office of Naval Research, or the U.S. government. The authors would like to thank Perla Velasco Elizondo, Jose Maria Fernandes, Diego Estrada Jimenez, Aparup Banerjee, Laura Gledenning, Mai Nakayama, Nina Patel, and Hector Rosas for their contributions to various aspects of this work.

References

1. Alion MA&D Operation. VIBES: Visualization of Belief Systems (May 2012), http://www.maad.com/index.pl/visualization_of_belief_systems
2. Bass, L., Clements, P., Kazman, R.: Software Architecture in Practice, 2nd edn. Addison Wesley (2007) ISBN 0-201-19930-0
3. Bavoil, L., Callahan, S.P., Scheidegger, C.E., Vo, H.T., Crossno, P., Silva, C.T., Freire, J.: Vistrails: Enabling interactive multiple-view visualizations. In: IEEE Visualization, vol. 18 (2005)
4. Biomedical Informatics Research Network. (BIRN), http://www.birncommunity.org
5. Brandt, J., Guo, P.J., Lewenstein, J., Dontcheva, M., Klemmer, S.R.: Two studies of opportunistic programming: interleaving web foraging, learning, and writing code. In: CHI, pp. 1589–1598 (2009)
6. Buschmann, F., Meunier, R., Rohnert, H., Sommerlad, P., Stal, M.: Pattern Oriented Software Architecture: A System of Patterns. John Wiley & Sons (1996)
7. Carley, K.M.: A dynamic network approach to the assessment of terrorist groups and the impact of alternative courses of action. In: Visualizing Network Information Meeting, RTO-MP-IST 2006, France (2006)
8. Clements, P., Bachmann, F., Bass, L., Garlan, D., Ivers, J., Little, R., Merson, P., Nord, R., Stafford, J.: Documenting Software Architectures: Views and Beyond, 2nd edn. Addison-Wesley Professional (October 2010)
9. Clements, P., Kazman, R., Klein, M.: Evaluating Software Architectures: Methods and Case Studies. Addison Wesley (2001)
10. Cypher, A. (ed.): Watch What I Do – Programming by Demonstration. MIT Press, Cambridge (1993)
11. Deelman, E., Singh, G., Su, M.-H., Blythe, J., Gil, Y., Kesselman, C., Mehta, G., Vahi, K., Bruce Berriman, G., Good, J., Laity, A.C., Jacob, J.C., Katz, D.S.: Pegasus: A framework for mapping complex scientific workflows onto distributed systems. Scientific Programming 13(3), 219–237 (2005)
12. Dwivedi, V., Velasco-Elizondo, P., Maria Fernandes, J., Garlan, D., Schmerl, B.: An Architectural Approach to End User Orchestrations. In: Crnkovic, I., Gruhn, V., Book, M. (eds.) ECSA 2011. LNCS, vol. 6903, pp. 370–378. Springer, Heidelberg (2011)
13. Eidelberg, D.: Metabolic brain networks in neurodegenerative disorders: A functional imaging approach. Trends Neurosci. 32, 548–557 (2009)

14. FMRIB Software Library (fsl), http://www.fmrib.ox.ac.uk/fsl/
15. Fowler, M.J.: Domain-Specific Languages. Addison-Wesley (2011)
16. Garlan, D., Carley, K.M., Schmerl, B., Bigrigg, M., Celiku, O.: Using service-oriented architectures for socio-cultural analysis. In: Proceedings of the 21st International Conference on Software Engineering and Knowledge Engineering (SEKE 2009), Boston, USA, July 1-3 (2009)
17. Garlan, D., Monroe, R.T., Wile, D.: Acme: Architectural description of component-based systems. In: Leavens, G.T., Sitaraman, M. (eds.) Foundations of Component-Based Systems, p. 47. Cambridge University Press (2000)
18. Garlan, D., Reinholtz, W.K., Schmerl, B., Sherman, N., Tseng, T.: Bridging the gap between systems design and space systems software. In: Proceedings of the 29th Annual IEEE/NASA Software Engineering Workshop (SEW-29), Greenbelt, MD, April 6-7 (2005)
19. Garlan, D., Schmerl, B.: Architecture-driven modelling and analysis. In: Cant, T. (ed.) Proceedings of the 11th Australian Workshop on Safety Related Programmable Systems (SCS 2006), Melbourne, Australia. Conferences in Research and Practice in Information Technology, vol. 69 (2006)
20. Garlan, D., Schmerl, B., Dwivedi, V., Banerjee, A., Glendenning, L., Nakayama, M., Patel, N.: Swift: A tool for constructing workflows for dynamic network analysis (2011), http://acme.able.cs.cmu.edu/pubs/show.php?id=333
21. Giardine, B., Riemer, C., Hardison, R.C., Burhans, R., Elnitski, L., Shah, P., Zhang, Y., Blankenberg, D., Albert, I., Taylor, J., Miller, W., Kent, W.J., Nekrutenko, A.: Galaxy: a platform for interactive large-scale genome analysis. Genome Res. 15(10), 1451–1455 (2005)
22. Gil, Y., Ratnakar, V., Deelman, E., Mehta, G., Kim, J.: Wings for Pegasus: Creating large-scale scientific applications using semantic representations of computational workflows. In: AAAI, pp. 1767–1774 (2007)
23. Goodell, H.: End-user computing. In: CHI 1997 Extended Abstracts on Human Factors in Computing Systems: Looking to the Future, CHI EA 1997, pp. 132–132. ACM, New York (1997)
24. Hellar, D.B., Vega, L.C.: The Ozone Widget Framework: towards modularity for C2 human interfaces. In: Proceedings of SPIE Conference on Defense Transformation and Net-Centric Systems, Baltimore, Maryland (2012)
25. Howison, J., Herbsleb, J.D.: Scientific software production: incentives and collaboration. In: CSCW, pp. 513–522 (2011)
26. Hutchins, E.L., Hollan, J.D., Norman, D.A.: Direct manipulation interfaces. Human Computer Interaction 1(4), 311–338 (1985)
27. Kim, J.S., Garlan, D.: Analyzing architectural styles. Journal of Software and Systems 83(7), 1216–1235 (2010)
28. Ko, A.J., Abraham, R., Beckwith, L., Blackwell, A.F., Burnett, M.M., Erwig, M., Scaffidi, C., Lawrance, J., Lieberman, H., Myers, B.A., Rosson, M.B., Rothermel, G., Shaw, M., Wiedenbeck, S.: The state of the art in end-user software engineering. ACM Comput. Surv. 43(3), 21 (2011)
29. Lee, C., Nordstedt, D., Helal, S.: Enabling smart spaces with osgi. IEEE Pervasive Computing 2, 89–94 (2003)
30. Letondal, C.: Participatory programming: Developing programmable bioinformatics tools for end-users. In: Lieberman, H., Paterno, F., Wulf, V. (eds.) End-User Development, pp. 207–242 (2005)
31. LexisNexis, http://www.lexisnexis.net
32. Ludäscher, B., Altintas, I., Berkley, C., Higgins, D., Jaeger, E., Jones, M.B., Lee, E.A., Tao, J., Zhao, Y.: Scientific workflow management and the Kepler system. Concurrency and Computation: Practice and Experience 18(10), 1039–1065 (2006)

33. McConahy, A.L., Herbsleb, J.D.: Platform design strategies: Contrasting case studies of two audio production systems. In: FutureCSD Workshop at CSCW (2011)

34. Medvidovic, N., Taylor, R.N.: A framework for classifying and comparing architecture description languages. In: ESEC / SIGSOFT FSE, pp. 60–76 (1997)

35. Monroe, R.T.: Rapid Develpomentof Custom Software Design Environments. PhD thesis, Carnegie Mellon University, School of Computer Science (July 1999)

36. Monroe, R.T., Garlan, D.: Style-based reuse for software architectures. In: Proceedings of the Fourth International Conference on Software Reuse (April 1996)

37. Monroe, R.T., Kompanek, A., Melton, R.E., Garlan, D.: Architectural styles, design patterns, and objects. IEEE Software 14(1), 43–52 (1997)

38. Moore, D.M., Crowe, P., Cloutier, R.: Driving major change: The balance between methods and people. Software Technology Support Center Hill AFB UT (2011)

39. Myers, B.A.: Taxonomies of visual programming and program visualization. J. Vis. Lang. Comput. 1(1), 97–123 (1990)

40. myExperiment, http://www.myexperiment.org/

41. Nardi, B.A.: A small matter of programming: perspectives on end user computing. MIT Press (1993)

42. neuGRID CNRS. N4u - neugrid for you, http://neugrid4you.eu

43. Oinn, T.M., Mark Greenwood, R., Addis, M., Nedim Alpdemir, M., Ferris, J., Glover, K., Goble, C.A., Goderis, A., Hull, D., Marvin, D., Li, P., Lord, P.W., Pocock, M.R., Senger, M., Stevens, R., Wipat, A., Wroe, C.: Taverna: lessons in creating a workflow environment for the life sciences. Concurrency and Computation: Practice and Experience 18(10), 1067–1100 (2006)

44. Pekar, J.J.: A brief introduction to functional MRI. IEEE Engineering in Medicine and Biology Magazine 25(2), 24–26 (2006)

45. Potomac Fusion. Ozone/Synapse download portal (2012),
http://widget.potomacfusion.com/main/home

46. Rex, D.E., Ma, J.Q., Toga, A.W.: The LONI Pipeline Processing Environment. Neuroimage 19, 1033–1048 (2003)

47. Schmerl, B., Aldrich, J., Garlan, D., Kazman, R., Yan, H.: Discovering architectures from running systems. IEEE Transactions on Software Engineering 32(7) (July 2006); also available from IEEE. Appendix A, Appendix B

48. Schmerl, B.R., Garlan, D., Dwivedi, V., Bigrigg, M.W., Carley, K.M.: SORASCS: a case study in SOA-based platform design for socio-cultural analysis

49. Segal, J.: Some problems of professional end user developers. In: VL/HCC, pp. 111–118 (2007)

50. Shaw, M., Garlan, D.: Software architecture - perspectives on an emerging discipline. Prentice Hall (1996)

51. de Smith, M.J., Goodchild, M.F., Longley, P.A.: Geospatial Analysis: A Comprehensive Guide to Principles, Techniques and Software Tools, 2nd edn. Troubador Publishing Ltd. (December 2007)

52. Spitznagel, B., Garlan, D.: A compositional formalization of connector wrappers. In: The 2003 International Conference on Software Engineering, ICSE 2003 (2003)

53. Strother, S.C.: Evaluating fMRI preprocessing pipelines. IEEE Engineering in Medicine and Biology Magazine 25(2), 27–41 (2006)

54. The Portuguese Brain Imaging Network Grid - IEETA. (BING),
http://www.brainimaging.pt

55. The University of Manchester and the European Bioinformatics Institute (EMBL-EBI). BioCatalogue. The Life Science Web Services Registry,
http://www.biocatalogue.org/

56. Elizondo, P.V., Dwivedi, V., Garlan, D., Schmerl, B., Fernandes, J.M.: Resolving data mismatches in end-user compositions (submitted for publication, 2012)
57. Villa, F., Athanasiadis, I.N., Rizzoli, A.E.: Modelling with knowledge: A review of emerging semantic approaches to environmental modelling. Environmental Modelling and Software 24(5), 577–587 (2009)
58. Yan, H., Garlan, D., Schmerl, B., Aldrich, J., Kazman, R.: DiscoTect: A system for discovering architectures from running systems. In: Proceedings of the 26th International Conference on Software Engineering, Edinburgh, Scotland, May 23-28 (2004)
59. Zhao, Y., Gallup, S.P., MacKinnon, D.J.: Lexical link analysis for the haiti earthquake relief operation using open data sources. In: International Command and Control, Research and Technology Symposium, Québec City, Canada, June 21-23 (2011)

Evolving Delta-Oriented Software Product Line Architectures

Arne Haber[1], Holger Rendel[1],
Bernhard Rumpe[1], and Ina Schaefer[2]

[1] Software Engineering, RWTH Aachen University, Germany
[2] Institute for Software Systems Engineering, TU Braunschweig, Germany

Abstract. Diversity is prevalent in modern software systems. Several system variants exist at the same time in order to adapt to changing user requirements. Additionally, software systems evolve over time in order to adjust to unanticipated changes in their application environment. In modern software development, software architecture modeling is an important means to deal with system complexity by architectural decomposition. This leads to the need of architectural description languages that can represent spatial and temporal variability. In this paper, we present delta modeling of software architectures as a uniform modeling formalism for architectural variability in space and in time. In order to avoid degeneration of the product line model under system evolution, we present refactoring techniques to maintain and improve the quality of the variability model. Using a running example from the automotive domain, we evaluate our approach by carrying out a case study that compares delta modeling with annotative variability modeling.

1 Introduction

Modern software systems simultaneously exist in many different variants in order to adapt to changing user requirements or application contexts. Software product line engineering [32] aims at developing a family of systems by managed reuse in order to decrease time to market and to improve quality. In addition to this variability in space, software systems are extremely long-lived and have to evolve over time in order to maintain, improve or update their functionality. This unanticipated variability in time [26] changes the system design, structure, and behavior in an unexpected manner, e.g., for adapting it to new customer requirements or technological conditions. Evolution of software systems needs to be managed, and gets particularly difficult if a family of systems is considered.

The design of the software architecture plays an essential role in software development [27,25]. The architecture allows decomposing a complex system into smaller hierarchically structured components. These can be developed independently. The change frequency of architectural descriptions is lower than the changes on the implementation level, where often bugs etc. need to be fixed. However, changes in the architecture have a wide range impact on the overall

R. Calinescu and D. Garlan (Eds.): Monterey Workshop 2012, LNCS 7539, pp. 183–208, 2012.

system such that architectural changes have to be planned, modeled and analyzed to ensure that the system quality is maintained despite of the changes. This is particularly complex for software product line architectures.

Most current ADLs [25] do not support the explicit representation of architectural change. The predominantly used approaches for architectural variability modeling use annotations to assign model elements to different variants. These *annotative variability modeling* approaches mostly use a so called 150%-percent model of the system architecture incorporating all possible variability in which specific elements are annotated to belong to specific product variants. The monolithic 150%-percent architecture description gets easily very complex for large product families and is hard to manage in case of evolutionary changes. Introducing a new variant will most likely require changes of the whole model, as modular development and implementation of variable parts is not possible. To counter this problem, ADLs should support variability modeling by representing changes to the architecture in space and in time as explicit first-class entities. The variability description in the ADL should be modular to facilitate tracing changes to particular functions, components, or features. Furthermore, the description should be readable, easy to comprehend, to evolve, and to maintain.

In this paper, we present Δ-MontiArc, an ADL with native support for architectural variability modeling in space and in time that allows defining variants of interactive distributed and Cyber-Physical systems in a modular manner. Δ-MontiArc is based on the concept of delta modeling software product lines [6]. A product line of architectures is described by a core architecture and a set of architectural deltas that encapsulate changes to the core architecture. In order to obtain a particular product variant, a set of suitable deltas defined in a product configuration is applied to the core. As variable parts of a model, e.g. functionality for new product variants, are encapsulated in deltas, this approach overcomes the aforementioned problems of annotative variability modeling. As complexity of models is decreased and modular modeling of variability is possible, delta models are easier to comprehend and to evolve. In previous work [16,14], Δ-MontiArc was used to represent spatial variability only. In this paper, we extend it to capture temporal variability with the same linguistic means. If new products should be included in a product family, new deltas can easily be added to a delta model to generate new variants. If a product variant is no longer supported, its product configuration and redundant deltas may be removed. Modifications to certain product functionalities, e.g., for bug fixing, can be realized by replacing a particular delta by another version. In order to avoid degeneration of a delta model after some evolution steps, it can be refactored to improve its structure without changing the generated products. The evolution of architectures as considered in this paper reflects the evolution of the features contained in a software product line. However, the presented approach solely works on the level of the product line artifacts modeling solution space variability [8], in contrast to problem space variability that is typically captured with product features on the requirements level.

In order to evaluate Δ-MontiArc, we carried out a case study to gain experience in spatial and temporal evolution of delta oriented product lines. This case study has been also modeled using a common annotative variability modeling approach to compare it with our approach. The case study describes a braking controller system which exists in variants for cars and motorcycles and allows the inclusion of several assistance system, like an anti-lock braking system or an electronic stability control. By considering several evolution and refactoring scenarios, we demonstrate that delta modeling is particularly well suited for representing architectural variability and architectural evolution.

The paper is structured as follows. Sect. 2 introduces Δ-MontiArc for representing spatial architectural variability. Sect. 3 demonstrates how Δ-MontiArc captures temporal architectural variability. Sect. 4 shows three refactoring strategies for delta models. Sect. 5 contains a qualitative and quantitative comparison of Δ-MontiArc and an annotative variability modeling approach based on the preformed case study. Related work is discussed in Sect 6. Sect. 7 concludes the paper and outlines future work.

2   Spatial Variability

Delta modeling [6,36] is a language-independent approach for modular modeling of variability in the solution space [8] and can be applied to different modeling and programing languages like, e.g., class diagrams [35] or Java [34,36]. In [16,14], the concept of delta modeling is applied to software architectures in order to obtain an ADL with native support for architectural variability in space. A Δ-MontiArc product line is specified by a designated core architecture that represents the architecture of a valid product variant, and a set of deltas that add, remove, or modify architectural elements to derive further product variants. An architectural variant is definied by a *variant configuration* that contains a set of application-specific deltas that are used in order to generate the variant. Therefore, the operations of these deltas are stepwise applied in a calculated order to transform the core to the architectural variant. After a variant is generated, its correctness is checked using mechanisms of the base language. To with an *application order constraint* (AOC) that determines which deltas must or must not be applied before. If, for example, a delta A modifies a model element, that has been introduced by another delta B and is not part of the core, the AOC of A has to claim that it must be applied after B. Hence, the application order of the deltas contained in a variant configuration is calculated by interpreting the attached AOCs. If more then one application order is valid for a product variant, all application orders are expected to generate the same product, not regarding the order of the model elements in the resulting variant. This is the case, if for example two or more deltas of a configuration do not have an attached AOC and their position in the application order may be arbitrary switched without influencing the generated product. However, it is yet unchecked, if several valid application orders really result in the sematically same product. Therefore the correctness of AOCs is assumed. According to [34] it is also possible to define product lines based on more than one valid core architecture. Then, however, the core model that is to be modified must be explicitly referenced in product configurations.

```
1  component BrakingSystem {
2    autoconnect port;
3
4    port
5      in BrakeCommand brake,
6      out BrakePressure wheelpressure1,
7      out BrakePressure wheelpressure2,
8      out BrakePressure wheelpressure3,
9      out BrakePressure wheelpressure4;
10
11   component PressureCalculator brakefunction;
12 }
```

Listing 1. Core architecture of BrakingSystem

Δ-MontiArc is based on the textual architectural description language (*ADL*) MontiArc [18] that allows modeling and simulation of interactive distributed and Cyber-Physical systems. Therefore it provides modeling elements to describe component type definitions that contain an interface description, an internal structure given by subcomponents, and the communication between subcomponents and the components interface. An example of a MontiArc architecture is given in Lst. 1. It depicts the definition of component type BrakingSystem that calculates the brake pressure for all four wheels of a car. MontiArc components communicate with their environment using their interface. The interface definition of component BrakingSystem is given by an incoming port brake with type BrakeCommand (l. 5) and four outgoing ports to emit the calculated brake pressure for each wheel (ll. 6–9). The BrakingSystem component contains a subcomponent brakefunction that is an instance of component type PressureCalculator (l. 11). The connections between the outer ports and the interface of the brakefunction subcomponent are created automatically using MontiArc's autoconnect statement (l. 2). Parametrized with keyword port, it automatically creates connections between all yet unconnected type-compatible ports with the same name.

Δ-MontiArc extends the MontiArc ADL with the concepts of delta modeling. Therefore it defines a language that allows modifications of component type definitions by adding or removing model elements like ports, subcomponents, or connections. Lst. 2 shows delta DTractionControl specified in Δ-MontiArc that adds a traction control functionality to component BrakingSystem by modifying the BrakingSystem component (c.f. ll. 3 ff). The delta adds an additional port accel to receive accelerate commands (l. 4). This port is implicitly connected to the added subcomponent stabilizer (l. 5). The aforementioned connections between the interface of component BrakingSystem and its subcomponent brakefunction are now explicitly redirected to the newly added

```
1  delta DTractionControl after
2      DAntiLockBrakingSystem && !DTwoWheel {
3    modify component BrakingSystem {
4      add port in AccelerateCommand accel;
5      add component TC stabilizer;
6
7      connect brakefunction.wheelpressure1 ->
8        stabilizer.fromabs1;
9      connect brakefunction.wheelpressure2 ->
10       stabilizer.fromabs2;
11     connect brakefunction.wheelpressure3 ->
12       stabilizer.fromabs3;
13     connect brakefunction.wheelpressure4 ->
14       stabilizer.fromabs4;
15   }
16 }
```

Listing 2. Delta adding traction control

subcomponent that itself is implicitly connected to the outer interface (c.f. ll. 7–14). In the example, the AOC given by keyword after in ll. 1 f defines that delta DTractionControl has to be applied after delta DAntiLockBrakingSystem (see Lst. 3) and not before delta DTwoWheel. To efficiently check the applicability of deltas and the consistency of the application order constraints during product generation, a family-based analysis of delta-oriented product lines is presented in [15].

Concrete product variants are defined in Δ-MontiArc by a product configuration that specifies which deltas have to be applied to the core architecture to generate a product variant. Lst. 4 shows product configuration CarWithTC for a braking system variant that contains an anti-lock braking system (added by delta DAntiLockBrakingSystem, see Lst. 3) and a traction control (added by delta DTractionControl, see Lst. 2) beside the basic brake functionality introduced by the core architecture which is depicted in Lst. 1.

```
1  delta DAntiLockBrakingSystem {
2    modify component BrakingSystem {
3      add port in WheelSensor wheelspeed1,
4              in WheelSensor wheelspeed2,
5              in WheelSensor wheelspeed3,
6              in WheelSensor wheelspeed4;
7      replace component brakefunction
8        with component ABS brakefunction;
9    }
10 }
```

Listing 3. Delta adding anti-lock braking system

```
1  deltaconfig CarWithTC {
2      DAntiLockBrakingSystem,
3      DTractionControl
4  }
```

Listing 4. Product configuration CarWithTC

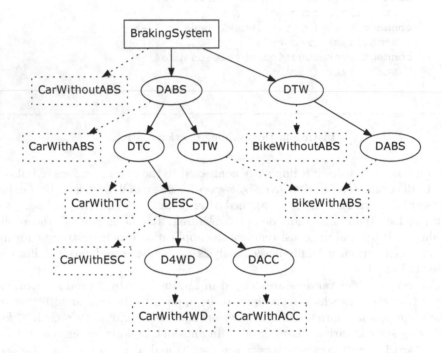

Fig. 5. Initial product line structure

As running example throughout this paper, we consider a product line of braking system controllers. In Fig. 5, the delta model of this controller product line is shown. The core architecture BrakingSystem (see Lst. 1) is depicted at the very top of the figure. Below, we see all deltas denoted by ellipses. The solid arrows show the possible application orders of the deltas according to the application order constraints in the after clauses. The supported product variants are shown in dashed boxes. The product line contains a braking system for cars without an anti-lock braking system (CarWithoutABS) as core architecture. By applying the delta DAntiLockBrakingSystem (short: DABS), a product variant CarWithABS can be obtained. Using the delta DTwoWheel (short: DTW), a braking system for motorbikes with only two wheels is generated (BikeWithoutABS). Using the delta DABS, a braking system for motorbikes with ABS is derived (BikeWithABS). For cars, a traction control can be added by delta DTractionControl (short: DTC), and afterwards an electronic stability control can be added by delta DElectronicStabilityControl (short: DESC). Finally, the architecture can be tailored to work with an adaptive cruise control system by applying delta DAdaptiveCruiseControl (short: DACC) or alternatively by a four wheel drive using delta DFourWheelDrive (short: D4WD). The initial product line of braking systems realized in Δ-MontiArc supports eight product variants with six deltas.

3 Temporal Variability

The difference between temporal and spatial variability is that spatial variability is anticipated and, thus, can be planned ahead while temporal variability is unanticipated and has to be integrated into the product line after its initial design. However, variability in time can be presented by the same means as variability in space using the concepts of delta modeling [6].

The evolution of a product line can be completely classified into three different scenarios: first, new product variants are added; second, product variants are removed; third, existing product variants are modified. In the following, we illustrate how these three evolution scenarios can be represented with Δ-MontiArc without re-engineering the delta models from scratch, but by evolving it via modular and local changes to deltas and product configurations.

Add Variants. A delta model in Δ-MontiArc consists of a designated core architecture, a set of architectural deltas and the set of supported product configurations which are selected subsets of the available deltas. When new architectural variants are added, this amounts to adding the respective deltas and product configurations that are required to generate the new product variants which are not yet contained in the delta model.

In our running example, we can add a new product variant to the braking system controller product line that includes support for a reduction gear. This variant is only for driving offroad and, thus, requires that four wheel driving is included in the product as well. To capture this change, a new delta DReductionGear (short: DRG) shown in Lst. 6 is added to the delta model. A new configuration CarWithRG (see Lst. 7) defines the new product variant.

Remove Variants. When product variants are removed, since they are now longer supported or maintained, the respective product configurations can simply be removed from the set of product configurations. If deltas are no longer required for product generation, because all product configurations using them have been removed, also the redundant deltas can be removed. The removal of deltas can require a modification of application order constraints of other remaining deltas. This can only be the case, if the removed delta is mentioned in the after clause as a conflicting delta that may not be applied together with this delta. Hence, constraints on removed deltas can be deleted without changing the remaining product variants.

```
1  delta DReductionGear after DFourWheelDrive {
2    modify component BrakingSystem {
3      add component BrakeAmplifier;
4      connect stabilizer.wheelpressure1
5        -> BrakeAmplifier.wheelpressurefromesp1;
6      connect stabilizer.wheelpressure2
7        -> BrakeAmplifier.wheelpressurefromesp2;
8      connect stabilizer.wheelpressure3
9        -> BrakeAmplifier.wheelpressurefromesp3;
10     connect stabilizer.wheelpressure4
11       -> BrakeAmplifier.wheelpressurefromesp4;
12   }
13 }
```

Listing 6. Delta for adding reduction gear

```
1  deltaconfig CarWithRG {
2    DAntiLockBrakingSystem,
3    DTractionControl,
4    DElectronicStabilityControl,
5    DFourWheelDrive,
6    DReductionGear
7  }
```

Listing 7. Configuration for product variant with reduction gear

In our running example, assume that the variants CarWithoutABS and CarWithTC should not be supported anymore, since all cars should now contain either ABS or ESC right away. These configurations can be removed from the product line without changing any delta, since all deltas are still required to generate the remaining variants. Now we assume, that the product portfolio should be consolidated such that only control units for cars are produced and motorbikes are not supported anymore. Hence, the variants BikeWithoutABS and BikeWithABS are removed and also delta DTwoWheel is removed since it is no longer required for generating a product variant. In delta DTractionControl, the negated reference to delta DTwoWheel is also deleted.

Modify Variants. The modification of existing product variants requires to change the implementation of one or more existing deltas. A reason for a modification of an existing delta may, for instance, be a bug fix or an improvement of performance by new component realizations.

In our running example, assume that the existing delta DAdaptiveCruise-Control (see Lst. 8) has to be modified by adding a new input port for a rainsensor which is necessary for its correct functioning. The new version of delta DAdaptiveCruiseControl is depicted in Lst. 9. As only the implementation inside this delta is changed, the general structure of the product line does not change. From now on, the new delta is used when generating product variants, such that the new corrected functionality of the adaptive cruise control system is contained in any newly generated product variant. Fig. 10 shows the structure of the product line after applying all three scenarios. Type safety of all deltas of a product line may be assured using a family-based analysis depending on MontiArcs checking facilities as described in [15] or by designing a constraint-based type system similar to the one presented in [33].

```
1  delta DAdaptiveCruiseControl after
2      DElectronicStabilityControl && !DFourWheelDrive {
3    modify component BrakingSystem {
4      add port in AccelerateCommand accelfromacc,
5              in BrakeCommand brakefromacc;
6      add component SignalHandler;
7      connect accel -> SignalHandler.accelfromdriver;
8      connect brake -> SignalHandler.brakefromdriver;
9    }
10 }
```

Listing 8. Original delta for adding adaptive cruise control

```
1  delta DAdaptiveCruiseControl after
2      DElectronicStabilityControl && !DFourWheelDrive {
3    modify component BrakingSystem {
4      add port in AccelerateCommand accelfromacc,
5              in BrakeCommand brakefromacc,
6              in RainIntensity rainsensor;
7      add component SignalHandler;
8      connect accel -> SignalHandler.accelfromdriver;
9      connect brake -> SignalHandler.brakefromdriver;
10   }
11 }
```

Listing 9. Modified delta for adaptive cruise control system

4   Refactoring Delta-oriented Product Lines

As we can observe in the previous section, evolving a delta-oriented product line includes the addition and removal of deltas and the addition and removal of product configurations. This may lead to a degeneration of the product line structure, e.g., deltas are factually separated, but always applied together, or sequences of deltas are always applied to the core without generating individual products. While this is not a problem for the generated product variants themselves, it unnecessarily complicates the product line structure and hinders further evolution and maintenance.

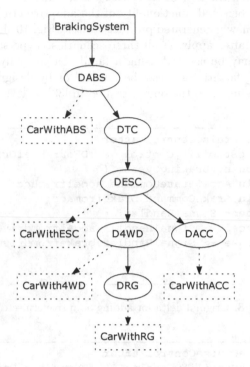

Fig. 10. Brake controller product line structure after evolution

Refactoring [11] is a well-known technique on the programming language level to improve the structure of code without changing its semantical meaning. The same idea can also be applied to product lines realized with Δ-MontiArc. *Product line refactorings* aim at reducing the overall complexity of the product line structure and at the same time increasing its comprehensibility. This is achieved by carefully changing the structure of a product line, but preserving the set of products that can be generated. Changes of the structure are accomplished by modifications of

1. the set of available deltas,
2. the content of existing deltas,
3. the application order constraints attached to deltas, and
4. the set of variant configurations.

In this section, we propose exemplary refactoring strategies to maintain the quality of the product line structure after product line evolution. In particular, we consider the *Compose-Deltas-Refactoring* where deltas that are always applied together are merged, the *Merge-With-Core-Refactoring* where deltas are integrated in the core to form a new core and *Merge-With-Core-Refactoring With Inverse Deltas* that extends the possibilities of the former refactoring.

This set of refactorings is not complete. Depending on the structure of a product line, more refactoring strategies might be possible.

Compose Deltas-Refactoring. The Compose-Deltas-Refactoring merges the content of a sequence of deltas and forms a new delta that contains the combined modifications of the delta sequence.

Situation: The precondition for this refactoring is that we have a sequence of deltas that are always applied together and where the intermediate products after applying any prefix of the sequence do not correspond to a supported product variant.

Mechanics: The Compose Deltas-Refactoring is carried out as follows:

1. Identify a sequence of deltas $D_1, ..., D_n$ satisfying the above conditions.
2. Construct a new delta D_n containing the modifications of the delta sequence:
   (a) Merge the modification operations of the composed deltas into D_n by putting all delta operations in sequence, starting from D_1 and ending with D_n. Delta operations targeting the same architectural element can be composed to a single operation. For example, if a component is first added, then removed in a subsequent delta, and finally added again, the three operations can be replaced by a single add operation.
   (b) Compute the new application order constraint AOC_n of D_n which is the union of the application order constraints of the merged deltas $AOC_1, ..., AOC_n$ where references to the deltas $D_1, ..., D_n$ are removed.
3. Adjust all supported product configurations that include the delta sequence $D_1, ..., D_n$ to only include D_n.
4. Remove $D_1, ..., D_{n-1}$ from the delta model, since they are no longer used to generate any product variant.

Effect: By the Compose-Deltas-Refactoring, product generation is simplified as only one delta instead of a sequence of deltas has to be applied. Additionally, the complexity of the product line decreases since deltas that are no longer required after the refactoring can be removed.

```
1  delta DElectronicStabilityControl after
2      DTractionControl && !DFourWheelDrive {
3    modify component BrakingSystem {
4      add port in LateralAcceleration lateralaccel;
5      replace component stabilizer with component ESC
             stabilizer;
6    }
7  }
```

Listing 11. Delta for adding an electronic stability control system

Example: In our running example, the deltas DTractionControl (set Lst. 2) and DElectronicStabilityControl (see Lst. 11) are always used together

```
1  delta DElectronicStabilityControl after
2      DAntiLockBrakingSystem && !DFourWheelDrive{
3    modify component BrakingSystem {
4      add port in AccelerateCommand accel,
5              in LateralAcceleration lateralaccel;
6      add component ESC stabilizer;
7
8      connect brakefunction.wheelpressure1 ->
9        stabilizer.fromabs1;
10     connect brakefunction.wheelpressure2 ->
11       stabilizer.fromabs2;
12     connect brakefunction.wheelpressure3 ->
13       stabilizer.fromabs3;
14     connect brakefunction.wheelpressure4 ->
15       stabilizer.fromabs4;
16   }
17 }
```

Listing   12.   Delta   composed   from   `DTractionControl`   and `DElectronicStabilityControl`

and the intermediate product after applying delta `DTractionControl` is not a supported product variant (see Fig. 10). To simplify the structure, these two deltas may be composed to a single delta which is again called `DElectronicStabilityControl` and shown in Lst. 12. It contains the delta operations of the two original deltas for adding the ports `accel` and `lateralaccel` and the respective connections. For the component `stabilizer`, there is only one delta operation adding the version of the component introduced by delta `DElectronicStabilityControl`. Delta `DTractionControl` adds subcomponent `stabilizer` to `BrakingSystem` (l. 5) that is replaced subsequently in the original delta `DElectronicStabilityControl` by another subcomponent (l. 4). Hence, in the composed delta it suffices to add the new version of the component, such that redundant delta operations can be removed. The new application order constraint of the delta `DElectronicStabilityControl` is (`DAntiLockBrakingSystem && !DFourWheelDrive`), since a reference to delta `DTractionControl` is no longer required. Afterwards, all product configurations containing the delta `DTractionControl` are adapted to only include the new version of delta `DElectronicStabilityControl` and delta `DTractionControl` is removed.

Merge-With-Core-Refactoring. The Merge-With-Core-Refactoring merges the core of a product line with the content of deltas to create a new core model.

Situation: After product line evolution, it can happen that the core itself is not a valid product anymore. All product variant configurations contain the same subset of deltas that transform the outdated core to a valid product variant.

Mechanics: The Merge-With-Core-Refactoring is carried out as follows:

1. If the core itself is no supported product variant, identify a delta sequence $D_1, ..., D_n$ that is directly applied to the core such that the intermediate products are also no supported product variants.
2. Apply the deltas $D_1, ..., D_n$ to the core to create a new core for the product line.
3. Adjust supported product variants by removing the deltas $D_1, ..., D_n$.
4. Adjust application conditions of remaining deltas by removing the deltas $D_1, ..., D_n$.
5. Remove the deltas $D_1, ..., D_n$ that are now integrated into the core from the product line.

Effect: After applying this refactoring, the core is valid product again. By reducing the amount of available deltas, comprehensibility of the product line has been increased while decreasing overall complexity.

```
1  component BrakingSystem {
2    autoconnect port;
3
4    port
5      in BrakeCommand brake,
6      out BrakePressure wheelpressure1,
7      out BrakePressure wheelpressure2,
8      out BrakePressure wheelpressure3,
9      out BrakePressure wheelpressure4,
10     in WheelSensor wheelspeed1,
11     in WheelSensor wheelspeed2,
12     in WheelSensor wheelspeed3,
13     in WheelSensor wheelspeed4;
14
15     component ABS brakefunction;
16 }
```

Listing 13. Core containing delta DAntiLockBrakingSystem

Example: In our case example (see Fig. 10), the core does not represent a supported product variant any more. Delta DAntiLockBrakingSystem has to be applied to the core before we obtain the product variant CarWithABS. Hence, the delta DAntiLockBrakingSystem can be integrated into the core. Fig. 14 shows the structure of the product line after applying the Merge-With-Core-Refactoring and the previous Compose-Deltas-Refactoring. The new core architecture is shown in Lst. 13.

Merge-With-Core-Refactoring with Inverse Deltas. In some cases, it can be useful to integrate a sequence of deltas into the core, although there is a product variant that is represented by the existing core.

Situation: A reason for this scenario may be that in the future the new core will become the basis for product development, but the old core should still

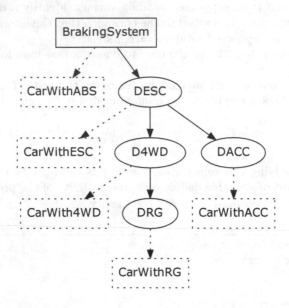

Fig. 14. Deltas and configurations after two refactorings

be maintained for a transitional period of time. After this time, it should be possible to easily remove the old core from the product line. The respective sequence of deltas can already be integrated into the new core, if the old core is reconstructable as long as necessary.

Mechanics: This transformation of the product line can be achieved using inverse deltas. An *inverse delta* [15] is a delta which reverts modifications carried out by another delta. An inverse delta of some existing delta is created by changing add operations to remove operations and vice versa. Modification operations have to be handled separately depending on the structure they alter. In [15], we show that for every delta in Δ-MontiArc a corresponding inverse delta exists.

A Merge-With-Core-Refactoring with Inverse Deltas is performed as follows (where the first 4 steps perform a Merge-With-Core-Refactoring):

1. Identify a delta sequence $D_1, ..., D_n$ which should be integrated into the core. The core represents an existing product, while there are no intermediate products generated by the delta sequence that correspond to supported product variants.
2. Apply the deltas $D_1, ..., D_n$ to the core to create a new core for the product line.
3. Update the remaining product configurations and the application order constraints of the remaining deltas by removing any references to the deltas $D_1, ..., D_n$.
4. Remove the deltas $D_1, ..., D_n$ from the product line.

5. Create an inverse delta for the sequence of deltas $D_1, ..., D_n$ by inverting the delta operations of the delta that is obtained by composing the sequence of deltas $D_1, ..., D_n$ (as described in the Compose-Deltas-Refactoring). The application order constraint of the inverse delta is the negation of all other deltas such that the inverse delta is always applied first in any product configuration. This delta transforms the new core to the old core. Although the application order constraint for the delta is not needed for this particular scenario, it is useful for further evolution steps.

6. Add a product configuration for obtaining the old core which only contains the inverse delta.

Effect: The refactoring merges a set of mostly used deltas with the core. For products that do not contain these deltas, the old core may be reconstructed by applying the created inverse delta. It is usefull, if the refactored deltas are part of the majority of product variants and the other products will be removed from the product line anytime soon. This way, development of new product variants is eased, as they may be build up on a richer core model.

```
1  delta DInverse after !DAdaptiveCruiseControl
2       && !DFourWheelDrive && !DReductionGear {
3    modify component BrakingSystem {
4      remove port accel;
5      remove port lateralaccel;
6      remove component stabilizer;
7
8      disconnect brakefunction.wheelpressure1 ->
9          stabilizer.fromabs1;
10     disconnect brakefunction.wheelpressure2 ->
11         stabilizer.fromabs2;
12     disconnect brakefunction.wheelpressure3 ->
13         stabilizer.fromabs3;
14     disconnect brakefunction.wheelpressure4 ->
15         stabilizer.fromabs4;
16   }
17 }
```

Listing 15. Inverse delta for delta DElectronicStabilityControl

Example: Assume that the variant CarWithESC should become the new core since every new car in the near future should be equipped with an electronic stability control. Hence, delta DElectronicStabilityControl shown in Lst. 12 can be integrated into the core. The new core shown in Lst. 13 is now serving as basis for all product variant generation. All product variants that previously used delta DElectronicStabiliyControl are adjusted as well as the application order constraints of the remaining deltas. The delta DElectronicStabiliyControl is removed from the product line. However,

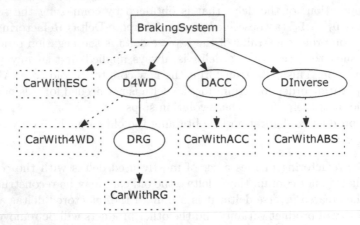

Fig. 16. Deltas and configurations after refactoring with inverse deltas

variant `CarWithABS` should still be supported for a transitional period of time. Hence, an inverse delta is required that reverts the modifications of delta `DElectronicStabilityControl`. This new delta `DInverse` is shown in Lst. 15. It is added to the product line, and a new product configuration for the product variant `CarWithABS` is added that applies the inverse delta to the new core. The resulting product line is depicted in Fig. 16.

The concept of inverse deltas is very flexible. Hence, it is possible to always include features into the core architecture and add inverse deltas to the product line to remove these features in order to generate specific product variants not containing these features. This is particularly advantageous if the core architecture is one of the main products of the product line since it can be thoroughly validated and verified using standard single application engineering techniques.

5   Comparison to Annotative Variability Modeling

The predominantly used approach in industrial applications for modeling architectural variability is annotative variability modeling [39]. Our experience shows that annotative variability modeling is the easiest way to add variability information to an existing software product. However, a subsequent change to another variability modeling method is mostly not realized since this is often very time consuming. Annotative variability modeling is based on a 150%-model capturing all possible variability and annotating specific elements with the variant(s) in which they are included. Elements of the core architecture have no annotations. In order to derive a particular variant, all elements annotated with only different variants are removed.

In order to compare Δ-MontiArc and its capabilities to capture product line evolution with annotative variability modeling, we realized all scenarios in Sec. 3 and Sec. 4 with Δ-MontiArc and also with annotative variability modeling.

We decided to compare Δ-MontiArc with an annotative modeling approach for MontiArc, since annotative variability modeling is the main variability modeling approach used current industrial practice. An annotative MontiArc dialect offers a good comparability to Δ-MontiArc, as both langauges are based on the same syntax and exclusively differ in its variability modeling technique. For our comparison, we do not consider compositional variability modeling approaches, such based on aspect-oriented implementation techniques [1,10], since these approaches do not natively support extractive product line development and the removal of modeling elements. The ability to explicitly represent removals is, however, essential for the direct representation of product line evolution without considering additional changes in the model structure, e.g., by refactorings before the evolution is carried out. Tool support for both modeling approaches, annotative and delta-based, is provided by the MontiCore framework for developing domain-specific languages [13] by extending the existing implementation of MontiArc [18].

Annotative Variability Modeling in MontiArc. For realizing annotative variability modeling in MontiArc, each architectural element is annotated by a stereotype denoting the variant(s) in which it is included. Variable parts of an architecture are ports, subcomponents, and connectors. Hence, these elements may be annotated to assign them to variants. The excerpt of an annotated MontiArc model in Lst. 17 shows an example of these stereotype annotations for architectural elements. Line 2 contains an incoming port without any annotation indicating that this element is part of the core architecture. The incoming port in l. 4 is only needed for bikes. The corresponding annotation in l. 3 states that this incoming port is only used in the variant BikeWithABS.

```
1  port
2    in BrakeCommand brake,
3    <<variant = "BikeWithABS">>
4    in BrakeCommand brakerear;
```

Listing 17. Example of model element annotation

In annotative variability modeling, *adding a product variant* to the product line means to add new architectural elements to the 150%-model and to annotate these and already existing architectural elements with the newly added variant. This can require to change the 150%-model in several places and might become fairly complex not to miss necessary additions. In delta modeling, simply new deltas and product configurations can be added that locally encapsulate the necessary modifications.

Removing variants in the annotative approach amounts to removing the respective variant annotations and also the architectural elements that are no longer required by any other variant. Here, again changes all over the variability model may be necessary. Also, it has to be taken care that architectural elements belonging to the core without annotations are not accidentally removed and that architectural elements of removed variants are not silently added to the core. In delta modeling, variants are removed locally by changing the respective product configurations and deleting redundant deltas.

The *modification of existing variants* in the annotative approach can have an impact on several architectural elements. New elements are added and annotated with the specific variant and redundant elements are removed. This is particularly difficult, since variants which are not affected by the modification should not be changed. In delta modeling, only the content of specific deltas has to be changed while the application order constraints, the other deltas and the product configurations remain unchanged.

The *refactorings* presented in Sec. 4 are specifically tailored to Δ-MontiArc. In particular, the Compose-Deltas-Refactoring and the Merge-With-Core-Refactoring with Inverse Deltas can only be applied in delta modeling. However, also in annotative variability modeling, it is possible to move certain variants to the core. This requires to determine all architectural elements which should belong to the core in the future. In a subsequent step, all annotations referring to these variants can be removed. This again might be a fairly complex and error-prone task, since it requires modifications in all parts of the variability model where architectural elements belonging to the considered variants occur. In delta modeling, only the deltas which should be included in the core have to be integrated, and application conditions of other deltas and specific product configurations can be changed locally.

Comparison with Δ-MontiArc. The modeling of the product line evolution scenarios in the annotative approach is very time consuming and error-prone since changes to product variants or the core architecture potentially require changes in all parts of the product line model. For every architectural modeling element, it has to be decided in which specific variants it appears. In delta modeling, changes are encapsulated modularly in deltas and can be performed locally. While in the annotative variability modeling approach, variability modeling is mixed with modeling of the functional architecture, in delta modeling, variability is a first-class entity. Deltas only focus on the representation of variability and are, thus, easier to comprehend and to evolve.

In order to quantitatively compare Δ-MontiArc with annotative modeling, we consider all implementations which are modeled in out case study. In total, we look at seven different product line scenarios: the base scenario is the initial product line depicted in Fig. 5; the first scenario is the product line after adding the product variant `CarWithRG`; the second scenario corresponds to the product line after removing variants which is depicted in Fig. 10 (p. 192); the third scenario is the product line after modification of variant `CarWithACC`. Scenarios 4 to 6 correspond to the three different refactoring strategies: the fourth scenario is the product line after the Compose-Deltas-Refactoring; the fifth scenario is the product line after also applying the Merge-With-Core-Refactoring as it is depicted in Fig. 14 (p. 196); the sixth scenario is the product line after the Merge-With-Core-Refactoring With Inverse Deltas depicted in Fig. 16 (p. 198).

Table 18. Quantitative comparisson of Δ-MontiArc and annotative modeling for temporal variability

| | base | | scenario 1 | | scenario 2 | | scenario 3 | |
	Δ	|150%	Δ	|150%	Δ	|150%	Δ	|150%
#components	6		7		6		5	
#ports	67		75		56		55	
#connections	6		10		10		10	
#variants	8		9		5		5	
#chars	4209	4156	5048	5111	3887	4056	3803	3956
#varchars	2437	1591	2954	1916	2238	1472	2264	1456
rel. variant inf.	57%	38%	58%	37%	57%	36%	59%	36%
#files	20	6	23	7	17	6	16	5
#maxchars	474	2087	474	2660	438	2284	438	2334
avg. chars p. file	210	692	219	730	228	676	237	791

Table 19. Quantitative comparisson of Δ-MontiArc and annotative modeling for refactoring scenarios

| | scenario 4 | | scenario 5 | | scenario 6 | |
	Δ	|150%	Δ	|150%	Δ	|150%
#components	5		5		5	
#ports	55		55		55	
#connections	10		10		10	
#variants	5		5		5	
#chars	3586	3956	3273	3219	3448	3219
#varchars	2047	1456	1649	719	1514	719
rel. variant inf.	57%	36%	50%	22%	43%	22%
#files	15	5	14	5	14	5
#maxchars	448	2334	438	1865	645	1865
avg. chars p. file	239	791	233	643	246	643

Tab. 18 and 19 show the results of our evaluation. For the overall sizes of the product lines in the different scenarios, we counted the total number of components (#components), ports (#ports), explicit connections (#connections), and supported product variants (#variants). Implicit connections created by the autoconnect statements are not counted. In the table, we see that all examples are mid-sized with 5 to 7 components and 5 to 9 supported product variants.

For quantitatively comparing the way variability is encoded in delta modeling and annotative variability modeling, we measured the overall sizes of the models, the total amount of variability information required to express all product variants, and the relative amount of variability information compared to the information necessary for encoding of functionality. We computed the overall model sizes by counting each visible character (except for comments) in the product line model (#chars). Since MontiArc allows many different formatting styles, visible characters give a more accurate measure of the model size than lines of

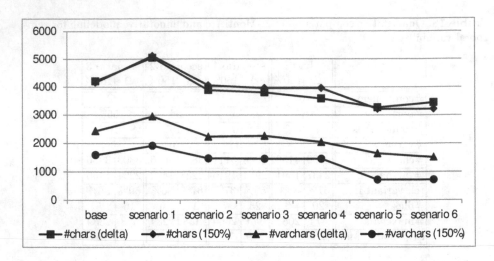

Fig. 20. Number of characters for model and variability representation

code. Also for the variability information, we counted the number of characters (#varchars) used for specifying deltas in Δ-MontiArc-models and the characters used for annotations in the annotative variability model. To compare the ratio between variability and functional parts of the models, the relative amount of variant information is calculated (rel. variant inf.) by dividing the number of characters used for encoding variability by the total number of characters used in the overall model. These metrics are suitable, as both languages use the same syntax and exclusively differ in modeling variability.

Fig. 20 visualizes the overall number of characters used for representing the product line architectures in the different scenarios and the number of characters used to specify variability, both for delta modeling and annotative variability modeling. Roughly, we can say that the sizes of both models are the same for both variability modeling approaches. Adding product variants in the first scenario increases the size of the model and also the amount of variability information in both approaches. Removing variants decreases the size of the model and the variability information. Modification of an existing product variant only changes the size of the model and the amount of variability information slightly. In the fourth scenario, which is the first refactoring scenario, we see the advantage for delta modeling if deltas are combined. The overall size of the model after refactoring is lower than for the annotative variability model. Since the Compose-Deltas-Refactoring and the Merge-With-Core-Refactoring with Inverse Deltas are not applicable for annotative variability modeling, the figures do not change from the third to the fourth scenario and from the fifth to the sixth scenario. The Merge-With-Core-Refactoring in the fifth scenario reduces the size of the model and also the amount of variability information for both approaches such that the model size is almost equal again. In scenario 6, after the Merge-With-Core-Refactoring with Inverse Deltas the size of the delta model is larger since the inverse delta is added to the product line model.

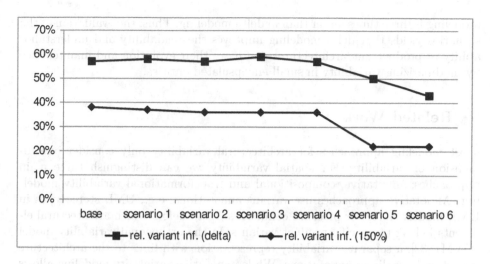

Fig. 21. Relative amount of variability information

The ratios of variability information compared to the overall model size stay roughly the same for both approaches independent of the evolution scenario for the base and the first four scenarios as it is visualized in Fig. 21. Only, when variants are merged into the core the ratio drops. The reason for this is that by merging deltas with the core or removing annotations variability information is removed while the overall size of the model stays the same. In general, the ratio of variability information is higher for delta modeling than for annotative variability modeling. From the figures, delta modeling seems to be very similar to annotative variability modeling when comparing the mere model size and its changes for the different evolution scenarios. However, when looking at the ratio of variability information, we can see that in annotative variability modeling roughly one third of all characters are used for expressing variability by annotations. If we now consider that in the annotative variability modeling approach we only have one 150%-model of all possible variability and that variability information is spread all over the model, having a third of all characters used for annotations renders the model very complex and difficult to comprehend and evolve. In contrast, in delta modeling, variability information is encapsulated in deltas which can be evolved locally.

To further analyze understandability and maintainability, we measured the average sizes of the files which make up the product line models for the single scenarios (see Tab. 18 and 19). A product line model is distributed over several files (#files) where each file defines a component, a delta or parts of it. In general, large files are harder to understand, to change and to maintain. Hence, we measured the maximum (#maxchars) and average characters per file (avg. chars p. file). We can see that in delta modeling the number of files is generally higher which results from the fact that each delta and the contained components are stored in separate files while in annotative variability modeling only each component has a separate file. Overall, the size of a file in annotative variability modeling is three times larger than in delta modeling. Thus, the evaluation of the scenarios yields that delta modeling improves the readability and understandability of product line architectures and eases their evolution and maintenance by modularizing variability in small encapsulated entities.

6 Related Work

Most modeling approaches for architectural variability only consider one dimension of variability. For spatial variability, we can distinguish three main approaches: annotative, compositional and transformational variability modeling. Annotative approaches use variant annotations, e.g., UML stereotypes in UML models [40,12] or presence conditions [7], to define which architectural elements belong to specific product variants. In the orthogonal variability model (OVM) [32], a separate variability representation with links to the architecture model replaces direct annotations. While annotative variability modeling allows fine-grained modifications, it relies on a monolithic product line representation.

Compositional approaches for modeling architectural variability [39] capture architectural variation by selecting specific component variants. In [10], Plastic partial components [31] model component variability by extending partially defined components with variation points and associated variants. Hierarchical variability modeling for software product lines [17] aims at combining component variability with the component hierarchy to foster component-based development of diverse systems during architectural design. Compositional variability modeling allows a modular description of variability, but limits the impact of changes to the applied composition technique.

Transformational approaches, such as delta modeling [6], represent variability by transformation of a base architectural model. In the common variability language (CVL) [19], elements of the base model are substituted according to a set of pre-defined rules. In [21], graph transformation rules capture the variability of a single kernel model comprising the commonalities of all systems. In [20], architectural variability is represented by change sets containing additions, removals or modifications of components and component connections that are applied to a base line architecture. All these approaches are only consider variability in space as the previous versions of Δ-MontiArc [16,14].

Temporal variability is usually specified with two mechanisms [29]: logical assertions or graph transformations. In the assertion-based approaches, e.g., [30,38], a transformation is characterized by a pre-condition defining when a transformation can be applied and a post-conditions specifying the properties that are ensured by the transformation. In graph transformation-based approaches, the product variants are represented by graphs. System evolution is specified by a graph transformation rule, see e.g. [28]. These approaches, however, represent temporal variability on a meta-level.

In order to be able to reason about architectural evolution, it has to be captured as first-class entity [27]. One approach towards this goal [24] defines new components by explicitly expressing the differences to the old component by adding, deleting, renaming or replacing elements. This is very similar to delta modeling where a delta encapsulates the differences from one product variant to the other. Aspect-oriented composition is also applied to model software architecture evolution [3] expressing variability by weaving selected aspects into a core architecture. However, these approaches only consider architectural evolution.

Refactorings of feature-oriented programming (FOP) product lines are presented in [37]. These refactorings that move fields or types between feature modules are mostly based on classical code refactorings like, e.g., pulling up fields or methods to parent types. In alignment with our approach, the authors suggest refactorings of a product line to be variant-preserving. Hence, such a refactoring only changes the structure of the product line, but not contained variants. However, the presented approach aims at the implementation of a software product line and not at its architecture.

In contrast to the above approaches, product line evolution [9] considers the combination of variability in space and variability in time. Extractive product line engineering [22] develops a product line from a set of legacy applications; the proactive approach aims at evolving an initial product line if new user requirements arise. In the PuLSE product line engineering methodology [4], product line evolution is defined as designated development phase. However, these approaches only focus on terminological issues and development processes. There is some work on feature model evolution [5] and evolution of feature-oriented [2] or aspect-oriented software product line implementations [1,10]. However, evolution in feature-oriented modeling and programming approaches is treated with different linguistic means than spatial variability, mostly due to the fact that features cannot remove model or program entities which is essential for capturing unexpected changes caused by evolution. Hence, a uniform modeling framework for architectural variability in space and in time is missing despite techniques, such as aspect-oriented composition and model transformations, that can factually express both dimensions of variability. Δ-MontiArc fills this gap by representing variability in space and in time as a first-class entity with the same linguistic means.

7   Conclusion

We have proposed Δ-MontiArc, an ADL with native support for variability based on delta modeling. Δ-MontiArc allows expressing architectural variability in space and in time in modular and easily maintainable manner as we demonstrated by a quantitative and qualitative comparison with annotative variability modeling. We presented exemplary refactorings that help cleaning up a degenerated product line. Variability by using delta modeling can also be applied to other modeling languages and is not restricted to modeling software architectures. Behavioral variability within the architectural descriptions can be realized by using deltas on state machines [23] or Java source code [34,36].

For future work, we aim at defining further refactorings that merge deltas with identical modification operations but different application order constraints and vice versa. Scalability and applicability has to be checked based on a more complex industrial-scale examples. We also plan to extend the conceptual ideas of Δ-MontiArc into a seamless software engineering process for software product lines that allows dealing with variability in space and in time by the same techniques.

References

1. Alves, V., Matos Jr., P., Cole, L., Vasconcelos, A., Borba, P., Ramalho, G.: Extracting and Evolving Code in Product Lines with Aspect-Oriented Programming. In: Rashid, A., Aksit, M. (eds.) Transactions on AOSD IV. LNCS, vol. 4640, pp. 117–142. Springer, Heidelberg (2007)
2. Apel, S., Leich, T., Rosenmüller, M., Saake, G.: Combining feature-oriented and aspect-oriented programming to support software evolution. In: RAM-SE, pp. 3–16 (2005)
3. Barais, O., Meur, A.F., Duchien, L., Lawall, J.: Software architecture evolution. In: Software Evolution. Springer (2008)
4. Bayer, J., et al.: PuLSE: a Methodology to Develop Software Product Lines. In: Symposium on Software Reusability (SSR), pp. 122–131 (1999)
5. Botterweck, G., Pleuss, A., Dhungana, D., Polzer, A., Kowalewski, S.: EvoFM: Feature-driven Planning of Product-line Evolution. In: 1st International Workshop on Product Line Approaches in Software Engineering, PLEASE 2010 (2010)
6. Clarke, D., Helvensteijn, M., Schaefer, I.: Abstract Delta Modeling. In: GPCE. Springer (2010)
7. Czarnecki, K., Pietroszek, K.: Verifying Feature-based Model Templates against Well-formedness OCL Constraints. In: Generative Programming and Component Engineering, GPCE (2006)
8. Czarnecki, K., Eisenecker, U.W.: Generative Programming: Methods, Tools, and Applications. Addison-Wesley (2000)
9. Elsner, C., Botterweck, G., Lohmann, D., Schröder-Preikschat, W.: Variability in time - product line variability and evolution revisited. In: VaMoS, pp. 131–137 (2010)
10. Figueiredo, E., Cacho, N., Sant'Anna, C., Monteiro, M., Kulesza, U., Garcia, A., Soares, S., Ferrari, F., Khan, S., Filho, F.C., Dantas, F.: Evolving software product lines with aspects: an empirical study on design stability. In: International Conference on Software engineering (ICSE), pp. 261–270. ACM (2008)
11. Fowler, M., Beck, K., Brant, J., Opdyke, W., Roberts, D.: Refactoring: Improving the Design of Existing Code. Addison-Wesley Professional (1999)
12. Gomaa, H.: Designing Software Product Lines with UML. Addison Wesley (2004)
13. Grönniger, H., Krahn, H., Rumpe, B., Schindler, M., Völkel, S.: MontiCore: a Framework for the Development of Textual Domain Specific Languages. In: 30th International Conference on Software Engineering (ICSE 2008), Leipzig, Germany, May 10-18, Companion Volume (2008)
14. Haber, A., Kutz, T., Rendel, H., Rumpe, B., Schaefer, I.: Delta-oriented Architectural Variability Using MontiCore. In: ECSA 2011 5th European Conference on Software Architecture: Companion Volume. ACM, New York (2011)

15. Haber, A., Kutz, T., Rendel, H., Rumpe, B., Schaefer, I.: Towards a Family-based
    Analysis of Applicability Conditions in Architectural Delta Models. In: Variability
    for You Proceedings of VARY International Workshop affiliated with ACM/IEEE
    14th International Conference on Model Driven Engineering Languages and Sys-
    tems (MODELS 2011). IT University Technical Report Series TR-2011-144, pp.
    43–52. IT University of Copenhagen (October 2011)
16. Haber, A., Rendel, H., Rumpe, B., Schaefer, I.: Delta Modeling for Software Ar-
    chitectures. In: Tagungsband des Dagstuhl-Workshop MBEES: Modellbasierte En-
    twicklung eingebetteterSysteme VII, pp. 1–10. Fortiss GmbH, Munich (2011)
17. Haber, A., Rendel, H., Rumpe, B., Schaefer, I., van der Linden, F.: Hierarchical
    Variability Modeling for Software Architectures. In: Proceedings of International
    Software Product Lines Conference (SPLC 2011). IEEE Computer Society (August
    2011)
18. Haber, A., Ringert, J.O., Rumpe, B.: MontiArc - Architectural Modeling of Inter-
    active Distributed and Cyber-Physical Systems. Tech. Rep. AIB-2012-03, RWTH
    Aachen (February 2012),
    http://aib.informatik.rwth-aachen.de/2012/2012-03.pdf
19. Haugen, Ø., Møller-Pedersen, B., Oldevik, J., Olsen, G., Svendsen, A.: Adding
    Standardized Variability to Domain Specific Languages. In: SPLC (2008)
20. Hendrickson, S.A., van der Hoek, A.: Modeling Product Line Architectures through
    Change Sets and Relationships. In: ICSE (2007)
21. Jayaraman, P., Whittle, J., Elkhodary, A.M., Gomaa, H.: Model Composition in
    Product Lines and Feature Interaction Detection Using Critical Pair Analysis. In:
    Engels, G., Opdyke, B., Schmidt, D.C., Weil, F. (eds.) MODELS 2007. LNCS,
    vol. 4735, pp. 151–165. Springer, Heidelberg (2007)
22. Krueger, C.: Eliminating the Adoption Barrier. IEEE Software 19(4), 29–31 (2002)
23. Lochau, M., Schaefer, I., Kamischke, J., Lity, S.: Incremental Model-Based Testing
    of Delta-Oriented Software Product Lines. In: Brucker, A.D., Julliand, J. (eds.)
    TAP 2012. LNCS, vol. 7305, pp. 67–82. Springer, Heidelberg (2012)
24. McVeigh, A., Kramer, J., Magee, J.: Using resemblance to support component
    reuse and evolution. In: SAVCBS, pp. 49–56 (2006)
25. Medvidovic, N., Taylor, R.: A Classification and Comparison Framework for Soft-
    ware Architecture Description Languages. IEEE Transactions on Software Engi-
    neering (2000)
26. Mens, T., Demeyer, S. (eds.): Software Evolution. Springer (2008)
27. Mens, T., Magee, J., Rumpe, B.: Evolving software architecture descriptions of
    critical systems. IEEE Computer 43(5), 42–48 (2010)
28. Mens, T., Taentzer, G., Runge, O.: Analysing refactoring dependencies using graph
    transformation. Software and System Modeling 6(3), 269–285 (2007)
29. Mens, T., Tourwé, T.: A survey of software refactoring. IEEE Trans. Software
    Eng. 30(2), 126–139 (2004)
30. Opdyke, W.: Refactoring: A Programm Restructuring Aid in Designing Object-
    Oriented Application Frameworks. Ph.D. thesis, Univ. of Illinois at Urbana-
    Champaign (1992)
31. Pérez, J., Díaz, J., Soria, C.C., Garbajosa, J.: Plastic Partial Components: A solu-
    tion to support variability in architectural components. In: WICSA/ECSA (2009)
32. Pohl, K., Böckle, G., van der Linden, F.: Software Product Line Engineering -
    Foundations, Principles, and Techniques. Springer, Heidelberg (2005)
33. Schaefer, I., Bettini, L., Damiani, F.: Compositional type-checking for delta-
    oriented programming. In: Intl. Conference on Aspect-oriented Software Devel-
    opment (AOSD 2011). ACM Press (2011)

34. Schaefer, I., Damiani, F.: Pure delta-oriented programming. In: Second International Workshop on Feature-oriented Software Development (FOSD 2010) (2010)
35. Schaefer, I.: Variability Modelling for Model-Driven Development of Software Product Lines. In: VaMoS (2010)
36. Schaefer, I., Bettini, L., Bono, V., Damiani, F., Tanzarella, N.: Delta-Oriented Programming of Software Product Lines. In: Bosch, J., Lee, J. (eds.) SPLC 2010. LNCS, vol. 6287, pp. 77–91. Springer, Heidelberg (2010)
37. Schulze, S., Thüm, T., Kuhlemann, M., Saake, G.: Variant-preserving refactoring in feature-oriented software product lines. In: VaMoS, pp. 73–81 (2012)
38. Tichelaar, S., Ducasse, S., Demeyer, S., Nierstrasz, O.: A meta-model for language-independent refactoring. In: Proc. of Principles of Software Evolution, pp. 154–164 (2000)
39. Völter, M., Groher, I.: Product Line Implementation using Aspect-Oriented and Model-Driven Software Development. In: SPLC (2007)
40. Ziadi, T., Hëlouët, L., Jézéquel, J.-M.: Towards a UML Profile for Software Product Lines. In: van der Linden, F.J. (ed.) PFE 2003. LNCS, vol. 3014, pp. 129–139. Springer, Heidelberg (2004)

Multi-view Modeling and Pragmatics in 2020*

Position Paper on Designing
Complex Cyber-Physical Systems

Reinhard von Hanxleden[1], Edward A. Lee[2],
Christian Motika[1], and Hauke Fuhrmann[3]

[1] Christian-Albrechts-Universität zu Kiel, Department of Computer Science
Olshausenstraße 40, 24118 Kiel, Germany
{rvh,cmot}@informatik.uni-kiel.de
[2] University of California at Berkeley, EECS Department
545Q Cory Hall, University of California, Berkeley CA 94720-1770
eal@eecs.berkeley.edu
[3] Funkwerk Information Technologies GmbH
Edisonstraße 3, 24145 Kiel, Germany
Hauke.Fuhrmann@funkwerk-it.com

Abstract. *Multi-view modeling* refers to a system designer constructing distinct and separate models of the same system to model different (semantic) aspects of a system. *Modeling pragmatics* also entails constructing different views of a system, but here the focus is on syntactic/pragmatic aspects, with an emphasis on designer productivity, and the views are constructed automatically by filtering and drawing algorithms.

In this paper, we argue that both approaches will have growing influence on model-based design, in particular for complex cyber-physical systems, and we identify a number of general developments that seem likely to contribute to this until 2020. This includes notably the trend towards domain-specific modeling and agile development, novel input devices, and the move to the cloud. We also report on preliminary practical results in this area with two modeling environments, Ptolemy and KIELER, and the lessons learned from their combined usage.

1 Introduction

A question prominently asked in computer science in model-based design is what kind of *model* (of computation) is particularly suitable for a given design problem. We here instead focus on the question of what *view* of a model might be best for a given task. When a designer creates two different models of the same system, e. g., one model for functional validation and another for deployment, this is referred to this as *multi-view modeling*. In this paper, we take a broader look at multi-view modeling than that traditional interpretation, and try to extrapolate recent developments, including existing products, into the mid-term

---

* This work was funded in part by the Program for the Future Economy of Schleswig-Holstein and the European Regional Development Fund (ERDF).

R. Calinescu and D. Garlan (Eds.): Monterey Workshop 2012, LNCS 7539, pp. 209–223, 2012.

future. We target the year 2020 as a time frame when not only the basic technologies are in place (in fact, much of these technologies are in place already today, as this paper aims to illustrate), but also have found their way into mainstream modeling tools and practices. We do so with particular consideration of *modeling pragmatics*, which refers to the practical aspects of handling graphical system models of complex systems, encompassing a range of activities such as editing, browsing or simulating models [8].

Contributions and Outline. We advocate in this paper to expand multi-view modeling to constructing different model views even if they refer to the same semantic aspects. We will argue in the following that this approach meshes well with current trends towards agile, domain-adapted modeling, and propose to employ *usage-specific views* and *hybrid views*. These do not only consider the domain of an application, but also the current design activity a modeler is pursuing (Sec. 3). This approach has an immediate benefit for designer productivity, and thus supports "pragmatics-aware modeling." We also investigate what consequences the trend towards "post-PC devices" and their novel user interfaces might have on today's modeling activities, and propose *touch-based editing and browsing* to increase designer productivity (Sec. 4). Furthermore, in the context of the increasingly pervasive "move to the cloud," we propose an *actor-oriented, distributed tooling* approach (Sec. 5). This tooling approach should foster synergies and could also support agility as addressed in Sec. 3. We conclude in Sec. 6.

2   Background and Related Work

A *graphical model* is a model that can have a graphical representation, like a Unified Modeling Language (UML) class model. A *view* onto the model is a concrete drawing of the model, sometimes also *diagram* or *notation model*, e. g., a UML class diagram. The abstract structure of the model leaving all graphical information behind is the *semantical* or *domain model*, or just *model* in short. E. g., a class model can also be serialized as an XML tree. Hence, the *model* conforms to the abstract syntax, while the *view* conforms to the concrete syntax. Fig. 1 shows three different views of the same class model.

Model-Driven Engineering (MDE), or alternatively Model Driven Software Development (MDSD), denotes software development processes where models are central artifacts that represent software entities at a high abstraction level [5]. *Multimodeling* is the act of combining diverse models, to model, e. g., different parts of a software system or physical systems [6]. One form of multimodeling is multi-view modeling, as exemplified in Model-Integrated Computing (MIC) [21].

Multimodeling is also closely related to the single vs. multiple model principle discussed by Paige and Ostroff [19]. The ISO/IEC/IEEE 42010:2011 standard [12], which is the latest edition of the original IEEE Std 1471:2000, *Recommended Practice for Architectural Description of Software-intensive Systems*, also defines *architecture views* (or simply, *views*) to address one or more of the

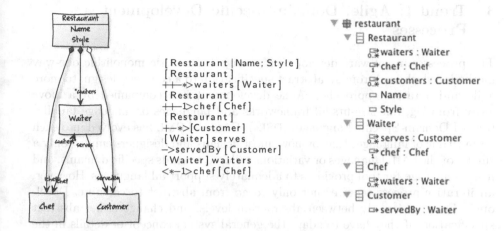

Fig. 1. Different Representations of a Class Model: Diagram, Text and Tree View (created with yUML (http://yuml.me) and Eclipse)

concerns held by the system's stakeholders, as no single view adequately captures all stakeholder concerns. Multimodeling is also related to *aspect-oriented modeling* [22], which focusses on identifying cross-cutting concerns; a central concept here are *join points*, which represent a concern element, i.e., an identifiable element of the language used to capture a concern. Brooks et al. [2] have also advocated the usage of multimodeling to separate concerns during a model-based design flow, e.g., to separate functional aspects from deployment and verification. This is particularly relevant in the real of cyber-physical systems, which have to consider physical deployment domains as well as the embedded control, and whose growing complexity necessitates a clean separation of concerns. The designer should be able to specify different aspects of the same system independently, to allow a clean separation of concerns while keeping a model consistent. However, multi-view modeling can be applied at different levels and in very different ways. For example, it can refer to the animation of a model during a simulation, or to the alternation between graphical and textual representations, or indeed also to the alternation between a monolithic Statechart model and an explicitly hierarchical syntax, as discussed in this paper.

However, Brooks et al. concluded: *At this point, it is still largely up to the modeler to construct different views of the same system. How best to harness a modeling system to assist the user with this task still seems to be a largely open problem.* While this problem still is certainly not completely solved yet, we here argue that modeling tools in 2020 should have made significant progress towards that goal. In fact, already today there are significant steps in that direction. To illustrate that point, we re-use in Sec. 3 the traffic light example from Brooks et al. [2], and present different views that are automatically synthesized.

3   Trend 1: Agile, Domain-Specific Development Processes

The processes in software development change from static monolithic one-way methods, which lead from an abstract specification to a concrete design, to more agile and iterative approaches. Agile development is accompanied by a move away from big, one-size-fits-all frameworks and languages or language families toward Domain-Specific Languages (DSLs). E. g., the UML has evolved into such a multitude of languages that by now, most designs and designers employ only a subset of the UML languages or variations tailored towards specific domains, and it is a challenge for tool providers to adequately support all languages. However, an iterative process requires not only to go from abstract to concrete. Developers jump arbitrarily between abstraction levels, and change either abstract specifications if they have to adapt the general system concept or details in the implementation if one iteration's prototype milestone needs to be finished. This *round-trip engineering* does not mesh very well with today's modeling tools.

3.1   2020 Vision: Usage-Specific Views

Agile processes require agile and lean tool support and languages that are not only tailored towards particular domains, but also towards particular design activities. This meshes with the concept of DSLs, which are also called "task-specific" languages [16], even if this interpretation is less common than the "(application) domain-specific" interpretation. Note that this does not necessarily require the invention of a host of new languages, but rather expresses that we want to be able to switch model views according to different model usages, and that these different views may employ different (graphical or textual) languages. We refer to this concept as *usage-specific views*.

To illustrate, consider the traffic light control example presented in Fig. 2, adapted from Brooks et al. [2]. The example is shown in three variants, which at first sight look quite different and employ different visual languages. The first variant, shown in Fig. 2a, employs a SyncCharts [1] model, developed in the Kiel Integrated Environment for Layout Eclipse Rich Client (KIELER)[1] modeling environment, to describe the behavior of the traffic light. As can be seen, there are two modes of operation, Normal and Error, and for each mode the behavior of the car light and the pedestrian light is specified. This *behavioral view* might be appropriate for a first specification of the traffic light. Fig. 2c now uses a very different language, or rather set of languages, namely a hierarchical combination of synchronous data flow with state machines, shown in the Ptolemy II[2] tool. This *structural view* (or *deployment view*) emphasizes what components the traffic light consists of, namely the car light and the pedestrian light, and through which signals they interact with the environment and with each other. However, even though these two views use different languages that have different semantics

---

[1] http://www.informatik.uni-kiel.de/rtsys/kieler/

[2] http://ptolemy.eecs.berkeley.edu/

and may be considered different models of a traffic light, they do express the same behavior, i. e., the semantics of these two models coincide. In fact, in this case the Ptolemy model that underlies the structural view has been synthesized automatically from the SyncChart model that underlies the behavioral view, with the original purpose of simulating the SyncChart model [17]. So, one may say that the model shown in Fig. 2c enhances the model from Fig. 2a in at least two ways, namely with a simulation capability and by illustrating to the user the structure of the traffic light.

A common criticism of SyncCharts (and Statecharts in general) is that they, due to their signal broadcast semantics, have only implied, hidden signal communication links. One possible answer to this is the structural view just presented. However, we also want to propose another, third alternative, which we will refer to as *hybrid view*. To that end, we now examine another means to better understand the *references* in a graphical model. The graphical representation depicts the main model objects as nodes, where the containment relations can be reflected by hierarchy in the model and containment of graphical symbols like rectangles. Therefore, the diagram exhibits intrinsic properties, and these properties directly correspond to properties in the represented domain [10]. Explicit connections display some other relations between the model objects. However, there is typically a set of model attributes that is hidden in simple property dialogs or simply represented by a label in the graphical representation. Relations between those attributes are usually not visible, such as the signal-based, name-bound broadcast communication in a Statechart.

3.2 Dual Modeling

We propose a dynamic extension of the graphical representation by its *dual model*, i. e., a graphical representation of the relations between referenced objects where this reference is not yet visualized. This dual model then results in a *hybrid view*, which emphasizes multiple semantic aspects of a model at once. The hybrid view in Fig. 2b reveals the rather simple communication of the traffic light example. The Error state has no inter-communication, hence focus&context [20] automatically collapses it. The structural view in Fig. 2c also shows this communication explicitly, however, the simplicity is more obvious in the hybrid view; this may also be due to the visible hierarchy there.

The *dual model* methodology should not only be helpful for Statecharts, but applies to very different types of models. References to other model parts are quite common where an explicit graphical representation is omitted for the sake of clarity in the original model. Two examples are:

Class Diagrams. The attributes of a class are presented more or less textually including the type of the field. However, the type may also reference another class or a data type definition node in the model. The dual model of a class diagram would reveal the data type usages of the classes and their attributes.

Ptolemy II. In Ptolemy one can define arbitrary parameters of actors. They are represented by an unconnected node only showing the key and the

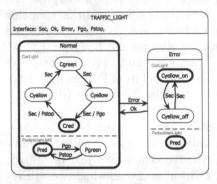
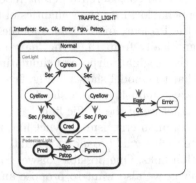

(a) Behavioral view (SyncChart)

(b) Hybrid view, revealing the communication via signals (SyncChart with dual modeling and focus&context filtering).

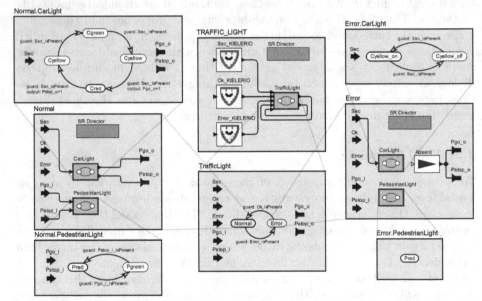

(c) Structural view (hierarchical data-flow + automata, from Motika et al. [17])

Fig. 2. Traffic light example, usage-specific views

value of the parameter. Then they get referenced by arbitrary expressions in Ptolemy's expression language, which is just text. They are often used to map parameters of lower-level actors to the top-level actor. The dual model could explicitly show which objects use which parameters. An example montage is shown in Fig. 3. Technically this would work best if the editor would use visible hierarchy, which the Ptolemy editor Vergil does not.

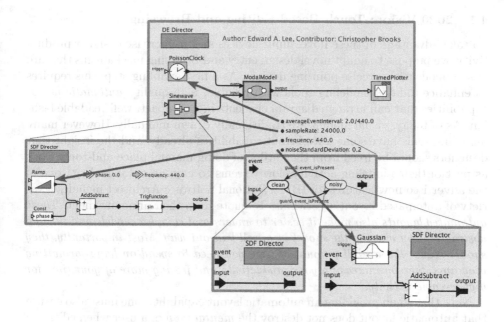

Fig. 3. A dual model for Ptolemy could show where parameters of an actor are used (from Fuhrmann [7])

Note that the structural view in Fig. 2c is also a kind of hybrid view that combines drawings of individual model components with an overall drawing (using gray lines) of how these components are related to each other. As of today, creating such drawings is again a manual, rather laborious process, which severely compromises designer productivity and thus goes against pragmatics-aware modeling. To do so automatically in a well-readable, compact fashion is an interesting layout problem that we are currently investigating, which leads to the concept of automatic layout also addressed in the next section.

4   Trend 2: Novel Input Devices

If we may believe innovation-leading companies in the field of ergonomic human-machine interaction, we are in the decade of "post-PC devices" [13]. Improvements in touch-display technology foster the success of smartphones and even new device categories like tablet computers that convince users with intuitive interaction paradigms. In professional environments such handheld devices or also bigger devices like computerized white boards may assist collaboration in team meetings and ease both the group access to data and capturing group results. Nonetheless the modeling community maintains traditional interaction paradigms for creating, navigating and maintaining models, notably What-You-See-Is-What-You-Get (WYSIWYG) Drag-and-Drop (DND) freehand editing that requires a precise instrument like the mouse.

4.1   2020 Vision: Touch-Based Editing and Browsing

To take advantage of these novel input devices and to increase designer productivity, we propose to adapt novel design entry and browsing mechanisms that are less dependent on precise pointing devices. As a first enabling step, this requires to enhance today's modeling tools with reliable, high-quality *automatic layout* capabilities that can arrange diagram elements in a compact, well-readable fashion. As of today, visual models are traditionally drawn manually. However many modeling tools have some auto-layout capabilities already, and the insight that designers should be freed from the burden of doing manual place-and-route work as part of their modeling activity slowly seems to gain acceptance. E. g., one of the advertised new features for IBM's Rational Software Architect includes a variety of automated layout algorithms. To quote from their announcement: *These automated layouts also make it easier to understand complex models and to build abstractions by viewing the model in a well-laid-out way. Most importantly, they should reduce the overall amount of time you need to spend on hand-formatting diagrams, thereby increasing your productivity and freeing more of your time for higher-value activity.*[3]

Note that when providing an automatic layout capability, one must also ensure that automatic layout does not destroy the *mental map* of a user when editing a model; for example, morphing mechanisms can help here significantly. We also acknowledge that designers, when confronted with the idea of automatic layout, are often at first reluctant to defer the drawing of a model to some algorithm that does not have any understanding of the application. As a compromise, there is also option of performing only *incremental* automatic layout, or to provide some *intentional* layout capability that allows the modeler to guide the automatic layout algorithm in certain ways. However, it is our experience that after getting used to a tool with high-quality automatic layout capabilities, designers are quite happy to make use of this capability, and become frustrated whenever they have to use a modeling tool without such a capability. This pattern is common whenever designers are asked to give up control of certain design aspects, and indeed it is often advisable to provide some escape mechanism. An analogy in the programming world is the capability of embedding assembler in a high-level language. However, carrying this analogy further, we also observe that today, most programmers appear to be glad to have been mostly freed from the task of manual assembler programmer, and are happy with the results that a compiler generates for them.

Note that the automated diagram drawing is by no means trivial, as many rather unusable auto-layout buttons can attest to, and there is an active research community that works on improving the state of the field [3]. However, the challenge here lies not only in the fundamental drawing problem, but also in smoothly integrating layout capabilities into the modeling tool. Here, the actor-oriented tooling approach outlined in Sec. 5 might also help. With automatic layout capabilities, it is possible to post-process imprecise drawing commands

---

[3] http://www.ibm.com/developerworks/rational/library/10/
whats-new-in-rational-software-architect-8/index.html

into high-quality diagram drawings. For a nice illustration of this approach, consider the Instaviz "pocket whiteboard,"[4] which uses advanced shape-recognition (Recog) and automatic drawing (GraphViz) capabilities. From the product description: *Sketch some rough shapes and lines, and Instaviz magically turns them into beautifully laid-out diagrams.* We are not aware of hard experimental data on the productivity of this software, but the subjective impression is that with this approach, working with a phone-size touch-sensitive display, one is faster to create a usable diagram than with a traditional model editor without layout capabilities installed on a full-size PC. This is not to advocate smart phones for productive system design, but the technologies developed there might very well be helpful. Multi-touch displays might allow more efficient and intuitive model manipulation and navigation than traditional pointing devices. For example, one might borrow from the effective navigation techniques that allow to browse photo libraries or web pages with very little screen real estate. Other examples of such inspiring innovations are dictionary-based predictive text entry (T9) or motion-based text entry (Swype).

4.2   Structure-Based Editing

Next, given a modeling platform that provides automated drawing capabilities, we can raise the abstraction level of editing activities to work on the structure of the model itself, rather than working on its representation. This *structure-based editing* [9] does not require precise pointing any more, so for example it does not require shape recognition. Instead, it suffices to select existing model elements and to specify the operation to apply to it, such as "add a successor state" or "invert transition direction".

   Such higher level, semantically oriented editing capabilities could also enhance traditional editing paradigms. For an example, consider the copy&paste operation, which originally was made possible by computer-based editing, but remains rather primitive until today. In a usual freehand editing environment, copy&paste requires numerous *enabling steps*. The user has to 1. select all objects to copy, 2. call the copy operation, 3. choose a target space, 4. free space at the target location, 5. select the target place (however, selecting an empty location usually is not possible in most tools), 6. call the paste operation, 7. move the pasted set of objects to the new empty space and finally 8. rearrange the surroundings such that the new objects seamlessly integrate. Especially steps 4, 7 and 8 may be arbitrarily effort-prone, and step 7 may be frustrating when the pasted objects do not appear at the target space of step 3 and the tool does not state explicitly about its target space policy. However, structure-based editing employing automatic layout can improve the situation considerably [7]. The editing steps would boil down to 1. select all objects to copy, 2. call the copy operation, 3. select a target *object*, and 4. call the paste operation. With automatic layout, the user should not specify any target *location*, but only a target *object* where the contents should be pasted. A generic transformation

---

[4] http://instaviz.com/

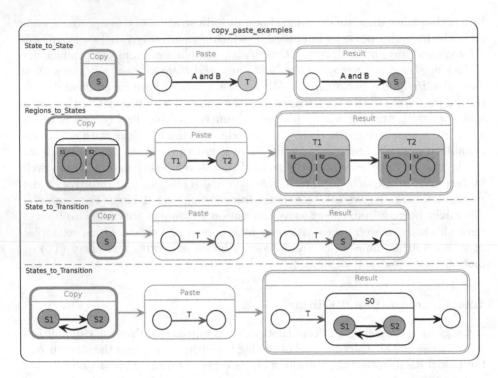

Fig. 4. Examples for copy&paste operations on a Statechart diagram. Each operation is illustrated with a sequence of three states: 1) the Copy state with a selected source to copy (e. g., state S), 2) the Paste state with the selected target (e. g., state T) into which the source should be pasted, and 3) the Result into which Paste gets transformed.

description should then specify how the elements are pasted *into* the target object and the automatic layout would do the rest.

To illustrate, Fig. 4 presents some possible copy&paste operations for State-charts. Each transformation rule has to consider the *copy sources* (labeled "S" in Fig. 4), i. e., the selected elements which get copied, and the *copy targets* ("T"). For Statecharts these objects may be states, regions, and transitions, and each set may be of arbitrary size. A good example is "copy multiple states to one transition". In a usual freehand editor, this is not possible and would do nothing. As implemented in KIELER, the transformation 1. cuts the target transition into two transitions, 2. adds a new state in-between both transitions, and 3. adds the selected nodes into a new region of the new state. Other similar transformations are possible, which the toolsmith would have to define according to experience in the context of the given DSL. Selecting multiple target objects is a fast way to replicate objects multiple times.

As a word of caution, these copy&paste effects go considerably beyond what designers are familiar with today. Also, some of these effects are probably needed only rarely, such as the "copy transitions to transitions". Still, extending the copy&paste paradigm in this fashion may significantly increase productivity, and is yet another example of the possibilities for harnessing automatic layout towards pragmatics-aware modeling.

5 Trend 3: The Move to the Cloud

Activities traditionally done locally become increasingly distributed and are moved to "the cloud." For example, to generate the class diagram drawing in Fig. 1, we did not install a UML tool, but visited a web page and pasted the textual description of the diagram into a text box. Not having to undergo lengthy installation procedures and always having a current tool version at one's disposal is appealing. We believe that this applies in particular to the world of MDE with its typically quite complex tool environments, and this also applies to other cloud-benefits such ease of design sharing (leading to *model mashups*) and designer mobility (consider google docs etc. that are already commonly integrated into mobile OSs such as Android). As another example, National Instruments' LabVIEW Web UI Builder is a cloud-based Rich Internet Application (RIA), which is hosted by Amazon Web Services and is basically a light-weight version of LabVIEW that allows to interface with hardware and/or web services. Similarly, NI offers a cloud version of a compiler that deploys LabVIEW models onto an FPGA. This application can be very compute-intensive, and there is a large variety of possible compilation targets; both factors make it attractive to move away from the local desktop into the cloud.

There already exist standards for web service interfaces, e. g., the Web Services Business Process Execution Language (WS-BPEL) [18] to describe business process activities as web services. However, such (mostly syntactic) standards are not enough, as they still exhibit semantic ambiguities that hamper tool compatibility. And, as Lapadula et al. state, the *design of WS-BPEL applications is difficult and error-prone also due to the presence of such intricate features as concurrency and race conditions, forced termination, [etc.]* [14].

5.1 2020 Vision: Actor-Oriented, Cloud-Based Modeling Tools

The idea of actor-oriented modeling is to break down complexity by decomposing a system into *actors* that communicate through well-defined interfaces [4]. The components interact not via control flow (such as a method-call in object-oriented design), but via data. This approach sidesteps many difficulties in the design of complex systems and supports the clean handling of concurrency [15].

We here claim that many of the arguments for actor-oriented design also apply to the modeling tools, and that this aligns well with the cloud-computing infrastructure already in place. This would not only make modeling tools more robust and versatile, but would also allow toolsmiths to focus on particular services, such as simulation or visualization, and not on having to re-develop everything else that is needed for a complete design environment. This would also go hand in hand with the trend towards more agile, customized design processes described earlier.

An interesting initiative in this regard is the ModelBus [11], which is built upon Web Services and follows a Service Oriented Architectures (SOA) approach. ModelBus provides an interaction pattern in order to enable model sharing in a distributed and heterogeneous model-driven development process. In comparison, actor-oriented design of modeling tool does not necessarily entail model sharing, but model sharing could be combined with the actor-oriented approach advocated here.

5.2   Example of a Service: Simulation

For example, as explained in Sec. 3, the KIELER modeling environment leverages Ptolemy as simulation engine. This is currently implemented by first transforming a KIELER model into a Ptolemy model. Then a Ptolemy instance is run in the background that processes simulation requests coming from KIELER and communicates simulation data back for proper visualization in KIELER.

One might as well move this simulation capability to a server that communicates through a standardized interface, e. g., based on XML. A non-trivial question here is what kind of information should be communicated. Traditionally, one is interested in the input/output behavior of the simulated component, and this is what most APIs (if tools have APIs for this purpose at all) offer. However, when using such a simulation service from within a modeling tool, one typically would like to know about the internal states of the simulated system as well. For example, the Ptolemy-SyncChart does communicate to KIELER the current state of the simulation; however, a modeler would typically also like to know which transition was taken to get to that state, which is not communicated. KIELER does remember the previous state, which can help to deduce the taken transition—but not if there are multiple transitions between the previous state and the current state. Conversely, one may not want to execute complete, externally visible reaction steps at once, but would like finer control over the simulation.

The lesson to be learned from there is that modeling frameworks should have open simulation interfaces, both for exporting and for importing simulations. These interfaces should not be limited to the externally visible behavior of the system under development (SUD), but should also include internal information that might be of interest to the modeler.

5.3   Example of a Service: Automatic Layout

As another example of a possible service to be provided in the cloud, KIELER provides layout capabilities to Ptolemy. A non-trivial issue there was to find a suitable user interface to access the auto-layout capabilities. E. g., initially, the user interface consisted of five buttons of different functionality. This proved too complicated to handle for the uninitiated. The current interface has just one button, which lead to much better user acceptance. The deeper reason for the initially too complicated user interface for the automatic layout was that, as is customary for today's editors, Ptolemy's graphical Vergil editor was not developed with externally provided automatic layout in mind. E. g., after the modeler has placed the nodes of a model, Vergil uses some heuristic to automatically route edges. This is a certain help to the human layouter, but conflicts with automatic layout, which needs control of both the node and the edge placement. The solution was to enhance Vergil to consider layout-annotations added by the KIELER layouter to the Ptolemy model.

Another issue turned out to be hyper edges. The Ptolemy way of connecting more than two actors is to add a relation node to the model, and adding a connection from each of the to-be-connected actor to the relation node. From the perspective of a generic layout algorithm, however, the relations look just like another actor. This typically leads to less compact layouts than would result from hyper edges that would directly connect the actors.

The lesson to be learned there is that editors should be developed with automatic layout in mind, and should provide simple interfaces to these. As a notable example in this direction, one of the five stated objectives of the Eclipse Graphiti project proposal was to provide *the ability to use any existing layout algorithms for auto layouting a diagram*[5]. There are further issues not discussed here, such as hyper edges, the handling of comments, and the efficient incorporation of layout results into a model (as it turns out, this is often more time consuming than the actual layout computation) [7].

A further issue was the handling of comments. Traditionally, comments are text boxes placed (manually, like everything else) at some convenient location in the visual model. These comments might refer to the whole diagram, e. g., to provide a general description or to identify the author. Often, however, comments refer to specific model elements. This reference is usually not anchored in the model itself, but only implicit in the spatial proximity of the comment to the referenced model element. This proximity usually gets lost when applying an automatic layout to the diagram. The lesson learned there was that comments should be anchored to model elements. This is already possible e. g. in Eclipse GEF.

6   Conclusions and Outlook

MDE, or software and systems engineering in general, keeps to be challenged by increasingly complex and powerful applications. In the past, this has fostered the development of similarly complex and powerful modeling tools and processes, often with little regard for the practical needs and limitations of the human developer.

We here advocate an approach that focuses on the different, concrete design activities of the developer and provides practical support for these activities. This proposal is driven mostly by the authors' experience in the design of cyber-physical systems, but we expect that much of this is of relevance beyond CPS design as well. Key aspects here are the tool-supported creation of different views

---

[5] http://www.eclipse.org/proposals/graphiti/

for these different activities, and pragmatic-aware model interaction paradigms. We sketched a vision, or at least fragments thereof, of how this approach might benefit from and provide support for a selection of current technological trends, and where this approach might lead to until the end of this decade. As it turns out, we here drew less from the established MDE community and more from other communities and from industry trends. So, a general conclusion might be that there is much innovation out there from which the MDE community could and should benefit from in the near future.

Acknowledgement. We thank the participants of the workshop and the reviewers for their very valuable comments.

References

1. André, C.: Computing SyncCharts reactions. Electronic Notes in Theoretical Computer Science 88, 3–19 (2004)
2. Brooks, C., Cheng, C.H.P., Feng, T.H., Lee, E.A., von Hanxleden, R.: Model engineering using multimodeling. In: Proceedings of the 1st International Workshop on Model Co-Evolution and Consistency Management (MCCM 2008), a Workshop at MODELS 2008, Toulouse (September 2008)
3. Di Battista, G., Eades, P., Tamassia, R., Tollis, I.G.: Algorithms for drawing graphs: An annotated bibliography. Computational Geometry: Theory and Applications 4, 235–282 (1994)
4. Eker, J., Janneck, J.W., Lee, E.A., Liu, J., Liu, X., Ludvig, J., Neuendorffer, S., Sachs, S., Xiong, Y.: Taming heterogeneity—the Ptolemy approach. Proceedings of the IEEE 91(1), 127–144 (2003)
5. Estefan, J.: Survey of model-based systems engineering (MBSE) methodologies, Rev. B. Technical report, INCOSE MBSE Focus Group (May 2008)
6. Fishwick, P.A., Zeigler, B.P.: A multimodel methodology for qualitative model engineering. ACM Trans. Model. Comput. Simul. 2, 52–81 (1992)
7. Fuhrmann, H.: On the Pragmatics of Graphical Modeling. Dissertation, Christian-Albrechts-Universität zu Kiel, Faculty of Engineering, Kiel (2011)
8. Fuhrmann, H., von Hanxleden, R.: On the Pragmatics of Model-Based Design. In: Choppy, C., Sokolsky, O. (eds.) Monterey Workshop 2008. LNCS, vol. 6028, pp. 116–140. Springer, Heidelberg (2010)
9. Fuhrmann, H., von Hanxleden, R.: Taming Graphical Modeling. In: Petriu, D.C., Rouquette, N., Haugen, Ø. (eds.) MODELS 2010, Part I. LNCS, vol. 6394, pp. 196–210. Springer, Heidelberg (2010)
10. Gurr, C.A.: Effective diagrammatic communication: Syntactic, semantic and pragmatic issues. Journal of Visual Languages & Computing 10(4), 317–342 (1999)
11. Hein, C., Ritter, T., Wagner, M.: Model-driven tool integration with ModelBus. In: Workshop Future Trends of Model-Driven Development (2009)
12. ISO/IEC JTC 1/SC 7: Systems and software engineering architecture description. ISO/IEC FDIS 42010, working document ISO/IEC JTC 1/SC 7 N (2011), http://www.iso-architecture.org/
13. Jobs, S.: Apple special event, keynote speech (March 2011)
14. Lapadula, A., Pugliese, R., Tiezzi, F.: A Formal Account of WS-BPEL. In: Lea, D., Zavattaro, G. (eds.) COORDINATION 2008. LNCS, vol. 5052, pp. 199–215. Springer, Heidelberg (2008)

15. Lee, E.A.: The problem with threads. IEEE Computer 39(5), 33–42 (2006)
16. Mernik, M., Heering, J., Sloane, A.M.: When and how to develop domain-specific languages. ACM Computing Surveys 37(4), 316–344 (2005)
17. Motika, C., Fuhrmann, H., von Hanxleden, R., Lee, E.A.: Executing domain-specific models in Eclipse (in preparation)
18. OASIS WSBPEL TC: Web Services Business Process Execution Language Version 2.0. (April 2007),
    http://docs.oasis-open.org/wsbpel/2.0/OS/wsbpel-v2.0-OS.html
19. Paige, R., Ostroff, J.: The single model principle. Journal of Object Oriented Technology 1 (2002)
20. Prochnow, S., von Hanxleden, R.: Statechart Development Beyond WYSIWYG. In: Engels, G., Opdyke, B., Schmidt, D.C., Weil, F. (eds.) MODELS 2007. LNCS, vol. 4735, pp. 635–649. Springer, Heidelberg (2007)
21. Sztipanovits, J., Karsai, G.: Model-integrated computing. Computer 30(4), 110–111 (1997)
22. Wimmer, M., Schauerhuber, A., Kappel, G., Retschitzegger, W., Schwinger, W., Kapsammer, E.: A survey on UML-based aspect-oriented design modeling. ACM Comput. Surv. 43(4), 28:1–28:33 (2011),
    http://doi.acm.org/10.1145/1978802.1978807

View-Based Development
of a Simulation Framework
for Multi-disciplinary Environmental Modelling*

Rolf Hennicker and Matthias Ludwig

Institut für Informatik, Ludwig-Maximilians-Universität München
{hennicker,mludwig}@pst.ifi.lmu.de

Abstract. We report on the development of a large-scale simulation framework for environmental modelling. The framework allows to couple various simulation models from natural and social science disciplines to perform integrative simulations. It has been constructed following a development methodology based on the identification of different functional views, which are concerned with data exchange, simulation space and coordination of distributed simulation models with respect to (logical) simulation time. On all levels of the development we have rigorously applied modelling and specification techniques including the last step, in which the different views are integrated into a component model of the full framework. The requirements for the correct coordination of simulation models have been formally specified in terms of the process algebra FSP and the design model has been model checked against the coordination requirements. Within the GLOWA-Danube project the framework has been successfully instantiated to construct the distributed simulation system DANUBIA which integrates up to 15 simulation models from various disciplines to model the consequences of global climate change for the water household on regional scales.

1 Introduction

Global climate change has an increasing impact on our natural and social environment. Therefore it is important to understand better the complex, mutually dependent processes occurring in nature and in socio-economic systems which calls for interdisciplinary research. Computer-based simulations have emerged as an appropriate means for studying possible scenarios for the future and to support the management of adaptation and/or prevention strategies. While in the past simulation models often were developed as monolithic applications by a particular discipline to provide specialised answers, nowadays the need for interdisciplinary modellling and integrative simulation has been recognized.

* This research has been partially supported by the GLOWA-Danube project 01LW0602A2 sponsored by the German Federal Ministry of Education and Research and by the EU project ASCENS, 257414.

R. Calinescu and D. Garlan (Eds.): Monterey Workshop 2012, LNCS 7539, pp. 224–250, 2012.

In an integrative simulation system several simulation models are coupled in order to analyse dependencies and transdisciplinary effects of the simulated processes. Following [20] and [8] environmental simulation models can be classified with respect to their basic modelling approach (process-, data- or agent-based modelling), treatment of simulation space (spatially distributed or lumped) and treatment of simulation time (discrete or continuous)[1]. Moreover, in a network of coupled simulation models one can distinguish whether the models are sequentially executed one after the other (possibly with iterations), whether they are concurrently executed and whether they are dependent from each other.

Coupling of simulation models from various disciplines is a non-trivial task, both conceptually and also from the implementation point of view. One has to cope, among others, with different simulation paradigms, different resolutions of space, and different local time scales to represent simulation time. For instance, in natural sciences often a process-based simulation approach is preferred, models typically use grid-based resolutions of space, and the time scale typically ranges from minutes to hours. In social sciences, however, an agent-based approach is most likely, space is often distributed into political units, and the time scale is usually more coarse ranging from months to years.

In this paper, we focus on process-based models which simulate spatially distributed processes and work on discrete time scales. We consider concurrently running simulation models which are dependent and exchange data at runtime. In this context, we report on the development of a generic framework for computer-based environmental modelling which has been constructed within the project GLOWA-Danube, cf. [22,26], which is part of a program on the consequences of climate change set up by the German Ministry of Education and Research. The framework is generic in the sense that it is, in principle, applicable to any kind of model which supports distributed geographical units of arbitrary size and arbitrary discrete time scales.

The development of the simulation framework has been guided by conceptual and architectural requirements. Conceptually, we have identified three major issues. The framework should support:

1. Data exchange between concurrently running simulation models.
2. Consistent treatment of simulation space for all models.
3. Coordination of simulation models with respect to simulation time.

From the architectural perspective, two logical layers are required, a *framework core* and a *developer interface* as indicated in Fig. 1. The framework core comprises all features that can be handled by the framework itself like, e.g., building simulation configurations and coordination of simulation models. Hence, it serves as a runtime environment for coupled simulations. The developer interface is intended to facilitate the implementation of single simulation models. It provides a programming interface, where particular elements exhibit so-called *plug-points*

---

[1] Our notion of simulation time does not refer to real time but to the specific date for which a simulation model actually computes data; e.g. the simulated temperature at 5 p.m. on July 5th, 2035.

(in the sense of [7]), which have to be filled with appropriate *plug-ins* in order to obtain an executable system. The plug-ins are provided by concrete simulation models, say M1, ..., M4, as indicated in Fig. 1. Hence, the simulation models instantiate the generic framework to a complete, coupled simulation system. The framework core is transparent for the model developer. Thus the developer of a simulation model is not concerned with administrative issues, like, e.g. model linking. On the other hand, all simulation models must adjust to general rules for common structure and behaviour which are implemented in the framework.

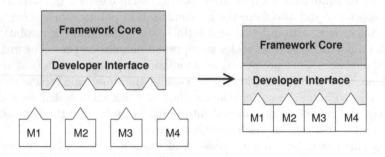

Fig. 1. Framework layers

For the development of the framework we have applied a rigorous methodology based on different functional views (or aspects) and on different abstraction levels. The view-based approach supports separation of concerns which is mandatory to understand the various tasks, in which an integrative simulation framework is involved. In our context, we have identified three views related to the three requirements from above: *data exchange*, *simulation space* and *simulation time*. These views are founded on a common *base view* which deals with basic properties of integrative simulations. We propose three abstraction levels for each view, dealing with *requirements*, with *design* and with the construction of a *component architecture*. Finally, on the component level, the single system views are integrated into an overall component model of the simulation framework. Fig. 2 gives an overview of our methodology which shows that the base view is extended on each abstraction level. As indicated in the picture, the diagrams must commute, i.e. extensions (denoted by ↪) and refinements (denoted by ⤳) must be compatible with each other.

For the representation of each view we use the Unified Modeling Language UML [15] as a graphical notation and the Object Constraint Language OCL [27] for specifying constraints. We have restricted the use of UML to an excerpt for which we have defined refinement relations between models on different abstraction levels, extension relations between models on the same abstraction level as well as a construction for model integration. We use structural models in the form of class and component diagrams and behavioural models in the form of sequence diagrams. For the most critical part of the framework, concerning the

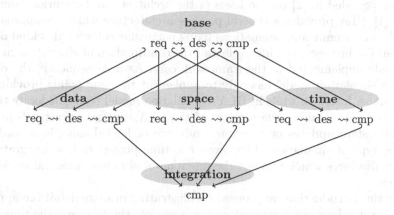

Fig. 2. View-based development

coordination of the simulation models w.r.t. simulation time, formal specifications in terms of the process algebra FSP [23] have been provided and the design model (using a timecontroller) has been model checked against the coordination requirements.

The framework implementation is systematically derived from the integrated component model by a pattern transforming components into Java packages which contain component managers to instantiate interfaces between components. The framework has been implemented as a distributed system relying on Java's Remote Method Invocation interface. Within the GLOWA-Danube project, the framework has been successfully applied to construct the distributed simulation system DANUBIA which integrates up to 15 simulation models from various disciplines, like meteorology, hydrology, plant physiology, glaciology, economy, agriculture, tourism, and environmental psychology. Actually, DANUBIA is already in use as a tool for decision makers to support the sustainable planning of the future of water resources in the Upper Danube basin.

A number of other frameworks and interfaces supporting integrated environmental modelling emerged since the GLOWA-Danube project started in 2001; for an overview see [16]. There are, e.g., the Object Modelling System OMS [18], ModCom [13], The Invisible Modelling Environment TIME [24], and the Open Modelling Interface OpenMI [9]. While TIME is a platform for the development of stand-alone modelling tools, OMS, ModCom, and OpenMI are frameworks which support the independent development of models and allow for execution of coupled simulations. In particular, OpenMI is designed to extend existing stand-alone models by standard interfaces for data exchange. In contrast to our approach, OpenMI allows only for sequential execution of dependent models. OMS supports also parallel execution, as long as models are independent from each other. ModCom and TIME are both not designed for distributed execution. Distributed simulations of dependent models are supported by the High Level Architecture HLA [6] which was set up in the nineties to define a structural basis for simulation interoperability. A formal model for the architecture of HLA has been provided in [2] on the basis of the architectural description language Wright [1]. HLA provides a general purpose architecture while our approach is tailored to environmental simulations fixing particular rules for this kind of application. For instance, the life cycle and the coordination of simulation models are already implemented in the framework core. As a consequence, the developer of a simulation model has only to implement the plug points provided by our developer interface while in HLA a simulation model (called federate there) must take care of calling the services of the HLA runtime infrastructure, e.g. to publish state updates or to request advance of logical time, in accordance with the type of simulation. Thus even real-time players can be integrated in HLA architectures which was not the intention of our environmental modelling approach.

After this introduction we proceed by illustrating in more detail the application of our development methodology for (parts of) the base and the time view of the simulation framework in Sects. 2 and 3. In Sect. 4 we describe briefly the requirements models for the data exchange and the simulation space view. We do not consider in detail the component models of the single views, but we give an overview of the final result of their integration in Sect. 5. Then we discuss the application of our framework to obtain the DANUBIA simulation system in Sect. 6 and we finish with some concluding remarks in Sect. 7.

2 Base View Development

2.1 Base View Requirements

Requirements analysis concerns the identification and modelling of concepts which are crucial for the envisaged system. To model the concept of an *integrative simulation* we use the class Simulation shown in Fig. 3. Any (integrative) simulation has a (non-empty) set of participating simulation models represented by instances of the class Model. We require that simulations and models can be identified by a unique simulationId and modelId, resp., expressed by the property {key}, which is a shorthand notation for a corresponding OCL invariant defined in an obvious way.

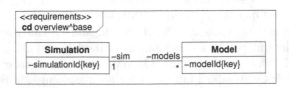

Fig. 3. Base view requirements: static model

Concerning basic dynamic behaviour of integrative simulations, the sequence diagram in Fig. 4 shows a minimal set of actions that are expected, when an integrative simulation is performed. By means of an appropriate user interface, which is not in the scope of the simulation framework and therefore is modelled as an actor, a Simulation object is created and started. Then instances of all participating models must be created and executed (as indicated in the loop fragment). When a model has finished its simulation run the Simulation object is notified by the message finished. If this notification has arrived from all participating models the end of the simulation is signalled to the UserInterface. All messages in the sequence diagram are asynchronous (indicated by an open arrowhead). Hence the single simulation models are executed in parallel after they have been started within the loop. Obviously, the static and the dynamic model are consistent, since all lifelines in the sequence diagram correspond to roles and types of the static model.

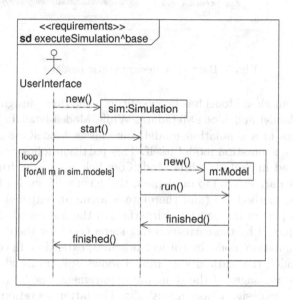

Fig. 4. Base view requirements: dynamic model

2.2   Base View Design

Design modelling concerns the development of solutions in order to realise the abstract concepts. In our case we discriminate active entities for controlling and descriptive objects that carry information. An overview of the structural design model of the base view is depicted in Fig. 5.

The class Simulation of the requirements model is split into the two classes SimulationAdmin and SimulationConfiguration. While a SimulationAdmin instance is supposed to act as a management entity for an integrative simulation and is therefore designed as an active class (indicated by a vertical double line on the border of the UML class box), the class SimulationConfiguration holds descriptive information about the simulation (indicated by the stereotype «data type»).

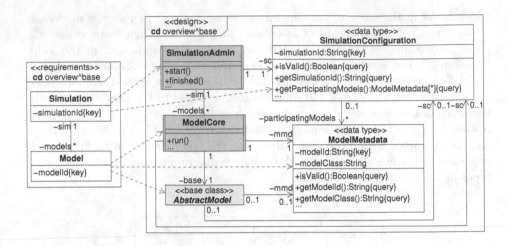

Fig. 5. Base view design: static model

The requirement class Model has been split into the three design classes ModelCore, AbstractModel and ModelMetadata. While ModelMetadata is a class for storing meta data of a simulation model, the classes ModelCore and Abstract-Model represent a simulation model itself. This partition follows the framework principle explained in Sect. 1: while ModelCore belongs to the framework core (indicated by the dark colour) to implement the general life cycle of a simulation model within the method run (and therefore is again an active class), the class AbstractModel is part of the developer interface of the framework. It constitutes a *base class* (depicted by the corresponding stereotype) for the development of an individual simulation model by (object-oriented) extension. In contrast to the requirements model, the static design model shows operations which are either derived from the messages of the dynamic requirements model (see Fig. 4) or identified during the design phase, like isValid. The latter operation occurs in the classes SimulationConfiguration and ModelMetadata, to determine the validity of simulation configurations and the validity of model meta data resp. In each case it is a query specified by OCL pre- and postconditions as expected.

```
context SimulationConfiguration :: isValid ()
  pre:   true
  post:  result = self . simulationId <> ""
    and  self . participatingModels <> null
    and  self . participatingModels—>forAll (m | m. isValid ())

context ModelMetadata :: isValid ()
  pre:   true
  post:  result = self . modelId <> "" and self . modelClass <> ""
```

There is also a refinement of the dynamic requirements model of Fig. 4 taking into account the new classes, see Fig. 6. The sequence diagram depicts preconditions that must be satisfied before an object is created and postconditions that must be valid after creation. It also contains a reference to a nested sequence diagram not shown here.

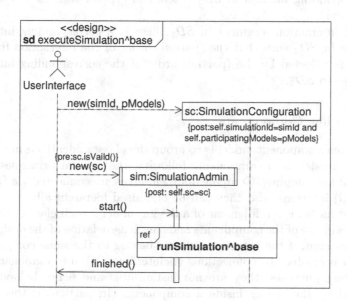

Fig. 6. Base view design: dynamic model

Refinement Rules. We have defined general rules for refinement which allow us to split requirement classes into sets of design classes and to rename and add model elements and behaviours. The rules are defined for class diagrams and sequence diagrams by taking into account their syntactic structure. Semantic refinement relations between sequence diagrams can be found, e.g., in [5], or in the STAIRS approach [11,10].

Structural Model. A structural model SM_2 is a refinement of a structural model SM_1, denoted by $SM_1 \rightsquigarrow SM_2$, if

- for each class A in SM_1 there exists a non-empty set Cor_A of corresponding refining classes in SM_2,
- for each attribute of a class in SM_1 there is a corresponding attribute in one of the refining classes of that class,
- for each association in SM_1 between two classes A and B there exists an association in SM_2 between two classes in Cor_A and Cor_B resp. such that multiplicities are respected, and
- for each invariant Inv occurring in SM_1 there exists an invariant Inv' in SM_2 such that $Inv' \Rightarrow Inv$.

Dynamic Model. Let SD_1 and SD_2 be sequence diagrams with corresponding structural models SM_1 and SM_2 resp. such that $SM_1 \rightsquigarrow SM_2$. Then SD_2 is a refinement of SD_1, denoted by $SD_1 \rightsquigarrow SD_2$, if

- for each lifeline L in SD_1 with type $A \in SM_1$ there is a non-empty set Cor_L of corresponding lifelines in SD_2 where the type of each $Ll \in Cor_L$ is in Cor_A, and
- for each interaction fragment in SD_1 there is a corresponding interaction fragment in SD_2 such that the (partial) order of the interaction fragments in SD_1 is reflected by the (partial) order of the corresponding interaction fragments in SD_2.

2.3 Base View Components

The goal of our component model is to group the classes, identified in the structural design model, into components following the general principles of high cohesion and low coupling. Components themselves are connected via (provided and required) interfaces and they can be organised hierarchically. We say that a component model is a refinement of a design model if each class of the design model occurs in one of the components and if each association of the design model is either preserved, if the associated classes belong to the same component, or otherwise, it is resolved by connections via interfaces. We use components solely for structuring purposes; they are not instantiable and hence behaviours are implemented by the classes inside a component. (In particular, this allows a straightforward implementation in object-oriented languages.) Hence the transition from design to components concerns only the static aspects while the dynamic model of the design remains still valid on the component level.

The UML component diagram in Figure 7 shows the component model for the base view. We use two components, Simulation and Model, containing the respective classes for simulations and for models occuring in the static design model in Fig. 5. The associations between simulation and model classes and the interactions between their instances have lead to the interfaces ModelAccess and ExceptionHandler which are implemented (depicted by the ball notation) and used (depicted by the socket notation) by the appropriate classes of the components. (The multiplicity * indicates that at runtime arbitrary many instances of model classes can interact with a simulation.) The interfaces SimulationAccess and UserInterface show the open connections to the user interface not being part of the framework.

3 Simulation Time and Coordination

A central role in integrative environmental simulations is played by the notion of time and by the coordination of the simulation models. As already mentioned in the introduction, our notion of time expresses logical simulation time and does not refer to execution time. In this section we show how the models of

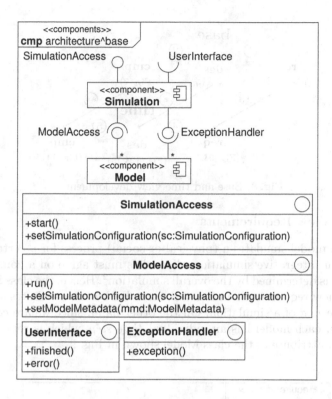

Fig. 7. Base view: component model

the time view are constructed by extensions of the corresponding levels of the base view. Fig. 8 gives an overview of the single extensions and refinements to be considered. The single steps are performed in the following order: Steps 1 and 2 concern the refinement from requirements to design and from design to components in the base case which have already been carried out in Sect. 2. In step 3, the requirements model of the time view is constructed as an extension of the requirements model of the base view. This requirements model is then refined, in step 4, into a design model of the time view. This leads to the proof obligation (*) that the resulting design model of the time view is an extension of the design model of the base view, i.e. the lefthand diagram commutes. Finally, in step 5, the design model of the time view is refined into a component model. This leads to the proof obligation (**) that the resulting component model of the time view is an extension of the component model of the base view, i.e. the righthand diagram commutes.

In our approach extension relations are defined by precise (syntactic) rules on the basis of an excerpt of the UML metamodel for class and sequence diagrams. In principle, an extension relation is a particular case of a refinement relation such that renaming of model elements and splitting of classes and lifelines is not allowed. For details see [21].

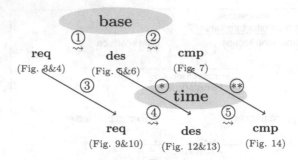

Fig. 8. Base and time view development

3.1   Time View Requirements

A simulation model simulates a (physical or social) process for a certain period of time. In an integrative simulation all models must agree on a common time period which is determined by the overall simulation[2]. Hence, the class Simulation of the base view requirements in Fig. 3 is extended by two attributes storing the *begin* and the *end* of a simulation. On the other hand, since we are considering discrete time, each model has an individual *time step*, which is represented by an additional attribute of the class Model shown in Fig. 9.

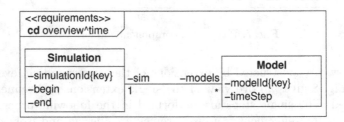

Fig. 9. Time view requirements: static model

Much more involved are the *behavioural* requirements concerning simulation time and coordination. In contrast to stand-alone simulation models, a coupled simulation model not only computes data, but has to perform activities concerning data exchange in accordance with the simulation time. The general life cycle a coupled simulation model must follow is described as follows.

- *initialise* model with basic data (e.g. about the simulation area)
- *provide* exported data at the model's export interfaces[3]
- while not at simulation end
    - *get data* from the model's import interfaces

---

[2] For instance, in the GLOWA-Danube project the common simulation time spans typically 50 years starting from the actual date.

[3] Which is necessary for other models to start their computation.

- • *compute* new data for the next time step
- • *provide* newly computed data at the model's export interfaces
- *finalise* the simulation (e.g. closing of open files or database connections)

This general life cycle of any simulation model is integrated into the sequence diagram of the base view (Fig. 4) resulting in the sequence diagram for the dynamic time view requirements shown in Fig. 10, which is an obvious behavioural extension of the former one.

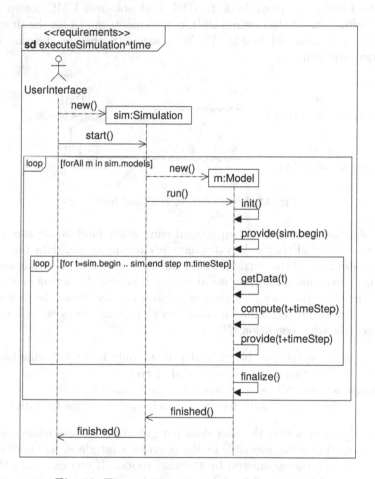

Fig. 10. Time view requirements: dynamic model

The sequence diagram in Fig. 10 models the parallel execution of all simulation models participating in an integrative simulation. But it allows much more (parallel) executions than desired since the single models are by no means coordinated w.r.t. simulation time yet. For instance, Fig. 10 would allow an execution where the first simulation model has already finished its getData - compute - provide loop, while some other model, whose exported data is needed by the first one, has not even provided data yet or has only provided data which is obsolete for the first model. Hence, we are faced with a non-trivial coordination problem which cannot be specified in UML. Our solution is to switch from the UML requirements model to a formal specification of the coordination problem. For this purpose we use the process algebra FSP (Finite State Processes FSP) introduced by Magee and Kramer [23] which allows us to formalise the coordination requirements in terms of so-called property processes[4]. Then we develop an FSP design model and check that the design model satisfies the coordination constraints. Finally, we move back to UML and obtain a UML design model which is a refinement of the original UML requirements model for the time view. Our procedure is depicted in Fig. 11. We start with the specification of the coordination problem.

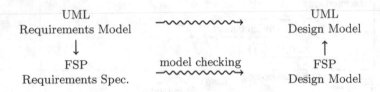

Fig. 11. From UML to FSP and back

The Coordination Problem. When several simulation models are executed in parallel, it is essential that only valid data is exchanged, i.e. data that fits to the local model time of the participating models. To specify this requirement we consider only two simulation models at a time, one, say U, acting as a user of data, and the other one, say P, acting as a data provider. From the user's point of view we obtain the coordination condition (U), from the provider's point of view the coordination condition (P).

(U) U gets data expected to be valid at time t_U only if the following holds:
    The next data that P provides is valid at time t_P with $t_U < t_P$.
(P) P provides data valid at time t_P only if the following holds:
    The next data that U gets is expected to be valid at time t_U with $t_U \geq t_P$.

Condition (U) ensures that the user does not get obsolete data while condition (P) guarantees that data, available at the provider's interface, will not be overwritten if it is not yet considered by the user model. If one can show that all (pairwise) combinations of all models participating in an integrative simulation considered in both roles, as user and as provider of data, satisfy the two coordination requirements, then the whole integrative simulation is coordinated correctly.

To specify the coordination conditions, we first formalise the general life cycle of a simulation model in terms of the following FSP process MODEL, which is

---

[4] An alternative formalisation of the coordination problem using purely mathematical notations is given in [3].

parameterised with respect to the model's time step. The actual simulation time, when a certain action happens, is modelled by an action index. The sequence of actions in line 5, getData[t] -> compute[t+Step] -> provide[t+Step], is iteratively performed with increasing time t and thus formalises the inner loop of the sequence diagram in Fig. 10. Let us remark that the computation of new data for time t+Step relies on data obtained for time t. This time difference avoids deadlocks of concurrently running models (in the case of feedback loops) but it may also lead to imprecisions whose relevance must be analysed in concrete cases and, if necessary, can be resolved by using smaller time steps.

```
1   range SimTime = SimStart .. SimEnd
2   MODEL(Step) = (run -> init -> provide[SimStart] -> M[SimStart]),
3   M[t:SimTime] =
4       if (t+Step <= SimEnd)
5       then (getData[t] -> compute[t+Step] -> provide[t+Step]
6       -> M[t+Step])
7       else (finalize -> finished -> STOP).
```

A particular simulation model with modelId m and time step sm is then formalised by the labelled FSP process [m]:MODEL(sm). In this process all actions are prefixed by the model identificator m, i.e. the actions are of the form [m].run, [m].init, [m].provide[t], m.get[t] etc.

On this basis we can formalise the coordination conditions in terms of the following FSP property process VALIDDATA. The first alternative of the process VALIDDATA formalises condition (U) from above such that the index variable nextUser corresponds to t_U, nextProv corresponds to t_P and therefore nextProv-StepProv corresponds to $last_P$. The second alternative formalises condition (P) from above.

```
1   property VALIDDATA(User, StepUser, Prov, StepProv) =
2       VD[SimStart][SimStart],
3   VD[nextGet:Time][nextProv:Time] =
4     (when (nextGet<nextProv)
5        [User].getData[nextGet] -> VD[nextGet+StepUser][nextProv]
6     |when (nextGet>=nextProv)
7        [Prov].provide[nextProv] -> VD[nextGet][nextProv+StepProv]).
```

For a system of coupled simulation models all requirements concerning the validity of data are now obtained by pairwise instantiations of the generic property process VALIDDATA such that, in different instantiations, the same simulation model occurs once in the role of a user and once in the role of a provider of data. To validate the property processes we have used the FSP-tool LTSA (Labelled Transition System Analyser) which translates FSP processes into labelled transition systems and visualises the transition systems if the property process is instantiated (by small parameters).

3.2   Time View Design

The formal specification of the coordination requirements is highly non-constructive. The basic idea of the formal design model is to introduce a global control process that coordinates appropriately all simulation models participating in an integrative simulation. In [12] we have constructed an explicit coordination process with FSP, called TIMECONTROLLER, which has actions of the form m.enterGet[t], m.exitGet[t], m.enterProv[t], m.exitProv[t] for all model identificators m and time steps t within the range of the simulation time. The enter actions are guarded by appropriate coordination conditions like, in the case of three simulation models to be coordinated,

```
when (t<nextProv1 & t<nextProv2 & t<nextProv3)
     [1..3].enterGet[t] -> ...
| when (nextGet1>=t & nextGet2>=t & nextGet3>=t)
     [1..3].enterProv[t] -> ...
```

The exit actions are not guarded but change the value of the nextGet and nextProv variables accordingly.

Moreover, the FSP process MODEL of the requirements model is extended such that any provide and get action is surrounded by appropriate enter and exit actions which are shared with the timecontroller. Since shared actions can only be executed together, the timecontroller process now monitors when a simulation model can execute its get and provide actions in the parallel composition

```
([1]:MODEL(s1)||...||[n]:MODEL(sn)||TIMECONTROLLER)
```

We have verified with LTSA that the FSP design model indeed satisfies the coordination conditions formalised by (instantiations of) the property processes of the FSP requirements model; see [12] for more details.

The formal FSP design model suggests a particular architecture of a design model on the UML level which introduces the class Timecontroller shown in the static UML design model in Fig. 12. Obviously, this model is a refinement of the static time view requirements model in Fig. 9 and also an extension of the static base view design model in Fig. 5, as required by the proof obligation (*) in Fig. 8.

During an integrative simulation run there is exactly one instance of the class Timecontroller which acts as a monitor that must be called by the simulation models (more precisely, by the ModelCore instances) before data delivery and data access can be performed. This is pointed out in Fig. 13 which shows an excerpt of the dynamic UML design model for the time view. In particular one can see in Fig. 13 that any enter message called on the timecontroller is equipped with an "enable" constraint which expresses a coordination condition derived from the FSP guards in the timecontroller process. We have introduced enable constraints, though not part of the OCL standard, to model situations in which a calling object will be blocked if the condition is not valid and then waits until the constraint becomes true. Let us remark that enable conditions are methodologically (and also from the implementation point of view) quite different from OCL preconditions, since preconditions are expected to hold when an operation is called. Indeed, when we use preconditions in our models, we express a requirement for the caller and our reference implementation will raise an exception if the precondition is not satisfied upon operation call. In contrast, if an operation call is constrained by an enable condition, say cond, then the operation, say op, will be implemented in Java by a synchronized method applying the following general pattern proposed in [23]:

```
public synchronized void op() throws InterruptedException {
    while (!cond) wait();
    ... // monitor state = nextState
    notifyAll();
}
```

If the condition cond is not satisfied, the calling thread will be blocked by wait. If the condition is satisfied the thread may enter the critical region and change the monitor state. After that it releases, if necessary, all waiting threads by notifyAll. The while loop ensures that the condition is checked again after a thread has been released which is necessary since Java follows the "signal and continue" principle.

The sequence diagram in Fig. 13 shows also that, after a simulation model has entered the monitor, the concrete execution of getting data and providing data is delegated to an instance of the class AbstractModel and similarly for computing new data. How the operations getData, provide and compute will finally be implemented is due to the developer of a concrete simulation model who has to extend the abstract model class. Therefore getData, provide and compute are declared as plug points in the class AbstractModel as indicated in Fig. 12.

As already mentioned, Fig. 13 shows only an excerpt of the dynamic design model for the time view. The full model is a hierarchically organised sequence diagram presented in all details in [21]. It is a refinement of the dynamic time view requirements model in Fig. 10 and also an extension of the dynamic base view design model in Fig. 6 (as required by the proof obligation (*) in Fig. 8).

3.3   Time View Components

The component model for the time view encapsulates the Timecontroller class in the component TimeCoordination, which is connected to the two components of the base view by appropriate interfaces, one to access the timecontroller monitor from a model and the other one to pass a simulation configuration from the simulation administrator. This corresponds to the refinement step 5 in Fig. 8.

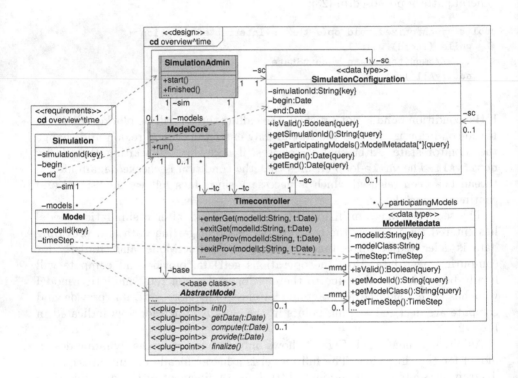

Fig. 12. Time view design: static model

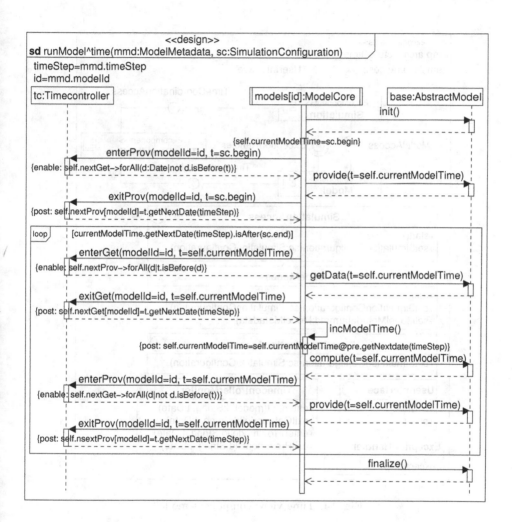

Fig. 13. Time view design: Excerpt of the dynamic model

Fig. 14 shows the component model of the time view. It extends the base view component model in Fig. 7 by the component TimeCoordination and by the two interfaces TimecontrollerMonitor and TimeCoordinationAccess together with their associated relationships for usage and implementation. Hence, the proof obligation (**) of Fig. 8 is satisfied.

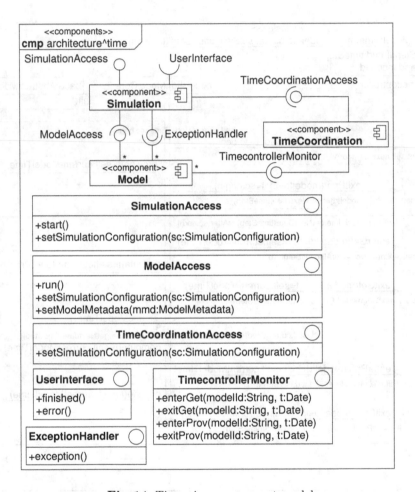

Fig. 14. Time view: component model

4   Data Exchange and Simulation Space

This section gives a short overview on the remaining system views concerning data exchange and simulation space. We only present the static requirements models as extensions of the base view to get an idea of the relevant concepts in these cases. For the complete development of the data exchange and simulation space aspects we refer to [21].

4.1   Data Exchange: Requirements

In a coupled simulation, the single simulation models exchange data at runtime. We require that for data exchange they use data interfaces. For each simulation model the interfaces appear in two different roles. First, a model must have a set of *export* interfaces to provide computed data for other models. Secondly, a model imports data that it needs for its own computations from other models. For this purpose it uses *import* interfaces (which at the same time are export interfaces of a providing model). Statically, we extend the requirements model of the base view (cf. Fig. 3) by the type DataInterface associated with the conceptual class Model by two directed associations, one for the exported and one for the imported interfaces of a simulation model, as shown in Fig. 15. A concrete example of an exported and imported interface of a groundwater simulation model is given later when we illustrate the framework instantiation in Fig. 19.

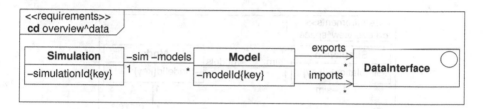

Fig. 15. Data exchange requirements: static model

The class diagram in Fig. 15 is enhanced by a consistency condition for integrative simulations which requires that for any model participating in a simulation and for each interface imported by the model there must exist exactly one simulation model which exports that interface. The following OCL invariant expresses this requirement.

```
context Simulation inv:
    self.models.forAll(m |
     m.imports->forAll(i |
       self.models->one(n |
         n.exports->includes(i)))))
```

The dynamic requirements model for data exchange is a simple extension of the basic one (Fig. 4), which integrates an activity to link models via their corresponding import/export data interfaces.

4.2   Simulation Space: Requirements

Any environmental simulation model operates on some simulation space. For integrative simulations we assume that all models use the same simulation space which consists of a set of so-called proxels. The term proxel (cf. [25]) stems from *process pixel* and suggests that a proxel does not only model a structural element of the simulation space, but it shows also dynamic behaviour by simulating the environmental processes on this particular geographical unit. The entire simulation area is then modelled by a set of (non-overlapping) proxels. The spatial requirements of an integrative simulation are described by the UML class diagram in Fig. 16. It says that a simulation concerns always exactly one simulation area which, in turn, consists of a set of proxels. The class Proxel requires that each proxel has a unique identifier pid and a number of properties which must be common to all simulation models (like, e.g., geographical coordinates, elevation, etc.). On the other hand, each simulation model has a set of proxels, on which it operates. These proxels must belong to the simulation area of the simulation, in which a model participates. This requirement is again expresses by an OCL invariant not shown here. Obviously, the static requirements model in Fig. 16 is an extension of the basic one in Fig. 3.

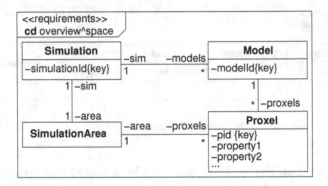

Fig. 16. Simulation space requirements: static model

5 Integration

In the last step of our development methodology the component models of the single views are integrated into an overall component model which is an extension of each view, as indicated in Fig. 17. Though we have not considered the component levels of the data exchange and space views, we still want to give an overview of the component architecture of the full simulation framework shown in Fig. 18. One can see that it extends the time view component model of Fig. 14 by the component ModelLinking, which stems from the data exchange component model, and by the two components Basedata and Proxel, both stemming from the simulation space view. The latter has been introduced as a subcomponent of the Model component. As indicated in the picture, all components are connected via appropriate provided and required interfaces.

Our integration follows a general integration procedure for static and dynamic models which produces a unique result up to renaming, similarly to a pushout construction, and which is independent of the order of the integration (up

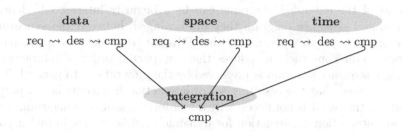

Fig. 17. Integration

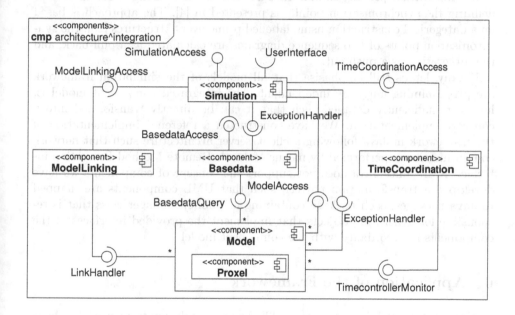

Fig. 18. Integrated component model: Overview

to renaming) in the case of more than two diagrams. For static models, our procedure works on an excerpt of the UML metamodel for class and component diagrams; it is widely adopted from the UML package merge construction as explained, e.g., in [14].

But we have also to consider the integration of dynamic models in the form of sequence diagrams, which we have used in the dynamic design models of each view and which are still valid in the single component models. The task is to describe how two sequence diagrams extending a common base sequence diagram are integrated. For this purpose we have defined general rules which work on an excerpt of the UML metamodel for sequence diagrams. An integrated sequence diagram comprises the lifelines, messages and interaction fragments of its constituent parts. During the integration process the interaction fragments of the base diagram act as synchronisation points whereas the other interaction fragments of the extended diagrams can be arbitrarily interleaved. Hence, in the integrated sequence diagram they are arranged, between the synchronisation points, in separate operands of the UML par construct to express parallel executions. Our construction ensures that the partial order of interactions of each single sequence diagram is preserved by the integration. In general, it may however happen, that the resulting set of interaction fragments is not partially ordered, i.e. the result is not necessarily a well-formed sequence diagram; cf. [17]. Thus our integration construction for dynamic models defines in fact a partial function. Concerning our simulation framework the integration of the sequence diagrams of the single views is rather involved and presented in detail in [21].

An integration process similar to ours, but without using a common base defining the synchronisation points, is presented in [4]. The approach is based on a categorical construction using labelled prime event structures [28]: the synchronisation points of two sequence diagrams are calculated as a pull-back, and the integration as a push-out.

Finally, let us still emphasise that all models of the simulation framework are programming language independent. The integrated component model is, however, sufficiently detailed such that it can be directly transformed into a concrete implementation. We have constructed a reference implementation of the framework in Java following a client/server architecture such that network communication is performed by means of Java's Remote Method Invocation interface RMI. Since Java does not support the concept of components we have developed a transformation pattern such that UML components are mapped to Java packages, each package containing a (public) manager class that is responsible for generating objects that implement the provided interfaces of the components in accordance with the component model.

6   Application of the Framework

Within the GLOWA-Danube project [22,26] our simulation framework has been instantiated to construct the integrative simulation system DANUBIA which integrates up to 15 simulation models for natural processes (like hydrology, plant physiology, groundwater, glaciology etc.) as well as socio-economic models. The latter have been developed to model the behaviour of the involved actors in the areas of agriculture, economy, water supply, private households, and tourism based on the structure of societies and their interests. The ultimate purpose of DANUBIA is to serve as a tool for decision makers from policy, economy, and administration for the sustainable planning of water resources in the Upper Danube basin under global change conditions. DANUBIA was validated with comprehensive data sets of the years 1970 to 2005. It is actually in use to run and evaluate coupled simulations which are driven by climatic as well as societal scenarios for the next 50 years.

How a concrete simulation model is integrated into the framework is shown in Fig. 19 in terms of a groundwater model. The upper layer indicates (part of) the framework core and the middle layer (part of) the developer interface as discussed in Sect. 1. One can see that all model classes (and interfaces) of the groundwater model extend the base classes (the base interface `DataInterface` resp.) of the developer interface by certain domain-specific properties, like the proxel attributes `gwWithdrawal, gwLevel` etc., and by providing implementations for the plug-in operations like, e.g., `compute` and `computeProxel`. Thereby the framework's core functionality concerning runtime coordination, management tasks and the like is completely hidden from model developers.

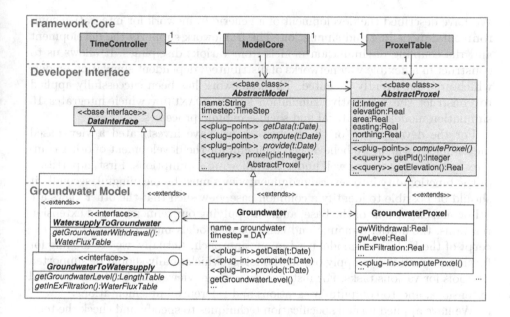

Fig. 19. Instantiation of the framework

While the framework is primarily intended for the development of new simulation models, legacy models can yet be integrated into the framework as long as their computation steps are controllable from the outside. In this case the legacy model is surrounded by a wrapper which must implement the (plug-in) operations like any other model. The concrete computation steps of the legacy model can then be initiated by using the Java Native Interface.

Of course, the performace of a coupled simulation run depends strongly on the number and type of the participating simulation models. For instance, a simulation that couples only socio-economic models (together with a groundwater model needed to interact with the water supplier model) runs actually between three and four days for a simulation period of 50 years. In this case the smallest local time step is one day. If, however, all 15 models participate in a simulation run, then for the same simulation period of 50 years the simulation execution takes approximately 70 days. Hence, performance is still an issue and the obvious approach to improve efficiency would be to figure out further parallelisation possibilities which may concern the framework as well as the implementations of the single simulation models. For instance, the coordination could be made more liberal if in addition to the local time steps individual dependencies and independencies of simulation models would be taken into account. The models themselves may also identify further parallelisable parts, though we have already provided templates for parallel computations of different proxels.

7   Conclusion

We have described the development of a generic framework for integrative environmental modelling and simulation. The framework supports the development and the coupling of simulation models from various disciplines. It allows us to construct in a flexible way networks of distributed, dependent simulation models which are concurrently executed. The framework has been successfully applied to construct the integrative simulation system DANUBIA which integrates 15 simulation models for natural and socio-economic processes.

For the development of the framework we have investigated a view-based methodology which, we believe, can be useful for the development of other complex software systems as well under the following assumptions: First, a partition of the functionality into several prominent views must be meaningful, secondly it should be possible to identify a common base view such that the other views are othogonal extensions of the base, and, for applying our refinement and extension relations, the static, dynamic and component models must conform to the excerpt of the UML metamodel used in our approach. Actually, we are looking for further case studies to apply our methodology which finally should be supported by tools for various tasks. For instance, to manage views, check refinements and extensions, and to compute integrations and reference implementations.

We have applied formal specification techniques to specify and check the temporal coordination being the heart of integrative simulations with dependable models. We are not aware of any other system of comparable complexity which has been completely modelled and specified in such a rigorous manner up to the last step, in which a full, implementation language independent model of the whole system is constructed. The models and specifications serve at the same time as a complete documentation for maintenance, furher developments and adaptations of the framework. The framework as well as the simulation models developed in the GLOWA-Danube project have been published under the name OPENDANUBIA under an Open Source Licence. Thus the framework is accessible for model developers for instantiation and also for framework developers, who may want to add further features (e.g., to support dynamic changes of simulation configurations). More information about OPENDANUBIA and a comprehensive list of publications discussing the application of the framework for particular scenarios and simulation results from various perspectives can be found at the GLOWA-Danube web page [26].

Acknowledgement. We would like to thank the anonymous reviewers of this paper for their careful reading and for their useful suggestions for improvement.

References

1. Allen, R., Garlan, D.: A formal basis for architectural connection. ACM Trans. Softw. Eng. Methodol. 6(3), 213–249 (1997)
2. Allen, R., Garlan, D., Ivers, J.: Formal modeling and analysis of the HLA component integration standard. In: Proceedings of the 6th ACM SIGSOFT International Symposium on Foundations of Software Engineering (SIGSOFT 1998/FSE-6), pp. 70–79 (1998)
3. Barth, M., Knapp, A.: A coordination architecture for time-dependent components. In: Proc. 22nd Int. Multi-Conf. Applied Informatics. Software Engineering (IASTED SE 2004), pp. 6–11 (2004)
4. Bowles, J.K.F., Bordbar, B.: A Formal Model for Integrating Multiple Views. In: International Conference on Application of Concurrency to System Design, pp. 71–79 (2007)
5. Cengarle, M.V., Knapp, A., Mühlberger, H.: Interactions. In: Lano [19], ch. 9, pp. 205–248
6. Dahmann, J.S., Fujimoto, R., Weatherly, R.M.: The department of defense high level architecture. In: Winter Simulation Conference, pp. 142–149 (1997)
7. D'Souza, D., Wills, A.: Objects, Components and Frameworks with UML – The Catalysis Approach. Addison-Wesley, Reading (1999)
8. Giupponi, C., Jakeman, A.J., Karssenberg, D., Hare, M.P. (eds.): Sustainable Management of Water Resources – An Integrated Approach. Edward Elgar Publishing, Cheltenham (2006)
9. Gregersen, J.B., Gijsbers, P.J.A., Westen, S.J.P.: OpenMI: Open modelling interface. Journal of Hydroinformatics 9(3), 175–191 (2007)
10. Haugen, Ø., Husa, K., Runde, R., Stølen, K.: STAIRS towards formal design with sequence diagrams. Software and Systems Modeling 4, 355–357 (2005), 10.1007/s10270-005-0087-0
11. Haugen, Ø., Stølen, K.: STAIRS – Steps To Analyze Interactions with Refinement Semantics. In: Stevens, P., Whittle, J., Booch, G. (eds.) UML 2003. LNCS, vol. 2863, pp. 388–402. Springer, Heidelberg (2003)
12. Hennicker, R., Ludwig, M.: Property-Driven Development of a Coordination Model for Distributed Simulations. In: Steffen, M., Zavattaro, G. (eds.) FMOODS 2005. LNCS, vol. 3535, pp. 290–305. Springer, Heidelberg (2005)
13. Hillyer, C., Bolte, J., van Evert, F., Lamaker, A.: The ModCom modular simulation system. European Journal of Agronomy 18(3), 333–343(11) (2003)
14. Hitz, M., Kappel, G., Kapsamer, E., Retschnitzegger, W.: UML@Work – Objektorientierte Modellierung mit UML 2 (3. Auflage). dpunkt.verlag, Heidelberg (2005)
15. Jacobson, I., Booch, G., Rumbaugh, J.: The Unified Modeling Language User Guide, 2nd edn. The Addison-Wesley Object Technology Series. Addison-Wesley (2005)
16. Jagers, H.R.A.: Linking Data, Models and Tools: An Overview. In: Swayne, D.A., Yang, W., Voinov, A.A., Rizzoli, A., Filatova, T. (eds.) Proceedings of the iEMSs Fifth Biennial Meeting: International Congress on Environmental Modelling and Software (iEMSs 2010), Ottawa, Canada. International Environmental Modelling and Software Society (July 2010)
17. Klein, J., Caillaud, B., Hélouet, L.: Merging Scenarios. In: 9th International Workshop on Formal Methods for Industrial Critical Systems (FMICS), Linz, Austria, pp. 209–226 (September 2004)

18. Kralisch, S., Krause, P., David, O.: Using the Object Modeling System for hydrological model development and application. Advances in Geosciences 4, 75–81 (2005)
19. Lano, K. (ed.): UML 2 Semantics and Applications. John Wiley & Sons (2009)
20. Letcher, R.A., Bromley, J.: Typology of Models and Methods of Integration. In: Giupponi, et al. [8], vol. 11, pp. 287–323
21. Ludwig, M.: Modelling and Architecture of a Generic Framework for Integrative Environmental Simulations. Berichte aus der Informatik. Shaker, Aachen (2011)
22. Ludwig, R., Mauser, W., Niemeyer, S., Colgan, A., Stolz, R., Escher-Vetter, H., Kuhn, M., Reichstein, M., Tenhunen, J., Kraus, A., Ludwig, M., Barth, M., Hennicker, R.: Web-based Modeling of Water, Energy and Matter Fluxes to Support Decision Making in Mesoscale Catchments – the Integrative Perspective of GLOWA-Danube. Physics and Chemistry of the Earth 28, 621–634 (2003)
23. Magee, J., Kramer, J.: Concurrency: state models & Java programming, 2nd edn. Wiley, Chichester (2006)
24. Rahman, J.M., Seaton, S.P., Perraud, J.-M., Hotham, H., Verrelli, D.I., Coleman, J.R.: It's TIME for a New Environmental Modelling Framework. In: Proceedings of MODSIM 2003 International Congress on Modelling and Simulation, Townsville, Australia, vol. 4. Modelling and Simulation Society of Australia and New Zealand Inc. (July 2003)
25. Tenhunen, J.D., Kabat, P. (eds.): Integrating Hydrology, Ecosystem Dynamics, and Biogeochemistry in Complex Landscapes. Wiley, Chichester (1999)
26. GLOWA-Danube Project Website, http://www.glowa-danube.de (last visited May 10, 2011)
27. Warmer, J., Kleppe, A.: The Object Constraint Language, 2nd edn. Addison-Wesley (2003)
28. Winskel, G., Nielsen, M.: Models for concurrency. In: Abramsky, S., Gabbay, D.M., Maibaum, T.S.E. (eds.) Handbook of Logic in Computer Science, vol. 4, pp. 1–148. Oxford University Press, Oxford (1995)

Revealing Complexity
through Domain-Specific Modelling and Analysis

Richard F. Paige[1], Phillip J. Brooke[2], Xiaocheng Ge[1],
Christopher D.S. Power[1], Frank R. Burton[1], and Simon Poulding[1]

[1] Department of Computer Science, University of York, York, YO10 5GH, UK
{paige,xchge,cpower,frank,smp}@york.ac.uk
[2] School of Computing, Teesside University, Middlesbrough, TS1 3BA, UK
pjb@scm.tees.ac.uk

Abstract. Complex systems exhibit emergent behaviour. The explanations for this explicit emergent behaviour are often difficult to identify, and usually require understanding of significant parts of system structure and component behaviour to interpret. We present ongoing work on a set of techniques, based on Model-Driven Engineering principles and practices, for helping to reveal explanations for system complexity. We outline the techniques abstractly, and then illustrate parts of them with three examples from the health care, system security and Through-Life Capability Management domains.

1 Introduction

Complex systems exhibit behaviour that is not directly predictable or traceable from the behaviour of their constituent components. For large-scale complex IT systems (LSCITS), complexity arises due to combinations of attributes: increasing system size; increasing rates of changing requirements that must be addressed; increasing numbers and types of stakeholders. The roots of complexity are typically *hidden*, and often these do not become apparent during the system engineering phase. When tested or deployed, emergent behaviour readily becomes apparent, as illustrated by some recent failures, e.g., the Mars Polar Lander.

The LSCITS initiative[1] has argued that existing reductionist approaches to engineering complex systems do not address essential complexity. Instead, new approaches, which allow engineers to understand and control complexity, are needed.

Model-Driven Engineering (MDE) is a systems engineering approach that promotes models —abstract descriptions of phenomena of interest— to first-class engineering artefacts. The 'engineering' in MDE focuses on constructing, analysing and manipulating models in rigorous ways, particularly with automated tools that support required tasks. MDE requires organisations to invest substantial effort into constructing models and supporting the modelling process.

---

[1] www.lscits.org

R. Calinescu and D. Garlan (Eds.): Monterey Workshop 2012, LNCS 7539, pp. 251–265, 2012.
© Springer-Verlag Berlin Heidelberg 2012

Models range from design artefacts (e.g., in UML, SysML, or bespoke domain-specific languages), to requirements, to documentation and reports, to what-if models, and beyond. The tasks that are typically applied to models in MDE include *calculations* (e.g., calculating a representative response time based on a model of a network), *transformations* (e.g., transforming a system model into a detailed design model), *comparisons* (e.g., comparing two versions of a model to identify the changes made during a configuration management process) and more. Numerous tools now exist to support MDE tasks, and MDE is now practiced in industry, and on very large complex systems engineering projects and problems.

MDE, as its name suggests, is most typically used for engineering complex systems. It is used less frequently for *understanding* systems, *explaining* systems, and *revealing inherent complexity* in systems. It is the latter that is the focus of this paper.

We contribute towards an approach for modelling complex systems, designed to help engineers better understand — and ultimately control — complexity. The approach, based on MDE principles, practices and tools, focuses on *domain modelling* and use of bespoke *simulation and analysis* of said models. The analyses and simulations are designed to help disentangle relationships – both structural and behavioural – between entities and components of complex systems. They are not intended to *hide* complexity but to reveal just enough detail for engineers to understand specific interactions between components. This, in turn, may help engineers understand (1) the impact of engineering decisions on overall system complexity; and (2) how to better manage and control complexity in a deployed system. The analyses and simulations are produced via use of MDE transformations, which, as a side-effect, produce traceability information that can be used to connect the results of analysis/simulation back to the models that capture essential characteristics of the problem domain. This "closing of the loop" can thus help to support evolution and change of models, as a deeper understanding of complexity develops.

The rest of the paper is structured as follows. We start with an abstract overview of the general approach for modelling complex systems (Section 2), which is inspired by approaches to domain-specific language design. Then, in Section 3, we present three modelling examples that focus on revealing different kinds of complexity. The examples are all related to LSCITS socio-technical problems and concepts; while not all LSCITS must exhibit socio-technical characteristics, many do, and in turn the complexity of such systems is significant (in part because of the increased number of events and nondeterminism that arises with humans and organisations involved). In Section 4 we provide pointers and concrete ideas for future work.

2   Domain-Specific Modelling Approach

The approach we take to modelling complex systems is inspired by domain-specific language approaches to MDE. The general strategy is to model domain concepts of interest (e.g., components, behaviours, requirements) in a language specifically developed for the domain. As such, the semantic gap between the domain and the language used for expressing that domain should be reduced (and therefore the complexity of the problem domain is the focus of the modelling problem and the engineers). After constructing a suitable domain-specific language (with supporting tools for manipulating models), task-specific simulations and analyses are specified and developed. These analyses, which are designed to make explicit views on the behaviour and structures of the complex system, are developed and encoded using MDE operations (e.g., the transformations or comparisons mentioned earlier). The analyses can then be used to ask questions of the complex system model, e.g., what is the source of a set of events, how do events get transformed through parts of the system, what is the cost associated with processing particular types of events. In some cases, these questions may generate a *view* on the original system model; in other cases, it may elaborate part of the system model that was previously left abstract or obscured from an engineer. It is, ultimately, the engineer's responsibility to decide how to make use of the elaborated system models that are produced as a result of applying the analyses. Importantly, by using MDE operations (particularly model-to-model transformations or model-to-text transformations) to implement the analyses and simulations, we obtain full traceability (via a trace model) to original (domain) models. As such, when an analysis is executed, its results (e.g., model checking counter-examples, simulation outputs) can be traced back to important modelling elements, thus helping to explain the output – and complexity – in a more precise and analytic way. The traceability information can also be used to elaborate or refine the source models to take into account any improvements that may be needed as a result of the analysis or simulation.

In summary, the general modelling approach is as follows.

1. Identify domain concepts and relationships of interest; this in turn identifies and clarifies the scope of the DSL to be used, and of the modelling that is to take place.
2. Encode domain concepts and relationships in a domain-specific language, including the language's abstract and concrete syntax. Ideally, provide an editor for the language; the tool support will help to reduce errors and increase trust in the models.
3. Encode analyses of interest, by transforming (via model transformations of different kinds) domain-specific models into models amenable to analysis. The transformations should effectively produce views or elaborations of the original model, e.g., by simulating algorithms or calculating values.
4. Present the results of analysis to engineers, ideally in a perspective similar to the original editor (where feasible). Exploit the traceability information generated from running the transformations to enable this (e.g., following the approach of [6]).
5. Exploit the same traceability information to refactor and evolve the domain-specific language, where needed.

We now illustrate parts of this approach with several small examples.

3   Illustrations

Our illustrations focus on constructing and analysing domain-specific languages, and thereafter models of complex systems, to help to reveal explanations for their emergent behaviour. We present three examples.

1. A process modelling example wherein complex behaviours (particularly exceptional behaviours) are revealed through the modelling approach;
2. A secure systems example wherein complex inter-relationships between actors are revealed through the modelling approach; and
3. A Through-Life Capability Management class of problem, wherein LSCITS must be obtained to satisfy disparate goals, where there are multiple (optimal) ways in which the goals can be satisfied.

3.1   Failures in Healthcare Processes

Healthcare is a complex system [1, 15, 16]. Here we use term *'system'* generically, to indicate a conceptual entity whose components interact in rich and fine-grained ways because they continually affect each other and operate towards a common sense of purpose. There are many factors which may contribute to the complexity of healthcare systems; the focus of our example is the structures of healthcare systems, and the patterns created by the interaction of their components. To describe these, a business process model can be constructed.

A *business process* [7] is a collection of tasks designed to produce a specific output (e.g., a product or service). A *business process model* defines a specific ordering of tasks across time and space. A business process may have a hierarchical structure, i.e., tasks may include or trigger further business processes. As such, they may also be recursive, i.e., a business process may invoke itself. A task is normally made up of activities (carried out by actors), resources (which support activities) and constraints.

A business process consists of a *normal* set of tasks and constraints, as well as *exceptional* tasks and constraints, designed to deal with situations outside the norm. Exceptions in business processes have been widely studied, including work on both identifying exceptions as well as exception handling. The traditional approach is to anticipate beforehand, and ideally exhaustively, all exceptional conditions that may arise, and augment business process models with the additional conditional elements that represent exception handling activities. This, however, makes business process models more complicated, and introduces complexity through interactions between normal conditions and so-called *exceptional* conditions, which model exceptional behaviour. This complexity is normally hidden from the modeller, until the process model is reviewed and validated. Even then, for large business process models, it is easy to overlook or misunderstand the complex interactions between normal tasks and exceptional tasks.

We applied the approach from Section 2 to the problem of understanding exceptional behaviour in complex business process models. The key concept that we chose to focus on in developing a DSL (according to the process of Section 2) was that of exceptional conditions. We chose to treat exceptional conditions (and hence, tasks that were executed following exceptional conditions) as *failures*, and carry out a *failure propagation analysis* on a business process model. This in turn would illustrate (a) the impact of an exception on the overall business process model; and (b) the sensitivity of the business process model to exceptional conditions (namely, by illustrating the types of exception that tended to consolidate in specific parts of the business process model). In a nutshell, our DSL would include many familiar concepts for business modelling, but would be targeted at modelling of exceptional behaviour.

In terms of the approach of Section 2, we commenced by producing a small DSL for modelling business processes; this was effectively a subset of the Business Process Description Metamodel (BPDM), tailored for the example we were planning to use for experiments. However, the subset of BPDM was extended to include concepts for modelling the possible *failure modes* of the business process. This requires elaboration, because it is non-trivial and also because it is the key modelling challenge associated with this problem.

The problem we are interested in solving is identifying the failure modes of a business process. Our claim is that most process faults have a direct association with a task in the process — i.e., we assume that in the majority of cases the failure of a business process is initiated by a failure in a task of the process, and the failures introduced by individual tasks propagate through the process until the process delivers failure behaviour. So, to start analysing the behaviour of a business process in the presence of exceptions, we must first identify the possible failure modes of each task in the business process.

Let us illustrate this with a small healthcare system example. Consider Figure 1, which shows parts of a prototypical healthcare (business) process. We focus particularly Task 15 (Investigations); this task consists of one activity. Briefly, this task is as follows.

> "Patients who have had a suspected stroke should have specialist assessment and investigation within 24 hours of onset of symptoms and be transferred to the acute stroke unit."

The activity associated with this task is to investigate the condition of the suspected stroke patient. Resources available include acute stroke/TIA specialists, required medical documents (e.g., results of early assessment, patient medical history), and the availability of an acute stroke unit. There is also a constraint to carry out this activity within 24 hours of the onset of symptoms.

Given the activities, resources and constraints, we can now identify failure modes, i.e., the ways in which the business process fails to deliver its service. In effect, failure modes identify mismatches between expected outcomes and desired qualities. Based on an analysis of the literature [8, 9, 14] and a domain analysis of health care [2, 5], we argue that the qualities of a business process have the following five dimensions:

- **completeness**, whether the outcome of the process is complete;
- **validity**, whether the outcome of the process meets its requirements;

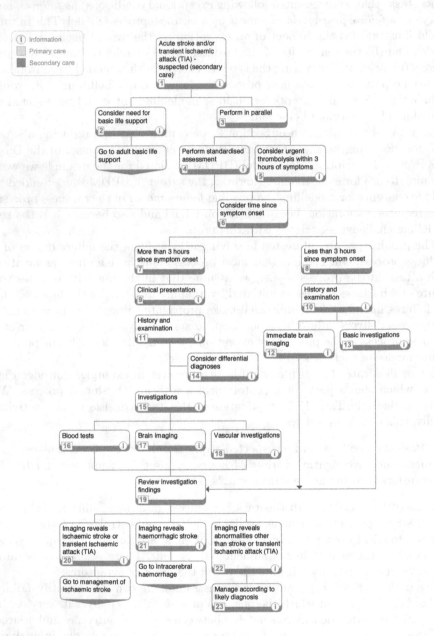

Fig. 1. Acute Stroke/TIA - suspected (secondary care) (derived from [13])

- **consistency**, whether the outcome of the process is consistent whenever the process is executed;
- **timeliness**, whether the outcome of the process is generated on time; and
- **adequacy**, whether the outcome of the process is fit-for-purpose.

In each quality dimension, we can determine the possible failure modes of each activity, resource and constraint of a task. For example, considering the human resources of Task 15, the possible failure modes might be:

- *incomplete*, the human resources assigned to the task are insufficient. For instance, the task requests a specialist and a nurse to assist the investigation, but in reality, there is no nurse available when the task is performed.
- *Late*, the team of specialists are late in carrying out the task.
- *Inadequate*, the task should be performed by a stroke specialist, but in reality, it is done by a different specialist.

Process models expressed in our DSL can be annotated with tokens indicating the type of potential failure for each kind of activity, resource or constraint. Importantly, this failure modelling is carried out on the *domain model*, in the vocabulary of process models. Additionally, these failures can then be elaborated to capture the *propagation* and *transformation* behaviour of activities, resources and constraints. For example, an activity may receive faulty outcomes from preceding activities. The new activity may compound the failure (by transforming it into a new failure), may simply propagate the failure, or may mitigate the failure in an appropriate way. Our modelling approach includes mechanisms for modelling such failure behaviours.

However, the (annotated) process model constructed as above only captures the component failure behaviour; it says nothing about the whole-system (emergent) failure behaviour. To understand and reveal this, we *transform* the annotated process model to a new model amenable to failure propagation analysis. The details of this are outside the scope of this paper, but the overall approach used is consistent with what was presented in Section 2: a model transformation maps the annotated process model into an interval timed coloured Petri Net, which can then be simulated to reveal the overall business process model failure behaviour. The overall algorithms used for simulation are inspired by those in the Failure Propagation and Transformation Calculus [17]. The transformation itself is not particularly complicated, requiring only several hundred lines of code (written in a specialised model transformation language); in part, the transformation is straightforward because of some similar structures arising in both the DSL for process modelling, and in the dialect of Petri nets.

We applied this approach to the health care example illustrated in Figure 1. This process includes sixteen key activities[2] We focused on one particular failure

---

[2] Excluding the final activity —i.e., determining whether the patient has experienced an acute stroke, TIA, haemorrhagic stroke, or other attack— because we are interested in analysing this example to identify key potential failures leading to incorrect judgement.

that was identified during the modelling stages: *incorrect judgement after activities related to reviewing the investigating results* (activity A19 in Figure 1). As a result of elaborating the business process model via transformation to a failure propagation model, we identified a number of reasons that could lead to this particular failure. Perhaps more importantly, we identified a number of 'vulnerable' activities that may be the ultimate cause of such a failure. These include A5 (judgement of application of urgent thrombolysis within 3 hours), A9 (clinical presentation), A10/11 (review history of health care and examinations) and A17 (brain imaging). During the analysis, the conclusion was that the quality of the services provided by these activities rely substantially on the skills of the personnel carrying them out. Thus, we can argue that to better mitigate such a failure, improvements should be concentrated on improving the skills and experience of the personnel carrying out these critical activities. These 'critical' activities were identified by expert analysis, assisted and supported by the traceability information derived from the model transformation mapping the process model into Petri nets. The results of the Petri net analysis was (manually) traced back, via the underlying trace model, to the activities of the process model. In this particular situation, the reflection of analysis results on the original model was not done automatically, but expert analysis was assisted by automated tools.

The modelling and analysis approach helped in this example to reveal inherent complexity due to failure behaviour. In turn, the analysis helped us identify critical parts of business processes, and how these parts contribute to overall failures and exceptional conditions.

Our second example uses a similar approach to modelling, but for different effect: to understand the complex inter-relationships that exist between actors.

3.2 Secure Transaction Problem

The recently cancelled UK National ID card programme was intended to introduce new large-scale complex IT systems, with particularly significant socio-technical concerns; similar (though not as controversial and pervasive) ID card systems exist in other countries world-wide. The intention for the UK ID card programme was to use a unified ID card, with secure transactions, to support many identification scenarios now currently supported by a collection of mechanisms (e.g., non-biometric cards). Many of the intended scenarios, and secure transactions, involve both network and cryptographic protocols and the interactions of different humans participants in a real-world environment. Modelling these scenarios is complex, in part due to the fuzziness of some of the properties involved. In this illustration, we use our modelling approach to unveil complexity in these scenarios, and by doing so address two other key contributors to complexity: *nondeterminism* and *unpredictability*.

Consider the following concrete example.

> *Alice has an identification card issued by her national government. She applies, in person, for a tax certificate for her car. The clerk takes Alice's identification card and tests it for various properties, related to Alice's*

identifying features (name, photograph, biometrics, address), which are needed to ensure that a tax certificate is properly issued to the person who should hold it. Specifically, the clerk at the tax office uses the identification card as a means of verifying any claims that Alice makes about herself (e.g., related to name and age).

Such scenarios occur widely. They appear to be simple (i.e., can Alice be issued a tax certificate for her car?) yet have significant inherent complexity. This complexity arises for at least two reasons.

1. decisions taken within the scenario are not based purely on boolean values (i.e., they are taken or not taken). Nor are they taken based on a probability (e.g., 75% of the time the certificate is issued, 25% of the time it is not[3]). Instead, decisions are taken based on probability distributions. A seemingly binary decision (*e.g.*, can Alice acquire a tax certificate?) is underpinned by a number of fuzzy decisions (*e.g.*, how accurately does the ID card presented identify Alice? To what extent does the clerk believe that the ID card represents Alice?).
2. the scenarios are inherently *generic* and must be *configured* to be fully analysable. For example, different mechanisms of different quality can be used within the scenario to support Alice demonstrating that she is at least 18. Such instantiations must take into account the scenario context (e.g., how effective will biometric scanners be in this particular building during these particular hours), and must be taken into account in any analysis process.

At different steps of the scenario (*e.g.*, when Alice enters the tax office, when the clerk first observes Alice), decisions are taken (*e.g.*, Alice is over 18, Alice's ID is valid). A simplistic view would be that these decisions are binary, and one branch of the decision structure (*e.g.*, Alice is over 18) is taken with probability p, and the other (*e.g.*, Alice is not over 18) taken with probability $1 - p$. Such a structure would naturally lend itself to state exploration and property checking using a probabilistic model checker, *e.g.*, PRISM [10] or a probabilistic process algebra, *e.g.*, pCSP [11]. A different view is that decisions are taken based on probability *distributions*. When Alice enters the office, the clerk forms a belief about Alice's age; conceptually, this belief is not that Alice is or is not 18, but that it can be represented as a distribution *around* Alice's age and represents the clerk's ability to perceive a person's age. Similarly, when Alice presents an ID card, there is a probability distribution associated with the clerk's perception of this ID card (*e.g.*, does the photo accurately depict Alice; does it appear that the card has been tampered with). This distribution is in turn dependent on the clerk's ability to perceive if a card has been tampered with. Later distributions may depend on an earlier perception, such as the ability of a third party to forge or modify a card.

Modelling scenarios like these as a set of binary decisions with real-valued probabilities hides much of the complexity of how decisions are made. By hiding

---

[3] Though post facto analysis of many instances of the scenario could lead to sufficient data about the probability of a decision being made.

this complexity, we make it difficult to understand the *impact* of changes in the scenario, *e.g.*, the use of ID cards that are claimed to provide fewer false positives. This in turn makes it more difficult to analyse scenarios and carry out *what-if* analyses, particularly to establish the benefit of improvements in the mechanisms used in specific configurations of scenarios.

We have applied the modelling approach of Section 2 to scenarios like the tax certificate one above. In [3] we identified the concepts for and the abstract syntax of a domain-specific language for modelling configurable scenarios. The DSL includes concepts for modelling actors (e.g., agents, subjects, cheats), mechanisms (e.g., cards, card readers), locations, and events (e.g., test a card, validate a transaction). As a result, the DSL contains slots for carrying out configurations, for example, to introduce particular cards or particular events.

Transformations have then been defined to map models written in the DSL to input to a probabilistic state exploration tool. This would allow the use of probabilistic model checkers such as PRISM, or state exploration tools like Casper, FDR2, or ProBE to do exhaustive runs of specific scenarios, or to work in an interactive mode. These would support probability distributions related to events, but it would not allow the manipulation of those distributions. In order to provide support such manipulations, we transform models to to serve as input into a bespoke state exploration tool. This tool allows us to exhaustively explore scenario instances, and as result obtain a better understanding of the inherent complexity of such scenarios. The transformation – in this case, a model-to-text transformation – is, like the previous example, not particularly complex. Much of the complexity arises with supporting the configuration of the scenario, e.g., to introduce cards with particular capabilities. In this particular case, because the number of configurations we needed to work with was relatively small – just a few different types of cards and around 10 different events – we configured the models interactively. In other words, we asked the end-user to select which configurations they wanted to execute (as the model-to-text transformation was running). For larger configurations we would likely re-implement the transformation to take two models as input – one for the scenario model, the other encoding configuration parameters. It is worth noting that the transformation tools we used support transformations involving multiple input models.

What does the elaboration of complex scenario models actually provide to us? For one, it allows us to determine the impact of mechanisms on outcome. For example, we might ask: what, truly, is the impact of biometric ID cards on identification scenarios such as this? Before biometric ID cards, successful completion of the scenario (i.e., offering Alice a tax certificate when she was legitimately entitled to one; and refusing when she shouldn't receive one) depended predominantly on the beliefs formed by the clerk. Do biometric ID cards offer any improvement? The work in [3] included a number of instances of similar scenarios and as a result made the following observations:

– use of biometric ID cards led to small, though noticeable increases in true positives and small, but noticeable reductions in false negatives (when compared with using no cards at all);

– when compared with alternative mechanisms (e.g., non-biometric ID cards), biometric ID cards made very small improvements (on the order of 1%).

While many more scenarios and experiments would need to be carried out to better bound the overall impact, it is arguable whether more expensive biometric ID cards add value when compared with less sophisticated, less accurate mechanisms of identification.

With this example, we were able to use modelling and overall approach to make explicit the relationships between actors in a scenario, and to tease out the semantics underpinning these relationships — i.e., that they were based on belief models instead of discrete probabilities. In constructing our domain-specific language and our analysis tools, we have configured the approach in a way that allows experiment with different semantics. For example, we could experiment with Bayesian models underpinning the belief systems set up in the scenarios, without having to change the overall DSL or the modelling approach — only the back-end state exploration or modelling tool would need to be changed.

3.3 Through-Life Capability Management

Large organisations typically manage LSCITS projects in terms of procuring the equipment, facilities, personnel and software that they require. Procurement exercises are invariably large and complex, requiring different entities (e.g., computers, lifeboats) to be compared in different ways.

It has been recognised by numerous government departments and large organisations that management of projects in terms of *capability* could potentially offer increased efficiencies. In classical procurement, an organisation may have defined a problem in terms of a *requirement* for a piece of equipment (e.g., a lifeboat); said equipment would then be acquired. In capability-based management, the problem would be defined in terms of a capability of *rescuing people and equipment at sea*, and a range of possible solutions could be considered. In effect, capability-based management means moving from defining problems in terms of concrete solutions, to defining problems in terms of abstract needs.

The challenge associated with capability-based management is that it opens up the solution space: a problem is now specified in terms of abstract needs, which can be met in a number of ways. Each potential solution must be identified and costed. Moreover, potential solutions are themselves capabilities, and are associated with their own individual requirements. To put it another way, solutions come with new problems, and as such understanding how solutions interact is difficult. Modelling – particularly with domain-specific languages – can help provide engineers with means to manage the solution space.

Through-Life Capability Management (TLCM) [12] is a specific instance of capability-based management, which also takes into account long-lived capabilities, e.g., logistics, personnel, training, deployment and decommissioning. It is of particular interest to military organisations (e.g., the UK Ministry of Defense). An example of a TLCM problem arises with acquisition of long-lived assets such as aircraft carriers: not only must the equipment (the carrier) be acquired, but so must airplanes, personnel, and fixtures and fittings. Moreover, personnel must be trained (at the right time) so that the aircraft carrier can be deployed on-time and on-budget. Furthermore, personnel and other equipment must be moved off the aircraft carrier in time for it to be decommissioned. There are, of course, multiple ways in which acquisition of these various assets can be implemented. In general, TLCM problems exhibit the following characteristics:

- They exhibit multiple objectives (e.g., protect a country, minimise costs).
- To solve them requires heterogeneous tradeoffs (e.g., between training and equipment). This is sometimes called the 'Apples and Wednesdays' problem, as it requires comparing and deciding between very different things.
- Different solutions may be optimal or near-optimal at different times.
- There may be multiple solutions, and understanding how each solution contributes to solving the overall problem may be difficult.

We applied the approach in Section 2 in a number of experiments that constructed DSLs for modelling TLCM problems. At the same time, we developed MDE techniques for calculating optimal and near-optimal solutions to these problems. The full details of our approach to calculating optimal solutions (based on search-based software engineering techniques) have recently been presented in [4], including a small example. We give a concise overview of our modelling approach here.

There are two basic modelling problems associated with TLCM.

1. Modelling TLCM problems in a domain-specific way, which reveals the complexity of the problem but says nothing about potential solutions. In this manner, we use abstraction and domain-specific concepts to allow us to focus on the challenges of *understanding the problem*, instead of concerning ourselves with characteristics of the solution space.
2. Modelling *components*, which are artefacts that can be used to (partially or fully) satisfy the goals inherent in a TLCM problem. In effect, the components are the basic building blocks of the solution space, and when components are – perhaps in combination or aggregation – used to satisfy goals, a solution to the overall TLCM problem is derived.

To support this, we used the approach in Section 2 and designed and implemented two domain-specific languages: one for modelling TLCM goals, and the other for modelling components. In the first DSL, goals can be decomposed further; moreover, each goal is itself associated with an arbitrary number of ways in which its satisfaction can be determined. For example, some goals may be satisfied in a probabilistic way (e.g., 100%, 75%); others may be satisfied in a measurable but discrete way (e.g., best, worst). The overall abstract syntax of the problem/goal DSL is illustrated in Fig. 2. We use UML's concrete syntax to represent the abstract syntax; in practice, we usually implement the abstract syntax using Ecore and the Eclipse Modelling Framework (EMF)[4]. For reasons of compliance with TLCM vocabulary, a goal is called a Capability in this diagram.

---

[4] www.eclipse.org/emf

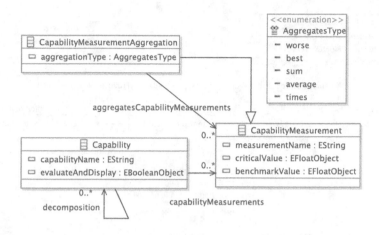

Fig. 2. Capability and goal DSL

The second DSL is used for modelling components that can be used to satisfy goals (capabilities). Components are associated with a particular cost, as well as a description of the capabilities they provide, and the capabilities they require (it is typical of TLCM problems that acquired capabilities require other assets to also be acquired). This is illustrated in Fig. 3

The first DSL is used by the TLCM expert who wishes to model and understand a TLCM problem; the second DSL may be used by a procurement expert who understands what assets are available, what they may cost, and what is required to acquire and deploy them. Models expressed in the two DSLs are then input in to an optimisation algorithm (implemented using the Epsilon model management framework[5], which will automatically calculate optimal ways in which the components can be configured to satisfy the overall TLCM objectives. The details of this algorithm can be found in [4]. Effectively, the implementation of the algorithm uses a chain of different kinds of model transformations to calculate optimal solutions. The chain of transformations maintains traceability between source models (scenarios and components) and optimal solutions; the chain is itself very complex, involving around 5K lines of transformation code. However, the traceability information is not specifically needed to trace the results from solution back to source models, because the way in which the transformations produce results, both solutions *and* relevant source models are presented to the end-user (in other words, the traceability information is captured explicitly in the output). Explicitly representing traceability information in this specific case is necessary to allow the end-user to consider the tradeoffs between solutions that are available.

---

[5] http://www.eclipse.org/epsilon

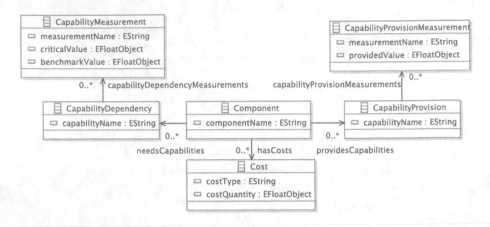

Fig. 3. Component and measurement DSL

We have applied the modelling approach and the optimisation algorithm to a number of TLCM problems, including the next-release problem (i.e., determining the optimal features to include in a next software release), a lifeboat problem, and a crisis management problem. With this approach we were able to make explicit the relationships between solutions and problems, particularly when those relationships were extremely complex (e.g., when an aggregate of components was used in a non-obvious way to satisfy a complex decomposition of goals). Effectively, the approach can be used to disentangle the most appropriate ways to satisfy goals, to exhaustively enumerate all possible optimal solutions to TLCM problems, and as a result guide TLCM practitioners through the process of making tradeoffs between these solutions. DSLs and modelling helped us to reveal complexity, but also manage it in efficient and controlled ways.

4   Conclusions

We have outlined a modelling approach, based on the construction of domain-specific languages, for improving understanding of complex systems. Typical approaches to use of domain-specific languages (e.g., as exemplified in Model-Driven Engineering) focus on generating new applications; we instead focus on using the principles of domain-specific languages to produce views of complex systems that help us better understand interactions between components. We have used this approach, in concert with model transformation technology, to better understand complex business processes (to help identify failure behaviour, both locally and in subsystems) and to better understand complex scenarios (to help identify the relationships between actors in scenarios). We are current applying domain-specific languages to wider search-related problems, particularly for validation and verification of models and mechanisms for manipulating models. One of the critical problems in modelling is determine the validity of the model; we are attempting to evaluate this by building tools that manipulate models (e.g., via transformation, code generation, or comparison) and then using search-based techniques to automatically test the tools, thus ideally giving us more confidence in the validity of the models, the DSLs themselves, and the tools.

References

1. Baxter, G.: White paper: Complexity in health care. Technical report, Large Scale Complex IT System, LSCITS (2010)
2. Brook, R.H., McGlynn, E.A., Cleary, P.D.: Quality of health care: measuring quality of care. New England Journal of Medicine 335, 966–970 (1996)
3. Brooke, P.J., Paige, R.F., Power, C.: State exploration and property checking for fuzzy scenarios (under review, 2012)
4. Burton, F.R., Paige, R.F., Rose, L.M., Kolovos, D.S., Poulding, S., Smith, S.: Solving Acquisition Problems Using Model-Driven Engineering. In: Vallecillo, A., Tolvanen, J.-P., Kindler, E., Störrle, H., Kolovos, D. (eds.) ECMFA 2012. LNCS, vol. 7349, pp. 428–443. Springer, Heidelberg (2012)
5. Donabedian, A.: The Definition of Quality and Approaches to Its Assessment. Health Administration Press (1980)
6. dos Santos, O.M., Woodcock, J., Paige, R.F.: Using model transformation to generate graphical counter-examples for the formal analysis of xuml models. In: ICECCS, pp. 117–126 (2011)
7. Object Management Group. Business process definition metamodel (BPDM), process definitions (2008), http://www.omg.org/cgi-bin/doc?dtc/2008-05-09
8. Haywood-Farmer, J., Alleyne, A., Duffus, B., Downing, M.: Controlling service quality. Business Quarterly 50(4), 62–67 (1986)
9. Haywood-Farmer, J.: A conceptual model of service quality. International Journal of Operations and Production Management 8(6), 19–29 (1988)
10. Kwiatkowska, M., Norman, G., Parker, D.: PRISM: Probabilistic Symbolic Model Checker. In: Field, T., Harrison, P.G., Bradley, J., Harder, U. (eds.) TOOLS 2002. LNCS, vol. 2324, pp. 113–140. Springer, Heidelberg (2002)
11. Lowe, G.: Probabilistic and prioritized models of timed CSP. Theoretical Computer Science 13(2), 315–352 (1995)
12. McKane, T.: Enabling acquisition change - an examination of the Ministry of Defence's ability to undertake Through Life Capability Management. Technical report (June 2006)
13. NHS. Acute stroke and transient ischaemic attack suspected (January 2010), http://healthguides.mapofmedicine.com/choices/map/stroke2.html
14. Parasuraman, A., Zeithaml, V.A., Berry, L.L.: A conceptual model of service quality and its implications for future research. Journal of Marketing 49, 41–50 (1985)
15. Plsek, P.E., Greenhalgh, T.: The challenge of complexity in health care. British Medical Journal 323, 624–628 (2001)
16. Sweeney, K., Griffiths, F. (eds.): Complexity and Healthcare: an introduction. Radcliffe Medical Press (2002)
17. Wallace, M.: Modular architectural representation and analysis of fault propagation and transformation. Electr. Notes Theor. Comput. Sci. 141(3), 53–71 (2005)

Information Requirements for Enterprise Systems

Ian Sommerville[1], Russell Lock[2], and Tim Storer[3]

[1] School of Computer Science, University of St. Andrews, St. Andrews, Scotland
[2] Department of Computer Science, Loughborough University, Leics., England
[3] School of Computing Science, Glasgow University, Glasgow, Scotland
ian.sommerville@st-andrews.ac.uk, r.lock@lboro.ac.uk,
timothy.storer@glasgow.ac.uk

Abstract. In this paper, we discuss an approach to system requirements engineering, which is based on using models of the responsibilities assigned to agents in a multi-agency system of systems. The responsibility models serve as a basis for identifying the stakeholders that should be considered in establishing the requirements and provide a basis for a structured approach, described here, for information requirements elicitation. We illustrate this approach using a case study drawn from civil emergency management.

Keywords: requirements engineering, requirements, enterprise systems, responsibility modeling, socio-technical systems.

1   Introduction

The derivation of requirements for complex systems has been recognized as a major problem in industry. The system requirements are a definition of what is expected of the system. They inform the system implementation and, in some cases, serve as a basis for a contract between a system procurer and a system provider. Historically, requirements have been expressed as statements of natural language text that have set out the functionality of the system that is expected. Modern agile methods have rejected the notion of requirements as descriptions of functionality and use approaches such as user stories to describe what is expected. However, these approaches are still primarily concerned with what the system should *do*.

Behavioural approaches to requirements engineering are appropriate when systems are to be developed from scratch. However, in most organization, new systems are now created by integrating functionality from existing systems and components. In such cases, it makes little sense to specify requirements in terms of what the system should do – the functionality is already defined in these systems. Rather, we argue that it is more appropriate to consider the system requirements from an informational perspective – what information should the system provide and who needs that information to do their job.

The derivation of requirements involves extensive discussions and consultations with system stakeholders – people who may be system users, their managers or who are influenced in some way by the system. An enduring problem in requirements engineering has been how to identify the stakeholders to be consulted and how to help

R. Calinescu and D. Garlan (Eds.): Monterey Workshop 2012, LNCS 7539, pp. 266–282, 2012.

them articulate their requirements for a system [1]. Requirements engineering methods such as Volere [2], say little about this problem – they highlight the importance of stakeholder consultation but their only guidance of stakeholder identification is to provide a list of stakeholder types. The problems of stakeholder identification are exacerbated in situations where the system to be developed spans several organizations and these stakeholders are distributed across these organizations.

To address this problem, we have developed the notion of responsibility modeling. We explicitly identify the responsibilities of organizational stakeholders in a problem setting and draw up a model showing these responsibilities and their assignment to agents. This then serves as a basis for both identifying stakeholders and for identifying whether or not there are inconsistencies in responsibility perception in the different organizations involved.

Once stakeholders have been identified, we can then enter into discussions with them about how they do their job and what information they require to do so. The responsibility model, along with a set of standard questions, is used to facilitate that discussion and to help the requirements engineer tease out the interactions between stakeholder responsibilities. This then leads to a statement of 'information requirements' which are then used to inform the system design and implementation.

In the remainder of the paper, we discuss enterprise systems and how these are typically created by composing and configuring existing software systems or components. We go on to explain why we think information requirements are the most important type of requirement for enterprise systems and follow this with an introduction to responsibility modeling. We explain how responsibility models are used to derive information requirements and illustrate our approach with a case study of an emergency management system. We conclude with a discussion of related work and our thoughts on how this work can be taken forward.

2   Enterprise Systems

The focus of our work for a number of years has been *enterprise systems* [3]. This term is widely used and is sometimes used synonomously with the term *ERP or enterprise resource planning systems*. Whilst ERP systems are certainly enterprise systems, we actually use the term more widely to denote systems that have the following characteristics:

1. They are multifunctional systems in that they deliver different classes of functionality. For example, an enterprise system may deliver functionality to support both sales and purchasing functions in an organization.
2. They are often oriented around one or more shared databases. The sharing of data means that data is not replicated in the organization and there are opportunities for data sharing across the different functions delivered by the system.
3. The different components of the system are self-contained systems so that they can operate with or without other components. An enterprise system may therefore be considered as a system of systems.

4. They are used by different classes of stakeholder who have different jobs in the organization. Users may have different levels of power and authority in the organization and different levels of technical expertise. The user base for these systems is therefore heterogeneous and drawn from different levels in the organization.

5. The system will have emergent behavior that cannot be predicted by an analysis of the system components. This behavior may be desirable or undesirable and is a consequence of the complexity of the relationships between the different systems in the enterprise system.

ERP systems, such as those marketed by SAP and Oracle, are enterprise systems where all of the system components are supplied by a single supplier. These ERP systems normally have a preferred mode of use and organizations that wish to use an ERP system are advised to adapt their processes to this mode of use. Typically, a single ERP system will replace a number of separate systems in an organization.

More generally, enterprise systems may include systems from a number of different suppliers. These may communicate through a shared database but may also maintain their own databases. Some component systems may be legacy systems – older systems based on obsolete technology that have been 'wrapped' with e.g. a service interface so that they can interact with other systems. Other components may be off-the-shelf systems from different manufacturers, specially written systems, etc.

Enterprise systems may be considered as technical software/hardware systems but they are an integral part of wider socio-technical systems in the enterprise. Socio-technical systems are systems that include people as well as technical elements and which are profoundly influenced by organizational policies, processes and culture, as well as external regulation. In essence, socio-technical systems are the ways in which work gets done in an organization.

Over the past decade of so, the notion of a virtual organization or virtual enterprise [4] has been developed. A virtual organization is temporary entity that is created with a particular mission and which involves a number of other organizations. For example, a virtual organization may be created to organize a major sporting event such as the Olympic Games. This encompasses many different partners, who each have their own IT systems.

Virtual organizations are enterprises in their own right and enterprise systems may therefore be created to support their operation. In this case, the component systems are distributed across the organizations in the virtual enterprise. These systems have all of the above enterprise system characteristics but with additional complications:

1. The system components in the system of systems are independently owned and managed. This means that there is no single authority that can control the functionality and development of the enterprise system.

2. There is no single shared database but rather a confederation of databases from the different organizations that are involved in the system. Inevitably there are syntactic and semantic incompatibilities between these systems.

3. The practices and cultures of the different organizations in the virtual organization are different. This has the consequence that the overall virtual enterprise system is perceived in quite different ways by stakeholders in these different organizations.

In this paper, we will draw on our experience of interacting with a virtual organization, which is created to deal with serious civil emergencies such as a terrorist attack, regional flooding, or a nuclear incident.

3 Requirements Engineering for Enterprise Systems

Requirements engineering (RE) is the process of understanding a system's environment with a view to deriving the requirements for the system – what has to be implemented to provide the business functionality that is required. For organizational systems, this inevitably means dealing with multiple stakeholders from different parts of the organization who have differing needs and priorities. The RE process therefore inevitably involves negotiations with and between these stakeholders to arrive at a set of requirements that is acceptable to all stakeholders. This is illustrated in Figure 1.

The requirements engineering team works with stakeholders to understand their requirements for a new or replacement system. These requirements are then documented, usually using natural language text, and system models of different kinds may be produced. These are then taken back to stakeholders for checking. Typically, this is an incremental process and there will be several rounds of the cycle completed before a comprehensive set of requirements have been produced.

Inevitably, there will be conflicts between these requirements as they will represent the wishes of stakeholders with diverse needs. Some of these conflicts will be resolved by the requirements engineering team but there is always a need for a period of negotiation to settle disagreements and to arrive at a set of compromise requirements. This negotiation may also involve the implementation team who provide information about the costs of implementing the requirements – if requirements are too expensive to implement, they may be discarded.

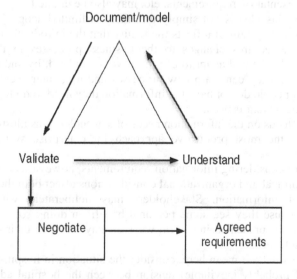

Fig. 1. The requirements engineering cycle

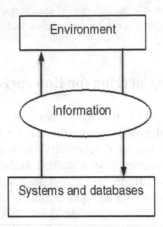

Fig. 2. Enterprise system requirements engineering

Most approaches to requirements engineering that have been developed have adopted a behavioural perspective – they focus on what the system should 'do', in terms of delivering functionality to stakeholders of different kinds. However, when we are considering enterprise systems, the detailed functionality is largely pre-defined by the system components that are used. Instead, we argue that the focus of requirements engineering process should be on identifying the information that is needed and used by stakeholders, rather than the specific functionality that is used.

In essence, the requirements engineering process should focus its analysis on the information that people need to do their work, the information that they create in the course of that work and the information that is shared with other people. Non-functional information requirements such as confidentiality requirements for shared information, presentation requirements, etc. may also be elicited .

The basis of this idea is not simply that there is limited scope for extending the functionality of the system. It reflects the reality that the introduction of an enterprise system normally requires changes to the business processes in the organization. People have to change and adapt to use the new system and, by and large, this is not really a problem. They can learn new processes and user interfaces. Problems arise, however, when people do not have the information they need to do their job, whatever the specific process that is used.

Therefore, a focus on the information needs of stakeholders, as illustrated in Figure 2, is likely to be the most productive approach for enterprise system requirements engineering.

When we are considering information requirements, however, we need to take into account that political and organizational considerations affect both the availability and the sharing of information. Stakeholders may deliberately withhold or delay information because they see some personal benefit in doing so; they may demand that information be presented in certain ways or may insist on their own information classification schemes.

To illustrate what we mean here, consider the situation in hospitals where there is perennial (and probably inevitable) tension between the hospital administrators and the senior doctors. Information that is required to support administration is inevitably different from clinical information and providing that information often requires doctors to do extra work. If doctors are in a strong position within the organization, they may simply refuse to provide that information, thus constraining the information system. On the other hand, if the power struggle favours the hospital managers, then the doctors may comply with the demands to change the way they capture patient information. The information requirements depend on the power relationships in the organization as well as what people need in order to do their job.

4   Responsibility and Responsibility Modelling

Our work over the past few years has been concerned with the notion of socio-technical systems engineering, where we are exploring how methods and techniques for socio-technical analysis of organizations can be used alongside systems and software engineering methods [5]. As part of this work, we have been investigating the abstractions that can be used to model complex socio-technical systems. Such systems include human and automated components, are significantly influenced by organizational policies, culture and politics and often involve participants and systems from a number of different organizations.

One abstraction that we have found to be particularly helpful is the notion of 'responsibility', which can be used to represent the expectations placed on both individuals and systems and which is a universal abstraction, used in all types of organization. We define a responsibility to be:

A duty, held by some agent, to achieve, maintain or avoid some given state,
subject to conformance with organizational, social and cultural norms.

The key points in this definition are

- a responsibility is a duty, which implies that the agent holding the responsibility is accountable to some authority for their actions,
- responsibilities may be concerned with avoiding undesirable situations and not just with accomplishing some actions
- in discharging responsibilities, agent behaviour is constrained by laws, regulations and social/cultural conventions and expectations. Therefore, the effectiveness of an agent in discharging their responsibility is not only judged by the outcome but also by the ways in which the agent has discharged that responsibility.

Responsibilities are a particularly helpful abstraction because they are firmly rooted in the world of work and are not abstract notions, such as goals, which are apparently internalized in individuals. The naturalness of responsibilities means that responsibility holders find it easy to communicate with people about their own responsibilities and also about the responsibilities of others.

Of course, it is often the case that there are different interpretations about what a responsibility means. Perceived differences in what a responsibility entails are often helpful in identifying sources of misunderstanding and, sometimes, requirement conflicts. For example, a responsibility to arrange seminars in a university may be interpreted as simply involving finding speakers and gaining their agreement to speak, but without any involvement in booking rooms, arranging refreshments, etc. The same responsibility may also be considered to be more inclusive so that it involves both finding speakers and making all other arrangements for the seminar presentation.

A responsibility model is a succinct description of the responsibilities that have been assigned to agents in one or more organizations. Our experience in modeling with client organizations is that modeling notations have to be simple, easy to explain and must avoid technical concepts that are alien to the people in the organization. For this reason, we believe that technical modeling notations such as the UML are not particularly useful for early-stage requirements engineering.

To make the models as simple as possible to explain, we have limited a responsibility model to three abstractions:

1. Responsibilities, as discussed above. Examples of responsibilities, drawn from an emergency response system, might be 'Establish local communications', 'Casualty evacuation' and 'Press liaison'.
2. Agents, which are organizational, human or system entities that may be assigned responsibilities. Therefore, an agent may be a named organization such as the ambulance service, a person or a role, such as the communication coordinator or a software-intensive system, such as an automated despatcher for emergency vehicles.
3. Resources, which are used by agents in discharging their responsibilities. We distinguish between two types of resource namely physical resources, which are 'consumed' in use and information resources, which are not. An example of a physical resource is an ambulance – there are a limited number of ambulances in an area and once these have all been allocated, the despatcher must wait until one has been released. By contrast, an information resource such as a geographical information system is not (normally) limited by demand – it can be used irrespective of the number of users.

Figure 3 illustrates a responsibility model that we developed as part of an analysis of response to a civil nuclear emergency at a power station by the coast. There are consequent responsibilities to inform shipping in the area. In this model:

1. Responsibilities are shown in round-edged rectangles.
2. Agent names are enclosed in angle brackets.
3. Physical resources are shown in square brackets.
4. The names of information resources are surrounded by vertical bars.
5. Arrows show the sources and destination of information.

From this model, you can see that responsibility to check on the safety of shipping falls on MRCC Clyde, the maritime rescue coordination center for the Clyde Estuary area and it relies on incident information provided by the police and the nuclear emergency liaison officer from the NAECC, the National Atomic Emergency Coordination Centre. Notice that we don't decompose this responsibility – how it is discharged is up to the organization assigned the responsibility and is of no concern to the emergency coordination team.

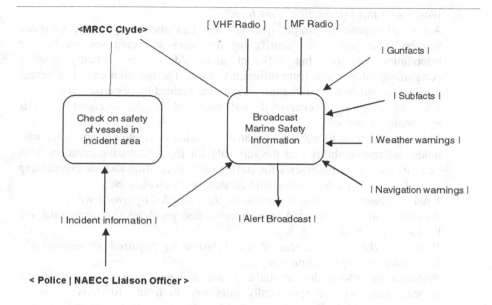

Fig. 3. An example of a responsibility model

The broadcasting of safety information relies on a number of information resources from various sources (not shown here) and the physical resources of VHF and MF radios, which are used to broadcast the information.

5   Deriving Information Requirements

Responsibility models document the responsibilities of the agents involved in a multi-agency virtual enterprise and so serve as a basis for identifying the sources of requirements and the stakeholders who need to be consulted to derive these requirements. Our approach to requirements derivation is based on a set of structured questions that are put to stakeholders in the system. These questions are based around the following topics:

1. *What information needs to be provided to discharge this responsibility?*
   Whilst an apparently simple question, it is not necessarily the case that stakeholders from different agencies require the same information. For example, a stakeholder in agency A may already have some information because it is generated in agency A but this needs to be provided in other agencies. So, as well as identifying specific information items, these questions identify information that may have to be shared between agencies.
2. *What channels are used to communicate this information?*
   This question identifies the ways in which information is communicated to stakeholders. In some organizational systems, this is simple and straightforward but in other circumstances such as emergency response, communication channels can be unreliable. We therefore may identify requirements for alternative communication channels that may be used.

3. *Where does this information come from?*
   Again, an apparently simple question that can elicit surprisingly complex answers. Our aim is to identify the databases and data sources for the information required but different stakeholders may actually acquire comparable information from different sources. The question can often reveal duplication and overlap in the information maintained by organizations.

4. *What information is generated and recorded in the discharge of this responsibility and why?*
   This question tries to tease out what information is created by an agent who holds and responsibility and the rationale for the information creation. This helps us identify requirements for storing that information and for maintaining meta-data for that information (who created, when created, etc.

5. *What channels are used to communicate this recorded information?*
   As above, we are interested in communication problems that may arise and backup requirements.

6. *What are the consequences if the information required is unavailable, inaccurate, incomplete, late, early?*
   Problems of information availability are common in multi-organizational systems Here we are specifically interested in trying to derive 'coping' requirements which allows the system to continue in effective operation when things go wrong. We have developed an approach based on HAZOPs [7], which we have discussed in some detail in a separate paper [8].

These questions are not formulaic – they are interpreted by the requirements engineering depending on local circumstances and the people being interviewed. Their purpose is to structure the discussion between a requirements engineer and system stakeholders. Typically, they lead to further questions and discussion about how stakeholders discharge their responsibilities. We expect the requirements engineer to deliver the results of that discussion in a form that is appropriate for the type of system being developed. This could be natural language requirements, diagrams or tables or even user stories.

6   Case Study – Emergency Coordination System

To illustrate the derivation of requirements from responsibilities, we use an example of a system that helps coordinate the responses of the different agencies that are involved in dealing with civil emergencies. In the UK (and we understand elsewhere), the emergency services each have their own command and control systems and they do not think that it is appropriate to integrate these into a single system for all of the emergency services. Systems from other agencies may also be required to support emergency coordination. These might include systems from government agencies, such as the environment agency for flood management, and systems from local and regional government that maintain information about the local area.

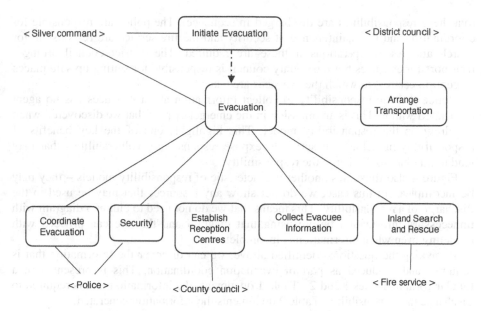

Fig. 4. Responsibility model of evacuation coordination

Therefore, the coordination system is primarily an information management system that draws information from other systems and databases. It serves a variety of different stakeholders - emergency service staff working at the site of the emergency, emergency service coordination and planning officers, press officers, local government officers, and so on.

We will focus in this case study on the information requirements for the evacuation of premises in an area that is threatened by flooding. The information here is drawn from an analysis of a flooding emergency in the north-west of England in 2005.

Figure 4 shows the responsibility model for area evacuation. Some terminology here may need to be explained:

1. Silver command is the command centre that is set up to deal with the emergency and is responsible for strategic decision making. It is located in a pre-allocated, networked control room. Officers from the different services are involved in Silver Command. It is generally located away from the source of the emergency and communicates by radio and telephone with the on-site command centre (Bronze Command).
2. In England, there are two levels of local government at the district level (District Council) and at the regional level (County Council). The allocation of functions to District and County councils is historical.

Given situation information such as the current and predicted level of local rivers and weather forecasts, Silver Command carries out a risk analysis and on the basis of that analysis may decide that an area should be evacuated (Initiate Evacuation). This is a legal decision that results in the handover of certain powers to the emergency services, such as the right to remove people from their homes, and this must be agreed by all of the services. Evacuation then proceeds (the dashed arrow in Figure 4 means that these responsibilities are discharged in sequence). The police are responsible for coordination and the maintenance of security and the fire service are responsible for search and rescue operations if these are required. The district council arranges transport for evacuees but the county council is responsible for setting up safe places (reception centres) to which the evacuees are taken.

Notice that the responsibility to collect information about evacuees has no agent associated with it. This is an omission in the emergency plan that we discovered when we drew up the responsibility model. This highlights one of the key benefits of responsibility modeling – it serves to expose responsibility vulnerabilities that may lead to a failure to discharge the responsibility.

Figure 4 also illustrates another characteristic of responsibility models – they may be incomplete. In this case, we do not show any resources that may be used in the discharge of a responsibility. This means that we do not need to clutter a diagram with unnecessary information before using that diagram and that we can proceed with modeling even when information is incomplete.

By asking the questions identified above, we can discover the information that is required and produced as part of evacuation coordination. This is presented in a tabular form in Tables 1 and 2. Table 1 documents the information that is required to discharge the responsibility. Table 2 documents the information generated.

Table 1. Information used in the discharge of the evacuation responsibility

Information required	Source	Communication channel
Area map	County council	Radio data link to printers in local command centre
Priority premises list	District Council	Radio data link to printers in local command centre
Assembly points list	District Council	Radio data link to printers in local command centre
Evacuated premises	Police, Fire Service	Radio from Silver Command
Unsafe routes	Police	Radio from Silver Command
Threat information	Environment agency	Radio from Silver Command
Transport capacity and availability	District Council	Radio from Silver Command
Police and other emergency service availability	Police, other services	Radio from Silver Command

The priority premises list is a list of premises, such as schools and care homes, where the occupants cannot be expected to evacuate themselves. The evacuation involves local residents going to local assembly points from which they are transported to a place of safety. Unsafe routes are those routes that must be closed off by the emergency services because they are already flooded or in imminent danger of flooding.

We have found that it is important to maintain information about the communication channels that are used. Communications are often a problem in emergency management so it is important to check that backup channels are available. In addition, the system being developed automatically generates and sends messages and so it is important to have information about how these should be transmitted.

Table 2. Information recorded in the discharge of the evacuation responsibility

Information created/recorded	Channels
Information about evacuated premises, evacuation time and units responsible for evacuation	Radio or verbal report from ground units to local Bronze Command. Email or fax to Silver Command if available, otherwise radio.
Information about unchecked premises	Radio or verbal report from ground units to local Bronze Command. Email or fax to Silver Command if available, otherwise radio
Information about unsafe routes	Radio or verbal report from ground units to local Bronze Command. Email or fax to Silver Command if available, otherwise radio

A critical part of the questioning process is the analysis of the consequences if information is not available as expected. We assess these consequences when the information required is unavailable, inaccurate, incomplete, delivered late or early? For example, consider the information relating to the list of priority premises to be evacuated:

1. *Information unavailable.* A manual premises check is required to see if there are vulnerable people who need help with evacuation. Evacuation delayed and additional effort required.
2. *Information inaccurate.* Again, a manual premises check may be required. There may be delay in evacuating vulnerable people and vulnerable people may not left behind.
3. *Information incomplete.* Delay in evacuation.
4. *Information late.* Information has to be communicated to units in the field by radio rather than to local coordination centre. This is time consuming and less reliable than written communications with Bronze Command.
5. *Information early.* No consequence.

The information on 'information hazards' may then be used as a basis for defining requirements for mitigation strategies that lessen the consequences of subsequent failure. We see examples of these in the requirements shown in the following section.

6.1   System Requirements

After the information about the information used by and generated by stakeholders has been collected, it is then the responsibility of the requirements engineer to generate system requirements in an appropriate form. If a formal requirements document is to be produced, this is likely to be a mix of natural language requirements and tables; if the requirements are expressed less formally, then tables such as Table 1 and Table 2, along with relevant commentary may be all that is required.

We show a subset of natural language requirements for an emergency response coordination system (ERCS) along with the rationale for these requirements below. These have been derived from the information documented in Tables 1 and 2.

1. The ERCS shall be able to import information from the District Council planning system, the Police emergency system and the Fire Service emergency system. (*Different types of information needs to be shared and this allows for information transfer between agencies*).

2. All information to be imported shall be available in either XML format or in PDF. (*This is intended to minimize the problems of importing information from different databases*).

3. The ERCS shall maintain its own list of priority premises to be evacuated for each town in the local area. This shall be updated by the local council when the coordination centre is established from the council's list. (*This is a critical asset for evacuation. The premises list is normally maintained by the local government authority but may not be immediately available outside of normal working hours; While an older list may be out of date, it is better than nothing*).

4. The ERCS shall maintain a list of premises evacuated along with the time of evacuation and the units involved in the evacuation. (*This allows units involved in the evacuation to be coordinated and maintains an audit trail of who did what and when*).

5. The ERCS shall notify all liaison officers of new information about the threat situation as it becomes available. (Different services may respond differently to changes in the threat situation e.g. local government staff may withdraw from a situation because they are not equipped to deal with search and rescue).

6. Alerts that threat information has changed should be displayed on all user screens and should be sent by SMS to all liaison officers (*Threat information is critical and should be sent on multiple channels. SMS can reach officers when they are not at their desk*).

7. ERCS operators should be able to update the Area Map with information about unsafe routes, without the need to access the source data for that map (*This allows maps to be distributed to emergency services but does not require operators to have access to the Council GIS*).

8. If information on evacuated premises is not available, the ERCS shall request the information from the Police liaison officer and send an SMS alert that this information has been requested. (*The Police are responsible for collecting this information and the Police liaison officer is then responsible for initiating a manual premises check if this is required*).

9. The ERCS shall maintain a list of all unchecked premises and shall automatically update this when information on evacuated premises is updated. (*If premises have been evacuated, they are no longer unchecked. This partially mitigates problems due to delays in updating the unchecked premises list*).

10. Transcripts of all incoming radio communications shall be maintained in the ERCS along with the time of these communications and the identifier of the source of the message (*This is required for auditing purposes if problems are subsequently reported*).

7   Related Work

The notion of using models of responsibility to support the requirements engineering process was first suggested by Dobson and Strens [8]. This was part of the ORDIT project [9, 10], which focused on organizational issues in software engineering. The work on requirements here was mostly concerned with what they termed 'organizational requirements' – requirements that are derived from organizational factors such as the power and authority relationships between people and departments in an organization.

Working in conjunction with Sommerville and others [11, 12], Dobson continued the work on responsibility models and documented this in a series of papers, which were published in a book that he co-edited with Dewsbury [13]. These were the basis for our own work on responsibility modeling where we have been concerned with responsibilities and system dependability and models of responsibility in virtual organizations [14, 15, 16] .

Responsibilities are an example of an abstraction that is clearly located in the world of system stakeholders rather than a technical abstraction such as an object or system function. The most closely related alternative abstraction to responsibility that has been proposed is the notion of a *goal*. A goal is seen as something that an agent is trying to achieve and goal-based approaches to requirements engineering such as i* and KAOS are intended to expose high level dependencies between the goals associated with agents in a given system [17, 18, 19].

Sub-goals may be derived from higher level objectives and assigned to agents for completion. Goals are achieved through the achievement of some or all sub- goals. Relationships between sub-goals express the possible ways in which the super-goal may be achieved. Analysis of such models can examine, for example, whether a super-goal may fail due to the failure of a single sub-goal (brittleness), or whether a particular agent has been overloaded with too many goals to achieve.

We argue that the key benefit of using responsibilities rather than goals comes from the naturalness of the abstraction. Goals, in the sense of something that is to be achieved, have 3 main problems:

1. The goals of individuals are usually internalised and people find these very difficult to articulate. This is particularly true in professional roles where the work to be done is left to the discretion of the individual.
2. Many, perhaps most organizations, do not have a coherent set of organizational goals and, where they do, it cannot be assumed that goals set by management are actually shared by the people in the organization.
3. The goals of individuals in an organization may be focused on personal advancement and this may, in fact, conflict with organizational goals.

In a review of research on goal-oriented approaches, Lapouchnian [20] rightly states "Identifying goals is not an easy task". He has found, in practice, that goals are normally derived from other information that is discovered from stakeholders rather than articulated directly from them.

8   Conclusions

The modeling approach proposed here, based on the responsibilities that have been assigned to agents in an enterprise, has been found to be useful in supporting the elicitation of 'information requirements'. We argue that for enterprise systems, which are systems of systems it is more appropriate to focus on the information required and created by system stakeholders rather than the behavioural characteristics of a system.

The key benefits of using responsibilities and responsibility models in this context are:

1. *Naturalness: can stakeholders without experience of requirements engineering relate to the approach?* The notion of responsibility and responsible behaviour is widely used in everyday discourse so people can readily discuss their responsibilities in some situation. The questions used to discover information requirements relate directly to the stakeholder's job and are therefore easy to understand.

2. *Scalability: Can the approach be used with real rather than simple example systems?* The problem with many RE methods is that they have been developed using relatively simple systems and when scaled up, unmanageable volumes of information are created. Our development has always relied on real system examples and we are confident that our approach scales – for example, we have developed responsibility models of 300-page emergency plans.

3. *Complementarity: can the approach be used alongside other requirements engineering methods?* Responsibility models offer a different perspective from the behavioural perspective used in other methods so there are no problems in practice in using these together.

There are practical and methodological problems in attempting to compare requirements engineering methods, which mean quantitative comparative evaluation is unreliable. Furthermore, comparison of methods is not the same as comparison of outcomes. Method A may be better than method B at eliciting requirements but until a system has been implemented and put into use, we really don't know if these requirements meet the needs of the system stakeholders.

Therefore, we cannot and do not claim here that the use of responsibility models in the RE process necessarily leads to the discovery of 'better' requirements. All we can say is that responsibilities are a good way of stimulating requirements discussions and this, we believe, increases the chances that the requirements are likely to be appropriate.

Responsibility models provide a technology-independent perspective on complex systems of systems, where the components are already in existence. We have explored how these models may also be used in the systems design phase [21]. In this work, we have found the need to enhance these models with the notion of a capability – a set of competences and resources – that defines the responsibilities that could be assigned to a system. This work is still at an early stage but it points the way to how responsibilities and capabilities could be used to support system of systems design.

References

1. Glinz, M., Wieringa: Stakeholders in Requirements Engineering: Guest Editors Introduction. IEEE Software 24(2), 18–20 (2007)
2. Robertson, S., Robertson, J.: Mastering the Requirements Process. Addison Wesley, Harlow (1999)
3. Giachetti, R.E.: Design of Enterprise Systems: Theory, Architecture and Methods. CRC Press, Boca Raton (2010)
4. Camarinha-Matos, L., Afsarmanesh, H.: The Virtual Enterprise Concept. In: Proc. IFIP TC5 WG5.3 / PRODNET Working Conference on Infrastructures for Virtual Enterprises: Networking Industrial Enterprises, pp. 3–14 (1999)
5. Baxter, G., Sommerville, I.: Socio-technical Systems: From design methods to systems engineering. Interacting with Computers 23(1), 4–17 (2011)
6. Redmill, F., Chudleigh, M., Catmur, J.: System Safety: HAZOP and Software HAZOP. Wiley, Chichester (1999)
7. Lock, R., Storer, T., Sommerville, I., Baxter, G.: Responsibility Modelling for Risk Analysis. In: Proc. ESREL 2009, Prague, pp. 1103–1109 (September 2009)
8. Dobson, J.E., Strens, M.R.: Responsibility modelling as a technique for requirements definition. Intelligent Systems Engineering 3(1), 20–26 (1994)
9. Blyth, A.J., Chudge, J., Dobson, J.E., Strens, M.R.: ORDIT: A new methodology to assist in the process of eliciting and modelling organizational requirements. In: Kaplan, S. (ed.) Proceedings on the Conference on Organizational Computing Systems, Milpitas, California, USA, pp. 216–227. ACM Press (1993)
10. Dobson, J.E., Strens, M.R.: Organizational requirements definition for information technology systems. In: Proceedings of the IEEE International Conference on Requirements Engineering (ICRE 1994), Colorado Springs, pp. 158–165. IEEE Press (April 1994)
11. Sommerville, I.: Models for responsibility assignment. In: Dewsbury, G., Dobson, J. (eds.) Responsibility and Dependable Systems, pp. 165–186. Springer (2007)
12. Sommerville, I.: Causal responsibility models. In: Dewsbury, G., Dobson, J. (eds.) Responsibility and Dependable Systems, pp. 187–207 (2007)
13. Dewsbury, G., Dobson, J. (eds.): Responsibility and Dependable Systems. Springer-Verlag London Ltd. (June 2007)
14. Sommerville, I., Storer, T., Lock, R.: Responsibility modelling for contingency planning. In: Workshop on Understanding Why Systems Fail, Contingency Planning and Longer Term Perspectives on Learning from Failure in Safety Critical Systems (June 2007)
15. Sommerville, I., Lock, R., Storer, T., Dobson, J.: Deriving Information Requirements from Responsibility Models. In: van Eck, P., Gordijn, J., Wieringa, R. (eds.) CAiSE 2009. LNCS, vol. 5565, pp. 515–529. Springer, Heidelberg (2009)
16. Sommerville, I., Storer, T., Lock, R.: Responsibility Modelling for Civil Emergency Planning. Risk Management 11, 179–207 (2009), doi:10.1057/rm.2009.11

17. Dardenne, A., Fickas, S., van Lamsweerde, A.: Goal-directed concept acquisition in requirements elicitation. In: Proceedings of the Sixth International Workshop on Software Specification and Design, pp. 14–21. IEEE Computer Society Press (October 1991)
18. Yu, E.S.: Towards modelling and reasoning support for early-phase requirements engineering. In: 3rd IEEE International Symposium on Requirements Engineering (RE 1997), pp. 226–235. IEEE Computer Society (1997)
19. Dardenne, A., van Lamsweerde, A., Fickas, S.: Goal-directed requirements acquisition. Science of Computer Programming 20, 3–50 (1993)
20. Lapouchnian, A.: Goal-oriented requirements engineering: An overview of the current research. Depth report, Department of Computer Science, University of Toronto (June 2005)
21. Lock, R., Sommerville, I.: Modelling and analysis of socio-technical system of systems. In: 15th IEEE International Conference on Engineering of Complex Computer Systems, Oxford, March 22-26, pp. 224–232 (2010)

A Counterexample-Based Incremental and Modular Verification Approach

Étienne André, Kais Klai, Hanen Ochi, and Laure Petrucci

LIPN, CNRS UMR 7030
Université Paris 13, Sorbonne Paris Cité
99 Avenue Jean-Baptiste Clément
93430 Villetaneuse, France
{first.last}@lipn.univ-paris13.fr

Abstract. Model checking is a powerful and widespread technique for the verification of finite state concurrent systems. However, the main hindrance for wider application of this technique is the well-known state explosion problem. In [16], we proposed an incremental and compositional verification approach where the system model is partitioned according to the actions occurring in the property to be verified and where the environment of a component is taken into account. But the verification at each increment might be costly. On the other hand, Symbolic Observation Graphs provide a compact analysis means for LTL\X properties. We have shown a purely modular construction of these in [15]. Therefore, in this paper, we combine both techniques to benefit from their pros. Also, we propose a novel approach for incrementally checking the validity of the counter-example.

1 Introduction

Model checking is a powerful and widespread technique for the verification of finite state concurrent systems. However, the main hindrance for wider application of this technique is the well-known state explosion problem. Modular and compositional approaches to verification are promising to tackle this problem. They are based on the "divide and conquer" principle and aim at deducing the properties of the system from those of its components analysed in isolation.

In [16], we proposed an incremental and compositional verification approach where the system model is partitioned according to the actions occurring in the property to be verified and where the environment of a component is taken into account using the linear place invariants of the system. The first component contains only the actions occurring in the formula, and each newly added component is obtained based on the neighbourhood of those already analysed.

However, the verification at each increment might be costly. On the other hand, Symbolic Observation Graphs (SOGs) [9,17] provide an abstraction-based approach leading to a compact representation of the system's state space graph, and allowing for the analysis of properties expressed using LTL\X (Linear Time

R. Calinescu and D. Garlan (Eds.): Monterey Workshop 2012, LNCS 7539, pp. 283–302, 2012.
© Springer-Verlag Berlin Heidelberg 2012

Logic [20] from which the "next operator" has been removed). We have shown a purely modular construction of these in [15].

Therefore, in this paper, we combine both techniques to benefit from their advantages. Since, it has been empirically shown that breaking up a system is a difficult task (see for instance [5]), we assume here that the system is already given as a set of components sharing global actions. In order to use an approach derived from [16], either all actions of the formula belong to a single component, or we compose all those containing such actions, to start with. Note that [16] considered Petri nets models, whereas the technique is here generalised to Labelled Transitions Systems (LTSs). In general, the LTS and a counterexample can be derived on-the-fly as long as an initial state and a transition relation are provided.

Related Work. During the last 20 years, many researchers have worked on the use of abstraction and/or modularity to tackle the explosion problem of model-checking properties on concurrent systems. On one hand, modularity refers to a wide range of techniques that make use of the fact that components have some intrinsic behavior of their own. Each component (subpart) of the global system is verified separately and the behavior of the main system is deduced from the behaviors of its components (see, e.g. [22,4]). Among modular techniques, authors of [18] present algorithms to exploit the modular analysis in the determination of reachable states with specified partial markings, to determine possible deadlocks, both global and local, and also liveness. The idea there was to start from a system designed in a modular way and construct the state space of the complete system in a similar way: one local state space per module and a synchronization graph showing their interactions. The technique was applied to a problem of controller design, where some of the actions could be controlled and others not. The approach advocated was also to lift these actions to the global (i.e. synchronization) level, so that both synchronized and controllable actions are visible in the synchronization graph and only there. Another related paradigm is compositional state space verification [26]. In this paradigm, systems are specified as a parallel composition of subcomponents, and the state space of the full system is computed from the state spaces of the subcomponents. Moreover, the state spaces of subcomponents can be replaced by smaller and behaviourally equivalent state spaces before constructing the state space of the full system. Authors use methods and models considering actions in the context of synchonous communicating systems.

On the other hand, abstraction-based techniques aim to build an abstract model of the system by getting rid of some of its irrelevant parts so that the analysis can be achieved on the abstract model instead of the original system. Depending on the property to be checked, the abstract model can either compeletely characterize the system, or represents a super set of its possible behaviors. In the first case, the abstraction satisfies the formula if and only if the original system does (e.g. [25,21,9,17,7]). In the second case, only a sufficient condition exists (i.e. if the abstract model is error-free, then so is the original system). Thus, when the abstract model does not satisfy the property, one can not decide about the verification result on the original system (e.g. [13]). Counterexample-driven abstraction refinement techniques (e.g. [1,3,6,24,10]) come with an iterative approach to face this weakness: when the abstract model does not satisfy the property, an abstract counterexample is automatically supplied and we check whether it corresponds to a concrete counterexample in the system. If this is the case, we conclude that the system does not satisfy the property. Otherwise, we start over using a new abstract model. In [10] as in the approach presented in this paper, the abstract model used in one pass is obtained using the one computed in the previous pass, while in [3,24,1,6] the abstract model is constructed from scratch and the new one is model-checked.

The approach we present in this paper has the advantage to combine modularity and counter-example abstraction refinement for the verification of temporal properties (generic properties, e.g. deadlock freeness, can also be considered in a similar way).

Benefits and Originality of the Approach. The approach presented in this paper enjoys several advantages. Firstly, SOGs are computed locally. This favours reuse of modules since once the SOG is computed, it can be used in another environment without need of calculating it again. Moreover, for confidentiality issues, a SOG showing only global actions can be provided instead of the module itself, thus hiding the details of the internal functioning to external users, and favouring the use of "black box" (or "gray box") modules. The verification process is incremental at all stages: not only the formula verification but also checking the counterexample. Thus, the whole LTS does not always require a complete analysis, and the satisfaction of the property can be decided on-the-fly.

Even though the combination of both techniques from [15] and [16] is quite easy, it also leads to improvements. The definition of aggregates contains a more elaborate structure for detecting internal deadlocks, making things way easier at the composition stage. Moreover, the validation of counterexamples is also incremental, sticking to the spirit of the overall approach.

Outline. The paper is structured as follows: after preliminary definitions and notations in Section 2, the approach is introduced in Section 3. It defines the different steps as well as the associated model checking algorithm. Section 4 presents the application of our approach to case studies. Finally, Section 5 concludes and gives perspectives for future work.

2   Preliminaries

The technique presented in this paper applies to different kinds of process models that can map to labelled transition systems, e.g. Petri nets. The techniques addressed here are of particular interest for the analysis of workflow Petri nets (WF-nets) as shown in [14]. For the sake of simplicity and generality, we chose to present it for labelled transition systems, since this formalism is well adapted to event-based approaches.

2.1   Labelled Transition Systems

Definition 1 (Labelled Transition Systems)
A labelled transition system (LTS for short) is a 4-tuple $\langle \Gamma, Act, \rightarrow, I \rangle$ where:

- Γ *is a finite set of* states;
- *Act is a finite set of* actions;
- $\rightarrow \subseteq \Gamma \times Act \times \Gamma$ *is a* transition relation;
- $I \subseteq \Gamma$ *is a set of* initial states.

In this paper, we restrict the set of states Γ to those that are reachable from an initial state in I. We distinguish observed actions, denoted by a set *Obs*, from unobserved actions, denoted by *UnObs* (with $Obs \cup UnObs = Act$ and $Obs \cap UnObs = \emptyset$). Observed actions include the set of actions occurring in an LTL formula to be verified and interface actions allowing for the synchronisation of two LTSs. Unobserved actions are the remaining ones. Therefore, unobserved actions can be seen as silent τ actions.

In the sequel, we use the following notations:

- For $s, s' \in \Gamma$ and $a \in Act$, we denote by $s \xrightarrow{a} s'$ that $(s, a, s') \in \rightarrow$.
- If $\sigma = a_1 a_2 \cdots a_n$ is a sequence of actions, $\overline{\sigma}$ denotes the set of actions occurring in σ, while $|\sigma|$ denotes the length of σ, and $s \xrightarrow{\sigma} s'$ denotes that $\exists s_1, s_2, \cdots s_{n-1} \in \Gamma : s \xrightarrow{a_1} s_1 \xrightarrow{a_2} \cdots s_{n-1} \xrightarrow{a_n} s'$.
- The set *Enable(s)* denotes the set of actions a such that $s \xrightarrow{a} s'$ for some state s'. For a set of states S, *Enable(S)* denotes $\bigcup_{s \in S} Enable(s)$.
- $\pi = s_0 \xrightarrow{a_1} s_1 \xrightarrow{a_2} \cdots$ denotes a path of an LTS.
- $s \nrightarrow$, for $s \in \Gamma$, denotes that s is a dead state, i.e., $Enable(s) = \emptyset$.
- $Reach_{UnObs}(s) = \{s' \mid s \xrightarrow{\sigma} s' \wedge \overline{\sigma} \subseteq UnObs\}$ is the set of states that are reachable from a state s by unobserved actions only. For $S \subseteq \Gamma$, $Reach_{UnObs}(S) = \bigcup_{s \in S} Reach_{UnObs}(s)$.
- $s \nRightarrow$, for $s \in \Gamma$, denotes that no state of $Reach_{UnObs}(s)$ enables an observed action, i.e., $Enable(Reach_{UnObs}(s)) \cap Obs = \emptyset$. Conversely, $s \Rightarrow$ denotes $\neg(s \nRightarrow)$, i.e. there is a state in $Reach_{UnObs}(s)$ enabling an observed action.
- A finite path $C = s_1 \xrightarrow{\sigma} s_n$ is said to be a *circuit* if $s_n = s_1$ and $|\sigma| \geq 1$. If $\overline{\sigma} \subseteq UnObs$ then C is said to be a *livelock*. If, in addition, $s_1 \nRightarrow$ then C is called a *strong livelock*. Otherwise it is called a *weak livelock*.

If $s \nRightarrow$ for $s \in \Gamma$, only a dead state or a *strong livelock* are reachable from s. In this paper we assume that a strong livelock behaviour is equivalent to a deadlock. These two behaviours are not distinguished and both are called deadlock. The reason for this is that if unobserved actions are local to a module, the system will somehow be stuck in this module, whatever the others' behaviour.

2.2   Model Checking LTL Formulae

Checking LTL formulae on an LTS is reduced to analyse its *maximal paths*. A *maximal path* is either a finite path (leading to a terminal state) or an infinite one.

Since we observe a subset of the LTS's actions, we distinguish the infinite paths where observed actions occur infinitely often from those where from some point, only unobserved actions occur infinitely often (called divergent paths). It is well known that preserving maximal paths suffices to preserve properties expressed using LTL\X. This corresponds to the CFFD semantics [12], which is exactly the weakest equivalence preserving LTL\X. The usual solution in automata theoretic approaches to check LTL formulae on an LTS is to convert each of its finite paths (leading to a terminal state) to an infinite one by adding a loop onto its last state.

Definition 2 (Maximal paths). *Let $\mathcal{T}$ be an LTS and $\pi = s_1 \xrightarrow{a_1} s_2 \xrightarrow{a_2} \cdots \xrightarrow{a_{n-1}} s_n$ a path of $\mathcal{T}$. Then, π is said to be* a maximal path *if one of the following two properties holds:*

- $s_n \not\rightarrow$,
- $\pi = s_1 \xrightarrow{a_1} s_2 \xrightarrow{a_2} \cdots s_m \xrightarrow{a_m} \cdots \xrightarrow{a_{n-1}} s_n$ and $s_m \xrightarrow{a_m} \cdots \xrightarrow{a_{n-1}} s_n$ is a circuit.

Observed Behaviour. In the following, we define a particular mapping (called *observed behaviour*) applied to states of an LTS $\mathcal{T}$. It will be established that it is the necessary and sufficient local information to be retained so that LTL\X properties can be checked on the composition of two processes.

Definition 3 (Observed behaviour mapping). *Let $\mathcal{T} = \langle \Gamma, Obs \cup UnObs, \rightarrow, I \rangle$ be an LTS. The observed behaviour is progressively defined by :*

1. $\lambda_{\mathcal{T}} : \Gamma \rightarrow 2^{Obs}$
   $\lambda_{\mathcal{T}}(s) = Enable(Reach_{UnObs}(s)) \cap Obs$
2. $\lambda_{\mathcal{T}} : 2^{\Gamma} \rightarrow 2^{Obs}$
   $\lambda_{\mathcal{T}}(S) = \{\lambda_{\mathcal{T}}(s) \mid s \in S\}$
3. $\lambda_{\mathcal{T}}^{min}(S) = \{X \in \lambda_{\mathcal{T}}(S) \mid \nexists Y \in \lambda_{\mathcal{T}}(S) : Y \subset X\}$.

Informally, the observed behaviour of a state s, $\lambda_{\mathcal{T}}(s)$, represents the set of observed actions which can be executed from s, possibly via a sequence of unobserved actions. The observed behaviour is then extended to sets of states: the observed behaviour $\lambda_{\mathcal{T}}$ of a set of states S is a set of sets of observed actions. This set contains the observed behaviour of the states of S. Finally, $\lambda_{\mathcal{T}}^{min}(S)$ is the minimal set of subsets (w.r.t. the set inclusion relation) of $\lambda_{\mathcal{T}}(S)$.

The following proposition establishes that deadlock-freeness of an LTS can be deduced from computing the observed behaviour associated with its states.

Proposition 1. *Let $\mathcal{T} = \langle \Gamma, Obs \cup UnObs, \rightarrow, I \rangle$ be an LTS. $\mathcal{T}$ is deadlock-free if and only if $\forall S \subseteq \Gamma : \emptyset \notin \lambda_{\mathcal{T}}^{min}(S)$.*

Note that it is actually sufficient to check that, for all individual states s, $\lambda_{\mathcal{T}}(s) \neq \emptyset$. In Section 3, we will need to consider sets of states (instead of states), and this is the reason why Proposition 1 is needed in this form.

2.3   Synchronisation of LTSs

In the following, we define the synchronised product of two LTSs. The synchronised product of n LTSs (for $n > 2$) can be built by iterative multiplication.

Definition 4 (LTS synchronised product). *Let $\mathcal{T}_i = \langle \Gamma_i, Act_i, \rightarrow_i, I_i \rangle, i = 1, 2$ be two LTSs. The synchronised product of $\mathcal{T}_1$ and $\mathcal{T}_2$ is the minimal LTS $\mathcal{T}_1 \times \mathcal{T}_2 = \langle \Gamma, Act, \rightarrow, I \rangle$ given by:*

1. $\Gamma \subseteq \Gamma_1 \times \Gamma_2$;
2. $Act = Act_1 \cup Act_2$;
3. $\rightarrow$ *is the transition relation, defined by:*
   $\forall (s_1, s_2) \in \Gamma : (s_1, s_2) \xrightarrow{a} (s_1', s_2') \Leftrightarrow$
   $\begin{cases} s_1 \xrightarrow{a}_1 s_1' \wedge s_2 \xrightarrow{a}_2 s_2' & \text{if } a \in Act_1 \cap Act_2 \\ s_1 \xrightarrow{a}_1 s_1' \wedge s_2 = s_2' & \text{if } a \in Act_1 \setminus Act_2 \\ s_1 = s_1' \wedge s_2 \xrightarrow{a}_2 s_2' & \text{if } a \in Act_2 \setminus Act_1 \end{cases}$
4. *The set of states Γ contains all (and by minimality only) reachable states:*
   $\Gamma = \{(s_1, s_2) \in \Gamma_1 \times \Gamma_2 \mid \exists (i_1, i_2) \in I_1 \times I_2, \exists \sigma \in Act^* : (i_1, i_2) \xrightarrow{\sigma} (s_1, s_2)\}$;
5. $I = I_1 \times I_2$;

Note that the parallel operator for synchronisation is similar to Hoare's classical alphabetised parallel operator for CSP [11], with the exception that τ actions are synchronised in our settings.

Every state of the synchronised product is a pair of states; the first component indicates the corresponding state of the first LTS; the second component indicates the one of the second LTS. Each LTS can still perform its own activities autonomously, i.e. only one component of the pair representing a state of the composed LTS is changed by such an action. For common activities, both components of the state are changed synchronously.

Consider the two examples of LTSs in Figure 1 (unobserved actions are denoted by τ). The synchronised product of these two LTSs is an LTS containing 24 reachable states, depicted in Figure 2.

Recall that even if two LTSs are deadlock free, their synchronised product is not necessarily. Both LTSs in Figure 1 are deadlock free; however, in the synchronised product in Figure 2, the path $(s_0, s_0') \xrightarrow{\tau} (s_0, s_2') \xrightarrow{\tau} (s_1, s_2')$ leads to the deadlock state (s_1, s_2').

Notations. Given n LTSs $\mathcal{T}_i$, for $i = 1 \ldots n$, we denote by $\mathcal{T}_{\langle i, \ldots, k \rangle}$, for $1 \leq i < k \leq n$, the LTS representing the synchronised product of the LTSs $\mathcal{T}_i, \mathcal{T}_{i+1}, \ldots, \mathcal{T}_k$. When $i = k$, $\mathcal{T}_{\langle i, \ldots, k \rangle}$ is denoted by $\mathcal{T}_{\langle i \rangle}$.

3   Approach

In this section we describe our incremental and modular approach for model checking LTL\X properties. In order to counter the state space explosion problem we propose to abstract each LTS involved in the whole system by a SOG.

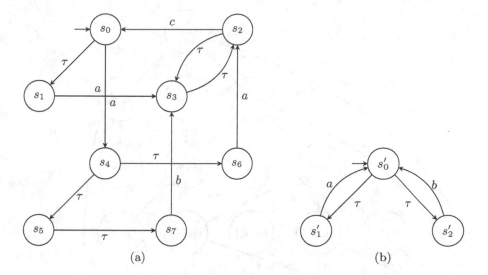

Fig. 1. Two LTSs

This allows for not considering local states, i.e. states (s_1, s_2) that permit the execution of neither interface actions nor actions occurring in the formula to be checked. We recall the notion of Symbolic Observation Graph in Section 3.1, and the preservation of LTL\X properties in Section 3.2. Then we present our approach on top of these notions in Section 3.3.

3.1   The Symbolic Observation Graph

The construction of the SOG corresponding to an LTS is guided by the set of actions occurring in an LTL\X formula expressing a property to be checked. Such actions are said to be observed while the other actions of the system are unobserved. Previous results [9,17] show that such a formula is satisfied by the LTS if and only if it is satisfied by the respective SOG. The SOG is defined as a graph where each node is a set of states linked by unobserved actions and each arc is labelled by an observed action. Nodes of the SOG are called *aggregates* and may be represented and managed efficiently using decision diagram techniques (BDDs, see e.g. [2]). In practice, due to the small number of actions in a typical formula, the SOG has a very moderate size and thus the time complexity of the verification process is negligible in comparison to the building time of the SOG (see [9,17,15] for experimental results). SOGs are used to abstract LTSs so that all internal behaviour is hidden. Additional information is attached to the aggregates so that the preservation of LTL\X formulae still holds by composition. The observed actions are of two kinds: the actions occurring in the LTL formula to be checked, and the interface actions.

Definition 5 (Aggregate). *Let* $\mathcal{T} = \langle \Gamma, Act, \rightarrow, I \rangle$ *be an LTS with* $Act = Obs \cup UnObs$. *An aggregate is a tuple* $a = \langle S, \lambda, l \rangle$ *defined as follows:*

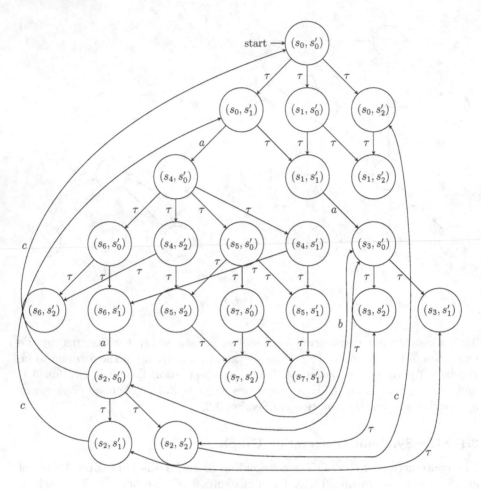

Fig. 2. Product of the 2 LTSs in Figure 1

1. *S is a nonempty subset of Γ satisfying: $Reach_{UnObs}(S) = S$;*
2. $\lambda = \lambda_{\mathcal{T}}^{min}(S)$
3. *$l \in \{true, false\}$; $l = true$ iff S contains a weak livelock.*

From now on, $a.S$, $a.\lambda$ and $a.l$ denote the corresponding attributes of a given aggregate a.

In the following definition, we inductively define a SOG associated with an LTS.

Definition 6 (Symbolic Observation Graph). *A symbolic observation graph (SOG for short) associated with an LTS $\mathcal{T} = \langle \Gamma, Obs \cup UnObs, \rightarrow, I \rangle$ is a 4-tuple $\langle \mathcal{A}, Act', \rightarrow', I' \rangle$ where:*

1. *$\mathcal{A}$ is a finite set of aggregates satisfying:*
   - *there is an aggregate $a_0 \in \mathcal{A}$ with $a_0.S = Reach_{UnObs}(I)$, and*

- if, for some $a \in \mathcal{A}$ and $o \in Obs$, the set $Ext(a, o) := \{s' \notin a.S \mid \exists s \in a.S, s \xrightarrow{o} s'\}$ is not empty, then it is a pairwise-disjoint union of non-empty sets $S_1 \ldots S_k$, and for $i = 1 \ldots k$, there is an aggregate $a_i \in \mathcal{A}$ with $a_i.S = Reach_{UnObs}(S_i)$;

2. $Act' = Obs$;

3. $\rightarrow' \subseteq \mathcal{A} \times Act' \times \mathcal{A}$ is the transition relation satisfying:
   - if $a \neq a'$ then $(a, o, a') \in \rightarrow'$ iff $a'.S = Reach_{UnObs}(S')$ for some $S' \subseteq Ext(a, o)$, and
   - $(a, o, a) \in \rightarrow'$ iff $Reach_{UnObs}(\{s' \in \Gamma \mid \exists s \in a.S, s \xrightarrow{o} s'\}) = a.S$;

4. $I' = \{a_0\}$ (where $a_0.S = Reach_{UnObs}(I)$).

Note that Definition 6 does not guarantee the uniqueness of a SOG for a given LTS. In fact, it offers some flexibility for its implementation. In particular, the SOG can be nondeterministic even if the original LTS is not. It is clear that the canonical minimal SOG is obtained when the SOG is deterministic. Actually, one can take advantage of such nondeterminism to obtain smaller aggregates. Even if the SOG obtained in this way has more aggregates than a deterministic one, its construction might consume less time and memory.

This is different from, e.g. determinisation of a process or specification with unobserved actions hidden used in some model checkers.

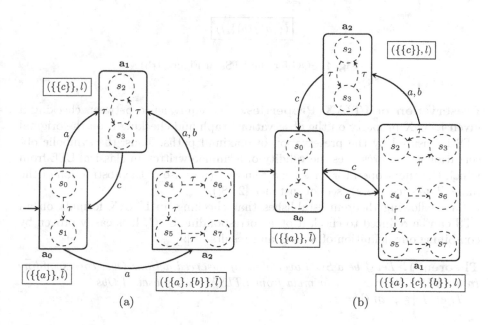

Fig. 3. Two possible SOGs for the LTSs in Figure 1(a)

The two SOGs (a) and (b) of Figure 3 correspond to two possible SOGs associated with the LTS of Figure 1(a) page 289, while the SOG of Figure 4 is a SOG of the LTS of Figure 1(b). Let us explain the first two SOGs. The set of observed actions is $\{a, b, c\}$ and the unobserved actions are represented by the mute action τ. Each aggregate a is indexed with a pair $(a.\lambda, a.l)$. The left part λ is the observed behaviour associated with a, and indicates whether a contains a deadlock state (viz. $\emptyset \in a.\lambda$). The symbol l (resp. $\bar{l}$) is used when a contains (resp. does not contain) a livelock. The first SOG (Figure 3(a)) is nondeterministic and the sets of states of the aggregates represent a partition of the LTS's states. In this SOG, one can regroup a_1 and a_2 leading to the deterministic SOG (Figure 3(b)) where s_2 and s_3 belong to two different aggregates.

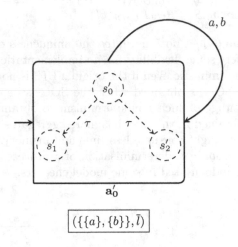

Fig. 4. SOG for the LTSs in Figure 1(b)

Preservation of LTL\X Properties. The equivalence between checking a given LTL\X property on the observation graph and checking it on the original LTS is ensured by the preservation of maximal paths. Thus, the symbolic observation graph preserves the validity of formulae written in classical LTL from which the "next operator" has been removed (because of the abstraction of the immediate successors) (see for instance [23,8]).

The following theorem establishes that checking an LTL\X formula on an LTS can be reduced to check it on a corresponding SOG. It is easily proven by combining our definition of a SOG and results of [9].

Theorem 1. *Let $\mathcal{G}$ be a SOG over a set of observed actions Obs, corresponding to an LTS $\mathcal{T}$. Let φ be a formula from LTL\X on a subset of Obs.*
Then $\mathcal{T} \models \varphi$ iff $\mathcal{G} \models \varphi$.

3.2   Composition of SOGs

Let us consider several LTSs which communicate synchronously. This section shows how to compose the SOGs of the individual LTSs so that the result is isomorphic to some SOG of the composition of the original LTSs. Thus, the composition of SOGs is correct (with respect to LTL\X formulae) if and only if the composition of the original LTSs is correct. However, it is well known that deadlock-freeness is not preserved by composition (e.g. the two LTSs of Figure 1 are deadlock-free but their synchronised product in Figure 2 is not).

The computation of the observed behaviour associated with an aggregate a can be done using symbolic operations exclusively (BDD operations). Moreover, it is not necessary to explore all the states of the aggregate but only analyse the observed transitions and the states that enable these states (immediately).

From now on, an aggregate a is identified by two attributes $a.l$ and $a.\lambda$. Also, the set of states $a.S$ of an aggregate a does not have to be stored explicitly within the aggregate. Once the SOG is built, it will not play any role in the composition process.

When composing several modules, a SOG corresponding to each module is computed locally and once and the obtained SOGs are then composed, leading to a new SOG. The observed behaviour and the livelock attributes of each aggregate of this SOG are deduced from those of the composed aggregates, as follows.

Definition 7 (Product aggregate). *Let* $T_i = \langle \Gamma_i, Obs_i \cup UnObs_i, \rightarrow_i, I_i \rangle$, *for* $i = 1, 2$, *be two LTSs. Let* $\mathcal{G}_1$ *and* $\mathcal{G}_2$ *be SOGs corresponding to* T_1 *and* T_2, *respectively. Let* a_i *be an aggregate of* $\mathcal{G}_i$. *The product aggregate* $a = a_1 \times a_2$ *is defined by:*

1. $a.l = a_1.l \lor a_2.l$
2. $a.\lambda = \{(x \cap y) \cup (x \cap (Obs_1 \setminus Obs_2)) \cup (y \cap (Obs_2 \setminus Obs_1)) \mid x \in a_1.\lambda,\ y \in a_2.\lambda\}$

Deducing the weak livelock attribute of the product aggregate from the involved aggregates is rather trivial: there exists a livelock in the product aggregate $a = a_1 \times a_2$ if and only if there exists a livelock in a_1 or there exists a livelock in a_2. Computing the observed behaviour $a.\lambda$ requires some explanation. First note that the sets of observed actions Obs_1 and Obs_2 are not necessarily identical. When we compose a_1 and a_2, if a_1 can progress in $\mathcal{G}_1$ by using local observed actions (i.e. actions that are observed in $\mathcal{G}_1$ but not shared by $\mathcal{G}_2$), the product aggregate a should be able to do the same. If this is not the case, then a has to have the same behaviour as a_1 and a_2 conjunctively. In this way, the observed behaviour associated with a product aggregate is helpful to deduce whether the involved set of (pairs of) states contains a deadlock.

Proposition 2. *Let* T_1 *and* T_2 *be two LTSs. Let* $T = \langle \Gamma, Obs \cup UnObs, \rightarrow, I \rangle$ *be their synchronised product. Let* $\mathcal{G}_1$ *and* $\mathcal{G}_2$ *be SOGs corresponding to* T_1 *and* T_2, *respectively. Let* a_1 *and* a_2 *be two aggregates of* $\mathcal{G}_1$ *and* $\mathcal{G}_2$, *respectively, such that* $a = a_1 \times a_2$. *Then* $\exists s \in (a_1.S \times a_2.S) \cap \Gamma : s \not\rightarrow$ *if and only if* $\emptyset \in a.\lambda$.

Given two SOGs $\mathcal{G}_1$ and $\mathcal{G}_2$, their synchronised product is a SOG $\mathcal{G}$. The synchronised product of two SOGs can be defined similarly to the synchronised product of two LTSs (Definition 4). The only difference is that we deal with aggregates (carrying additional information) instead of states. Definition 7 allows for deducing the attributes of a product attribute $a = a_1 \times a_2$ from the attributes of a_1 and a_2. In particular, the observed behaviour computation allows to detect new deadlock situations, i.e. deadlocks due to the composition process.

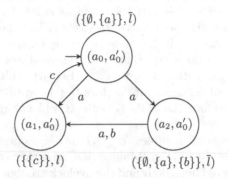

Fig. 5. Product of the SOGs in Figures 3(a) and 4

For instance, the synchronised product between the SOGs of Figures 3(a) and 4 is a SOG (presented in Figure 5) containing three aggregates (a_0, a_0'), (a_2, a_0') and (a_1, a_0') where the first two contain a deadlock. Indeed, by composing their observed behaviour we obtain the empty set as a member of the observed behaviour of the product aggregate.

The following theorem will be a basis for our approach. We give an informal illustration of this theorem in Figure 6.

Theorem 2. *Let $\mathcal{T}_1$ and $\mathcal{T}_2$ be two LTSs with synchronised product $\mathcal{T}$. Let $\mathcal{G}_1$ and $\mathcal{G}_2$ be SOGs corresponding to $\mathcal{T}_1$ and $\mathcal{T}_2$ with respect to observed actions Obs_1 and Obs_2 respectively. Let $\mathcal{G}$ be the synchronised product of $\mathcal{G}_1$ and $\mathcal{G}_2$. Then, $\mathcal{G}$ is a SOG of $\mathcal{T}$ with respect to the observed actions $Obs_1 \cup Obs_2$.*

Corollary 1. *Let $\mathcal{T}_1$ and $\mathcal{T}_2$ be two LTSs with synchronised product $\mathcal{T}$. Let $\mathcal{G}_1$ and $\mathcal{G}_2$ be SOGs corresponding to $\mathcal{T}_1$ and $\mathcal{T}_2$ with respect to observed actions Obs_1 and Obs_2 respectively. Let $\mathcal{G}$ be the synchronised product of $\mathcal{G}_1$ and $\mathcal{G}_2$. Then $\mathcal{T} \models \varphi$ iff $\mathcal{G} \models \varphi$.*

3.3 Verification Algorithm

We suppose that a decomposition of the system $\mathcal{T}$ into n LTSs $(\mathcal{T}_1, \ldots, \mathcal{T}_n)$, and an LTL\X formula φ are given. We also suppose that this decomposition is such that all actions appearing within φ appear only in $\mathcal{T}_1$. If this is not the case, we compose all components containing such actions, so that such actions appear only in $\mathcal{T}_1$.

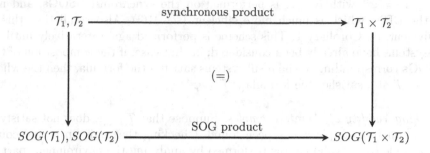

Fig. 6. Illustration of Theorem 2

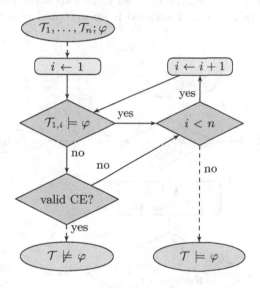

Fig. 7. Our approach (general scheme)

We give the general scheme of our approach in Figure 7. The main principle is that we will check φ on the synchronisation of the SOGs corresponding to an iteratively growing number of LTSs. Starting with $i = 1$, we first check whether $\mathcal{T}_1 \models \varphi$, viz. whether the first subsystem satisfies φ (test "$\mathcal{T}_{\langle 1,...,i \rangle} \models \varphi$" in Figure 7, with $i = 1$). If not, we then check the validity of the counterexample exhibited (test "valid ce" which will be explained below); if the counterexample is indeed valid, the global system $\mathcal{T}$ does not satisfy the property ("$\mathcal{T} \not\models \varphi$"). If the counterexample is not valid, or if the first subsystem satisfies φ, we go one step further ("$i \leftarrow i + 1$") by considering the system obtained by composition of the first and the second subsystems. Note that the satisfiability test (test

"$\mathcal{T}_{\langle 1,...,i\rangle} \models \varphi$" with $i = 2$) is performed on the synchronised SOGs, and not on the LTSs, which is much more efficient (see [16]). Also recall that this is equivalent, by Corollary 1. This scheme is performed again iteratively until all subsystems have already been considered; in that case, if the composition of the n SOGs corresponding to the n subsystems satisfies the formula, then the whole system $\mathcal{T}$ also satisfies the formula ("$\mathcal{T} \models \varphi$").

Checking Validity of Counterexamples. Suppose that $\mathcal{T}_{\langle 1,...,i\rangle}$ does not satisfy φ and a counterexample σ has been found. Checking that σ is an actual counterexample (test "valid ce") is performed by analysing the environment part of the system, i.e. $\mathcal{T}_{\langle i+1,...,n\rangle}$. This can be achieved in an incremental way as well, as depicted in Figure 8. Let σ_k be the projection of σ on the actions shared by $\mathcal{T}_{\langle 1,...,i\rangle}$ and $\mathcal{T}_{\langle i+1\rangle}$. If σ_k is not an accepted run of $\mathcal{T}_{\langle i+1\rangle}$, then the counterexample is not valid. Otherwise, we iteratively check the validity of σ on the LTS $\mathcal{T}_{\langle i+1,...,k\rangle}$, for $k = (i + 2)...n$. If all iterations show that the projection of σ (on the appropriate sets of actions) is an accepted run, then σ is a valid counterexample.

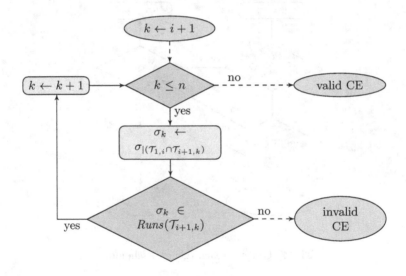

Fig. 8. Approach for checking validity of counterexamples

Advantages. The main interest of our scheme relies on the iterative composition of SOGs instead of LTSs (by Corollary 1). Furthermore, such SOGs are computed locally: one SOG corresponds to one LTS, independently of any information concerning neighbouring systems except their shared actions. As a consequence, one can reuse SOGs; even better, one can provide a SOG instead of an LTS, and thus allow for confidentiality (the original system is not provided, only its abstraction with respect to its neighbouring systems is). Similarly, refinement of one subsystem is possible without reverifying the whole system, as long as the SOG of the refined subsystem is the same as the original one.

Also note that our scheme is more general than the one of [16] in the sense that we do not give any assumption on the decomposition: we suppose for the sake of simplicity that it is given *a priori*.

4   Case Study: The Clients/Servers Example

4.1   Description of the Model

Our approach based on an incremental and modular verification is illustrated on the well known Clients/Servers problem. This is a distributed application which partitions tasks between the providers of a service (called servers), and the requesters of this service (called clients). Clients and servers communicate by sending and receiving messages. This system can be modelled by a composition of clients and servers LTSs depicted in Figure 9. Each client can issue service requests by sending messages to any of the servers, and each server can provide the service to the requesting clients, sending it an answer message.

When a client i is ready (state $CReady_i$), it sends a message (action $CSend_i^j$) to a server j which is also in a ready state, $SReady^j$ (for sake of clarity, we use subscript for clients and superscript for servers). The client is then in a pending state ($CWait_i$) waiting for a response from the server to move to the ready state again by enabling $CRec_i^j$. Until then, the server is in a busy state ($SBusy_i^j$) to proceed the received message, and then sends a response message to the corresponding client before returning to its initial state.

Each client has an internal behaviour: After receiving message, the client decrypts and verifies it according to its own rules (actions $decrypt_i$ and $verify_i$). If the message is valid, the client stores it in a local database (action $store_i$); otherwise, the client rejects it (action $reject_i$).

4.2   First Property

We are interested in checking whether the first client receives a response from each server to whom it sends a message. This can be expressed by the LTL formula $\varphi_1 = \Box(CSend_1^j \Rightarrow \Diamond CRec_1^j)$, where $\Box$ reads "always" and $\Diamond$ reads "eventually".

We consider the case where the first client sends a message to server 1, and receives a response from server 1; other cases can be obtained similarly. As mentioned in the previous section, we propose to compose all components such that all actions of the formula appear only in the first LTS (first client $\mathcal{T}_{C1}$): the second client and the servers are denoted respectively $\mathcal{T}_{C2}$, $\mathcal{T}_{S1}$ and $\mathcal{T}_{S2}$ so that $\mathcal{T} = (\mathcal{T}_{C1}, \mathcal{T}_{S1}, \mathcal{T}_{C2}, \mathcal{T}_{S2}) = \mathcal{T}_{<1,2,3,4>}$. This case can easily be generalized to an arbitrary number of servers and clients.

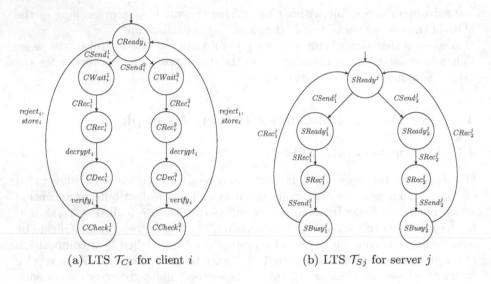

(a) LTS $\mathcal{T}_{Ci}$ for client i (b) LTS $\mathcal{T}_{Sj}$ for server j

Fig. 9. LTSs composing the Clients/Servers model

Step 1. In order to check the LTL formula φ_1 using our approach, we start with the first subsystem $\mathcal{T}_{C1}$. As we can see in Figure 9(a), we obviously have $\mathcal{T}_{C1} \models \varphi_1$ since once a message is sent to the first server (action $CSend_i^1$), this client eventually receives an answer from that server (action $CRec_i^1$). Let us verify this on the corresponding SOG, that we give in Figure 10(a). Observe that only the actions of φ_1 (viz., $CSend_1^1$, $CRec_1^1$, $CSend_1^2$ and $CRec_1^2$) are observable. It is straightforward to verify that φ_1 holds for this SOG.

Step 2. Following our approach in Figure 7, the second step is to synchronise SOGs associated with $\mathcal{T}_{C1}$ and the next subsystem (the first server component, viz. $\mathcal{T}_{S1}$). We give in Figure 10 the SOG of $\mathcal{T}_{S1}$, where only the actions of φ_1 (viz., $CSend_1^1$ and $CRec_1^1$) and the interface actions (viz. $CSend_2^1$ and $CRec_2^1$) are observable.

The obtained synchronised product of SOGs, denoted by $(\mathcal{T}_{C1}, \mathcal{T}_{S1})$, is represented in Figure 11. Note that, for the sake of clarity, we abbreviated some state names; for example, $CReady_1$ is abbreviated with CR_1, and $SRec_1^2$ is abbreviated with SV_1^2 (V is used for $ReceiVe$, other letters are straightforward). For this subsystem, the formula holds, viz. $(\mathcal{T}_{C1}, \mathcal{T}_{S1}) \models \varphi_1$.

Step 3. We give the rest of the analysis with less details. The verification process is applied to the synchronised product by composing one more subsystem. We get the synchronised product of SOGs $(\mathcal{T}_{C1}, \mathcal{T}_{S1}, \mathcal{T}_{C2})$, that we do not represent here. It can be shown that the formula φ_1 is satisfied by this product.

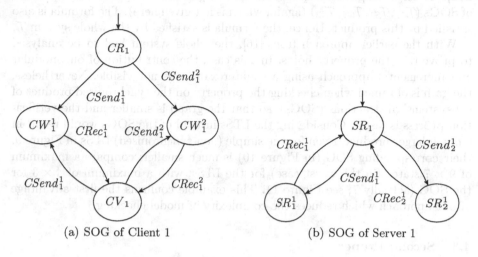

(a) SOG of Client 1   (b) SOG of Server 1

Fig. 10. SOGs of Client 1 and Server 1 for φ_1

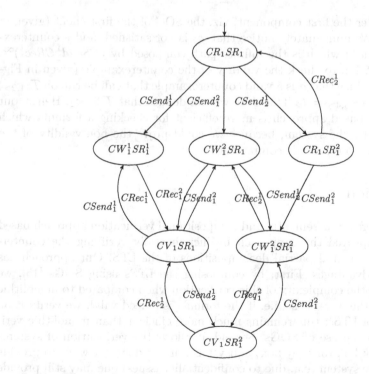

Fig. 11. Synchronised product of SOGs $\mathcal{T}_{<1,2>} = (\mathcal{T}_{C1}, \mathcal{T}_{S1})$

Step 4. Then, we go one step further, and we perform the synchronised product of SOGs ($\mathcal{T}_{C1}, \mathcal{T}_{S1}, \mathcal{T}_{C2}, \mathcal{T}_{S2}$) (again, which is not given here). The formula is also satisfied by this product. Hence, the formula is satisfied by the whole system $\mathcal{T}$.

With the earlier approach from [16], the whole system had to be analysed to prove that the property holds. In this case, the contribution of our modular and incremental approach using a counterexample is not visible. Nevertheless, the gain is obtained when checking the property on the synchronised product of subsystems' abstractions (SOGs), so that the graph is smaller and the verification process is faster. Considering the LTSs instead of the SOGs would result in a much larger product. Even for the simple (non-synchronised) LTSs in Figure 9, their corresponding SOG (in Figure 10) is much smaller: compare a maximum of 9×7 states (in the worst case) for the LTSs, with a maximum of 4×3 for the SOG (actually 7, see Figure 11. This example confirms the first advantage of our approach which reduces the complexity of model checking.

4.3   Second Property

Let us now consider another property to verify: the first client has to alternate between the two servers at least once when sending messages. This property can be expressed by the LTL formula $\varphi_2 = \Box(CSend_1^i \Rightarrow \Diamond CSend_1^j)$ with $i \neq j$ and $i, j \in \{1, 2\}$.

Let us consider the first component, viz. the SOG of the first client (given in Figure 10(a)). We immediately notice that φ_2 is not satisfied, and a counterexample σ is deduced which is the infinite path composed by $(CSend_1^1 CRec_1^1)^\infty$. Using our algorithm to check the validity of the counterexample (given in Figure 8), we can deduce that σ is a valid counterexample that can be run on $\mathcal{T}_{<1,2>}$, $\mathcal{T}_{<1,2,3>}$ and $\mathcal{T}_{<1,2,3,4>} = \mathcal{T}$. Therefore we can deduce that $\mathcal{T} \not\models \varphi_2$. Hence, our counterexample-based approach is more efficient for checking a formula which is not satisfied by the system, because we could prove the non-validity of the formula directly from a single component.

5   Conclusion

We proposed here an incremental and compositional verification approach based on [16]. We improved that approach by incrementally verifying the counterexample on incremental partial decompositions of the LTS. Our approach has the following advantages. First, by composing the LTSs using SOGs [15], we strongly reduce the complexity of this verification when compared to monolithic verification. In the worst case, i.e. if the formula is indeed valid, we verify it on the whole set of LTSs; this remains much more efficient than monolithic verification, due to the use of SOGs. Second, it allows the verification of systems containing black box (or gray box) subsystems: if one does not want to provide some part of the system (e.g. due to confidentiality issues) one may still provide the corresponding abstraction under the form of its SOG, thus allowing verification without disclosing the precise implementation. This also allows for reusing some components under the form of their SOG. Several issues can be investigated in the future: Given a decomposition $\langle \mathcal{T}_1, \ldots, \mathcal{T}_n \rangle$, we considered so far that the actions of the LTL\X formula φ all appear in $\mathcal{T}_1$ only (see Section 3.3). If these actions appear in further LTSs, one idea would be to decompose the formula in subformulae, as for instance in [19], each to be checked on the underlying sub-compoenent. Also, we suppose that the decomposition of the system is already given. As done in [16], one can build a decomposition of the system which is guided by the formula to be checked.

An efficient implementation of our approach is ongoing. It will both strengthen the initial results on examples of moderate size and allow for comparing the approach developed here with the monolithic verification on the one hand, and with the approach of [16] on the other hand.

References

1. Ball, T., Rajamani, S.K.: Automatically Validating Temporal Safety Properties of Interfaces. In: Dwyer, M.B. (ed.) SPIN 2001. LNCS, vol. 2057, pp. 103–122. Springer, Heidelberg (2001)
2. Bryant, R.E.: Symbolic boolean manipulation with ordered binary-decision diagrams. ACM Computing Surveys 24(3), 293–318 (1992)
3. Clarke, E.M., Grumberg, O., Jha, S., Lu, Y., Veith, H.: Counterexample-Guided Abstraction Refinement. In: Emerson, E.A., Sistla, A.P. (eds.) CAV 2000. LNCS, vol. 1855, pp. 154–169. Springer, Heidelberg (2000)
4. Clarke, E.M., Long, D.E., McMillan, K.L.: Compositional model checking. In: LICS 1989, pp. 353–362 (1989)
5. Cobleigh, J.M., Avrunin, G.S., Clarke, L.A.: Breaking up is hard to do: An evaluation of automated assume-guarantee reasoning. ACM Trans. Softw. Eng. Methodol. 17(2), 7:1–7:52 (2008)
6. Das, S., Dill, D.L.: Successive approximation of abstract transition relations. In: Proceedings of the 16th Annual IEEE Symposium on Logic in Computer Science, LICS 2001, p. 51. IEEE Computer Society, Washington, DC (2001)
7. Duret-Lutz, A., Klai, K., Poitrenaud, D., Thierry-Mieg, Y.: Self-Loop Aggregation Product — A New Hybrid Approach to On-the-Fly LTL Model Checking. In: Bultan, T., Hsiung, P.-A. (eds.) ATVA 2011. LNCS, vol. 6996, pp. 336–350. Springer, Heidelberg (2011)
8. Goltz, U., Kuiper, R., Penczek, W.: Propositional Temporal Logics and Equivalences. In: Cleaveland, W.R. (ed.) CONCUR 1992. LNCS, vol. 630, pp. 222–236. Springer, Heidelberg (1992)
9. Haddad, S., Ilié, J.-M., Klai, K.: Design and Evaluation of a Symbolic and Abstraction-Based Model Checker. In: Wang, F. (ed.) ATVA 2004. LNCS, vol. 3299, pp. 196–210. Springer, Heidelberg (2004)
10. Henzinger, T.A., Jhala, R., Majumdar, R., Sutre, G.: Lazy abstraction. SIGPLAN Not. 37(1), 58–70 (2002)
11. Hoare, C.A.R.: Communicating sequential process. Communication of the ACM 21(8), 666–677 (1978)
12. Kaivola, R., Valmari, A.: The Weakest Compositional Semantic Equivalence Preserving Nexttime-less Linear Temporal Logic. In: Cleaveland, W.R. (ed.) CONCUR 1992. LNCS, vol. 630, pp. 207–221. Springer, Heidelberg (1992)

13. Klai, K., Haddad, S., Ilié, J.-M.: Modular Verification of Petri Nets Properties: A Structure-Based Approach. In: Wang, F. (ed.) FORTE 2005. LNCS, vol. 3731, pp. 189–203. Springer, Heidelberg (2005)
14. Klai, K., Ochi, H.: Modular verification of inter-enterprise business processes. In: eKNOW, pp. 155–161 (2012)
15. Klai, K., Petrucci, L.: Modular construction of the symbolic observation graph. In: Billington, J., Duan, Z., Koutny, M. (eds.) ACSD, pp. 88–97. IEEE (2008)
16. Klai, K., Petrucci, L., Reniers, M.: An Incremental and Modular Technique for Checking LTL\X Properties of Petri Nets. In: Derrick, J., Vain, J. (eds.) FORTE 2007. LNCS, vol. 4574, pp. 280–295. Springer, Heidelberg (2007)
17. Klai, K., Poitrenaud, D.: MC-SOG: An LTL Model Checker Based on Symbolic Observation Graphs. In: van Hee, K.M., Valk, R. (eds.) PETRI NETS 2008. LNCS, vol. 5062, pp. 288–306. Springer, Heidelberg (2008)
18. Lakos, C., Petrucci, L.: Modular analysis of systems composed of semiautonomous subsystems. In: ACSD, pp. 185–194. IEEE Computer Society Press (2004)
19. Lehmann, A., Lohmann, N., Wolf, K.: Stubborn Sets for Simple Linear Time Properties. In: Haddad, S., Pomello, L. (eds.) PETRI NETS 2012. LNCS, vol. 7347, pp. 228–247. Springer, Heidelberg (2012)
20. Manna, Z., Pnueli, A.: The temporal logic of reactive and concurrent systems. Springer-Verlag New York, Inc., New York (1992)
21. Peled, D., Valmari, A., Kokkarinen, I.: Relaxed visibility enhances partial order reduction. Formal Methods in System Design 19(3), 275–289 (2001)
22. Pnueli, A.: In transition from global to modular temporal reasoning about programs. In: Logics and Models of Concurrent Systems, pp. 123–144. Springer-Verlag New York, Inc. (1985)
23. Puhakka, A., Valmari, A.: Weakest-Congruence Results for Livelock-Preserving Equivalences. In: Baeten, J.C.M., Mauw, S. (eds.) CONCUR 1999. LNCS, vol. 1664, pp. 510–524. Springer, Heidelberg (1999)
24. Saïdi, H.: Model Checking Guided Abstraction and Analysis. In: Palsberg, J. (ed.) SAS 2000. LNCS, vol. 1824, pp. 377–396. Springer, Heidelberg (2000)
25. Valmari, A.: On-the-fly Verification with Stubborn Sets. In: Courcoubetis, C. (ed.) CAV 1993. LNCS, vol. 697, pp. 397–408. Springer, Heidelberg (1993)
26. Valmari, A.: Compositionality in State Space Verification Methods. In: Billington, J., Reisig, W. (eds.) ICATPN 1996. LNCS, vol. 1091, pp. 29–56. Springer, Heidelberg (1996)

Compositional Reverification of Probabilistic Safety Properties for Large-Scale Complex IT Systems

Radu Calinescu[1], Shinji Kikuchi[2], and Kenneth Johnson[1]

[1] Department of Computer Science
University of York, Deramore Lane, York YO10, UK
{radu.calinescu,kenneth.johnson}@york.ac.uk
[2] Fujitsu Laboratories Limited
4-1-1 Kamikodanaka, Nakahara-ku, Kawasaki, Kanagawa 211-8588, Japan
skikuchi@jp.fujitsu.com

Abstract. Compositional verification has long been regarded as an effective technique for extending the use of symbolic model checking to large, component-based systems. This paper explores the effectiveness of the technique for large-scale complex IT systems (LSCITS). In particular, we investigate how compositional verification can be used to reverify LSCITS safety properties efficiently after the frequent changes that characterise these systems. We identify several *LSCITS change patterns*—including component failure, join and choice—and propose an approach that uses *assume-guarantee compositional verification* to reverify *probabilistic safety properties* compositionally in scenarios associated with these patterns. The application of this approach is illustrated using a case study from the area of cloud computing.

1 Introduction

A variant of symbolic model checking termed *compositional verification* has proved particularly effective in extending the applicability of formal verification to large, component-based systems [1,2,14,21,25,27,29]. This technique analyses the components of a system independently, and derives global system properties through verifying a composition of its component-level properties. The state-transition models verified in both steps of the technique are often orders of magnitude smaller than a monolithic model of the same system.

However, traditional compositional verification is less effective for a class of IT systems of growing practical importance, namely *large-scale complex IT systems* (LSCITS). LSCITS are affected by regular component failures, joins and departures, and by frequent modifications in environment and requirements [9,28,31]. This continual change has the effect of quickly invalidating the result of any compositional verification, which is based on a set of models that are accurate for only a short period of time.

Recent research has used (quantitative) model checking techniques at runtime, to ensure that IT systems continue to comply with their requirements after

R. Calinescu and D. Garlan (Eds.): Monterey Workshop 2012, LNCS 7539, pp. 303–329, 2012.

changes similar to those experienced by LSCITS [5,6,12,17,20,24]. The approach proposed in this work involves monitoring the running system, and verifying an updated model of its behaviour whenever an environment or system change is identified. If the runtime verification confirms that the system continues to comply with its requirements, no further action is required. Otherwise, the verification results are used to guide a *self-adaptation* process through which the system adjusts its parameters to reinstate the compliance with its requirements. While the approach proved effective in applications ranging from dynamic power management [4,11,12] to quality-of-service optimisation in service-based systems [5,6,17], none of the systems in these applications was an LSCITS.

This paper presents the results of our work to integrate techniques from the areas of compositional verification and runtime model checking. We envisage that a successful integration of the two types of techniques will extend the benefits of our recent work on runtime model checking [5,6,8,10,12] to larger systems, and ultimately to certain classes of LSCITS.

The rest of the paper is organised as follows. In Section 2, we overview existing compositional verification techniques, focusing on the probabilistic assume-guarantee approach used in our work. In Section 3, we identify several *LSCITS change patterns*, and we explain how *assume-guarantee compositional verification* can be used reverify compliance with safety properties *incrementally* in scenarios associated with these patterns. A running example from the area of cloud computing is used to illustrate these results throughout this section. Finally, Section 4 summarises the contributions of our work and discusses a number of future research directions.

2   From Monolithic to Compositional Verification

2.1   Running Example

We will illustrate the concepts and verification techniques discussed in the paper using the three-tier software service whose deployment on cloud infrastructure is depicted in Figure 1. Several instances of each of the three components (or *functions*) of this service—Web, Application and Database—are run on different virtual machines (VMs) that are located on four physical servers.

Note that while the system in Figure 1 is not a large system, it can be easily scaled up to become one by using standard cloud infrastructure functionality to increase the number of servers, virtual machines and "function" instances, potentially by many orders of magnitude. Indeed, some of the discussion later in the paper assumes this to be the case. Likewise, running a scaled-up version of the service across multiple cloud data-centres (an increasingly common practice for some users of cloud infrastructure [16,33]) can augment the system with LSCITS-specific characteristics.

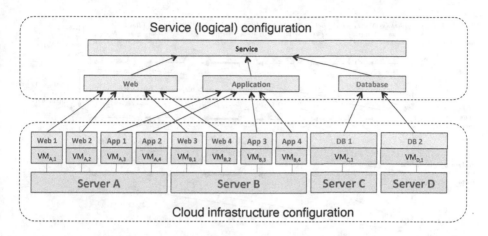

Fig. 1. Three-tier service deployed on cloud infrastructure

2.2 Background

Model checking a component-based system involves verifying if the parallel composition of $n > 1$ interdependent models of the system components and environment M_1, M_2, ..., M_n satisfies a set of requirements R:

$$M_1 \parallel M_2 \parallel \ldots \parallel M_n \models R. \tag{1}$$

Each model M_i, $1 \le i \le n$, comprises a finite set of states S_i and a *state transition relation* $T_i \subseteq S_i \times S_i$ with the property that for every state $s \in S_i$ there is at least a state $s' \in S_i$ such that $(s, s') \in T_i$. The states in S_i correspond to possible states of the modelled real-world component or environment element, and T_i encodes the possible transitions between these states. A *labelling function* $L_i : S_i \to AP_i$ is used to associate each state with a set of *atomic propositions* that are true in that state, and $s_i^0 \in S_i$ denotes the initial state of M_i. Formally,

$$M_i = (S_i, s_i^0, T_i, L_i), \quad 1 \le i \le n, \tag{2}$$

is termed a *Kripke structure* over the set of atomic propositions AP_i.

The requirements R are formulae defined over $\cup_{i=1}^{n} AP_i$ and expressed in extensions of propositional logic that support reasoning about the timing of events in the system. These *temporal logics* are used to specify desirable sequences of transitions between system states without referring to time explicitly. In particular, temporal logic formulae can specify *safety properties* (e.g., "the server failure state is *never* entered") and *liveness properties* (e.g., "the VM is *eventually* migrated to an operational server").

These concepts are illustrated in Figure 2, which depicts a model of a single physical server from our running example from Figure 1. We assume that the server has initially N_{DISK} disks, N_{CPU} CPUs and N_{MEM} memory blocks that are operational, but that each of these components can fail over time. To ensure that such component failures do not lead to failures of the VMs running on the

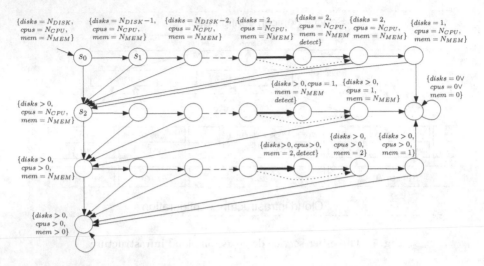

Fig. 2. State transition model of a physical server. The states labelled with the atomic proposition *detect* are reached if multiple component failures render the server "unsafe" *and* the failure detection mechanism operates correctly. For our running example, the server is deemed unsafe when it is left with only two disks or one CPU or two memory blocks that are operational.

server, the server is provided with a hardware failure detection mechanism. When multiple failures of components of the same type make the server "unsafe", this mechanism triggers the migration of the VMs to another physical server.

The model in Figure 2 supports the verification of safety properties such as "it is never the case that the failure of all server components of the same type (i.e., all disks or all CPUs or all memory blocks) is not detected" over a fixed time period (e.g., one year). The state transitions of this model correspond to:

- individual components failures (e.g., the transition (s_0, s_1) corresponds to the failure of the first disk within the analysed time period);
- individual components being operational at the end of the considered time period (e.g., the transition (s_0, s_2) is taken if the first disk is operational throughout the considered time period);
- the failure detection mechanism operating correctly (i.e., the three transitions depicted using thick lines in the transition graph from Figure 2);
- if applicable, the incorrect operation of the failure detection mechanism (i.e., the three transitions represented with dotted lines).

To keep the model small, the first two types of state transitions are included for a component only when the failure or correct operation of that component has an impact on the safety properties that we are interested in. For instance, state s_2 is reached if at least one of the disks remains operational throughout the considered time period. Therefore, the model does not include any transitions leaving s_2 or a state reachable from s_2 and modelling the failure or correct operation of a disk; and all these states are labelled with the atomic proposition "$disks > 0$". Choosing the right *level of abstraction* for the model in this way is essential in order to reduce the size of its state space.

The safety property "it is never the case that the failure of all disks or all CPUs or all memory blocks is not *detect*-ed" can be expressed formally using the G (globally) and U (until) linear-time temporal logic (LTL) operators:

$$G[\neg(\neg detect \text{ U } disk = 0 \vee cpu = 0 \vee mem = 0)]. \tag{3}$$

This property is satisfied by the server model if and only if the state transitions represented with dotted lines in Figure 2 are not present. We make this observation by examining every single *path* (i.e., sequence of transitions) from the initial state s_0 to the state labelled with the atomic proposition "$disk = 0 \vee cpu = 0 \vee mem = 0$", and noting that it includes a state labelled "*detect*" if and only if the dotted-line transitions are not part of the model.

Various modelling formalisms support the verification of reliability, performance and cost-related properties by additionally annotating the model transitions and/or states with probabilities, transition rates and costs/rewards, respectively. For instance, annotating the state transitions from our server model in Figure 2 with probabilities allows the verification of *probabilistic safety properties* such as "the probability that the failure of all server components of the same type is detected is at least 0.999". This property can be expressed formally in probabilistic computation tree logic (PCTL) as

$$P_{\geq 0.999}[G[\neg(\neg detect \text{ U } disk = 0 \vee cpu = 0 \vee mem = 0)]], \tag{4}$$

where P is the probabilistic PCTL operator.

Finally, component interactions are modelled by annotating the state transitions of the models $M_i = (S_i, s_i^0, T_i, L_i)$ from (2) with *actions* from an *action alphabet* α_i, $1 \leq i \leq n$. When a transition $(s, s') \in T_i$ is annotated with action $a \in \alpha_i$, it can be taken when model M_i is in state s only at the same time with an a-annotated transition in every other model $M_j \neq M_i$ whose action alphabet also includes a, $1 \leq j \leq n$.

Figure 3 shows a variant of the server model in which transitions are annotated with both probabilities and actions. The former support the verification of the probabilistic safety property (4). The latter enable the modelling of the interaction between the server and the other components of the system in Figure 1, e.g., through the parallel composition of the server model M_{server} with the model $M_{web+app}$ of the two Web and two App(lication) instances running on Server A or on Server B. This model (shown in Figure 4) comprises state transitions annotated with the actions "server_down", "warn" and "server_up" that also belong to the action alphabet for the server model. The $M_{web+app}$ state transitions corresponding to the actions shared between the two models are not annotated with probabilities like all the other $M_{web+app}$ state transitions, as these probabilities depend on the server behaviour and are unknown until the two models are composed.

The way in which we established the safety property (3) by examining every path starting at the initial state s_0 of the model in Figure 2 is applicable only

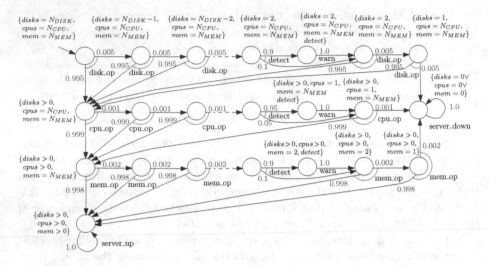

Fig. 3. Model M_{server} for the running example: annotating the state transitions of the server model with probabilities and actions enables the verification of probabilistic safety properties and the modelling of component interactions, respectively

to models that are relatively small or have a particularly regular structure. Advanced model checking techniques including *symbolic model checking* and *partial order reduction* overcome this limitation by avoiding the exhaustive enumeration and analysis of all such paths through the model [13].

2.3   Compositional Verification

Even though symbolic model checking extends the applicability of formal verification to some very large models, this is still insufficient for many models associated with today's IT systems. A complete model of our service from Figure 1, for instance, requires the parallel composition of:

- Four instances of the server model M_{server} from Figure 3 (one for each of Servers A, B, C and D). These model instances—denoted M_{server_A}, M_{server_B}, M_{server_C} and M_{server_D}—are obtained from the model M_{server} in Figure 3 by subscripting all its actions and atomic proposition parameters with A, B, C and D, respectively (e.g., server_down$_A$ or $disk_B$).
- Two instances of the "Web-Application" model $M_{web+app}$ from Figure 4 (corresponding to the web and application instances deployed on Server A and Server B, and denoted $M_{web+app_A}$ and $M_{web+app_B}$).
- Two instances of the "Database" model M_{db} from Figure 5 (M_{db_C} and M_{db_D}, corresponding to the Database instances on Servers C and D, respectively).
- The three-tier architecture model $M_{service}$ from Figure 6.

We implemented this composition as a monolithic model

$$M = M_{server_A} \parallel M_{server_B} \parallel M_{server_C} \parallel M_{server_D} \parallel M_{web+app_A} \parallel \\ M_{web+app_B} \parallel M_{db_C} \parallel M_{db_D} \parallel M_{service} \tag{5}$$

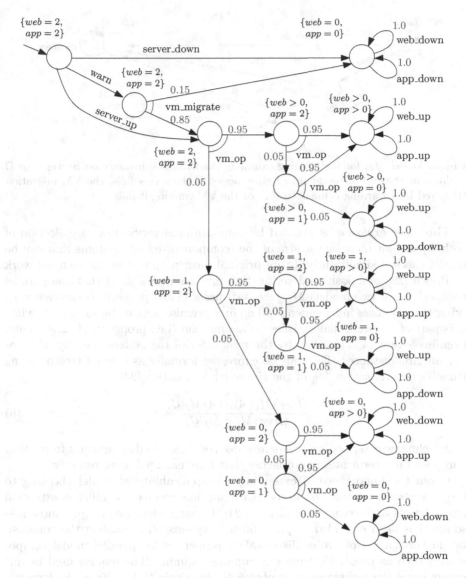

Fig. 4. Model $M_{web+app}$ for the running example: the two Web and the two App(lication) instances on Server A or B are down at the end of the analysed time period if the server fails, the VM migration triggered by a warning is unsuccessful, or the VMs running them fail

for the probabilistic symbolic model checker PRISM [22], and the tool ran out of memory when attempting to verify if the resulting 176,381,406,182,650-state model satisfied the property "the probability that the service fails within a one-year time interval is under 0.0005".

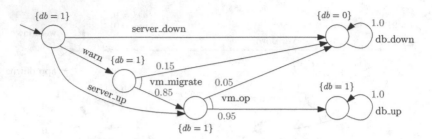

Fig. 5. Model M_{db} for the running example: the Database instance on Server C or D is down at the end of the analysed time period if the server fails, the VM migration triggered by a warning is unsuccessful, or the VM running it fails

This *state explosion* is avoided by compositional verification, a collection of techniques that increase the size of the (component-based) systems that can be model checked significantly. In its original form proposed in the seminal work of Pnueli [29], compositional verification involves establishing that the parallel composition of two models $M_1 \parallel M_2$ satisfies a global property $\mathcal{G}$ through verifying two premises independently. The first premise is that M_2 satisfies $\mathcal{G}$ when it is part of a system that satisfies an *assumption* (i.e., property) $\mathcal{A}$. The second premise is that $\mathcal{A}$ is satisfied by the remainder of the system (i.e., by M_1) under all circumstances. This can be expressed formally as a proof tree by using Pnueli's generalisation [29] of the Hoare triple notation [23]:

$$\frac{\langle true \rangle M_1 \langle \mathcal{A} \rangle, \ \langle \mathcal{A} \rangle M_2 \langle \mathcal{G} \rangle}{\langle true \rangle M_1 \parallel M_2 \langle \mathcal{G} \rangle}. \tag{6}$$

The technique is termed *assume-guarantee reasoning*, to distinguish it from other compositional verification approaches that have emerged more recently.

Given the importance of extending the applicability of model checking to larger systems, assume-guarantee reasoning has received significant attention from the research community [3,14,15,21]. In particular, assume-guarantee reasoning has been extended to probabilistic systems [27], enabling the compositional verification of probabilistic safety properties for parallel model compositions such as model (5) from our running example. The models used in this extension of the technique are *probabilistic automata* (PAs) [30] of the form

$$M_i = (S_i, s_i^0, \alpha_i, \delta_i, L_i). \tag{7}$$

As before, S_i, $s_i^0 \in S_i$, α_i and L_i represent a finite set of states, the initial state, the action alphabet and an atomic-proposition labelling function, respectively. However, the state transition relation T_i from the definition of the Kripke model in (2) is replaced by a *probabilistic state transition relation* $\delta_i \subseteq S_i \times (\alpha_i \cup \{\tau\}) \times Dist(S_i)$, where $Dist(S_i)$ denotes the set of all discrete probability distributions over the state set S_i. The possible transitions from a generic state $s \in S_i$ to another state in S_i are given by the set $\delta_i(s) = \{(s, a, d) \mid (s, a, d) \in \delta_i\}$. When the system is in state s, an element

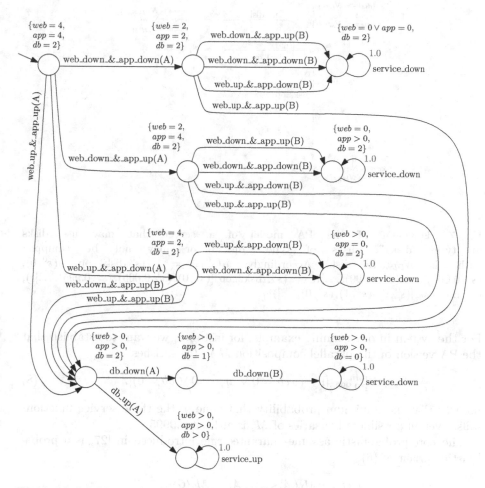

Fig. 6. Model $M_{service}$ for the running example: the service fails if all instances of any of the Web, Application and Database "functions" fail

$(s, a, d) \in \delta_i(s)$ is chosen nondeterministically, and the next state s' is selected randomly according to the distribution $d \in Dist(S_i)$. This characteristic of probabilistic automata is particularly useful for modelling LSCITS components, as illustrated in Figure 7 for a physical server from our running example.

The analysis of PA properties requires the resolution of its nondeterministic choices by means of *adversaries*, i.e., functions that map any finite path ending in a generic state $s \in S_i$ to one of the discrete probability distributions in $\delta_i(s)$ or "decide" to remain in state s. Given the set of all adversaries Adv_i of a PA model M_i, we are typically interested in verifying a property related to the minimum and/or maximum probability of an event over all adversaries in Adv_i.

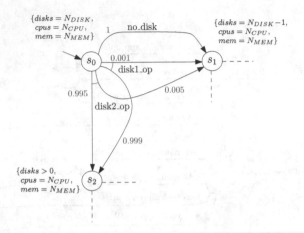

Fig. 7. Fragment of the PA model of a server that may use disks of type "disk1", disks of type "disk2" or may not be equipped with the N_{DISK}'th disk. Accordingly, $\delta_1(s^0)$ = $\{(s^0,\text{disk1\_op}, [(s^0, 0),$ $(s^1, 0.001),$ $(s^2, 0.999), \ldots]),$ $(s^0, \text{disk2\_op}, [(s^0, 0), (s^1, 0.005), (s^2, 0.995), \ldots]]),$ $(s^0, \text{no\_disk}, [(s^0, 0), (s^1, 1), (s^2, 0), \ldots])]\}$.

For the system in our running example, for instance, we want to establish that the PA version of the parallel composition M in (5) satisfies

$$\text{P}^{min}_{\geq 0.9995}[\text{F} \neg(web = 0 \vee app = 0 \vee db = 0)], \tag{8}$$

namely that the minimum probability that none of the three service functions fails, over all possible adversaries of M, is at least 0.9995.

The core probabilistic assume-guarantee rule introduced in [27] is a probabilistic variant of (6):

$$\frac{\langle true \rangle M_1 \langle \mathcal{A} \rangle_{\geq p_1}, \ \langle \mathcal{A} \rangle_{\geq p_1} M_2 \langle \mathcal{G} \rangle_{\geq p_2}}{\langle true \rangle M_1 \parallel M_2 \langle \mathcal{G} \rangle_{\geq p_2}}, \tag{9}$$

where, given a model M and a *probabilistic safety property* $\langle \mathcal{X} \rangle_{\geq p}$, $M \models \langle \mathcal{X} \rangle_{\geq p}$ holds iff the minimum probability that $\mathcal{X}$ is satisfied over all adversaries of M is at least p. A probabilistic safety property $\langle \mathcal{X} \rangle_{\geq p}$ is specified by means of:

- A *deterministic finite automaton* (DFA) $\mathcal{X}^{\text{err}} = (Q, \alpha_\mathcal{X}, \delta_\mathcal{X}, q_0, F)$ with the state set Q, alphabet $\alpha_\mathcal{X}$, transition function $\delta_\mathcal{X} : Q \times \alpha_\mathcal{X} \to Q$, initial state q_0 and accepting states $F \subseteq Q$. The finite words accepted by $\mathcal{X}^{\text{err}}$ specify the sequences of actions associated with prefixes of paths that do not satisfy $\mathcal{X}$.
- The rational probability bound p.

Consider, for instance, the server model M_{server} from Fig. 3, its action alphabet $\alpha_{server} = \{\text{disk\_op, cpu\_op, mem\_op, detect, warn, server\_up, server\_down}\}$, and let $\langle \mathcal{A}_1 \rangle_{\geq 0.999}$ be the probabilistic safety property from eq. (4). The DFA $\mathcal{A}_1^{err}$ and its regular language $L(\mathcal{A}_1^{err})$ of "bad prefixes" are shown in Fig 8(a).

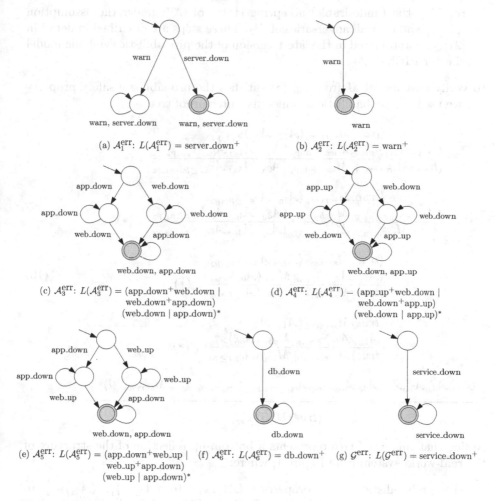

(a) $\mathcal{A}_1^{\mathrm{err}}$: $L(\mathcal{A}_1^{\mathrm{err}}) = \mathrm{server\_down}^+$

(b) $\mathcal{A}_2^{\mathrm{err}}$: $L(\mathcal{A}_2^{\mathrm{err}}) = \mathrm{warn}^+$

(c) $\mathcal{A}_3^{\mathrm{err}}$: $L(\mathcal{A}_3^{\mathrm{err}}) = (\mathrm{app\_down}^+\mathrm{web\_down} \mid$
$\mathrm{web\_down}^+\mathrm{app\_down})$
$(\mathrm{web\_down} \mid \mathrm{app\_down})^*$

(d) $\mathcal{A}_4^{\mathrm{err}}$: $L(\mathcal{A}_4^{\mathrm{err}}) - (\mathrm{app\_up}^+\mathrm{web\_down} \mid$
$\mathrm{web\_down}^+\mathrm{app\_up})$
$(\mathrm{web\_down} \mid \mathrm{app\_up})^*$

(e) $\mathcal{A}_5^{\mathrm{err}}$: $L(\mathcal{A}_5^{\mathrm{err}}) = (\mathrm{app\_down}^+\mathrm{web\_up} \mid$
$\mathrm{web\_up}^+\mathrm{app\_down})$
$(\mathrm{web\_up} \mid \mathrm{app\_down})^*$

(f) $\mathcal{A}_6^{\mathrm{err}}$: $L(\mathcal{A}_6^{\mathrm{err}}) = \mathrm{db\_down}^+$

(g) $\mathcal{G}^{\mathrm{err}}$: $L(\mathcal{G}^{\mathrm{err}}) = \mathrm{service\_down}^+$

Fig. 8. Deterministic finite automata and regular expressions defining for the probabilistic safety properties from the running example

Given the DFAs $\mathcal{A}^{\mathrm{err}}$ and $\mathcal{G}^{\mathrm{err}}$ for the assumed and guaranteed probabilistic safety properties in the proof rule (9), the verification of its two premises is carried out as follows [27]:

- To verify $\langle\mathit{true}\rangle M_1\langle\mathcal{A}\rangle_{\geq p_1}$ quantitatively, the parallel composition of M_1 and $\mathcal{A}^{\mathrm{err}}$ is model checked to obtain $1 - p_1$, the maximum probability of reaching the (undesirable) accepting states of $\mathcal{A}^{\mathrm{err}}$, over all adversaries of M_1.
- To verify $\langle\mathcal{A}\rangle_{\geq p_1} M_2\langle\mathcal{G}\rangle_{\geq p_2}$, M_2 is composed with both $\mathcal{A}^{\mathrm{err}}$ and $\mathcal{G}^{\mathrm{err}}$. Because the satisfaction of $\mathcal{A}$ with probability p_1 and of $\mathcal{G}$ with probability p_2 must be analysed together, a technique called *multi-objective model checking* [18] is then used. This technique produces $1 - p_2$, the maximum probability of

reaching the (undesirable) accepting states of $\mathcal{G}^{err}$, under the assumption $\langle \mathcal{A} \rangle_{\geq p_1}$ and over all adversaries of M_2. These steps are described in detail in [27], and automated in the latest version of the probabilistic symbolic model checker PRISM [26].

To verify that model M from eq. (5) satisfies the probabilistic safety property (8), we used the probabilistic assume-guarantee proof tree

$$\frac{\langle true \rangle M_{server_A} \langle \mathcal{A}_{1_A}, \mathcal{A}_{2_A} \rangle_{\geq p_1, p_2} \quad \langle \mathcal{A}_{1_A}, \mathcal{A}_{2_A} \rangle_{\geq p_1, p_2} M_{web+app_A} \langle \mathcal{A}_{3_A}, \mathcal{A}_{4_A}, \mathcal{A}_{5_A} \rangle_{\geq p_3, p_4, p_5}}{\langle true \rangle M_{server_A} \parallel M_{web+app_A} \langle \mathcal{A}_{3_A}, \mathcal{A}_{4_A}, \mathcal{A}_{5_A} \rangle_{\geq p_3, p_4, p_5}}, \quad (*)$$

$$\frac{\langle true \rangle M_{server_B} \langle \mathcal{A}_{1_B}, \mathcal{A}_{2_B} \rangle_{\geq p_1, p_2} \quad \langle \mathcal{A}_{1_B}, \mathcal{A}_{2_B} \rangle_{\geq p_1, p_2} M_{web+app_B} \langle \mathcal{A}_{3_B}, \mathcal{A}_{4_B}, \mathcal{A}_{5_B} \rangle_{\geq p_3, p_4, p_5}}{\langle true \rangle M_{server_B} \parallel M_{web+app_B} \langle \mathcal{A}_{3_B}, \mathcal{A}_{4_B}, \mathcal{A}_{5_B} \rangle_{\geq p_3, p_4, p_5}}, \quad (*)$$

$$\frac{\langle true \rangle M_{server_C} \langle \mathcal{A}_{1_C}, \mathcal{A}_{2_C} \rangle_{\geq p_1, p_2} \quad \langle \mathcal{A}_{1_C}, \mathcal{A}_{2_C} \rangle_{\geq p_1, p_2} M_{db_C} \langle \mathcal{A}_{6_C} \rangle_{\geq p_6}}{\langle true \rangle M_{server_C} \parallel M_{db_C} \langle \mathcal{A}_{6_C} \rangle_{\geq p_6}}, \quad (*) \qquad (10)$$

$$\frac{\langle true \rangle M_{server_D} \langle \mathcal{A}_{1_D}, \mathcal{A}_{2_D} \rangle_{\geq p_1, p_2} \quad \langle \mathcal{A}_{1_D}, \mathcal{A}_{2_D} \rangle_{\geq p_1, p_2} M_{db_D} \langle \mathcal{A}_{6_D} \rangle_{\geq p_6}}{\langle true \rangle M_{server_D} \parallel M_{db_D} \langle \mathcal{A}_{6_D} \rangle_{\geq p_6}}, \quad (*)$$

$$\frac{\langle \mathcal{A}_{3_A}, \mathcal{A}_{4_A}, \mathcal{A}_{5_A}, \mathcal{A}_{3_B}, \mathcal{A}_{4_B}, \mathcal{A}_{5_B}, \mathcal{A}_{6_C}, \mathcal{A}_{6_D} \rangle_{\geq p_3, p_4, p_5, p_3, p_4, p_5, p_6, p_6} M_{service} \langle \mathcal{G} \rangle_{\geq p_7}}{\langle true \rangle M \langle \mathcal{G} \rangle_{\geq p_7}} \quad (\#)$$

Notice that this proof tree represents a bottom-up reflection of the structure of the real-world system from Figure 1, where:

- the probabilistic safety properties $\langle \mathcal{A}_{1_A} \rangle_{\geq p_1}$ to $\langle \mathcal{A}_{1_D} \rangle_{\geq p_1}$, $\langle \mathcal{A}_{2_A} \rangle_{\geq p_2}$ to $\langle \mathcal{A}_{2_D} \rangle_{\geq p_2}$, etc. are defined by the DFAs in Figure 8 (with the appropiate subscript—A, B, C or D—applied to their action names);
- the probabilities p_1 to p_7 were obtained using the probabilistic model checker PRISM as described earlier;
- (*) denotes the application of the ASYM-MULT probabilistic assume-guarantee proof rule from [27];
- (#) marks the application of the new assume-guarantee proof rule that we introduce in Appendix A.

We executed the verification steps for all premises in (10) on a Macbook Pro laptop with 2.66 GHz Intel Core 2 Duo processor and 8GB of memory, using the hardware failure probabilities reported in [32,34] ($p_{disk\_fail} = 0.0231$, $p_{cpu\_fail} = 0.0018$ and $p_{mem\_fail} = 0.0231$ for a one-year period of operation).[1]

---

[1] The component failure probabilities in Figs. 3 and 7 were used only for illustration.

Table 1. Experimental results for the probabilistic assume-guarantee proof tree (10). The probabilities associated with the assumed and guaranteed properties in (10) were calculated for a one-year time interval, based on the hardware component failure probabilities reported in [32,34].

Verified model	Number of states	Result
$M_{server_{A-D}}$	570	$p_1 = 0.999998$
		$p_2 = 0.999544$
$M_{web+app_{A-B}}$	54	$p_3 = 0.999946$
		$p_4 = 0.997452$
		$p_5 = 0.997452$
$M_{db_{C-D}}$	13	$p_6 = 0.949954$
$M_{service}$	1035	$p_7 = 0.997482$

The results of the verification and the size of the models verified are shown in Table 1. As indicated by these results, the size of the state space for the verified models ranged between 13 and 1035, which explains why each of the verification steps completed in under one second. We anticipate that safety properties for systems comprising much larger numbers of servers, VMs per server, and function instances per service could be verified using the approach, and we are planning to confirm this experimentally in the future.

3 Reverification of Safety Properties for LSCITS

We showed in the previous section how compositional verification can be used to verify safety properties of a class of systems that can potentially be very large. However, size is not the only defining characteristic of LSCITS. LSCITS can be seen as *coalitions of systems* whose components join and leave continually, and within which frequent component selection and failure represent the norm rather than an exception [9,28,31].

In this section, we present techniques for the calculation of the minimal sequence of assume-guarantee premises that need to be reverified in response to several of these key *patterns of LSCITS change*. To describe these techniques, we will use the following additional notation:

- $\mathcal{M}$, the set of PA models (7);
- $\mathcal{P}$, the set of probabilistic safety properties;
- DFA, the set of deterministic finite automata;
- $dfa : \mathcal{P} \to DFA$, the function that maps each probabilistic safety property to its defining deterministic finite automaton;
- $prob : \mathcal{P} \to [0,1]$, the function that maps each probabilistic safety property to its associated probability (i.e., $\forall \langle \mathcal{X} \rangle_{\geq p} \in \mathcal{P} \bullet prob(\langle \mathcal{X} \rangle_{\geq p}) = p$);
- $mc : 2^{\mathcal{P}} \times \mathcal{M} \times DFA \to [0,1]$, the quantitative model checking function that, given a set of assumptions $A \in 2^{\mathcal{P}}$, a model $M \in \mathcal{M}$ and a deterministic finite automaton $\mathcal{G}^{err} \in DFA$, ensures that $\langle \mathcal{G} \rangle_{\geq p}$, i.e., $M \models \langle \mathcal{G} \rangle_{\geq mc(A,M,\mathcal{G}^{err})}$ under the assumptions A;

- $\mathcal{V} \subset 2^{\mathcal{P}} \times \mathcal{M} \times 2^{\mathcal{P}}$, the set of all *verification steps* that can appear as premises in a probabilistic assume-guarantee proof tree; $(A, M, G) \in \mathcal{V}$ iff A and G are finite sets of assumed and guaranteed probabilistic safety properties for the PA model M, respectively.

Note that $\langle true \rangle$ is a special element of $\mathcal{P}$; when it is used as an assumption for a model $M \in \mathcal{M}$, $dfa(\langle true \rangle)$ is the one-state DFA that has the same alphabet α_M as M and does not accepts any word, i.e., $dfa(\langle true \rangle) = (\{q_0\}, \alpha_M, \{a \in \alpha_M \bullet (q_0, a) \mapsto q_0\}, q_0, \{\})$ and $prob(\langle true \rangle) = 1$. In the definition of the transition function for $dfa(\langle true \rangle)$, we used the set comprehension notation $\{a \in \alpha_M \bullet (q_0, a) \mapsto q_0\}$ to build the set of mappings "$(q_0, a) \mapsto q_0$" for all possible values $a \in \alpha_M$. This notation, including its generalised form $\{declaration \mid predicate \bullet expression\}$ will be used again in this section as a concise way of specifying sets such as $\{x \in \mathbb{N} \mid 5 \leq x \leq 20 \bullet \sqrt{x}\}$, the set comprising the square root of all natural numbers between 5 and 20.

We are interested in the finite sequences of verification steps $(v_1, v_2, \ldots, v_n) \in seq\mathcal{V}$ that correspond to probabilistic assume-guarantee proof trees, which we term *compositional verification tasks*. A sequence $(v_1, v_2, \ldots, v_n)$, where $v_i = (A_i, M_i, G_i) \in \mathcal{V}$ for all $1 \leq i \leq n$, is a compositional verification task iff the set of assumed properties for each of its verification steps comprises only the special property $\langle true \rangle$ and properties guaranteed by preceeding verification steps: $A_i \subseteq \{\langle true \rangle\} \cup G_1 \cup G_2 \cup G_{i-1}$, for $1 \leq i \leq n$.

Using the notation introduced above, the compositional verification task (9) from our running example can be specified as a nine-element sequence of verification steps $(v_1, v_2, \ldots, v_9)$, where

$$
\begin{aligned}
v_1 &= (\{\langle true \rangle\}, M_{server_A}, \{\langle A_{1_A} \rangle_{\geq p_1}, \langle A_{2_A} \rangle_{\geq p_2}\}) \\
v_2 &= (\{\langle true \rangle\}, M_{server_B}, \{\langle A_{1_B} \rangle_{\geq p_1}, \langle A_{2_B} \rangle_{\geq p_2}\}) \\
v_3 &= (\{\langle true \rangle\}, M_{server_C}, \{\langle A_{1_C} \rangle_{\geq p_1}, \langle A_{2_C} \rangle_{\geq p_2}\}) \\
v_4 &= (\{\langle true \rangle\}, M_{server_D}, \{\langle A_{1_D} \rangle_{\geq p_1}, \langle A_{2_D} \rangle_{\geq p_2}\}) \\
v_5 &= (\{\langle A_{1_A} \rangle_{\geq p_1}, \langle A_{2_A} \rangle_{\geq p_2}\}, M_{web+app_A}, \{\langle A_{3_A} \rangle_{\geq p_3}, \langle A_{4_A} \rangle_{\geq p_4}, \langle A_{5_A} \rangle_{\geq p_5}\}) \\
v_6 &= (\{\langle A_{1_B} \rangle_{\geq p_1}, \langle A_{2_B} \rangle_{\geq p_2}\}, M_{web+app_B}, \{\langle A_{3_B} \rangle_{\geq p_3}, \langle A_{4_B} \rangle_{\geq p_4}, \langle A_{5_B} \rangle_{\geq p_5}\}) \\
v_7 &= (\{\langle A_{1_C} \rangle_{\geq p_1}, \langle A_{2_C} \rangle_{\geq p_2}\}, M_{db_C}, \{\langle A_{6_C} \rangle_{\geq p_{A_6}}\}) \\
v_8 &= (\{\langle A_{1_D} \rangle_{\geq p_1}, \langle A_{2_D} \rangle_{\geq p_2}\}, M_{db_D}, \{\langle A_{6_D} \rangle_{\geq p_{A_6}}\}) \\
v_9 &= (\{\langle A_{3_A} \rangle_{\geq p_3}, \langle A_{4_A} \rangle_{\geq p_4}, \langle A_{5_A} \rangle_{\geq p_5}, \langle A_{3_B} \rangle_{\geq p_3}, \langle A_{4_B} \rangle_{\geq p_4}, \\
&\quad \langle A_{5_B} \rangle_{\geq p_5}, \langle A_{6_C} \rangle_{\geq p_6}, \langle A_{6_D} \rangle_{\geq p_6}\}, M_{service}, \{\langle G \rangle_{\geq p_7}\})
\end{aligned}
\tag{11}
$$

3.1   Reverification of a Sequence of Verification Steps

Consider a compositional verification task $cv = (v_1, v_2, \ldots, v_n) \in seq\mathcal{V}$ that was completed successfully as described in the Section 2.3. The rest of this section describes a technique for the derivation of the minimal sequence of verification steps $\Delta cv \in seq\mathcal{V}$ that need to be carried out to reverify the safety properties associated with cv after different types of changes in the verified system.

We start by introducing a *reverify* function that takes as parameters:

1. a sequence of verification steps $vs \in \text{seq}\mathcal{V}$; and
2. a set of guaranteed property *changes* of the form $(g, g') \in \mathcal{P} \times \mathcal{P}$ (where g and g' are related properties before and after a system change, respectively)

and produces the minimum sequence of verification steps that need to be carried out in order to reestablish the probabilistic safety properties from vs. We define the function

$$reverify : \text{seq}\mathcal{V} \times 2^{\mathcal{P} \times \mathcal{P}} \to \text{seq}\mathcal{V} \qquad (12)$$

recursively on the size of the sequence of verification steps vs:

$$reverify((), changes) = ()$$

$$reverify((A, M, G) \frown vs, changes) =$$
$$= \begin{cases} reverify(vs, changes), & \text{if } A \cap \{(g, g') \in changes \bullet g\} = \emptyset \\ (A', M, G') \frown reverify(vs, changes'), & \text{otherwise} \end{cases}$$
$$(13)$$

where:

(i) $A' = \{a \in A \mid \neg(\exists(g, g') \in changes \bullet a = g)\} \cup \{(g, g') \in changes \mid g \in A \bullet g'\}$ is obtained by updating all the assumptions from A that changed;

(ii) $G' = \{x \in \mathcal{P} \mid (\exists g \in G \bullet dfa(x) = dfa(g)) \wedge prob(x) = mc(A', M, dfa(g))\}$ is the new set of probabilistic safety properties guaranteed by the model M given the changed assumed property set A';

(iii) $changes' = changes \cup \{(g, g') \in G \times G' \mid dfa(g) = dfa(g') \wedge prob(g') < prob(g)\}$ represents the new set of guaranteed property changes, which is obtained by extending the old *changes* set with all pairs from $G \times G'$ that correspond to a decrease in a safety probability bound.

Throughout this section we assume that the goal of the reverification is to establish whether the analysed system continues to satisfy given probabilistic safety properties after changes. If the aim is instead to find the new probability bounds for all safety properties, then $prob(g') < prob(g)$ should be replaced with $prob(g') \neq prob(g)$ in the calculation of *changes'* above.

The cost of executing the *reverify* function has two components:

1. the cost of running the verification steps (A', M, G') from (13);
2. the cost of performing the set intersection from (13) and the calculations from steps (i)–(iii) described above.

For each use of *reverify* in handling one of the LSCITS change patterns covered later in this section, we will prove that *reverify* yields the minimum sequence of verification steps required to reverify the analysed probabilistic safety properties. Therefore, we focus here only on the second cost component. To evaluate this cost component, we consider the execution of $reverify(cv, changes)$ for a generic compositional verification task cv and a generic property change set *changes*. Without loss of generality, we assume that cv comprises $n > 0$ verification steps, and that these n verification steps and the *changes* set taken together contain $m > 0$ assumed and guaranteed probabilistic safety properties. Under these assumptions, the set intersection $A \cap \{(g, g') \in changes \bullet g\}$ from (13) requires at most $O(m^2)$ time. Likewise, the two set comprehensions from step (i) take at most $O(m^2)$ time even for the most basic implementation of set membership queries. Building the set G' in step (ii) requires $O(m)$ time (in addition to the cost of executing $mc(A', M, dfa(g))$, but this is part of the first cost component). Finally, the cost of updating $changes$ to $changes'$ in step (iii) requires again at most $O(m^2)$ time for the examination of the elements in $G \times G'$. Due to the recursive $reverify$ invocations, the operations analysed above are performed n times, so the overall time complexity for the operations covered by the second cost component is $O(nm^2)$. Note that, even for large values of n and m, this represents a modest overhead compared to the first cost component, which corresponds to executing the model checking operations $mc(A', M, dfa(g))$ from (13). Since we will prove that the minimal set of such model checking operations is executed in each scenario in which $reverify$ is used in the remainder of the section, we conclude that $reverify$ is cost effective for the scenarios in which it is used.

Having introduced and analysed the generic $reverify$ function in (12)–(13), we are ready to calculate the minimum sequences of verification steps required after different types of LSCITS changes.

3.2 LSCITS Component Failure (or "Departure")

Suppose that the system component associated with model M_i from the verification step v_i of the compositional verification task $cv = (v_1, v_2, \ldots, v_n)$ failed (or left the system), where $1 \le i \le n$. In this scenario, appropriately modified variants of some or all of the verification steps $v_{i+1}, v_{i+2}, \ldots, v_n$ need to be redone. The theorem below provides a method for the derivation of these verification steps.

Theorem 1. The minimal sequence of verification steps that needs to be carried out to reverify a compositional verification task $cv = (v_1, v_2, \ldots, v_n)$ after the failure of the component associated with its i-th verification step is

$$\Delta cv = reverify((v_{i+1}, v_{i+2}, \ldots, v_n), \{g \in G_i \bullet (g, \langle true \rangle)\}). \tag{14}$$

The proof of this theorem is included in Appendix A.

Returning to our running example, suppose that the database function on server D is removed from the system because the service workload no longer justifies maintaining two instances of the database. Since the verification step associated with this component in (11) is v_8, the sequence of verification steps that need to be redone is given by

$$\Delta cv = reverify((v_9), \{(\langle \mathcal{A}_{6_D} \rangle_{\ge p_6}, \langle true \rangle)\}). \tag{15}$$

According to the *reverify* definition in (13), this is

$$\Delta cv = reverify((\{\{\langle\mathcal{A}_{3_A}\rangle_{\geq p_3}, \langle\mathcal{A}_{4_A}\rangle_{\geq p_4}, \langle\mathcal{A}_{5_A}\rangle_{\geq p_5}, \langle\mathcal{A}_{3_B}\rangle_{\geq p_3}, \langle\mathcal{A}_{4_B}\rangle_{\geq p_4},$$
$$\langle\mathcal{A}_{5_B}\rangle_{\geq p_5}, \langle\mathcal{A}_{6_C}\rangle_{\geq p_6}, \langle\mathcal{A}_{6_D}\rangle_{\geq p_6}\}, M_{service}, \{\langle\mathcal{G}\rangle_{\geq p_G}\}),$$
$$\{(\langle\mathcal{A}_{6_D}\rangle_{\geq p_6}, \langle true\rangle)\})$$
$$= (\{\{\langle\mathcal{A}_{3_A}\rangle_{\geq p_3}, \langle\mathcal{A}_{4_A}\rangle_{\geq p_4}, \langle\mathcal{A}_{5_A}\rangle_{\geq p_5}, \langle\mathcal{A}_{3_B}\rangle_{\geq p_3}, \langle\mathcal{A}_{4_B}\rangle_{\geq p_4}, \langle\mathcal{A}_{5_B}\rangle_{\geq p_5},$$
$$\langle\mathcal{A}_{6_C}\rangle_{\geq p_6}, \langle true\rangle\}, M_{service}, \{\langle\mathcal{G}\rangle_{\geq p_7'}\}) \frown reverify((), changes')$$
$$= (\{\{\langle\mathcal{A}_{3_A}\rangle_{\geq p_3}, \langle\mathcal{A}_{4_A}\rangle_{\geq p_4}, \langle\mathcal{A}_{5_A}\rangle_{\geq p_5}, \langle\mathcal{A}_{3_B}\rangle_{\geq p_3}, \langle\mathcal{A}_{4_B}\rangle_{\geq p_4}, \langle\mathcal{A}_{5_B}\rangle_{\geq p_5},$$
$$\langle\mathcal{A}_{6_C}\rangle_{\geq p_6}\}, M_{service}, \{\langle\mathcal{G}\rangle_{\geq p_7'}\}) \frown ()$$
$$= (\{\{\langle\mathcal{A}_{3_A}\rangle_{\geq p_3}, \langle\mathcal{A}_{4_A}\rangle_{\geq p_4}, \langle\mathcal{A}_{5_A}\rangle_{\geq p_5}, \langle\mathcal{A}_{3_B}\rangle_{\geq p_3}, \langle\mathcal{A}_{4_B}\rangle_{\geq p_4}, \langle\mathcal{A}_{5_B}\rangle_{\geq p_5},$$
$$\langle\mathcal{A}_{6_C}\rangle_{\geq p_6}\}, M_{service}, \{\langle\mathcal{G}\rangle_{\geq p_7'}\})$$

$$(16)$$

where the probability bounds p_1 to p_7 are those in Table 1,

$$p_7' = mc(\{\{\langle\mathcal{A}_{3_A}\rangle_{\geq p_3}, \langle\mathcal{A}_{4_A}\rangle_{\geq p_4}, \langle\mathcal{A}_{5_A}\rangle_{\geq p_5}, \langle\mathcal{A}_{3_B}\rangle_{\geq p_3}, \langle\mathcal{A}_{4_B}\rangle_{\geq p_4}, \langle\mathcal{A}_{5_B}\rangle_{\geq p_5},$$
$$\langle\mathcal{A}_{6_C}\rangle_{\geq p_6}\}, M_{service}, dfa(\langle\mathcal{G}\rangle_{\geq p_7}))$$

and

$$changes' = \begin{cases} \{(\langle\mathcal{A}_{6_D}\rangle_{\geq p_6}, \langle true\rangle), (\langle\mathcal{G}\rangle_{\geq p_7}, \langle\mathcal{G}\rangle_{\geq p_7'})\}, & \text{if } p_7' < p_7 \\ \{(\langle\mathcal{A}_{6_D}\rangle_{\geq p_6}, \langle true\rangle)\}, & \text{otherwise} \end{cases}$$

Redoing the only verification step in (16) yields $p_7' = 0.949943$. Since $p_7' < p_7 = 0.997482$ (cf. Table 1), $changes' = \{(\langle\mathcal{A}_{6_D}\rangle_{\geq p_6}, \langle true\rangle), (\langle\mathcal{G}\rangle_{\geq p_7}, \langle\mathcal{G}\rangle_{\geq p_7'})\}$ (although this updated set of changes is not used in the recursive invocation of *reverify*, which is applied to the empty sequence of verification stepss).

3.3   LSCITS Component Change

Assume that the system component associated with model M_i, $1 \leq i \leq n$, from the verification step v_i of compositional verification task $cv = (v_1, v_2, \ldots, v_n)$ changed. The theorem below specifies the minimum sequence of verification steps that need redone to re-establish the properties corresponding to cv.

Theorem 2. The minimal sequence of verification steps that needs to be carried out to reverify a compositional verification task $cv = (v_1, v_2, \ldots, v_n)$ after a change in the component associated with its i-th verification step is

$$\Delta cv = (A_i, M_i', G_i') \frown$$
$$reverify((v_{i+1}, v_{i+2}, \ldots, v_n),$$
$$\{(g, g') \in G_i \times G_i' \mid dfa(g) = dfa(g') \wedge prob(g') < prob(g)\}),$$

$$(17)$$

where M_i' represents the updated model for the changed system component and $G_i' = \{x \in \mathcal{P} \mid (\exists g \in G_i \bullet dfa(g) = dfa(x)) \wedge prob(x) = mc(A_i, M_i', dfa(x))\}$.

Proof. The proof is similar to that of Theorem 1.

$$\square$$

To illustrate the application of the result in Theorem 2, suppose that the service functions running on Server A from our running example are redeployed on a different type of server (perhaps located in a different data centre). Suppose that the new server has $N'_{DISK} = 4$ disks instead of $N_{DISK} = 3$ disks for the server from our original scenario, but that the N'_{DISK} new disks are less reliable, i.e., $p'_{disk\_fail} = 0.0250$ compared to $p_{disk\_fail} = 0.0231$ previously. According to (17), the sequence of verification steps that need to be redone is

$$\Delta cv = (\{\langle true\rangle\}, M'_{serverA}, \{\langle \mathcal{A}_{1A}\rangle_{\geq p'_1}, \langle \mathcal{A}_{2A}\rangle_{\geq p'_2}\})^\frown$$
$$reverify((v_2, v_3, \ldots, v_9), changes),$$

where $M'_{serverA}$ is the updated model for Server A,

$$p'_1 = mc(\{\langle true\rangle\}, M'_{serverA}, dfa(\langle \mathcal{A}_{1A}\rangle_{\geq p_1})),$$
$$p'_2 = mc(\{\langle true\rangle\}, M'_{serverA}, dfa(\langle \mathcal{A}_{2A}\rangle_{\geq p_2})),$$

the probabilities p_1 and p_2 are those in Table 1, v_2 to v_9 are defined in (11), and

$$changes = \{i \in \mathbb{N} \mid 1 \leq i \leq 2 \wedge p'_i < p_i \bullet (\langle \mathcal{A}_{iA}\rangle_{\geq p_i}, \langle \mathcal{A}_{iA}\rangle_{\geq p'_i})\}.$$

Executing the first verification step in Δcv yields

$$p'_1 = 1 - 5.85\text{E-}8 \quad \text{(which is larger than } p_1 = 0.999998)$$
$$p'_2 = 0.999984 \quad \text{(which is larger than } p_2 = 0.999544)$$

hence $changes = \{\}$ and, since $reverify((v_2, v_3, \ldots, v_9), \{\}) = ()$, no further verification step needs to be carried out.

3.4   LSCITS Component Joining

Suppose that a new component with model M_{new} joins the system. Re-establishing the probabilistic safety properties of the system requires updating any component models that depend on M_{new}, and carrying out verification steps for M_{new}, these updated models, and any other models whose verification steps include assumed properties that have changed. The minimal sequence of verification steps that need to be carried out is given by the theorem below.

Theorem 3. Let M_{new} be the model of a new component that joins a system for which a composition verification task $cv = (v_1, v_2, \ldots, v_n)$ was completed successfully before this operation. Also, let $M_{i_1}, M_{i_2}, \ldots, M_{i_m}, m > 0$, be the models of the components that depend on $M_{new}, 1 \leq i_1 < i_2 < \ldots < i_m \leq n$, and assume that their updated versions reflecting the presence of the new component are $M'_{i_1}, M'_{i_2}, \ldots, M'_{i_m}$. Under these circumstances, the minimal sequence of verification steps that needs to be carried out to reverify cv is

$$
\begin{aligned}
\Delta cv = &(A_{new}, M_{new}, G_{new})^\frown \\
&reverify(((A'_{i_1}, M'_{i_1}, G_{i_1}), v_{i_1+1}, v_{i_1+2}, \ldots, v_{i_2-1}, \\
&\quad (A'_{i_2}, M'_{i_2}, G_{i_2}), v_{i_2+1}, v_{i_2+2}, \ldots, v_{i_3-1}, \\
&\quad \ldots \\
&\quad (A'_{i_m}, M'_{i_m}, G_{i_m}), v_{i_m+1}, v_{i_m+2}, \ldots, v_n), \\
&\quad \{(g, g_{new}) \in \mathcal{P} \times G_{new} \mid dfa(g) = dfa(g_{new}) \wedge prob(g) = 0\}),
\end{aligned}
\tag{18}
$$

where $A_{new} \subseteq \cup_{j=1}^{i_1-1} G_j \cup \{\langle true \rangle\}$ is the set of assumed properties for the verification of the new system component, and $A'_{i_j} \subseteq A_{i_j} \cup \{a \in \mathcal{P} \mid (\exists g \in G_{new} \bullet dfa(a) = dfa(g)) \land prob(a) = 0\}$ represents the new set of assumed properties for the model M'_{i_j}, $1 \le j \le m$. Note that $A'_{i_j} \setminus A_{i_j} \ne \{\}$ for all $1 \le j \le m$ since M'_{i_j} depends on M_{new}.

Proof. We note first that the minimal sequence of verification steps must include the verification step for the new component, i.e., $(A_{new}, M_{new}, G_{new})$. Moreover, this step can appear at the beginning of the sequence since its assumed property set, A_{new}, consists of properties already established by the previously executed compositional verification task cv. We also note that the assumed property sets for the verification tasks v_1 to v_{i_1-1} are unchanged after the new component joined the system. Accordingly, the use of a sequence of verification steps that start at the i_1-th component as the first argument for the *reverify* invocation from (18) is correct. The rest of the proof shows that this invocation of *reverify* yields the sequence of verification steps required to re-establish the probabilistic safety properties in cv for the system components associated with the models M'_{i_1}, M_{i_1+1}, M_{i_1+2}, $\ldots$, M_{i_2-1}, M'_{i_2}, M_{i_2+1}, M_{i_2+2}, $\ldots$, M_{i_m-1}, M'_{i_m}, M_{i_m+1}, M_{i_m+2}, $\ldots$, M_n after the execution of the verification step $(A_{new}, M_{new}, G_{new})$. This part of the proof is similar to the proof of Theorem 1, and therefore not included in the paper.

$\square$

Returning to our running example, suppose that the service is augmented with a third database instance running on an additional server (Server E). The first verification step from $(v_1, v_2, \ldots, v_9)$ that is affected by this change is v_9, whose model needs to be updated to $M'_{service}$. The new verification step for the component that joined is

$$v_{new} = (A_{new}, M_{new}, G_{new}) = (\{\langle \mathcal{A}_{1_E} \rangle_{\ge p_1}, \langle \mathcal{A}_{2_E} \rangle_{\ge p_2}\}, M_{db_E}, \{\langle \mathcal{A}_{6_E} \rangle_{\ge p_6}\}),$$

so, according to Theorem 3,

$$\Delta cv = (\{\langle \mathcal{A}_{1_E} \rangle_{\ge p_1}, \langle \mathcal{A}_{2_E} \rangle_{\ge p_2}\}, M_{db_E}, \{\langle \mathcal{A}_{6_E} \rangle_{\ge p_6}\})^\frown$$
$$reverify(((A'_9, M'_{service}, \{\langle \mathcal{G} \rangle_{\ge p'_7}\})), \{((\langle \mathcal{A}_{6_E} \rangle_{\ge 0}\}, \langle \mathcal{A}_{6_E} \rangle_{\ge p_6}\})\})$$

with $A'_9 = \{\langle \mathcal{A}_{3_A} \rangle_{\ge p_3}, \langle \mathcal{A}_{4_A} \rangle_{\ge p_4}, \langle \mathcal{A}_{5_A} \rangle_{\ge p_5}, \langle \mathcal{A}_{3_B} \rangle_{\ge p_3}, \langle \mathcal{A}_{4_B} \rangle_{\ge p_4}, \langle \mathcal{A}_{5_B} \rangle_{\ge p_5}, \langle \mathcal{A}_{6_C} \rangle_{\ge p_6}, \langle \mathcal{A}_{6_D} \rangle_{\ge p_6}, \langle \mathcal{A}_{6_E} \rangle_{\ge 0}\}$. As a result,

$$\Delta cv = (\{\langle \mathcal{A}_{1_E} \rangle_{\ge p_1}, \langle \mathcal{A}_{2_E} \rangle_{\ge p_2}\}, M_{db_E}, \{\langle \mathcal{A}_{6_E} \rangle_{\ge p_6}\})^\frown$$
$$(\{\langle \mathcal{A}_{3_A} \rangle_{\ge p_3}, \langle \mathcal{A}_{4_A} \rangle_{\ge p_4}, \langle \mathcal{A}_{5_A} \rangle_{\ge p_5}, \langle \mathcal{A}_{3_B} \rangle_{\ge p_3}, \langle \mathcal{A}_{4_B} \rangle_{\ge p_4},$$
$$\langle \mathcal{A}_{5_B} \rangle_{\ge p_5}, \langle \mathcal{A}_{6_C} \rangle_{\ge p_6}, \langle \mathcal{A}_{6_D} \rangle_{\ge p_6}, \langle \mathcal{A}_{6_E} \rangle_{\ge p_6}\}, M'_{service}, \{\langle \mathcal{G} \rangle_{\ge p'_7}\})$$

Carrying out the two verification steps yields $p_6 = 0.949954$ (as for the other database instances) and $p'_7 = 0.999861$.

3.5   LSCITS Component Choice

Assume that the functionality of the i-th system component, $1 \leq i \leq n$, can be provided by $m > 1$ new concrete implementations of this component, each characterised by different performance, reliability and cost. Let $M_i^1, M_i^2, \ldots M_i^m$ be the models associated with these functionally equivalent component implementations. Assume that the implementation that helps the system satisfy its requirements with minimum cost needs to be identified.

Theorem 4. The minimal sequence of verification steps that needs to be carried out to select the least expensive i-th component in the scenario described above is

$$
\begin{aligned}
\Delta cv = (A_i, M_i^1, G_i^1)^\frown \\
reverify((v_{i+1}, v_{i+2}, \ldots, v_n), \\
\{(g, g') \in G_i \times G_i^1 \mid dfa(g) = dfa(g') \wedge prob(g') < prob(g)\})^\frown \\
(A_i, M_i^2, G_i^2)^\frown \\
reverify((v_{i+1}, v_{i+2}, \ldots, v_n), \\
\{(g, g') \in G_i \times G_i^2 \mid dfa(g) = dfa(g') \wedge prob(g') < prob(g)\})^\frown \\
\ldots^\frown \\
(A_i, M_i^m, G_i^m)^\frown \\
reverify((v_{i+1}, v_{i+2}, \ldots, v_n), \\
\{(g, g') \in G_i \times G_i^m \mid dfa(g) = dfa(g') \wedge prob(g') < prob(g)\}),
\end{aligned}
$$
(19)

where $G_i^j = \{x \in \mathcal{P} \mid (\exists\, g \in G_i \bullet dfa(g) = dfa(x)) \wedge prob(x) = mc(A_i, M_i^j, dfa(x))\}$ for $1 \leq i \leq m$.

Proof. Selecting the least expensive component requires the independent examination of the effect of changing M_i with each of the models $M_i^1, M_i^2, \ldots M_i^m$, in order to identify the options that satisfy the requirements of the system. Therefore, the minimal sequence of verification steps is obtained by concatenating the minimal sequences of verification steps from Theorem 2 for models M_i^1 to M_i^m, as shown in (19).

□

Returning again to our running example, suppose that the version of the virtualisation middleware installed on Server A from Figure 1 can be selected from three options. Assume that these options are associated with different levels of functionality/configurability, and with different levels of reliability, reflected in the probability p_{VM_fail} that a VM fails to operate correctly during a given time period:

1. The latest stable version of the virtualisation software, which is characterised by $p_{VM\_fail} = 0.05$ for a one-year time period. As shown by the probabilities annotating the state transitions associated with vm_op actions in Figure 4, this is the option used by model $M_{web+app_A}$ from our case study.

2. The latest beta version of the virtualisation middleware, which provides the richest functionality and configurability, but which is also the least reliable, with $p_{VM\_fail} = 0.1$ for a one-year time period.

3. A highly reliable old version of the middleware that is characterised by $p_{VM\_fail} = 0.01$ over one year, but which lacks some of the monitoring capabilities of the other two options.

The last two options mentioned above correspond to two new models $M^1_{web+app_A}$ and $M^2_{web+app_A}$ for verification step v_5 from our compositional verification task cv from eq. (11). According to Theorem 4, the minimal sequence of verification steps required to assess the suitability these two new options is

$$\Delta cv = (\{\langle \mathcal{A}_{1_A}\rangle_{\geq p_1}, \langle \mathcal{A}_{2_A}\rangle_{\geq p_2}\}, M^1_{web+app_A}, \{\langle \mathcal{A}_{3_A}\rangle_{\geq p_3^1}, \langle \mathcal{A}_{4_A}\rangle_{\geq p_4^1}, \langle \mathcal{A}_{5_A}\rangle_{\geq p_5^1}\})^\frown$$
$$reverify((v_6, v_7, v_8, v_9),$$
$$\{(g, g') \in G_5 \times G_5^1 \mid dfa(g) = dfa(g') \wedge prob(g') < prob(g)\})^\frown$$
$$(\{\langle \mathcal{A}_{1_A}\rangle_{\geq p_1}, \langle \mathcal{A}_{2_A}\rangle_{\geq p_2}\}, M^2_{web+app_A}, \{\langle \mathcal{A}_{3_A}\rangle_{\geq p_3^2}, \langle \mathcal{A}_{4_A}\rangle_{\geq p_4^2}, \langle \mathcal{A}_{5_A}\rangle_{\geq p_5^2}\})^\frown$$
$$reverify((v_6, v_7, v_8, v_9),$$
$$\{(g, g') \in G_5 \times G_5^2 \mid dfa(g) = dfa(g') \wedge prob(g') < prob(g)\})$$

Carrying out the two verification steps shown explicitly above yields: $p_3^1 = 0.999852$, $p_4^1 = p_5^1 = 0.989953$, $p_3^2 = 0.999952$ and $p_4^2 = p_5^2 = 0.999852$. Since the probability bounds for the original compositional verification task were $p_3 = 0.999946$ and $p_4 = p_5 = 0.997452$, we have

$$\Delta cv = (\{\langle \mathcal{A}_{1_A}\rangle_{\geq p_1}, \langle \mathcal{A}_{2_A}\rangle_{\geq p_2}\}, M^1_{web+app_A}, \{\langle \mathcal{A}_{3_A}\rangle_{\geq p_3^1}, \langle \mathcal{A}_{4_A}\rangle_{\geq p_4^1}, \langle \mathcal{A}_{5_A}\rangle_{\geq p_5^1}\})^\frown$$
$$reverify((v_6, v_7, v_8, v_9),$$
$$\{(\langle \mathcal{A}_{3_A}\rangle_{\geq p_3}, \langle \mathcal{A}_{3_A}\rangle_{\geq p_3^1}), (\langle \mathcal{A}_{4_A}\rangle_{\geq p_4}, \langle \mathcal{A}_{4_A}\rangle_{\geq p_4^1}), (\langle \mathcal{A}_{5_A}\rangle_{\geq p_5}, \langle \mathcal{A}_{5_A}\rangle_{\geq p_5^1})\})^\frown$$
$$(\{\langle \mathcal{A}_{1_A}\rangle_{\geq p_1}, \langle \mathcal{A}_{2_A}\rangle_{\geq p_2}\}, M^2_{web+app_A}, \{\langle \mathcal{A}_{3_A}\rangle_{\geq p_3^2}, \langle \mathcal{A}_{4_A}\rangle_{\geq p_4^2}, \langle \mathcal{A}_{5_A}\rangle_{\geq p_5^2}\})^\frown$$
$$reverify((v_6, v_7, v_8, v_9), \{\})$$
$$= (\{\langle \mathcal{A}_{1_A}\rangle_{\geq p_1}, \langle \mathcal{A}_{2_A}\rangle_{\geq p_2}\}, M^1_{web+app_A}, \{\langle \mathcal{A}_{3_A}\rangle_{\geq p_3^1}, \langle \mathcal{A}_{4_A}\rangle_{\geq p_4^1}, \langle \mathcal{A}_{5_A}\rangle_{\geq p_5^1}\})^\frown$$
$$(\{\langle \mathcal{A}_{3_A}\rangle_{\geq p_3^1}, \langle \mathcal{A}_{4_A}\rangle_{\geq p_4^1}, \langle \mathcal{A}_{5_A}\rangle_{\geq p_5^1}, \langle \mathcal{A}_{3_B}\rangle_{\geq p_3}, \langle \mathcal{A}_{4_B}\rangle_{\geq p_4},$$
$$\langle \mathcal{A}_{5_B}\rangle_{\geq p_5}, \langle \mathcal{A}_{6_C}\rangle_{\geq p_6}, \langle \mathcal{A}_{6_D}\rangle_{\geq p_6}\}, M_{service}, \{\langle \mathcal{G}\rangle_{\geq p_7^1}\})^\frown$$
$$(\{\langle \mathcal{A}_{1_A}\rangle_{\geq p_1}, \langle \mathcal{A}_{2_A}\rangle_{\geq p_2}\}, M^2_{web+app_A}, \{\langle \mathcal{A}_{3_A}\rangle_{\geq p_3^2}, \langle \mathcal{A}_{4_A}\rangle_{\geq p_4^2}, \langle \mathcal{A}_{5_A}\rangle_{\geq p_5^2}\})^\frown$$
$$()$$
$$= (\{\langle \mathcal{A}_{1_A}\rangle_{\geq p_1}, \langle \mathcal{A}_{2_A}\rangle_{\geq p_2}\}, M^1_{web+app_A}, \{\langle \mathcal{A}_{3_A}\rangle_{\geq p_3^1}, \langle \mathcal{A}_{4_A}\rangle_{\geq p_4^1}, \langle \mathcal{A}_{5_A}\rangle_{\geq p_5^1}\})^\frown$$
$$(\{\langle \mathcal{A}_{3_A}\rangle_{\geq p_3^1}, \langle \mathcal{A}_{4_A}\rangle_{\geq p_4^1}, \langle \mathcal{A}_{5_A}\rangle_{\geq p_5^1}, \langle \mathcal{A}_{3_B}\rangle_{\geq p_3}, \langle \mathcal{A}_{4_B}\rangle_{\geq p_4},$$
$$\langle \mathcal{A}_{5_B}\rangle_{\geq p_5}, \langle \mathcal{A}_{6_C}\rangle_{\geq p_6}, \langle \mathcal{A}_{6_D}\rangle_{\geq p_6}\}, M_{service}, \{\langle \mathcal{G}\rangle_{\geq p_7^1}\})^\frown$$
$$(\{\langle \mathcal{A}_{1_A}\rangle_{\geq p_1}, \langle \mathcal{A}_{2_A}\rangle_{\geq p_2}\}, M^2_{web+app_A}, \{\langle \mathcal{A}_{3_A}\rangle_{\geq p_3^2}, \langle \mathcal{A}_{4_A}\rangle_{\geq p_4^2}, \langle \mathcal{A}_{5_A}\rangle_{\geq p_5^2}\}).$$

The only remaining verification step to carry out is the one in the middle, which yields $p_7^1 = 0.997494$, a value that is slightly lower than the probability bound $p_7 = 0.997482$ provided by the original choice of a virtualisation middleware version for Server A.

4   Conclusion and Future Work

Large-scale complex IT systems (LSCITS) are notoriously difficult to verify formally. Their extremely large state spaces, continual changes and nondeterministic behaviour challenge not only the scalability of existing verification techniques, but also the validity of the traditional approach of performing the verification offline, typically at design time. While an increasing number of compositional verification techniques address the scalability challenge, less research has explored the effect that continual change has on the verification of LSCITS.

This paper overviewed assume-guarantee compositional verification in the context of a case study from the area of cloud computing, and presented a formalism for specifying several classes of change that are common to LSCITS. We showed how this formalism can be used to generate the sequence of verification steps that need to be (re-)done after each type of change, and illustrated the application of this approach for several scenarios from our case study.

Our future work will focus on extending the change specification formalism to other classes of LSCITS change (e.g., changes in requirements), and on validating it in additional case studies. In the longer term, we envisage the integration of the approach with online learning techniques supporting change detection [7,17] and with techniques for learning the assumptions for its sequence of compositional verification steps [15,19].

Finally, an important challenge for our compositional reverification approach is the availability of suitable models for the components of the analysed LSCITS. In the work presented in this paper, we assumed that such models were available for all LSCITS components, including those joining the system "on the fly". Clearly, this assumption does not hold in many real-world scenarios. Significant future research is therefore needed to devise techniques that can learn these models from observations of the running system, or at least automate their synthesis from domain-specific descriptions of the LSCITS components.

Acknowledgements. This work was partly supported by the UK Engineering and Physical Sciences Research Council grant EP/H042644/1.

References

1. de Alfaro, L., Henzinger, T.A.: Interface automata. SIGSOFT Softw. Eng. Notes 26(5), 109–120 (2001),
   http://doi.acm.org/10.1145/503271.503226
2. Berezin, S., Campos, S.V.A., Clarke, E.M.: Compositional Reasoning in Model Checking. In: de Roever, W.-P., Langmaack, H., Pnueli, A. (eds.) COMPOS 1997. LNCS, vol. 1536, pp. 81–102. Springer, Heidelberg (1998),
   http://dl.acm.org/citation.cfm?id=646738.701964
3. Blundell, C., Giannakopoulou, D., Pasareanu, C.S.: Assume-guarantee testing. ACM SIGSOFT Software Engineering Notes 31(2) (2006)
4. Calinescu, R.: General-purpose autonomic computing. In: Denko, M., et al. (eds.) Autonomic Computing and Networking, pp. 3–30. Springer (2009)

5. Calinescu, R., Ghezzi, C., Kwiatkowska, M., Mirandola, R.: Self-adaptive software needs quantitative verification at runtime. Communications of the ACM (September 2012)
6. Calinescu, R., Grunske, L., Kwiatkowska, M., Mirandola, R., Tamburrelli, G.: Dynamic QoS management and optimization in service-based systems. IEEE Transactions on Software Engineering 37, 387–409 (2011)
7. Calinescu, R., Johnson, K., Rafiq, Y.: Using observation ageing to improve Markovian model learning in QoS engineering. In: Proceedings 2nd ACM/SPEC International Conference on Performance Engineering, pp. 505–510 (2011)
8. Calinescu, R., Kikuchi, S., Kwiatkowska, M.: Formal methods for the development and verification of autonomic IT systems. In: Cong-Vinh, P. (ed.) Formal and Practical Aspects of Autonomic Computing and Networking: Specification, Development and Verification, pp. 1–37. IGI Global (2012)
9. Calinescu, R., Kwiatkowska, M.: Software Engineering Techniques for the Development of Systems of Systems. In: Choppy, C., Sokolsky, O. (eds.) Monterey Workshop 2008. LNCS, vol. 6028, pp. 59–82. Springer, Heidelberg (2010)
10. Calinescu, R., Kikuchi, S.: Formal Methods @ Runtime. In: Calinescu, R., Jackson, E. (eds.) Monterey Workshop 2010. LNCS, vol. 6662, pp. 122–135. Springer, Heidelberg (2011)
11. Calinescu, R., Kwiatkowska, M.: CADS*: Computer-Aided Development of Self-* Systems. In: Chechik, M., Wirsing, M. (eds.) FASE 2009. LNCS, vol. 5503, pp. 421–424. Springer, Heidelberg (2009),
    http://qav.comlab.ox.ac.uk/papers/fase09.pdf
12. Calinescu, R., Kwiatkowska, M.Z.: Using quantitative analysis to implement autonomic IT systems. In: 31st International Conference on Software Engineering, pp. 100–110 (2009), http://dx.doi.org/10.1109/ICSE.2009.5070512
13. Clarke, E.M., Grumberg, O., Peled, D.A.: Model Checking. MIT Press (1999)
14. Clarke, E.M., Long, D.E., McMillan, K.: Compositional model checking. In: Proc. 4th Intl. Symp. Logic in Computer Science, pp. 353–362 (1989),
    http://ieeexplore.ieee.org/xpl/freeabs_all.jsp?arnumber=39190
15. Cobleigh, J.M., Giannakopoulou, D., Păsăreanu, C.S.: Learning Assumptions for Compositional Verification. In: Garavel, H., Hatcliff, J. (eds.) TACAS 2003. LNCS, vol. 2619, pp. 331–346. Springer, Heidelberg (2003),
    http://dl.acm.org/citation.cfm?id=1765871.1765903
16. Dikaiakos, M.D., Katsaros, D., Mehra, P., Pallis, G., Vakali, A.: Cloud computing: Distributed internet computing for it and scientific research. IEEE Internet Computing 13(5), 10–13 (2009)
17. Epifani, I., Ghezzi, C., Mirandola, R., Tamburrelli, G.: Model evolution by runtime adaptation. In: Proceedings of the 31st International Conference on Software Engineering, pp. 111–121. IEEE Computer Society (2009)
18. Etessami, K., Kwiatkowska, M., Vardi, M.Y., Yannakakis, M.: Multi-objective Model Checking of Markov Decision Processes. In: Grumberg, O., Huth, M. (eds.) TACAS 2007. LNCS, vol. 4424, pp. 50–65. Springer, Heidelberg (2007)
19. Feng, L., Kwiatkowska, M.Z., Parker, D.: Automated Learning of Probabilistic Assumptions for Compositional Reasoning. In: Giannakopoulou, D., Orejas, F. (eds.) FASE 2011. LNCS, vol. 6603, pp. 2–17. Springer, Heidelberg (2011)
20. Filieri, A., Ghezzi, C., Tamburrelli, G.: A formal approach to adaptive software: continuous assurance of non-functional requirements. Formal Asp. Comput. 24(2), 163–186 (2012)

21. Grumberg, O., Long, D.E.: Model checking and modular verification. ACM Trans. Program. Lang. Syst. 16(3), 843–871 (1994), http://doi.acm.org/10.1145/177492.177725

22. Hinton, A., Kwiatkowska, M., Norman, G., Parker, D.: PRISM: A Tool for Automatic Verification of Probabilistic Systems. In: Hermanns, H. (ed.) TACAS 2006. LNCS, vol. 3920, pp. 441–444. Springer, Heidelberg (2006)

23. Hoare, C.A.R.: An axiomatic basis for computer programming. Commun. ACM 12(10), 576–580 (1969), http://doi.acm.org/10.1145/363235.363259

24. Inverardi, P., Patrizio, Tivoli, M.: Towards an assume-guarantee theory for adaptable systems. In: Proceedings of the Software Engineering for Adaptive and Self-Managing Systems Workshop (SEAMS), pp. 106–115 (2009)

25. Kesten, Y., Pnueli, A.: A compositional approach to ctl* verification. Theor. Comput. Sci. 331(2-3), 397–428 (2005), http://dx.doi.org/10.1016/j.tcs.2004.09.023

26. Kwiatkowska, M., Norman, G., Parker, D.: PRISM 4.0: Verification of Probabilistic Real-Time Systems. In: Gopalakrishnan, G., Qadeer, S. (eds.) CAV 2011. LNCS, vol. 6806, pp. 585–591. Springer, Heidelberg (2011)

27. Kwiatkowska, M., Norman, G., Parker, D., Qu, H.: Assume-Guarantee Verification for Probabilistic Systems. In: Esparza, J., Majumdar, R. (eds.) TACAS 2010. LNCS, vol. 6015, pp. 23–37. Springer, Heidelberg (2010), http://qav.cs.ox.ac.uk/bibitem.php?key=KNPQ10

28. Northrop, L., et al.: Ultra-large-scale systems - the software challenge of the future. Tech. rep., Software Engineering Institute, Carnegie Mellon University (June 2006)

29. Pnueli, A.: In transition from global to modular temporal reasoning about programs. In: Apt, K.R. (ed.) Logics and Models of Concurrent Systems, pp. 123–144. Springer-Verlag New York, Inc., New York (1985), http://dl.acm.org/citation.cfm?id=101969.101977

30. Segala, R., Lynch, N.A.: Probabilistic simulations for probabilistic processes. Nord. J. Comput. 2(2), 250–273 (1995)

31. Sommerville, I., Cliff, D., Calinescu, R., Keen, J., Kelly, T., Kwiatkowska, M., McDermid, J., Paige, R.: Large-scale complex IT systems. Communications of the ACM 55(7), 71–77 (2012)

32. Thomas, K.: Solid state drives no better than others, survey says, http://www.pcworld.com/businesscenter/article/213442/solid_state_drives_no_better_than_others_survey_says.html

33. Tordsson, J., Montero, R.S., Moreno-Vozmediano, R., Llorente, I.M.: Cloud brokering mechanisms for optimized placement of virtual machines across multiple providers. Future Generation Computer Systems 28(2), 358–367 (2012)

34. Vishwanath, K.V., Nagappan, N.: Characterizing cloud computing hardware reliability. In: Proceedings of the 1st ACM Symposium on Cloud Computing, SoCC 2010, pp. 193–204. ACM, New York (2010), http://doi.acm.org/10.1145/1807128.1807161

Appendix A

A.1 Additional Probabilistic Assume-Guarantee Proof Rule

The proposition below introduces the assume-guarantee proof rule (#) that we used in eq. (9). To prove the rule we use the following additional notation:

- $Pr_{M_i}^{\sigma_i}(A_i)$ represents the probability that model M_i satisfies the safety property A_i for a fixed adversary $\sigma_i \in Adv_i$.
- Given an adversary $\sigma \in Adv_{M_1 \| M_2 \| ... \| M_x}$, $\sigma \upharpoonright_{M_i} \in Adv_i$ denotes the projection of σ onto M_i, $1 \leq i \leq x$.

Proposition 1. If M_1, M_2, ..., M_k are probabilistic automata, and $\langle A_1 \rangle_{\geq p_1}$, $\langle A_2 \rangle_{\geq p_2}$, ..., $\langle A_k \rangle_{\geq p_k}$ are probabilistic safety properties such that $\alpha_{A_i} \subseteq \alpha_{M_i}$ for all $1 \leq i \leq k-1$ and $\alpha_{A_k} \subseteq \alpha_{M_k} \cup \alpha_{A_1} \cup \alpha_{A_2} \cup ... \cup \alpha_{A_{k-1}}$, then the following proof rule holds:

$$
\begin{array}{c}
\langle true \rangle M_1 \langle A_1 \rangle_{\geq p_1} \\
\langle true \rangle M_2 \langle A_2 \rangle_{\geq p_2} \\
... \\
\langle true \rangle M_{k-1} \langle A_{k-1} \rangle_{\geq p_{k-1}} \\
\langle A_1, A_2, ..., A_{k-1} \rangle_{\geq p_1, p_2, ..., p_{k-1}} M_k \langle A_k \rangle_{\geq p_k} \\
\hline
\langle true \rangle M_1 \parallel M_2 \parallel ... \parallel M_k \langle A_k \rangle_{\geq p_k}
\end{array}
\tag{20}
$$

Proof. Starting from the hypothesis, we have:

$\forall i \in \{1, 2, ..., k-1\} \bullet \forall \sigma_i \in Adv_{M_i} \bullet Pr_{M_i}^{\sigma_i}(A_i) \geq p_i$
$\qquad$ (according to the definition of $\langle true \rangle M_i \langle A_i \rangle_{\geq p_i}$)

$\Rightarrow$

$\forall i \in \{1, 2, ..., k-1\} \bullet \forall \sigma \in Adv_{M_1 \| M_2 \| ... \| M_{k-1}} \bullet Pr_{M_i}^{\sigma \upharpoonright_{M_i}}(A_i) \geq p_i$
$\qquad$ (since $\sigma \upharpoonright_{M_i} \in Adv_{M_i}$)

$\Rightarrow$

$\forall i \in \{1, 2, ..., k-1\} \bullet \forall \sigma \in Adv_{M_1 \| M_2 \| ... \| M_{k-1}} \bullet Pr_{M_1 \| M_2 \| ... \| M_{k-1}}^{\sigma}(A_i) \geq p_i$
$\qquad$ (by part (a) of Lemma 1 from [27], since $\alpha_{A_i} \subseteq \alpha_{M_i}$)

$\Rightarrow$

$\forall \sigma \in Adv_{M_1 \| M_2 \| ... \| M_{k-1}} \bullet Pr_{M_1 \| M_2 \| ... \| M_{k-1}}^{\sigma}(A_1) \geq p_1 \wedge ... \wedge$
$\qquad \wedge Pr_{M_1 \| M_2 \| ... \| M_{k-1}}^{\sigma}(A_{k-1}) \geq p_{k-1}$
$\qquad$ (rewrite of the previous step)

$\Rightarrow$

$\langle true \rangle M_1 \| M_2 \| ... \| M_{k-1} \langle A_1, A_2, ..., A_{k-1} \rangle_{\geq p_1, p_2, ..., p_{k-1}}$
$\qquad$ (by definition)

$\Rightarrow$

$\langle true \rangle M_1 \parallel M_2 \parallel ... \parallel M_k \langle A_k \rangle_{\geq p_k}$
$\qquad$ (by applying the ASYM-MULT rule from [27])

$\qquad\qquad\qquad\qquad\qquad\qquad\qquad\qquad\qquad\qquad\qquad\qquad\qquad$ □

A.2. Proof of Theorem 1

Theorem 1. The minimal sequence of verification steps that needs to be carried out to reverify a compositional verification task $cv = (v_1, v_2, \ldots, v_n)$ after the failure of the component associated with its i-th verification step is

$$\Delta cv = reverify((v_{i+1}, v_{i+2}, \ldots, v_n), \{g \in G_i \bullet (g, \langle true \rangle)\}). \qquad (21)$$

Proof. We start by observing that, according to the recursive definition of *reverify* from (13), Δcv can be rewritten as:

$$
\begin{aligned}
\Delta cv &= \Delta cv_1 \frown reverify((v_{i+1}, v_{i+2}, \ldots, v_n), changes_0) \\
&= \Delta cv_2 \frown reverify((v_{i+2}, v_{i+3}, \ldots, v_n), changes_1) \\
&= \ldots \\
&= \Delta cv_{n-i+1} \frown reverify((), changes_{n-i+1}),
\end{aligned}
\qquad (22)
$$

where $\Delta cv_1 = ()$, $changes_1 = \{g \in G_i \bullet (g, \langle true \rangle)\}$ and, for $1 < j \leq n - i + 1$, Δc_j and $changes_j$ are obtained by carrying out the calculations defined by (13). We will prove the following intermediate results by induction on the value of j:

1. Δc_j is the minimal sequence of verification steps required to re-establish the probabilistic safety properties associated with the first $i + j - 1$ elements of cv;
2. $changes_j$ is the set of all changes in the probabilistic safety properties guaranteed by models $M_1, M_2, \ldots, M_{i+j-1}$,

for $j = 1, 2, \ldots, n - i + 1$. The theorem will then follow immediately from the fact that Δcv_{n-i+1} is "the minimal sequence of verification steps required to re-establish the probabilistic safety properties associated with the first $i + (n - i + 1) - 1 = n$ elements of cv", since $\Delta cv = \Delta cv_{n-i+1} \frown reverify((), changes_{n-i+1}) = \Delta cv_{n-i+1} \frown () = \Delta cv_{n-i+1}$.

The base case, corresponding to $j = 1$, is straightforward:

1. $\Delta cv_1 = ()$ since the verification steps $v_1, v_2, \ldots, v_{i-1}$ do not need to be redone (as their assumption sets $A_1, A_2, \ldots, A_{i-1}$ do not contain any properties guaranteed by the failed component), and v_i does not need to be redone (because we already know that it corresponds to the failed component);
2. $changes_1 = \{g \in G_i \bullet (g, \langle true \rangle)\}$ since none of the properties guaranteed by $M_1, M_2, \ldots, M_{i-1}$ has changed, and all properties in G_i, which were guaranteed by the failed component, need to be replaced with the property that does not offer any guarantees, i.e., $\langle true \rangle$.

Suppose now that Δc_j and $changes_j$ satisfy our two properties for a value of j such that $1 \leq j < n - i + 1$. We will prove that the two properties are also satisfied by Δc_{j+1} and $changes_{j+1}$.

According to the notation introduced in (22) and to the definition of *reverify* from (13),

$$
\Delta c_{j+1} = \Delta c_j \frown \begin{cases} (), & \text{if } A_{i+j} \cap changes_j = \emptyset \\ (A'_{i+j}, M, G'_{i+j}), & \text{otherwise} \end{cases}
\qquad (23)
$$

and

$$changes_{j+1} = changes_j \cup$$

$$\begin{cases} \{\} & \text{if } A_{i+j} \cap changes_j = \emptyset \\ \{(g, g') \in G_{i+j} \times G'_{i+j} \mid dfa(g) = dfa(g') \wedge \\ \quad prob(g') < prob(g)\} & \text{otherwise} \end{cases} \quad (24)$$

where

- $A'_{i+j} = \{a \in A_{i+j} \mid \neg(\exists(g, g') \in changes_j \bullet a = g)\} \cup \{(g, g') \in changes_j \mid g \in A_{i+j} \bullet g'\}$;
- $G'_{i+j} = \{x \in \mathcal{P} \mid (\exists g \in G_{i+j} \bullet dfa(x) = dfa(g)) \wedge prob(x) = mc(A'_{i+j}, M_{i+j}, dfa(g))\}$.

We analyse each of the two cases above in turn, recalling the fact that, according to the inductive hypothesis, $changes_j$ is the set of all changes in the probabilistic safety properties guaranteed by models M_1 to M_{i+j-1}:

- The case $A_{i+j} \cap changes_j = \emptyset$ corresponds to the scenario in which the assumptions for the verification step v_{i+j} are unchanged. Therefore, the minimal sequence of verification steps for models M_1 to M_{i+j} coincides in this case with the minimal sequence of verification steps for models M_1 to M_{i+j-1}, i.e., with Δcv_j (according to the inductive hypothesis). Since $\Delta cv_{j+1} = \Delta cv_j$, it follows that, in this case, Δcv_{j+1} satisfies the first required property. Finally, no probabilistic safety properties guaranteed by M_{i+j} changed, so $changes_{j+1} = chages_j$ satisfies the second required property.
- The second case (i.e., $A_{i+j} \cap changes_j \neq \emptyset$) corresponds to the scenario in which at least one of the assumptions for the verification step v_{i+j} changed, hence the model M_{i+j} needs to be reverified against the updated set of assumptions A'_{i+j} defined above, yielding the new guaranteed probabilistic safety properties in G'_{i+j}. The minimal set of verification steps to be redone for models M_1 to M_{i+j} consists of all the verification steps that need to be redone for models M_1 to M_{i+j-1} (i.e., Δcv_j) and the additional step $(A'_{i+j}, M_{i+j}, G'_{i+j})$. This is precisely Δcv_{j+1}, so the first required property is also satisfied in the second case. Finally, we note again that $changes_j$ the set of all changes in the probabilistic safety properties guaranteed by M_1 to M_{i+j-1}, and that the set $\{(g, g') \in G_{i+j} \times G'_{i+j} \mid dfa(g) = dfa(g') \wedge prob(g') < prob(g)\}$ contains precisely the changes to the probabilistic safety properties guaranteed by M_{i+j}. Therefore, the union of these two sets (i.e., $changes_{j+1}$) represents the set of all changes in the probabilistic safety properties guaranteed by models M_1 to M_{i+j}.

□

Extreme Symmetries in Complex Distributed Systems: The Bag-Oriented Approach*

Maximilien Colange[1], Lom-Messan Hillah[2], Fabrice Kordon[1], and Pierre Parutto[1]

[1] LIP6, CNRS UMR 7606, Université P. & M. Curie – Paris 6
4, Place Jussieu, F-75252 Paris Cedex 05, France
{Maximilien.Colange,Fabrice.Kordon}@lip6.fr
[2] LIP6, CNRS UMR 7606 and Université Paris Ouest Nanterre La Défense
200, Avenue de la République, F-92001 Nanterre Cedex, France
Lom-Messan.Hillah@lip6.fr

Abstract. Model checking is widely used as an automatic exhaustive verification technique to check properties of complex systems. However, it is difficult to operate in the context of today's emerging systems that combine distribution (and asynchronous communications) together with a large size (and a hierarchical composition of components – and thus, of specifications).

This paper combines existing techniques tackling the known combinatorial explosion of model checking. To achieve this, we exploit the structure of such distributed systems (symmetries and hierarchical composition), thus allowing a better compression factor and calculus factorization in favorable cases. We present these techniques and assess their impact on some benchmark examples.

Keywords: Symmetric Nets with Bags, formal method, model checking, state space generation, Symmetries-based techniques, Hierarchical Set Decision Diagrams.

1 Introduction

Context. Model checking is now widely used as an automatic and exhaustive verification technique to check properties of complex systems. However, this approach suffers from an intrinsic combinatorial explosion issue that must be tackled. One trend is to take full advantage of the characteristics of the class of system being analyzed. A first example of this was, in the 1990's, the exploitation of the characteristics of hardware systems [7].

Today's emerging complex systems have two main characteristics. Firstly, they are more and more distributed: numerous entities, often sharing the same code (only the context differs), communicate asynchronously. Secondly, these entities are often hierarchically organized: systems are composed of systems (SoS *for Systems of Systems*).

Moreover, these emerging systems handle more and more critical functions and need to be trusted. Their complexity prevents traditional test or simulation based approaches to reach a satisfactory level of confidence, formal methods, such as those based on state space analysis, must be operated. However, the asynchronous nature of such systems,

---

* This work was partially supported by a grant from the Direction Générale pour l'Armement.

R. Calinescu and D. Garlan (Eds.): Monterey Workshop 2012, LNCS 7539, pp. 330–352, 2012.

as well as their size, increase the combinatorial explosion of these analysis techniques, thus preventing their use in satisfactory conditions.

Problem. One issue in tackling the combinatorial explosion related to state space analysis is to combine existing reduction techniques. Among them, several are commonly involved in the analysis of distributed systems:

1. Partial Orders: this technique aims at fighting the interleaving introduced when several execution flows are running in parallel. When several paths lead from state A to state B in the state space, only one is stored. This technique may reduce the explored state space by orders of magnitude in favorable cases [16,3].
2. Symmetries: this technique aims at identifying the possible permutations of actors in a system (i.e. all clients are identical up to a permutation of identity). Instead of building the explicit state space, symmetries allow to compute a *quotient* state space that can be exponentially smaller in favorable cases. This technique was introduced for Petri nets in the early 1990's [6] and then adapted in a more general case [23]. A variant, called "counter abstraction" [2], also allow to consider as a whole groups of processes.
3. Locality: this technique aims at exploiting the locality of the system's evolution. Typically, when one process evolves, the set of variables to be changed is very small compared to the state of the full system. This locality property allows to share the representation of common parts in the state space. The use of appropriate data structures to represent the state space such as decision diagrams leads to exponential gains in favorable cases [5].

Preliminary experiments [28,10] have demonstrated that the two last techniques can be combined, despite the fact that they appear to be independent. The idea is to achieve this in a more efficient way and reduce the need for the partial order reduction by using a dedicated modeling technique, since it seems difficult to combine the three techniques together.

Contribution. This paper proposes a method for structuring symmetries in a system model by means of bags. The idea is to make a link between potentially useful modeling constructs and efficient model checking mechanisms in order to improve the combination of reduction techniques. The objective is twofold:

- Reducing again the potential interleaving, thus decreasing the need for partial order techniques,
- Exploiting the hierarchical structure of symmetries for a better encoding of the quotient state space into decision diagrams, and thus, increasing the combined efficiency.

Altogether, these combined techniques should help us provide efficient state space generation and state space analysis for distributed systems.

To achieve this, we rely on the use of bags to structure data carried out in a system. Thus, we use Symmetric nets with Bags (SNB) [18] that are a compact and readable dialect of colored Petri nets, allowing structured specification of complex systems. However, we claim it can be generalized to other notations dedicated to concurrent systems as soon as a structural analysis, allowing to detect permutations and a hierarchical structuring, can be performed.

We call this approach *"extreme symmetries"* because we make an intensive use of these in different ways, as it is explained in the discussion part of section 2.1.

Contents. Section 2 presents basic definitions of the formal concepts the presented method relies on. Then, section 3 details the main principles of our contribution. Finally, section 4 presents an early performance evaluation of the method by means of selected examples.

2   Definitions

This section provides the definitions needed in this paper: Symmetric Nets with Bags (SNB) and Decision Diagrams (DD). The goal of this section is to provide an overview for the understanding of the paper only. However, there are references to formal and precise definitions.

Symmetric Nets with Bags are used to model systems with the possibility to structure data in a new way where hierarchical information can be exploited to tackle complexity. Decision Diagrams is a commonly accepted technique to represent state spaces in a very compact way. In this paper, we focus on a specific class of decision diagrams: Set Decision Diagrams (SDD), that can be composed hierarchically.

2.1   Symmetric Nets with Bags

Petri Nets [15]. They are a well-known formalism for the modeling of asynchronous systems. Basically, a Petri Net (or P/T net) consists in a set of places and a set of transitions. Places contain tokens, and transitions move tokens from place to place. More precisely, when it *fires*, a transition consumes tokens from its input places, and produces tokens to its output places, thus reaching a new marking (vector of tokens in places). By applying a fixed point on the firing relation, one can theoretically generate the full state space for finite systems.

Colored Petri nets [21,22] extend P/T nets by adding typed data in tokens. Colored Petri nets may have a better expressive power (sometimes leading to undecidability) but the specification is smaller, thus increasing readability.

Among several variants of colored Petri nets, Symmetric Nets (SN) [6] define a simple typing mechanism (discrete types, cartesian product) allowing the exploitation of symmetries in a system. The expressive power of SNs is the same as P/T nets.

Symmetric Nets with Bags (SNB). This is a recent extension of SN [18]. SNBs propose a new mechanism allowing to avoid some interleaving, by enabling multisets (or bags, see definition 3 in section 3.3) of colors in tokens. SNBs allow to express the same symmetries as SNs do, thus enabling similar exploitation of symmetries.

The SNB presented in Fig. 1 models a simple deadlock-free resource manager based on the global allocation of all required resources before entering a critical section [26]. There are two discrete types of color respectively describing the processes ids (Proc) and the critical resources (Res). Then, the type representing the set of bags of resources is defined (BagR), as well as its cartesian product with processes ids (P_BagR).

Initially, marking M_r in R contains the available resources of the system (there can be several copies of some resources, i.e. several tokens of the same value) and M_p in outCS

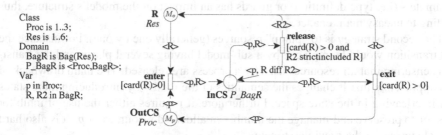

Fig. 1. An example of SNB: the Resource Manager. $M_p = \langle \text{Proc}.all \rangle$ and $M_r = n \times \langle \text{Res}.all \rangle$, with n being a positive value. Class.*all* is the function that generates generates one token per possible value in Class.

represents all the processes (they are represented by their identity) that are initially out of the critical section. Transition enter assigns to a process p a *bag* of resources R. As indicated by the guard of the transition, a process is assigned at least one resource. Place InCS holds the processes using at least one resource (in the critical section). Transition release allows to release resources. However, its guard prevents from releasing all the resources, which is done when firing transition exit.

SNB do not extend the expressive power of SN but lead to a more compact model as illustrated below.

SNB versus SN. This system could be modeled using SN too. However, the resulting model is then more complex. Two strategies to unfold a SNB into an equivalent SN are considered.

The first one relies on the *unfolding* of places and transitions in which bags occur. It is illustrated in Fig. 2. Let us detail the process for transition enter when $1 < card(\text{R}) \leq N$. First, the cartesian product P_BagR is replaced by N cartesian products (one per possible cardinality of R in enter bindings). Transition enter and place InCS must also be duplicated N times since tokens and bindings are typed by the new cartesian products types. The main problem of this modeling technique is that an upper bound of the bag cardinality must be known a priori (here, $N = 3$ was chosen). Also, changing the model

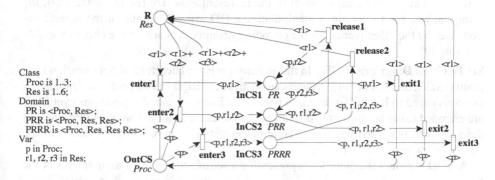

Fig. 2. Unfolding the model of Fig. 1 for $1 < card(\text{R}) \leq N, with\ N = 3$

parameters (i.e. type definition) or guards has an impact on the model's structure, thus leading to uneasy maintenance.

The second strategy is to "pump" resources (generally one by one). For instance the exit transition would be replaced by a sub-model having several places and the transitions ensuring that all resources used by a process are released. The main drawback of this approach is that it changes the semantics of the model by introducing more states and interleaving in the state space. Furthermore, it requires either the use of inhibitor arcs, or to preserve and manage the number of allocated resources to p. It is also hard to scale up, as for the previous strategy.

The SNB model is therefore much more compact and scalable than its SN equivalent. Indeed, modification on the model parameters does not require structural changes.

Benefits of SNBs. Bags in SNBs allow to abstract complex constructs such as the aforementioned pumping scheme. The encapsulation of bags in tokens also allows a better structuring of the model. This is illustrated in our example where they encode quite clearly the allocation of resources to a process. Bags in SNB thus offer to the modeler two tools: an abstraction mechanism, along with a structuring mechanism, that may be combined.

Moreover, by avoiding situations that generate interleaving, bags reduce the need for partial order techniques that are difficult to stack on top of decision diagrams and symmetries without paying the price of not using this technique.

This is what we call *"extreme symmetries"*: a way to structure symmetries in the system specification to enable the activation of efficient encoding of the state space generation and analysis (in the decision diagram meaning of it). This structuring information is transparently provided by the modeler instead of being guessed by the model checker.

2.2 Decision Diagrams

Principle. Shared Decision Diagrams (DD) [4] are a data structure to compactly represent sets. There are many variants of decision diagrams used for model-checking, but they all rely on the same underlying principles: *i)* nodes of the decision tree are unique in memory thanks to a canonical representation; *ii)* the number of paths through the diagram (states) can be exponential in the representation size (nodes in the DD); *iii)* using caches, most operations manipulating a DD are polynomial in the representation size; *iv)* the effectiveness of the encoding strongly depends on the chosen variable ordering [9].

Set Decision Diagrams (SDD). In this paper we rely on Hierarchical Set Decision Diagrams (SDD, defined in [14]), which extend classical BDD in two respects: *1)* variables are considered to have a set domain instead of a Boolean one; *2)* operations over SDD are encoded using homomorphisms instead of the usual fashion where another decision diagram with two variables per variable of the state signature is used. Definitions are taken almost verbatim from [29].

A SDD is a data structure for representing a set of sequences of assignments of the form $\omega_1 \in s_1; \omega_2 \in s_2; \cdots; \omega_n \in s_n$, also noted $\omega_1 \xrightarrow{s_1} \omega_2 \xrightarrow{s_2} \cdots \omega_n \xrightarrow{s_n} 1$, where ω_i are variables and s_i are sets. These sets can themselves be represented by SDD: in that case, we think of SDD as hierarchical decision diagrams. We assume no implicit variable ordering and the same variable can occur several times in an assignment sequence. We define the terminal **1** to represent the empty assignment sequence, terminating any valid sequence. The terminal **0** represents the empty set of assignment sequences. Let *Var* be a set of variables, and for any ω in *Var*, let $\mathrm{Dom}(\omega)$ be the domain of ω, that may be infinite.

Definition 1 (SDD). *The set* $\$$ *of SDD is defined inductively by* $\delta \in \$$ *if either:*

- $\delta \in \{0,1\}$ *or*
- $\delta = \langle \omega, \pi, \alpha \rangle$ *with:*
  - $\omega \in$ *Var,*
  - $\pi = \{s_0; \dots ; s_n\}$ *a finite partition of* $\mathrm{Dom}(\omega)$
  - α *an injective mapping from* π *to* $\$$

By convention, paths terminated by the SDD **0** *are not represented.*

Let us note that SDD or other variants of DD can be used as the domain of variables, thus introducing hierarchy in the data structures.

Example of State Encoding. Let us illustrate the use of SDD with a simple example: the encoding of two states in the model of Fig. 1:

$$S_0 = \mathsf{InCS}(0) + \mathsf{OutCS}(\langle 1_p \rangle + \langle 2_p \rangle + \langle 3_p \rangle) + \mathsf{R}(\langle 1_r \rangle + \langle 2_r \rangle + \langle 3_r \rangle + \langle 4_r \rangle + \langle 5_r \rangle + \langle 6_r \rangle)$$
$$S_1 = \mathsf{InCS}(\langle 1_p, \{1_r, 2_r, 3_r, 4_r, 5_r, 6_r\} \rangle) + \mathsf{OutCS}(\langle 2_p \rangle + \langle 3_p \rangle) + \mathsf{R}(0)$$

S_0 is the initial state where all resources are available and all processes out of the critical section. S_1 is a state where process 1 is in the critical section and uses all resources. Figure 3 shows a possible encoding of these two states. Let us first provide some notation convention in this figure:

- $1_p, 2_p, 3_p$ (respectively $1_r, 2_r, 3_r, 4_r, 5_r, 6_r$) correspond to the values in Proc (respectively Res),
- double lines correspond to the encoding of the marking structure, single lines to a piece of marking and dotted lines to a hierarchical relation,

The main part of this SDD has two paths: the left one encodes S_1, the right one encodes S_0. The encoding of S_1 must be read as follows: place InCS holds a composed token

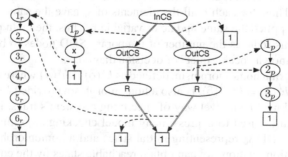

Fig. 3. Example of hierarchical encoding of some markings from the net of Fig. 1

represented by another SDD on the left. This SDD refers itself to a second one that represents the bag containing one occurrence of each element in Res. Then, continuing the path, place outCS holds two tokens: 2_p and 3_p. Finally, place R is empty (the underlying SDD is reduced to its terminal). A similar interpretation can be performed for S_0.

Figure 3 illustrates several types of sharing with SDD. First, as for traditional decision diagrams, common nodes are represented only once (let us note that the terminal node is represented several times to make the figure clearer but there is only one occurrence in memory). Second, sub-SDD introduce a new type of sharing. Typically, the marking of R in S_0 and the bag contained in the token of InCS in S_1 are represented once in a sub-SDD. Similarly the rightmost SDD encodes two markings: $\{\langle 1_p \rangle, \langle 2_p \rangle, \langle 3_p \rangle\}$ and $\{\langle 2_p \rangle, \langle 3_p \rangle\}$ that share a common part.

SDD Operations. SDD support standard set operations: $\cup, \cap, \setminus$. The semantics of these operations are based on the sets of assignment sequences that the SDD represent.

SDD also offer a concatenation $\delta_1 \cdot \delta_2$ which replaces terminal **1** of δ_1 by δ_2. This corresponds to a cartesian product. Basic and inductive homomorphisms are also introduced to define application-specific operations. A more detailed description of SDD homomorphisms can be found in [13].

A basic homomorphism is a mapping $\Phi : \mathbb{S} \mapsto \mathbb{S}$ satisfying $\Phi(\mathbf{0}) = \mathbf{0}$ and $\forall \delta, \delta' \in \mathbb{S}, \Phi(\delta \cup \delta') = \Phi(\delta) \cup \Phi(\delta')$. Many basic homomorphisms are hard-coded. The sum $+$ operation between two homomorphisms $(\forall \delta \in \mathbb{S}, (\Phi_1 + \Phi_2)(\delta) = \Phi_1(\delta) \cup \Phi_2(\delta))$ and the composition of two homomorphisms $\circ$ $(\Phi_1 \circ \Phi_2(\delta) = \Phi_1(\Phi_2(\delta)))$ are themselves homomorphisms.

A homomorphism c is a *selector* iff. $\forall \delta \in \mathbb{S}, c(\delta) \subseteq \delta$. This allows to represent boolean conditions, as c selects states satisfying a given condition; thus the negation of c is $\bar{c}(\delta) = \delta \setminus c(\delta)$. As a shorthand for "if-then-else", we use $\mathtt{IfThenElse}(c, h_1, h_2) = h_1 \circ c + h_2 \circ \bar{c}$, where h_1 and h_2 are homomorphisms.

This mechanism is generalized with a variant called "multi-linear" homomorphisms. Such a homomorphism splits a SDD into several parts, for which it applies a specific operation.

Multi-linear homomorphisms are particularly useful when one wants to change the value of a variable x depending on the value of a variable y that has not been read yet (e.g. in tokens containing bags). Since SDD represent a set, several values for y may exist. Multi-linear homomorphisms split the SDD into several subsets $s_1 \ldots s_n$, one for each value of y. Thus, for each i, all the elements of s_i have the same value for y and can therefore be applied the same update of variable x. Thus, the main part (x) remains unchanged and this reduces the number of temporary SDD nodes to be merged later; this reduced the known "peak-effect" of decision diagrams.

The *fixpoint* $h^\star$ of a homomorphism, defined as $h^\star(\delta) = h^k(d)$ where k is the smallest integer such that $h^k(\delta) = h^{k+1}(\delta)$, is also a homomorphism provided k exists.

Besides providing a high level way of specifying a system's transition relation, homomorphisms can be used to express many model checking algorithms directly. For instance, given a SDD s_0 representing initial states and a homomorphism *succ* representing the transition relation, we can obtain reachable states by the equation $Reach = (succ + Id)^\star(s_0)$.

Specifying model checking problems as homomorphisms allows the software library to enable automatic rewritings that yield much better performances, such as the saturation algorithm [19].

Discussion on SDD. When hierarchical structuring is possible, SDD allow a better sharing than traditional "flat" decision diagrams. The main reason is that hierarchy introduced flexibility in the encoding, thus reducing the known effect of variable ordering on the performances of this technique. They also enable partial reuse of local encoding patterns (as shown in Fig. 3)

Finally, the homomorphism notion and the associated rewriting techniques allow an intensive use of caches and the activation of efficient resolution algorithms such as automatic saturation [19]. Therefore, SDD are a good candidate to be stacked with the symmetry-based optimizations brought by SNB.

In this specific framework, multi-linear homomorphisms are of particular interest to canonize marking. This is because the structure of the marking may not respect the locality of the operations where decision diagrams are usually very efficient. Such homomorphisms could help to reduce the drawback of this lack of locality.

3 Formal Analysis of Extreme Symmetric Systems

Formal analysis consists in verifying expected properties of a system modeled in an appropriate formalism. We focus here on state-based analysis. Thus, expected properties usually are specified as reachability formulas, deadlock detection, LTL or CTL formulas, etc. over the model state space. The drawback of these approaches is the so-called combinatorial explosion of the number of states that hinders analysis.

3.1 Existing Approaches for the Analysis of Symmetric Systems

Several approaches have been proposed to tackle this combinatorial explosion. We focus on two of them, namely symmetry reduction, and decision diagrams. We then associate these two techniques with bag-based modeling.

Symmetries. Concurrent systems often exhibit symmetries: the typical example consists in n identical processes that behave asynchronously. A state in such systems is then characterized by the states of these n processes, up to a renaming of the processes: the processes are all behaviorally equivalent.

Formally, two components are said to be symmetrical if they can be permuted without changing the behavior of the system. In most systems, there are several groups of components with similar behavior: each component can be permutable with any component in the same groups. In SNB, such behavioral groups are defined as *equivalence classes* on C.

Definition 2 (Color Equivalence Classes). *Let us consider a discrete data type (i.e. a color in a SNB) C. Two colors in C are symmetrical if the behavior of the system is not affected when they are swapped.*

The "is symmetrical to" is an equivalence relation over C. Its equivalence classes
$C_1, \ldots, C_n$ *partition C in the following way:*

$$C = \bigcup_{i=1..N} C_i$$

The symmetries on the colors naturally extend to symmetries of system states. The relation "is symmetrical to" is also an equivalence relation over the set of system states, whose equivalence classes are also called *symbolic states*. The *quotient* state space is defined as the quotient of the reachability graph by this equivalence relation [6]. In favorable cases, the quotient state space is exponentially smaller than the state space.

Decision Diagrams. We mentioned decision diagrams in section 2.2 as a compact structure. They were first used in model checking [5] to successfully handle large state spaces. Several variants have been used since then for the efficient representation of large state spaces.

Symmetry reduction and decision diagrams can be used together. Although previous works have shown their efficiency, decision diagrams still require specific algorithms because their optimal use is not straightforward. [8] has shown that the traditional approach for the representation of complex operations on decision diagrams fails at providing an efficient solution to the computation of a quotient state space. However, the notion of homomorphism presented in section 2.2 appears to be a promising way to overcome this obstacle, as several investigations show [13,28,10]. Nevertheless, the design of algorithms for symmetry reduction using decision diagrams is still a challenging problem.

3.2 Using Bags Information to Optimize State Space Generation

Bags provide an abstraction mechanism, especially for subsystems that generate interleaving. They thus decrease the need for partial order techniques that are incompatible with decision diagrams. This can be observed on transition enter in Fig. 1 and its unfolding presented in Fig 2. In the SNB, there is only one possible transition to be fired while, in the second model, several exist. So, if the number of symbolic states in the quotient state space remains the same, the number of firings is dramatically reduced in the case of SNB [10]. Then, we avoid several type of situations where partial order techniques could be operated.

At this stage, several techniques can be activated, based on the information carried out by bags, as provided in SNB. We list these techniques before showing how they are applied to implement the transition relation.

Technique 1: Dedicated Representation of Guards. together with the definition of Symmetric nets, a dedicated representation for guards was introduced [6]. The objective was to preserve the information about equivalence classes in color types and thus, to enable the implementation of the so-called *symbolic firing* of transitions.

For instance, an expression like $v < V$ (where v represents a variable and V a constant in the color class C) implicitly defines two color equivalence classes. The first one C_1 contains all the values of C that are smaller than V, and C_2 contains the other values of C. Once the color equivalence classes have been computed, such an expression can be rewritten $v \in C_1$.

This rewriting can be generalized to any relation between a variable and a constant provided that equivalence classes are computed. Guards are then expressed using a disjunction of membership test to selected equivalence classes. For instance, inequalities between two variables leads to a partition of C into $N = |C|$ singleton subclasses (i.e. such an expression breaks all the symmetries) while $=$ and $\neq$ preserve the equivalence relation.

Such a representation is painful to explicit by the modeler but it can be automatically computed on Symmetric Nets [27]. Extensions of this algorithm can be provided, considering extra operators to manage bags cardinalities.

Technique 2: Deducing a Hierarchical Representation from the Bag Structure. This idea has been introduced in a first reachability analysis tool for SNB [10] and its principle is roughly presented in the example for marking encoding in Fig. 3. It can also be extended to the manipulation of bags.

Technique 3: Recursive Unfolding. this technique is efficient when a system (or parts of a system) can be defined recursively [19]. Let us sketch its principle on the dining philosophers problem. Instead of considering symmetries "horizontally" (e.g. all philosophers share the same behavior), the idea is to consider them "vertically". Then, T_n the table of n can be decomposed in a recursive way:

$$
\begin{aligned}
T_n = 2\times \quad & \overbrace{ T_{\frac{n}{2}} } & + \text{ interactions} \quad & = 2 \times \tfrac{1}{2}\text{tables} \\
= 2\times \quad & \overbrace{2 \times T_{\frac{n}{4}} + \text{interactions}} & + \text{ interactions} \quad & = 4 \times \tfrac{1}{4}\text{tables} \\
= 2\times \, 2\times \, & \overbrace{2 \times T_{\frac{n}{8}}} + \text{interactions} + \text{ interactions} & + \text{ interactions} \quad & = 8 \times \tfrac{1}{8}\text{tables} \\
\vdots \quad & & & \vdots
\end{aligned}
$$

until T_2 (the "elementary" table with 2 philosophers) is reached. This technique, when it applies for regular systems, proved to be extremely efficient thanks to a recursive hierarchical encoding (which is possible with SDD). We show, later in this paper, that bags can be encoded recursively in a similar way to the example provided here.

Technique 4: Anonymization. this technique was introduced to deal with the computation of a hierarchical order to encode a state space with SDD [20]. The principle is to reuse similar patterns with a new interpretation. For instance, if we consider two sequences of affectations ($x = 4 \rightarrow y = 2 \rightarrow 1$) and ($t = 4 \rightarrow u = 2 \rightarrow 1$), one can observe that x, y for the first one and t, u for the second one can be considered as "contextual information", thus reducing those two patterns to a single one.

This technique, associated with a hierarchical representation, can dramatically reduce the number of different SDD patterns, and thus, lead to a more compact storage of the state space.

These four techniques are exploited to elaborate an efficient representation in memory of the state space, as well as performant computation of the quotient state space.

Class   Var

Res is Res$_1$ = [1..3] ∪   r1 in Res$_1$;

Res$_2$ = [4..6];   r2 in Res$_2$;

(M) —⟨r1⟩+ 2*⟨r2⟩ ⟶ ||—⟨r1⟩+ 2*⟨r2⟩ ⟶ $\bigcirc$

free *Res*   **assign**   **busy** *Res*

Fig. 4. illustration of the symbolic firing, $M = \langle Res_1.all \rangle + 4 \times \langle Res_2.all \rangle$

3.3   Computing the Transition Relation in SNB

We detail here how efficient algorithms dedicated to SNB can be deduced from the techniques identified in the previous section.

The Transition Relation. Models usually are specified in terms of a transition system, with initial states and a generic transition relation. The verification of a property then consists in an exploration of the state space. Algorithm 1 is typical of the state space generation for a model given as a set of initial states and the transition relation. Once the state space has been generated, several properties (reachability, deadlock detection, LTL, CTL formulae ...) can be checked against it.

Depending on the type of property to be verified, this algorithm can be tweaked for improved performance. For instance, reachability and LTL formulae can be checked on-the-fly (the algorithm returns as soon as the property is verified or a counter-example is found). We do not focus on such optimizations but on the "core generation" of the state space instead.

The Transition Relation in SN. The transition relation is quite straightforward in this case. [6] introduces a framework for an efficient use of symmetries in SN. Formally, colors are separated into *color equivalence classes* that express the possible symmetries, as explained earlier.

Let us illustrate this framework with the SN of Fig. 4 that illustrates the affectation of resources in a system. There are two types of resources: Res$_1$ (one is hold at a time) and Res$_2$ (two copies are hold simultaneously).

Since all resources in Res$_1$ (resp. Res$_2$) are symmetrical, there are several symmetrical bindings for the variables r1 and r2 that lead to symmetrical markings.

The color equivalence classes are partitioned into dynamic subclasses, depending on the marking. For instance, Res$_1$ could be split into Z_1, the free resources (tokens in place free), and Z_2 the busy ones (tokens in place busy). A symbolic marking is thus expressed in terms of such dynamic subclasses. Similarly, binding the variables of a transition to dynamic subclasses rather than explicit values allows to capture several symmetrical

Require: a model M given as a set of initial states S_0 and the transition relation *Next*

    $S \leftarrow S_0$

   repeat

      $S \leftarrow S \cup Next(S)$

   until a fixpoint is reached

   return S

Ensure: S is the state space of M

Algorithm 1. The state space generation algorithm

bindings at once. For instance, considering that $\mathsf{Res}_1 = Z_1 \cup Z_2$ and $\mathsf{Res}_2 = Z_3 \cup Z_4$, r1 and r2 have two possible bindings each, leading to four symbolic bindings. This number is to be compared to the nine possible explicit bindings (9 in the example).

Variables can only be bound to dynamic subclasses Z such that $card(Z) = 1$. This may lead to a preprocessing of the symbolic marking, called *splitting* in order to obtain such dynamic subclasses. Similarly, once the symbolic firing occurred, a postprocessing operation called *grouping* recomputes the dynamic subclasses.

Let us note that, in this case, both the description of markings and the description of bindings are represented using equivalence classes as basic representation of values. The larger the color equivalence classes, the fewer values are evaluated during the firing of transitions, and the fewer states in the quotient state space.

The Transition Relation in SNB. [18] extends the notion of symbolic markings and symbolic firing to SNB. The sole difference between the SN and SNB transition relations is the binding of bag variables, and the efficient computation of all the possible bindings. In SNB, classical variables are instantiated as in SN, and bag variables are instantiated with bags over dynamic subclasses. The same processes of splitting and grouping the dynamic subclasses, adapted for bags, occur.

Finding all the bindings of a transition with bag variables is always reducible to the enumeration of bags over a finite domain (the dynamic subclasses) with bounded cardinality. A naive enumeration would however suffer from the interleaving that was supposed to be avoided. We propose an appoach for the efficient computations of such bindings.

A bag (or multiset) is a set where there can be several instances of some elements.

Definition 3. *Bag Let $C = \{c_1 \ldots c_n\}$ be a finite set. A bag b over C is a formal sum $b = \Sigma_{i=1}^{n} a_i c_i$ where $a_i \in \mathbb{N}$ is the multiplicity of the element c_i.*
The cardinal of b is $|b| = \Sigma_{i=1}^{n} a_i$, and the support of b is the set of elements with non-zero multiplicity: $Supp(b) = \{c_i | a_i > 0\}$.
The multiplicity of c_i may also be denoted by $b(c_i)$.

$Bag(C)$ denotes the set of multisets over C. $Bag_n(C)$ denotes the set of multisets over C having a cardinality of n. The union, intersection and difference on sets extend naturally to multisets:

- $b_1 \cup b_2 = \Sigma_{i=1}^{n}(b_1(c_i) + b_2(c_i))c_i$
- $b_1 \cap b_2 = \Sigma_{i=1}^{n} \min(b_1(c_i), b_2(c_i))c_i$
- $b_1 - b_2 = \Sigma_{i=1}^{n} \max(b_1(c_i) - b_2(c_i), 0)c_i$
- $b_1 \subset b_2$ if and only if $b_1(c) \leq b_2(c)$ for all $c \in C$

Note that when all the multiplicity are 0 or 1, then the bag is a set, and that all definitions above fall back to classical set definitions. Further optimizations can be obtained when the encountered bags are actually restricted to be sets, but are not detailed here as they mainly rely on classical computations over sets.

Application of technique 1 is then trivial (canonization of guards). However, it required some extensions for bags. In order to compute the set of bags having cardinal n over a set C, one may use recursive definitions concerning either the cardinality of, or the support of the bags, thus applying technique 2.

Property 1. *Recursion over the cardinal*
$$Bag_{m+n}(C) = Bag_m(C) \uplus Bag_n(C) = \{b_1 \cup b_2 | b_1 \in Bag_m(C), b_2 \in Bag_n(C)\}$$

Property 2. *Recursion over the support*
$$Bag_n(C_1 \cup \ldots \cup C_k) = (\bigcup_{i=1}^{k} Bag_n(C_i)) \cup Bag_n^*(C_1, \ldots, C_k) \text{ where } Bag_n^* \text{ represents the bag}$$
of cardinality n over mixed supports (i.e. involving several C_i).

Properties 1 and 2 allow to represent a set of bags of a given cardinality in terms of sets of bags of smaller cardinality or smaller support.

When colors classes are split into equivalence classes, the use of property 2 reduces the problem in terms of generating sets of bags over color classes. Then, we use the recursion over bags cardinality. All together, these properties allow for an efficient divide-and-conquer generation strategy.

For instance, by carefully choosing the parameters n and m in property 1, one can represent $Bag_n(C)$ in $O(log(n))$ SDD nodes. This leads to the type of recursive encoding over the structure of the bags as done by technique 3 (its principle is sketched in Fig. 5). Thus, as soon as we detect an upper bound for the cardinality of a bag over C, its representation is easily elaborated based on this scheme.

Finally, technique 4 (Anonymization) can be applied to increase the sharing of common patterns. This can be applied to the markings structure (see the example presented in Fig. 3) or to the net structure (as illustrated in [20]).

It is also applicable to the recursive bag representation as illustrated in Fig. 6. The idea is to have a representation of the bag cardinalities for a generic class $\mathfrak{C}$ that can be mapped to any C or $C_i \subset C$. Then, values in $\mathfrak{C}$ are only referenced by their position and the maximum cardinality of $\mathfrak{C}$ is the one of the largest type (or equivalence class). When a reference is made to $\mathfrak{C}$, the associated context is expressed using a reference to the effective class $\mathfrak{C}$ is mapped to. This relation is done at runtime when effective markings or transition bindings in the SNB are computed. By applying this principle to the recursion over bag cardinalities in Fig. 5 we get the reduced representation of Fig. 6. This technique also applies to the recursion over bag support.

All together, these techniques allow to contain the combinatorial explosion of the state space in terms of memory, as well as CPU consumption, since less calculus are needed.

Overview of the State Space Representation. The representation of a SNB state space is divided in three parts (see Fig. 7):

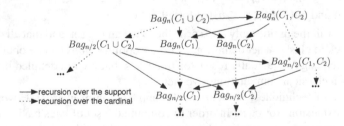

Fig. 5. Recursion over the definition of bags

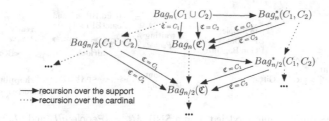

Fig. 6. Optimized representation of bags (anonymization over bag cardinalities)

1. the structure of the system states,
2. a sets of bags "heap",
3. representation of bag values.

Structure of the system states encodes the structure of states as they are expressed in the SNB. A naive way to encode this is to list the net places in a given order. However, the hierarchy supported by SDD allows a better reuse of patterns describing parts of the SNB structure.

The representation of tokens in places refers to a "heap" storing sets of bags as a unique and shared data structure.

Sets of bags "heap" encodes the bags of color that can be referenced to represent tokens in places. Once again, the representation can be hierarchical, especially when bags are hold in colored tokens.

The representation of bags in tokens refers to common representation of bag.

Representation of bag values recursively encodes the bags referenced in the state space.

The four techniques mentioned in section 3.2 can be activated there. In particular, anonymization allows a better reuse of representation patterns in any part of the state space.

Implementation of the Transition Relation. As explained earlier, one of the main characteristics of SDDs is the ability for developers to use dedicated operations (homomorphisms). To take full advantage from SDDs, the transition relation is encoded with homomorphisms. There are four steps in the transition relation [18]:

1. splitting dynamic subclasses,
2. binding the variables of each transition to splitted dynamic subclasses,
3. firing the transition,
4. canonizing the symbolic markings to group and rename dynamic subclasses.

Fig. 7. Structure of the state space representation

Fig. 8. The SaleStore example modeled with a SNB. $M_p = \langle \text{People}.all \rangle$ and $M_g = \langle \text{Gifts}.all \rangle$, $\text{P} = \text{G} = n$ is the scaling parameter of this example.

Each step is encoded as a homomorphism, and the transition relation is the composition of these four homomorphisms. Each step is theoretically independent, but it is of interest to propagate some information from one step to the next one for optimization purposes. In our implementation for instance, the two first steps are almost merged, in order to compute as few bindings as possible.

Building these operations on top of SDDs allows to profit from the shared structure. For instance, splitting the dynamic subclasses in the marking of a place is done only once for all the markings that share it. This significantly optimizes each step, especially the costly canonization.

The presented data structures are generated on the fly by the homomorphisms when needed. Thus, the SDD representation of the system acts like a cache itself.

4   Assessment

In this section, we take several examples for which the use of SNB is of interest for modeling purpose. We then provide some performances compared to the reference tool on Symmetric Nets: GreatSPN [17].

4.1   The Examples

We selected three examples that illustrate the interest of bag-based modeling as well as the interest of bags in the optimization of state space based analysis: the deadlock-free resource manager, the salestore, and the distributor. The two first models are "toy examples" emphasizing the use of bags in tokens. The last model also benefits from the use of bags but it was designed from a case study found in the litterature.

The Resource Manager Model. This is the model presented in Fig. 1 (see section 2.1). However, for the need of performances analysis, we constrained it to let processes have a maximum of three resources in their critical section. To do so, we changed the guard of transition enter into [card(R) > 0 and card(R) < 4]. The scaling parameter of this example is n in the initial marking M_r.

This model shows how bags can help to preserve symmetries. In order to discriminate between the transition exit (where a process and all its allocated resources are released) and the transition release (where some resources are released, but the process remains in he critical section), the SN unfolding breaks a few symmetries. This explains the difference of the number of symbolic states found by Crocodile and by GreatSPN in Table 1 (section 4.2). This is also an example of the interest of the bags in such models.

The Salestore Model. This model was introduced in [10] and is shown in Fig. 8. People enter the sale store through an airlock (transition airlock) with a capacity of two (of course, a single person may enter too). Then, people may buy items (at most two but possibly zero if none fits their need) and leave with the acquired items. Let us note that this example has two scalable parameters: P, the number of involved people in the system and G, the number of possible gifts in the warehouse. In our example, the model has been explicitly constrained: the airlock has a maximum capacity of 2 people and each customer cannot leave with more than 2 gifts.

The Distributor Model. This model of a coffee dispenser machine and optional features (e.g. milk, sugar, etc.) was introduced in [25] as a Feature Petri Net. We present in Fig.9 a SNB version of this model. The machine dispenses products (place theProducts) like coffee or tea. When brewing (transition elaborate) one of these products, it may add options (place theOptions) like milk or sugar, on demand.

The machine is refilled with products and options according to the conditions on transitions addProduct and addOption respectively. Options may be enabled (transition enable) or disabled individually (transition disable) and dynamically.

The original work in [25] presenting Feature Petri nets is intended to model the behavior of Software Product Lines (SPL). That approach was proposed as a means to *"ensure that all products[1] meet their specifications without having to check each product individually"*. A modular modeling framework is then proposed to incrementally build larger feature nets from smaller ones. The Feature nets are based on P/T nets. New features are thus added as new net fragments.

Our model is an adaptation of this example, showing SNB suitability to model a SPL: the specification is much more compact since, instead of adding pieces of Nets, only the definition of color types is changed. Moreover, thanks to the use of bags, scalability over the sets of features and their multiplicity in the machine configurations is guaranteed.

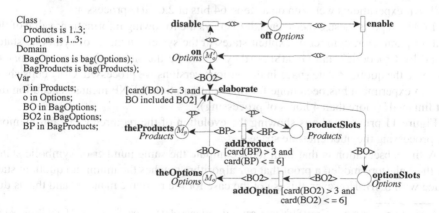

Fig. 9. The distributor example modeled with a SNB. $M_p = x \times \langle \text{Products}.all \rangle$, $M_o = x \times \langle \text{Options}.all \rangle$ and $M'_o = \langle \text{Options}.all \rangle$, x is the scaling parameter of this example.

---

[1] i.e. an assembly of selected features to build a specific model (e.g. {Coffee, Tea, Milk}).

Fig. 10. The unfolded equivalent SN from the model of Fig. 8

4.2   Performances

A first version of Crocodile was implemented and compared to GreatSPN [17] in [10]. GreatSPN is a well-known model checker for various classes of Petri Nets. Among its various capabilities, we only use its quotient state space generation features. It works with SN only, and does not use decision diagrams [2].

This first study revealed that the combination of symmetries and decision diagrams is of interest: our tool was more performant than GreatSPN. However, at this stage, the management of bags was not optimized at all. This impeded performances when bags were used in tokens, while sets in tokens were appropriately handled.

For the *resource manager* and the *salestore*, we compare Crocodile2 to GreatSPN once again. We compute the quotient state space of the SNB and the unfolded SN with Crocodile2, and the quotient state space of the unfolded SN with GreatSPN. The unfolded SN of the *resource manager* is presented in Fig. 2 and the one of the *salestore* is presented in Fig. 10.

Since the *distributor* is too complex to unfold, we only compute the quotient graph with Crocodile2 from the SNB version. The idea is to show its capability to scale-up well. All experiments were run on a Xeon 64 bits at 2.6 GHz processor.

Table 1 reports these experiments. It displays the following information: value of the scaling parameter, number of explicit states in the system, number of symbolic states found by Crocodile2 and GreatSPN (they should be the same), time and memory to compute the quotient state space in the various versions we processed. Gray cells show that no experiment has been done for this configuration. EDNF means "execution did not finished" (more than 4 hours of processing).

Figure 11 provides charts showing the evolution of the required CPU and memory for processing the quotient state space.

A first observation is that both tools compute the same number of symbolic states for the Salestore model, a proof that our algorithm reaches the minimum quotient state space with SNB. However, this is not the case for the resource manager and this is due

---

[2] A prototype version of GreatSPN uses several variants of decision diagrams [1]: multi-way DD (MDD), multi-terminal MDD (MTMDD), and edge-valued MDD (EV+ MDD). None of these are hierarchical and they encode Stochastic P/T nets so far. Their results also show significant gain from the original version. However, we could not use this version of GreatSPN against our prototype.

Table 1. Performances of state space generation using Crocodile2 and GreatSPN

scaling parameter	# Explicit States	# Symbolic States Crocodile2 on SNB	GreatSPN on SN	Time (s) Crocodile2 SNB	SN	GreatSPN SN	Memory (KB) Crocodile2 SNB	SN	GreatSPN SN
				Resource manager					
02	1.8×10^{01}	4	8	ε	0.02	ε	80	80	80
04	2.2×10^{03}	12	38	0.04	0.48	0.05	80	3112	80
06	7.2×10^{05}	27	116	0.24	4	0.67	4008	4716	1156
08	4.5×10^{08}	53	289	1	23	44	8188	8816	9076
10	4.8×10^{11}	94	621	6	120	5892	19120	16820	851596
15	8.2×10^{19}	295	EDNF	165	3185	EDNF	245212	101860	EDNF
20	7.7×10^{28}	717		2941	EDNF		3059216	EDNF	
22	4.3×10^{32}	973		6131			4192604		
23	3.5×10^{34}	EDNF		EDNF			EDNF		
				Salestore					
02	2.9×10^{01}	13	13	0.01	0.01	ε	80	80	80
04	4.2×10^{03}	60	60	0.13	0.14	0.04	2864	3128	80
06	1.5×10^{06}	180	180	0.94	0.97	0.63	5720	6028	1132
08	9.4×10^{08}	425	425	5	4	40	12292	14108	9056
10	9.7×10^{11}	861	861	23	18	4798	32056	34352	851452
15	1.6×10^{20}	3336	EDNF	500	242	EDNF	222764	221192	EDNF
20	1.3×10^{29}	9196		5010	2157		1076816	910444	
22	7.0×10^{32}	12948		10003	4596		1811008	1398944	
23	5.6×10^{34}	EDNF		EDNF	6339		EDNF	1730348	
24	4.5×10^{36}				9357			2419028	
25	3.8×10^{38}				EDNF			EDNF	
				Distributor					
01	2.2×10^{04}	64		0.11			2740		
02	1.4×10^{06}	560		0.84			3936		
03	1.6×10^{07}	2400		4			7064		
04	8.9×10^{07}	7700		14			13760		
05	3.4×10^{08}	20384		43			26768		
06	1.0×10^{09}	47040		108			46224		
07	2.5×10^{09}	97920		236			71436		
08	5.7×10^{09}	188100		472			111144		
09	1.1×10^{10}	338800		918			171040		
10	2.2×10^{10}	578864		1596			239684		
11	3.8×10^{10}	946400		2894			420620		
12	6.5×10^{10}	1490580		4553			699408		
13	1.0×10^{11}	2273600		7763			1070832		
14	1.6×10^{11}	EDNF		EDNF			EDNF		

to the unfolding that breaks some hierarchical symmetries as we already mentioned in section 4.1.

We also observe that, for small values of the scaling parameter, greatSPN outperforms Crocodile2 both in time and memory consumption. This is typical of the involved techniques (both decision diagram-based and symmetries-based) that have an "initial cost" due to the management of data structures, that is not compensated in the case of small state spaces. Then, curves cross when the gain in memory and CPU compensates this overhead.

For the two models we also compare with GreatSPN, we reach a stage where greatSPN exceeds the maximum computation time. As observed in [10], the combinatorial explosion of firings is greater for GreatSPN since it canonizes more states than Crocodile2. When both are working on SN, Crocodile2 benefits from the fact that decision diagrams allow to fire and canonize a set of states at the same time. SNB bring a strong reduction of the interleaving that should increase efficiency. In fact the smaller

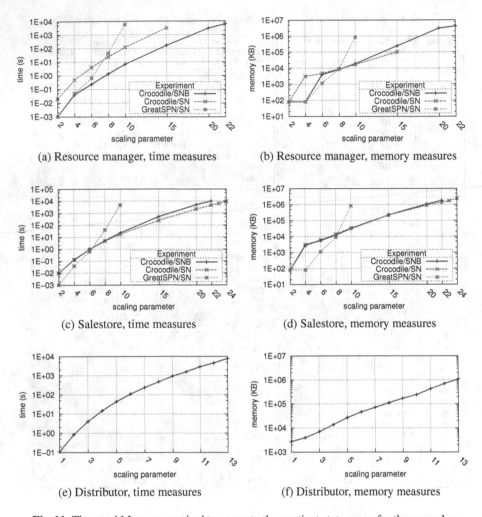

Fig. 11. Time and Memory required to generate the quotient state space for the examples

number of symbolic states for the SNB version of the resource manager leads to an increased efficiency of the state space generation in time (see Fig. 11a).

For those two models, we observe no increase of performances between the SNB version and the unfolded SN one (for Crocodile2). This seems mostly due to the fact that multi-linear homomorphisms have been recently implemented in libDDD and probably require some optimization when associated with hierarchical representations. We guess (this must be investigated) that there are some side effects on the cache management that impede CPU gains and memory consumption.

The distributor model is difficult to model easily with SN while its structure would depend on the numbers of products and options which is the scaling parameter (this SNB structure remains constant). However, our tool is able to scale up quite well with respect to the number of generated states.

4.3 Discussion

Evaluation of Reachability Properties. So far, our prototype only provides analysis of reachability properties. Such properties are constraints that can be checked during state space generation. This does not bring extra complexity (just a constant due to the property evaluation). Evaluation of a reachability property is done using the following schema:

- translation of the property into constraint c on the symbolic markings (expressed as a SDD),
- for each new symbolic state s, compare the canonical representation of s with c (since both are SDDs, this is a fast operation).

So far, once a state verifying the property is found, the tool must reexecute the state space generation algorithm to store the list of symbolic firings leading to the identified state. Thus, verification of a reachability property may lead to building twice the state space in the worst case. This complexity is compensated by the gain in the state space generation.

Towards Evaluation of CTL Formulas. CTL formulas can be evaluated on symmetric systems provided that, either it respects the system symmetries, or the equivalence relation is computed including constraints of both the model and the property (this may degrade the model symmetries).

Crocodile2 is implemented on top of libITS [24], that provides access to SDD via high-level structuring mechanisms (synchronizations and hierarchy). This library supports the evaluation of CTL formulas when atomic propositions they refer to are expressed in a symbolic way.

CTL evaluation heavily relies on the transition relation of the system. This is why we focus on the efficiency of its implementation since it is a key issue to provide efficient CTL analysis.

Usability of Bags in Tokens. One could have some skepticism about the usability of SNB. In fact, they are good to capture some dynamic aspects that are commonly found in distributed systems when a variable number of resources is handled by an actor of the system. This is typically the case for resources in the resource manager model (Fig. 1). As shown in section 2.1, modeling of such parts with SN requires to manually bound the number of handled resources. On top of the fact that symmetries are more difficult to capture, this makes the model more complex, and each state to be handled more difficult to encode in memory.

A domain that is very suitable for SNB-based modeling is games where players carry out a variable number of objects or features. The resulting model is much simpler and its analysis benefits from the use of Bags.

Moreover, the handling of SN being included in the handling of SNB, Crocodile2 remains a good tool to perform analysis on such models.

5   Conclusion

This paper presents a method that links a modeling concept recently introduced in Petri nets, the use of bags in tokens, to some efficient state space generation techniques. This modeling concept helps the modeler increase the structuring of symmetries in a specification in a relatively "natural" manner. This bag concept (as introduced in SNB) is of particular interest when associating a variable number of items to an entity (e.g. the critical resources in the resource manager model – see Fig. 1). Such a modeling issue often occurs when modeling distributed systems. This structuring information is reused in the back-end of a model checker tool to tackle the combinatorial explosion.

One main interest of the proposed modeling concept is to reduce the need for partial order techniques. Another originality is to increase the efficiency of the combined use of symmetries-based techniques, together with hierarchical decision diagrams. This association of techniques is of interest when performing state space-based analysis of complex and distributed systems.

We have implemented the presented strategies in a tool, Crocodile2, which outperforms the previous version thanks to the intensive use of efficient data representation techniques and operations. This tool is to be integrated in the *CosyVerif* verification environment [12].

Early assessment of this method by means of SNB models shows increased performance of reachability analysis versus a reference tool like GreatSPN. These promising results strengthen the idea that, in order to tackle complex distributed systems analysis, combined techniques must be activated together with enabling model-level optimized constructs. However, this requires some structural analysis capabilities such as the ones provided by Petri nets.

So far, we have experimented this association on Symmetric Nets with Bags (SNB). A further objective is to generalize this concept in order to apply it to other types of notations dedicated to classes of systems exhibiting symmetries such as peer-to-peer applications or Software Product Lines. A first study in that direction [11] showed interesting results.

Another objective is the optimization of the multi-linear homomorphisms that aim at tackling the cost of non-locality when using decision diagrams. Such an improvement would benefit to all application based on decision diagrams.

References

1. Babar, J., Beccuti, M., Donatelli, S., Miner, A.S.: GreatSPN Enhanced with Decision Diagram Data Structures. In: Lilius, J., Penczek, W. (eds.) PETRI NETS 2010. LNCS, vol. 6128, pp. 308–317. Springer, Heidelberg (2010)
2. Basler, G., Mazzucchi, M., Wahl, T., Kroening, D.: Symbolic Counter Abstraction for Concurrent Software. In: Bouajjani, A., Maler, O. (eds.) CAV 2009. LNCS, vol. 5643, pp. 64–78. Springer, Heidelberg (2009)
3. Bošnački, D., Holzmann, G.J.: Improving Spin's Partial-Order Reduction for Breadth-First Search. In: Godefroid, P. (ed.) SPIN 2005. LNCS, vol. 3639, pp. 91–105. Springer, Heidelberg (2005)
4. Bryant, R.E.: Graph-based algorithms for boolean function manipulation. IEEE Transactions on Computers 35(8), 677–691 (1986)

5. Burch, J.R., Clarke, E.M., Mcmillan, K.L., Dill, D.L., Hwang, L.J.: Symbolic model checking: 10^{20} States and beyond. Information and computation 98(2), 142–170 (1992)
6. Chiola, G., Dutheillet, C., Franceschinis, G., Haddad, S.: Stochastic well-formed coloured nets for symmetric modelling applications. IEEE Transactions on Computers 42(11), 1343–1360 (1993)
7. Clarke, E.M.: The Birth of Model Checking. In: Grumberg, O., Veith, H. (eds.) 25 Years of Model Checking. LNCS, vol. 5000, pp. 1–26. Springer, Heidelberg (2008)
8. Clarke, E., Enders, R., Filkorn, T., Jha, S.: Exploiting symmetry in temporal logic model checking. Formal Methods in System Design 9(1), 77–104 (1996)
9. Clarke, E., Grumberg, O., Peled, D.: Model Checking. MIT Press, Cambridge (1999)
10. Colange, M., Baarir, S., Kordon, F., Thierry-Mieg, Y.: Crocodile: A Symbolic/Symbolic Tool for the Analysis of Symmetric Nets with Bag. In: Kristensen, L.M., Petrucci, L. (eds.) PETRI NETS 2011. LNCS, vol. 6709, pp. 338–347. Springer, Heidelberg (2011)
11. Colange, M., Kordon, F., Thierry-Mieg, Y., Baarir, S.: State Space Analysis using Symmetries on Decision Diagrams. In: 12th International Conference on Application of Concurrency to System Design (ACSD 2012), pp. 164–172. IEEE Computer Society, Hamburg (2012)
12. Cosyverif: a verification environment (2012), http://www.cosyverif.org
13. Couvreur, J.-M., Encrenaz, E., Paviot-Adet, E., Poitrenaud, D., Wacrenier, P.-A.: Data Decision Diagrams for Petri Net Analysis. In: Esparza, J., Lakos, C. (eds.) ICATPN 2002. LNCS, vol. 2360, pp. 101–120. Springer, Heidelberg (2002)
14. Couvreur, J.-M., Thierry-Mieg, Y.: Hierarchical Decision Diagrams to Exploit Model Structure. In: Wang, F. (ed.) FORTE 2005. LNCS, vol. 3731, pp. 443–457. Springer, Heidelberg (2005)
15. Girault, C., Valk, R.: Petri Nets for Systems Engineering. Springer (2003) ISBN: 3-540-41217-4
16. Godefroid, P., Wolper, P.: A partial approach to model checking. In: Proceedings of Sixth Annual IEEE Symposium on Logic in Computer Science, LICS 1991, pp. 406–415 (July 1991)
17. GreatSPN: Petri nets suite (2012), http://www.di.unito.it/~greatspn
18. Haddad, S., Kordon, F., Petrucci, L., Pradat-Peyre, J., Treves, L.: Efficient state-based analysis by introducing bags in petri nets color domains. In: American Control Conference, ACC 2009, pp. 5018–5025. IEEE (2009)
19. Hamez, A., Thierry-Mieg, Y., Kordon, F.: Building efficient model checkers using hierarchical set decision diagrams and automatic saturation. Fundamenta Informaticae 94(3-4), 413–437 (2009)
20. Hong, S., Kordon, F., Paviot-Adet, E., Evangelista, S.: Computing a Hierarchical Static Order for Decision Diagram-Based Representation from P/T Nets. In: Jensen, K., Donatelli, S., Kleijn, J. (eds.) ToPNoC V. LNCS, vol. 6900, pp. 121–140. Springer, Heidelberg (2012)
21. Jensen, K.: Coloured Petri nets and the invariant-method. Theor. Comput. Sci. 14, 317–336 (1981)
22. Jensen, K., Kristensen, L.: Coloured Petri Nets: Modelling and Validation of Concurrent Systems. Springer (2009) ISBN: ISBN 978-3-642-00283-0
23. Junttila, T.: On the Symmetry Reduction Method for Petri Nets and similar formalisms. Ph.D. thesis, Helsinki University of Technology, Espoo, Finland (2003)
24. libits (2012), http://move.lip6.fr/software/DDD
25. Muschevici, R., Proença, J., Clarke, D.: Modular Modelling of Software Product Lines with Feature Nets. In: Barthe, G., Pardo, A., Schneider, G. (eds.) SEFM 2011. LNCS, vol. 7041, pp. 318–333. Springer, Heidelberg (2011)
26. Tanenbaum, A.: Operating Systems: Design and Implementation. Prentice Hall (1987)

27. Thierry-Mieg, Y., Dutheillet, C., Mounier, I.: Automatic Symmetry Detection in Well-Formed Nets. In: van der Aalst, W.M.P., Best, E. (eds.) ICATPN 2003. LNCS, vol. 2679, pp. 82–101. Springer, Heidelberg (2003)
28. Thierry-Mieg, Y., Ilié, J.-M., Poitrenaud, D.: A Symbolic Symbolic State Space Representation. In: de Frutos-Escrig, D., Núñez, M. (eds.) FORTE 2004. LNCS, vol. 3235, pp. 276–291. Springer, Heidelberg (2004)
29. Thierry-Mieg, Y., Poitrenaud, D., Hamez, A., Kordon, F.: Hierarchical Set Decision Diagrams and Regular Models. In: Kowalewski, S., Philippou, A. (eds.) TACAS 2009. LNCS, vol. 5505, pp. 1–15. Springer, Heidelberg (2009)

Towards Communication-Based Steering of Complex Distributed Systems

Klaus Dräger and Marta Kwiatkowska

Department of Computer Science, University of Oxford, Oxford, UK

Abstract. Quantitative verification is an established automated technique that can ensure predictability and dependability of software systems which exhibit probabilistic behaviour. Since offline usage of quantitative verification is infeasible for large-scale complex systems that continuously adapt to the changing environment, quantitative runtime verification was proposed as an alternative. Using an illustrative case study of communicating, distributed probabilistic processes, we formulate the problem of quantitative steering, a runtime technique that involves system monitoring, prediction of future errors, and enforcement of system's behaviour away from the error states. We consider a communication-based variant of steering where enforcement is achieved by modifying the contents of communication channels. Our approach is based on stochastic games, where one player is the system and the other players assume the role of the controller, and hence steering reduces to finding a controller strategy that meets the given quantitative goal. We discuss the solution to the quantitative steering problem and its extensions inspired by complex real-world scenarios.

1 Introduction

Software systems underpin the vast majority of our activities, from commerce, to manufacturing, transport and healthcare. Typical requirements for such systems are that they run in distributed and de-centralised environments; must be fault-tolerant, since devices may fail and communication media may be unreliable; and are expected to run continuously, adapting to the changes in the environment, for example user demand. Being deployed in business-critical setting, they must also behave in a predictable and dependable manner.

Formal verification techniques such as model checking [10] have proved particularly useful in preventing errors in the deployed software. Formal verification is used mainly in an offline fashion, though there have been recent efforts to integrate it within autonomic systems [9], where adaptive behaviour can be handled by applying concepts from control such as feedback loops. In this context, software is monitored at runtime, its behaviour analysed against given requirements, and, if deviation is detected, instructions are issued to steer its behaviour accordingly. In cases where software systems can exhibit failure and must comply with resource limitations, the modelling frameworks typically allow for probabilistic behaviour and annotation with appropriate quantities to represent the

R. Calinescu and D. Garlan (Eds.): Monterey Workshop 2012, LNCS 7539, pp. 353–368, 2012.
© Springer-Verlag Berlin Heidelberg 2012

incurred cost, e.g. energy usage. *Quantitative verification* [19] is a technique which combines formal verification with numerical computation, and is able to automatically answer the questions such as "what is the maximum probability of reaching an error state?", and "what is the expected energy usage in the start up phase?". Quantitative verification techniques have been implemented, e.g., within the PRISM model checker [20]. PRISM has been successfully used to verify a range of quantitative/probabilistic temporal properties, in some cases discovering critical flaws.

The offline application of quantitative verification, however, is usually infeasible in the context of *large-scale complex systems* [24]. The main culprit is state-space explosion in conjunction with the inherent complexity of the analysis methods that are involved. A *quantitative runtime verification* approach was recently proposed [2,16,1] as an alternative, complementary analysis method. We adopt this approach, and focus on the following system characteristics:

- adaptivity in presence of probabilistic choice: we explicitly model failure using probability distributions, and allow for continuous changes as the system evolves, including changes to probability values and system transitions;
- resource limitations: we model resource limitatations, for example finite message queue sizes, by placing quantitative bounds on them;
- partial observability: we assume that, while we have a formal model overapproximating the behaviour of the processes, we know nothing about their current internal state other than what we can infer from the model and the communication history.

In this paper we formulate the problem of *quantitative runtime steering* for large-scale complex systems that exhibit the above characteristics. The (non-quantitative) steering problem has been earlier solved in the context of distributed systems [26], where a model checker has been used to predict and prevent future inconsistencies. As a representative setting, we consider systems comprising a number of distributed probabilistic processes, communicating through message channels. We assume that each process is modelled as a Markov decision process (see the next section for details) and the system is constructed through parallel composition of those. To enable steering, we allow an explicit controller process who can use the channels both as a source of information (to try to determine the actual system state) and as a steering medium (by altering the channel contents). We then take a *stochastic game* view [8] of the system, where, in addition to a randomised player that deals with probabilistic transitions, we have:

- player 1 representing the decisions of a controller, striving to ensure that the required quantitative property holds; and
- player 2 representing the combined decisions of the system components, which in order to cover the worst possible scenario is usually assumed to be malicious.

In [8], a reward-based temporal logic and verification algorithms were proposed for turn-based stochastic games and implemented as an extension of PRISM [23].

The logic can express properties such as "player 1 has a strategy to ensure that the maximum probability of reaching a final state is at least 0.99, regardless of the strategy of any other player". Here, for simplicity, we assume that the controller's goal is to ensure a *safety* objective, namely the avoidance of a given set of *error* states. As a secondary goal, we want the controller to achieve this objective in the least intrusive way possible. We model this requirement by associating a *cost* with every alteration of the channels; this naturally leads to the definition of the steering problem in terms of a generation of a controller strategy that meets the stated *quantitative goal*.

To illustrate our approach, we introduce a motivating case study which forms the basis of our discussions. We then describe how to solve the steering problem outlined above, at first treating a simplified variant which can be solved exactly using existing methods. As mentioned above, due to the adaptivity and partial observability, this exact solution will be inappropriate for very large systems; in the following sections we discuss how to adapt the method to a variety of harder scenarios inspired by real-world complex systems. We conclude the paper by summarising future research in this area.

Related Work. The idea to incorporate the use of formal methods at runtime dates back to the work of Crow and Rushby [11] on fault detection, identification and reconfiguration. Subsequent developments include the framework of [22]. In [26] a model checker executed from the current local state has been used to predict and prevent future inconsistencies in a distributed system. In the quantitative runtime setting, a number of approaches have been proposed for different types of models, to mention the autonomic approach of [2,1] for discrete- and continuous-time Markov chains, parametric techniques of [15,16] for discrete time Markov chains and the incremental approach of [21] for Markov decision processes. Partially observable Markov decision processes are known to be infeasible, but a promising partial approach to adversary generation was recently proposed in [18]. Stochastic games have been a very active research topic, see e.g. [13,7,3]. A survey of results can be found in [5] and an overview of partially observable stochastic games in [4]. The majority of the work has been theoretical, and we are aware of only two implementations, GIST [6] for synthesis and PRISM-games for quantitative verification [8,23]. Our paper is the first to propose stochastic game techniques as a solution to quantitative runtime steering.

1.1   Case Study

Consider the following example, motivated by a cloud computing scenario, for distributing a workload of tasks among a number of processing units. We are given processing units $P_1, \ldots, P_n$ arranged in a network (see Figure 1). For the sake of simplicity, the network topology we use in this example is a ring of processes, each of which can communicate with other processes up to two positions away, and with an *environment* process.

Figure 2 shows the abstract specification for process $P_r, r \in \{1, \ldots, n\}$. The process executes the following main loop:

- In the idle location q_1, it can receive requests to perform some computation, either as a req_r message from the environment, or as a $a_{i,r}$ or $b_{i,r}$ message from another process P_i, representing some subtask which P_i generated to distribute the workload. Note that i serves as a free variable, which parameterizes families of actions ($a_{i,r}$ and $ack_{i,r}$) and locations ($q_{11,i}$) in P_r. The process moves to q_2, storing the client process id in variable m (a value of 0 representing the environment).
- In each of the *busy* locations q_2, q_3, q_4, further requests from another P_i are rejected using a $nack_{r,i}$ message.
- In locations q_2 and q_3, the process makes a probabilistic decision about whether or not to issue a subrequest of type a or b, respectively. If the answer is positive, it then chooses a recipient, by calling the auxiliary function *pick j* (resp. *pick k*), which
  - assigns to j (resp. k) a neighbour id chosen uniformly at random, excluding the current values of j, k, m, and
  - increases the counter *tries*,
  and sending an $a_{r,j}$ (resp. $b_{r,k}$) message.
- In q_4, the process checks and acts on responses:
  - if *tries* exceeds a given bound, give up and send a $nack_{r,m}$ message,
  - if an *ack* arrives from P_j (or P_k), set j (respectively k) to zero,
  - if both j and k are zero, there are no pending subrequests; send an *ack* message,
  - if either P_j or P_k send a *nack*, choose a new recipient for the failed subrequest (again using *pick j*/*pick k*).

Note that the system is driven by user demand and does not offer a guarantee that the workload will be successfully distributed; in fact, it may fail to do so and this can be expressed using probability. This system therefore exhibits two problems. Firstly, in the case when a process fails to distribute the workload despite having tried the specified number of times, it is possible that *ack* or *nack* messages arrive after the *tries* counter has exceeded the bound; these messages are not cleaned up and can confuse the process in subsequent computations. Secondly, the system may enter a configuration in which failure is unacceptably high, for example, if the workload is distributed badly between the units. Suppose the initial request leads to generation of subtasks as in Figure 3, where in the rightmost configuration processes $P_1, \ldots, P_7$ are all busy (note that these are only a subset of the full system, and some of them may still have subrequests to send). Then in that rightmost column:

- P_5 has only busy neighbours, so if it generates any subrequests, it will fail (after 5 attempts). The probability for this case is 0.64.
- If P_5 does fail, P_3 receives the resulting $nack_{5,3}$ and re-sends its subrequest up to 4 times; the recipient is chosen randomly from $\{P_1, P_2, P_5\}$, subject to the condition that the same recipient cannot be chosen in two successive attempts. Since all neighbours other than P_5 are busy, this will lead to a failure of the overall request with probability 0.4672 (see the case $k = 5, tries = 2$ in Figure 4).

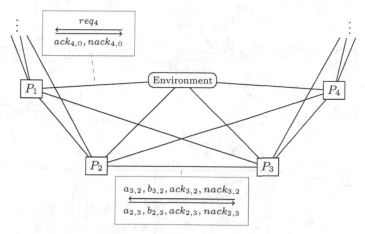

Fig. 1. A simple cluster of computing units. Processes $P_1, \ldots, P_n$ are arranged in a ring, each able to directly communicate with processes up to two positions away, and with the environment, which can generate requests req_i for each process P_i. Messages $a_{i,j}, b_{i,j}$ represent subrequests from P_i to P_j; $ack_{i,j}$ and $nack_{i,j}$ are success and failure notifications (in the latter case, j can be 0, representing a notification to the environment).

Our goal is to prevent the above scenario through using a controller which cancels requests responsible for creating such contiguous overloaded regions by deleting them and injecting a *nack* message. The idea is that the controller is able to predict that congestion is reachable in the near future, and can then select an appropriate strategy to avoid it. In the example scenario, the congestion problem could be addressed by trying to get P_6 to send its second subrequest to a process further down the chain, instead of its direct neighbour. In order to do this, the controller would delete the request ($a_{6,7}$ or $b_{6,7}$) and inject a $nack_{7,6}$ message.

2   Preliminaries

In this section, we formally describe the class of systems we are interested in, together the corresponding quantitative verification and steering problems. The systems comprise a number of distributed, probabilistic processes, each modelled as a Markov decision process, communicating through (bounded) channels.

2.1   Words and Word Distances

As usual, the sets of finite and infinite *words* over an alphabet Σ are denoted by Σ^* and Σ^ω, respectively. The empty word is ϵ, and the length of a word $w \in \Sigma^*$ is $|w|$.

In order to represent the intrusiveness of a steering strategy, we use a *distance* between words, based on the number of steps needed to transform one into the other, where a step consists of deleting or inserting a symbol (corresponding to interception or injection of a message). Specifically, we have the following definition.

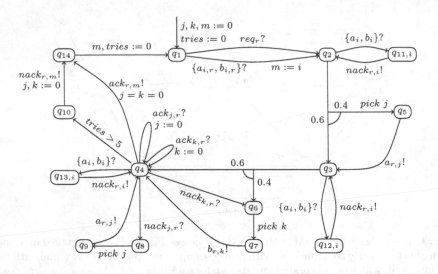

Fig. 2. One process P_r in the cluster. Variables m, j, and k are used to store the ids of neighbours whose subrequest P_r is currently processing (m) and to which subrequests have been sent (j, k). The auxiliary actions *pick j* and *pick k*, called before sending a subrequest, assign a neighbour index other than the current values of j, k, m to j or k, respectively, and increment the *tries* counter.

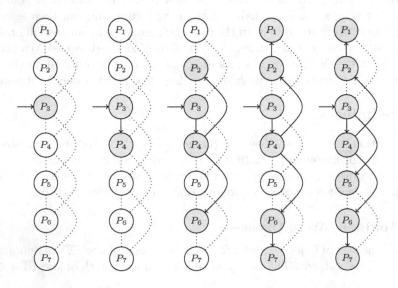

Fig. 3. Buildup of congestion in part of the network. Arrival of a request leads to a cascade of subrequests, eventually rendering all processes in the segment $P_1, \ldots, P_7$ busy (indicated by shading). In particular, P_5 is effectively isolated in the final state (rightmost column), since it has only busy neighbours. This leads to a failure probability for the overall task which is unnecessarily high.

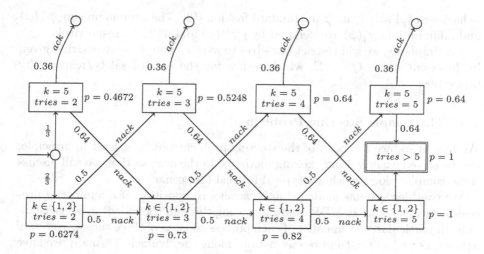

Fig. 4. Probabilities of overall failure in the situation shown in Figure 3, starting in the next-to-last column and abstracting away all details except the values of $k \in \{1, 2, 5\}$ and the $tries$ counter in P_3. The subrequest can only succeed (with probability 0.36) when $k = 5$; the value of k must change in each iteration.

Definition 1. *Let Σ be an alphabet, and let $\gamma = (\gamma_-, \gamma_+)$ consist of the* cost *functions $\gamma_-, \gamma_+ : \Sigma \to \mathbb{N} \cup \{\infty\}$. This gives rise to a weighted directed graph $G_{\Sigma, \gamma} = (\Sigma^*, E, w)$, where E consists of all pairs of the form $(xay, xy), (xy, xay)$ for $a \in \Sigma$ and $x, y \in \Sigma^*$, and the edge weight w is given by $w(xay, xy) = \gamma_-(a)$ and $w(xy, xay) = \gamma_+(a)$.*

The (weighted edit) distance *$d_\gamma(u, v)$ between words $u, v \in \Sigma^*$ is the minimal weight of a path from u to v in $G_{\Sigma, \gamma}$.*

2.2 Markov Decision Processes

Definition 2. *Given a set S, a* finitely supported *probability distribution on S is a function $\Delta : S \to \mathbb{R}_{\geq 0}$ such that $\Delta(s) = 0$ for all but finitely many $s \in S$ and $\sum_{s \in S} \Delta(s) = 1$. We denote the set of all such distributions on S by $\mathcal{D}(S)$.*

Definition 3. *A* Markov decision process (MDP) *is a tuple $A = (Q, \Sigma, q^0, T)$, where*

- *Q is a set of* states, *including the* initial state *$q_0 \in Q$,*
- *Σ is an alphabet of* actions, *and*
- *$T : Q \times \Sigma \to \mathcal{D}(Q)$ is a partial* transition function.

The action alphabet represents the possibility of nondeterministic choices in A, which can be resolved by an *adversary*. In its most general form, this adversary makes a probabilistic choice between actions based on the history, i.e. it is given as a function $\sigma : Q^* \to \mathcal{D}(\Sigma)$. For any such adversary and any temporal property φ defining a measurable set $[\![\varphi]\!] \subseteq Q^\omega$ of paths, we get a probability $p_A^\sigma(\varphi)$ of the behaviour of A satisfying φ in standard fashion [19]. The supremum $\sup_\sigma p_A^\sigma(\varphi)$ and infimum $\inf_\sigma p_A^\sigma(\varphi)$ are denoted by $p_A^{\max}(\varphi)$ and $p_A^{\min}(\varphi)$, respectively.

For simplicity, we will restrict ourselves to *pure memoryless* adversaries, given by functions $\sigma : Q \to \Sigma$, which suffice for the case of safety/reachability properties.

2.3   The Simple Steering Problem

We first introduce a version of the steering problem which, at least in principle, can be solved exactly using existing methods. In the next section, we will discuss some complications which are typical for real-life scenarios.

We consider systems modelled as a parallel composition of a number of processes, each given as an MDP, communicating through (bounded) message channels. In particular, the alphabet of each process consists of three subsets: *internal* actions, as well as *send* and *receive* actions along the channels. Formally, we have the following.

Definition 4. *A* Probabilistic Bounded Channel System (PBCS) *is given by* $S = (A, C, \beta, \gamma)$, *where*

- $A = \{A_1, \ldots, A_k\}$ *is a finite set of MDPs* $A_i = (Q_i, \Sigma_i, q_i^0, T_i)$,
- $C = \{\Gamma_{i,j} \mid i, j \in \{1, \ldots, k\}, i \neq j\}$ *is a set of* message alphabets, *whose disjoint union we denote by* Γ,
- $\beta : C \to \mathbb{N}$ *is a channel bound* function, *and*
- $\gamma = (\gamma_-, \gamma_+)$ *is a pair of cost functions on* Γ,

such that, for $i = 1, \ldots, k$, *the alphabet* Σ_i *in* A_i *is the union of a set* Λ_i *of local actions,* $\{a? \mid a \in \Gamma_{j,i} \text{ for some } j\}$, *and* $\{a! \mid a \in \Gamma_{i,j} \text{ for some } j\}$.

A (global) state $s = (l, c)$ *of* S *consists of*

- *a tuple* $l = (l_i)$ *of local states* $l_i \in Q_i$ *for each* i, *and*
- *a tuple* $c = (c_{i,j})$ *of channel contents* $c_{i,j} \in \Gamma_{i,j}^*$ *for all* $i \neq j$.

We denote the set of global states by Q_S. *The initial global state* s^0 *is given by* $l_i = q_i^0$ *for all* i *and* $c_{i,j} = \epsilon$ *for all* $i \neq j$.

A transition of this system corresponds to a transition in one of its processes, which, as a side effect, may add a new message to an outgoing channel (if the action was a *send*) or consume a message from an incoming channel (if it was a *receive*). These two types of non-local transitions may only happen if the channel in question is not full or empty, respectively. Formally, we define the transition relation of the composed system S.

Definition 5. *Let* $S = (A, C, \beta, \gamma)$ *be a PBCS and* $s = (l, c)$ *its global state.*

- *For* $q \in Q_i$, $s[q] = (l', c)$ *is obtained by replacing the location* l_i *of* A_i *in* l *with* q, *i.e.* $l_i' = q$ *and* $l_j' = l_j$ *for* $j \neq i$.
- *For* $\Delta \in \mathcal{D}(Q_i)$, $s[\Delta] \in \mathcal{D}(Q_S)$ *is the distribution defined by* $s[\Delta](s[q]) = \Delta(q)$ *for* $q \in Q_i$ *and* $s[\Delta](s') = 0$ *otherwise.*

- *For $a \in \Gamma_{i,j}$, $a.s = (l, c')$ and $s.a = (l, c'')$ are obtained by appending a to the front or back, respectively, of the channel contents $c_{i,j}$:*
  - *$c'_{i,j} = a.c_{i,j}$ and $c''_{i,j} = c_{i,j}.a$;*
  - *$c'_{r,s} = c''_{r,s} = c_{r,s}$ otherwise.*

Then the transitions in A_i translate into the following system transitions for all $s = (l, c)$:

- *if $a \in \Lambda_i$ and $T_i(q_i, a) = \Delta$, then $T(s, a) = s[\Delta]$;*
- *if $a \in \Gamma_{i,j}$, $|c_{i,j}| < \beta(\Gamma_{i,j})$ and $T_i(q_i, a!) = \Delta$, then $T(s, a!) = (s.a)[\Delta]$;*
- *if $a \in \Gamma_{j,i}$ and $T_i(q_i, a?) = \Delta$, then $T(a.s, a?) = s[\Delta]$.*

Thus the composed system induces an MDP (Q_S, Σ, s^0, T) over the global states, and our goal is to ensure that this MDP satisfies a given safety property, expressed as a subset $E \subseteq Q_S$ of error states to be avoided.

In order to do this, we assume a *controller* whose task is to steer the system away from the bad states. This controller cannot directly influence the decisions of the system processes, but has access to the communication channels, and can remove or insert messages. The set of *controller transitions* is thus given by $(l, c) \Rightarrow (l, c')$ for all l, c, c'. The *cost* of such a transition is the sum of the distances between the channel contents in c and c', i.e. $d((l,c),(l,c')) = \sum_{i \neq j} d_\gamma(c_{i,j}, c'_{i,j})$.

This gives rise to a *stochastic game* structure between the system and the controller. One round of this game consists of the system executing an enabled system transition, followed by a probabilistic choice according to the resulting distribution, and the controller executing one of its transitions, i.e. altering the channel contents.

Definition 6. *The steering game $G_S = (N, I, M, c)$ for a PBCS $S = (A, C, \beta, \gamma)$ consists of:*

- *the set $N = N_S \cup N_C$ of nodes, where*
  - *$N_S = Q_S \times \{0\}$ is the set of system nodes, containing the initial node $I = (s^0, 0)$,*
  - *$N_C = Q_S \times \{1\}$ is the set of controller nodes,*
- *the set $M = M_S \cup M_C$ of moves, where*
  - *M_S is the set of system moves*
    $\{((s,0), \Delta') \mid s \to \Delta, \Delta'(s, 1) = \Delta(s) \text{ for all } s\}$,
  - *M_C is the set of controller moves $\{((s,1), (s', 0)) \mid s \Rightarrow s'\}$,*
  and
- *$\pi : M \to \mathbb{N}$ gives the cost of a move, where $\pi(m) = 0$ for $m \in M_S$ and $\pi((s,1), (s',0)) = d_\gamma(s, s')$ represents the total cost of steering operations to obtain s' from s.*

A play of G_S is an infinite sequence of nodes $p = n_0, n_1, \ldots$ such that $n_0 = I$ and, for all i, $(n_i, n_{i+1}) \in M$.

We are interested in the long-run cost of such plays. Since a play is in general infinite, we cannot simply add up all the costs of its moves, because this sum would diverge. A standard solution to this problem is to use the *discounted payoff* of p, which is defined in terms of a suitably chosen *discount factor* $\lambda \in (0,1)$, as the infinite sum $\sum_{k=1}^{\infty} \lambda^k c(n_{k-1}, n_k)$.

The behaviour of the system and controller players is given in terms of strategies $\sigma_S : N_S \to \mathcal{D}(N_C)$ and $\sigma_C : N_C \to N_S$ such that $(n, \sigma_S(n)) \in M_S$ for all $n \in N_S$ and $(n, \sigma_C(n)) \in M_C$ for all $n \in N_C$. Any choice $\sigma = (\sigma_S, \sigma_C)$ of strategies turns the game into a Markov chain $M_\sigma = (N, n^0, T)$ in the standard fashion [8], with the probability distribution $T(n)$ given by $T(n) = \sigma_S(n)$ for $n \in N_S$ and $T(n)(\sigma_C(n)) = 1$ for $n \in N_C$.

The *expected* discounted payoff for σ_S, σ_C and discount factor λ is then given by the limit $\eta_\lambda(\sigma_S, \sigma_C) = \lim_{k \to \infty} p_k$ of the sums

$$p_k = \sum_{n_1, \ldots, n_k \in N} T(n_0, n_1) \cdots T(n_{k-1}, n_k)(\lambda^1 c(n_0, n_1) + \cdots + \lambda^k c(n_{k-1}, n_k)).$$

In order to solve the steering problem described above, we need to find a controller strategy σ_C with two properties, as defined below.

Definition 7. *A λ-optimal strategy for a steering game G and a set E of error states is a controller strategy σ_C which*

1. *avoids the error states, i.e. reaches E with probability 0 in $M_{(\sigma_S, \sigma_C)}$ for all system strategies σ_S, and*
2. *among the strategies satisfying the first property, minimizes the worst-case expected discounted payoff, i.e. the supremum $\sup_{\sigma_S} \eta_\lambda(\sigma_S, \sigma_C)$.*

In the next section we discuss ways of finding a λ-optimal strategy, if it exists (which it may not, if the safety condition cannot be guaranteed).

3   Attacking the Steering Problem

3.1   The Simple Version

We will first consider the simplest version of the steering problem as presented in the previous section, assuming a fixed system and full observability, by which we mean that the controller is aware of the internal state of the system processes. In this case, the problem has a straightforward solution using existing methods:

1. Compute the full game graph $G_S = (N, I, M, c)$.
2. Determine the unsafe region U, starting from the set E of error nodes and iteratively adding the following sets until a fixpoint is reached:
   - all system nodes $n \in N_S$ for which there is $\Delta \in \mathcal{D}(N)$ and $n' \in U$ with $(n, \Delta) \in M_S$ and $\Delta(n') > 0$;
   - all controller nodes $n \in N_C$ such that $n' \in U$ for all n' with $(n, n') \in M_C$.

3. If U contains I, give up: we cannot avoid the error. Otherwise, remove U and all incident transitions from G_S, and use the existing algorithms [12] to find an optimal strategy for the resulting discounted payoff game on $N \setminus U$.

Unfortunately, the case of large-scale complex systems is much more complicated, and this simple solution is no longer appropriate. Some prominent difficulties are:

1. The state space, even if finite, (for example, because the processes are actually finite-state abstractions), is huge, making the explicit construction of the full game graph impractical.
2. If we allow for continuous system adaptation, this would, in our setting, manifest itself as changes to parameters such as transition probabilities, channel sizes, or cost functions. This calls for incremental quantitative verification techniques [21], which can be executed at runtime, reacting to system changes.
3. Full observability is unrealistic: all we can really expect the controller to see is the communication behaviour of the processes, i.e. the channel contents. In particular, we have to assume that processes could perform arbitrarily many unobservable internal transitions between communications, i.e. a system move would consist of a sequence of local transitions followed by a *send* or *receive* transition.

Note that the latter two points also imply that we can no longer hope to guarantee the safety property. Instead, we aim at a best-effort approach, which, in this context, we take to mean an attempt to avoid (or, in the partial observability scenario, minimize the probability of reaching) the error states within some number of steps.

We will now describe an approach which addresses the first two points; partial observability introduces some rather fundamental issues and will be discussed in Section 4.

3.2 Runtime Verification

In order to tackle the more general case, we use a runtime approach, which only explores a bounded part of the state space in any given step. Specifically, we assume given a suitable *lookahead* $L \in \mathbb{N}$ such that the goal in each step is to find a minimum-cost controller strategy to avoid the error states for *at least L* steps, starting from the current state s. Note that, in this case, we can simply add up the costs of a play with no need for a discount factor.

This problem can be formalized using the techniques developed in [8]. For the original game $G_S = (N, I, M, c)$ and the error states E, define the set of error nodes $N_e := \{(s,i) \mid s \in E, i \in \{0,1\}\}$, and consider the modified game $G'_{S,E,L,s} = (N', I', M', c')$ starting in s, where

- $N' = N \times \{0, \dots, L\}$,
- $I' = (s, 0, 0)$,
- $M' = M'_S \cup M'_C$ with

- the system moves M'_S given by
  $$\{((n,i) , \Delta') \mid n \notin N_e, (n,\Delta) \in M_S, \Delta'((n',i)) = \Delta(n') \text{ for all } n'\}, \text{ and}$$
- the controller moves M'_C given by
  $$\{((n,i) , (n',i+1)) \mid n \notin N_e, (n,n') \in M_C, i < L\},$$
- $c'((n,i),(n',i')) = c(n,n')$ for all n,n',i,i'.

Intuitively, we have augmented the original game with a counter which is incremented on each controller move. The error states become sinks from which no escape is possible. The controller then strives to reach the states where the counter has the value L, avoiding the error states up to this bound on the number of states, but without guaranteeing that the error states will be avoided in future.

We thus need to find the minimum-cost controller strategy to reach the set of goal nodes $G = \{(n,L) \mid n \in N\}$, where the cost of not reaching them (due to a failure to avoid the error states) is infinite. In the logic $rPATL$, which is an extension of the logic ATL with the probabilistic and reward operators, this can be expressed as $\varphi \equiv \langle\langle\{C\}\rangle\rangle R^c_{\min=?}[F^\infty g]$, where C is the controller player, and g is an atomic proposition labelling the goal states.

The overall solution then proceeds as follows: in each step, use the model checking algorithm from [8] to find the strategy[1] solving the $rPATL$ formula φ on the game $G'_{S,E,L,s}$ starting in the current state (note that this includes taking into account any changes in the model); make any changes which are immediately required by this strategy; and await the next system transition.

If the error condition is based on the states of just a small number of processes, this approach can be augmented using a form of *target enlargement* by first computing, for this subsystem, the set U of unsafe states (as defined in the simple case). The cylinder over U (i.e. the system states where the relevant processes are in an U-state) is then used in place of E.

4   Extensions

The game-based approach to the quantitative runtime steering problem that we introduced in the previous section is sufficient for the simplified setting, but not for many realistic large-scale complex systems scenarios. In this section, we use our framework as a basis to discuss a number of challenging variations. We briefly describe them and suggest possible solutions.

4.1   Compositional Analysis

In case the error condition is given in terms of some local error states in a subset of processes, it is tempting to try analysing these processes in isolation. If the bound L is relatively small, it may well be possible that the message channels to some of these processes are sufficiently full so that the behaviour of the other

---

[1] An implementation of strategy generation for the logic $rPATL$ is in progress, extending the functionality of [23].

processes cannot influence them within this number of steps. Even if this is not the case, there may only be a small number of messages which could be both sent and received before the time bound, allowing us to restrict the analysis of the processes not contributing to the error.

4.2 Partial Observability

In order to cope with partial observability, the controller needs to keep track of the states in which the system processes might be, and the corresponding probabilities. The recent paper [4] gives a good overview of the complexity of this problem in general stochastic games.

The classic approach to this problem occurs in the case of partially observable Markov decision processes (POMDPs) $M = (Q, \Sigma, O, \Delta^0, T, o)$, which are MDPs extended with a set O of observables and an observation function $o : Q \to O$. The idea is that an observer infers at each step a distribution D_i based on D_{i-1}, the action a_i, and the observation $o(q_i)$; these distributions are referred to as *belief states*.

The channel systems we are considering are an extreme case, in that we only have the actions available, corresponding to a trivial (singleton) O. The controller could then maintain a sequence of belief states Δ_i, starting with the Dirac distribution Δ_0 such that $\Delta_0(s^0) = 1$, and updating based on the observed actions c_i. Let $S_i \subseteq Q$ be the *support* of c_i, i.e. the set of states q for which $T(q, c_i)$ is defined, and let p_i be the probability $\sum_{q \in S_i} \Delta_i(q)$ of S_i in Δ_i. After c_i is observed, the new belief state is

$$\Delta_{i+1}(q) = \sum_{q' \in S_i} \Delta_i(q')T(q', c_i, q)/p_i.$$

This could then be combined with the steering game as described in the previous section, where we now have an initial distribution (Δ_i) instead of an initial state. One problem with this approach is that the support of the distributions involved might grow substantially over time. For the belief states, this can be addressed to some extent by realizing that we can maintain individual distributions for the processes instead of one distribution over product states, which could complement the compositional approach when it is viable.

So far, while we have treated the internal state of processes as unobservable, we were still assuming that the controller knows about all actions which occur. There are two quite realistic deviations from this which make the analysis much harder:

- There may be a delay between the time when an action occurs and the time when the controller becomes aware of it. This can be treated as a special case of incomplete information and dealt with as in [25].
- Some or all internal actions can be *silent*. In particular, since the controller cannot know about their occurrence, in this case a system step would actually consist of some number of such silent transitions followed by an observable one. The example in Figure 5 illustrates this situation: when

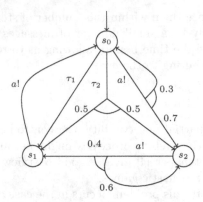

Fig. 5. State inference in systems with silent transitions. Even if the process is known to be in s_0 initially, the presence of τ-transitions means that, when observing an $a!$-event, we only know that the state was in $\{s_0, s_1, s_2\}$ before.

observing an action, there are several possible sequences of silent actions which might have occurred (in this case, τ_1, τ_2, or neither) resulting in several possible belief states $\{s_0, s_1, 0.5s_1 + 0.5s_2\}$, with the successor states $\{0.3s_0 + 0.7s_2, s_0, 0.5s_0 + 0.2s_1 + 0.3s_2\}$. Pursuing this naive extension of the belief state-based analysis leads to exponentially growing sets of distributions, which suggests the need for more compact (and less precise) representations for the possible process states.

4.3   Multi-way Communication Channels

The communication in our system model uses point-to-point channels, each with a dedicated sender and receiver. It would be interesting to generalize this to channels with arbitrary sets of readers and writers. Adapting the basic algorithms to this setting is straightforward (it changes the set of system transitions, which just needs to be reflected in the game structure), but the compositional approach described above becomes more difficult, since the assumptions about the possible interactions within the chosen time frame are no longer valid.

4.4   Soft Errors

We have so far used the assumption that the error states should be avoided if at all possible. Alternatively, one can consider situations in which they are merely undesirable and can be recovered from. In this case, instead of a safety property, the goal of the controller could, for example, be to minimize the time spent in these error states; more generally, we could assign a separate cost function to states and look for controllers minimizing the discounted long-term cost. If combined with the action-based cost function, this leads to multi-objective properties for stochastic games, about which very little is currently known; see [14,17] for multi-objective model checking algorithms and implementation for MDPs.

5   Conclusion and Future Work

In this paper we have formulated the problem of quantitative runtime steering for large-scale complex systems modelled as a parallel composition of Markov decision processes communicating through bounded channels. We have shown how the simplified setting can be solved by employing stochastic games, and reduces to finding a controller which meets a given quantitative goal by manipulating the channel contents. Real-world scenarios are, however, more complex, and we have outlined the challenges and possible solutions in this case.

Quantitative runtime verification and steering are powerful new techniques that have the potential to significantly enhance fault prevention and therefore predictability and dependability of software systems. In future we will work on adding these techniques to the repertoire of automated verification.

Acknowledgements. This research is supported by EPSRC project EP/F001096.

References

1. Calinescu, R., Ghezzi, C., Kwiatkowska, M., Mirandola, R.: Self-adaptive software needs quantitative verification at runtime. Communications of the ACM (to appear, 2012)
2. Calinescu, R., Kwiatkowska, M.: Using quantitative analysis to implement autonomic it systems. In: Proc. ICSE 2009, pp. 100–110. IEEE (2009)
3. Chatterjee, K., de Alfaro, L., Henzinger, T.A.: The Complexity of Stochastic Rabin and Streett Games'. In: Caires, L., Italiano, G.F., Monteiro, L., Palamidessi, C., Yung, M. (eds.) ICALP 2005. LNCS, vol. 3580, pp. 878–890. Springer, Heidelberg (2005)
4. Chatterjee, K., Doyen, L.: Partial-observation stochastic games: How to win when belief fails. In: Proc. LICS 2012 (to appear, 2012)
5. Chatterjee, K., Henzinger, T.A.: A survey of stochastic omega-regular games. Journal of Computer and System Sciences (2011)
6. Chatterjee, K., Henzinger, T.A., Jobstmann, B., Radhakrishna, A.: GIST: A Solver for Probabilistic Games. In: Touili, T., Cook, B., Jackson, P. (eds.) CAV 2010. LNCS, vol. 6174, pp. 665–669. Springer, Heidelberg (2010)
7. Chatterjee, K., Jurdzinski, M., Henzinger, T.: Quantitative stochastic parity games. In: Proc. SODA 2004, pp. 121–130 (2004)
8. Chen, T., Forejt, V., Kwiatkowska, M., Parker, D., Simaitis, A.: Automatic Verification of Competitive Stochastic Systems. In: Flanagan, C., König, B. (eds.) TACAS 2012. LNCS, vol. 7214, pp. 315–330. Springer, Heidelberg (2012)
9. Cheng, B.H.C., de Lemos, R., Giese, H., Inverardi, P., Magee, J., Andersson, J., Becker, B., Bencomo, N., Brun, Y., Cukic, B., Di Marzo Serugendo, G., Dustdar, S., Finkelstein, A., Gacek, C., Geihs, K., Grassi, V., Karsai, G., Kienle, H.M., Kramer, J., Litoiu, M., Malek, S., Mirandola, R., Müller, H.A., Park, S., Shaw, M., Tichy, M., Tivoli, M., Weyns, D., Whittle, J.: Software Engineering for Self-Adaptive Systems: A Research Roadmap. In: Cheng, B.H.C., de Lemos, R., Giese, H., Inverardi, P., Magee, J. (eds.) Software Engineering for Self-Adaptive Systems. LNCS, vol. 5525, pp. 1–26. Springer, Heidelberg (2009)
10. Clarke, E., Grumberg, O., Peled, D.: Model Checking. The MIT Press (1999)

11. Crow, J., Rushby, J., Struss, P.: Model-based reconfiguration: Diagnosis and recovery (1994)
12. de Alfaro, L., Henzinger, T., Majumdar, R.: Discounting the Future in Systems Theory. In: Baeten, J.C.M., Lenstra, J.K., Parrow, J., Woeginger, G.J. (eds.) ICALP 2003. LNCS, vol. 2719, pp. 1022–1037. Springer, Heidelberg (2003)
13. de Alfaro, L., Majumdar, R.: Quantitative solution of omega-regular games. In: STOC 2001, pp. 675–683. ACM Press (2001)
14. Etessami, K., Kwiatkowska, M., Vardi, M., Yannakakis, M.: Multi-objective model checking of Markov decision processes. Logical Methods in Computer Science 4(4), 1–21 (2008)
15. Filieri, A., Ghezzi, C., Tamburrelli, G.: Run-time efficient probabilistic model checking. In: Proc. ICSE 2011, pp. 341–350. ACM, New York (2011)
16. Filieri, A., Ghezzi, C., Tamburrelli, G.: A formal approach to adaptive software: continuous assurance of non-functional requirements. Formal Aspects of Computing 24, 163–186 (2012)
17. Forejt, V., Kwiatkowska, M., Parker, D.: Pareto curves for probabilistic model checking. In: Proc. 10th International Symposium on Automated Technology for Verification and Analysis (ATVA 2012). LNCS. Springer (to appear, 2012)
18. Giro, S., Rabe, M.: Verification of partial-information probabilistic systems using counterexample-guided refinements. In: Proc. 10th International Symposium on Automated Technology for Verification and Analysis (ATVA 2012). LNCS. Springer (to appear, 2012)
19. Kwiatkowska, M.: Quantitative verification: Models, techniques and tools. In: Proc. 6th joint meeting of the European Software Engineering Conference and the ACM SIGSOFT Symposium on the Foundations of Software Engineering (ESEC/FSE), pp. 449–458. ACM Press (September 2007)
20. Kwiatkowska, M., Norman, G., Parker, D.: PRISM 4.0: Verification of Probabilistic Real-Time Systems. In: Gopalakrishnan, G., Qadeer, S. (eds.) CAV 2011. LNCS, vol. 6806, pp. 585–591. Springer, Heidelberg (2011)
21. Kwiatkowska, M., Parker, D., Qu, H.: Incremental quantitative verification for Markov decision processes. In: Proc. DSN-PDS 2011, pp. 359–370. IEEE (2011)
22. Oreizy, P., Medvidovic, N., Taylor, R.N.: Runtime software adaptation: framework, approaches, and styles. In: Proc. Companion of ICSE 2008, pp. 899–910. ACM (2008)
23. PRISM-games, http://www.prismmodelchecker.org/games/
24. Sommerville, I., Cliff, D., Calinescu, R., Keen, J., Kelly, T., Kwiatkowska, M., McDermid, J., Paige, R.: Large-scale Complex IT Systems. Communications of the ACM 55(7), 71–77 (2012)
25. Stoller, S.D., Bartocci, E., Seyster, J., Grosu, R., Havelund, K., Smolka, S.A., Zadok, E.: Runtime Verification with State Estimation. In: Khurshid, S., Sen, K. (eds.) RV 2011. LNCS, vol. 7186, pp. 193–207. Springer, Heidelberg (2012)
26. Yabandeh, M., Knezevic, N., Kostic, D., Kuncak, V.: Crystalball: predicting and preventing inconsistencies in deployed distributed systems. In: Proceedings of the 6th USENIX Symposium on Networked Systems Design and Implementation, NSDI 2009, pp. 229–244. USENIX Association, Berkeley (2009)

Evolution, Adaptation, and the Quest for Incrementality*

Carlo Ghezzi

Politecnico di Milano
Dipartimento di Elettronica e Informazione
DeepSE Group
Piazza Leonardo da Vinci, 32, 20133 Milano (MI), Italy
carlo.ghezzi@polimi.it

Abstract. Software is constantly evolving. Evolution becomes necessary to respond to changes that may occur in the requirements and/or in the environment in which it is embedded. A consequence of changes is that several activities (such as analysis, verification, code generation, deployment) need to be redone, over and over. This paper focuses on verification. Incrementality comes into play because often changes are local to restricted parts. In order to save time, it would be beneficial if instead of redoing activities from scratch after each change, the results of previous processing may be reused and composed with the results of processing restricted portions of the changed software. Incrementality becomes even more necessary when changes occur at runtime and the software itself is responsible for reacting in a self-managed manner. In this setting, the processing that needs to be performed after each change is subject to severe time constraints. The paper is a position statement on incrementality in the context of self-adaptive systems. It starts by motivating the need for incrementality and then reviews three main approaches to incremental verification that have been proposed earlier, compares their potential, and outlines promising research directions.

1 Introduction

Modern software systems are embedded in an increasingly dynamic and open world [10], which is a source of continuous change. The requirements the system is expected to satisfy change because the goals one tries to achieve through the system change over time. The domain assumptions upon which the software is built may also change, and the change may lead to violations of the requirements. The consequence of these exogenous changes is that the software system is also required to change in order to fulfil its goals.

This phenomenon is traditionally known as *software evolution*. Its initial recognition dates back to the 1970s (see [5,27]). In the recent years, however, change became even more pervasive and manifested itself in new forms. Changes

---
* This research has been partially funded by the European Commission, Programme IDEAS-ERC, Project 227977-SMScom.

R. Calinescu and D. Garlan (Eds.): Monterey Workshop 2012, LNCS 7539, pp. 369–379, 2012.
© Springer-Verlag Berlin Heidelberg 2012

occur at runtime and must be handled at runtime. Indeed, there is a need for systems that can recognize changes and react to them in a self-managed manner, as they are running and providing service. The goal of *self-adaptive software* leads to the notion of *software adaptation* as a new form of software evolution.

Software engineering has long been concerned with supporting software evolution. Research has been focusing on developing design methods that would facilitate software evolution. The foundational work by David Parnas on *design for change* [28] lead to the notions of modularity, encapsulation, interface abstractions, contracts, and so on. Languages—object- and then aspect-oriented— were also invented to effectively support program changes.

There has been also research on supporting change through incremental methods and tools. The systematic design of a software system, in fact, goes through a number of steps, which generate certain artifacts. Typically, high-level models are developed, analyzed, and transformed into increasingly more detailed descriptions and verified against certain properties. Eventually, an executable form is generated and deployed for execution. A change in the requirements or in the domain assumptions implies that the development process needs to be revisited to accommodate changes. A naive approach would consist of viewing the changes as defining a new system. An incremental approach instead would try to characterize exactly what changed and reuse as much as possible of the results of previous processing steps in the steps that must be replayed after the change. The main motivation is of course time efficiency. Time is in fact a very critical factor in change management. It is very important in the case of software evolution, to support timely development of new versions of an existing system. Because many modern systems are large, redoing the processing from scratch after each change may in fact have a severe impact on the development process. Time becomes even more important in the case of adaptation, because changes in the running system may be subject to very tight time constraints to react in order to prevent requirements violations.

Existing approaches to incrementality are unfortunately still partial, rather ad-hoc, and only cover a few steps of software development. In this paper, we argue that in order to support software evolution, we should revisit all steps of the development process with the goal of making them incremental. This becomes a fundamental issue if we wish to support software adaptation. As we will motivate in Section 2, adaptive software requires that certain activities that are normally conceived as off-line development steps must extend their scope to runtime, to provide full support to self-adaptive reactions. But to in order to comply with the tight time constraints that characterize the runtime environment, execution efficiency becomes very critical, and therefore it asks for incrementality.

This paper is a position statement on incrementality in the development of adaptive software, focusing on analysis and verification activities. In this context, the goal of incrementality may be stated as follows: Let S be a system and let P be a property against which S has been verified. A change is a new pair $\langle S', P' \rangle$. An incremental verification reuses partial results of the analysis of S against P

to analyze S' against P'. The main objective is to improve time efficiency of verification.

The goal of this position statement is to provide arguments that support this view, mostly based on the author's past and current work and planned future research. As such, it lacks completeness of the analysis of related work and avoids entering into technical details of the presented techniques, which can be found in referenced papers. The paper is organized as follows. Section 2 provides more background discussion on change, evolution, and adaptation and how they affect verification. Section 3 discusses three main approaches to incremental verification. Finally, Section 4 outlines a possible research agenda and draws some conclusions.

2   Motivations

A software system is built to satisfy certain *requirements* R, which derive from some overall *goals* G. The software system is embedded in an environment (also called *domain*) whose properties D must be understood in order to derive the software *specification* S, which must be satisfied by the software system to ensure that the requirements R are actually met. According to M. Jackson and P. Zave ([20,30]), the software engineers who are responsible for deriving S and implementing a system that satisfies S must fulfill a satisfaction argument, expresed as $S, D \models R$, which can be read as:

> *If the specification defined by S is satisfied by the software and the domain properties D hold and both S and D are satisfied and consistent with each other, then the requirements R are satisfied by the system.*

The satisfaction argument must be fulfilled by software engineers when the system is initially developed. This is normally achieved by reasoning on suitable *models* of the software system (which correspond to S) and of the environment (which correspond to D) and providing convincing arguments that these entail satisfaction of R. Because of possible changes, however, these arguments are very fragile, and may be broken whenever R and/or D change. R may change because the goals change over time, for example due to turbulence in the stakeholders' world. D may change because some of the assumptions made initially later change, or because the behavior of the environment we are dealing with intrinsically changes. In many practical cases, it is possible to predict at development time what in the environment may change at runtime. For example, we may know that in a mobile application the kind of localization method may change depending on whether the user will be indoor or outdoor. Some other times, certain environment properties that may affect the behavior of the application are hard to predict exactly at design time. As an example, the access rate to certain functions from end-users, which may affect the overall requested response time, may be difficult to predict when the system is initially designed: they may change, for example in certain seasonal peak conditions.

In all the previous cases, the assumptions D made by designers when the system is initially developed may be invalidated at runtime, and may continue to change, when the system is operational. In all these cases, the reasons that may require changes in the system are discovered dynamically, by observing the running system. This is the situation in which adaptation comes into play. Adaptation deals with changes in the environment that may be detected and can be handled in a self-managed manner[1]. The application itself must be capable of monitoring the data that may indicate a change in the environment's behavior. Often, the collected data must be abstracted —e.g., through a machine-learning step— into higher-level phenomena on which the software itself can reason to understand whether an adaptation is required to continue to satisfy the requirements. And finally —if necessary— the adaptation must take place as the system is running.

In previous work [4,7], it has been shown that in order to support the above reasoning features, a model of the system and of the environment must be kept alive at runtime. Models at runtime must be checked to prove the same satisfaction arguments that were verified at design time and may now be violated at runtime, leading to an adaptation. The need for runtime verification to possibly detect requirements violation and decide proper reactions asks for efficient verification procedures, which must decide within stringent time constraints. Often,the very nature of the application requires self-adaptation (and hence verification) to be completed within hard deadlines. Because runtime changes are by their nature incremental (only a few phenomena change at each time point) and because changes may occur very frequently, the opportunities for incrementality should be fully exploited.

Although our main motivations originate from the need for continuous adaptation at run time, incrementality would be highly beneficial also in the context of agile software development and explorative design, where change is an intrinsic and distinctive feature.

3   Approaches

In this section we review three approaches to incrementality. The review is not meant to be complete, in the sense of coverage of all possible approaches that were proposed in the past. Also, it does not aim at providing a taxonomy of possible approaches. It does, however, try to provide a perspective in which the author's past and future work in this area can be positioned. The approaches we are going to present fall under the following three broad categories: incrementality by change encapsulation, incrementality by change anticipation, and syntax-driven incrementality.

---

[1] The reader may refer to [6] for an excellent discussion of the precise meaning of the term *adaptive software*.

3.1   Incrementality by Change Encapsulation

The first approach we discuss is a direct consequence of design for change. It applies compositional reasoning to a modularized system through an approach that commonly is called *assume-guarantee*. The system is viewed as a parallel composition of modules, each of which has to guarantee a certain property, that corresponds to its *contract* subscribed with the other modules. The key idea of *assume-guarantee reasoning* [22,29] is that we show that module M_1 guarantees certain properties P_1 on the assumption that module M_2 delivers certain properties P_2, and vice versa for M_2, and then claim that the system composed of M_1 and M_2 (i.e., both running and interacting together) guarantees P_1 and P_2 unconditionally. Verification methods of this kind are called compositional because they allow one to reason about M_1 and M_2 separately and deduce properties about the parallel composition of the two modules $M_1 \| M_2$ without having to reason about the composed system directly. This direction is perhaps the most widely studied in the literature and leads in general to compositional approaches that can help dominate the complexity of reasoning on a large system.

Assume-guarantee approaches can be applied to manage verification incrementally. That is, whenever the effect of a change can be *encapsulated* within the boundary of a module (i.e., that module, after the change that affected it, can be proved to continue to guarantee its contract property), the other modules are not affected, and their verification does not need to be redone. Success of this approach depends on how well the initial design that defined the module boundaries ensures that anticipated possible changes do not percolate through the module's interface, affecting its guaranteed property (i.e., its contract). Compositional reasoning fails whenever the consequence of a change is that a module does not guarantee the specified property any more. Often, in fact, the effect of certain changing phenomena care cross-cutting. As a final remark, because if its reliance on the modular structure of the system, incrementality by change encapsulation is intrinsically a large-grain technique. As such, it only partly fits the requirements of runtime adaptation.

3.2   Incrementality by Change Anticipation

The second approach we describe is also based on anticipating the changes that may occur, but it does not rely on the modular structure. It is not necessary to state a-priori boundaries to prevent change propagation and it does not suffer from limitations due to percolation of change effects through interfaces. The approach is based on the concept of *partial evaluation* (PE), initially proposed by [12]. PE was originally defined for programs, and supports program specialization when some input values are known statically (i.e., before runtime).

PE can be intuitively defined as follows: Let P be a program, which defines a function from an input domain I to an output domain O ($P : I \to O$). Suppose that I can be partitioned in two subsets, I_s and I_d, where I_s is the set of input data that are known statically, before runtime. Partial evaluation transforms the program P into a new program $\hat{P}$, called *residual program*, by precomputing all static input before runtime. The residual program is more specialized and it is executed more efficiently than the original program.

Partial evaluation meets incremental change management quite naturally: the binding to concrete information that is known before runtime can be propagated through the program. The method postpones to runtime evaluation only the part that depends on runtime information (the residual program).

The principle of partial evaluation can be generalized to a much wider context than just programs. For example, we have been working, and still are, on *incremental probabilistic model checking* through parameterization[2]. The artifacts we focus on in this work are Markov models, which may be used to represent – and reason about – nonfunctional properties of systems, expressed in a probabilistic setting. Examples of such properties are reliability, performance, or costs of any kinds (including, for example, energy consumption). For the sake of simplicity, let us consider a specific formalism: *Discrete Time Markov Chains* (DTMCs). A DTMC can be viewed as a finite state machine where each transition is labeled by a probability value that represents the probability that the transition is taken to exit the state (of course, the sum of the probabilities associated with the transitions existing any given state must be equal to 1.)

A DTMC can be verified against a property the model is expected to satisfy, expressed in a temporal logic language, such as PCTL [3]. Verification can be performed by a model checker (notable examples are PRISM [25] and MRMC [23]). Suppose now that some changes occur in the world which imply that the model also has to change. We assume here that changes only affect the probabilities associated with the transitions. A non-incremental approach implies that verification through model checking should be applied to the modified model, and re-applied after any subsequent change from scratch. The incremental approach we have been working on ([14]) is called *parametric*. This means that the transitions representing phenomena that can change are labeled by variables, not constants. Constants model phenomena that are fully known before execution and cannot change, whereas variables model changeable phenomena. Evaluation of the required PCTL properties on the model (which contains constant and variable parts) is a partial evaluation, which involves both numeric and symbolic processing. The result is a (polynomial) formula that represents the residual verification condition corresponding to the partially evaluated PCTL property. This verification condition is kept and used at runtime to support continuous verification. In fact, as the real values become known at runtime, the evaluation of the verification condition can tell us whether the system behaves as specified or not. The proposed method is extremely efficient at runtime, at the obvious expense of a high pre-runtime complexity, which we are generally willing to pay to achieve runtime efficiency[3].

---

[2] Other approaches to incremental analysis of Markov models are described by [26,9,18].

[3] The design-time complexity heavily depends on the number of variables (i.e., changeable phenomena).

Let us move on a more concrete ground, to provide glimpse of the practical use of the approach. A DTMC can be used to model a system from a reliability viewpoint. The paths on the state diagram from the initial to the final states represent the possible different use cases. Final states are states having a self-transition labeled with probability 1. They are also called *absorbing states*. Some of these absorbing states represent *success*, some represent *failure*. The probabilities used to label transitions represent domain assumptions about distributions of user requests to the system or the expected probability of successful completion (vs. failure) of certain computational steps. For example, the DTMC in Figure 1, taken from [17], models an e-commerce system, which integrates external services for user authentication (offering *Login* and *Logout* operations), normal shipping of goods (operation *NrmShipping*), express shipping (operation *ExpShipping*) and payment (operation *CheckOut*). The DTMC shows that these operations, offered by external service providers, may fail: for example, *Login* and *Logout* fail with probability 0.03, leading to the final state *FailedLg*. The DTMC also shows that after successful login, users are recognized as belonging to two possible customer categories, *ReturningCustomer* or *NewCustomer*, that differ in terms of quality of service to be guaranteed by the e-commerce application. The expected usage profile is that the probability that a user is a *ReturningCustomer* is 0.35. Similarly, expected usage profiles give us the values of probabilities that *ExpShipping* is chosen instead of *NrmShipping*. Finally, suppose that the global requirements to be satisfied by the model include the following ones:

- $\mathcal{P}_{>0.8}$ [$\Diamond$ $s = 16$]: the probability of eventually reaching state 16, which corresponds to the successful completion of the session (see Figure 1) is greater than 0.8.
- $\mathcal{P}_{<0.035}$ [$\Diamond$ $s = 13$ $\{s = 1\}$]: the probability of eventually reaching state 13 (representing a failed express shipping) given that the DTMC starts its execution in state 1 (*Returning Customer*) is less than 0.035.
- $\mathcal{P}_{<0.06}$ [$\Diamond$ $s = 5$]: the probability of eventually reaching the *FailedLg* state is less than 0.06.

By using the probabilistic model checker PRISM [25] on the DTMC, it is easy to verify the satisfaction of the requirements. If, however, we assume that usage profiles actually may change at runtime, we may replace the constants that label exit transitions from states 2, 14 with x and $1 - x$, respectively (and do similarly for states 7, and 9). Verification of the above PCTL formulae on the model yield polynomial formulae to be evaluated on the variables we introduced to label transitions. These polynomials are carried on to runtime to support runtime verification.

A main limitation of this approach is that it can deal with a limited class of variability; in the DTMC case, the structure of the model cannot change, just transition labels.

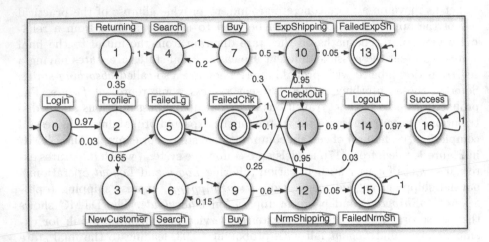

Fig. 1. Example DTMC Model (taken from [17]), representing initial assumptions. To anticipate possible future changes, transitions exiting states 2, 7, 9, and 14 may be labeled by variables.

3.3 Syntax-Driven Incrementality

Syntax-driven incrementality assumes that the artifact to be analyzed incrementally has a syntactic structure that is described by a formal grammar. Analysis algorithms are then developed as incremental syntax-driven algorithms. The best known and most basic examples of syntax-driven incrementality can be found in the domain of syntax-driven compilation, and date back to the 1970s. The author, together with D. Mandrioli, developed a theory of *incremental parsing* [15,16]. The goal of this past work was to improve the time efficiency of syntax analysis of programs by allowing a parser to reuse knowledge from a previous analysis (the saved syntax tree) in order to limit the amount of re-analysis that needs to be done after any change. Changes may be insertions and/or deletions of text in the program. Incremental parsing algorithms can automatically detect the minimum portions of text that need to be re-parsed and can then produce a new syntax tree that weaves the newly built portion with reused portions of the previous one. Incremental algorithms have also been devised for the semantic evaluations that can be expressed in terms of *attribute grammars* [21].

The benefit of syntax-driven incrementality is that the possible changes are not constrained a-priori in any sense. The incremental algorithm is able to automatically decide which is the minimum portion of text that needs to be re-analyzed (i.e., the new portion of parse tree that needs to be built). This also automatically determines the portion of semantic attribute evaluation that needs to be performed.

In [11], we applied attribute grammars to the verification of workflows. Assume that an implementation of a high-level model like the one shown in Figure 1) is given in a workflow language, like BPEL [1], which orchestrates a number of services. These services, which provide authentication, payment, and shipping, are characterized by their failure profiles, which take into account multiple failure mode. The usage profile related with the selection of paths of the workflow is also given. The goal is to evaluate the overall reliability of the workflow that coordinates the independent services. The failure profile of the composition is described in terms of an attribute grammar that allows the workflow's failure profile to be synthesized as an attribute of the entire workflow (the program). The interesting finding of this paper is that a verification process (in the specific example, reliability analysis) can be expressed as an attribute grammar and executed as attribute evaluation. The next natural research step, which we are currently undertaking, is making this evaluation incremental. In the specific example, if the failure profile of certain components changes over time, the incremental algorithm is able to update the overall reliability attribute of the workflow by recomputing only parts of the attributes, reusing the values computed earlier for other unchanged parts, and then propagating attribute values through the tree up to the root. The same algorithm would be incremental if changes are applied to the structure of the workflow dynamically [13].

Notice that in a syntax-driven approach changes can be of any kind. The change can only be in some elementary attribute (the failure profile of an external component), in which case only the attribute evaluation process needs to be performed incrementally. The change can also be in the workflow, with the addition/deletion of parts. In this latter case, incrementality of syntax analysis determines the portion of the syntax tree to be newly built and the portion to be reused, and attributes are evaluated incrementally according to the changes in the syntactic structure.

4 Future Work and Conclusions

This position paper has given motivations for incremental strategies to support continuous verification of evolving and, in particular, self-adaptive software. It also went through three general approaches that can help moving in the direction of incrementality: incrementality by change encapsulation, incrementality by change anticipation, and syntax-driven incrementality. The three classes do not cover all current and previous work on incremental verification. Moreover, other work than the one presented here exists in each class. Although an extensive state-of-art analysis falls beyond the scope of this position statement, a few references to other relevant work are given next.

An assume-guarantee approach to probabilistic model checking of Markov models is presented in [26]. Parametric model checking of Markov models has also been studied by [9] and [18]. As for contributions to incremental program model checking, one may refer to [19,8,24].

As for future work, significant research advances are needed, for example, to further exploit the approach we called "incrementality by change anticipation" in cases where we are currently unable to generate a closed verification formula at development time (e.g., for models described as Continuous Time Markov

Chains and properties expressed in CSL [2]). More work is also needed to assess the potentials of "syntax-driven incrementality". We are actually engaged in this line of research, and our goal is to show that most existing analysis algorithms can be expressed as syntax-driven algorithms. As such, they can benefit from the incrementality that is inherent in the approach.

Another interesting research can be address the issue of better understanding and possibly deriving a taxonomy of different approaches to incrementality, clearly identifying the benefits and pitfalls, and clarifying where the different approach overlap and how they can be combined.

Finally, we would like to remark that the all the approaches we discussed in this paper date back to seminal theoretical work that was done in the 1970s. They can provide now mature results to solve practical problems that are becoming crucial due to continuous evolution and runtime adaptation.

Acknowledgments. Many contributed to shaping these ideas and provided useful comments on the initial draft. I would like to thank, in particular, Dino Mandrioli, Raffaela Mirandola, Domenico Bianculli, Giordano Tamburrelli and Antonio Filieri. The participants in the Monterey workshop provided comments and engaged me in very useful discussions that will guide my future work. The anonymous reviewers also provided very useful comments.

References

1. Alves, A., Arkin, A., Askary, S., Bloch, B., Curbera, F., Goland, Y., Kartha, N., Sterling, König, D., Mehta, V., Thatte, S., van der Rijn, D., Yendluri, P., Yiu, A.: Web services business process execution language version 2.0. OASIS Committee Draft (May 2006)
2. Baier, C., Haverkort, B., Hermanns, H., Katoen, J.-P.: Model-checking algorithms for continuous-time markov chains. IEEE Transactions on Software Engineering 29, 524–541 (2003)
3. Baier, C., Katoen, J.-P.: Principles of Model Checking. The MIT Press (2008)
4. Baresi, L., Ghezzi, C.: The disappearing boundary between development-time and run-time. In: FoSER 2010, New York, USA (2010)
5. Belady, L., Lehman, M.: A model of large program development. IBM Systems Journal (1976)
6. Bruni, R., Corradini, A., Gadducci, F., Lluch Lafuente, A., Vandin, A.: A Conceptual Framework for Adaptation. In: de Lara, J., Zisman, A. (eds.) FASE 2012. LNCS, vol. 7212, pp. 240–254. Springer, Heidelberg (2012)
7. Calinescu, R., Ghezzi, C., Kwiatkowska, M., Mirandola, R.: Self-adaptive software needs quantitative verification at runtime. Communications of the ACM (accepted for publication)
8. Conway, C.L., Namjoshi, K.S., Dams, D.R., Edwards, S.A.: Incremental Algorithms for Inter-procedural Analysis of Safety Properties. In: Etessami, K., Rajamani, S.K. (eds.) CAV 2005. LNCS, vol. 3576, pp. 449–461. Springer, Heidelberg (2005)
9. Daws, C.: Symbolic and Parametric Model Checking of Discrete-Time Markov Chains. In: Liu, Z., Araki, K. (eds.) ICTAC 2004. LNCS, vol. 3407, pp. 280–294. Springer, Heidelberg (2005)

10. Di Nitto, E., Ghezzi, C., Metzger, A., Papazoglou, M., Pohl, K.: A journey to highly dynamic, self-adaptive service-based applications. In: ASE (2008)
11. Distefano, S., Filieri, A., Ghezzi, C., Mirandola, R.: A compositional method for reliability analysis of workflows affected by multiple failure modes. In: Proceedings of the 14th International ACM Sigsoft Symposium on Component Based Software Engineering, CBSE 2011, pp. 149–158. ACM, New York (2011)
12. Ershov, A.: On the partial computation principle. Information Processing Letters (1977)
13. Filieri, A., Ghezzi, C., Mandrioli, D.: Sidecar: Syntax-driven incremental compositional verification (unpublished internal report, 2012)
14. Filieri, A., Ghezzi, C., Tamburrelli, G.: Run-time efficient probabilistic model checking. In: Proceedings of the 33rd International Conference on Software Engineering (2011)
15. Ghezzi, C., Mandrioli, D.: Incremental parsing. ACM Transactions on Programming Languages and Systems (1979)
16. Ghezzi, C., Mandrioli, D.: Augmenting parsers to support incrementality. Journal of the ACM (1980)
17. Ghezzi, C., Tamburrelli, G.: Reasoning on non-functional requirements for integrated services. In: RE 2009. Proceedings of the International Conference on Requirements Engineering (2009)
18. Hahn, E.M., Hermanns, H., Zhang, L.: Probabilistic Reachability for Parametric Markov Models. In: Păsăreanu, C.S. (ed.) Model Checking Software. LNCS, vol. 5578, pp. 88–106. Springer, Heidelberg (2009)
19. Henzinger, T.A., Jhala, R., Majumdar, R., Sanvido, M.A.A.: Extreme Model Checking. In: Dershowitz, N. (ed.) Verification: Theory and Practice. LNCS, vol. 2772, pp. 332–358. Springer, Heidelberg (2004)
20. Jackson, M., Zave, P.: Deriving specifications from requirements: An example. In: ICSE 1995, p. 1005 (1995)
21. Jalili, F.: A general incremental evaluator for attribute grammars. Science of Computer Programming (1985)
22. Jones, C.: Tentative steps toward a development method for interfering programs. ACM Transactions on Programming Languages and Systems (1983)
23. Katoen, J.-P., Khattri, M., Zapreev, I.S.: A Markov reward model checker. In: QEST, pp. 243–244. IEEE Computer Society, Los Alamos (2005)
24. Krishnamurthi, S., Fisler, K.: Foundations of incremental aspect model-checking. ACM Trans. Softw. Eng. Methodol. 16(2) (2007)
25. Kwiatkowska, M., Norman, G., Parker, D.: Prism 2.0: a tool for probabilistic model checking. In: Proceedings. First International Conference on the Quantitative Evaluation of Systems, QEST 2004, pp. 322–323 (2004)
26. Kwiatkowska, M., Norman, G., Parker, D., Qu, H.: Assume-Guarantee Verification for Probabilistic Systems. In: Esparza, J., Majumdar, R. (eds.) TACAS 2010. LNCS, vol. 6015, pp. 23–37. Springer, Heidelberg (2010)
27. Lehman, M.: Life cycles, and laws of software evolution. Proceedings of the IEEE (1980)
28. Parnas, D.: On the criteria to be used in decomposing systems into modules. Communications of the ACM (1972)
29. Rushby, J.: An Overview of Formal Verification for the Time-Triggered Architecture. In: Damm, W., Olderog, E.-R. (eds.) FTRTFT 2002. LNCS, vol. 2469, pp. 83–105. Springer, Heidelberg (2002)
30. Zave, P., Jackson, M.: Four dark corners of requirements engineering. ACM Trans. Softw. Eng. Methodology (1997)

Independent Implementability of Viewpoints

Thomas A. Henzinger[1],[*] and Dejan Ničković[2]

[1] IST Austria, Klosterneuburg, Austria
[2] AIT Austrian Institute of Technology, Vienna, Austria

Abstract. Interface theories provide a formal framework for component-based development of software and hardware which supports the incremental design of systems and the independent implementability of components. These capabilities are ensured through mathematical properties of the parallel composition operator and the refinement relation for components. More recently, a conjunction operation was added to interface theories in order to provide support for handling multiple viewpoints, requirements engineering, and component reuse. Unfortunately, the conjunction operator does not allow independent implementability in general.

In this paper, we study conditions that need to be imposed on interface models in order to enforce independent implementability with respect to conjunction. We focus on multiple viewpoint specifications and propose a new compatibility criterion between two interfaces, which we call orthogonality. We show that orthogonal interfaces can be refined separately, while preserving both orthogonality and composability with other interfaces. We illustrate the independent implementability of different viewpoints with a FIFO buffer example.

1 Introduction

Component-based design is a common design methodology, where complex systems are developed by assembling individual components. It usually involves a combination of *bottom-up* and *top-down* design techniques. In bottom-up design, the designer assembles the overall system by integrating already available components. Top-down design starts from the specification of the overall system that is decomposed and refined into requirements for the subsequent design stages.

Interface theories [6] were developed as a formal framework that supports both bottom-up and top-down approaches in component-based design. An *interface* is an abstract specification that describes the interaction of a component with its environment. In particular, an interface captures both the *assumptions* that the component makes about its environment, and the *guarantees* that the component provides when used in the intended design context. In order to support bottom-up design, interface theories provide a *composition* operator that satisfies

---

[*] This work was supported in part by the ERC Advanced Grant QUAREM (Quantitative Reactive Modeling) and by the FWF National Research Network RISE (Rigorous Systems Engineering).

R. Calinescu and D. Garlan (Eds.): Monterey Workshop 2012, LNCS 7539, pp. 380–395, 2012.

the *incremental design* property. Two interfaces are *compatible* for composition if their port types match and there exists a design context in which they can interact without violating their mutual guarantees. Incremental design requires the possibility of checking the compatibility of two interfaces and composing them, without considering the precise design context in which the composition will be used. The composition operator is both *associative* and *commutative*, thus ensuring that compatible interfaces can be developed independently and composed in any order. In top-down design, the notion of *refinement* plays a central role. This design flow starts with a system-level interface that is iteratively decomposed and refined into sub-system interfaces, until implementations of respective components are obtained. Top-down design, illustrated in Figure 1, is subject to the *independent implementability* property, that requires the possibility of refining compatible interfaces separately, while still maintaining compatibility between them.

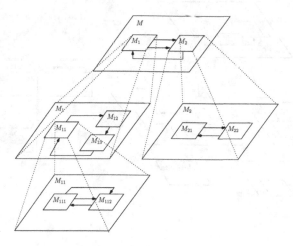

Fig. 1. Top-down design

The properties of the composition operator and the refinement relation, provide necessary basic support for bottom-up and top-level design in interface theories. However, composition alone does not cover all the aspects that are encountered in component-based design, such as:

1. Specification of component's *multiple viewpoints*, where each viewpoint is modeled as an interface, and specifies a particular (behavioral, timing, power consumption, etc.) aspect of the component;
2. *Requirement engineering*, by formal modeling of requirement documents that consist of a conjunction of individual requirements;
3. *Component reuse* in different parts of a design.

In order to provide additional support for the above aspects of component based design, the *conjunction* operator was introduced in [8], in the context of stateless and Moore interfaces [4]. The conjunction is a partial function defined on pairs of interfaces and is the most general refinement of individual interfaces, i.e. the greatest lower bound in the refinement lattice on interfaces. The conjunction between two interfaces is defined if they are *consistent*[1], i.e. if their input variables do not overlap with the output variables and the output guarantees do not contradict each other. The conjunction operator was subsequently added to modal interfaces [10], assume/guarantee contracts [2] and synchronous relational interfaces [12]. Top-down design with conjunction is illustrated in Figure 2 in the context of multiple viewpoints and component reuse, where components can be reused in different parts of a design, without being restricted to be trees of components, but they can also be directed acyclic graphs.

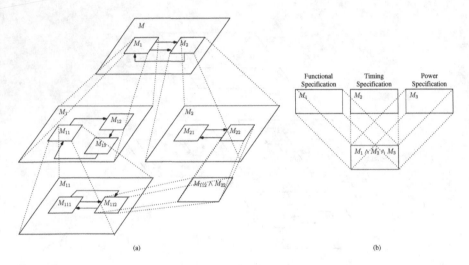

Fig. 2. Top-down design with conjunction for: (a) component reuse, and (b) multiple viewpoints

The conjunction of specifications plays an important role in top-down design. A natural requirement for the conjunction operator would be to support independent implementability and allow separate stepwise refinement of individual interfaces. Unfortunately, conjunction does not satisfy the independent implementability property, in general. We illustrate this point with the following example.

Example 1. Let M, M' and N be three stateless interfaces shown in Figure 3. The input variables of M and N do not overlap with their respective output variables. Furthermore, the output guarantees of M and N do not contradict, i.e. there always exists an output ($y = 2$), such that both the guarantees of M

---

[1] In [8], consistency is called shared refinability.

and N are satisfied. It follows that M and N are consistent. Moreover, M' refines M because the two interfaces accept the same inputs and the output guarantee of M' implies the output guarantee of M. However, M' and N are not consistent, because the conjunction of their output guarantees is unsatisfiable, hence the conjunction of M' and N is not defined. It follows that M and N cannot be refined independently, given that the consistency property is not preserved by refinement.

$$M : \begin{cases} \text{var:} \begin{cases} \text{in: } x \ : \ \mathbb{B} \\ \text{out: } y \ : \ \mathbb{N} \end{cases} \\ \text{A: TRUE} \\ \text{G: } y \leq 2 \end{cases} \quad M' : \begin{cases} \text{var:} \begin{cases} \text{in: } x \ : \ \mathbb{B} \\ \text{out: } y \ : \ \mathbb{N} \end{cases} \\ \text{A: TRUE} \\ \text{G: } y < 2 \end{cases} \quad N : \begin{cases} \text{var:} \begin{cases} \text{in: } x \ : \ \mathbb{B} \\ \text{out: } y \ : \ \mathbb{N} \end{cases} \\ \text{A: TRUE} \\ \text{G: } y \geq 2 \end{cases}$$

Fig. 3. Single-state interfaces M, M' and N: M and N are consistent, M' refines M, but M' and N are not consistent

In this paper, we study sufficient conditions that need to be imposed on stateless and Moore interfaces, in order to guarantee their independent implementability with respect to the conjunction operator. We focus in particular on the context where conjunction is used to combine multiple viewpoints of the same component. Independent implementability of viewpoints is a highly desirable requirement of an interface theory, because different aspects of a component are often specified and developed by different design teams, and are not effectively combined until a late stage in the design process. We first observe that different viewpoints of a component usually specify non-overlapping aspects, and the guarantees that are provided by individual viewpoints are rarely conflicting. It follows that the notion of consistency is not well adapted to conjunction of viewpoints. We instead propose a different criterion, that we call *orthogonality*, for conjunction of two interfaces to be defined. We say that two interfaces are orthogonal if their input variables do not overlap with their output variables, and if the intersection of their output variables is empty. While this condition is not realistic for specifying multiple requirements of the same view of a component, we believe it is reasonable for expressing multiple view requirements. We show that for every two interfaces that are orthogonal, they can be refined separately, while maintaining orthogonality between them.

2   Stateless Interfaces

A stateless interface consists of a set of input and output variables, an input assumption predicate and an output guarantee predicate.

Definition 1 (Stateless interface). *A stateless interface* $M = \langle X^I, X^O, \varphi, \psi \rangle$ *consists of the following components:*

- X^I *and* X^O *are disjoint sets of* input *and* output *variables. We define* $X = X^I \cup X^O$;
- φ *is a predicate over* X^I *called* input assumption; *and*
- ψ *is a predicate over* X^O *called* output guarantee.

We require the stateless interface to be *well-formed*, i.e. to accept at least one input value and generate at least one output value.

2.1   Connection, Composition and Refinement

In this section, we define standard connection and parallel composition operators, as well as the refinement relation, as in [7], and recall the incremental design and independent implementability properties that are supported by stateless interfaces.

A connection consists of a set of interface variable pairs and defines which variables in an interface are interconnected after application of the connection operator. For all pairs, the first component is an output and the second component an input variable of the stateless interface to which the output is connected. Formally, we have the following:

Definition 2 (Connection). *A connection* θ *is a set of pairs* (x, y), *consisting of a* source *variable* x *and a* target *variable* y, *such that for all pairs* $(x, y), (x', y') \in \theta$, *if* $x \neq x'$, *then* $y \neq y'$.

We denote by $\mathcal{S}_\theta$ the set of source variables in θ, by $\mathcal{T}_\theta$ the set of target variables in θ, and by ρ_θ the predicate $\bigwedge_{(x,y)\in\theta}(x = y)$.

We say that a connection θ is *compatible* with a stateless interface M, if the following conditions hold: (1) the source variables in θ are all output variables of M; (2) the target variables in θ are all input variables in M; and (3) when source variables are connected to target variables, there exists a valuation of remaining input variables in M for which the assumption φ of M is satisfied for all values of output variables of M that satisfy the guarantee ψ of M.

Definition 3 (Compatibility for connection). *A stateless interface* $M = \langle X^I, X^O, \varphi, \psi \rangle$ *is compatible with a connection* θ *if the following conditions hold:*

- $\mathcal{S}_\theta \subseteq X^O$;
- $\mathcal{T}_\theta \subseteq X^I$;
- *the predicate* $\hat{\varphi} = \forall X^O. \forall \mathcal{T}_\theta.((\psi \wedge \rho_\theta) \rightarrow \varphi)$ *is satisfiable.*

Given an interface M and a connection θ such that M is compatible with θ, the result of applying θ to M is the stateless interface $M\theta = \langle \hat{X}^I, \hat{X}^O, \hat{\varphi}, \hat{\psi} \rangle$, where

- $\hat{X}^I = X^I \backslash T_\theta$;
- $\hat{X}^O = X^O \cup T_\theta$; and
- $\hat{\psi} = (\psi \wedge \rho_\theta)$

Example 2. The application of a connection θ to a stateless interface M is illustrated in Figure 4. In this example, $\theta = \{(z, x)\}$ and the predicate $\hat{\varphi} = (\forall x, z)((z < 2 \wedge z = x) \rightarrow (x < 3 \wedge y \neq 0))$ is satisfiable and can be simplified to $y \neq 0$.

$$M : \begin{cases} \text{var:} \begin{cases} \text{in: } x, y \ : \ \mathbb{N} \\ \text{out: } z \ : \ \mathbb{N} \end{cases} \\ \text{A: } x < 3 \wedge y \neq 0 \\ \text{G: } z < 2 \end{cases} \qquad M\theta : \begin{cases} \text{var:} \begin{cases} \text{in: } x \ : \ \mathbb{N} \\ \text{out: } y, z \ : \ \mathbb{N} \end{cases} \\ \text{A: } y \neq 0 \\ \text{G: } z < 2 \wedge x = z \end{cases}$$

Fig. 4. Stateless interfaces M and $M\theta$, where $\theta = \{(z, x)\}$

Theorem 1 ([7]). *Let M be a well-formed stateless interface and θ be a connection. If M is compatible with θ, then $M\theta$ is a well-formed stateless interface.*

Parallel composition operator supports combination of compatible stateless interfaces. We say that two stateless interfaces are compatible for parallel composition if (1) their output variables are disjoint; (2) the input variables of each stateless interface are disjoint of the output variables of the other stateless interface; and (3) the conjunction of their guaranteed is satisfiable.

Definition 4 (Compatibility for composition). *Two stateless interfaces $M = \langle X_M^I, X_M^O, \varphi_M, \psi_M \rangle$ and $N = \langle X_N^I, X_N^O, \varphi_N, \psi_N \rangle$ are compatible for parallel composition if*

- $X_M^O \cap X_N^O = \emptyset$;
- $X_M^I \cap X_N^O = X_N^I \cap X_M^O = \emptyset$; and
- $\varphi_M \wedge \varphi_N$ is satisfiable.

Formally, parallel composition of two compatible stateless interfaces is defined as follows:

Definition 5 (Parallel composition). *Given two stateless interfaces $M = \langle X_M^I, X_M^O, \varphi_M, \psi_M \rangle$ and $N = \langle X_N^I, X_N^O, \varphi_N, \psi_N \rangle$ which are compatible for parallel composition, their parallel composition is the interface $M \parallel N = \langle \hat{X}^I, \hat{X}^O, \hat{\varphi}, \hat{\psi} \rangle$, where*

- $\hat{X}^I = X_M^I \cup X_N^I$;
- $\hat{X}^O = X_M^O \cup X_N^O$;
- $\hat{\varphi} = (\varphi_M \wedge \varphi_N)$; and
- $\hat{\psi} = (\psi_M \wedge \psi_N)$.

Theorem 2 ([7]). *Let M and N be two well-formed stateless interfaces. If M and N are compatible for parallel composition, then $M \parallel N$ is a well-formed stateless interface.*

We say that a stateless interface N *refines* the stateless interface M if it has more permissive assumption and more restrictive guarantees.

Definition 6 (Refinement). *Given two well-formed stateless interfaces $M = \langle X_M^I, X_M^O, \varphi_M, \psi_M \rangle$ and $N = \langle X_N^I, X_N^O, \varphi_N, \psi_N \rangle$, we say that N refines M, denoted by $N \preceq M$, if*

- $(X_M^I \cup X_N^I) \cap (X_M^O \cup X_N^O) = \emptyset$;
- $\varphi_M \rightarrow \varphi_N$ *is valid; and*
- $\psi_N \rightarrow \psi_M$ *is valid.*

Following definitions of refinement, compatibility for connection, connection, compatibility for composition and parallel composition, we have that stateless interfaces satisfy the independent implementability with respect to both connection and composition, as stated in the following theorem.

Theorem 3 ([7]). *Let M and N be two well-formed stateless interfaces and θ be a connection. If $N \preceq M$ and M is compatible with θ, then N is compatible with θ and $N\theta \preceq M\theta$.*

Let M, N and S be three well-formed stateless interfaces such that $X_N \cap X_S \subseteq X_M$. If M and S are compatible for composition and $N \preceq M$, then N and S are compatible for composition and $N \parallel S \preceq M \parallel S$.

2.2   Conjunction

The conjunction $M \wedge N$ of two stateless interfaces M and N was introduced in [8] as an interface meant to work in two environments based on separate descriptions of each environment. The interface $M \wedge N$ allows inputs that satisfy assumptions of either M or N, and provides the guarantees of both M and N. In order to ensure that the conjunction of two interfaces is well-formed, the notion of consistency was introduced. Two stateless interfaces are said to be consistent if (1) the input variables do not overlap with the output variables and (2) their output guarantees do not contradict each other.

Definition 7 (Conjunction). *Given two consistent stateless interfaces $M = \langle X_M^I, X_M^O, \varphi_M, \psi_M \rangle$ and $N = \langle X_N^I, X_N^O, \varphi_N, \psi_N \rangle$, the conjunction of M and N is the stateless interface $M \wedge N = \langle \hat{X}^I, \hat{X}^O, \hat{\varphi}, \hat{\psi} \rangle$, where*

- $\hat{X}^I = X_M^I \cup X_N^I$;
- $\hat{X}^O = X_M^O \cup X_N^O$;
- $\hat{\varphi} = (\varphi_M \vee \varphi_N)$; *and*
- $\hat{\psi} = (\varphi_M \wedge \varphi_N)$.

Theorem 4 ([8]). *Let M and N be two well-formed stateless interfaces. If M and N are consistent, then $M \wedge N$ is a well-formed stateless interface.*

The conjunction of two stateless interfaces subsumes all behaviors of the given interfaces, as stated in the following theorem.

Theorem 5 ([8]). *Let M and N be two well-formed stateless interfaces. If M and N are consistent, then $M \wedge N \preceq M$ and $M \wedge N \preceq N$, and for all well-formed stateless interfaces S, if $S \preceq M$ and $S \preceq N$, then $S \preceq M \wedge N$.*

Unfortunately, conjunction does not support independent implementability of stateless interfaces, as demonstrated in Figure 3. The reason comes from the consistency condition between two stateless interfaces, that is not preserved by refinement. Given consistent stateless interfaces M and N, the output guarantees of M and N do not conflict by definition. However, another interface M' that refines M may strengthen its guarantees in a way that makes the output guarantees of M' and N conflicting. Thus, stateless interfaces M' and N may not be consistent. However, we observe that in the case that the conjunction operator is used to combine multiple viewpoints of the same component, the output variables of the individual viewpoints are usually disjoint, hence their output guarantees cannot contradict each other. In fact, the consistency between two stateless interfaces is not preserved by refinement. Following this observation, we propose a new condition between two stateless interfaces, that we call *orthogonality*.

Definition 8 (Orthogonality). *Let M and N be two well-formed stateless interfaces. We say that M and N are orthogonal if $(X_M^I \cup X_N^I) \cap (X_M^O \cup X_N^O) = \emptyset$ and $X_M^O \cap X_N^O = \emptyset$.*

We believe that in the context of multiple viewpoint specifications, the orthogonality is a realistic requirement. Note that while the output variables of two orthogonal interfaces are disjoint, the two interfaces are interacting with each other through common input variables. In the following lemma, we show that orthogonal interfaces are consistent.

Lemma 1. *Let M and N be two well-formed stateless interfaces. If M and N are orthogonal, then M and N are consistent.*

Proof. Assume that M and N are well-formed and orthogonal. It follows that both ψ_M and ψ_N are satisfiable. By definition, we have that ψ_M is a predicate over X_M^O and ψ_N is a predicate over X_N^O, and by assumption we have that $X_M^O \cap X_N^O = \emptyset$. It follows that there exists a valuation over $X_M^O \cup X_N^O$ that satisfies both ψ_M and ψ_N, hence $\hat{\psi}$ is also satisfiable.

□

Following Lemma 1, we are ready to state the result that establishes the independent implementatibility property for the conjunction operator between orthogonal stateless interfaces.

Theorem 6 (Independent implementability of conjunction). *Let M, N and S be three well-formed stateless interfaces such that $X_N^O \cap X_S = X_N \cap X_S^O = \emptyset$. If M and S are orthogonal and $N \preceq M$, then N and S are orthogonal and $N \wedge S \preceq M \wedge S$.*

Proof. Assume that M and S are orthogonal and $N \preceq M$. By Lemma 1, M and S are consistent, hence $M \wedge S$ is defined.

We have by definition of a stateless interface that (1) $X_N^I \cap X_N^O = X_S^I \cap X_S^O = \emptyset$. By the assumption that $X_N^O \cap X_S = \emptyset$ and $X_N \cap X_S^O = \emptyset$, we have that (2) $X_N^I \cap X_S^O = X_N^O \cap X_S^I = \emptyset$. By (1) and (2), it follows that $(X_N^I \cup X_S^I) \cap (X_N^O \cap X_S^O) = \emptyset$.

Furthermore, by the assumption that $X_N^O \cap X_S = \emptyset$, we have that $X_N^O \cap X_S^O = \emptyset$. It follows that N and S are orthogonal, hence by Lemma 1 consistent, and $N \wedge S$ is defined.

By the assumption, we have that (3) $N \preceq M$ and by Theorem 5, we have that (4) $N \wedge S \preceq N$. By (3) and (4), we have that (5) $N \wedge S \preceq M$. By Theorem 5, we have that (6) $N \wedge S \preceq S$. Finally, by (5), (6) and Theorem 5, we can conclude that $N \wedge S \preceq M \wedge S$. □

Example 3. Consider stateless interfaces M and N shown in Figure 5. The two interfaces do not share output variables, hence they are orthogonal. Stateless interface N' refines N, by constraining its guarantee predicate. It is not hard to see that the conjunction $M \wedge N'$ refines $M \wedge N$, illustrating the independent implementability property of the conjunction operator.

$$M : \begin{cases} \text{var:} \begin{cases} \text{in: } x \; : \; \mathbb{B} \\ \text{out: } y \; : \; \mathbb{N} \end{cases} \\ \text{A: TRUE} \\ \text{G: } y \leq 2 \end{cases} \quad N : \begin{cases} \text{var:} \begin{cases} \text{in: } x \; : \; \mathbb{B} \\ \text{out: } z \; : \; \mathbb{N} \end{cases} \\ \text{A: TRUE} \\ \text{G: } z \geq 0 \end{cases} \quad M \wedge N : \begin{cases} \text{var:} \begin{cases} \text{in: } x \; : \; \mathbb{B} \\ \text{out: } y, z \; : \; \mathbb{N} \end{cases} \\ \text{A: TRUE} \\ \text{G: } y \geq 2 \wedge z \geq 0 \end{cases}$$

$$N' : \begin{cases} \text{var:} \begin{cases} \text{in: } x \; : \; \mathbb{B} \\ \text{out: } z \; : \; \mathbb{N} \end{cases} \\ \text{A: TRUE} \\ \text{G: } z \bmod 2 = 0 \end{cases} \quad M \wedge N' : \begin{cases} \text{var:} \begin{cases} \text{in: } x \; : \; \mathbb{B} \\ \text{out: } y, z \; : \; \mathbb{N} \end{cases} \\ \text{A: TRUE} \\ \text{G: } y < 2 \wedge z \bmod 2 = 0 \end{cases}$$

Fig. 5. Stateless interfaces M, N and N': M and N are orthogonal, and $N' \preceq N$, hence M and N' are orthogonal and $M \wedge N' \preceq M \wedge N$

3   Moore Interfaces

In this section, we consider *Moore interfaces*, a synchronous interface model, that was first introduced in [4]. Moore interfaces have internal states, that are decorated with assumption predicates over input variables, and guarantee predicates over output variables. We consider Moore interfaces with deterministic transition relation, where transitions are guarded by predicates over input and output variables of the interface.

Definition 9 (Moore interface). *A Moore interface* $M = \langle X^I, X^O, Q, \hat{q}, \varphi, \psi, \rho \rangle$ *consists of the following components:*

- X^I *and* X^O *are disjoint sets of* input *and* output *variables. We define* $X = X^I \cup X^O$;
- Q *is a finite set of* locations, *and* $\hat{q} \in Q$ *is the* initial *location;*
- φ *is a labeling that associates with each location* $q \in Q$ *an input assumption predicate over* X^I;
- ψ *is a labeling that associates with each location* $q \in Q$ *an output guarantee predicate over* X^O;
- ρ *is a transition guard that associates with each pair of locations* $q, q' \in Q$ *a predicate* $\rho(q, q')$ *over* X.

Given a set X of variables, a *valuation* v over X is a function that assigns to each $x \in X$, a value $v(x)$ of the appropriate type. We denote by $\mathcal{V}[X]$, the set of all valuations v over X. Given a predicate φ on X, we write $v \models \varphi$ if the valuation v satisfies φ.

An *execution* of M is a sequence $q_0, v_0, q_1, \ldots, q_n, v_n, q_{n+1}$ of states $q_i \in Q$ and valuations $v_i \in \mathcal{V}[X]$ such that: (1) $q_0 = \hat{q}$ is the initial state of M, and (2) $v_i \models \varphi(q_i) \wedge \psi(q_i) \wedge \rho(q_i, q_{i+1})$. We say that the sequence $v_0, \ldots, v_n$ is the *trace* of M, and that the states $q_0, \ldots, q_{n+1}$ are *reachable* in M.

The Moore interfaces can in general be non-deterministic, or even block in some executions. Thus, we consider only *well-formed* interfaces, where the well-formedness criterion is defined as follows:

Definition 10 (Well-formedness). *A Moore interface* $M = \langle X^I, X^O, Q, \hat{q}, \varphi, \psi, \rho \rangle$ *is well-formed if for all states* q *that are reachable in* M: *(1) both* $\varphi(q)$ *and* $\psi(q)$ *are satisfiable; (2)* $(\varphi(q) \wedge \psi(q)) \rightarrow \exists q'. \rho(q, q')$ *is valid, and (3)* $((\rho(q, q') \wedge (\rho(q, q''))) \rightarrow q' = q''$ *is valid for all* $q', q'' \in Q$.

Well-formedness ensures that the interface is non-blocking by conditions (1) and (2), and deterministic by (3).

3.1   Composition and Refinement

In this section, we define standard parallel composition operator and refinement relation in the lines of [4], and recall the incremental design and independent implementability properties that are supported by Moore interfaces.

The parallel composition is a partial function on pairs of Moore interfaces, that is defined if the two interfaces are compatible. We say that two interfaces are compatible if their variable types match and if there exists a design context in which the two interfaces can interact in a way that preserves their individual guarantees.

Definition 11 (Compatibility and parallel composition). *Given two Moore interfaces* $M = \langle X_M^I, X_M^O, Q_M, \hat{q}_M, \varphi_M, \psi_M, \rho_M \rangle$ *and* $N = \langle X_N^I, X_N^O, Q_N, \hat{q}_N, \varphi_N, \psi_N, \rho_N \rangle$, *let* $X^O = X_M^O \cup X_N^O$, $X^I = (X_M^I \cup X_N^I) \backslash X^O$, $Q = Q_M \times Q_N$, $\hat{q} = (\hat{q}_M, \hat{q}_N)$, *and for all* $q, q' \in Q_M$ *and* $r, r' \in Q_N$, $\psi(q, r) = \psi_M(q) \wedge \psi_N(r)$ *and* $\rho((q, q'), (r, r')) = \rho_M(q, q') \wedge \rho_N(r, r')$. *We say that* M *and* N *are compatible, if* $X_M^O \cap X_N^O = \emptyset$, *and there exists a labeling* $\varphi_\otimes$ *such that for all executions* $(q_0, r_0), v_0, \ldots, v_{n-1}, (q_n, r_n)$ *of* $\langle X^I, X^O, Q, \hat{q}, \varphi_\otimes, \psi, \rho \rangle$, *we have that* $v_i \models (\varphi_M(q_i) \wedge \varphi_N(r_i))$ *for all* $0 \leq i \leq n$.

The parallel composition $P = M \parallel N$ *is defined if and only if* M *and* N *are compatible, in which case* $P = \langle X^I, X^O, Q, q_0, \varphi, \psi, \rho \rangle$, *where* φ *is the* weakest labeling *that satisfies the above conditions.*

The parallel composition operator is associative, thus supporting incremental design, i.e. ensuring that the compatible interfaces of a system can be put together in any order.

Theorem 7 ([4]). *Given three Moore interfaces* M, N *and* S, *either* $M \parallel (N \parallel S)$ *and* $(M \parallel N) \parallel S$ *are both undefined, or they are both defined and equal.*

The refinement of two Moore interfaces is defined as an alternating simulation relation R, and we say that R is a *witness* for $N \preceq M$.

Definition 12 (Refinement). *Given two Moore interfaces* $M = \langle X_M^I, X_M^O, Q_M, \hat{q}_M, \varphi_M, \psi_M, \rho_M \rangle$ *and* $N = \langle X_N^I, X_N^O, Q_N, \hat{q}_N, \varphi_N, \psi_N, \rho_N \rangle$, *we say that* N *refines* M, *denoted by* $N \preceq M$, *if*

1. $(X_M^I \cup X_N^I) \cap (X_M^O \cup X_N^O) = \emptyset$, *and*
2. *there exists a relation* $R \subseteq Q_M \times Q_N$ *such that: (1)* $(\hat{q}_M, \hat{q}_N) \in R$, $\varphi_M(q) \rightarrow \varphi_N(r)$ *is valid; (2)* $\psi_N(r) \rightarrow \psi_M(q)$ *is valid, and (3) for all* $q' \in Q_M$ *and* $r' \in Q_N$, *if* $\varphi_M(q) \wedge \psi_N(r) \wedge \rho_M(q, q') \wedge \rho_N(r, r')$ *is satisfiable, then* $(q', r') \in R$.

Following definitions of refinement, compatibility and composition, it follows that Moore interfaces satisfy the independent implementability requirement, as stated in the following theorem:

Theorem 8 ([4]). *Let* M, N *and* S *be three well-formed Moore interfaces such that* $X_N \cap X_S \subseteq X_M$. *If* M *and* S *are compatible, and* $N \preceq M$, *then* N *and* S *are also compatible and* $N \parallel S \preceq M \parallel S$.

3.2   Conjunction

The conjunction $M \wedge N$ of two Moore interfaces M and N was also introduced and defined in [8] as the weakest interface that refines both M and N, similarly to the stateless case. In the context of a conjunction of Moore interfaces M and N, as long as the inputs satisfy both the assumptions of M and N, the outputs must satisfy both the guarantees of M and N. If the assumption of M (N) is violated, then the conjunction interface does not need anymore to satisfy the guarantees of M (N) and jumps to a copy of N (M). The conjunction does not allow inputs that violate both assumptions of M and N.

Definition 13 (Conjunction). *Given two Moore interfaces* $M = \langle X_M^I, X_M^O, Q_M, \hat{q}_M, \varphi_M, \psi_M, \rho_M \rangle$ *and* $N = \langle X_N^I, X_N^O, Q_N, \hat{q}_N, \varphi_N, \psi_N, \rho_N \rangle$, *let* P *be the Moore interface* $\langle X^I, X^O, Q, \hat{q}, \varphi, \psi, \rho \rangle$, *where*

- $X^I = X_M^I \cup X_N^I$
- $X^O = X_M^O \cup X_N^O$
- $Q = (Q_M \times Q_N) \cup Q_M \cup Q_N$
- $\hat{q} = (\hat{q}_M, \hat{q}_N)$
- φ *and* ψ *are defined for all* $q \in Q_M$ *and* $r \in Q_N$, *by*

$$\begin{aligned}
\varphi(q,r) &= (\varphi_M(q) \vee \varphi_N(r)) & \psi(q,r) &= (\psi_M(q) \wedge \psi_N(r)) \\
\varphi(q) &= \varphi_M(q) & \psi(q) &= \psi_M(q) \\
\varphi(r) &= \varphi_N(r) & \psi(r) &= \psi_N(r)
\end{aligned}$$

- ρ *is defined for all* $q, q' \in Q_M$ *and* $r, r' \in Q_N$, *by*

$$\begin{aligned}
\rho((q,r),(q',r')) &= (\varphi_M(q) \wedge \varphi_N(r) \wedge \rho_M(q,q') \wedge \rho_N(r,r')) \\
\rho((q,r),q') &= (\varphi_M(q) \wedge \neg\varphi_N(r) \wedge \rho_M(q,q')) \\
\rho((q,r),r') &= (\neg\varphi_M(q) \wedge \varphi_N(r) \wedge \rho_N(r,r')) \\
\rho(q,q') &= \rho_M(q,q') \\
\rho(r,r') &= \rho_N(r,r') \\
\rho(q,(q',r')) &= \rho(r,(q',r')) = \bot
\end{aligned}$$

We say that M *and* N *are consistent if: (1)* $X^I \cap X^O = \emptyset$, *and (2)* $\psi(q)$ *is satisfiable for all states* q *that are reachable in* $M \wedge N$.

When M *and* N *are consistent, the conjunction* $M \wedge N$ *is the well-formed Moore interface* P.

Theorem 9 ([8]). *Let* M *and* N *be two well-formed Moore interfaces. If* M *and* N *are consistent, then* $M \wedge N \preceq M$ *and* $M \wedge N \preceq N$, *and for all well-formed Moore interfaces* S, *if* $S \preceq M$ *and* $S \preceq N$, *then* $S \preceq M \wedge N$.

In Section 1, we have seen that the conjunction operator does not support independent implementability in general, and hence similarly to the stateless interface case, we introduce the same orthogonality condition for Moore interfaces.

Definition 14 (Orthogonality). *Let* M *and* N *be two well-formed Moore interfaces. We say that* M *and* N *are orthogonal, if* $(X_M^I \cup X_N^I) \cap (X_M^O \cup X_N^O) = \emptyset$ *and* $X_M^O \cap X_N^O = \emptyset$.

In the following lemma, we show that two orthogonal Moore interfaces are also consistent:

Lemma 2. *Let* M *and* N *be two well-formed Moore interfaces. If* M *and* N *are orthogonal, then* M *and* N *are consistent.*

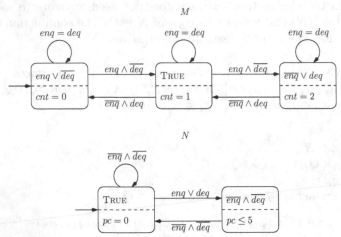

Fig. 6. FIFO buffer - functional specification M and functional/power consumption specification N

Proof. The proof is identical to the one of Lemma 1.

$\square$

Following Lemma 2, we are ready to state the result that establishes the independent implementability property for the conjunction operator between orthogonal Moore interfaces.

Theorem 10 (Independent implementability of conjunction). *Let M, N and S be three well-formed interfaces such that $X_N^O \cap X_S = X_N \cap X_S^O = \emptyset$. If M and S are orthogonal and $N \preceq M$, then N and S are orthogonal and $N \wedge S \preceq M \wedge S$.*

Proof. The proof follows the same line as the proof of Theorem 6. $\square$

4   FIFO Buffer Example

We illustrate independent implementability of viewpoints with a FIFO buffer example. The FIFO buffer specification consists of two interfaces, M and N that describe two different aspects of the buffer. These two specifications are extensions of the example presented in [8], and are depicted in Figure 6.

The interface M specifies a buffer of size 2. M has two Boolean input variables *enq* and *deq*, that model the enqueue and dequeue operations and one integer variable *cnt* that gives the current number of items that are stored in the buffer. The assumption (guarantee) predicates are depicted in the upper (lower) part of locations, and transitions are labeled by their guards. Initially, the buffer is empty, hence $cnt = 0$. Every exclusive enqueue (dequeue) operation increases (decreases) the *cnt* variable by one. However, in the initial state, the buffer is not allowed to dequeue, and in the state where the buffer is full ($cnt = 2$), the

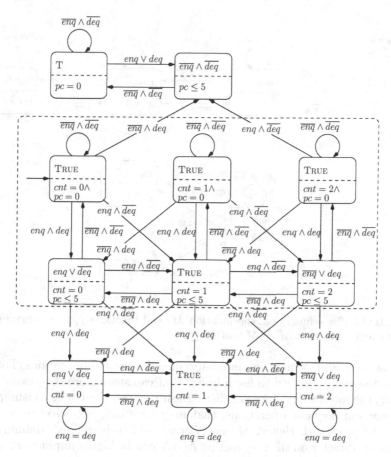

Fig. 7. FIFO buffer - conjunction $M \wedge N$

buffer is not allowed to enqueue new items. Note that simultaneous enqueue and dequeue operations are allowed, but have no effect.

Interface N specifies a power consumption and another behavioral aspect of a FIFO buffer. It has the same input variables as N (enq and deq), and an integer output variable pc that models the power consumption of a buffer. This interface forbids two consecutive enqueue or dequeue operations to happen. Additionally, it specifies the power consumption needed to process enqueue and dequeue requests. We can see that the absence of enqueue/dequeue requests results in no power consumption. On the other hand, any combination of the presence of enqueue and dequeue operations is bounded by 5 power units.

The interfaces M and N are naturally combined by the conjunction operator. The two interfaces are consistent, hence their conjunction $M \wedge N$ is defined and is shown in Figure 7. To obtain the conjunction $M \wedge N$, we need additional transitions leaving the dashed line box when the assumptions of M (N) are violated, and from then on only assumptions and guarantees of N (M) need to be satisfied.

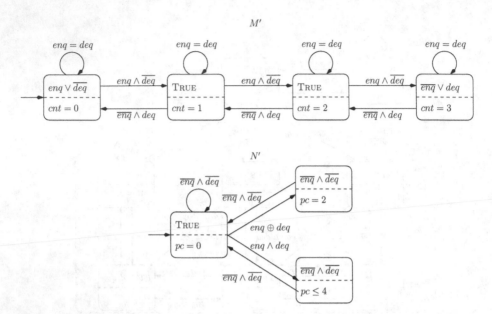

Fig. 8. FIFO buffer - functional specification M' and functional/power consumption specification N' such that $M' \preceq M$ and $N' \preceq N$

Interfaces M and N may be under-specified for many applications. For example, a designer may need to use a buffer that can store more than two items. Moreover, the interface N does not distinguish between the power consumption of enqueue and dequeue operations, that may have different resource requirements to be processed. Hence, M and N may need to be refined. Refining the requirements directly on the conjunction $M \wedge N$ can be highly impractical, given the relative complexity of $M \wedge N$ with respect to M and N. This can be appreciated by comparing Figures 6 and 7.

In this example, interfaces M and N are not only consistent, but also orthogonal. In fact, their output variables are disjoint, that is the number of items in the buffer does not depend on its power consumption, and vice versa. The orthogonality of M and N allows us to postpone taking an explicit conjunction of M and N, and to refine them separately and independently. In Figure 8, we show two interfaces, M' and N', where M' refines the interface M, and N' refines the interface N. M' specifies a buffer that can store up to three elements. It provides the same guarantees as M, while the number of items in the buffer is bounded by two, but is also able to process an additional enqueue request and store a maximum of three items.

On the other hand, the interface N' refines the power consumption guarantees, by distinguishing between the presence of an exclusive enqueue or dequeue request, that consumes exactly 2 power units, and a simultaneous enqueue/dequeue request that requires up to 4 power units. We leave to the reader the exercise to checking that M' and N' are indeed orthogonal and that $M' \wedge N'$ refines $M \wedge N$.

5   Conclusion

In this paper, we proposed orthogonality as a new condition between two Moore interfaces that ensures the independent implementability with respect to the conjunction operator. We believe that the orthogonality is the right notion when considering conjunction of multiple viewpoints. We demonstrated the stepwise refinement property of orthogonal interfaces with an example of a FIFO buffer that combines behavioral and power consumption specifications.

The power consumption specification of the FIFO buffer corresponds to a pure threshold resource interface in [5], but it was encoded as a Moore interface in our example. We believe that the next important step would be to study conjunction of fully heterogeneous interface models, a problem closely related to heterogeneous composition [1,3]. In particular, we are interested in models where the non-functional properties are expressed as Büchi threshold, pure energy and reward energy interfaces from [5] or real-time interfaces [9,11].

References

1. Benveniste, A., Caillaud, B., Carloni, L.P., Caspi, P., Sangiovanni-Vincentelli, A.L.: Composing heterogeneous reactive systems. ACM Trans. Embed. Comput. Syst. 7, 43:1–43:36 (2008)
2. Benveniste, A., Caillaud, B., Ferrari, A., Mangeruca, L., Passerone, R., Sofronis, C.: Multiple Viewpoint Contract-Based Specification and Design. In: de Boer, F.S., Bonsangue, M.M., Graf, S., de Roever, W.-P. (eds.) FMCO 2007. LNCS, vol. 5382, pp. 200–225. Springer, Heidelberg (2008)
3. Caspi, P., Benveniste, A., Lublinerman, R., Tripakis, S.: Actors without Directors: A Kahnian View of Heterogeneous Systems. In: Majumdar, R., Tabuada, P. (eds.) HSCC 2009. LNCS, vol. 5469, pp. 46–60. Springer, Heidelberg (2009)
4. Chakrabarti, A., de Alfaro, L., Henzinger, T.A., Mang, F.Y.C.: Synchronous and Bidirectional Component Interfaces. In: Brinksma, E., Larsen, K.G. (eds.) CAV 2002. LNCS, vol. 2404, pp. 414–427. Springer, Heidelberg (2002)
5. Chakrabarti, A., de Alfaro, L., Henzinger, T.A., Stoelinga, M.: Resource Interfaces. In: Alur, R., Lee, I. (eds.) EMSOFT 2003. LNCS, vol. 2855, pp. 117–133. Springer, Heidelberg (2003)
6. de Alfaro, L., Henzinger, T.A.: Interface automata. In: ESEC / SIGSOFT FSE, pp. 109–120 (2001)
7. de Alfaro, L., Henzinger, T.A.: Interface Theories for Component-Based Design. In: Henzinger, T.A., Kirsch, C.M. (eds.) EMSOFT 2001. LNCS, vol. 2211, pp. 148–165. Springer, Heidelberg (2001)
8. Doyen, L., Henzinger, T.A., Jobstmann, B., Petrov, T.: Interface theories with component reuse. In: EMSOFT, pp. 79–88 (2008)
9. Henzinger, T.A., Matic, S.: An interface algebra for real-time components. In: IEEE Real Time Technology and Applications Symposium, pp. 253–266 (2006)
10. Raclet, J.-B., Badouel, E., Benveniste, A., Caillaud, B., Legay, A., Passerone, R.: A modal interface theory for component-based design. Fundam. Inform. 108(1-2), 119–149 (2011)
11. Thiele, L., Wandeler, E., Stoimenov, N.: Real-time interfaces for composing real-time systems. In: EMSOFT, pp. 34–43 (2006)
12. Tripakis, S., Lickly, B., Henzinger, T.A., Lee, E.A.: A theory of synchronous relational interfaces. ACM Trans. Program. Lang. Syst. 33(4), 14 (2011)

Understanding Specification Languages through Their Model Theory

Ethan K. Jackson and Wolfram Schulte

Microsoft Research, Redmond, WA
{ejackson,schulte}@microsoft.com

Abstract. This paper studies the design of specification languages through their model theory. We show how language constructs and specification idioms are deeply rooted in the underlying model theory. We also show that some problems are fundamentally difficult to specify due to the underlying foundation of the language. The languages we study are *Alloy*, *Maude*, and *FORMULA*. FORMULA attempts to handle a large class of specifications problems while utilizing constraint solvers for formal analysis.

1   Introduction

Formal specification languages can be understood through their *model theory*. The *models relation* $\models_{Th}$ pairs a structure with a formula whenever the structure gives a valid interpretation to the formula under the theory Th. Consider the theory of Boolean algebra without quantifiers (i.e. SAT). The structures are functions from variables to Booleans and the formulas are propositions over Boolean variables:

$$\nu(x) \mapsto true, \nu(y) \mapsto false \quad \models_{SAT} \quad x \wedge \neg y.$$

The models relation also suggests the various types of formal reasoning. *Model checking* is to decide if $M \models_{Th} \varphi$, given M and φ. *Model finding* is to generate a model M given a formula φ such that $M \models_{Th} \varphi$.

One might imagine that the details of $\models_{Th}$ are far removed from the specifications users write. In this paper we show how the underlying model theory impacts the language level as much as it impacts the formal analysis:

- The structures determine what can be represented.
- The formulas determine the properties that can be expressed.
- The analyses (model checking / finding) determine the questions that can be asked.

In practice, users must have a deep understanding of the shapes of models and formulas in order to write specifications. Many standard concepts such as functions, relations, trees, and expressions require non-trivial encodings leading to various language idioms and specification patterns.

R. Calinescu and D. Garlan (Eds.): Monterey Workshop 2012, LNCS 7539, pp. 396–415, 2012.
© Springer-Verlag Berlin Heidelberg 2012

The goal of this paper is to illustrate how the model theory impacts common encoding tasks and language idioms. First, we review two well-known and dissimilar specification languages: *Alloy*[1] and *Maude*[2]. In *Alloy* models are finite relations over a universe of constants and the theory is first-order logic over relational algebra *FOL(RA)*. In *Maude* models are terms and theories are user-defined *equational theories*. In Alloy it is simple to represent relational structures and search problems; in Maude it is simple to represent recursive structures and language semantics.

Finally, we discuss the approach taken by the *FORMULA* language, which attempts to combine the benefits of both styles [3]. In FORMULA models are finite sets of well-typed terms and the theory is a subclass of fixpoint logic (FPL). The goal of FORMULA is to easily represent heterogeneous abstractions consisting of both:

- Relational structures such as finite graphs, system configurations and sets of objects in a heap;
- Recursive structures such as finite trees, instances of algebraic data types and fragments of expression languages.

This paper explores the impact of model theory on specification languages through two examples encoded in three languages. The running examples are the *homomorphism pair problem* and a *Boolean expression problem*. The homomorphism pair problem is to specify pairs of homomorphically-related finite graphs. The Boolean expression problem is to specify the evaluation semantics of a small Boolean expression language using a definition for disjunction based on De Morgan's law. Each example presents its own challenges. Section 2 reviews the Alloy specifications, Section 3 presents the Maude specifications, and Section 4 illustrates the FORMULA specifications. Finally, we conclude in Section 6.

2   Finite Relations and Alloy

There are variety of formal specification languages based on finite relations, including *Alloy* and Datalog languages [4,5,6]. These languages gives rise to signatures with the following shape:

$$\Sigma_{FR} \doteq \langle U, R_1, \ldots, R_k \rangle,$$

where U is a (possibly infinite) set of constants and each R_i is a finite n-ary relation over U. In symbols, $R_i \subseteq U^n$ and $\exists m \in \mathbb{N}. \ |R_i| = m$. Alloy specifications place constraints on the relations. A constraint φ is a first-order formula where all variables are quantified over relations. The formulas can also contain relational operators such as reflexive and transitive closure. Alloy's main analysis engine is a *finite model finder*; it searches for interpretations of the relations satisfying constraints [7]. We write x for a vector of variables $(x_1, \ldots, x_n)$ and $R(x)$ for $x \in R$. We also write $R()$, $R(,)$ etc... to indicate a unary, binary, etc... relation.

2.1   Finite Functions

A finite function is encoded by introducing unary relations for the (co-) domain, and then constraining the relation so it behaves like a function. Given unary relations $Dom_1, \ldots, Dom_m$ and $Cod_1, \ldots, Cod_n$, then R encodes a function from $\prod Dom_i$ to $\prod Cod_j$ if $arity(R) = m + n$, it is *left-total* and *right-unique*. If R is also *left-unique* it encodes an injection. If it is also *right-total* it encodes a surjection. Below are the first-order constraints for these properties.

(Left-total) $\forall x \in \prod Dom_i.\ \exists y \in \prod Cod_j.\ R(x, y).$
(Right-total) $\forall y \in \prod Cod_j.\ \exists x \in \prod Dom_i.\ R(x, y).$
(Left-unique) $\forall x, x' \in \prod Dom_i.\ \forall y \in \prod Cod_j.\ R(x, y) \wedge R(x', y) \Rightarrow x = x'.$
(Right-unique) $\forall x \in \prod Dom_i.\ \forall y, y' \in \prod Cod_j.\ R(x, y) \wedge R(x, y') \Rightarrow y = y'.$

Alloy's model theory uses finite relations for structures, which impacts the language. There is no function application and function declarations are shorthands for the previous constraints. The language simulates classes, objects and field accessors through finite relations, constraints and the relational join operator. For example, the Alloy specification in Figure 1 describes a data structure called *HomPair*; each instance must contain a homomorphic pair of graphs (G, H). The **sig** block simulates a class definition by introducing a unary relation *HomPair*(). The elements of *HomPair* correspond to the unique IDs of HomPair instances. Intuitively, HomPair instances contain other relations, such as the unary vertex relation Gv. Containment is simulated by increasing the arity of contained relations. For example, the vertex set Gv corresponds to the binary relation $Gv(,)$ where $Gv(x, y)$ holds if the HomPair instance with ID x has a vertex labeled y in its set Gv. The arrow operator $->$ is relational product; hence the edge relations Ge and He are subsets of Gv × Gv and Hv × Hv. The homomorphism witness Hom (Line 7) uses the cardinality constraint **one** to indicate it is functional. This introduces the left-total and right-unique axioms (appropriately adjusted for the hidden HomPair ID argument).

Finite relations impact how constraints are written in Alloy. The axiom that every instance of HomPair contains a pair of homomorphic graphs is shown in

```
1. sig HomPair              9.  fact {
2. {                        10.     all p : HomPair,
3.      Gv : Int,           11.         u, v : p.Gv, u', v' : p.Hv |
4.      Ge : Gv -> Gv,      12.     u -> v in *(p.Ge) and
5.      Hv : Int,           13.     u -> u' in p.Hom and
6.      He : Hv -> Hv,      14.     v -> v' in p.Hom =>
7.      Hom : Gv -> one Hv  15.     u' -> v' in *(p.He) }
8. }                        16. }
```

Fig. 1. Specifying homomorphic graphs using Alloy

Lines 9 - 16. Variables are quantified over relations; field accesses are simulated by relational join. For instance, the notation u, v: p.Gv uses the relational join operator '.' to construct a unary relation $p.GV()$ satisfying $p.Gv(y) \Leftrightarrow Gv(p, y)$. The operator $^*R$ generates the reflexive closure of a binary relation R. Figure 2 shows the overall signature of the HomPair specification and a model satisfying constraints.

$$\Sigma_{\mathsf{HomPair}} \doteq (U,\ HomPair(),\ Gv(,),\ Hv(,),\ Ge(,,),\ He(,,),\ Hom(,,)).$$

$HomPair \doteq \{c\}.$	$Hom \doteq \{(c, 1, 3), (c, 2, 3)\}.$
$Gv \doteq \{(c, 1), (c, 2)\}.$	$Ge \doteq \{(c, 1, 2)\}.$
$Hv \doteq \{(c, 3)\}.$	$He \doteq \{(c, 3, 3)\}.$

Fig. 2. A model of the HomPair specification

2.2 Recursive Structures

Finite relations easily encode class-like data types; relational joins simulate field accesses naturally. However, some finite structures are not encoded so easily. Consider the language of Boolean expressions in a grammar-like form:

$$e := x \mid not(e) \mid or(e, e) \mid and(e, e).$$

Boolean expressions are directed acyclic graphs (DAGs) so they are representable. Rather, the difficulty is operating on DAGs, which often requires recursive definitions outside of $FOL(RA)$. Consider this constraint on the $eval()$ function:

$$\forall e, e'.\ eval(or(e, e')) = eval(not(and(not(e), not(e')))). \tag{1}$$

It constrains the $eval()$ function to evaluate $or(e, e')$ in the same way as it evaluates the negation of De Morgan applied to $not(or(e, e'))$.

```
 1. abstract sig Expr {}              10. one sig Eval {
 2. sig And extends Expr              11.    eval: Expr -> one Bool
 3. { arg1: Expr, arg2: Expr }        12. }{
 4. sig Or extends Expr               13.    all o : Or, n, n', n" : Not, a : And |
 5. { arg1: Expr, arg2: Expr }        14.    some b : Bool |
 6. sig Not extends Expr              15.    (n.arg = a and a.arg1 = n' and
 7. { arg: Expr }                     16.    a.arg2 = n" and n'.arg = o.arg1 and
 8. sig Var extends Expr              17.    n".arg = o.arg2) =>
 9. { name: Int }                     18.    (o -> b in eval <=> n -> b in eval ) }

19. fact {
20.    not (some e: Expr | e -> e in
21.    ^(And <: arg1 + Or <: arg1 + And <: arg2 + Or <: arg2 + Not <: arg))
22. }
```

Fig. 3. Partial specification of an expression language using Alloy

Figure 3 shows one attempt to embed the language of Boolean expressions into finite relations. It uses the signatures And, Or, Not, and Var to encode expressions. Lines 19-22 encode acyclicity of expressions. This is accomplished by first forming binary restrictions of the expression relations. For instance, And $<:$ arg1 is a relation R satisfying $R(x,y) \Leftrightarrow arg1(x,y) \wedge And(x)$. An expression is cyclic if there is some sub-expression e where (e,e) is in the transitive closure $(\hat{R})$ of the union of these binary restrictions. Lines 12-18 attempt to encode Equation 1, but the attempt is flawed. In particular, the implication is activated only when the expressions hold for the *same objects* (e.g. n'.arg = o.arg1). Instead, the LHS should be true whenever both fields contain structurally equal subexpressions. Whether or not *structural equality* ($\sim$) is definable depends on the particular specification language. In the case of Alloy, structural equality is outside of the scope of the language, which permits only first-order logic over relations and several built-in relational operators. Equation 1 cannot be encoded, but we only provide an semi-formal argument that this is the case.

The transitive closure operator can be viewed as a built-in recursive function on binary relations, as follows:

$$F_{trans}(R) \doteq \begin{cases} R & \text{if } trans(R) \subseteq R, \\ F_{trans}(R \cup trans(R)) & \text{otherwise.} \end{cases} \qquad (2)$$

where $trans(R) \doteq \{(x,y) \mid R(x,y) \wedge R(y,z)\}$. The question is whether structural equality can be rephrased as a recursive function in the form of Equation 2. Consider the problem of defining structural equality between binary trees encoded with binary relations $lft(,)$ and $rt(,)$. If $lft(x,y)$ holds then the node named x has left child y, for $x \in node$ and $y \in node \cup \{nil\}$. The rt relation has an analogous interpretation for the right children. The first step towards an encoding is to rephrase the problem on a single relation. This is accomplished by tagging the relations and combining them into a single ternary relation:

$$R_0 \doteq (l \to lft) \cup (r \to rt) \cup \{(\sim, nil, nil)\}$$

for constants l, r, and $\sim$. Structural equality is computed by the following recursive function:

$$F_{\sim}(R) \doteq \begin{cases} R & \text{if } trans_{\sim}(R) \subseteq R, \\ F_{\sim}(R \cup trans_{\sim}(R)) & \text{otherwise.} \end{cases} \qquad (3)$$

where:

$$trans_{\sim}(R) \doteq \left\{ (\sim, x, x') \;\middle|\; \begin{array}{l} R(l,x,y) \wedge R(r,x,z) \wedge \\ R(l,x',y') \wedge R(r,x',z') \wedge \\ R(\sim,y,y') \wedge R(\sim,z,z') \end{array} \right\} \qquad (4)$$

Although Equations 2 and 3 have a similar form, structural equality cannot be rephrased into transitive closure unless $trans_{\sim}$ can be rephrased as $trans$ over a suitable binary relation. We claim this not possible.

However, structural equality is definable in languages supporting *fixpoint logic* (FPL) over finite relations, such as Datalog languages [8]. Figure 4 shows the definition of structural equality in Datalog, assuming the same signature as the Alloy specification. Structural equality can be encoded with FPL but at a cost. First, expression languages are essentially *algebraic data types* (ADTs), and users must have a full understanding of how relations simulate algebraic data types. This is particularly true if some ADT-like relations contain IDs of object-like relations. Second, the model finder must still work to produce IDs even though structural equality is insensitive to their values. At the same time, there are many isomorphic models satisfying the constraints, and it is non-trivial to avoid these isomorphic models. In conclusion, model theory based on finite relations and FOL(RA) or FPL significantly impacts the language-level encoding strategies and idioms.

3 Algebraic Data Types and Maude

ADTs are useful. At the other end of the spectrum are languages based entirely on ADTs. Most noteworthy are term rewriting systems (TRS) such as *Maude*. These languages give rise to signatures with the following shape:

$$\Sigma_{ADT} \doteq \langle U, C, f_1, \ldots, f_k, \tau_1, \ldots, \tau_l \rangle,$$

such that $C \subseteq U$ is a (possibly infinite) set of constants. Each f_i is an n-ary function $f_i : U^n \to U$ for $n \geq 1$. The *Peano axioms* are implicitly assumed for these functions:

- $f(x) \neq c$, for all $c \in C$.
- $f_i(x) = f_j(y) \Leftrightarrow i = j \wedge x = y$.
- $U = \bigcup_{i \geq 0} C_i$, where $C_0 \doteq C$ and $C_{i>0} \doteq \bigcup_{j=1}^{k} f_j(C_{i-1})$.

The Peano axioms yield *term algebras*. An element of U is called a *term*; all terms can be uniquely expressed using a combination of constants and function applications. Usual equality of terms ($=$) is equivalent to structural equality by the Peano axioms. The functions f_i are called *data constructors* and τ_j are called *data types*. Data types are subsets of terms: $\tau_i \subseteq U$; the expressiveness of the types depends on the specification language. With ADTs instances of expression languages can be written without introducing object IDs. For example, a Boolean expression is just a term:

$$not(and(not(true), not(var(0))))$$

1. $\sim$(id, id') :- Var(id), Var(id'), name(id, x), name(id', x).
2. $\sim$(id, id') :- Not(id), Not(id'), arg(id, x), arg(id', x'), $\sim$(x, x').
3. $\sim$(id, id') :- And(id), And(id'), arg1(id, x), arg2(id, y),
4.   arg1(id', x'), arg2(id', y'), $\sim$(x, x'), $\sim$(y, y').
5. $\sim$(id, id') :- Or(id), Or(id'), arg1(id, x), arg2(id, y),
6.   arg1(id', x'), arg2(id', y'), $\sim$(x, x'), $\sim$(y, y').

Fig. 4. Defining structural equality over finite relations using Datalog

3.1   Equational Theories

We still need a way to write meaningful specifications over ADTs. Extend Σ_{ADT} with a binary relation on terms called *theory equality* ($\approx$). Users give semantics to terms by a set of axioms $\mathcal{A}$ over theory equality and types; axioms must have the form:

$$\forall \boldsymbol{x}. \ s \approx t \Leftarrow \bigwedge \varphi_i. \quad \forall \boldsymbol{x}. \ \tau(s) \Leftarrow \bigwedge \varphi_i,$$

where φ_i is either $s_i \approx t_i$ or $\tau_i(s_i)$. The subformulas s, s_i and t, t_i may contain constructor applications, constants and variables. The axiom $\forall \boldsymbol{x}. \ x \approx x$ is always in $\mathcal{A}$. The key result is there exists a unique *least congruence relation* $\approx_{Th(\mathcal{A})}$ and least sets $\tau_1^{Th(\mathcal{A})}, \ldots, \tau_l^{Th(\mathcal{A})}$ satisfying the axioms.

The axioms $\mathcal{A}$ can be viewed as a user-defined theory $Th(\mathcal{A})$, called an *equational theory*. In the resulting model theory formulas have the following grammar:

$$formula := term \approx term. \quad term := var \mid c \in C \mid f(\boldsymbol{term}), \ f \in \Sigma_{ADT},$$

models are functions ν from variables to terms, and the models relation is defined as:

$$\nu \models_{Th(\mathcal{A})} s \approx t \quad \text{if} \quad s[\boldsymbol{x}/\nu(\boldsymbol{x})] \approx_{Th(\mathcal{A})} t[\boldsymbol{x}/\nu(\boldsymbol{x})],$$

where $s[\boldsymbol{x}/\nu(\boldsymbol{x})]$ is the Σ-term obtained by substituting all occurrences of the variables $\boldsymbol{x}$ in s with the Σ-terms $\nu(\boldsymbol{x})$. Maude (ignoring extensions) is a model finder for formulas of the form $x \approx t$, where t is variable-free:

$$x \models_{Th(\mathcal{A})} x \approx t. \tag{5}$$

Finding an x equivalent to t under $Th(\mathcal{A})$ is accomplished by rewriting t using axioms until t is reduced to a term where no further rewrites are applicable. Unlike Alloy, which uses a fixed theory, users must design their own theories so meaningful questions can be phrased in the form of Equation 5.

3.2   Recursive Structures

Equational theories fit well with ADTs because they immediately generalize to all subexpressions, as shown in Figure 5. Lines 2 - 8 introduce the constants True, False, the data constructors Var, Not, And, Or, and the types Bool, Expr (called *sorts*). The data constructors and constants are declared with type constraints, e.g. Var : Nat Bool –> Expr. (The Bool value given to the Var constructor indicates the value assigned to that variable.) Actually, type constraints are compiled into axioms on type membership:

$$\forall x, y. \ Expr(Var(x, y)) \Leftarrow Nat(x) \wedge Bool(y).$$

1.	**fmod** Expr **is**	12.	**vars** B : Bool .
2.	**sort** Bool Expr .	13.	**eq** And(X, X) = X .
3.	**op** True : –> Bool [ctor] .	14.	**eq** Var(N, B) = B .
4.	**op** False : –> Bool [ctor] .	15.	**eq** Or(X, Y) =
5.	**op** Var : Nat Bool –> Expr .	16.	Not(And(Not(X), Not(Y))).
6.	**op** Not : Expr –> Expr .	17.	**eq** And(False, X) = False .
7.	**op** And : Expr Expr –> Expr .	18.	**eq** And(X, False) = False .
8.	**op** Or : Expr Expr –> Expr .	19.	**eq** And(True, True) = True .
9.	**subsort** Bool < Expr .	20.	**eq** Not(True) = False .
10.	**vars** X Y : Expr .	21.	**eq** Not(False) = True .
11.	**vars** N : Nat .	22.	**endfm**

Fig. 5. Semantics of Boolean expression as an equational theory

Similarly, the **subsort** statement (Line 9) introduces the axiom:

$$\forall x.\ Expr(x) \Leftarrow Bool(x).$$

Lines 13 - 21 introduce axioms about theory equality. For instance, Lines 15 - 16 correspond to Equation 1. It introduces the axiom:

$$\forall x, y.\ Or(x, y) \approx Not(And(Not(x), Not(y))) \Leftarrow Expr(x) \wedge Expr(y).$$

The remaining equations encode the semantics of the Boolean operators Not, And.

Maude evaluates queries of the form $x \models_{Th(A)} x \approx t$ by rewriting t according to the axioms. Term rewriting is an operational semantics and requires more than just equations. First, the equations must be *terminating*, i.e. all sequences of rewrites must eventually terminate. For this reason, rewrites only replace LHSs with RHSs, otherwise every equation implies a trivial sequence of non-terminating rewrites. Second, equational theories must be *confluent*, i.e. every term must reduce to the same final form regardless of the order of rewrites. Without confluence, occasionally an equation $s \approx t$ might be judged as true and occasionally it might be judged as false. (Note, these rules are relaxed for badly-typed terms.) Below is a sequence of writes:

$$Or(Var(0, True), False) \rightarrow Not(And(Not(Var(0, True)), Not(False))) \rightarrow$$
$$Not(And(Not(True), Not(False))) \rightarrow \ldots \rightarrow Not(And(False, True)) \rightarrow$$
$$Not(False) \rightarrow True.$$

In the case of Boolean expressions, every expression should eventually be rewritten to True / False. This intent is expressed by the annotations [ctor] on the declarations of True, False (Lines 3 - 4). If the specifications have been written correctly, every well-typed term should be rewritten to a final form containing only [ctor] constants / constructors.

3.3   Relational Structures and Search

Earlier we showed that encoding ADTs into finite relations is non-trivial. Conversely, issues arise when axiomatizing finite relations using equational theories.

```
1.  fmod Graphs is
2.    sorts Edge EdgeSet Graph. subsort Edge < EdgeSet .
3.    op <_,_> : NzNat EdgeSet—> Graph [ctor] .
4.    op [_,_] : Nat Nat —> Edge [ctor comm] .
5.    op _,_ : EdgeSet EdgeSet —>  EdgeSet [ctor assoc comm idem] .
6.    op _in_ : Edge EdgeSet —> Bool .
7.    vars E : Edge . vars S : EdgeSet .
8.    eq E in E = true .
9.    eq E in E,S = true .
10.   eq E in S = false [owise].
11. endfm
```

Fig. 6. Defining graphs in Maude

Consider the binary set union operator $\cup$, e.g. $1 \cup (2 \cup 3)$ yields the set $\{1, 2, 3\}$. Axiomatizing $\cup$ requires axioms for associativity (A), commutativity (C), and idempotence (I). However, the AC axioms are non-terminating so they cannot be written in the standard way. Instead, Maude provides the special attributes [assoc], [comm] and [idem] for introducing these axioms and handles them specially during rewriting.

Figure 6 shows a Maude specification for graphs. Edges are constructed by the commutative [_,_] operator and edge sets are built using the ACI operator _,_. (We assume every graph has at least one edge.) The in operator determines if an edge is present in an edge set. Notice the equations for in are simple, because the operators have been declared to be C and ACI. In Line 8, the pattern E,S is sufficient because the AC axioms allow Maude to rewrite the edge set until E is at the front. The shorthand [owise] expands to a conditional equation handling the remaining cases. A graph is constructed by <_,_>, which takes the number of vertices in the graph and the edge set.

Another consequence of terminating and confluent equational theories is the difficultly of encoding search problems. Consider the NP-complete problem of checking if there exists a homomorphism from one graph to another. We can encode this problem into Maude by defining the operator CheckHom : Graph Graph —> Witness. The CheckHom term will be reduced to a term representing the homomorphism function from V_G to V_H, if it exists. However, the only way to define a confluent CheckHom is via a systematic generate and test scheme. This encoding is likely to be inefficient and it will require many axioms to implement search. (See Appendix A.) In our opinion, this shows a trade-off between specifications as constraints over a fixed theory (Alloy) and specifications as theories over a fixed constraint formula (Maude). Equational theories are a powerful specification tool, but encoding hard search problems within equational theories is challenging. (Maude also supports non-deterministic transition systems via non-confluent rewriting rules. An explicit state model checker for temporal logic is available, but this is outside the scope of our paper.)

```
1.   domain BoolExpr {
2.    Var    := new (name: Natural, val: Boolean).
3.    Not    := new (arg: any Expr).
4.    And    := new (arg1: any Expr, arg2: any Expr).
5.    Or     := new (arg1: any Expr, arg2: any Expr).
6.    Expr   := Boolean + Var + Not + And + Or.
7.    sub    := (exp: Expr).
8.    eval   := (exp: Expr, val: Boolean).

9.    sub(x) :- x is Expr; sub(Not(x)).
10.   sub(x), sub(y) :- sub(And(x, y)); sub(Or(x, y)).
11.   sub(Not(And(Not(x), Not(y)))) :- sub(Or(x, y)).

12.   eval(true, true). eval(false, false).
13.   eval(e, x) :- sub(e), e = Var(_, x).
14.   eval(e, x) :- sub(e), eval(e', x), e = Not(e'), y = !x.
15.   eval(e, x) :- sub(e), eval(e', x), eval(e'', y), e = And(e', e''), z = x & y.
16.   eval(e, x) :- sub(e), eval(e_dm, x), e = Or(e', e''),
17.                 e_dm = Not(And(Not(e'), Not(e''))).
18. }.
```

Fig. 7. Defining Boolean expressions in FORMULA

4 The FORMULA Approach

We now describe the hybrid approach taken by the specification language FOR-MULA. Like Maude, FORMULA begins with ADTs, but instead of theory equality it extends the signature with a single unary relation K over terms, called the *knowledge relation*. Like Alloy, FORMULA specifications are understood as constraints on relations; specifically as constraints on the single relation K. The logic of FORMULA is a class of fixpoint logic (FPL), similar to (but more general than) Datalog. First-class ADTs and FPL allow recursive reasoning over terms, while the knowledge relation supports direct encoding of relational structures. Like Alloy, FORMULA provides finite model finding so users do not have to encode search strategies.

We now introduce the approach with an informal discussion of the Boolean expression language encoded with FORMULA. Figure 7 shows the relevant code. Lines 3 - 9 are *data type declarations*; they simultaneously introduce data constructors and data types into the specification. Ignoring the keywords **new** and **any**, then a type declaration can have the form:

$$f := (l_1: T_1, \ldots, l_n: T_n)$$

in which case it introduces an n-ary constructor f and a data type τ_f. In FOR-MULA the corresponding data type has the same name as the constructor and the two are distinguished by context. The pairs $l_i: T_i$ give the names and types of constructor arguments. For example, the type declaration

$$\text{Var} := \textbf{new} \ (\text{name:} \ \textbf{Natural}, \ \text{val:} \ \textbf{Boolean})$$

gives Var two arguments called name and val that are expected to be of types **Natural** and **Boolean**. The data type τ_{Var} contains all the Var terms conforming to type constraints:

$$\tau_{Var} \doteq \{Var(x, y) \mid x \in \mathbb{N} \wedge y \in \mathbb{B}\}.$$

An f-term t is said to be *well-typed* if $t \in \tau_f$. Additionally, auxiliary data types can be declared using set-theoretic union $(+)$ as shown in Line 6. The Expr declaration does not introduce a constructor, but introduces a new data type τ_{Expr} that is equal to the union of other data types:

$$\tau_{expr} \doteq \tau_{Boolean} \cup \tau_{Var} \cup \tau_{Not} \cup \tau_{And} \cup \tau_{Or}.$$

These are useful to define more complex recursive data types, as in the cases of Not / And / Or.

4.1   Writing Constraints

The data type declarations required for the FORMULA encoding are similar to the Maude encoding, except for the two additional constructors sub and $eval$. As with the Alloy encoding, these extra constructors are needed to axiomatize evaluation of expressions. Alloy specifications constrain user-defined relations by FOL(RA). FORMULA specifications constrain the knowledge relation K through a set of rules. For example, the rule:

$$\text{sub}(x) \ :\text{-} \ x \ \textbf{is} \ \text{Expr}.$$

explains that if $x \in \tau_{Expr} \cap K$, then the term $sub(x)$ is also in K. The LHS of a rule is called the *head* and the RHS is called the *body*. Operationally, a FORMULA program defines a fixpoint operator that monotonically extends K by applying rules until K can be extended no further. The least fixpoint of this operator identifies a unique K, which is the interpretation of the program. The model theory is more subtle, and we shall discuss it shortly.

The intent of Lines 9-11 is to extend K with all the subexpressions appearing within elements of K. These rules use some syntactic sugar explained in Table 1. Unlike Maude, which simplifies away terms by rewriting, FORMULA must saturate K with all the subexpressions that need to be evaluated. Line 11 introduces the extra subexpressions for evaluating Or expressions with De Morgan. Suppose K contains the expression $Or(Var(0, true), Not(Var(1, false)))$. Then these rules extend K with the following terms:

$$\begin{gather} sub(Or(Var(0, true), Not(Var(1, false)))), \\ sub(Var(0, true)), \quad sub(Not(Var(1, false))), \quad sub(Var(1, false)) \\ sub(Not(And(Not(Var(0, true)), Not(Not(Var(1, false)))))), \hspace{2em} (6) \\ sub(And(Not(Var(0, true)), Not(Not(Var(1, false))))), \\ sub(Not(Var(0, true))), \quad sub(Not(Not(Var(1, false)))) \end{gather}$$

Table 1. Some syntactic sugar in FORMULA programs

Syntactic sugar	Example	Translation
A rule with a variable called '_'	h :- x = g(_, _).	h :- x = g(x_{fresh}, y_{fresh})
A rule without **is**	h :- f(y).	h :- x_{fresh} **is** f, x_{fresh} = f(y).
A rule with several heads	h$_1$, h$_2$:- B.	h$_1$:- B. h$_2$:- B.
A rule with several bodies	h :- B$_1$; B$_2$.	h :- B$_1$. h :- B$_2$.

Lines 12-17 gives the rules for evaluating subexpressions. They extend K with terms of the form $eval(e, x)$ whenever the subexpression e is known to evaluate to x. Line 12 contains special rules called *facts*, which do not contain any constraints in the body. Facts must appear in K. In particular *true* always evaluates to *true* and *false* always evaluates to *false*. Lines 14-15 illustrate some built-in operators. For instance, the evaluation of *Not* and *And* utilize the built-in operators ! and &.

4.2 Domains and Models

The logic program in Figure 7 defines a fixpoint operator; executing the logic program computes the least fixpoint of this operator by repeatedly applying rules starting from facts. The only facts in BoolExpr are $eval(true, true)$ and $eval(false, false)$, and the least fixpoint contains exactly these two terms. One way to evaluate more complex expressions is to extend the program with more facts. Consider adding the fact:

$$Or(Var(0, \textbf{true}), Not(Var(1, \textbf{false}))).$$

Adding this fact produces a larger fixpoint containing the *sub*-terms from Equation 6 along with many *eval*-terms. In particular, the fixpoint contains the evaluation of the previous expression: $eval(Or(Var(0, true), Not(Var(1, false))), true)$. Thus, instead of giving the program "input" in the traditional sense, it can be extended with more facts to cause various computations. But the basic rules of evaluation are fixed across all extensions.

This observation can be formalized by treating a logic program as *open* for some types of facts; we call these *open-world* programs. A program is *closed* by extending with a finite set of facts. We call such an extension a *world*. Once a program is closed by a world it computes a unique least fixpoint; before this the least fixpoint is underspecified. In FORMULA open-world programs are placed within *domain* blocks when they serve to axiomatize abstractions. A legal extension of a domain is a set of variable-free well-typed facts. The type declarations of a domain further constrain the possible extensions. Only constructors declared with the *new* keyword can appear in extended facts. In the Boolean expression example, the *sub* and *eval* constructors are declared without *new*, which effectively fixes their semantics, i.e. *sub* and *eval* terms can only be produced by the domain rules.

```
1.  model Expr1 of BoolExpr {          4.  model Expr2 of BoolExpr {
2.    Or(Var(0, true), Not(Var(1, false))).  5.    Or(Var(0, false), Not(Var(1, true))).
3.  }                                   6.  }
```

Fig. 8. Several FORMULA models of Boolean expressions

FORMULA worlds are called *models*, which close domains. Models describe instances of abstractions by listing a set of variable-free well-typed facts containing only *new*-modified constructors, as shown in Figure 8. The knowledge relation K of a model is obtained by closing the domain with model facts and computing the least fixpoint. Notice that the models Expr1 and Expr2 assign the variables 0 and 1 in different ways. This is not contradictory, because each model defines its own extension of the domain. Each model is an independent instance of the Boolean expression abstraction.

4.3   Model Theory and Open-World Reasoning

The model theory needs to be adjusted to account for open-world reasoning. To avoid confusion, we shall use the phrase *world* to describe extensions of programs. Let Π be an open-world program and $lfp(\Pi \cup W)$ be the least fixpoint of the program after it is closed by a finite set of variable-free well-typed facts W. Then the models relation between knowledge relations and open-world programs is:

$$K \models \Pi \text{ iff there exists } W \text{ s.t. } K = lfp(\Pi \cup W). \tag{7}$$

Though the full formalization of FORMULA is outside the scope of this paper, it is important to note that FORMULA programs must compute a unique finite least fixpoint for every world W. The uniqueness property is obtained by syntactic restrictions on programs, but the finiteness property is equivalent to program termination (hence undecidable) and must be guaranteed by the user. For the remainder of this paper we shall assume all programs exhibit these properties.

FORMULA is a finite model finder for open-world programs. It constructs both K and W witnessing that $K \models \Pi$. However, unconstrained search is rarely useful, so model finding can be further constrained with *goals* and *partial models*:

1. **Goal.** A goal g is rule of the form c_{fresh} :- B. K satisfies g if $c_{fresh} \in K$ and $K \models \Pi \cup g$.
2. **Partial Model.** A partial model is a constraint on the structure of worlds. Partial models limit search to a subset of worlds.

Model checking can be rephrased as constrained model finding by choosing an appropriate goal g.

Consider the NP-complete problem of finding an assignment of Boolean variables so a given expression evaluates to true. Unlike Maude, where search procedures were encoded as confluent rewrites, the SAT problem can be rephrased as a model finding problem over an open-world program. Like Alloy, FORMULA also

```
1.  domain BoolSAT extends BoolExpr {
2.    prob := new (exp: Expr).
3.    badAsn :- sub(Var(x, y)), sub(Var(x, z)), x != z.
4.    isSat    :- prob(e), eval(e, true), no badAsn.
5.  }

6.  partial model Problem of BoolSAT {
7.    requires atmost 1 prob.
8.    prob(Or(Var(0, x), Not(Var(1, y)))).
9.  }

10. model Solution of BoolSAT {
11.    prob(Or(Var(0, true), Not(Var(1, true)))).
12.    Or(Var(0, true), Not(Var(1, true))).
13. }
```

Fig. 9. Encoding Boolean satisfiability with open-world programs

uses a powerful solver (Z3 [9]) to search for solutions. Unlike Alloy, the FOR-
MULA specification is able to embed the recursive definition of expression evaluation. Figure 9 shows the FORMULA specification. The BoolSAT domain includes
all the declarations / rules of BoolExpr via the *extends* keyword. It adds the
open constructor prob to hold an expression that should be solved. Line 3 checks
for contradictory assignments of the same variable. Line 4 produces the isSat
constant if there is some problem $prob(e) \in K$ such that e evaluates to true
without any bad assignments (**no** badAsn).

The partial model in Lines 6-9 represents a subset of the possible extensions
of BoolSAT. The intent is to limit the search so exactly one specific Boolean
expression is solved. Line 7 is a *cardinality constraint* limiting the number of
prob-facts that can appear in any extension to one. Line 8 immediately introduces
a *prob*-fact containing the variables x and y. For every fact in a partial model
there must exist a corresponding fact in a world for some substitution of the
variables. Therefore, this partial model describes a set of worlds with exactly
one *prob*-fact resembling the fact in Line 8. The command:

solve Problem isSat

initiates the model finder on the partial model Problem with the goal c_{fresh}
:- isSat. The model finder must instantiate variables x and y so the problem
expression evaluates to true. Lines 10-13 show one solution where $x \mapsto true, y \mapsto$
true. Notice the model Solution contains an expression fact, which is necessary
to cause evaluation of the problem expression. Only the FORMULA model (i.e.
world) is returned, because K can be uniquely reconstructed. In summary, the
open-world approach using strongly typed logic programs can handle recursive
structures and fixpoints while supporting flexible model finding.

4.4   Finite Relations

Relations can also be encoded. Consider the following undirected graph:

$$G \doteq \langle \{1,2\}, \{(1,1),(1,2)\} \rangle.$$

The vertex and edge relations V_G/E_G can be encoded by declaring data constructors of matching arity, and then enumerating the relations as facts within a model. First, the data type declarations might be:

V := **new** (lbl: **Integer**). E := **new** (src: **Integer**, dst: **Integer**).

And the contents of the model might be:

{ V(1). V(2). E(1, 1). E(1, 2). }

Any place the specification would test for $(x, y) \in E_G$, instead it tests for $E(x, y) \in K$. For example, this rule computes the reflexive closure of the edge relation, assuming the edge relation has been point-wise enumerated in a FORMULA model.

rflx(y, x) :- E(x, y).

By allowing K to contain complex terms, an arbitrary number of finite relations can be encoded without introducing the ACI axioms as required for Maude.

However, the data declarations do not capture the complete relationship between V_G and E_G; namely $E_G \subseteq V_G \times V_G$. This relationship needs to be axiomatized. FORMULA provides a convention for axiomatizing the intended relationship between data types via a special rule of the form:

conforms :- B.

The conformance rule produces the special constant **conforms** for those models obeying the intended relationships between data types. For example:

badEnd   :- E(x, _), **no** V(x); E(_, y), **no** V(y).
conforms :- **no** badEnd.

The first rule produces badEnd if there is some $E(x, y) \in K$ where $V(x) \notin K$ or $V(y) \notin K$. This occurs precisely if $E_G \nsubseteq V_G \times V_G$. Thus, the conformance rule produces **conforms** only if the relationship is satisfied. The FORMULA model finder automatically assumes the subgoal **conforms** to restrict search to conforming models.

As with Alloy, finite relations and functions are so common that language support is highly desirable. FORMULA provides similar idioms, which are most convenient when using the following encoding pattern: Suppose $R \subseteq R_1 \times \ldots \times R_n$ for unary relations R_i. Then every relation must have a corresponding constructor. In particular, the declaration of R should use the types of the constituent constructors:

R := **new** (arg$_1$: R$_1$, ..., arg$_n$: R$_n$).

Instead of integer arguments, which could appear in any other relation-like constructor, the argument types identify the intended constituent relations. For these declarations FORMULA automatically introduces rules of the form:

$$\text{badArg} :\text{- } R(x_1, \ldots), \text{ } \textbf{no } x'_1 \textbf{ is } R_1, x'_1 = x_1;$$
$$\vdots$$
$$R(\ldots, x_n), \textbf{ no } x'_n \textbf{ is } R_n, x'_n = x_n.$$

Then **no** badArg is automatically conjuncted onto the conformance rule. Actually, this encoding generalizes to relations of arbitrary arity and argument types. In the cases where the arguments are built-in constants, then these values are ignored and are outside this idiom. Thus, the previous declarations for undirected graphs can be rewritten as:

$$V := \textbf{new } (\text{lbl: } \textbf{Integer}). \text{ } E := \textbf{new } (\text{src: } \textbf{V}, \text{dst: } \textbf{V}).$$

and the user does not have to write additional conformance rules. The contents of a model might be:

$$\{ \text{ } V(1). \text{ } V(2). \text{ } E(V(1), V(1)). \text{ } E(V(1), V(2)). \text{ } \}$$

Finally, in the case where a type is not used to encode a relation, then a *new*-modified constructor accepting this type should marked its field with the *any* modifier. This modifier causes the compiler to skip generation of argument constraints for that field. Recall the data type declarations for the Boolean expression language use the **any** modifier, because they are not encoding relations (Figure 7, Lines 3-5). (The compiler does not generate constraints for non-new constructors.)

Similar constraints can be generated for partial/total functions. As with Alloy, finite functions are specified by introducing uniqueness and totality constraints. Again consider a finite function $F : I_1 \times \ldots \times I_m \to O_1 \times \ldots \times O_n$. Assuming F is represented as:

$$F := \textbf{new } (\text{in}_1\text{: } I_1, \ldots, \text{in}_m\text{: } I_m, \text{out}_1\text{: } O_1, \ldots, \text{out}_n\text{: } O_n \text{ }).$$

Then the relevant totality and uniqueness constraints can be added according to Table 2. The function modifiers in Table 3 instruct the compiler to automatically introduce these constraints. All constructors annotated with function modifiers are implicitly modified with **new**.

4.5 Finding Homomorphism Pairs

We now return to the problem of finding homomorphic pairs of graphs. In Alloy the encoding was succinct and declarative, but in Maude the encoding was verbose and necessitated writing a confluent search strategy. The FORMULA encoding uses the aforementioned conventions on constructors to encode the finite relations as shown in Figure 10. Lines 2-6 encode the same relations as the Alloy specification. Lines 7-8 introduce the rflx constructor for computing the reflexive closure of the edge sets. The reflexive closure is then computed in Line 9.

```
1.  domain HomPair {              9.    rflx(y, x) :- Ge(x, y); He(x, y).
2.    Gv   := new (id: Integer).  10.   badHom :- Hom(x1, y1), Hom(x2, y2),
3.    Ge   := new (src: Gv, dst: Ge). 11.           rflx(x1, x2), no rflx(y1, y2).
4.    Hv   := new (id: Integer).  12.   conforms :- no badHom.
5.    He   := new (src: Hv, dst: He). 13.   }
6.    Hom  := fun (gv: Gv =>hv: Hv).
7.    rflx := (e1: V, e2: V).
8.    V    := V.
```

Fig. 10. Specification of HomPair problem with FORMULA

Table 2. Rules for totality and uniqueness constraints

(Not-left-total)	nlt :- $I_1(x_1)$, ..., $I_m(x_m)$, no $F(x_1, ..., x_m, \_, ..., \_)$.
(Not-right-total)	nrt :- $O_1(y_1)$, ..., $O_n(y_n)$, no $F(\_, ..., \_, y_1, ..., y_n,)$.
(Not-left-unique)	nlu :- e is F, e = $F(\_,...,\_,y_1,...,y_n)$,
	e' is F, e' = $F(\_,...,\_,y_1,...,y_n)$,
	e != e'.
(Not-right-unique)	nru :- e is F, e = $F(x_1,...,x_m,\_,...,\_)$,
	e' is F, e' = $F(x_1,...,x_m,\_,...,\_)$,
	e != e'.

Table 3. Examples of function modifiers. Complete set of modifiers is **fun, sur, inj, bij** and ->/ =>

Modifiers	Example	Description
fun, ->	F := **fun** (i: A -> o: B).	A partial function from $A \cap K$ to $B \cap K$. Gets argument and right-unique constraints.
fun, ->, any	F := **fun** (i: A -> o: **any** B).	A partial function from $A \cap K$ to B. Gets argument constraint only on i field. Gets right-unique constraint.
fun, =>	F := **fun** (i: A => o: B).	A total function from $A \cap K$ to $B \cap K$. Gets argument, right-unique, and left-total constraints.
sur, =>, any	F := **sur** (i: **any** A => o: B).	A total surjection from A to $B \cap K$. Gets argument constraint on field o. Gets right-unique, left-total, and right-total constraints.

Finally, a bad homomorphism is one where vertices x_1 and x_2 are connected, but are mapped to vertices y_1 and y_2 that are not connected (Lines 10-11). The user-defined conformance rule for the domain is **no** badHom. But the compiler will automatically extend this rule with more conjuncts due to the use of **new** and function modifiers.

1. **model** Solution **of** HomPair {
2.   Gv(1). Gv(2).
3.   Ge(Gv(1), Gv(2)).
4.   Hv(3).

5.   He(Hv(3), Hv(3)).
6.   Hom(Gv(1), Hv(3)).
7.   Hom(Gv(2), Hv(3)).
8. }

Fig. 11. Example of generated homomorphism pair

The model finder can be used to find homomorphic pairs. Because the model finder always includes **conforms** as a subgoal, it may be invoked directly on the domain without an explicit goal: **solve** HomPair. A result is a model like the one shown in Figure 11. In summary, the FORMULA approaches combines ADTs with strongly-typed open-world logic programming to declaratively specify recursive and relational structures. Model finding over open-world programs uses state-of-the-art solvers to implement search. Users do not implement search within the program.

5   Conclusion

This paper studied the design of specification languages through their model theory. We showed that everything from basic syntax to complex specification idioms are deeply rooted in the underlying model theory. In practice, users must have a deep understanding of the shapes of models and formulas in order to write specifications. Many standard concepts such as functions, relations, trees, and expressions require non-trivial encodings. We showed that Alloy provides succinct specifications for search problems over finite relations. On the other hand, Maude provides succinct specifications for recursive definitions, such as evaluation semantics. Finally, we introduced the FORMULA approach, which attempts to handle both of these problems while retaining automated formal analysis by constraint solving.

References

1. Jackson, D.: Alloy: A New Technology for Software Modelling. In: Katoen, J.-P., Stevens, P. (eds.) TACAS 2002. LNCS, vol. 2280, p. 20. Springer, Heidelberg (2002)
2. Clavel, M., Durán, F., Eker, S., Lincoln, P., Martí-Oliet, N., Meseguer, J., Quesada, J.F.: Maude: Specification and Programming in Rewriting Logic. Theor. Comput. Sci. 285(2), 187–243 (2002)
3. Jackson, E.K., Kang, E., Dahlweid, M., Seifert, D., Santen, T.: Components, platforms and possibilities: towards generic automation for MDA. In: EMSOFT, pp. 39–48 (2010)
4. Lifschitz, V.: Datalog Programs and Their Stable Models. In: de Moor, O., Gottlob, G., Furche, T., Sellers, A. (eds.) Datalog 2010. LNCS, vol. 6702, pp. 78–87. Springer, Heidelberg (2011)

5. Alvaro, P., Marczak, W.R., Conway, N., Hellerstein, J.M., Maier, D., Sears, R.: DEDALUS: Datalog in Time and Space. In: de Moor, O., Gottlob, G., Furche, T., Sellers, A. (eds.) Datalog 2010. LNCS, vol. 6702, pp. 262–281. Springer, Heidelberg (2011)
6. Becker, M.Y., Fournet, C., Gordon, A.D.: Secpal: Design and semantics of a decentralized authorization language. Journal of Computer Security 18(4), 619–665 (2010)
7. Torlak, E., Jackson, D.: Kodkod: A Relational Model Finder. In: Grumberg, O., Huth, M. (eds.) TACAS 2007. LNCS, vol. 4424, pp. 632–647. Springer, Heidelberg (2007)
8. Dantsin, E., Eiter, T., Gottlob, G., Voronkov, A.: Complexity and expressive power of logic programming. ACM Comput. Surv. 33(3), 374–425 (2001)
9. de Moura, L., Bjørner, N.: Z3: An Efficient SMT Solver. In: Ramakrishnan, C.R., Rehof, J. (eds.) TACAS 2008. LNCS, vol. 4963, pp. 337–340. Springer, Heidelberg (2008)

A   CheckHom Specification

```
1.  fmod Configs is
2.     including Graphs .
3.     sorts Config Placement .
4.
5.     *** A placement describes a map from GV to HV.
6.     *** It has the form v1 => u1, v2 => u2, end ...
7.     op init : Nat --> Placement .
8.     op end : --> Placement [ctor].
9.     op _,_ : Placement Placement --> Placement [ctor assoc] .
10.    op _=>_ : Nat Nat --> Placement [ctor].
11.
12.    *** A configuration [ N | P ] states the number of vertices in H
13.    *** and gives a placement from GV to HV.
14.    op [_|_] : Nat Placement --> Config [ctor] .
15.
16.    *** An initial configuration is generated using [ N | init(M) ],
17.    *** which expands into the default placement for the M vertices of G
18.    vars S T : EdgeSet . vars E : Edge . vars N : Nat .
19.    ceq init(N) = (N + -1 => 0), init(N + -1) if N > 0 .
20.    eq init(0) = end .
21.
22.    *** The inc operator generates a new placement: inc([N | P]).
23.    *** In turn, the pinc operator increments a placement.
24.    op inc : Config --> Config .
25.    op pinc : Nat Placement --> Placement .
26.    vars P : Placement . vars I I' J : Nat .
27.    eq inc([ N | P, end ]) = [ N | pinc(N, P), end ] .
28.    ceq pinc(N, (P, I => J)) = P, (I => J + 1) if J < N + -1 .
```

```
29.   ceq pinc(N, (P, I => J)) = pinc(N, P), (I => 0) if J = N + -1 .
30.   ceq pinc(N, I => J) = I => J + 1 if J < N + -1 .
31.   ceq pinc(N, I => J) = I => N if J >= N + -1 .
32.
33.   *** Placements can be applied to vertices an edges.
34.   *** This returns the vertex / edge under the placement.
35.   op _[_] : Placement Nat -> Nat .
36.   op _[_] : Placement Edge -> Edge .
37.   eq ((I => J), P)[I] = J .
38.   ceq ((I' => J), P)[I] = P[I] if I' =/= I .
39.   eq P[[I,J]] = [P[I], P[J]] .
40.
41.   *** The IsPlaced operator checks if an edge from G is in H
42.   *** under the current placement.
43.   op IsPlaced : EdgeSet Placement EdgeSet -> Bool .
44.   ceq IsPlaced((E,S), P, T) = false if not P[E] in T .
45.   ceq IsPlaced(E, P, T) = false if not P[E] in T .
46.   eq IsPlaced(S, P, T) = true [owise] .
47. endfm
48.
49. fmod Hom is
50.   including Configs .
51.   sort Witness .
52.
53.   op CheckHom : Graph Graph -> Witness .
54.   op CheckHom : Config EdgeSet EdgeSet -> Witness .
55.   op Wit : Config EdgeSet EdgeSet -> Witness [ctor] .
56.   vars P : Placement . vars S T : EdgeSet . vars N M I J : Nat .
57.   eq CheckHom(<(M),(S)>, <(N),(T)>) = CheckHom([N | init(M)], S, T) .
58.   ceq CheckHom([N | (I => J), P], S, T) = CheckHom(inc([N | (I => J), P]), S, T)
59.     if not IsPlaced(S, (I => J), P, T) and J < N .
60.   ceq CheckHom([N | (I => J), P], S, T ) = Wit([N | (I => J), P], S, T)
61.     if IsPlaced(S, (I => J), P, T) and J < N .
62.   ceq CheckHom([N | (I => J), P], S, T ) = Wit([N | (I => J), P], S, T) if J >= N .
63. endfm
```

Author Index